THE CHILD
WITH A DISABILITY

The Child with a Disability

DAVID M. B. HALL

MB, BS, BSc, FRCP
Professor of Community Paediatrics
University of Sheffield
Sheffield Children's Hospital
Sheffield

PETER D. HILL

MA, MB, BChir, FRCP, FRCPsych
Professor of Child and Adolescent Psychiatry
Department of Mental Health Sciences
St George's Hospital Medical School
London

SECOND EDITION

**Blackwell
Science**

© 1984, 1996 by
Blackwell Science Ltd
Editorial Offices:
Osney Mead, Oxford OX2 0EL
25 John Street, London WC1N 2BL
23 Ainslie Place, Edinburgh EH3 6AJ
238 Main Street, Cambridge
  Massachusetts 02142, USA
54 University Street, Carlton
  Victoria 3053, Australia

Other Editorial Offices:
Arnette Blackwell SA
  1, rue de Lille, 75007 Paris
  France

Blackwell Wissenschafts-Verlag GmbH
  Kurfürstendamm 57
  10707 Berlin, Germany

  Feldgasse 13, A-1238 Wien
  Austria

First published 1984
Second Edition 1996

Set by Setrite Typesetters, Hong Kong
Printed and bound in Great Britain
at the University Press, Cambridge

DISTRIBUTORS

Marston Book Services Ltd
PO Box 87
Oxford OX2 0DT
(*Orders*: Tel: 01865 791155
         Fax: 01865 791927
         Telex: 837515)

North America
Blackwell Science, Inc.
238 Main Street
Cambridge, MA 02142
(*Orders*: Tel: 800 215-1000
            617 876-7000
         Fax: 617 492-5263)

Australia
Blackwell Science Pty Ltd
54 University Street
Carlton, Victoria 3053
(*Orders*: Tel: 03 9347-0300
         Fax: 03 9349-3016)

A catalogue record for this title
is available from the British Library

ISBN 0-86542-850-6

Library of Congress
Cataloging-in-Publication Data

Hall, David M.B.
    The child with a disability/
    David M.B. Hall, Peter D. Hill. — 2nd ed.
      p. cm.
    Rev. ed. of: The child with a handicap. 1984.
    Includes bibliographical references and index.
    ISBN 0-86542-850-6
    1. Handicapped children — Development.
    2. Child development deviations.
    I. Hill, P.D. (Peter David)
    II. Hall, David M.B. Child with a handicap.
    III. Title.
    [DNLM: 1. Child Development Disorders.
    2. Disabled. WS 350.6 H175c 1996]
RJ137.H35   1996
362.4′083 — dc20
DNLM/DLC
for Library of Congress   95-14060

Contents

Preface to the Second Edition, vii

Preface to the First Edition, ix

Acknowledgements, xi

1   The Nature of Disability, 1

2   Intelligence, Development and Assessment, 4

3   A Review of Normal Development, 21

4   Practical Aspects of Assessment, 51

5   Hearing Tests, 67

6   Assessment of Visual Function, 86

7   Coping with Disability, 101

8   Services for Disabled Children, 116

9   Behaviour Problems and their Management, 131

10   Learning Disability, 147

11   Communication Disorders, 173

12   Hearing Loss, 210

13   Visual Impairment, 224

14   Cerebral Palsy, 237

15   Neural Tube Defects and Other Motor Disorders, 277

16   Educational Underachievement, 306

17   Fits, Faints and Funny Turns, 334

Glossary, 363

Appendix: Addresses for Equipment, 375

Index, 377

Preface to the Second Edition

The first edition of *The Child with a Handicap* was based on a popular account of the subject by Grace Woods, entitled *The Handicapped Child*. The late Hugh Jolly, who wrote the Foreword for the first edition, suggested that the change in title would 'emphasise that we were writing about ordinary children who have to contend with disability rather than a special breed of children'. In this, as in so much else, he was ahead of his time. We think he would have approved of our decision to change the title again, to *The Child with a Disability*. This reflects the views of the international disability movement, which stresses that much handicap is the result not just of biological impairments but also of society's unwillingness to adapt its structures and attitudes.

We thought that the production of this second edition would be a relatively simple task; a matter of updating the occasional paragraph as a result of advances in knowledge. This was a naïve view. It soon became clear that the task of writing a single author textbook on disability, which was just about manageable for the first edition, had now become all but impossible and Peter Hill therefore joined David Hall as co-author.

In this past decade there have been spectacular advances in knowledge. The most dramatic have of course been in the new genetics, which hardly existed in 1984. Other examples of progress include classification and understanding of dysmorphic syndromes, new insights into birth asphyxia, technical advances in communication and mobility aids, better equipment for testing hearing and useful developments in early intervention programmes.

Nevertheless, the care of children with a disability, and their families, is still a challenge to the traditional skills of clinical medicine. In every study so far published on the views and experiences of the parents, the topic to which they return over and over again is the way in which they first heard the news of their child's disability. The care, empathy and skill with which the task of news-breaking is undertaken sets the scene for the whole relationship between the professionals and the family. No amount of expertise in medical science can compensate for failures in this vital task. It is this fine balance between caring and communication on the one hand, and sophisticated technical knowledge on the other, which makes the care of children with disabilities so fascinating.

DAVID HALL
Professor of Community Paediatrics
University of Sheffield

PETER HILL
Professor of Child and Adolescent Psychiatry
St George's Hospital Medical School
London

Preface to the First Edition

The first edition of *The Handicapped Child*, by Dr Grace Woods, was published in 1976. At that time it was, to the best of my knowledge, the only single-author British book to offer a comprehensive introduction to the medical aspects of childhood disability and handicap, and it has retained this unique position.

During the eight years since publication of *The Handicapped Child* there have been rapid advances in knowledge and a more gradual evolution in the philosophical aspects of handicap. More attention is now devoted to the child's needs as a person and to the development of his assets and abilities instead of emphasising his disability. This shift in emphasis was recognised in the Warnock Report on Special Education and subsequently in the 1981 Education Act.

The change in title of this book from *The Handicapped Child* to *The Child with a Handicap* reflects these changing attitudes. Although it retains links with Grace Woods' book, and was conceived as a second edition, it has been completely revised and rewritten with much new material, to take account of recent advances in our knowledge of child development, assessment and related subjects.

The Child with a Handicap will be of particular value to doctors who, having undertaken some training in acute paediatric medicine, wish to expand their knowledge of developmental paediatrics as practised both in Child Development Centres, and outside the hospital in general practice, clinics, nurseries and schools. Students in related specialties such as speech therapy, psychology, special education and social work may also find it useful. As plain English has been used in preference to technical language wherever possible, I hope that parents of handicapped children will also find it a helpful source of information.

It is difficult to decide what to include and what to omit in a book on handicap. I elected to concentrate on neurological handicaps, and have not discussed disorders such as juvenile arthritis or haemophilia, which are well described in standard text books and monographs. Some may object to the inclusion of epilepsy and non-accidental injury, and to my suggestion that the paediatrician should undertake basic audiological testing; but I believe that these aspects of paediatrics will increasingly be managed by the new breed of paediatrician, the Consultant in Community Paediatrics. The contents of this book reflect my views as to the work and breadth of knowledge required of this new specialist, and the circumstances in which he will call on the greater expertise of the paediatric audiologist or neurologist.

The inevitable apology must be made for the deficiencies of the English language which lacks a unisex pronoun and has forced me to use the male pronoun for both doctor and child. The latter at least can be justified; liberated female readers can take comfort from the fact that in all studies of developmental problems there is a preponderance of boys!

I am grateful to many friends and colleagues who have helped me in various ways. I owe my interest and training in handicap to J.A.M. Martin, the paediatricians and neurologists at Baragwanath Hospital, Soweto, Johannesburg and to Dr Hugh Jolly, Nancie Finnie and the staff at the Child Development Centre at Charing Cross Hospital. In particular I value the enthusiasm and skill of my colleagues, both medical and non-medical, at St George's Hospital and in the community we serve.

I would like to thank all those who read portions of the manuscript and/or made valuable suggestions: Mike Berger, Peter Hill, Tony Martin,

Alison Hutchinson, Peter Depla, Dorothy Klein, Andrea Pugh, David Taylor, Heather Hunt, Sheila Henderson, Joan Bicknell, Marion Levick, Michael Baraitser, Nick Carter, June Lloyd, Krystina Summers, Matgorzata Borzyskowski, and my wife Sue. Needless to say, the opinions expressed and any errors that remain are my own.

The manuscript was typed by Sandra Garrett, Mary Mitchell, Christine Ryan and Pat Baldwin; Shirley Wheeler prepared the excellent illustrations; Per Saugman provided moral support and J. Russell guided the book through its production stages. I thank them all. Lastly I thank my family for their patience while this book was written. Without their love and support, the task would certainly not have been completed; it might not even have been started.

DAVID HALL
Department of Child Health
St George's Hospital, London

Acknowledgements

So many people have offered help and advice with the second edition that it is difficult to thank them all. If we have inadvertently omitted any of our advisers, we apologise in advance.

Particular thanks go to our colleagues over the years. Peter Hill and David Hall (who worked at St George's Hospital from 1978 to 1993) wish to acknowledge their great debt to all the staff of the Child Development Centre and the departments of Child Psychiatry and Psychology; and to many other members of the St George's staff. In addition, many valuable discussions with friends in the education and social services sectors, and in voluntary organizations, are reflected in this book.

In the first edition we listed the colleagues who helped by reading parts of the manuscript. For this second edition, we particularly wish to thank the following: Mike Berger, Eric Holroyd, Barry McCormick, Judith Dawkins, Tracey Twomey, Tony Martin, David Taylor, Jeremy Turk, Susan Hall, Donald Barltrop, Gillian Baird, Alison Wintgens, Karen Finnie, Tony Moss, Prudence Fuller, Hilary Rattue, Christine Bungay, David Scrutton, Henry Marsh, David Gardner-Medwin, Judith Middleton, Elizabeth Gordon, Claus Newman, Richard Robinson, Michael Patton and Neil Buchanan. We are grateful to the parents and children for permission to use the photographs taken by Christine Bungay (Chapters 14 and 15).

In addition the members and medical advisers of many voluntary organizations sent literature and helpful comments. Special thanks are due to the following: LINK, Tuberose Sclerosis Association, Sturge–Weber Foundation, Child Growth Foundation, REACH, Brittle Bone Society, Spastics Society (now SCOPE) and the Muscular Dystrophy Group.

Lastly, we thank Katrina McCallum at Blackwell Science for her patience and fortitude in dealing with endless revisions and changes to the manuscript.

Needless to say, the opinions expressed and any errors that remain are our responsibility.

CHAPTER 1
The Nature of Disability

Tolstoy opened his novel *Anna Karenina* with the provocative observation that 'Happy families are all alike; every unhappy family is unhappy in its own way.' He might have gone on to remark that every family with a disabled member is disadvantaged in its own way. Some families cope well with the most distressing problems, whereas others are devastated by disabilities that in purely medical terms are far less severe. The differences are to be found in the personalities and life experiences of the child and their parents, the functioning and strength of the family unit and the effectiveness of their network of support among relatives, friends and professional services.

The problems of the disabled child are often complex and multiple. No single profession can have the requisite knowledge and skills to deal with all of them. For example, the diagnosis and management of a child with a language disorder or learning disability might involve a speech therapist, psychologist and teacher. In these disciplines there is less emphasis on, or expectation of, a unitary diagnosis and more emphasis on defining problems that are amenable to intervention; in fact, there are many situations in which the precise medical diagnosis is of little relevance and is of considerably more interest to the doctor than to the child, their family or their teacher! An increasingly vocal body of opinion, particularly those working with learning-disabled adults, believes that disability is not primarily a medical problem and that treating it as such merely creates handicap.

When parents are told that their child is disabled, their perceptions of the child and of themselves are changed. There is still a stigma attached to disability. Goffman (1963) in his classic study described the concept of stigma thus:

the Greeks, who were apparently strong on

visual aids, originated the term stigma to refer to bodily signs designed to expose something unusual and bad about the moral status of the signifier. The signs were cut or burnt into the body and advertised that the bearer was a slave, a criminal, a traitor — a blemished person, ritually polluted, to be avoided, especially in public places . . .

today the term is widely used in something like the original literal sense, but is applied more to the disgrace itself than to the bodily evidence of it.

Parents may reject any medical term which implies disability or handicap; it seems that medical labels and therapy may stigmatize the child as much as their actual disability. An opposite phenomenon may also occur; parents may seek eagerly for a medical label, since our society has come to believe that modern medicine is powerful enough to have an answer for all problems if they can be defined in medical terms.

Some definitions

The terms *disorder, impairment, disability* and *handicap* have distinct meanings and professionals should not use them as if they were interchangeable (Table 1.1). These definitions are valuable since they illustrate an important philosophical point. In recent years the international disability movements have emphasized the social, financial and political aspects of disability and various alternative uses of these terms have been proposed. For example, 'disability' rather than 'handicap' has been used to describe the total experience of being disabled, including the impact of the environment and the role of society. The term 'disadvantage' has also been proposed to encompass the negative effects of discrimination

Table 1.1 Terminology derived from *International Classification of Impairments, Disabilities and Handicaps* (World Health Organization, Geneva, 1980). See text for further discussion

A *Disorder* is a medically definable condition or disease entity (e.g. meningomyelocele)

An *impairment* is any loss or abnormality of psychological, physiological or anatomical structure or function (e.g. paralysis of the legs)

A *disability* is any restriction or lack (resulting from an impairment) of ability to perform an activity in the manner or within the range considered normal for a human being (e.g. inability to walk)

A *handicap* is the impact of the impairment or disability on the person's pursuit or achievement of the goals which are desired by him/her or expected of him/her by society (e.g. unable to undertake any employment that requires mobility or access to public buildings)

The extent to which a disorder, impairment or disability impose a handicap on an individual depends not only on severity but also on:
- the attitudes and ambitions of the child and family
- the financial resources of the family
- secondary or iatrogenic problems created by professionals
- the prejudices of society
- adaptations of the physical environment
- legislation in support of the disabled

against disabled people. Nevertheless, the definitions given in Table 1.1 are still generally accepted by most health professionals in the UK and we do not think they should be abandoned until agreement can be reached on an alternative terminology.

The debate over terminology reflects a deeper dissatisfaction about attitudes to disability. The 'medical model' of disability, which locates the 'problem' within the individual, is caricatured as being obsessed with the pursuit of normality, the search for the perfect body and mind. It is a 'personal tragedy theory', a restricted view of disability as some terrible misfortune which occurs at random to certain individuals. In contrast, the

'social model of disability' locates the problem in society. Individual limitations are acknowledged but are seen as less important than society's failure to ensure that the needs of disabled people are taken into account in its organizations and facilities.

These radically different views are of practical importance. The paediatrician who understands them will recognize that, while medical skills have a part to play, the search for 'the cure' or 'normality' may, contrary to the usual perception, be a preoccupation of the professionals rather than the child or parents.

A practical distinction

For the purposes of this book, it is useful to separate three main groups of clinical problems as they present in practice. The first contains those uncommon, serious and usually disabling conditions which are likely to have a substantial and permanent effect on the child's future development. Blindness, sensorineural deafness, cerebral palsy and intellectual impairment fall into this group. Almost without exception these are of organic origin and are caused by lesions of the central or peripheral nervous system. They are commonly apparent to the parents very early in the child's life and it is most often the parents who first seek professional advice. They can be categorized as *high-severity, low-prevalence conditions*.

The second group includes minor defects which are also of organic origin but do not usually have a profound effect on the child's future. Examples include squint, myopia and conductive hearing loss due to otitis media. Although these conditions may be suspected by parents, they are easily overlooked unless specifically sought, and are often detected as the result of developmental surveillance programmes.

The third group consists of conditions known variously as developmental or neurodevelopmental disorders, developmental delays or learning disabilities. Examples include speech delay, clumsiness and reading difficulties. These do not fit neatly into precise diagnostic categories and there is seldom any readily demonstrated organic basis for them, although there is much speculation in the literature. There may be contributory environmental factors but it is often difficult to decide to what extent a particular problem should be attributed to these. The second and third groups together can be categorized as *low-severity, high-prevalence conditions*.

We recognize, of course, that some children in the second and third categories may have more severe functional problems than some of those in the first; there is inevitably some overlap between them. Nevertheless, we have found that the distinction is of some practical value, since it has implications for epidemiological research, service planning and clinical management.

Mental impairment and learning disability

There have been many changes over the years in the terminology used to describe children with low intellectual capacity — for example, mental handicap, mental retardation, educational subnormality, etc. The currently accepted term in the UK is *learning disability*. In this book we use the term *general (global) learning disability* to denote the presence of lower than normal intelligence (intelligence quotient (IQ)) and *specific learning disability* for conditions such as 'dyslexia', where one particular function or skill is involved. See Chapter 16 for further discussion.

References and further reading

Brechin, A. (ed). (1991) *Handicap in a Social World*. Hodder and Stoughton/The Open University, London/Milton Keynes.

Coleridge, P. (1993) *Disability, Liberation, and Development*. Oxfam (UK and Ireland), Oxford.

Goffman, E. (1963) *Stigma — Notes on the Management of Spoiled Identity*. Pelican Books, Harmondsworth.

CHAPTER 2
Intelligence, Development and Assessment

When intelligence tests were first introduced, around the turn of the century, they were thought to be measuring an innate and inherited quality, determined by the genes received from one's parents. In the late 1920s and early 1930s it was realized that substantial changes in intelligence could sometimes occur in response to changes in the environment. This discovery provoked intense speculation on the relative importance of heredity and environment in determining intelligence; this 'nature vs. nurture' debate still continues today, although it has become very much more sophisticated. It is now clear that there are both genetic and environmental contributions to intelligence, personality and temperament, and that there is a lifelong interaction between them.

It is difficult to define intelligence. It can be regarded as 'the ability to solve unfamiliar problems'. Cynics observe that it is nothing more than the quantity measured by intelligence tests. Some psychologists believe that there is a common factor in all mental processes, irrespective of the nature of the task, and that this can be identified in intelligence tests and distinguished from the influence of individual skills. Spearman, the psychologist who introduced this concept in 1904, called the common factor or underlying intelligence 'g'. Neurophysiological studies show that some brains do process information more rapidly than others, suggesting that there might indeed be a 'g' factor, analogous to the overall processing power of a computer.

On the other hand, the human brain is capable of an amazing range of skills and only a few of these are assessed in standard intelligence tests; the manual dexterity of a craftsman, musical and artistic creativity and excellence in sport are just a few examples of skills which are often ignored when intelligence is assessed and which are not invariably accompanied by other evidence of exceptional intellectual prowess. Questions about the nature of intelligence have also been raised by observations on so-called 'idiot savant' children, who have an extraordinary ability to carry out mathematical processes at high speed or perform prodigious feats of memory and transcription, and yet in all other respects have very limited intellectual powers. Whatever the truth of the matter, it is evident that any psychological assessment which ignores talents outside the narrow domains of traditional intelligence testing is likely to do the child a disservice.

Readers who require a detailed analysis of these issues should consult one of the many comprehensive volumes on the subject. For the developmental paediatrician, the following issues are of immediate clinical relevance.

1 Is the genetic contribution the major determinant of development and intellect? If it is, a child's developmental progress would be expected to follow a predetermined trajectory which could not easily be altered by environmental factors, therapy or teaching.

2 How much do biological influences such as intrauterine malnutrition or birth trauma affect intellectual development?

3 If environmental factors are important, what aspects of the environment are most closely related to development?

4 How can the clinician assess a child's development and the interactions between the factors which affect it?

5 How should the results of this assessment be summarized and presented to the parents and to other professionals?

6 Is intervention effective, and in which form, and for what indications?

Much of the following discussion will focus on

intelligence, since this has been more extensively studied than other parameters; however, similar points can be made about the development of language, personality, temperament, etc. The issues listed above will be briefly examined in turn.

Issues of clinical relevance

The genetic contribution

Heredity makes a significant contribution to intellect and also to other qualities such as temperament and personality, but the exact extent of the genetic contribution is controversial.

The inheritance referred to here is biological, that is, it is carried on the genes rather than transmitted socially through the quality of the environment created by the parents. The distinction between biological and social inheritance has always presented difficult research problems. Data which show a relationship between the intelligence quotient (IQ) of parents and that of their offspring could indicate either biological transmission or the effects of social and environmental variables. Studies of identical and non-identical twin pairs reared separately and together suggest that up to 80% of the variance in intelligence in a Western European or North American population can be attributed to genetic transmission. It must be emphasized that this is a statistical statement about a population selected for study. It does not preclude the possibility that, in one particular subject or subpopulation at a particular point in time, the environment may be of much greater or much less importance in determining intelligence. For instance, very wide variation in environmental stimulation in a particular population would increase the environmental effect. The genetic influence is not confined to the effect on total IQ scores; see Table 2.1 for examples.

Pathological influences on intelligence

Intrauterine and postnatal pathological factors

Table 2.1 The genetic influence is not confined to the effect on total IQ scores

1 A correlation between the abilities of children and their parents can be shown not only for total IQ scores but also for the strengths and weaknesses revealed by individual subtests

2 The correlation between the IQ scores of children and those of their parents changes over time. It is lowest in infancy and rises steadily throughout childhood, adolescence and adult life

3 Unusual patterns of development such as bottom shuffling or late language development often run in families (pp. 49 and 188)

4 Personality types and temperamental traits may also show familial traits — for example, hyperactivity (p. 329)

5 In 'gifted' twins there is also a strong genetic influence on intelligence, indicating that this operates at the upper end of the IQ distribution as well as within the 'normal' range

6 Some dysmorphic syndromes (p. 149) are associated with particular patterns of behaviour and development — 'behavioural phenotypes'. Although not invariable, these occur with sufficient frequency to suggest that there is a genetic influence at work. Examples: Angelman's syndrome, Williams' syndrome (see Glossary)

such as malnutrition must be regarded as environmental influences on brain development, and therefore on neurological and intellectual function. Pathological factors which affect the physical structure and growth of the nervous system could be responsible both for developmental disorders and for at least a part of normal variation. For example, some developmental problems might result from subtle perinatal brain damage, which could be either focal or diffuse. The literature relating brain disorders to problems of intellect, learning and behaviour is diverse and confusing and is summarized in Table 2.2. Clearly, the relationships are very complex. It is naïve and misleading to attribute developmental disorder to ill-defined 'brain damage' without considering what this means. The interactions with the child's psychosocial background are also crucial;

Table 2.2 The neurological contribution to understanding problems of intellect, learning and behaviour in children

---

1 Organically based psychological sequelae of brain damage can occur in the absence of neurological physical signs

2 Behaviour and psychiatric disorders are more commonly seen in children with brain pathology than in those without, and this is in part a function of the pathology itself, rather than any functional disability which it may have caused

3 There is no distinctive pattern of behavioural or psychiatric disorder which can be attributed to brain pathology. All patterns of disturbance can be found in children with and in those without brain pathology. The exception is the syndrome of gross social disinhibition, which may be associated with frontal lobe damage

4 Primate experiments suggest that the functions of damaged areas of the brain (excluding motor areas and vital centres) are not immutable and the intact areas can often make up for any deficiencies, although at the cost of a slight reduction in overall intellectual capacity. Head injury studies support the idea that, in children, brain injury is more likely to result in a global intellectual deficit than in a specific developmental or learning disability. Nevertheless, although the young child's brain shows considerable plasticity of function, some hemisphere specialization is present very early in life (p. 317)

5 Disturbances in psychological functioning are probably more likely to result from abnormal brain activity (e.g. epilepsy) than from loss of brain substance

6 A threshold phenomenon appears to govern the relationship between the severity of brain damage and the sequelae; the damage must reach a certain degree of severity before sequelae become detectable

7 Severe intrauterine malnutrition is associated with mild reduction in all parameters of intelligence and particularly motor function; possibly this is due to reduction of neuronal numbers and connections, notably in the cerebellum. Similar effects may result from prolonged postnatal malnutrition. There is an association between early growth faltering (first 6 months) and fine motor and speech impairment

8 Whatever the nature of the biological insult to the brain, psychosocial factors strongly affect the outcome by interacting with the child's intrinsic problems and become an increasingly important influence as the child grows older. An adverse environment greatly exaggerates the effects of brain damage, whereas a good one minimizes them

9 Severe asphyxial brain damage in the neonate can cause cerebral palsy and learning disability but rarely causes severe learning disability *without* cerebral palsy. However, impaired concentration, learning and motor co-ordination, without cerebral palsy, may be associated with other forms of brain injury, such as may occur in association with extreme prematurity or hypoglycaemia

10 If one excludes cases of identifiable perinatal brain damage associated with obvious neurological abnormality in the neonatal period, some relationship still exists between perinatal disorder and intellectual and learning deficits, but the correlations are weak and it is far from certain that the relationship is causal. In studying such relationships it is vital to control for the numerous psychosocial factors which contribute both to the occurrence of perinatal disorder (e.g. prematurity) and to the outcome

11 Many developmental disorders are probably due not to focal brain lesions but to other types of dysfunction. For example, in attention deficit disorder there may be an abnormality in the handling of neurotransmitters (p. 315). New imaging methods such as positron emission tomography (PET) scans and echo-planar imaging, developed from magnetic resonance techniques, suggest that in this condition and in obsessive compulsive disorder there are atypical patterns of brain activity, which can be corrected by medication

12 Some learning problems, for example dyslexia, may occasionally be associated with abnormal neuronal migration (the process by which neurons align themselves into columns and layers during early brain development). These abnormalities may be under genetic control. Similarly, there are structural asymmetries between the left and right hemisphere which have some relationship to the development of language and reading skills

13 Brain function can be considered in terms of circuits and systems which share and exchange information at so-called 'convergence zones'. It seems likely that differences in the structure and function of these circuits and zones may ultimately explain the genetic influences set out in Table 2.1.

14 Children with brain damage may receive drugs (e.g. anticonvulsants) which may adversely affect behaviour

furthermore, it is only the latter which might be amenable to change.

Environmental influences

In some circumstances intelligence is clearly related to environmental factors. For example, Rutter noted that 'there is abundant evidence that mild mental retardation is extremely common among children brought up in city slums. Intelligence develops and is not a "given" capacity. Its development is a social process strictly dependent upon the quality and organisation of the human environment in which it evolves.'

In extreme circumstances, environmental manipulation can lead to substantial gains in intelligence; some relevant studies are described later in this chapter. It is more difficult to discover if this is also true in families where the parents are of normal intelligence, material conditions are adequate and family life is stable. Environmental measures such as social class, income or quality of housing are no more than crude indicators of child-rearing styles and are too insensitive to be useful in unravelling this problem. It seems likely that the skill of the parents in encouraging and extending their child's development throughout childhood is the key factor. The term 'microenvironment' is useful to describe the innumerable small details of daily child-rearing and experience, the extent to which the child is encouraged to play and to practise skills, and so on (see also pp. 31–5).

Measurement and analysis of the microenvironment are difficult, but various methods have been devised, such as the home stimulation inventory. Correlations are found between environmental measures and the child's abilities and developmental progress, but the nature of the association is not always clear. The correlation may simply indicate that parents find it more rewarding to teach a child who is good-natured and intelligent. Nevertheless, there is some evidence that microenvironmental factors do influence intellect, personality and temperament.

The concepts of interaction and resilience

The development of any child is determined not by genetic or environmental factors in isolation but by the interaction between them. The child's temperament and abilities affect the parents' responses to the child — in other words, the child contributes to the creation of his/her own environment. Parental responses and interactions are also influenced by the extent to which the child matches their own preconceived ideas about the kind of child they hoped to have. This has been called the 'goodness of fit' between parental expectations and the child's actual temperament and personality.

All children are exposed to some degree of stress and adversity, but they vary in their resilience or vulnerability in response to life experiences. The differences are partly dependent on genetic factors such as temperament but are also affected by protective factors in the environment (Table 2.3).

Assessment

To many people 'assessment' has come to mean administration of a developmental or psychological test, but this is only a small part of the assessment process, and in many cases it may even be irrelevant to the presenting complaint. Assessment has been defined as 'the systematic collection, organization and interpretation of information about a person and their situation'. It should be conducted for a purpose rather than as a ritual. Table 2.4 summarizes the various circumstances in which assessment may be undertaken. A very different approach is needed in each of these situations and it is vital to identify and deal with the real problem — for example, a conflict over management.

A complete assessment might include the following components: definition of the main problem(s); evaluation of the genetic, biological, environmental and pathological factors which contribute to the problem; an estimate of the child's present development status — this may

Table 2.3 Model of interrelations between risk, stress, sources of support, and coping (based on data from the Kauai Longitudinal Study). From Werner and Smith (1982)

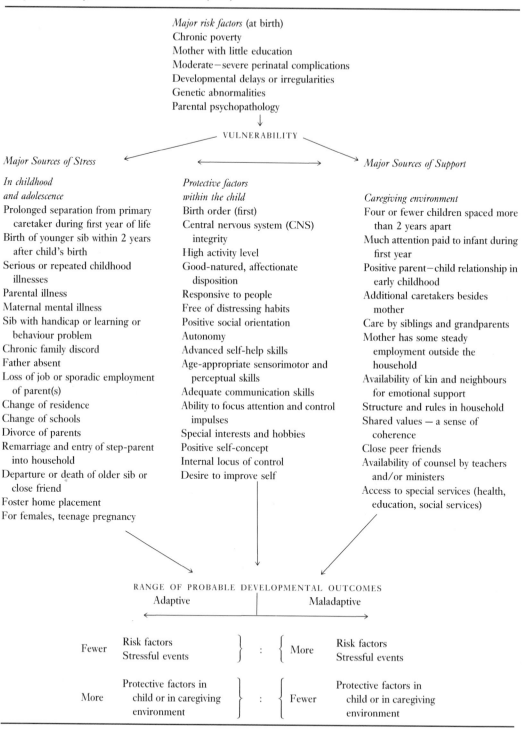

Major risk factors (at birth)
Chronic poverty
Mother with little education
Moderate–severe perinatal complications
Developmental delays or irregularities
Genetic abnormalities
Parental psychopathology
↓
VULNERABILITY

Major Sources of Stress   *Major Sources of Support*

*In childhood
and adolescence*
Prolonged separation from primary
   caretaker during first year of life
Birth of younger sib within 2 years
   after child's birth
Serious or repeated childhood
   illnesses
Parental illness
Maternal mental illness
Sib with handicap or learning or
   behaviour problem
Chronic family discord
Father absent
Loss of job or sporadic employment
   of parent(s)
Change of residence
Change of schools
Divorce of parents
Remarriage and entry of step-parent
   into household
Departure or death of older sib or
   close friend
Foster home placement
For females, teenage pregnancy

*Protective factors
within the child*
Birth order (first)
Central nervous system (CNS)
   integrity
High activity level
Good-natured, affectionate
   disposition
Responsive to people
Free of distressing habits
Positive social orientation
Autonomy
Advanced self-help skills
Age-appropriate sensorimotor and
   perceptual skills
Adequate communication skills
Ability to focus attention and control
   impulses
Special interests and hobbies
Positive self-concept
Internal locus of control
Desire to improve self

Caregiving environment
Four or fewer children spaced more
   than 2 years apart
Much attention paid to infant during
   first year
Positive parent–child relationship in
   early childhood
Additional caretakers besides
   mother
Care by siblings and grandparents
Mother has some steady
   employment outside the
   household
Availability of kin and neighbours
   for emotional support
Structure and rules in household
Shared values — a sense of
   coherence
Close peer friends
Availability of counsel by teachers
   and/or ministers
Access to special services (health,
   education, social services)

RANGE OF PROBABLE DEVELOPMENTAL OUTCOMES
Adaptive   Maladaptive

Fewer   Risk factors   } : {   More   Risk factors
        Stressful events   Stressful events

More   Protective factors in } : {   Fewer Protective factors in
        child or in caregiving   child or in caregiving
        environment   environment

Table 2.4 Reasons for assessment

1 There is parental or professional concern over the development of a child previously thought to be normal

2 A child is under regular supervision because he/she is 'at risk', e.g. because of a family history of a handicapping disorder or a previous cerebral insult

3 A child with a known disability attends for routine review

4 A child with a known disability attends because the parents wish to discuss a new problem

5 A child with a known disability needs an up-to-date report to facilitate assessment of special educational needs

vary from a rough approximation to a detailed set of measurements using a psychometric test battery; tests of hearing and vision; evaluation by speech therapist, physiotherapist or occupational therapist; the organization of an intervention programme; and a review of the response to intervention.

Methods of assessment

For the paediatrician, the usual approach would be an interview with the parents, followed by involvement of the child in simple play and/or observation of their spontaneous activities. The information obtained in this way is interpreted using a developmental scale, together with one's general knowledge of child development. A developmental scale is simply a means of arranging information about the mean ages at which children achieve various milestones. The way in which information is elicited about the items in the scale is left to the discretion of the clinician, and the extent of normal variation is indicated only in the most general terms. Items are classified into convenient, though arbitrary, categories, for example: (i) posture and large movements; (ii) vision and fine movement; (iii) hearing and speech; and (iv) social behaviour and play.

There are many clinical situations in which it might be sufficient for the paediatrician to state,

for example, that a child aged 3 years is functioning at the level of an 18 month old. Parents find it easy to understand this concept and can state whether or not they agree with the doctor's estimate. This information can also be expressed as a developmental quotient:

$$\frac{\text{Developmental age}}{\text{Chronological age}} \times 100$$

However, this practice has some disadvantages; it has an aura of accuracy which is not justified by the precision of the test procedures used, it conceals variations between different aspects of development, and it is mistaken by parents and sometimes other professionals for an IQ and is interpreted accordingly.

Using parents as a source of information

There is a widespread belief that, to parents, 'all their geese are swans', and that therefore their report of the child's abilities is likely to be hopelessly exaggerated and quite unreliable. As a result, excessive reliance is placed on the small and often unrepresentative sample of behaviour which can be elicited during a brief assessment session, and the parents' vast store of knowledge about their child is ignored. Yet only the parents can know whether the child's performance is representative of his/her true abilities or can explain the history of individual items of behaviour — why, for example, a word is used in a particular way or why the child shows an unexpected reaction to a task. Furthermore, the way in which they describe the child and his/her activities gives some insight into the quality of the child's microenvironment.

There are several reasons for the apparent unreliability of developmental information obtained from parents. Firstly, retrospective recall of the times at which milestones were achieved in the past is known to be unreliable. Secondly, where the child's current abilities are concerned, the questions put to the parents are often ambiguous and their replies are not subjected to further critical probing. Thirdly, it is usually the parents' interpretation of what they observe rather than their observations which is unreliable; resentment is generated by the failure of doctors and other professionals to recognize this distinction. Agreement must be established first with the parents on what the child can and cannot do, with specific examples being cited. Only then can the significance of the child's abilities be discussed.

Occasionally, parental accounts do seem to substantially over- or underestimate a child's abilities, in comparison with what is seen during assessment. This discrepancy is itself of considerable diagnostic importance, for the parents' lack of understanding may explain many management problems and might be a contributing cause in some developmental disorders. We have seen a small number of parents whose self-deception about their child's abilities is so extreme that it takes on the quality of a delusional system (Chapter 7). A few parents are more consciously manipulative and their description is distorted in order to obtain the opinion they desire. Even more rarely, they may deliberately try to mislead the doctor, perhaps for medicolegal reasons. All of these situations are uncommon, but they must be recognized if the family is to be helped. The parents' view of the child's problem is every bit as important as an 'objective' assessment of the child's development.

Psychological tests

Many doctors regard assessments based on interview and observation as crude and inaccurate, and feel that 'proper' tests, using more structured procedures, are essential for diagnostic precision. It is therefore worth noting that psychologists define a test as 'any systematic procedure for observing a person's behaviour and describing it with the aid of a numerical scale or a category system'. A systematic interview or an observation session constitutes a test in terms of this definition. The important question to ask is not 'Is this test accurate enough?' but 'Will this procedure provide reliable information relevant to the problem in hand?'

When it does seem necessary to quantify one's observations accurately, a formal test procedure may be used. For example, it may be useful to decide whether a deaf child has normal intelligence when confronted with non-verbal tasks, or to assess how much a child's IQ has changed following a brain injury. The mechanics of test administration are not difficult to master; the skill lies in the interpretation of the results, which calls for a knowledge of the psychological literature. For this reason, the supply of many test kits is restricted to qualified clinical or educational psychologists, who will normally be responsible for the detailed assessment of these more complex problems.

Psychological tests are designed to make systematic observations and quantify them. The results are then related to normative data; in other words, they are compared either with the individual's own previous performance or, more often, with the results obtained by a group of similar individuals. The first of these approaches is useful in, for example, planned teaching programmes for children with learning disabilities (e.g. Portage, p. 127), as a means of evaluating progress. The majority of the psychometric tests used in clinical assessment are of the second type, and the most familiar are those used to measure intelligence (IQ tests) and language development. Procedures are also available for the examination of personality, behaviour, brain damage, and many other factors. Table 2.5 summarizes some of the tests in common use. An important distinction is made between tests of IQ and tests of attainment, such as reading or writing (p. 310). Table 2.5 also includes examples of procedures for measuring the quality of the child's environment and for assessing daily living skills and independence.

Many psychometric tests are standardized. This means that they require a specified set of materials, the instructions and mode of presentation are precisely stated and the results are assessed by comparison with the known performance of normal children from a comparable background. The tester may of course use their discretion to depart from the specified procedure

Table 2.5 Psychometric tests and scales in common use (with age range in parentheses)

Tests of mental ability and developmental scales
Bayley Scales of Infant Development (2 months–2.5 years)
British Ability Scales (2.5 years–17 years)
Gesell Development Schedule (4 weeks–6 years)
Goodenough–Harris drawing test (3–15 years)
Griffiths Scales (0–8 years)
Kaufman test (2.5–12.5 years)
McCarthy Scales of Infant Development (2.5–8.5 years)
Merrill–Palmer Preschool Performance Test (1.5–5.25 years)
Miller test battery (2–6 years)
Raven's Progressive Coloured Matrices (young children and people with learning
    disabilities)
Bellman and Cash — schedule of growing skills (0–5 years)
Stanford–Binet Intelligence Scale (2 years–adult)
Wechsler Preschool and Primary Scale of Intelligence (WPPSI) (4–6.5 years)
Wechsler Intelligence Scale for Children (WISC) (6.5–16 years)

Specialized tests and applications
Bender Gestalt Test (visual motor perception) (4 years and over)
Callier–Azusa scale (visual impairment)
Columbia Mental Maturity Scale (verbal and physical handicaps) (3–10 years)
Frostig Developmental Test of Visual Perception (learning disabilities)
Hiskey–Nebraska Test of Learning Aptitude (hearing defects) (3–17 years)
HOME Inventory (measurement of environment)
Illinois Test of Psycholinguistic Abilities (speech and language problems)
    (2–10 years)
Leiter international scale (intelligence in the presence of communication defects and
    multiple impairments) (2–16 years)
Movement assessment battery for children (motor disability, clumsiness)
    (5–14 years)
Reynell–Zinkin scales (vision defects) (0–5 years)
Snijders–Oomen Non-verbal Intelligence Scales (all forms of verbal communication
    handicap) (2.5–7 years)
Williams Intelligence Test (vision defects) (5–15 years)

Language and vocabulary tests
British Picture Vocabulary Scale (2.5–18 years)
Clinical Evaluation of Language Fundamentals (CELF)
Edinburgh Articulation Test
Lowe–Costello Symbolic Play Test (1–3 years)
Macarthur Scale
Peabody Picture Vocabulary Test (2.5–18 years)
Renfrew Articulation Test
Reynell Development Language Scale (1.5–6 years)
Stycar Language Test (up to 7 years)
Test for the Reception of Grammar (TROG)

continued on p. 12

Table 2.5 (*continued*)

Attainment tests
Holborn Reading Test
Neale Analysis of Reading Ability (6–12 years)
Schonell Graded Word Reading Test
Wide-range Achievement Test (5 years–adult)
Wechsler Objective Reading Dimensions (WORD) (6–16 years)

Assessment scales linked to remedial programmes
Behaviour Assessment Battery (children and adults)
Parent Involvement Project
Portage Project
Progress Assessment Chart (PAC)

Functional scales of disability
Barthel Scale
Scale devised by Office of Population Censuses and Surveys (OPCS)
Townsend scale

---

but the more this is done, the less accurate the result will be.

New tests are checked for reliability, to ensure that comparable results would be obtained by different observers or on different occasions. The most important characteristic of a test procedure is its validity. Validity is concerned with questions such as: what is this test actually measuring? does this test give a true measure of the child's abilities in this particular area? what deductions can be made from the results? and do these results imply that the child has a problem which can be expected to interfere with future progress and prospects?

In general, any assessment of a young child should be regarded primarily as a measure of current functioning, a method of quantifying what the child has learnt up to the present moment. Prediction of future progress or ultimate intellectual potential from measures made in early childhood is unwise, unless the child's abilities are repeatedly found to be in the severely learning-disabled range. Many factors contribute to the difficulties of prediction, including the intrinsic deficiencies of the test; variations in the skill of the tester; anxiety, shyness, lack of motivation or undiagnosed hearing loss in the child; and unusual patterns or temporary setbacks in development. The tester has to make a subjective judgement of the extent to which these factors might invalidate the results. Also, since the child's ultimate abilities depend to some extent on experiences yet to come, it is intrinsically unlikely that one could predict their future on the basis of their performance in the first few years of life.

Several studies have shown that by 2½ years of age there begins to be some correlation between the test scores and later intelligence. The ability of an IQ score to predict academic and career progress increases throughout childhood. In the majority of children IQ is a surprisingly stable quantity; significant and occasionally dramatic changes can occur, but these are exceptional. Furthermore, it is not possible to predict how a particular life event or experience will affect the IQ of an individual child. Most children will tend to seek activities and environments in which they feel most comfortable, so that their intellectual powers are not encouraged to grow; but a few may deliberately engage in tasks which stretch their capacity and perhaps increase their IQ as a result.

Tests available to doctors. The Griffiths test is the most readily available formal test for the paediatrician. It is a standardized scale for children aged 0–8 years. It requires a special test kit, which is only supplied when a training period has been completed. The results are presented as a developmental profile (Fig. 2.1). The doctor who can use only this test is at a definite disadvantage compared with the psychologist, who can select the most appropriate procedure from an extensive repertoire. Furthermore, some aspects of this test are open to criticism on technical grounds. In particular, the construction of the test does not allow easy separation of language from non-verbal items.

Information from other sources

Further information from playgroup or nursery leaders, speech therapists or the health visitor may be very revealing, particularly where the quality of parental care is suspect. Serious diagnostic errors may result from neglecting to cross-check information in this way. Placement in a suitable playgroup or nursery, preferably with experienced and well-trained staff, provides an opportunity for more prolonged assessment, and the child's progress in this new environment may throw further light on their problems. Indeed, the response to specialized and expert teaching is of such diagnostic importance that it may be unwise to venture any final opinion until this has been undertaken.

Misconceptions about developmental assessment

Many errors in developmental assessment are made through failure to consider the reasons for, and diagnostic implications of, the child's failure on a particular item. For example, drawing is classified as a fine motor skill, but inability to draw a recognizable figure of a man at the appropriate age could be due to learning disability, poor vision, ataxia or lack of previous experience with drawing materials. No developmental tests

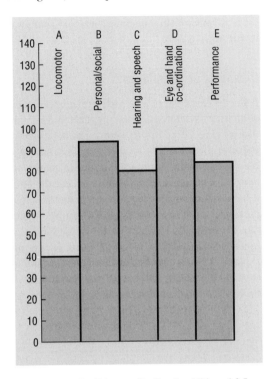

Fig. 2.1 The Griffiths test. Profile of a child aged 3.5 years with 'delayed motor development'. Diagnosis: muscular dystrophy (Duchenne).

will reliably reveal defects of vision or hearing. Specific tests must be done to detect these. Inability to climb stairs might indicate immature motor development or the much more serious diagnosis of Duchenne muscular dystrophy; observation and physical examination would be essential in differential diagnosis.

There is a very wide range of both ability and co-operation among normal young children. The limits are so wide that children with major impairments may achieve important milestones within the normal time; for example, a child with spastic hemiplegia may walk well before 18 months; conversely, many children whose milestones fall outside the 'normal' range (i.e. the slowest 3%) turn out to be normal. Also, few developmental scales make provision for describing children whose behaviour patterns are

14   *Chapter 2*

deviant rather than immature, as, for example, in autism.

Diagnosis or formulation?

A doctor is trained to approach clinical problems with what is known as 'the medical model' of disease (Fig. 2.2). This has proved to be a highly effective model and is responsible, for example, for the discovery and prevention of the causes of congenital rubella and kernicterus. Nevertheless, it has serious limitations in the care of the disabled person. Even if an exact diagnosis can be made, the condition is unlikely to be susceptible to medical treatment. It is often more useful to explain a child's disability to the parents at three separate diagnostic levels. The first is the type of problem — for example, hearing loss or learning

disability. The second is the cause or causes — for example, congenital rubella or tuberose sclerosis. The parents may have to be told that the cause cannot be determined even after extensive investigation, but they must at least be clear about the distinction between the type of problem and its cause (see also pp. 1–3). The third level of diagnosis is the severity and functional effects of the disability — in other words, the extent to which the impairment or disability may lead to handicap. These three levels are useful in the preparation of written reports for parents and for those assessing special educational needs.

When dealing with high-prevalence, low-severity conditions (p. 3), the limitations of the medical model become much more apparent. The cause of concern is the child's failure to perform in one or more areas of development at

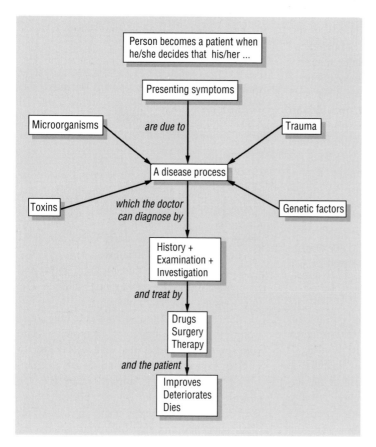

Fig. 2.2 The medical model.

the level expected for their age. So-called diagnoses such as 'minimal brain dysfunction' are really no more than circular definitions (Fig. 2.3) and add nothing to the understanding or management of the problem.

The questions which must be asked about the child with a 'developmental disorder' are different from those relevant to more serious impairments. Firstly, why has this particular child been brought for consultation at this point in time, whereas the parents of others with identical levels of ability may never seek professional advice? For example, a parent may complain about a boy's clumsiness, but the real problem may be their own depression which makes it hard to cope with the child's natural exuberance.

Secondly, how does one define a developmental disorder? A child might be said to have a developmental disorder if he/she scored more than 2 standard deviations below the mean (i.e. below the 3rd centile as an approximation) on a particular measure, for example a language test such as the Reynell (p. 11); but this finding does not necessarily predict future problems. The variations in normal development are such that a developmental disorder is almost impossible to define with any degree of precision.

Thirdly, it is commonly assumed that a child of unintelligent parents who performs poorly is slow because of genetically determined low intellect. The parents of such children make less effective use of available services than more fortunate families, and yet it is in precisely this area of 'subcultural deprivation' that efforts to improve the environment and enrich the child's experiences may be most beneficial.

Fourthly, when faced with a child whose development and behaviour are deviant, one has to consider to what extent these observations are explained by an interaction between inborn factors in the child and the responses of the child's family; it must not be assumed that the parents are the sole cause of the child's problem!

Lastly, there is the question of 'labelling'; will it be helpful or detrimental to the family and to the child to use terms such as specific language delay or learning disability? The advantages and disadvantages of labelling have already been mentioned (p. 2).

There is no single solution to these difficulties, but a change of orientation may help. Instead of thinking in terms of diagnosis and treatment, it may be more profitable to adopt an 'educational model' (Fig. 2.4). The multidisciplinary team can

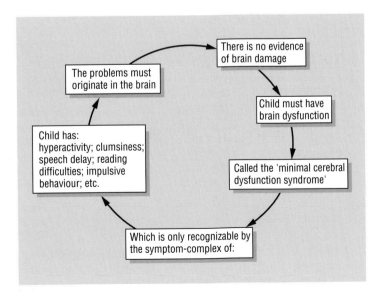

Fig. 2.3 Circular definitions.

formulate the child's problems in such a way that, while the question of diagnosis is not ignored, the emphasis is on setting goals and working towards them.

Intervention

The term 'intervention' is preferable to therapy and treatment, which have narrow medical connotations. It encompasses speech therapy, occupational therapy and physiotherapy; nursery experience; specialized education; behavioural or psychotherapeutic management by a psychologist or a psychiatrist; and social support of all kinds. Most intervention programmes for children with disabilities have more in common with education than with the medical tradition of a specific treatment for a particular disease. Sometimes an assessment is in itself a useful intervention even if no further help is needed. A good intervention programme should consist of four stages:

1 definition of the problem and of the child's current developmental status;
2 the setting of realistic goals;
3 devising and executing a means of achieving these goals;
4 evaluation of the result.

Is intervention effective?

The effectiveness of intervention programmes is important not only to practitioners but also to health planners and economists. The medical and educational models generate different research questions. Medical approaches to research favour the use of the classic randomized controlled trial (RCT), but few acceptable RCTs have been conducted in the field of childhood disability. There are several reasons for this: it is very difficult to find children with similar characteristics and disabilities; it is almost impossible, for both practical and ethical reasons, to assign a

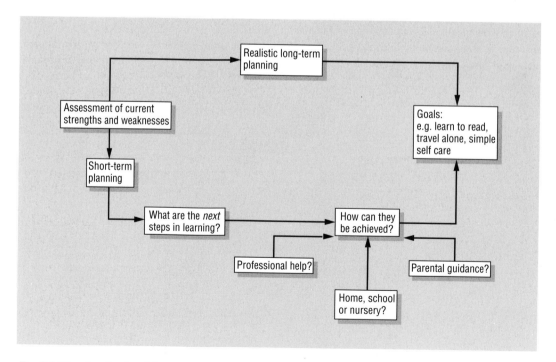

Fig. 2.4 The educational model.

disabled child to a 'no-treatment' group; the skill with which the intervention is carried out may be a more important variable than the potential effectiveness of the technique, so that the results cannot be generalized to other therapists in other situations; prevention of deterioration is an important outcome but is rarely measured; and often the time-scale over which changes might be seen is too long for most research programmes to encompass. The fact that evidence is difficult to accumulate does not mean, however, that intervention is ineffective.

Research in social sciences and in education utilizes other strategies; the RCT is seldom used. Often the outcomes to be measured are different from those used in medical research. For example, parent satisfaction, family functioning, the mental health of the child and siblings, or the capacity of the family to perceive their experiences in a positive light may be considered more relevant than changes in the range of movement of a joint or the number of yards a child can walk.

Medical staff, whose views are influential, need to be aware of the differences in the ways professionals perceive their role and their goals in the care of the disabled child; they must not undermine their colleagues by a narrow and often negative focus on the immediate benefits of an activity or programme.

Five aspects of intervention will be considered here:
1 the possibility of making major increases in the low intellectual capacity of children from a poor environment ('subcultural deprivation');
2 the potential for improving the development of children with learning disability;
3 the effects of nursery education;
4 the differences between schools;
5 the effects of therapy.

Subcultural deprivation

Poverty, poor housing, frequent rehousing or homelessness, domestic violence and lack of parental education all have an adverse effect on a child's school progress. These conditions affect poor indigenous people, new immigrants, refugees and families afflicted by misfortune, illness or alcoholism. In some parts of the country, entire communities have lived in poverty for several generations and see no hope of improving their situation; this has given rise to the concept of 'subcultural deprivation'.

From a social and political perspective, the most important studies on intervention with such families are programmes like Head Start in the USA, initiated by Presidents Kennedy and Johnson. The motivation for these programmes was a belief that poor, unintelligent parents would produce children who would follow the same pattern — the 'cycle of disadvantage'. It was hoped, perhaps naïvely, that a short period of intensive intervention with the child would enable him/her to make better use of schooling so that the child would not be at a disadvantage compared with their better-off peers. Many of the early Head Start programmes found that improvement was produced by interventions such as enthusiastic nursery teaching, but it was poorly sustained, although there were some small gains in motivation and parental attitudes.

Subsequently, more ambitious programmes provided an intensive programme of daily infant stimulation followed by high-quality day care with nursery school teaching; they also offered mothers instruction in child care and training for employment. Other schemes have addressed the needs of the mother rather than those of the child. For example, interventions by health visitors have been shown to reduce postnatal depression (which has an adverse effect on child development) and increase self-esteem.

Even the most ambitious intervention programmes failed to bring about dramatic gains in IQ scores. However, parental attitudes to education improved; for the child, progress and achievement in school, drop-out rates, teenage pregnancy rates, criminal offences, college attendance and stability of relationships all changed for the better. Such interventions are expensive, but are good value for money.

Children who start life with a biological

disadvantage (extreme prematurity, chronic ill-ness, malformations, etc.) may be at increased risk of developmental and behavioural problems, particularly in poor social circumstances. Early intervention programmes are probably highly cost-effective in this situation.

Learning disability

In the famous Brooklands experiment (Tizard, 1960), children with severe learning disability were removed from a featureless institutional routine and placed in a normal stimulating house-hold environment. This classic study laid the foundation for modern ideas on learning disability by demonstrating that, even in the most severely impaired child, important gains can be made by providing appropriate experiences.

The benefits of preschool nursery experience

Placement in nursery or nursery school is often prescribed as a means of overcoming early social disadvantage and 'treating' developmental delay. This provides valuable experience and enjoyable social contact for the children and is a great help to parents. These benefits alone would be reason enough to regard universal access to preschool provision as a desirable goal. In addition, nursery school education may provide the child with a better start in formal schooling, although day nurseries, which tend to provide less structure and lack coherent teaching objectives, do not offer the same advantage and are less likely to compensate for inadequate exposure to language at home. The benefits of early nursery experiences are greater and more persistent if parents are involved in the programme from the start.

The role of the school

The importance of the school in the development and progress of the individual child is discussed on p. 309.

The effectiveness of therapy

Few evaluation studies have been done, but re-search does suggest some basic principles. Firstly, if the child's developmental disorder appears to be related to environmental factors, intervention needs to be intensive and prolonged if sustained progress is to be achieved. Secondly, whatever the child's problem may be, programmes which involve the parent are more likely to be effective; professional time may often be better spent on counselling, instructing and demonstrating than on direct treatment of the child. Thirdly, it is vital to specify the goals of treatment and therapy and to review them from time to time. Sometimes, an apparently small improvement in function, obtained only after considerable effort, may greatly improve the child's quality of life and the parents' morale. Thus, without specified goals, it is im-possible to assess the impact of any intervention.

Is there a 'sensitive period' for intervention?

One striking feature of developmental paediatrics has been the emphasis on the preschool child. This has come about for two reasons. Firstly, children with disability come to the attention of paediatricians at an early age, whereas educational services until recently have only been available from the age of 5 onwards. The second and more fundamental reason for concentrating attention on preschool children arises from an implicit assumption about child development: not only that environmental influences are important, but that they are of overriding importance and have irreversible effects in the first few years of life.

The early work of John Bowlby in the 1950s dealt specifically with mother−infant attachment but had a profound effect on ideas about all aspects of child development. His findings implied that inadequate or adverse early experiences inevitably led to irreversible intellectual and emotional damage and it followed that services for the young child should have a major impact on performance through the school years into adult life. A parallel concept was the 'sensitive period' (also called 'critical period'). This meant that, if a child failed to acquire a particular ability or level of development by a certain age, he/she might never do so.

To some extent, the apparent importance of early experience may be an artefact. Most children who start life in a poor environment remain in that environment throughout childhood, and there is therefore a built-in correlation between early childhood adversity and ultimate outcome. Of course, experiences in the first few years of life are very important, particularly with respect to the development of secure attachments and of language; but the environment can be changed with beneficial effects at any point in childhood. Several lines of evidence support this view.

Firstly, further research has shown that early, brief separation of the infant and parent or main carer is not necessarily damaging and can even be beneficial, as mildly stressful experiences may help the child to cope with adversity later on in life. The effects depend on the circumstances and handling of the separation, the quality of substitute care, the previous experiences of the child, and perhaps the child's temperament and adaptability.

Secondly, there are at least two reports of children adopted in mid-childhood (7–9 years) from orphanages in Korea and Vietnam. These children showed substantial gains in both intellect and emotional maturity. Although the outcome was probably not quite as favourable as with very early adoption, the results show that the damage caused by early adversity, even if severe and prolonged, is not irreversible. Further evidence regarding recovery after severe deprivation in early childhood comes from individual case-studies, of whom the Koluchova twins and Genie are the most famous.

Learning to see and hear is associated with fundamental changes in the structure and function of the developing nervous system. In experimental animals, there is for some functions a sensitive period of development; if the animal does not acquire the necessary exposure to visual and auditory stimuli during this period, it will never do so thereafter. In humans, it seems likely that the same principle applies, but the duration of the sensitive period is not yet known; it is almost certainly measured in years rather than months, and is unlikely to have a sharply defined end-point. See Chapters 12 and 13, and Bishop and Mogford (1988) for further discussion.

The fear that a sensitive period of development might be 'missed', with disastrous consequences, has sometimes resulted in an unjustified sense of urgency when dealing with suspected developmental problems in early childhood. Of course, there are some situations where a child's development is being avoidably neglected or impaired and in these circumstances urgent action may be imperative. In many cases, however, discussion and negotiation with the parents will secure their understanding and co-operation. In comparison with this advantage, a few months' delay are of little consequence.

Conclusion

Professional skills are scarce and it is reasonable to devote them to the children who lag behind the majority, but in the long run the universal availability of a preschool educational system which encourages parents' involvement and offers adequate remedial teaching would greatly reduce the need to make arbitrary judgements about developmental disorders and learning disabilities.

References and further reading

Ball, C. (1994) *Start Bright: the Importance of Early Learning.* Royal Society of Arts, London.

Bishop, D. and Mogford, K. (1988) *Language Development in Exceptional Circumstances.* Churchill Livingstone, Edinburgh.

Conner, J.P. (1988) Educating poor minority children. *Scientific American,* **259**(5), 24–30.

Fonagy, P., Steele, M., Steele, H., Higgitt, A. and Target, M. (1994) The Emanuel Miller Memorial Lecture 1992: the theory and practice of resilience. *Journal of Child Psychology and Psychiatry,* **35**(2), 259–83.

Meisels, S.J. and Shonkoff, J.P. (1992) *Handbook of Early Childhood Intervention.* Cambridge University Press, Cambridge.

Murray, L. (1992) The impact of postnatal depression in infant development. *Journal of Child Psychology and Psychiatry*, **33**, 543−61.

O'Connor, N. and Hermelin, B. (1988) Low intelligence and special abilities. *Journal of Child Psychology and Psychiatry*, **29**, 391−6.

Pearce, J. (1992) Behavioural disturbance and organic brain dysfunction. *Current Paediatrics*, **2**(3), 151−8.

Plomin, R. (1994) The Emanuel Miller Memorial Lecture 1993. Genetic research and identification of environmental influences. *Journal of Child Psychology and Psychiatry*, **35**(5), 817−35.

Pollitt, E., Gorman, K.S., Engle, P.L., Martorelli, R. and Rivera, J. (1993) *Early Supplemental Feeding and Cognition: Effect over two Decades* (Monographs of the Society for Research in Child Development, Serial No. 235, Vol. 58, No. 7, 1993), p. 122. University of Chicago Press, Chicago.

Rutter, M. (ed). (1980) *Scientific Foundations of Developmental Psychiatry*. Heinemann, London.

Rutter, M., Bolton, P., Harrington, R., Le Couteur, A., Macdonald, H. and Simonoff, E. (1990) Genetic factors in child psychiatric disorders − I: a review of research strategies. *Journal of Child Psychology and Psychiatry*, **31**, 1−37.

Rutter, M., Macdonald, H., Le Couteur, A., Harrington, R., Bolton, P. and Bailey, A. (1990) Genetic factors in child psychiatric disorders − II: empirical findings. *Journal of Child Psychology and Psychiatry*, **31**, 39−83.

Rutter, M. and Hay, D.F. (1994) *Development Through Life: A Handbook for Clinicians*. Blackwell Science, Oxford.

Skuse, D., Pickles, A., Wolke, D. and Reilly, S. (1994) Postnatal growth and mental development: evidence for a 'sensitive period'. *Journal of Child Psychology and Psychiatry*, **35**(3), 521−47.

Sylva, K. (1994) School influences on children's development. *Journal of Child Psychology and Psychiatry*, **35**(1), 135−71.

Tizard, J. (1960) Residential care of mentally handicapped children. *BMJ*, **1**, 1041−4.

Walzer, S. (1985) X chromosome abnormalities and cognitive development: implications for understanding normal human development. *Journal of Child Psychology and Psychiatry*, **26**, 177−84.

Werner, E.E. and Smith, R.S. (1982) *Vulnerable but Invincible: A Longitudinal Study of Resilient Children and Youth*. McGraw Hill, New York.

CHAPTER 3

A Review of Normal Development

The development of the normal child has been described in detail by a number of authors. For assessment purposes, numerous scales and tests are available and every developmental paediatrician must have access to at least one of these, as discussed in the previous chapter. It would be superfluous to duplicate these here and no attempt will be made to provide a detailed list of developmental milestones or a comprehensive review of normal development. The purpose of this chapter is to consider, particularly in the light of recent advances in psychology and linguistics, some of the numerous influences on and variations in normal development which account for many of the differences between children. Developmental paediatrics, developmental psychology and child psychiatry are inseparable; many aspects of a child's development can only usefully be measured and altered within the context of their family environment.

The development of social and interpersonal behaviour

The child's place in the family

There are many clinical situations in which parental behaviour only makes sense when the significance of the child within the family is understood. The notion that all children are wanted and are planned at times of social and economic convenience for the family unit is a Western middle-class ideal which is not always realized. Numerous factors influence the decision to embark upon or continue with a pregnancy. At least part of the urge to reproduce derives from cultural pressures. For example, couples are often made to feel peculiar or deficient if they announce their intention of remaining childless. Would-be grandparents, in particular, are powerful persuaders! In other families, conception may be deliberately planned to save a deteriorating relationship or to manipulate the partner. In poor communities, the birth of a child sometimes brings status to a young woman, the chance of obtaining accommodation of her own and acceptance as an adult by other women. Being a mother may be the only 'career' in which she can anticipate any chance of success. Children are seen in some cultures as an inevitable part of family life, necessary to the family economy and bringing security in old age.

Some children are conceived for special reasons or come to assume a special significance in the family. A baby conceived after the death of a previous child or after a stillbirth may be expected to take on the attributes, real or imagined, of the deceased child. These 'replacement' children are at special risk of emotional and developmental problems, particularly if conceived while the parents are still mourning their loss. In some families, one child, usually the first son, is expected to fulfil the family's academic or financial ambitions or to compensate for their parents' failure in those fields. Conversely, the youngest child of a large family may be encouraged to remain a baby for as long as possible, perhaps to avoid the 'empty nest' when the parents return to life as a couple after their children have left home.

The concepts of bonding and attachment

These terms have become increasingly confused and are sometimes used interchangeably. This is unhelpful because the way in which a close relationship between child and parents is established is complex and involves at least three processes.

Before and shortly after birth, parental feelings of anticipation and recognition of their baby as an

21

individual commonly (but not consistently) expand and deepen. This is paralleled by a newborn baby's development of an ability to recognize their mother and differentiate her from other women. These early processes are largely to do with parental, especially maternal, feelings and are at their peak in the first week after childbirth. In this chapter they are referred to as *neonatal bonding*.

At about 6 months, the baby begins to show clinging behaviour towards one or two particular individuals. This is evidence of a selective emotional *attachment*, usually to the mother in the first instance, and is something which is largely to do with the baby's emotions rather than the parents' feelings. It is, of course, usually reciprocated by a deepening of parental feelings towards the baby, triggered in part by the baby's selection of the parents for preferential affection and his/her display of helplessness which they alone can relieve. It does not depend upon earlier neonatal bonding.

A further consideration in the development of closeness in an emotional relationship is the need for both parties to develop an empathic relationship, within which they can recognize each other's feelings and develop an easiness about being together in each other's company, trusting each other's responses and being able to anticipate them sensitively. This is an extension of the early acquisition of turn-taking skills but is more than learning how to alternate behaviours. There is no single term which is generally recognized for this, but *intersubjectivity* and *mesh* have been employed. Probably several processes interact in its development. One is the ability to conceive of the other person as having a separate, private, unique set of experiences, perceptions and memories. This has been referred to as possessing a *theory of mind*.

Primary maternal preoccupation

During pregnancy, most mothers-to-be find themselves increasingly preoccupied with the forthcoming birth and an increasing amount of their thoughts become centred around the future baby and their needs. This is the start of the character-istic mental process which determines a child's central place in their mother's mind and is termed *primary maternal preoccupation*. Sometimes this period of mental preparation is disrupted, for example by complications of pregnancy, or unavoidable iatrogenic anxieties such as abnormal ultrasound scan results, which strengthen parental fears that the infant may be abnormal. It is very common for parents to have ambivalent feelings about pregnancy and about the influence of the baby on their lifestyle. Where the pregnancy was not desired or was undertaken for reasons no longer valid, the mother may sometimes even refuse to admit to herself that she is pregnant. She may reveal her state of mind by adverse comment on the unborn baby or on babies in general. Difficulties in child-rearing and child abuse can sometimes be traced to disturbances in the normal process of mental preparation which occurs in pregnancy.

Parental responses to the infant

The antenatal mental preparation for the infant's arrival normally equips the parents to weather any crisis that may occur. There may be disappointments, for example in the sex or appearance of the infant or alarm at the baby's premature arrival. Most of these are rapidly overcome, although on occasion they may continue to be a source of distress and resentment. When the infant's survival or normality is in doubt, many parents deliberately distance themselves from the baby; sometimes to the extent of not handling or visiting him/her. They feel that they dare not allow themselves to love the infant, for fear that they would be unable to tolerate his/her loss. If the baby then survives, it may be very hard to reverse these inhibitions. Any of these events may have a profound effect on the child's development, and may be manifest in disturbances of behaviour and relationships.

A stable marriage is ultimately strengthened by the birth of a child, but a poor parental relationship can deteriorate as a consequence of paternal jealousy of the child's capacity to engage the mother's attention. Equally, the stress of sleepless nights, cumulative fatigue, lack of social activities or lowered female sexual interest and consequent irritable discord between parents in the early stages of looking after a baby can weaken a marriage. Either way, fathers may leave. The mother may extend the bitterness she feels at being deserted to her child, blaming him/her, particularly if he is male and resembles the father physically or if the child has a disability. It is worth noting, nevertheless, that the rate of marital breakdown in families with a child with a disability is not particularly raised during the child's school years compared with families of normal children.

The effect of disability on bonding

During pregnancy, most parents consider the possibility that the child might be abnormal, and may mentally rehearse their reactions to such an event in advance. For example, mothers in their 40s are well aware of the high risk of Down's syndrome and may explain their apparently bland reaction to the birth of a Down's syndrome child on the basis that they 'half expected it'. Conversely some conclude during pregnancy that under no circumstances could they tolerate an abnormal child, and in these rejection may be all but inevitable, even before the child is born.

Not surprisingly, a disabled child is more easily accepted if the parents have other normal children, if the child was wanted, and if there is a supportive extended family. Impairments associated with obvious external deformity are initially hardest to accept, but sometimes this external marker makes adjustment easier. Conversely, the parents find it hard to believe that their child is disabled when the external appearance is totally normal, as may be the case with learning disability or deafness. Problems which only become apparent at a later date seem likely to be associated with more intense grief but much less likelihood of rejection (see Chapter 2).

Some apparent handicaps may actually be welcomed by parents, for example prelingual deafness by some deaf parents; the 'handicap' is actually an indicator of membership of a subculture.

The infant's contribution to bonding

In the first hour after birth, the neonate exhibits a peaceful wide-eyed alertness, gazing intently at the mother's face. This behaviour is virtually universal, although it is readily disrupted by obstetric interventions such as sedative medication; it is presumably a neurologically 'programmed' aid to bonding.

An ability known as 'turn-taking' appears very early, within the first few weeks or even days. Both mother and baby participate, either taking the lead. For instance, sucking during feeding occurs in bursts. As the baby stops sucking at the end of each burst, the mother will jiggle the nipple and may talk encouragingly to the baby until he/she takes up sucking again. The mother remains passive until this burst comes to an end, and then moves into active encouragement once more. A rhythm of alternating activity is established between mother and baby with the mother's responsiveness being the determining factor in this instance. The baby's responsiveness to the mother can be demonstrated most easily when the baby is in a peaceful and relaxed state. The mother makes a sound to the baby; in response the baby reduces gross, random movements, and instead makes small movements of the limbs synchronously with the mother's voice. When the mother stops, the baby vocalizes and increases bodily movement. Trevarthen noted that 'if the mother stops responding and just makes a blank face at the baby, the infant is clearly puzzled by the change in the mother and makes exaggerated solicitations as if to get her attention back. Some quickly become dejected-looking and withdrawn, a state of acute depression that takes minutes to abate' (see Martlew, 1987). Turn-taking appears to be a very fundamental behaviour pattern and is a reassuring sign of normal development.

The extent, range and persistence of turn-taking behaviour may well be as important a factor in development as the mothering skill of the parent. A study of babies in an orphanage showed that some babies were much more successful than others in obtaining mothering from the nurse in charge. It seems likely that the more skilful parent can provide increased stimulation for a baby who is relatively sluggish or unresponsive. Conversely, an immature or uncertain mother with an unresponsive infant is an unpromising combination.

Newborn babies differ in their style of behaviour. Differences in temperament cannot be attributed solely to differences in obstetric practice or maternal handling. There are variations in sleep requirements, irritability, and the speed at which feeding routines are developed. These temperamental differences are of great importance in determining parental responses; not everything that goes wrong with child development is due to bad management by the parents.

Attachment behaviour

Between 3 and 12 months, usually at about 6−7 months, the baby begins to show attachment behaviours which clearly serve to maintain one particular person, usually the mother, in close proximity to him/her. Thus the baby will cry when separated from the mother, will attempt to follow her (depending on locomotor capacity), and generally cling to her, especially if tired, frightened or in pain. This is normal and the sign that the baby is beginning to forge a deep emotional relationship with her; she is the baby's first attachment object (the term 'object' is unfortunate psychiatric jargon for a thing or person with which or whom one has an emotional relationship). In most family groups, the first attachment is to the mother, although in a minority of instances it is shared between father and mother, or is even to another person completely. That person, whether mother or not, will be someone who has been intensely involved socially with the baby. The attachment process is not secondary to being fed by someone but stands in its own right as an emerging piece of behaviour and emotional development. It is less evident (but still present) in large families where a number of people, adults and children, are involved with the baby. A number of small children also develop an attachment to

an inanimate comfort object and derive the same sort of comfort from its presence and apprehension at its absence as they do with their mother. Given that, in the vast majority of instances, the infant's first attachment is to the mother, it is convenient to use 'mother' as a shorthand term for the child's main attachment object.

When a young child is relaxed and feels secure, he/she may enjoy the company and attention of strangers or, indeed, may temporarily prefer them to the mother, but anxiety, stress, fatigue, pain and fear invariably demonstrate the child's need for the security provided by the mother, revealed by anxious glances and clinging in infancy, and active seeking, following and sometimes pestering in the mobile toddler or older child. The mother is used as a secure emotional base from which to make exploratory forays and to embark on play activities. Her presence rather than her active involvement provides the necessary security, helping the child to resolve anxiety or distress. Enforced separation of the child from the mother causes intense distress or 'separation anxiety'. Provision of this secure base is a vital part of the mother's task. If she is unable to do this, because of depression, inadequate comprehension of the child's needs or inability to love him/her, the relationship between parent and child becomes distorted or attenuated, leading to depression, withdrawal or failure to thrive.

The strength and frequency of attachment behaviour patterns and the vigour of separation protest are not necessarily related to the quality of parenting, the degree of parent/child empathy or the amount of time spent in each other's company; nevertheless, misinterpretation of attachment behaviours is commonplace among inexperienced medical and nursing staff. For example, a tendency to make indiscriminate casual attachments with any available adult is often seen among children in care who have been unable to make strong bonds with a permanent caregiver; it is not a sign of a pleasant friendly nature or an indication of the adult's personal charm! Strong attachment behaviours are not always inhibited by punishment or physical abuse. Excessive clinging and separation protests are not necessarily a sign of an intensely loving relationship; indeed, in older infants they are more likely to be a sign of insecurity and are often seen in unhappy and unstable families. Conversely, a strong attachment to a comfort object is not, as one might imagine, a sign of insecurity; rather surprisingly, it helps the child tolerate separations from the mother and is unusual in institutionalized children.

In young families, changes of job or housing, the birth of siblings, temporary absence of one parent, marital breakdown and death of a grandparent are all common life events. It is often tempting to attribute a whole variety of clinical problems to these events, and a variety of behavioural changes such as minor regression or increased clinging may occur at such times, but these are usually transient and are readily understood by most parents. There is substantial evidence that such events are not in themselves damaging to young children. The social context of adverse experiences is crucial. In a normal family environment, the infant is generally protected to some extent from these disruptions by the continuation of the normal routine or supported through them by parental comfort and encouragement. In such circumstances, minor adversities can become 'steeling' experiences which strengthen emotional resilience. Conversely, an insecure or unsupported child might be overwhelmed by such experiences, sensitizing him/her to future adversity and creating a vulnerability to future stress.

Many young children react to separation from their main attachment figures with intense distress. Should this figure fail to return after a few days, this is followed by a period of apathy and despair (often mistaken by hospital staff for 'settling down'). This is followed by indifference to or rejection of the parent when the separation is over, with a degree of insecurity in the relationship — the child no longer trusts the mother not to disappear. If the parent recognizes what is happening and does not overreact, normal affectionate behaviour is soon restored. The parent who responds with anger and disappointment may perpetuate a prolonged and mutual antagonism which may eventually require professional help. If separation for several days is unavoidable, as may happen if the child is hospitalized in an emergency, it is essential to encourage free and regular contact between parent and child, and to warn the parent of the likelihood of temporary behaviour disturbances when the child is discharged.

With increasing age and emotional maturity, the child becomes better able to tolerate separation. As language develops, an internal representation of the parent is developed and concepts of time and place are established which enable the child to maintain the bond with the absent parent. With the approach of adolescence, the child will often actively seek and relish the independence offered by temporary separation. Marital discord, the fear of family disintegration, parental illness or emotional immaturity in one or other parent may all inhibit this process of maturation so that the child is fearful of even brief separations, resulting in social inhibitions, school phobia and a variety of other psychological problems.

The child who is brought up in residential care or a seriously neglectful family may have no opportunity to develop normal attachment behaviours. The end result of such deprivation has been described as affectionless psychopathy, the features of which include emotional immaturity, indiscriminate friendliness and intimacy, failure to learn social rules, inability to tolerate and maintain close relationships, a lack of guilt feelings, and antisocial behaviour. The complete syndrome is rare, although individual components of this picture are common and may be seen amongst chronically abused children.

An understanding of attachment behaviour is vital in the interpretation of many developmental and behavioural disorders, and particularly in the management of pervasive developmental disorders.

Temperament and personality

There are constitutional, largely inherited determinants of a child's style of behaviour, which are referred to as their 'temperament'. This is a way of describing the child in terms of how he/she goes about things and is roughly equivalent to the notion of personality, a term usually reserved for adults and including, among other things, the effects of personal experience. Temperament is initially relatively independent of experience (newborn babies differ from one another) but is moulded slowly and partially by it. Temperamental traits are not necessarily fixed for all time. Some continuity can be observed between temperament styles in infancy and those in later childhood, but considerable changes can also occur gradually, particularly in the first year of life. Temperament can be assessed and classified according to various schemes but the most widely known is that developed by Thomas and Chess (1957) (Table 3.1), based on an interview study with parents. The fact that parents were the source of information in this study means that the descriptions of children were derived from the parents' perception of their child rather than objective measures of individual differences between children. Nevertheless, the scheme has obvious appeal to clinicians, possibly because of this.

Perhaps the most important aspect is the 'difficult' category, which represents a very problematic child for any parent to live with and may be commoner among children with neurodevelopmental disabilities. Most parents subscribe to the contemporary myth that their child's disposition is solely the product of their handling. They thus feel guilty and even angry at having a difficult child in spite of their best attempts. They need to be told that their child's temperament is not the result of their parenting.

Another source of stress is when the child's style is so different from the parents' own personalities that all family members become exasperated. The easygoing, unfastidious child with the intense, inflexible, punctilious parent is one instance. The 'goodness of fit' concept refers to the extent of match or mismatch between the parents' expectations and personalities and their child's temperament. A poor fit is a potential source of friction, since the parents attempt unsuccessfully to change

Table 3.1 Scheme developed by Thomas and Chess for assessing and classifying temperament

THE VARIABLES
Activity level
Regularity of biological functions (sleep, hunger, etc.)
Approach to or withdrawal from novelty
Adaptability to imposed changes
Threshold of responsiveness
Intensity of emotional reaction
Quality of general mood
Distractibility
Attention span or persistence

TEMPERAMENTAL STYLES

Easy
Regular biological rhythm
Positive approaches to novel situations
Rapid positive adaptability to change
Predominantly sunny mood
Mild intensity of emotional reactions

Slow to warm up
Withdrawing responses to novel situations
Slow adaptability

Difficult
Irregular biological rhythms
Withdrawing responses to novel situations
Slow to adapt to change
Predominantly negative mood (whines, grumbles, feels cheated)
Intense, extreme emotional reactions

the child, rather than their attitude to him/her. In most instances, parents need to be cautioned that they can only expect to alter their child's personality by a very small degree, and extremely slowly at that.

Learning the rules of social behaviour

Although children are born with the ability to initiate social attachments, the complex rules which govern social behaviour have to be learnt. The child has to extract these rules from observations of everyday life by a process which is presumably very similar to that described for language, later in this chapter.

Certain patterns of social behaviour are regarded as typical of particular age-groups. For example, the 6–12-month infant is often rather suspicious of strangers; the 18-month toddler is shy and clinging, perhaps hiding their face against the mother; whereas the 3 year old is much more easily involved in games and has acquired considerable social poise. These are, of course, generalizations and social behaviour is determined by numerous environmental and temperamental factors such as the social class and attitudes of the parents, their own degree of introversion and extroversion and the extent to which the child has met adults other than parents or been cared for by them. Advanced language development tends to be associated with more mature and outgoing social behaviour. Parental attitudes to authority are also significant, both in general development and in the particular context of a consultation with a doctor or other professional person. Lower-social-class families tend to be more aware of hierarchies of authority and their children develop more acquiescent attitudes to instruction and information, whereas in middle-class families self-confidence and a critical faculty are encouraged. These differences are often very apparent in the ways in which both children and adults behave when using professional services.

For professional people such as doctors and psychologists, the standard of 'normal' social behaviour is that seen in the happy, well-adjusted child of their own social class. The child is vocal, open and friendly after a brief period of initial shyness. He/she has learnt, by the age of $2\frac{1}{2}$, and often very much earlier than this, to sit down, listen carefully to instructions, and await the next item in a game or test without fidgeting. The child is eager to please. This behaviour pattern certainly makes clinical assessment easier! It is doubtless also an enormous advantage to the child when starting school, and middle-class parents are well aware of this and try to develop an organized attitude to learning from a very early age. Originality is encouraged and indeed highly prized. Small games are extended and developed, and creative efforts with bricks or paint are proudly displayed. It is almost impossible for any child-minder or nursery to re-create this atmosphere for the child who lacks it at home, and it may be that this is one of the fundamental problems of most intervention programmes for disadvantaged children.

Many other social behaviour patterns are seen in the course of developmental assessment. Although they are different from the one described above, and often make the clinician's task more difficult, they are not necessarily abnormal. The child may be excessively shy, perhaps because he/she has little contact with other adults, or because the atmosphere of a clinic is so unfamiliar. The child may be extremely active, incapable of sitting and awaiting instructions and comprehending a sequence of events. He/she may only enjoy destructive games, or the play may be fragmentary, lacking in originality and perhaps limited to lining up and pushing toy cars.

The role of genetic factors

The relative contributions of genes and child-rearing styles in creating social behaviour are impossible to disentangle. Behavioural genetics is a rapidly developing field. Among its contributions is the revelation that some of the behaviours inherited have a selecting and shaping effect on the environment, which in turn provides experience and other ways of influencing personal development. For instance, children who chatter are more likely to be talked back to and thus to enrich their linguistic environment. Clinical observations and some research evidence suggest that microenvironmental factors are as important here as with global intelligence or language, both in the development and in the manifestation of behaviours. Although temperamental characteristics observed early in life do persist to some extent, behaviour patterns are very dependent on the situation in which the child is seen. For this reason, teachers' and parents' assessments of behaviour problems differ to a remarkable extent, while minor changes in a play setting can lead to dramatic changes in activity levels. Therefore it is very unwise to draw firm conclusions or to use words like 'hyperactivity' or 'distractable' on the basis of behaviour seen only in the very artificial surroundings of a clinic.

There are sex differences both in child behaviour and in child-rearing practices. These arise both from inherited behaviour patterns and from social attitudes. Even when parents deliberately try to minimize these distinctions in the interests of sex equality, differences can still be observed. These can also affect parental handling — a prickly, difficult child elicits prickly parenting. Parents are often less in control of their own behaviour towards their children than they think.

It is sometimes hard for parents to realize that children's social behaviour is not entirely the result of their upbringing. They overestimate their power in socializing their child and conversely blame themselves if their child behaves badly. This can rapidly develop into blaming the child. Yet many behaviour problems in childhood arise out of deficiencies in skills, the child being unable to achieve what he/she wants by orthodox, civilized means and needing to resort to more primitive methods of demanding, taking, hitting, evading or giving vent to emotional displays.

Although the standards of adequate ('good enough') parenting can be set out, most parents are quite capable of implementing these on common-sense grounds. They sometimes need to be reminded that encouragement and praise for desired behaviours must balance attempts to discipline unacceptable behaviour. Similarly it may be necessary to help them remain child-centred and appreciate the child's point of view. Not uncommonly, the parents of children with disabilities have on occasion to be reminded to look after themselves and their marriage rather than subvert their own selves in caring for their child and being no more than full-time parents; otherwise, bringing a child up to cope successfully with a social world is something most parents do well. Some children make this easier than others.

Development from 1 to 5

Between the first and second birthdays the child makes rapid strides in understanding. He/she recognizes and comprehends in considerable detail the daily routine of life at home, and becomes increasingly aware of their own rights and identity as an individual. Clashes of will with their parents are frequent. When placed in unfamiliar surroundings their behaviour may be more diffident, and the child may still cling to the mother but will gradually make increasingly daring forays into unfamiliar territory — a behaviour pattern which is very typical of the middle of the second year. Evidence of the extent of the child's understanding begins to be seen in their play, both in imitation of domestic activities and in the use of toys and symbolic play.

In the third year, the child firmly establishes his/her identity. The child sees him/herself as distinct from the world around and uses the pronoun 'I'. Children of this age are completely mobile and can explore where they will; they have worked out all the important relationships and functions of their surroundings and familiar adults, and have the language to describe them. This understanding gives them confidence to deal with new situations much more readily than the 18-month-old child. By the age of 4, children have often acquired such confidence in their own abilities and importance that they become somewhat exuberant and bumptious. They are nevertheless still vulnerable in new situations, subject to sudden changes of mood and inexplicable fears, but in familiar surroundings are able to join in complex games and activities with other children.

Most parents actively foster this growing independence in their child, in preparation for school. They may provide playgroup experiences or other opportunities to play with young children. Some parents (the socially isolated, depressed or agoraphobic) are less able to help their children to learn to mix and play with others, or to master the social rules which govern play and peer activities. A warm relationship with an adult may be lacking, or alternatively the child may have to take on the role of an adult companion to the parent. In such circumstances, the child may present with a variety of developmental or behavioural problems, and later is likely to show considerable difficulties of adjustment in school.

Some parents have very unrealistic expectations; for example, they may imagine that speech appears as if by magic without any contribution from them. Thus a child with delayed speech comes to be regarded as a chronic disappointment and is subjected to neglect or harsh discipline which do nothing to promote speech development.

The early school years

At school the child is introduced to a new world of learning and discipline, and the previous typical exuberance of the 4 year old may disappear as the child becomes rather more sober and subdued. Provided that their initial experiences are happy, their innate capacity and enthusiasm for learning enable the child to master numerous new areas of intellectual and physical skill. Fear of failure and of disappointing the adults around them and diffi- culties in adjusting to the demands of their peers may be apparent in less fortunate children. A degree of anxiety, minor obsessions, episodes of lying and stealing, and moodiness due to quarrels with friends or dislike of teachers are all common- place. Many of the mild problems experienced by children in this age-group are transient, and should be seen as part of normal development. However, behaviour problems of moderate or severe degree can be strikingly persistent and will not abate without specific intervention. The capacity of parents to encourage and support the child seems particularly important.

With increasing maturity, there is more aware- ness of major events such as marital discord or the death of a near relative, but the effects on the child's behaviour, personality and performance are unpredictable, and apparent links between life events and clinical problems often turn out to be spurious. In the school years, the peer group becomes rapidly more influential, but the stability, interest and support of the family remain as essential as ever. Children expect their parents to listen to their news from school, and to champion them when in difficulties. The ability of parents to respond in this way appears to correlate with progress in school. It probably also determines whether many of the commonplace problems mentioned above are self-limiting or escalate to the point of requiring professional intervention.

The development of language

The science of linguistics now encompasses the whole of human communication, by words, ges- tures, signs and social behaviour. Figure 3.1 summarizes the terminology used in describing spoken language. For the clinician, the distinc- tions between 'speech' and 'language' and between expression and comprehension are of particular significance.

Chomsky is acknowledged as the leader of the modern revolution in linguistics, but much of his work is difficult to apply to the everyday problems of paediatrics. Crystal (1976 and 1981) has made a major contribution to linguistic theory and its application to clinical work. Pinkers' account of modern linguistics offers the most readable intro- duction to the subject.

Speech sounds

From early infancy the baby produces an ever- increasing range of sounds. At first only vowel sounds are made, but from about 6 months on- wards consonants can be recognized. Individual sounds are repeated and strung together and vari- ations in intonation, volume and pitch gradually come under voluntary control. It is important to distinguish between the random sounds made by the baby's early experimenting and the increasing voluntary control over production of specific con- sonants. This natural progression sometimes worries parents because they notice that some

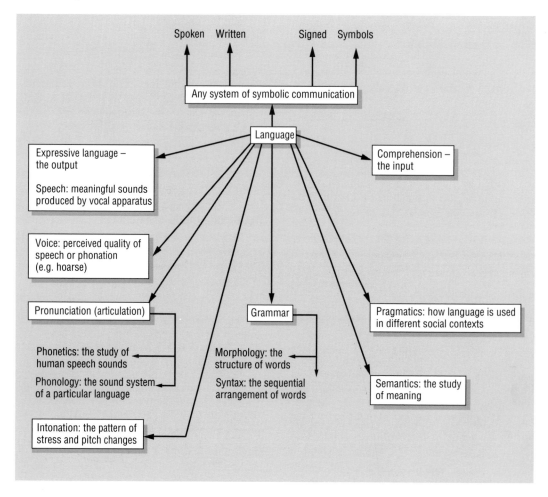

Fig. 3.1 Linguistic terminology.

sounds, for example l and r, have disappeared from the child's repertoire.

Consonant sounds are made in a variety of ways and places. Some are made by the sudden release of air pressure, producing a single sound called a plosive (e.g. p); others are made by the passage of air through a narrow space producing a continuous hissing noise, called a fricative (e.g. s). The place of articulation may be the lips (labials), the teeth (dentals) or the palate (palatals). Air may be allowed to pass at the side of the tongue (laterals) or through the nose (nasals). There are wide variations in the rate at which

children acquire the various sounds of speech, and the order is also unpredictable, although certain generalizations can be made. Firstly, sounds made at the front of the mouth appear before back sounds (p, b, m before k, g). Secondly, plosives usually appear before fricatives. Thirdly, oral sounds seem easier to make than nasal sounds. Fourthly, consonant clusters appear at the end of words before the beginnings. Correct articulation of all sounds may not be achieved until after the child starts school (Table 3.2) and errors are very common. For example, banana is produced as 'nana'; dog as 'gog'; plate as 'pate'; cup as 'top';

Table 3.2 Acquisition of consonants

Age	Sounds mastered
By $3\frac{1}{2}$	b p m w h
By $4\frac{1}{2}$	d t n g k j n (as in 'long')
By $5\frac{1}{2}$	f
By $6\frac{1}{2}$	v l th (as in 'though') sh (as in 'show') s (as in 'measure')
By $7\frac{1}{2}$	s z r th (as in 'think')

or red as 'wed'. Mastery of intonation patterns may take even longer.

Long strings of partially organized babble or 'jargon' talk take on the intonation patterns of the child's native language, so that by 1 year of age an observer can distinguish the babble of an English from that of a Chinese baby. Jargon varies greatly in quantity and complexity and some babies seem very silent until they start to use true words. Deaf babies produce jargon which is less complex, has fewer intonational changes and tends to be rather harsh; also the total amount of jargon may be less than normal and is decreasing by the first birthday. However, very careful observation is needed in order to recognize these differences.

The origins of communication

The behavioural pattern known as turn-taking undoubtedly provides the framework within which language can develop. The capacity to listen to and discriminate between sounds is present at birth. Very young babies can copy facial gestures, such as tongue protrusion, and it can be shown that they make efforts to imitate sounds long before their imitations are easily recognizable. By 6 or 7 months the primitive turn-taking capability has developed into more sophisticated reciprocal vocal games between parent and child. It is a simple matter for the parent to select sounds produced by the baby and to develop them in these auditory games. An important promoter of communication is the parents' tendency to attribute meaning to their baby's utterances and respond

accordingly ('Yes, you want teddy — here you are').

Referential looking

The phenomenon of referential looking may partly explain the emergence of the first words. When a baby's gaze falls on an interesting object or person, the mother glances at her baby and follows their line of sight to see what has caught their attention. She then describes and comments on the object of the baby's interest. In this way the child learns to associate word labels with the object or person they describe.

Baby talk ('motherese')

The use of baby words is frowned upon by many standard baby books, but they are widely used in other cultures, and there are good reasons to support their use to promote communication between mother and child. Baby words are usually simple stressed two-syllable pairs (e.g. tum-tum, gee-gee) which are easy for the child to learn, so that he/she rapidly masters the link between words and objects. Even if baby words are avoided, deliberate simplification of language, clear voice, slower speed of delivery and a raised pitch (register) are so widely adopted by adults and even young children talking to babies that 'motherese' seems to be an instinctive and natural response to a baby's efforts to communicate.

Acquisition of grammar

It is often impossible to decide at what point the infant's utterances can be called words. Probably parental enthusiasm is the main determinant of when the first word is recognized. The first few words are often used in a variety of ways (Table 3.3); they do not have a single specific meaning or use but are used to cover a range of meaning ('holophrases'). The joining of words to make two-element sentences usually occurs at around 18–24 months but it is doubtful whether grammatical terms like subject or verb are appropriate

Table 3.3 Overgeneralization of word meanings. From work by Eve V. Clark of Stanford University

Child's lexical item	First referents	Other referents in order of occurrence	General area of semantic extension
MOOI	Moon	Cake Round marks on windows Writing on windows and in blocks Round shapes in books Tooling in leather book covers Round postmarks Letter O	Shape
KOTIBAIZ	Bars of cot	Large toy abacus Toast rack with parallel bars Picture of building with columns	Shape
VOV-VOV	Dog	Kittens Hens All animals at zoo Picture of pigs dancing	Shape
KOKO	Cockerel's crowing	Tunes played on a violin Tunes played on a piano Tunes played on an accordion Tunes played on a gramophone All music Merry-go-round	Sound

at this stage. These can only be applied with confidence when three-element sentences appear. Crystal (1976) has neatly summarized these and subsequent stages of grammatical development (Table 3.4). Comprehension of language develops along similar lines but is generally some months in advance of expressive ability.

At one time it was thought that language development was dependent on the parent reinforcing, by praise and encouragement, the random utterances of the infant, whenever he/she utters a word-like sound. Modern linguists have rejected this simple explanation for language development for many reasons, of which the most compelling is the fact that so many early utterances of young children are clearly invented by them. Indeed, the parent often copies the utterances of the baby, rather than vice versa. Children extract the rules of grammar from adult speech and build on them

themselves. They do this so successfully and so universally that Chomsky proposed that the brain must be programmed to carry out this analytic feat; he called this hypothetical brain circuit the 'language acquisition device'. Alternatively, it may be that the need for the basic classes of word, names (nouns) and actions (verbs), is so fundamental that no other system of symbolic communication is conceivable, and this discovery is made afresh by every child in every culture. Certainly the distinction is recognized by mentally retarded children learning to communicate by sign systems, where the noun–verb distinction is equally essential.

Children frequently learn a word without fully understanding its significance. They overgeneralize its meaning and then refine it as their knowledge of the world develops. The same process can be recognized with grammatical rules (Table 3.5).

Table 3.4 Crystal's seven stages in expressive language development. From Crystal (1976)

𝕉	Stage 1 9–18 months	Single element: e.g. dada, there, no, gone, more
	Stage 2 18–24 months	Two elements: e.g. dada there, all gone car
	Stage 3 24–30 months	Three elements: e.g. daddy kick ball, where man gone
	Stage 4 30–36 months	Four or more elements: e.g. Where my mummy's bag gone
	Stage 5 36–42 months	Complex sentences: use of 'and' and 'but', multiple clauses, comparisons, e.g. Daddy gone in the garden and he felled over — and he hurted his knee
	Stage 6 42–54 months	Refinement of grammar: irregular verbs and plurals, passive structures, etc., e.g. I just been stung by a wasp
	Stage 7 Beyond 54 months	Increasing sophistication of language use: continues at least until puberty

Table 3.5 Learning the rules about plurals

1	Boy	Cat	Man	House	Foot Feet
2			Men		
3	Boys	Cats	Mans	House	Foots Feets
4	Boysez	Catsez	Mansez Mensez	House	Footsez Feetsez
5	Boys	Cats	Mans	Houses	Feets
6	Boys	Cats	Men	Houses	Feet

In clinical assessment of language development, overgeneralization often accounts for the apparent 'errors' made by children in labelling objects or describing pictures. Often the parent can explain how the particular use of the word came about.

Characteristics of parent–child conversation

Parents characteristically comment on their baby's behaviour and facial expressions, inferring motive or emotion: 'Ooh, you didn't like that, did you?' or 'You're trying to talk to kitty, aren't you?' This tends to be conducted in motherese (see above) and follow a turn-taking pattern, interspersing with the baby's responses or initiatives. The intensity of parental talk and excitement escalates as the baby begins to babble and subsequently utter first words. It appears to offer encouragement to communicate and provides a conversational framework in which language, both comprehensive and expressive, can be learned. Correction of the child's statements is usually related to content and factual accuracy more than grammatical style or pronunciation. Emphasis on the latter types of error is futile and may even inhibit language development. For example, it is more productive to correct 'Grandad are a lady' to 'No, grandad is a *man*'. Paraphrase and expansion give the child a correct model to copy, without being discouraged by constant correction or negative responses: (child) 'Car ... red car', (mother) 'Yes, it's a big red car.' Competent parents manage to interpret many utterances that would be incomprehensible to a stranger, and feed these back to the child in the corrected form.

Imitation plays a part in the rapid acquisition of

vocabulary and syntax. Many children pass through a phase of repeating much of what is said to them, as if this helps them to understand the meaning and rehearse the use of the word. This is known as 'echolalia'; it seldom persists much beyond the third birthday.

Higher levels of language learning

The essentials of basic grammar are generally mastered by the end of the fourth year but the more sophisticated constructions and the ability to remember and integrate a series of ideas, as in a story, continue to develop throughout the school years. The child also has to learn about the more subtle aspects of social communication: sarcasm, understatement, the concealment of orders within questions (e.g. 'would you like to . . .'), the difference between formal and informal conversation, the rules for addressing important adults such as teachers and so on.

Factors affecting language development

The frequency of verbal exchanges between parent and child is likely to affect progress. It would be surprising if the child of a depressed, uncommunicative parent progressed as fast as one who is constantly talked to by parents, siblings and relatives. In many societies children do not acquire language from their parents, but from contact with their siblings and peers. This does not seem to cause any disadvantage in their normal surroundings but, when such families are transplanted to an unfamiliar society and children are deprived of much contact with their peers, they may be in serious difficulty.

Bernstein (1971) described some interesting differences in the usage of language between social groups (although the distinction is not as sharp as his original description suggested). Middle-class families were said to use language extensively to discuss, plan, argue and describe — 'the extended code'. The lower social classes limited the use of language only to conveying instructions and essential information — 'the re-

stricted code'. It is a characteristic of Western middle-class culture that children are encouraged in critical questioning and abstract thought. A high value is placed on imagination, creative thought and play. Nevertheless, these class distinctions were later realized to be partly artefactual. The social circumstances in which professional assessments of language are made are inhibiting to lower-class children; furthermore, they may have a style of communication which, though different from that of middle-class families, is not necessarily inferior.

The importance of empathy, putting oneself in another's shoes, is revealed in numerous daily exchanges, e.g. 'How would you feel if I pulled *your* hair?' Empathy facilitates the function of the close-knit nuclear family, and probably makes for greater success in business and professional life, but it is not necessarily so highly prized by other cultures, where there may be more emphasis, for example, on conformity to group behaviour, or on independence and strength. It is foolish to apply Western norms to children from other cultures without recognizing these differences. At the same time, they inevitably put the child at a disadvantage if he/she has to compete in the educational system and later the labour market in Western society.

Some parents, particularly professional people, overestimate their child's intelligence and language ability and their conversation with the child is pitched at too high a level of complexity. This seems particularly likely to occur with children with less intrinsic ability than their older siblings. Conversely, parents may persistently underestimate a child's expressive language, refusing to credit him/her with saying a word unless the pronunciation is clear. Such parents fail to recognize that the conveying of meaning is the most vital aspect of communication and they make repeated attempts to make the child speak more clearly. The child may react with stubborn silence; this negativistic behaviour is quite normal in the young child, although it is seldom, if ever, an adequate explanation on its own for severe delay in language development.

Variations in language acquisition

Both production and comprehension of speech vary widely in young children. The scatter is so wide that at the age of 4 about one in six children have a language level 1 year below the mean (Fig. 3.2a). Some of the children whose early rate of language acquisition is slow continue to lag behind, but many others catch up (Fig. 3.2b). These observations explain why the detection of children with potentially serious language impairments is so difficult in the preschool period (see also p. 186).

There are also variations in the route by which children acquire language. Some quickly master and use a large number of nouns, while others seem to concentrate more on words that express personal desires or are used for social interaction. The latter group are more likely to use long strings of incomprehensible babble as a prelude to the formation of mature sentences. The effects

of deprivation, exposure to more than one language and other miscellaneous factors are discussed in Chapter 11.

Non-verbal communication

Humans communicate by numerous non-verbal signals, involving auditory, visual and tactile channels. Speakers convey information not only by their words, but by tone of voice, intonation and the use of pauses and 'punctuation' noises (er, um, you see, etc.). Visual signals include gestures such as pointing, changing facial expressions, body posture or movement. 'Turn-taking' behaviour is learned by both auditory and visual channels, and can also be mastered by the deaf–blind, using tactile cues. Much has been written about non-verbal communication in adults, but less is known about the way that this is learned in childhood; presumably the same processes are at work as in spoken language.

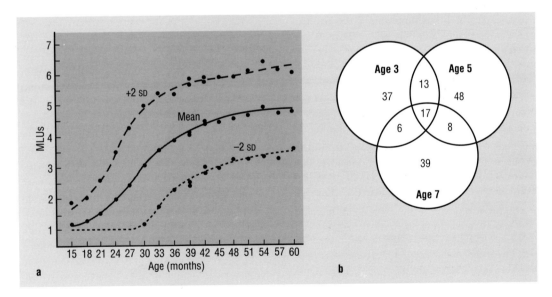

Fig. 3.2 **a,** Mean length of utterance (MLU) is a convenient measure of the increasing complexity of language production. This figure shows that at the age of, for example, 4 years, 16% of children score 1 SD below the mean. This corresponds to around the 3-year level. In other words, one in six of all 4 year olds have language

skills 1 year or more below age level. From Wells (1985) **b,** Showing how children may be designated 'language-delayed' at one age but not at another. Only 17 were 'delayed' at all three assessments. Total sample = 857; children assessed at 3, 5 and 7 years. From Silva (1987).

Relevance of linguistic research

Linguistic knowledge is expanding very rapidly and the clinical applications are not yet finally established. The features highlighted in this chapter are those which already seem to have some clinical value. Thus, turn-taking and referential looking provide valuable evidence of a satisfactory parent—infant relationship. Observation that a parent uses language teaching strategies such as expansion and paraphrase might suggest that a poor linguistic environment is not primarily responsible for a child's difficulties in language acquisition. An apparently bizarre use of words or grammar may sometimes be explained by the principle of overgeneralization. A child's familiarity with the social rules of language use — making a request, awaiting instructions or recounting an experience — is an encouraging sign when grammar or articulation seem deficient. The close relationship between language usage and the social situation means that interpretation of assessment results must be very circumspect.

Recent research has emphasized the need to consider communication in the context of the environment. Measures of language development such as the vocabulary count and sentence length are not adequate in themselves. An 'effective environment' also includes aspects of social behaviour such as the use of praise by parents and adequate listening to what the child says; this goes way beyond mere 'exposure' to spoken language. It must be remembered, however, that language is biologically robust and that substantial differences in the genetic endowment of intelligence and of language skills still remain. It would be a serious error to explain all disturbances of language development purely in terms of an inappropriate linguistic environment.

Clinical assessment of communicative ability

Language competence

When parents are questioned about a child's language abilities, it should be remembered that they often *under*estimate the extent of the child's speech output, because they do not credit unclear utterances with meaning. The opposite error may occur when parents are exceptionally astute at interpreting the child's attempts at speech. Comprehension is usually *over*estimated and parents often reply 'everything' when asked how much the child understands, because they automatically keep their conversation with him/her within the limits of the child's understanding. More searching questions are needed to define the true extent of the child's comprehension (Tables 3.6 and 3.7).

Any unusual features of the child's language should be noted. There may be bizarre grammatical constructions: difficulties in word selection: echolalia of whole sentences irrelevant to the situation: obsessional concentration on one theme: or inability to deal with abstract ideas. Parents are often well aware of their child's abnormal behaviour patterns and if asked appropriate questions can provide some useful information.

Deviant social behaviour

Some children exhibit patterns of development and behaviour which are not merely delayed, but qualitatively abnormal. In extreme cases, the presenting parental complaint may be of deafness or blindness. Yet these children may well turn out to have learning disability or a communication disorder. They seem unable to relax or enjoy being cuddled and fail to adapt their body posture to the parent's body when held. Responses to sound may be inconsistent and localization poor, so that one has difficulty in capturing the baby's attention by voice alone. Exaggerated movements and gestures are needed. Their vocalizations may be abnormal in quality or lacking in modulation or variety, and they may show no appreciation of 'turn-taking'. Eye contact, which should be direct and intent, is often deficient in abnormal infants. The baby may seem to avoid eye contact or look past the examiner, or he/she may simply have a

Table 3.6 Clinical assessment of communicative ability

QUESTIONS AND OBSERVATIONS ABOUT COMPREHENSION

Does the child understand by non-verbal means — pointing, gestures, facial expression?

Does the child understand everyday noises? e.g. feeding bottle being shaken, dinner being prepared, bath water running, dog barking

Does the child understand pat-a-cake, wave bye-bye or similar instructions?

How much does the child understand when you talk to him/her?

Does the child understand better if he/she can see your face or if you point to the thing you are talking about?

Does the child understand:

    names of objects, people or pets?

    simple instructions, e.g. shut the door, get your coat?

    two-part instructions, e.g. go and get your coat from the kitchen?

    more complicated instructions?

Can you make a bargain with the child? e.g. let me finish this and I will play with you

Can you tell the child what is going to happen? e.g. we are going out in the car to the hospital

Can you tell the child a story? Does he/she follow it?

QUESTIONS AND OBSERVATIONS ABOUT EXPRESSIVE LANGUAGE AND COMMUNICATION

If not yet talking

Does the child use other means of communication — pointing, pulling parent to show something, non-verbal sounds, gestures, bringing something to show you? (cf. Table 3.8)

If talking

How much can the child say?

    any sounds that you understand?

    any words that you recognize?

    how many words: a few, up to 10, 10−20, or too many to count?

    does the child join words? If so, how many?

    can the child make up long sentences?

    does the child tend to copy what you say?

Are you worried because

    the child doesn't say very much?

    the child's speech is hard to understand?

    both?

Does the child try to make you understand what he/she wants? If so, how?

What language(s) do you speak at home? Which does the child speak and understand best?

Which language do you use most of the time?

Does the child ask for things?

Does the child ask questions?

Can the child tell you what he/she has been doing, e.g. at playgroup?

vacant expression. In such cases, it is not possible to interpret the baby's 'feelings' with changing facial expression as one can do so easily in a normal child. Whenever there is any doubt about a child's attachment to their caregivers or about their social responsiveness, further questions should be asked to determine whether the behaviour in this area of function is outside the wide range of normal (Table 3.8). These questions may be useful when autism is suspected (p. 192).

Table 3.7 Using simple toys, pictures and books to detect impaired comprehension

Age	Comprehension level
12–18 months	Recognition of objects by name: 'Show me the …'
2–2½ years	Relating two ideas: 'Put the … in the …' 'Give the … to Mummy' Understanding action words: 'Show me someone sweeping'
2½–3 years	Recognition of objects by function: 'Which one is for eating/kicking/drinking with?' The beginnings of negatives and concepts of size and colour: 'Show me a big/little …' 'Show me a round/long …' 'Find a red one'
3–3½ years	More complicated ideas: 'Which one is the same as that one?' 'Show me a different one.' 'Are you a boy or a girl?' 'Which one is behind/underneath …?'
4 years +	Abstract questions involving concepts of time, place, reasoning, etc.: 'How did you come here today?'

Table 3.8 Questions about attachment, social interaction and unusual social behaviours

How does the child respond to the parents?
Does the child respond differently to them as compared with other familiar and unfamiliar people?
Does the child recognize close relatives, siblings?
Does the child like to be picked up, cuddled, bounced, swung?
Does the child come to the parents for comfort when upset, tired or hurt?
Could the parents walk away and leave the child – would he/she mind?
How does the child get on with other children – of the same age? older children?
Does the child play? with toys? with other children? with real 'pretending'? Give examples
Does the child realize when a parent is upset? or angry?
Does the child try to comfort a friend or sibling who is crying?
Does the child have any favourite activity that is repeated over and over again? Give examples
Does the child have any particular rituals or habits that he/she must follow?

NB. Specifically enquire about, and look for: pretend play using objects as if they have other properties or identities; attribution of human motives and feelings to toys; joint attention behaviour of proto-declarative pointing (use of finger to indicate to another person an object of interest as an end in itself) – this is distinguished from proto-imperative pointing solely to attain a desired object). Pretend play and joint attention as defined are normally present by 15 months but may be delayed or absent in autism (Baron-Cohen *et al.*, 1992).

Cognitive development

This term is used to describe the understanding of concepts about functions and relationships. Under normal circumstances cognitive and linguistic development are intimately related. Some theorists argue that language is a necessary tool for the acquisition of concepts, while others believe that language can only advance when the necessary concepts have already been formed. It seems more likely that the two usually develop simultaneously, but they may be dissociated in conditions such as deafness or aphasia. Whatever the exact learning process may be, the presence of a particular language skill can be taken as evidence that the underlying concept is present; thus, if a child says, 'This doll bigger 'n that one', he/she clearly understands the concept of size. A severely deaf child with no spoken language might also understand the concept of big and little, but this would need to be demonstrated by non-verbal means. For example, the child could be given a set of dolls and chairs of differing sizes; if the child selects the appropriate size for each, it may be assumed that he/she has some understanding of the concept of size.

Learning in infancy

The infant's ability to learn is demonstrated by their preference for novel and interesting stimuli and their decreased interest in repeated present-ations of the same stimulus. This latter phenom-enon is known as habituation. For example, if a bell is rung gently behind a resting baby, he/she responds with a startle, but each successive rep-etition elicits a decreasing response. After the third or fourth presentation, the baby may ignore it altogether, but will respond again to a new and different sound. By presenting test stimuli which are similar but not identical, it is possible to determine how fine a discrimination can be achieved by the baby. Habituation has also been used as a clinical measure of nervous system integrity in the newborn.

The importance of vision

The visual channel is of great significance to the infant, long before he/she is mobile, in the con-struction of their own mental map of their sur-roundings. It is vision which later provides the main spur for the infant to reach, creep, crawl and walk. Even in the first months, the infant's behaviour towards inanimate objects is different from that reserved for humans. Inanimate objects are inspected with detached interest. The infant attempts to grasp and explore them by hand and mouth. Objects which make a noise are of particu-lar importance. By 3 months an infant has learnt to pay attention and turn to a noise 'in the expec-tation of seeing a spectacle', as Piaget put it.

In contrast, humans elicit the complicated be-havioural pattern called turn-taking, described previously. Facial patterns and contours arouse the infant's interest at a very early age. By $2\frac{1}{2}$ months, a human face regularly elicits a smile. During the next 3 months the infant learns to distinguish the mother from other adults, and familiar people from unfamiliar. Certain additions to a familiar face, such as spectacles, may alarm and upset the baby. Distinction between male and female faces and a wariness of strangers can be demonstrated by 7 months of age. The increas-ing recognition of human voice patterns parallels that of faces and the infant learns to associate the mother's voice with her facial appearance, and sounds with the objects that make them.

The importance of vision in social and cognitive development is best illustrated by the responses of blind babies, and the problems experienced by their parents in developing normal attachments to them. This is discussed on p. 231.

Acquisition of concepts and skills

Children do not learn to speak unless they are exposed to spoken language but, however poor the environment may be, they can acquire some understanding of their surroundings, of spatial relationships and of their own abilities to influence the world around them, by observation and exper-imentation. The opportunity to explore and ma-nipulate objects helps intellectual development but, given a suitably structured task, even a severely physically disabled child may reveal a surprisingly advanced level of understanding gained entirely by observation.

The Swiss psychologist, Piaget, has had a major influence on modern ideas about cognitive devel-opment. His theories were based on observation of the spontaneous activities of his own children. Piaget realized that the infant is not merely the passive recipient of auditory and visual sensations; he/she has to organize and make sense of them. This is achieved in a series of developmental stages characterized by increasing sophistication of logical thought.

Piaget's work has stimulated a vast amount of research, which in turn has generated alternative explanations for his original observations. Some of the tasks used in his studies have been incor-porated into various psychometric scales, and three examples of Piagetian concepts which are of immediate value to the clinician are mentioned below. In general, however, Piaget's work in its original form is not easily adapted to clinical assessment.

Object permanence

This means that objects continue to have an existence of their own even when they cannot be seen. This is a concept of fundamental import-ance, discovered by each normal infant for

a   b   c

d   e   f

Fig. 3.3 Development of object permanence: **a**, adult shows baby the toy so he/she wants it; **b**, adult hides toy under a cloth; **c**, baby can retrieve toy if only partly covered; **d**, baby can retrieve toy even if fully covered; **e**, if it is hidden several times under the same cloth and then under a second cloth, the baby searches under the first cloth; **f**, baby searches under correct cloth even with a choice of three.

him/herself in the first year of life. In the first few months any object which is out of sight is out of the baby's mind, as far as ordinary clinical observation can tell. The evolution of the concept of object permanence is illustrated in Fig. 3.3. This is the concept underlying many familiar milestones and assessment tasks, including peep-bo games, searching for a fallen object, retrieving a pellet covered by a box or cup, and (at a more advanced level) having a regular place for storing toys and searching systematically for one that is missing. It is also a necessary concept for language development; before an object can be labelled, it must be recognized to have an independent existence. Emotional security and maturation are dependent on the child's discovery that their parents continue to exist even when not immediately visible.

Causality

This refers to the child's ability to deduce the link between an action and its consequence. Between 4 and 8 months, a baby observing an interesting spectacle will indicate their desire for a repeat performance by what Piaget called 'procedures' — for example, generalized excitement, vocalization or banging their hands on their table. Procedure games help the infant to learn that their actions influence the world around them and make things happen. From 8 to 12 months, the baby becomes more certain of the link between spectacle and performer and the procedures become more complex — for example, touching the adult's hand. Between 12 and 18 months, if presented with an interesting toy, the child is likely to explore it, but will not be able to operate it and will therefore return it to the adult with an eloquent unspoken request for the toy to be reactivated. From 18 months onwards, the child is likely to make a more prolonged, determined and systematic effort to solve such problems on their own.

Generalization

Normal children can use previous experience to solve unfamiliar problems. For example, they can recognize a hairbrush or a cup even though it may be of a different shape, size, colour and material from the one they have at home. The parents of learning-disabled infants often report that they recognize such objects at home and are surprised that they obviously do not recognize a similar item presented to them in the clinic. Similarly, the parents may teach their learning-disabled child to complete a difficult jigsaw, but when they are asked to complete a slightly different puzzle it becomes clear that they have not generalized this learning and that they have no idea of the significance of the task or of the picture on the puzzle. It is important to recognize this situation, since it is a common source of confusion among parents.

Attention and attention control

Advances in play, in logical thought and in language skills are associated with increasing maturity of attention control. Attention, the ability to focus only on selected stimuli, is a difficult function to measure and it certainly cannot be adequately described in terms of duration alone. Even very young babies sometimes show intense and prolonged concentration on an object or a social game. The young child has difficulty retaining and processing information from auditory and visual channels simultaneously. He/she cannot await sequential instructions or switch their attention easily back and forth between, for example, a play activity and an adult's comments; these abilities gradually develop, in the third and fourth years. With increasing maturity, the child becomes less readily distracted by irrelevant stimuli. There is good reason to believe that attention is a skill which is to some extent determined by environmental factors and can be taught. In clinical practice, observations of attention control are invaluable and are easily made during the course of hearing and language assessments. The clinical problems of hyperactivity (p. 327) are widely regarded as a consequence, at least in part, of an impairment of selective attention control.

Play

Some play is concerned with discovery; it enables the child to explore their environment by experimentation with objects and ideas and to rehearse various activities, real or imagined, without any external pressure to achieve a particular goal. It may be a way of thinking, using representational toys with which the child can re-enact a memory or explore a puzzling situation. Other play activities are more obviously concerned with the mastery of skills.

The role of parents

There are conflicting views on whether adults should intervene and help a child with their play. Some authorities feel that this robs the child of the satisfaction of making discoveries for him/herself. However, there is some evidence that judicious help from an interested adult can accelerate the child's mastery of ideas and methods of reasoning.

> Some parents show a superb capacity to break tasks down so that they are always offering the child problems to solve as he tries to learn something, but problems which are neither too difficult nor too easy. When the child starts to experience difficulty, they immediately step in and structure the situation more tightly; as he shows signs of success they back off, leaving him greater scope for initiative. In simple laboratory situations at least, this performance by the parent correlates with the child's ultimate ability to solve the problem alone. The strategy of teaching does have a causal influence on the child's learning. (D.J. Wood in Rutter, 1980; pp. 241–2)

Adult interventions in play may involve spoken instructions and suggestions but are probably more effective if the point at issue is also demonstrated, since young children appear to have some difficulty in learning by purely verbal instruction.

Pictures, story-books and toys all stimulate parent–child interactions with both visual and auditory components. In a favourable environment, play becomes increasingly complex and imaginative in the early years of life, as summarized in Table 3.9. The Lowe and Costello Symbolic Play test offers a standardized method of assessing play in children under the age of 3.

Play is not synonymous with toys and in many cultures children invent their own games without any purpose-designed props. Nor is it dependent on internal verbalization, although it is sometimes said to require 'inner language'. The play of a newly-diagnosed deaf child may reveal an extensive understanding of everyday events and ideas, even though the child has no verbal language.

The motivation to explore and learn seems to be inborn. This can be encouraged and reinforced by the parents, so that the child discovers that learning is a pleasurable experience. Not all motivation is dependent on reinforcement from other people or on material rewards; discovery and problem-solving bring their own satisfaction.

Persistence of immature patterns of play and behaviour

It is normal for an infant to mouth objects, but this does not usually continue much beyond 18 months, except for comfort or in moments of boredom. Hand regard, the practice of intently observing their own hands, should also have subsided well before this age. Similarly, 'casting' or throwing objects away as soon as they have been inspected briefly, is common at 1 year, but by 18–21 months should have more or less disappeared except, perhaps, as part of a temper tantrum. Shaking a toy is a normal response at 9–12 months, but is likewise unusual by 18 months, except with rattles and noise-makers, where the behaviour is appropriate. The repeated occurrence of such activities in a child over the age of 2 is cause for concern.

A normal child of 2 and upwards can concentrate on an activity or toy and explore its possibilities methodically. Flitting rapidly from one toy

Table 3.9 Development of play

1 year	3 years
Indiscriminate response to all toys (e.g. mouthing, handling, banging)	Actions which demonstrate understanding of properties (e.g. balls roll, cars can be pushed)
Random series of actions	Sequential investigation (touching, manipulating, activating)
Items used one at a time	Use of toys as a group (building bricks; cup and saucer; toy cars and garage)
Brief episodes of attention	Organized game with a theme and time sequence
Imitates adult actions on self (pretends to eat), then on doll (feeds doll)	Objects interacting, e.g. doll feeds another doll
Functional use of toy (brick used to build)	Toy can represent something else (e.g. brick becomes a car)
Dependence on adult for ideas	Can invent a game and direct its execution

to another, constant opening of cupboards, and fiddling with taps and light switches in spite of reprimands are disturbing behaviour patterns that are often associated with learning disability, autism or severe emotional disturbance. It may be tempting to describe these children as 'hyperactive', but this is a much abused term which is best avoided unless a firm diagnosis of hyperactivity is being considered (p. 327).

Clinical assessment

The evaluation of cognitive ability forms part of any developmental assessment. The distinction between language-based skills and non-verbal abilities is particularly important when the child has a hearing loss or other communicative impairment (Chapters 11 and 12). The concept of non-verbal intelligence should be explained to the parents; they need to understand that a child who is unable to hear or comprehend spoken language can nevertheless learn through visual observation and can demonstrate their intelligence by what he/she does.

Assessment procedures should be used which test the child's ability to form concepts and solve problems without any dependence on spoken language. Standard intelligence quotient (IQ) tests and developmental scales do not always make this distinction; items often test both verbal and non-verbal concepts simultaneously. Specialized psychometric tests have been designed for this purpose (p. 12), but in practice psychologists often use the more readily available standard tests and omit items which have a significant verbal component, or they make allowances for the child's communication difficulty.

Similar but even more difficult problems are encountered when the child's cognitive abilities are masked by a severe motor disorder, as in cerebral palsy; these children can neither communicate by speech nor reveal their intellectual capacity by gestures or movements. See p. 269 for further discussion.

Information obtained from the parents and informal observation are often sufficient to form at least a tentative opinion of the child's non-verbal abilities, prior to more formal psychometric assessment if the latter seems indicated. Table 3.10 gives examples.

Three very rough indicators may be useful for the rapid exclusion of serious developmental disorder. Firstly, the achievement of normal developmental milestones (unless the child has some impairment such as cerebral palsy or hearing loss); secondly, the size of the child's vocabulary correlates quite well with other markers of normal development (assuming there is no evidence of hearing loss or specific language difficulty); thirdly, the level of curiosity is a helpful indicator, although it is important not to be misled by aimless flitting from one object to another, which is related to attentional problems rather than curiosity.

Table 3.10 Questions and observations about non-verbal abilities

Self-help skills
Does the child understand about daily routines (bathtime, bedtime, mealtimes)?
Can the child hold his/her bottle or cup/feed him/herself/use a spoon?
Does the child try to help when being dressed/undress him/herself/dress him/herself?
Does the child try to help with tasks in the home? Give examples
Can the child wash and dry his/her hands without help?

Play
How does the child spend most of his/her time?
Does the child have favourite toys and know their use?
Does the child know where to find his/her toys?
Does the child put objects in and out of containers?
Does the child have any bricks or similar toys? What does he/she do with them?
What does the child do with a pencil or crayon — scribble, do circles, try to draw something?
Does the child play any imaginary games?
Does the child have any puzzles? What sort and how well does he/she do them?
Can the child select a favourite tape or video? Can he/she play it without help?*

* NB. This skill is acquired by many normal children before the second birthday and is not indicative of high intelligence!

Self-representation

The developing child acquires an idea about him/herself. In part this is descriptive — their self-concept: what sort of person he/she is, what sex, their name and other ways in which he/she shares characteristics with others or is different from them. In this context, children with a disability may come to realize what their disability is and what it means for them. They may misunderstand the nature of their problem — a child with dyslexia is highly likely to believe him/herself to be unintelligent. Particularly in adolescence, there is an issue as to whether they see themselves as predominantly handicapped or essentially normal:

'I am deaf' versus 'I've got a hearing problem.' It is not always clear which the more beneficial position is. Although a common ideological orthodoxy is to encourage children with disabilities to see themselves as essentially normal but with an impairment, in this instance being deaf may allow the teenager to feel part of the community of deaf people and to draw some sense of identity and solidarity from that.

There is also an evaluative dimension in terms of the level of self-esteem possessed by the child. Children with a normal sense of self-worth have a measure of confidence in themselves which enables them to try new things, to persevere and to expose themselves to a wider range of experiences than those who have poor self-esteem, think themselves useless and fear failure. Good self-esteem therefore facilitates development and the acquisition of skills. Repeated failure is common, almost by definition, in children with disabilities and those around them need to recognize how susceptible they are to low self-esteem, which, in turn,

handicaps them further. Disparagement or ridicule may emanate from the peer group, but is not unknown within the home or classroom, where it should not be tolerated. The importance of using encouragement, accurate feedback and incentive schemes is hard to exaggerate.

Motor development

The movement patterns of normal infants show a remarkable uniformity, implying that some neural pathways are 'preprogrammed'. A number of 'primitive' reflexes can be demonstrated (Fig. 3.4) and these gradually disappear as the baby matures and develops cortical mastery of movement. The biological importance of these reflexes is uncertain and the rate at which they disappear is variable, so they are of limited usefulness in clinical assessment. Because their movements appear at first glance to be random, uncoordinated and purposeless, neonates were for many years regarded as 'purely reflexive beings'. It is now

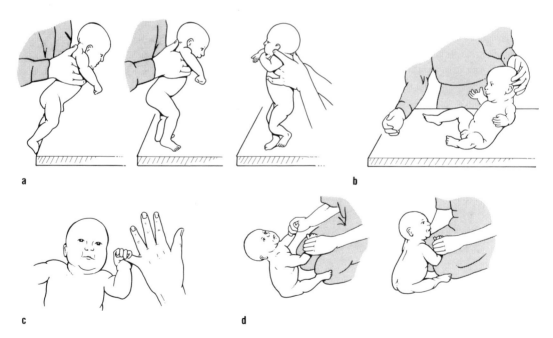

Fig. 3.4 Motor development — the primitive responses of the first 2 weeks: **a**, placing and stepping; **b**, Moro reflex; **c**, grasp; **d**, head lag.

known that purposeful movement does occur even in the early weeks of life, for example visually guided reaching for an object is present as early as 11 days, although a carefully contrived experimental situation is needed to demonstrate this.

The development of posture and movement is dependent on two physiological functions, tone and reciprocal innervation. Postural tone is the degree of muscular tension at a particular point in time; it is constantly altering in response to movement and changes in posture. Reciprocal innervation means that, whenever a movement is performed, there is a change in the tone not only of the muscles performing the movement but also of opposing muscle groups and of those that provide fixation for the active part of the body, for example stabilization of the shoulder while performing a skilled movement with the fingers. Both the early motor development of infancy and the later acquisition of complex motor skills depend on increasingly refined cortical control of tone and reciprocal innervation.

The righting reactions and equilibrium reactions are reflex postural mechanisms which are believed to be essential to normal motor function. Righting reactions are active responses which maintain normal alignment of the head and face with the body, trunk and limbs. They are dependent on sensory information through visual, labyrinthine, tactile and proprioceptive stimuli. Equilibrium reactions are complex responses to changes in posture and involve continuing changes in muscle tone to maintain posture and balance. When handling a young infant, these are often better felt than seen. Sudden changes in posture elicit the saving or parachute reactions.

While there is no doubt that complex reflex mechanisms of movement do develop as the infant matures, it should be remembered that much of the experimental work on which their original description was based was carried out on animals with extensive brain lesions. In this situation, the reflex patterns which can be elicited are stereotyped and the normal control of movement is totally abolished. In contrast, motor development in the normal infant is smooth and integrated. The value of describing it in terms of discrete reflex patterns must be questioned.

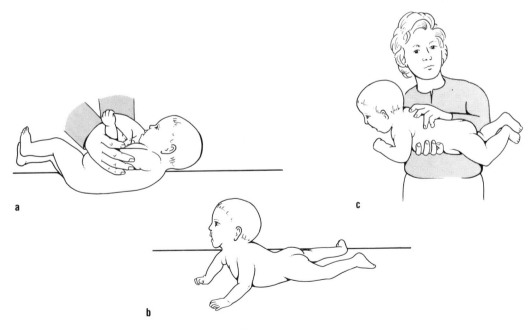

Fig. 3.5 Motor development — 5 months of age: **a**, pull to sitting; **b**, prone; **c**, ventral suspension.

The first 6 months

The flexed posture of neonates gradually changes over the first few months to one of predominant extension. There is increasing control of head and trunk as the postural reflexes develop (Fig. 3.5). In the prone position, they push themselves up on their hands and by 4 or 5 months show eager but usually ineffectual attempts to crawl towards desired objects. They learn to pivot round in this position and gradually discover the creeping posture. At 5–7 months the protective reflexes appear (Fig. 3.6) and these remain for life. Independent safe sitting is only possible when these are present.

In the early weeks, the hands are often fisted, but extension of the wrist and fingers occurs in periods of activity. The asymmetric tonic reflex posture (Fig. 3.7), in which the head and eyes turn towards the extended arm, encourages infants to view their hands and they become fascinated by the movements of their fingers, using vision to supply feedback in the development of more complex manual skills.

By 3 months they are examining the fingers of both hands together in the midline (Fig. 3.8) and by $4\frac{1}{2}$ months they can control them enough to pick up objects. They then learn to hold two objects simultaneously and to transfer from one hand to the other. By 7–8 months they acquire the skill of opposing finger and thumb but, when presented with a small object, a raking movement of all four fingers may be used, a movement which is characteristic of this stage of development. Manual dexterity improves throughout the second year with increasing control over delicate finger/thumb movements.

In the early years, initiation of fine movements in one limb causes similar movements in the opposite limb and other associated movements, such as tongue protrusion and facial grimacing, also occur during the performance of skilled motor tasks. With increasing competence movement becomes more concise and economical and associated movements diminish, but they may still be observed at times even in adult life and are of doubtful significance. Motor control depends not only on the level of maturity but also on emotional status at the time of examination.

Hand skills and the suppression of unwanted associated movements continue to mature throughout childhood, and this can be demonstrated using the neurodevelopmental examination techniques described on p. 66.

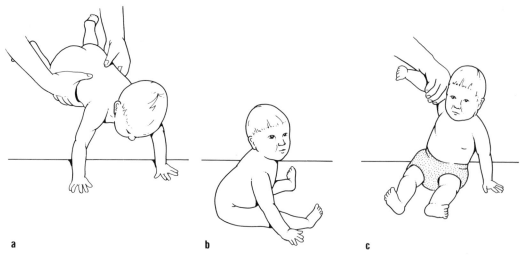

a   b   c

Fig. 3.6 Protective reflexes at 10 months old:
a, downwards parachute reaction; b, forwards reaction;
c, sideways reaction.

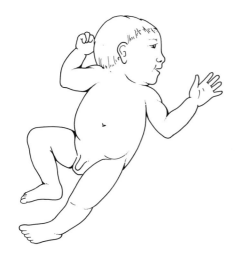

Fig. 3.7 Asymmetric tonic neck reflex (ATNR) (age 6 weeks).

Fig. 3.8 Hand use in midline (age 5 months).

Motor learning

In the early stages of learning a motor task, performance is slow, jerky and inaccurate and is monitored by visual and proprioceptive feedback as the results of the movement are observed. With mastery of the task, the execution becomes smooth, continuous and organized and is no longer dependent on feedback. Specific examples, such as learning to play a musical instrument or mastering a sport like skating, are familiar to everyone. Undoubtedly the same learning process increases the economy and efficiency of movement in all motor development. One striking feature of motor learning is that, once a skill has been mastered, it can be executed in a variety of ways. For example, when a child has acquired the skill of signing their name, this unique signature can be reproduced in an endless variety of ways: with a pencil on paper, a paint brush on a wall or a stick in the sand. The muscles used are different, but the pattern is the same. Probably the effects of encouragement and opportunity to practise motor skills are cumulative and become more evident as motor activity becomes more complex, as with language and cognitive development. Some children, however, appear to have exceptional difficulties in organizing their movement patterns and making the transition from the jerky to the smooth level of performance, as seems to be the case in 'clumsy' children.

Factors affecting motor development

There are wide variations between individuals in the rate of motor maturation, and examples of this are shown in Fig. 3.9. There are probably also racial differences in the speed of maturation, which are only partly explained by different methods of child rearing. Certainly there are familial differences. Many of the children with isolated motor delay show a particular pattern of motor development known as bottom-shuffling (Fig. 3.10), which runs in families, providing good evidence for the existence of genetically determined variations in development. Some children walk as early as 7 months, whereas shufflers may not walk until 30 months, and yet subsequently no difference can be found between the early and the later walkers, either in motor competence or in intelligence.

As with other aspects of development, much of the variation in motor progress must be attributed to genetic factors, affecting both specific motor pathways and temperamental characteristics of

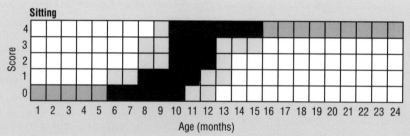

Sitting

Score:
0 The infant was unable to sit without support
1 The infant was able to sit free for some seconds
2 The infant was able to sit free for about 30 s
3 The infant was able to sit free for about 1 min
4 The infant was able to sit free for longer than at least 1 min

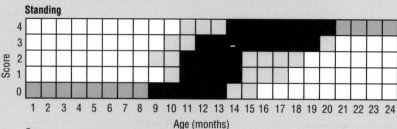

Standing

Score:
0 The infant was unable to stand up
1 The infant was able to get into a kneeling position while supporting him/herself with one or both hands
2 The infant was able to get into a standing position while supporting him/herself during standing
   The infant was not able to sit down without help
3 The infant was able to get into a standing position while supporting him/herself during standing
   The infant was able to sit down without help
4 The infant was able to stand free

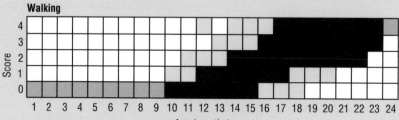

Walking

Score:
0 The infant was unable to walk
1 The infant could walk if mother held him/her by both hands
2 The infant could walk if mother held him/her by one hand
3 The infant walked free for a few paces
4 The infant walked free for at least seven paces consecutively

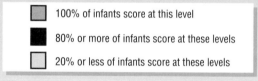

100% of infants score at this level

80% or more of infants score at these levels

20% or less of infants score at these levels

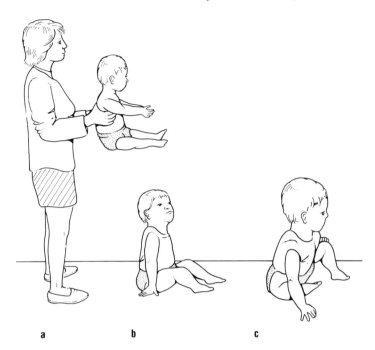

Fig. 3.10 Bottom shufflers. These babies are often slightly low-toned; they dislike the prone position. **a,** When held vertically they do not weight bear but adopt a 'sitting on air' posture; **b,** they are often late to walk and instead of crawling they shuffle; or **c,** hitch using one hand. There is often a family history suggestive of dominant inheritance.

        a   **b**   **c**

curiosity and drive. Under normal circumstances environmental influences do not seem to have much effect on the rate of early motor development, although teaching of specific motor skills is certainly possible even in infancy. In cases of extreme emotional deprivation, for example when a child has been left unattended in a cot for hours at a time, there may be an apparent marked delay in motor development, associated with general apathy. The motor development of blind babies is also delayed, probably because the motivation for movement is reduced (p. 231).

Anatomical variations affecting motor development

There are marked variations in the degree of internal and external rotation of the femur and tibia in early childhood. There may be an extreme degree of external rotation at the hips, so that the feet can be turned 90° outwards. This may be asymmetric (Birch and Wenger, 1981). In femoral internal torsion, the femoral neck points slightly anteriorly, causing the feet to point inwards. The tibia may show medial torsion with similar results.

Bow legs (genu varum) are normal in the infant but should correct by 18 months of age. At this age there should not be more than 4 cm between the femoral condyles when the ankles are placed together. Knock-knees (genu valgum) are common in childhood, but also rarely need treatment. *Anterior* bowing of the tibia is abnormal and is associated with bone defects which predispose to fracture. With the exception of the last, most of these deformities correct spontaneously. Their importance to the paediatrician is that, although they are normal variants, they may present with an 'awkward' gait or a complaint of excessive falling.

References and further reading

Baron-Cohen, S., Allen, J. and Gillberg, C. (1992) Can autism be detected at 18 months? The needle, the

---

Fig. 3.9 (*Facing page*) Variations in the motor development of normal infants. From Touwen (1976).

haystack and the CHAT. *British Journal of Psychiatry*, **161**, 839–43.

Bernstein, B. (1971) *Class, Codes and Control*, Vol. 1. Routledge & Kegan Paul, London.

Birch, R. and Wenger, J. (1981) Unilateral outward-turning leg in infancy. *BMJ*, **282**, 776–7.

Bishop, D.V.M. (1990) *Handedness and Developmental Disorder*. Clinics in Developmental Medicine, No. 110. Mackeith Press, London.

Chomsky, N. (1959) A review of B.F. Skinner's 'Verbal Behaviour'. *Language*, **35**, 26–58.

Clark, H.H., Clark, E.V. (1977) *Psychology and Language: An Introduction to Psycholinguistics*. Harcourt, Brace, Jovanovich, New York.

Combes, G. and Schonveld, A. (1992) *Life Will Never be the Same Again: Learning to be a First Time Parent*. Health Education Authority, London.

Crystal, D. (1976) *Child Language, Learning and Linguistics*. Edward Arnold, London.

Crystal, D. (1981) *Clinical Linguistics*. Disorders of Human Communication, No. 3. Springer Verlag, Berlin.

Goodyer, I.M. (1990) Family relationship, life events and childhood psychopathology. *Journal of Child Psychology and Psychiatry*, **31**, 161–92.

Hopkins, B. and Kalverboer, A.F. (1983) Symposium on mother infant interaction (4 papers). *Journal of Child Psychology and Psychiatry*, **24**, 113–62.

Kalverboer, A.F., Hopkins, B. and Geuze, R. (1993) *Motor Development in Early and Later Childhood: Longitudinal Aproaches*. Cambridge University Press, Cambridge.

Lukeman, D. and Melvin, D. (1993) The preterm infant: psychological issues in childhood. *Journal of Child Psychology and Psychiatry*, **34**(6), 837–50.

Martlew, M. (1987) Prelinguistic communication. In *Language Development and Disorders*, (ed. W. Yule and M. Rutter), pp. 53–69. Mackeith Press, London.

McFadyen, A. (1994) *Special Care Babies and their Developing Relationships*. Routledge, London.

McGuire, J. and Earls, F. (1987) Prevention of psychiatric disorders in early childhood. *Journal of Child Psychology and Psychiatry*, **28**, 215–22.

Moscowitz, B.A. (1978) Learning to speak. *Scientific American*, **239**, 84.

Paediatric Clinics of North America. (1977) *Symposium on Orthopaedics*, Vol. 24, No. 4. W.B. Saunders, Philadelphia.

Pinker, S. (1994) *The Language Instinct*. Allen Lane, Penguin Press, London.

Pollak, E. (1993) *Textbook of Developmental Paediatrics*. Churchill Livingstone, Edinburgh.

Pugh, G., De'Ath, E. and Smith, C. (1994) *Confident Parents, Confident Children*. National Children's Bureau, London.

Robson, P. (1970) Shuffling, hitching, scooting or sliding: observations in 30 otherwise normal children. *Developmental Medicine and Child Neurology*, **12**, 608.

Robson, P. (1968) Persisting head turning in the early months: some effects in the early years. *Developmental Medicine and Child Neurology*, **10**, 82–92.

Rolf, J., Masten, A.S., Cicchetti, D., Nuechterlein, K.H. and Weintraub, S. (1993) *Risk and Protective Factors in the Development of Psychopathology*. Cambridge University Press, Cambridge/New York.

Rutter, M. (ed.) (1980) *Scientific Foundations of Developmental Psychiatry*. Heinemann, London.

Rutter, M. (1992) *Developing Minds: Challenge and Continuity Across the Life Span*. Penguin Books, London.

Rutter, M. (1995) Clinical implications of attachment concepts: retrospect and prospect. *Journal of Child Psychology and Psychiatry*, **36**(4), 549–72.

Schorr, L.B. (1989) *Within our Reach: Breaking the Cycle of Disadvantage*. Anchor Books (Doubleday), New York.

Silva, P.A. (1987) Epidemiology, longitudinal course and associated factors: an update. In *Language Development and Disorders*, (ed. W. Yule and M. Rutter), pp. 1–15. Mackeith Press, London.

Staheli, L.T. (1986) Torsional deformity. *Pediatric Clinics of North America*, **33**(6), 1373–83.

Thomas, A. and Chess, S. (1957) An approach to the study of sources of individual differences in child behaviour. *Journal of Clinical and Experimental Psychopathology*, **18**, 347–57.

Thomas, A. and Chess, S. (1977) *Temperament and Development*. Brunnel/Mazel, New York.

Tizard, B. and Harvey, D. (1977) *Biology of Play*. Clinics in Developmental Medicine, No. 62. Mackeith Press, London.

Touwen, B.C.L. (1976) *Neurological Development in Infancy*. Clinics in Developmental Medicine, No. 58. Mackeith Press, London.

Trevarthen, C. (1974) Conversations with a two-month-old. *New Scientist*, May 2nd, 230–4.

Wells, G. (1985) *Language Development in the Pre-school Years*. Cambridge University Press, Cambridge.

Wenger, D.R. and Leach, J. (1986) Foot deformities in infants and children. *Pediatric Clinics of North America*, **33**(6), 1411–27.

CHAPTER 4

Practical Aspects of Assessment

Organization

The organization of assessments depends on the facilities available and on the personal styles of the staff, but several authors have described their personal approach and shown how their resources have been adapted to meet the particular needs of their patients. There is no evidence that any one method of assessment is superior. One essential on which all authors agree is an efficient secretary and organizer to co-ordinate assessments and ensure smooth communication between staff and parents.

In some units, assessment of a disabled child may last for 3 weeks, whereas in others it is completed in a few hours. No information is available on the relative efficiency or value of varying styles of assessment. It is not possible to outline any one approach which can be used as a recipe for every clinical problem, and flexibility and imagination are essential if time and skill are to be used economically. In many districts, children with 'straightforward' problems such as language delay are assessed in community clinics and only those children with severe or complex problems are referred to a Child Development Centre. Frequently, however, one finds that the policy has never been clearly articulated and often it is chance rather than logic which determines how resources are used.

Assessment of developmental problems is time-consuming. The initial consultation can seldom be completed in less than 30 minutes and may often require an hour or more. Failed appointments are therefore both irritating and very expensive in terms of wasted professional time. Paediatricians should encourage their colleagues who refer children for assessment to write directly rather than use a hospital or clinic appointment system, since only by knowing the details of referrals in advance can they make optimum use of time and resources. All available details about the child should be collected in advance, except in the rare cases where parents request a second opinion 'blind' to the views of other doctors. A letter outlining practical details of the assessment is sent to the parents with the appointment, and a reply-paid card is enclosed so that parents can indicate whether they will keep the appointment offered. Sometimes, if the family is socially incompetent or disorganized, the health visitor or social worker may help to ensure that the appointment is kept. An interpreter may be needed for families from ethnic minorities.

Introduction to the family

The doctor should usually collect the parents and the child from the waiting area him/herself, as much can be learnt about the child by discreet eavesdropping while casually strolling in the waiting area. Older children should be greeted by name. It is easy to be seduced by the charm of a smaller normal sibling and to ignore the disabled child if he/she is not very active or vocal. This mistake commonly irritates parents, since it reflects the attitudes of society in general to the disabled, and parents feel that doctors specializing in this field should know better!

If a behavioural or emotional problem seems to be the main cause for concern, older children may sometimes conveniently be left in the waiting area to play or read, so that the parents feel less inhibited in explaining their worries. The child should always be recalled and given a résumé, appropriately edited, of what has been discussed. An individual session with the child on their own may also be illuminating.

51

Parents should sit in comfortable chairs, beside the doctor rather than on the far side of the desk. Colleagues should be introduced, and permission obtained beforehand for the presence of non-essential observers such as professional visitors or students. Young children are often shy and clinging on arrival in a strange place. Social overtures should not be made too soon; even looking at some children may provoke tears. The production of a few interesting toys, particularly wind-up clockwork items, often works wonders, but they should be handed casually to the child without comment or eye contact. Nothing should be said to a young child that demands a reply until confidence is established.

'Difficult children'

It is frequently valuable to share the first consultation with one colleague, most commonly a speech therapist or physiotherapist. The therapist concentrates on involving the child in relevant activities while the doctor interviews the parents. It is then possible to compare notes immediately and to proceed to physical examination, hearing tests, etc., so that a preliminary combined opinion on diagnosis and management can be offered.

Observation facilities consisting of a large playroom and a smaller room separated by a one-way mirror are often useful. Good sound transmission is essential, and a table microphone or a portable radio-microphone, which can be worn by the child or carried by the therapist, gives better results than all but the most expensive fixed ceiling microphone systems. These facilities can be used in two ways. A child may happily separate from the parents, indeed may perform better in their absence, and their play and language abilities can be demonstrated by a therapist or psychologist, while the doctor and parents watch from the observation room. This system enables the parents to comment on the significance of the child's activities, and on whether they are representative. It has an additional unexpected advantage; many parents find that the one-way mirror enables them to take a more objective view

of their child's disability than has hitherto been possible.

Alternatively, one or both parents may be asked to play with the child in the playroom, while the doctor and colleagues watch from the observation room. This is sometimes the only way of assessing an extremely shy child, and is invaluable in cases of severe language disorder or selective mutism. It is surprising how well most parents cope with this experience.

Overactive, restless and fidgety children can be very distracting and may make interviewing impossible. It is helpful to fix a handle high on the door of the consulting-room to prevent the child from absconding every few moments. Cupboards should be locked, shelves high and taps isolated by stopcocks! When the paediatrician fails dismally in attempts to control the child, he/she can say to the parents, 'How would you normally deal with this at home?' This gives them freedom to carry out any course of action and may, at the same time, throw more light on behaviour problems. When all else fails, one must either find an alternative child-minder while the interview is completed or make another appointment to see the parents unencumbered.

Sometimes a restless or fretful child may be used by the parents as a 'prop' to pace the interview. If the discussion is distressing, for example at the time of diagnosis of a disabling condition, they may welcome opportunities to comfort the child or intervene in their bad behaviour or play, while they regain control of their emotions and digest each item of information.

Video- and tape-recording

These can be useful in several ways. Video facilities are invaluable for making a permanent record of motor and language disorders. A portable camera is sometimes helpful for the analysis of puzzling behavioural problems which only occur in specific situations. Video is also a powerful tool in some training regimes, for example social skills training. The bizarre language and behaviour of autistic children can also be captured in this way.

A tape-recorder may be loaned to parents of children who refuse to talk in a clinic, for example in selective mutism. Some parents welcome being able to take away a tape-recording of the assessment, particularly the discussion of findings.

Assessment at home

Children are seldom seen at their best in unfamiliar clinic surroundings and there is much to be said for assessing children at home, at their playgroup or in nursery school. The extra time spent may be justified by the additional information gained and the reduced need for further consultations. On the other hand, hearing and vision tests are more difficult to perform at home, and some parents feel that an opinion delivered in a hospital consulting-room is more authoritative than one given at home.

Non-attendance and non-compliance

Parents may fail to attend because they are unconvinced that there is anything wrong with their child; they only agreed to visit the paediatrician to placate their general practitioner or clinic doctor! Others fear that something really is wrong, but cannot face the possible bad news. Follow-up appointments are often failed for different reasons. Parents may need time to adjust to the bad news before facing the doctor again, or they may feel dissatisfied with the opinion given, or may be despondent about the limited ability of medical knowledge to help their child. It should not be forgotten that there are other genuine reasons for non-attendance, such as muddled appointments and long delays in clinics.

For people of limited means, without transport of their own, the usual social orbit is very restricted, and a visit to a paediatric unit only a few miles away may require a great personal effort of organization, enquiries about bus routes, etc., which may be more than the inadequate parent can manage. The paediatric team must be sufficiently flexible to be able to respond to such cases in the most appropriate way, for example by visiting the child at home or at school. Contact may be made via the health visitor or social worker.

Some parents are criticized by therapists for not complying with the recommended treatment programme, either by non-attendance or by not following instructions at home. Often this is interpreted as a form of non-acceptance or rejection of the child. While this may be so, other reasons include the demands of other members of the family, doubt about the effectiveness of the measures recommended, and inadequate instruction or explanation.

Structure of the interview

A consultation for a developmental problem can be divided into the following stages: (1) definition of the problem; (2) background history; (3) present developmental abilities and problems; (4) physical and neurological examination; and (5) preliminary exposition of the findings to the parents. These may be followed by: (6) further assessment by members of the multidisciplinary team; (7) investigations, if indicated; and (8) further discussion and/or case conference with parents. Most readers of this book will be familiar with routine paediatric interviewing and physical examination. It would be superfluous to describe these in detail and the following discussion is confined to points of particular relevance in developmental problems.

Definition of the problem

The first questions to ask are: 'Why have the parents brought the child?', 'Who is worried, and about what?' and 'Why has the child been referred at this particular time?' It is not always the parents who are the most worried; it may be the teacher, school doctor or grandparent. For example, the main object of an assessment is sometimes to reassure other professionals that they are managing the child's disability correctly. The parents should be asked where they have been for previous advice, whom they have consulted, who is currently responsible for the child's care and what they understand of the child's problems. Often the parents' view of the situation is remarkably different (and sometimes more accurate!) than that of the referring professional. Whatever the problem may be, it is essential to establish whether it is improving, deteriorating or merely becoming more obvious as the child gets older. The distinction between progressive and non-progressive or static disorders is a vital and early stage in differential diagnosis.

The background history

In developmental problems it is often easier and more logical to begin the history in the past and work forwards. This gives an immediate understanding of family background, attitudes and function. Crucial information, such as a family history of an inherited disorder or severe maternal depression, emerges early in the interview; and parents are less likely to suspect that this detailed history means that the doctor attributes their child's problems to bad management.

Family structure

A family tree should be constructed, using the conventional symbols (Fig. 4.1). This clearly defines family relationships, at the same time providing the basis for recognizing inherited disorders. Now that there are so many one-parent families, it may be diplomatic to ask an unaccompanied parent 'Who else is there in the family?' and 'Who lives at home?'; it is important to know about both parents, both to avoid embarrassing mistakes in relation to genetic aspects and also to understand family reactions. Other children with their dates of birth are listed. The question 'Any other pregnancies?' will elicit details of babies who have died, miscarriages and stillbirths. This information may not otherwise be volunteered, but it is often relevant in the genesis of parental depression and conflict, and may also help in aetiological diagnosis.

Consanguinity should be noted, particularly among Asian families. The question 'Are you related to your husband?' usually causes some confusion or amusement and should be supplemented 'For example, are you cousins or second cousins?' The point may need to be pursued still further, e.g. 'Do you come from quite separate families?' There are often distant relationships which may be thought insignificant by the family.

The parents' occupations are recorded. Specific enquiries should be made of their health, and about relevant familial disorders, including muscle disease, backwardness or learning problems in school, fits, delay in speech or motor development, and a history of bottom-shuffling in parents or siblings.

Social background

The parents' geographic and ethnic origins and religion should be established as they are of importance in understanding both child-rearing practices and attitudes to disability. Isolation from family support makes it harder for parents to cope with stressful situations. Religious beliefs may explain unexpected response to bad news; Catholics, Moslems, Hindus and non-believers may react in very different ways to the birth of a disabled child.

Family relationships

Many of the common developmental disorders, notably speech and language delay, are associated with behavioural disturbances — indeed, it may be largely chance that determines whether the child is first seen by a paediatrician, speech therapist or child psychiatrist. Some insight into family function is essential for optimal counselling. It is not always necessary or desirable to ask explicit questions. One can often 'read between the lines' and the doctors may do better to keep their insights to themselves rather than alienate the parents by probing too deeply, before they feel ready to discuss private matters. Some psychopathology can be found in most families

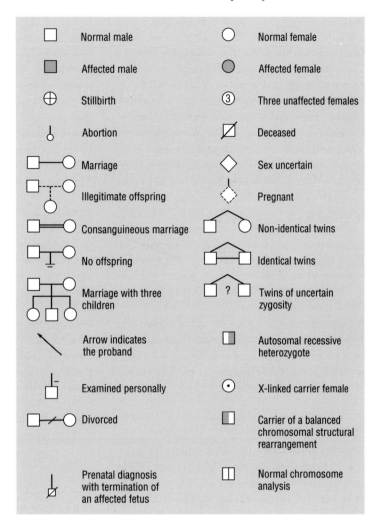

□	Normal male	○	Normal female
■	Affected male	◉	Affected female
⊕	Stillbirth	③	Three unaffected females
⌀	Abortion	⬚	Deceased
□—○	Marriage	◇	Sex uncertain
□┈○	Illegitimate offspring	◈	Pregnant
□═○	Consanguineous marriage	□ ○	Non-identical twins
□⊤○	No offspring	□—□	Identical twins
□—○	Marriage with three children	□ ? □	Twins of uncertain zygosity
↖	Arrow indicates the proband	▯	Autosomal recessive heterozygote
□	Examined personally	⊙	X-linked carrier female
□⧸○	Divorced	▮	Carrier of a balanced chromosomal structural rearrangement
⌀	Prenatal diagnosis with termination of an affected fetus	▯▯	Normal chromosome analysis

Fig. 4.1 Symbols used in pedigree construction. The affected individual who caused the family to seek advice is called the proband.

and it may be tempting to exaggerate the parental contribution to a disturbed relationship and to ignore the relevance of deviant language development or difficult temperamental characteristics in a child. Abnormalities in the child can cause abnormalities in parent–child relationships as well as vice versa.

Obstetric history

In addition to the usual medical information, the obstetric history can provide an opportunity to probe parental attitudes to the child. For example, 'What was pregnancy like?', 'How did you feel about being pregnant?', 'How did the child's father feel about it?' The usual enquiries about viral illnesses, drugs and smoking should include alcohol and exposure to any other drugs or noxious substances.

The birth history should include the parents' recollection of the early minutes of the baby's life. Minor obstetric interventions and abnormalities such as forceps delivery may acquire an exaggerated importance to the layman, but details must be carefully recorded so that misconceptions can be eliminated later. Abnormal birth and neonatal behaviour may be of great diagnostic importance, but the parents' recollections are often hazy and inaccurate, and a report from the place of birth is usually essential to evaluate the significance of perinatal events. Postnatal depression is common and well known, and many mothers will admit to having been depressed, although they may disguise its severity. Sometimes the nature of the clinical problem makes it unlikely that perinatal events are relevant. In these cases, the history may be curtailed by asking 'screening' questions such as 'Were the doctors worried about the baby?' or 'Did you go home with the baby at the usual time?'

Past medical history

Specific questions should be asked about fits, faints and funny turns, head injuries and pertussis immunization. The doctor may well consider these events irrelevant, but the family often regard them as highly significant.

Important events

Life events such as births, deaths, marital breakdown or moving house should be noted. They may well not be relevant to the child's disability but sometimes account for management problems and may seem to the parents to have aetiological significance. A convenient question is 'Did anything important happen in the family around this time: for example, serious illness, moving, a death in the family and so on?'

Developmental history

Retrospective recall of the ages at which milestones were achieved is known to be unreliable, so little time should be spent on this unless it seems likely to be crucial, as may be the case when a progressive disease is suspected. One can enquire about the child's progress at specific points, e.g. their second birthday, Christmas or a

period of hospitalization. Comparisons with siblings or children of relatives or neighbours may also jog the memory.

Although parents may rapidly forget dates and ages, they never forget the growing feeling of anxiety that something was wrong. Useful questions are: 'Were you, or anyone else, ever worried about his/her development at that time?' or 'If you look back over his/her early months now, do you think there was any problem at all?' (Table 4.1).

Interview with the child

In appropriate cases children should be interviewed, either alone or with their parents. Suitable topics for conversation include: their family and pets; whether they like school, whether they ever wish they need not go to school, and what they like most and least at school; the names of their friends; what they do at home; what they did last Saturday; what they worry about; what makes them happy and sad; what other people think of them; and what they would wish for if they had three wishes. Often a brief conversation along these lines will enable the developmental paediatrician to recognize situations where the help of a

Table 4.1 General questions about development

How does the child compare with other children of the same age?
How much do you think the child is behind other children in development?
Do you think the child is getting further behind as he/she gets older?
Is the child losing the ability to do things he/she could do before?
Is this what the child is like at home?
Have I seen a fair picture of what the child can do?
What do you think is the child's biggest problem?
If the child could tell us, what would he/she say his/her biggest problem is?
Is the child able to concentrate when he/she is interested in something?
How does the child spend his/her time at home?
Does the child pretend or show any imagination?

child psychiatrist might be useful. Conversely, it can be reassuring when a parent is desperately worried about the effects of a disability on the child's emotional well-being.

Developmental assessment

In developmental assessment an initial profile of the child's abilities is obtained by combining information obtained from the parents, with observations of the child's behaviour, as discussed in Chapter 3. A guide to normal attainments and milestones is useful. The Denver test (Fig. 4.2), although originally devised for screening rather than assessment, provides a useful systematic introduction to child development. The information obtainable from the parents is limited mainly by the ingenuity of the interviewer. Equipment can be purchased very cheaply and expensive test kits, though useful, are not essential. A restricted range of toys should be reserved for the actual assessment and the paediatrician should become familiar with the range of normal responses to them. Other toys should be available for the child to use while the parents are interviewed.

The majority of children with developmental disorders have non-progressive problems. Although progress may be slow, the parents are quite clear that they are not getting worse (although the gap between the child and their peers may be getting wider). A history of loss of skills is always worrying and must be elucidated with care. Some children with moderate or severe learning difficulties (p. 148) learn a few new words, use them briefly and then apparently lose them; this situation is common and is usually associated with non-progressive learning problems, but can be wrongly interpreted as evidence of progressive brain disease or hearing loss or acquired aphasia (p. 190).

Children under 1 year of age will usually respond quickly to friendly overtures. In this age-group, most developmental scales overemphasize motor development and it is essential to look carefully at social and communicative behaviour

as well. In the 12–21 months age-group, children can initially be presented with four or five familiar items, such as a cup, spoon, brush and shoe. They are more likely to demonstrate their understanding by appropriate action ('definition by use') than by speech (Fig. 4.3). The child is then asked to point out the items, using a normal voice level. If their co-operation can be sustained, a very simple hearing test can be attempted (p. 77), but many toddlers become engrossed in one or two objects and ignore all further spoken instructions. Patience and skill are needed to divert attention to new tasks.

Beyond 21 months of age, even shy children can usually be persuaded to respond to instructions, although it may be a long time before they will speak and even longer before the speech produced is representative of their competence. No pressure should be put on the children to talk, and parents who try to do so must be asked to desist. When toys are offered to them, they are told the name of each, but are *not* asked to say the word. Once they seem relaxed and interested, they can be casually asked 'What is this one?' but if they do not reply they should be told at once, or they may well dissolve into tears or retreat to the parent. A game can often be developed using, for example, doll's-house furniture or a toy garage, and this will reveal the extent of their understanding and symbolic play. Alternatively, books and pictures can be used as a stimulus for conversation.

An approximate assessment of non-verbal skills can be made, using familiar tests such as the copying of models built from bricks; copying a line, circle, cross, square and triangle; colour matching; the 'draw a man test'; a three-piece form board, or a more complex board with up to a dozen pieces. Toys which can be activated in various ways often produce more co-operation and interest. Simultaneously the attention control and social maturity are estimated.

Hearing tests

A hearing test is a routine part of developmental

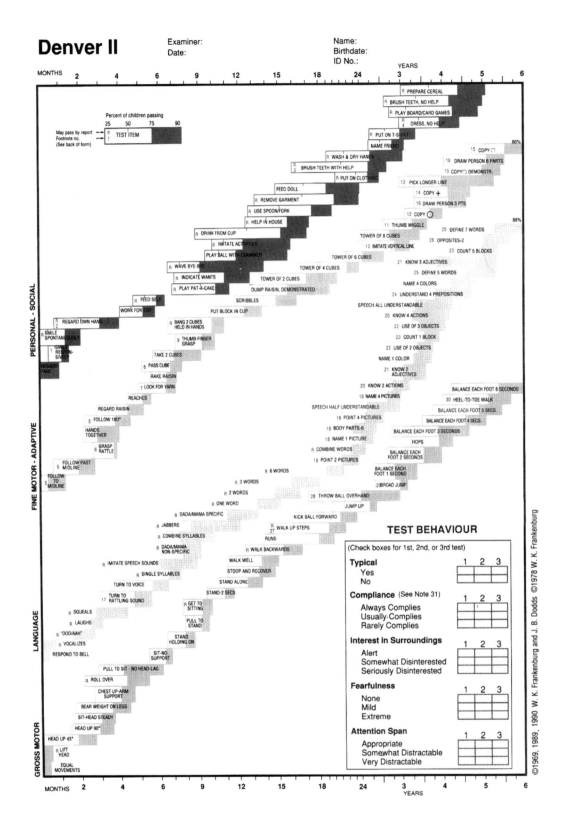

assessment. For descriptive convenience, however, the techniques are discussed in Chapter 5. There are several reasons why developmental paediatricians may wish to undertake hearing tests, if appropriately trained. Firstly, they have the necessary skills in handling young children. Secondly, the differential diagnosis of abnormal language development includes deafness; conversely, the assessment of suspected deafness includes an evaluation of language development. Furthermore, the child's reactions to a hearing test are in themselves a useful developmental test.

Physical examination

Physical examination is often deferred until the developmental assessment is completed. Measurement and charting of height, weight and head circumference, and a general examination should be routine. More comprehensive accounts of physical and neurological examination will be found elsewhere.

Physical anomalies

So many dysmorphic syndromes have now been described that no one can or should try to remember them all. In many cases, the features are so striking that they immediately prompt further enquiry, but this is not always the case. It is therefore essential to cultivate the habit of careful observation; all minor anomalies, however trivial, should be recorded and, if their significance is uncertain, standard reference works should be consulted (see Glossary). The fact that an anomaly is trivial in appearance does not always imply that its significance is also trivial; for example, ear pits may be a genetic marker of severe deafness. Some defects can occur either as isolated anomalies or as part of a more serious

---

Fig. 4.2 (*Facing page*) The Denver Developmental Screening Test provides a convenient reference summary of important developmental milestones. Courtesy of Denver Developmental Materials, Inc., Denver, USA.

Fig. 4.3 Definition by use.

disorder, for example pes cavus may be the first sign of Friedreich's ataxia.

Single minor anomalies, such as those listed in Table 4.2, occur in 14% of infants and are seldom significant. They are often also present in other family members. However, only 0.5% of babies have three or more minor defects and 90% of these have a major defect as well. Thus, although they may not suffice to make an exact diagnosis, minor dysmorphic features are a useful pointer to the prenatal origin of a child's problems. Abnormal dermatoglyphics (fingerprints) are found in some conditions but as a diagnostic aid have proved to be very disappointing.

Neurological examination

Delayed motor milestones are usually obvious even to unsophisticated parents. Motor development and the disorders which affect it are easier to assess than language or intellect, because they can be analysed by means of the classical neurological examination and investigations. Because of the wide variations of normality, developmental assessment can never be a substitute for the neurological evaluation. The distinction between gross and fine motor function, recognized in all

Table 4.2 Minor anomalies (these may be indications of more serious malformations and suggest a prenatal origin for a child's problems)

Large fontanelle (particularly posterior fontanelle; suggestive of delay in ossification)
Third fontanelle
Wide-spaced eyes (hypertelorism)
Slanted palpebral fissures
High palate and prominent lateral palatal ridges (suggestive of hypotonia with weakness of tongue)
Preauricular tags and pits
Prominent, slanted or low-set ears
Clinodactyly (curved finger)
Camptodactyly (bent finger)
Syndactyly
Hypoplasia of nails
Abnormal skin creases
Anomalous hair patterns
Dimples over bony points
Shawl scrotum (scrotum extends above and around base of penis)
Scalp defects

Variants not classed as anomalies
Minor variations in folding of ear
Shallow sacral dimple
Syndactyly of second and third toes

---

developmental scales, has no *neurological* validity. Both may be, and usually are, affected by any disorder of the central or peripheral nervous system. Nevertheless, the motor items found in these scales offer useful ways of eliciting and documenting motor behaviour.

Neurological assessment is intended to answer two questions: firstly, where is the lesion? and, secondly, what is the lesion? Traditionally, it is said that the first of these is more likely to be answered by the physical findings, and the second by the history. The principles underlying the adult neurological examination are applicable to children of all ages but with two additional complications: the young child's inability to co-operate and the need to distinguish between signs due to organic nervous system disease and those associated simply with immaturity. A distinction is

sometimes made between hard and soft signs. Hard signs are those which would provide unequivocal evidence of damage to neurological pathways at any age. Soft signs are more subjective and their interpretation more variable. They indicate immaturity rather than disease of the nervous system and they largely disappear by the age of 9 or 10 years. The neurodevelopmental examination is designed to demonstrate these signs (p. 66).

Preliminary observations

Abnormalities of posture, poverty of movement and unwanted movement patterns can be recognized simply by watching the infant. Hemiplegia, ataxia and athetosis are demonstrated by presenting the child with a toy at arm's length. Building a tower with bricks is a poor test of intellect but a good way of demonstrating unwanted movements. If old enough, the child is asked to walk, run, climb on a chair, hop, walk heel-to-toe and rise from the supine position (Fig. 4.4). These can all be done before the child is touched, and if they are made into a game subsequent examination is simplified. If these manoeuvres show no weakness or abnormality of posture, gait or fine hand function, the child is unlikely to have any major neuromuscular disease.

Cranial nerves

Examination of the eyes, eye movements and visual fields is described on p. 86 and hearing testing on p. 69. Facial movements and asymmetry can be recognized when the child smiles or cries. In upper motor neuron lesions, the forehead movements are spared. Facial involvement and asymmetry may be seen in hemiplegia but, surprisingly, are often minimal or undetectable. In lower motor neuron lesions, the whole face is involved. The asymmetric crying facies syndrome, which is due to congenital absence of the depressor anguli oris muscle, is often mistaken for a lower motor neuron lesion. Bilateral facial

Fig. 4.4 Gower's manoeuvre. To rise from supine, the child turns into the prone position, and 'walks' the hands up the thighs. The manoeuvre indicates proximal muscle weakness. From Dubowitz (1978).

weakness occurs in myopathies and in the Moebius syndrome. A brisk jaw jerk is found when upper motor neuron lesions affect the facial and oral musculature. Neurological examination of facial sensation, tongue, lips and palate rarely reveals hard signs in developmental problems but 'soft' signs are common.

Primitive reflexes

Assessment of the primitive reflexes is usually included in the routine examination of infants under 6 months of age, although their value is limited. Prolonged persistence of these reflexes is seen in severe cerebral palsy (p. 247), but is rarely, if ever, the first or main clue to the diagnosis. The age at which they disappear is very variable even in normal babies. Minor asymmetries of movement, posture and reflexes are often detectable in the first weeks of life. Some authors consider that these 'hemisyndromes' are often followed by developmental problems, but the physical signs are very subtle and errors are easily made.

Protective and postural reflexes

The positive supporting reaction and the sideways and forwards saving reactions appear around 6–8 months, as weight-bearing and independent sitting become established. The feel of the baby as he/she attempts to correct their posture during the sideways saving reaction should be noted. The forwards response is a sensitive way of demonstrating sluggish and asymmetric hand function in cerebral palsy. The Landau reaction may be abnormal in any neurological or muscular disorder which impairs muscle strength or control of the trunk postural reflexes. These reflexes are often difficult to demonstrate if the child is very tense, fearful or screaming and, in these situations, the hands may be fisted and the arms flexed, even in the normal baby.

Examination of the limbs

The limbs are inspected for muscle bulk, texture, pseudohypertrophy, fasciculation and equality of size and length. Asymmetry may be recognized by a need for different-size shoes (half a size difference is common and is not necessarily significant), unequal wear or unequal size of the feet and hands, often best demonstrated by comparing the finger- or toenails and if necessary by measuring limb circumference.

Tone can be assessed by flapping the limb, by flexing and extending at the elbow and knee and abducting the hip, and by pronating or supinating the forearm while holding the child's hand as in a handshake. The characteristic catch of spasticity (the clasp-knife phenomenon) and continuous rigidity through the full range of movement (lead-pipe rigidity) may be distinguished by these manoeuvres.

Power in the major muscle groups can be examined even in very young children with a little ingenuity. Observation of spontaneous activity is usually adequate to rule out gross weakness. Trying to take a toy away from the child or tickling their feet while holding them still may help to assess muscle power in toddlers and babies. By the age of 3, many children will try to co-operate with detailed muscle testing, but their limbs often need to be moved passively to demonstrate each action, rather than relying on verbal instructions. Little boys, in particular, will often co-operate better if the examination is made into a 'trial of strength' game.

Tendon reflexes can be difficult to evaluate in small children. Muscle tone and reflexes depend very much on the child's state of mind. These may appear to be markedly increased in a hungry crying baby or in a frightened young child. Even very brisk reflexes and a few beats of ankle clonus may be within normal limits. Babinski responses are unpredictable and of little clinical value before the second birthday. Even if one is extensor and the other flexor, this may be of no significance. Asymmetry of tendon jerks is more likely to be clinically important, but is usually only unequivocally present when other physical signs are also obvious. Complete areflexia is found in some neuromuscular disorders, such as Werdnig–Hoffmann disease, but tendon reflexes may be difficult to elicit in some normal babies. The

presence of brisk reflexes does not rule out the possibility of muscle disease. In very severe spasticity or rigidity, it may be difficult to elicit any reflexes at all.

Problems of movement control

A mild symmetrical tremor is quite commonly seen in 2 and 3 year olds. It may be worse when the child is anxious. If there is little or no functional difficulty, and there are no other signs or complaints, a long-standing but non-progressive tremor in this age-group is unlikely to indicate either ataxic cerebral palsy or any other serious neurological disorder.

A broad-based gait with exaggerated balancing movements of the arms is normal when a child first begins to walk, but in an older child may be evidence of ataxia. In children old enough to co-operate, a poor performance on classical tests, such as the 'finger–nose test' and rapid alternating hand movements, is more commonly associated with 'clumsiness' (see below) than with cerebellar disease.

Excessive choreiform movement is best revealed by asking the child to hold their arms outstretched, palms up, fingers spread, mouth open and eyes closed. It may be very marked, particularly in boys of around 4 or 5 years of age. These movements gradually resolve with increasing maturity and, unless the history suggests unusual severity, recent onset or progression, they should not be regarded as evidence of nervous system disease.

Sensation

In young children, major sensory deficits may be delineated by watching for changing facial expression or withdrawal reactions when unpleasant stimuli such as tickling, pinprick or pinch are applied. Even with co-operative older children, sensory examination is tedious, and several attempts are usually needed. Situations where this is necessary are uncommon in general paediatric practice. Children with hemiplegic cerebral palsy often have a deficiency in cortical sensation, best assessed by 'writing' shapes and letters on the palm (graphaesthesia) or by placing objects in the hand for tactile recognition (stereognosis).

*Orthopaedic examination**

The full length of the spine must be exposed to reveal short-neck syndromes, midline cutaneous anomalies and scoliosis. Limbs are inspected for deformities such as syndactyly. Rotation deformities of the lower limbs and normal variations in posture of the feet are easily mistaken for neurodevelopmental disorders. Two common complaints are that the child falls too often and that the feet do not 'look right'. Common minor orthopaedic problems which can be recognized by the developmental paediatrician or physiotherapist and do not usually require orthopaedic referral are described below.

Intoeing. Intoeing is due to femoral neck anteversion, tibial torsion or metatarsus adductus. In infancy, the angle between the femoral neck and head, and the femoral shaft, is different from that observed in the older child and adult. Instead of pointing inwards, the head and neck point forwards. As the child grows, the femur spirals until the adult position is reached. If the child starts to walk while the femoral heads are still pointing forwards, the child rotates the leg inwards as he/she walks, in order to maintain the position of the femoral head firmly in the acetabulum. The child therefore walks with the kneecaps facing each other and the feet pointing inwards.

This can be demonstrated by placing the child prone (Fig. 4.5a–c) and showing that the legs can be rotated inwards often to 90°, whereas the outward or external rotation is greatly reduced (Fig. 4.5d). This apparently alarming 'deformity' almost always resolves with growth, usually by the

* This section is adapted from Hall, Hill and Elliman (1994) by kind permission of Radcliffe Medical Press, Abingdon.

age of 8 or 9 years, and no treatment should be given or suggested.

Tibial torsion. The tibia spirals as it grows in the same way as the femur. If the growth and rotation of the tibia is out of step with that of the femur, the foot may be either inwardly or outwardly rotated. Inward rotation of the foot is associated with internal tibial torsion and leads to intoeing. It is usually associated with outward curving of the tibia, giving an apparent bow-leg appearance. Clinical assessment is rather more difficult than in the case of the thigh. It is necessary to assess the thigh–foot angle as shown in Fig. 4.6.

Metatarsus adductus (varus). Some children have feet with an inward curve between the heel and the toes, giving the foot the appearance of a banana (Fig. 4.7). The condition is distinguished from clubfoot by the normal position and appearance of the heel. In most cases the deformity is minor and corrects spontaneously.

Outtoeing. When the child stands and begins to walk, the feet turn out, sometimes to nearly 90°. The hips are externally rotated and internal rotation is much reduced (Fig. 4.5e). Spontaneous correction occurs in most cases and no treatment is needed.

Flat feet. The child should be asked to stand on tiptoe. If the arch is seen to form normally when the child does this the foot is normal and no treatment is required.

High arched or 'cavus' feet, and clawing of the toes. These are more likely to be abnormal and may have a neurological cause.

Overriding of the fifth toe over the fourth. This is common and though not serious can be a troublesome problem to treat. Attractive simple solutions, such as strapping, do not help. If necessary, the toe can be straightened by surgery.

Knock knees and bow legs. A mild degree of bow

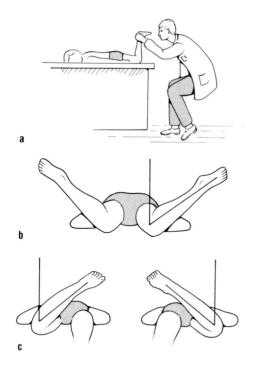

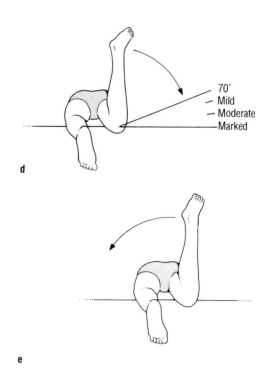

Fig. 4.5 Hip rotation. **a,** Assessment of hip rotation — the child lies prone. **b,** Assessment of internal rotation. **c,** Assessment of external rotation — each hip is checked separately. **d,** Increased internal rotation. **e,** Increased external rotation. From Hall, Hill and Elliman (1994), redrawn from *Pediatric Clinics of North America* (1977), **24** (4).

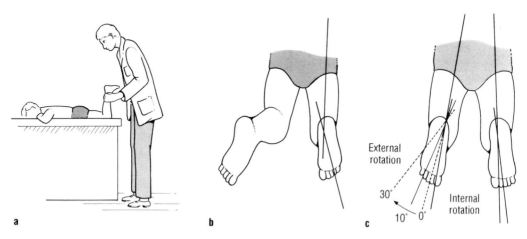

Fig. 4.6 Tibial torsion. **a,** and **b,** Assessment of thigh — foot angle. **c,** Normal range of thigh — foot angle is 0–30° of external rotation with a mean of 10°. From Hall, Hill and Elliman (1994), redrawn from *Pediatric Clinics of North America* (1977), **24** (4).

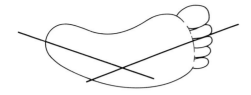

Fig. 4.7 Metatarsus adductus (varus). From Hall, Hill and Elliman (1994).

legs (genu varus) is common up to the age of 2 years (Fig. 4.8a). Between 2 and 4 years old, knock knees (genu valgus) is a normal finding (Fig. 4.8b). The degree of rotation of the hips should be checked because internal rotation of the hips leads to the appearance of knock knees.

The extent of the deformity is easily determined. For bow legs, the ankles are brought together until they just touch and the distance between the knees is measured. To assess the degree of knock knees, the knees are brought together until the inside of the knees just touch and the feet are pointing straight forward. The distance between the malleoli of the ankles is measured and recorded. Up to 6 or 7 cm is generally accepted as normal in each case.

The neurodevelopmental examination

This is designed to reveal the 'soft signs' sometimes found in young children with learning disabilities, clumsiness, etc. It is not a substitute for conventional neurological examination. Soft signs are rarely indicative of neurological disease, nor do they reliably predict educational progress. The main value of the neurodevelopmental examination is in demonstrating to parents and teachers some possible reasons why a child is having so much difficulty with certain tasks, particularly those involving motor functions. Many versions of this examination have been described. Selected test items are listed in Table 4.3.

Head circumference

Measurement of the head circumference is always included in the developmental examination but, as small children dislike it, this may be left until

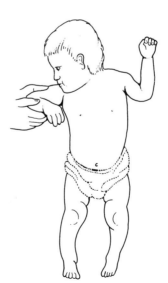

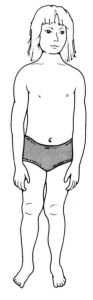

Fig. 4.8 a, A mild degree of bow legs (genu varus). **b,** Knock knees (genu valgus). From Hall, Hill and Elliman (1994).

a   b

Table 4.3 Neurodevelopmental examination: looking for 'soft' signs

---

Ask child to eye-track a moving target: observe whether, when asked to do so, he/she can do this without moving the whole head

Ask child to rapidly protrude and retract tongue several times: observe rapidity and smoothness of movements

Place tip of tongue on lip in various specified positions

Say 'lalala', 'p-p-p', 'k-k-k', 'p-t-k', several times

Stand still with eyes closed, mouth open, arms outstretched and hands supinated: watch for choreiform movements

Tap table with each finger in turn, like playing scales on the piano: watch smoothness and rhythm of movement. Observe ability to improve with practice. A marked difficulty with this task often emphasizes to the parent that a child's problems with writing or drawing are genuine and not just laziness

Hopping, heel–toe walking and standing on one leg: as in conventional neurological examination. Also ability to dribble and kick ball

Fog test: the child is asked to stand on the outer edges of the feet. Marked supination of the arms is normal in children under the age of 9 or 10

NB. These signs have been found to be clinically useful for interpretation and demonstration, but should not be construed as evidence of any specific entity. There are no absolute norms for different ages and each examiner must develop their own standards by experience.

last. It is essential to record the *maximum* occipito-frontal circumference, and the measurement should be taken twice to ensure accuracy. Paper and steel tapes do not stretch but they have sharp edges, and cloth tapes lengthen with prolonged use. Fibreglass tapes are best. The measurement is meaningless unless it is plotted on a head circumference chart and is related to the child's height and weight.

Conclusion

What the parents want is a diagnosis and an opinion as to whether the child really does have a problem that will significantly affect the child's and their own lives. It must never be forgotten that assessment is only the means by which this question may be answered. It has no intrinsic therapeutic merits!

The success of the consultation depends not only on the accuracy of the assessment and diagnosis, but also on the way in which the results are presented to the parents. This topic is discussed in more detail in Chapters 7 and 8. When the child has been seen and assessed by those members of the multidisciplinary team whose skills are relevant to the problem, a further consultation is arranged so that the conclusions can be discussed with the parents. It may sometimes be useful to hold a 'case conference' to plan management. In some areas, with well-developed services, the parents' biggest problem may be the proliferation of professionals who are all eager to help their child. One person may be named as key worker or case manager (p. 118), to provide a reliable contact for the parents in the event of further problems or concerns.

References and further reading

Baird, H.W. and Gordon, E.C. (1983) *Neurological Evaluation of Infant and Children*. Clinics in Developmental Medicine, No. 84/85. Mackeith Press, London.

Berger, M. (1991) Psychological testing. Current Paediatrics, 1(4), 233–5.

Dubowitz, V. (1995) *Muscle Disorders in Childhood*, (2nd edn). W.B. Saunders, Philadelphia.

Egan, D.F. (1990) *Developmental Examination of Infants and Preschool Children*. Clinics in Developmental Medicine, No. 112. Mackeith Press, London.

Hall, D.M.B., Hill, P. and Elliman, D. (1994) *Child Surveillance Handbook*. Radcliffe Medical Press, Abingdon.

Johnson, J.H. and Goldman, J. (1990) *Developmental Assessment in Clinical Child Psychology*. Pergamon, New York.

CHAPTER 5

Hearing Tests

Acoustics is the science of sound and its properties; audiology is the clinical study of hearing and its disorders. If the paediatrician is to diagnose communication disorders, recognize children who may have a hearing loss and perhaps undertake hearing tests when appropriate, some familiarity with the basic principles of acoustics and phonetics is essential.

Acoustic and phonetic principles

Sounds can be divided into two main types — pure tones and noises. A *pure tone* is a periodic sound with a waveform showing regularly repeating patterns. A *noise* is a sound in which pressure changes are random and do not show repeated patterns. Noises may be continuous, like hissing steam, or discrete, like the crack of a rifle.

Most clinical hearing tests in paediatrics require the child to respond by some means either to speech, to familiar non-speech sounds (for example, rattles) or to pure tones. In acoustic terms, the first two of these are complex sounds containing many different frequencies, whereas a pure tone is a simple sound consisting of a single tone of fixed frequency and variable intensity.

Frequency and pitch

Frequency of a soundwave is measured in cycles per second or hertz (Hz). Pitch is the subjective impression of frequency. The human ear is able to perceive frequencies of between 16 Hz and 20 000 Hz (20 kHz). The very low frequencies may be perceived partly as vibration. The ear is not equally sensitive to all frequencies. The greatest sensitivity is in the middle of the frequency range, around 1000 Hz. Higher sound-pressure levels are needed in the low and high frequencies to exceed the audibility threshold (Fig. 5.1).

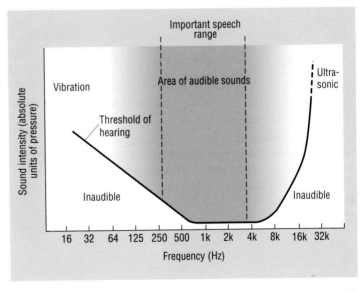

Fig. 5.1 Absolute threshold of hearing depends on frequency. After Newby (1979).

At each frequency, 0 dBHL (see below) is taken as the normal person's threshold of hearing for that frequency, and audiometers are calibrated accordingly, so the clinician does not need to make any adjustments for the differences in absolute sensitivity.

Intensity and loudness

The intensity of a soundwave refers to the transmission of sound energy, measured either as a pressure or as a flow of power. Loudness refers to the *subjective experience* of the intensity of a sound. The human ear is sensitive to a wide range of intensities; the loudest tolerable sound (the pain threshold) has about 100 million million (10^{14}) times the intensity of the softest sound audible to the average person (the audibility threshold) (Fig. 5.2).

Because this range is so wide, it is inconvenient to measure sound intensity in absolute units of pressure or power. Instead, it is customary to describe intensity as a ratio between the pressure of the sound and a reference pressure which corresponds approximately to the audibility threshold. The logarithm of this ratio is the number of bels. One bel is divided into 10 decibels (dB). An increase in intensity from 0 to 10 dB or from 30 to 40 dB represents a 10-fold increase. Intensity decreases in inverse proportion to the square of the distance from the sound source. Several different scales are used, depending on the situation (dBA for sound-level meters; dBHL for pure-tone audiometry (PTA); dBnHL for brainstem-evoked response (BSER) audiometry, etc. (see audiology texts for details)).

Measurement of intensity

Subjective estimates of sound intensity are unreliable and it is essential to measure intensity of the speech and other sounds used in audiological testing of young children by using a sound-level meter, which measures sound-pressure levels, in the range between 30 and 100 dB. Sound intensity falls off with the square of the distance so, when

Intensity (dB)	
0	Audibility threshold
20 – 30	Whisper
40 – 50	Background noise in average home/office
60	Conversational voice
75 – 80	Cocktail party voice
90 – 100	Discotheque
105 – 110	Shout
110 – 120	Low-flying aircraft
120 – 140	Jet engines, heavy machinery
140	Threshold of pain

Fig. 5.2 Sound intensities related to everyday experiences.

the intensity of sounds is checked, the meter must be placed at the same distance from the source as was the child during the test. It should also be in the same position since there may be variations in sound intensity at different points in a room.

Speech sounds

Speech sounds contain both tones and noises. *Tones* are generated in the larynx by the vibration of the vocal folds, produced by the passage of air from the lungs. The laryngeal tone is a high-energy, low-frequency carrier wave. The fundamental frequency is lower in men than in women and is around 100–200 Hz. There is no laryngeal tone in a whisper, which has a higher frequency spectrum and is therefore acoustically different from a quiet voice.

The pharyngeal space and oral cavity act as resonators and filters which alter sounds so that speech sounds can be differentiated and each person's voice is unique. Vowels are a homogeneous group of sounds produced at the larynx, with the largest energy peak in the lower frequencies (Fig. 5.3). In speech, hissing noises

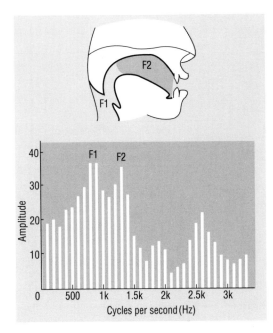

Fig. 5.3 Oral cavities: formants of 'a' as in 'bard'. From Whetnall and Fry (1964).

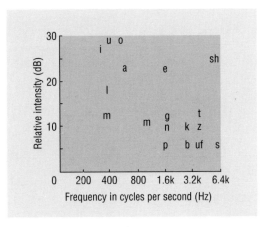

Fig. 5.4 Intensity and frequency of some common English sounds. From Whetnall and Fry (1964).

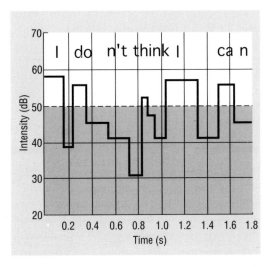

Fig. 5.5 Changes in mean intensity during the sentence 'I don't think I can'. Only the sounds whose intensity is above the shaded area would be audible to a child with an overall hearing loss of 50 dB. From Whetnall and Fry (1964).

such as the 's' sound (fricatives) and sudden noises like the 'b' sound (plosives) are superimposed on the basic laryngeal tone. Consonant sounds in general have a lower energy content but a higher frequency than vowels (Fig. 5.4). Analysis of connected speech shows that the intensity is not constant but varies over a 30–40 dB range (Fig. 5.5).

Characteristics of non-speech sounds

Responses to sounds made by sound-producing toys and musical instruments may be useful in detecting hearing loss in young children, but they give no information about the hearing loss at different frequencies. Casual testing with broad-spectrum sounds will 'miss' children who have hearing loss only in some frequencies. Two rattles, the Manchester and the Nuffield, are specially designed to produce only high-frequency sound. Most sounds should be assumed to produce mixed frequencies, however 'high-pitched' they may

sound to the listener (Fig. 5.6). Pure tones generated electronically for headphone testing have the advantage of precision in intensity and frequency. Warble-tone generators are preferred for children who are too young to wear headphones.

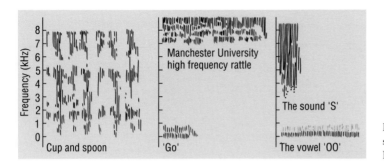

Fig. 5.6 Frequency spectrum of sounds used to test hearing. From Nolan and Tucker (1981).

Hearing loss

A person with impaired hearing will only hear sound when the intensity is raised beyond their audibility threshold. The sound intensity required to reach the threshold of the impaired ear is the threshold hearing level or *hearing loss* for that ear. Thus a person who cannot hear any sound quieter than 30 dB has 30 dB hearing loss. *Sensation level* is the level in dB of a sound, relative to the threshold of audibility for that sound for a particular individual. For example, a child with a 30 dB hearing loss perceives a sound of 70 dB intensity at a sensation level of 40 dB.

Audiometry

Adults or older children will co-operate in establishing their threshold by means of an audiometer, which generates pure tones, each having a single fixed frequency and known intensity. The tones are delivered via headphones. The method is called pure-tone audiometry (PTA). The results are plotted graphically, as an audiogram. At each frequency, one records the quietest sounds which the subject can hear, using a standardized procedure. By definition, the average normal person can hear a sound of 0 dBHL intensity at each frequency. The normal audiogram and the audiograms of two subjects with hearing loss are shown in Fig. 5.7.

Speech discrimination

Most of the information content of speech is carried in the consonants. Even a modest degree of hearing loss impairs the perception of consonants and therefore causes difficulties in the comprehension of speech. Children who have a high-frequency hearing loss may seem to respond normally to speech and other sounds because of their low-frequency components, and their hearing defect may only be diagnosed when they are old enough for the impaired speech comprehension to be recognized. The diagnosis of high-frequency hearing loss will inevitably be overlooked unless hearing tests always include high-frequency sounds.

Hearing tests in preschool children

Until children reach a developmental age of 3 or 4 years, they cannot be expected to co-operate in determining their threshold of hearing by PTA, and it is therefore not usually possible to establish the exact extent of a hearing loss using this technique. Nevertheless, a reasonably accurate estimate of hearing can be made. In some circumstances, when the child is very young, has other impairments, or is hard to test clinically for any reason, 'objective' electrophysiological methods may be invaluable (p. 80).

Sound-field testing

Clinical hearing testing in this age-group is performed in 'sound field', i.e. without headphones. The child indicates that he/she has heard the sound by a variety of behavioural responses, such as turning to locate the sound or selecting the

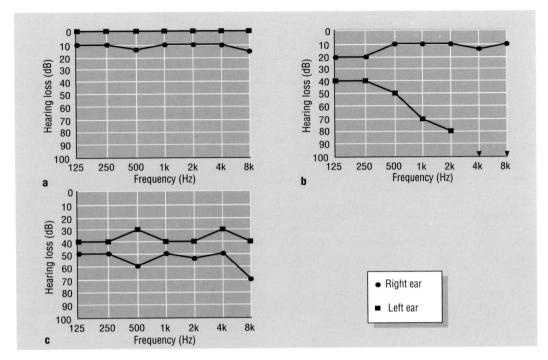

Fig. 5.7 Examples of audiograms: **a**, normal audiogram (left ear) and insignificant hearing loss (right ear); **b**, minimal hearing loss in right ear, severe high-frequency loss in left ear; **c**, bilateral hearing loss, averaging 40 dB in left ear and 50 dB in right ear.

named toy. The object is to determine, and to measure on a sound-level meter, the quietest sound level at different frequencies at which an unequivocal response can be obtained.

Sound-field tests are capable of producing an estimate of hearing loss which correlates remarkably well with the results obtained when the child is old enough to co-operate with audiometric testing. The apparent simplicity of the equipment and techniques used in free-field testing disturbs many parents and they may feel that the results should be confirmed with 'proper' tests using more sophisticated equipment. They can best be reassured that the findings are valid by an explanation of the principles underlying sound-field testing.

It is usual to assume that, if hearing responses can be obtained at levels of 30–35 dBA, there is unlikely to be a hearing loss of major clinical significance, although middle-ear disease may still be present. If responses are only obtainable at 40–45 dBA or above, a hearing loss must be suspected.

Background noise

When sound-field tests are performed, no response can be expected from the child if the test sounds are obscured by background noise. There is then an almost irresistible temptation to raise the intensity of the test sounds. The diagnosis of hearing loss is too important for casual testing in bad conditions and a sound-treated room is essential.

Practical aspects of hearing tests

The purpose of the diagnostic hearing tests described below is to establish or confirm the presence, severity and significance of a hearing loss and also, if possible, the anatomical site of the lesion. Diagnostic tests should not be confused with screening tests, which are intended only to separate children into two categories: the normally hearing and those with possible hearing loss. This topic is discussed on p. 83.

The history

Children with hearing loss usually present with one of the following: parental suspicion, family history of deafness, other high-risk factors (p. 83), delayed language development, failed screening test, symptoms of middle-ear disease or behaviour disturbance. A detailed ear, nose and throat (ENT) history is important. A family history of hearing loss, minor illnesses in pregnancy, perinatal problems and a history of viral illness, meningitis or head injury may be relevant.

Whatever the age of the child, always ask the parents, 'What do you think about their hearing?' *If the parents think that their child has a hearing defect, they are right until proved otherwise.* Sometimes their diagnosis is incorrect — for example, global learning difficulties (p. 148) or auditory agnosia (p. 186) may be the correct explanation of their observations — but when the parents suspect a hearing loss there is usually something wrong with the child. Conversely, if they are sure that the child can hear and can give reasons why they are sure, he/she is unlikely to have a profound hearing loss, although parents may easily overlook a moderate or high-frequency impairment. The lack of external stigmata of hearing defects and the child's ability to make sense of visual clues and behave in a socially normal fashion together deceive many parents (and doctors) into doubting that their child could possibly have a hearing problem.

The next question should be: '*Why* do you think the child can/cannot hear?' The parents'

observations should be noted in detail; if they are hesitant, questions such as those listed in Table 5.1 may be used to prompt them. If the child has age-appropriate comprehension of spoken language, without the aid of raised voice level, lip-reading or gestural clues such as pointing, he/she is unlikely to have any serious hearing problem.

Techniques of hearing testing

The blink reflex

This is also known as the acousticopalpebral reflex (APR). The blink is produced by a sudden loud noise. A positive response to a noise of 80–90 dB is good evidence that the child has useful hearing, but it is, of course, vital to ensure that the infant does not *see* the sound source. The reflex cannot be used to establish the hearing level.

Table 5.1 Useful questions about hearing

What do *you* think about the child's hearing?
Why do you think the child can/cannot hear? e.g.
  listens and turns to voices
  wakes when bedroom door opens
  hears dog bark, father's keys in lock, etc.
  hears rustling of sweet or biscuit paper
  responds to name
  carries out instructions when called from another room
      or without accompanying gesture
  hears loud noises, such as aircraft, sirens, etc.
  turns TV up loud
How long have you been worried about the child's
    hearing?
Can the child tell where a sound is coming from?
Does the child respond better if you raise your voice?
Does the child try to see your face when you speak to him/
    her?
Does the child watch your lips when you speak?
Does the child say 'eh', 'what' or 'pardon' frequently?
Does the child sometimes seem to deliberately ignore you?
Does the child's hearing seem to vary from day to day?

Distraction tests and visual-response audiometry

These tests rely on changes in behaviour and activity in response to a sound whose source is outside the child's visual field.

The ability to localize sound can sometimes be demonstrated even in the first weeks of life, by a gradual head turn towards human voice. Localization becomes increasingly accurate during the first year. By 6−8 months babies have learnt to control sitting balance and head posture, and can turn their gaze directly and precisely to a sound source in any position, except immediately above, below or behind their head. Babies who can hear the sound, but cannot turn to localize it because of visual or motor handicap, developmental immaturity or asymmetric hearing difficulty, may respond in other ways: for example, by cessation of motor activity or vocalization, or widening of the palpebral fissure. These responses may be genuine indicators of hearing but are more easily misinterpreted than a head turn.

As the concepts of object and person permanence develop, babies become increasingly aware of the tester's presence behind them and they may decide to ignore further stimuli; or else they regard the whole performance as a game, and try to outguess the tester by turning before the sound stimulus is presented. From about 15 months onwards, children are increasingly likely to become so engrossed in play that they may ignore even very loud sounds, making distraction testing difficult. Since most babies have adequate localizing and motor abilities by 6−9 months of age, but do not yet have a sophisticated concept of object permanence, this is regarded as the ideal age for distraction testing; however, the techniques can be applied throughout infancy, or, indeed, at any age, and are particularly useful in testing children with learning difficulties.

Technique

It is important to involve the mother or other carer who is holding the baby, by explaining the steps and purpose of the test. It is vital to ensure that the baby is properly positioned, that inadvertent clues are not given by bodily movements and that the mother herself does not startle if loud sounds need to be used.

The participants are arranged as shown in Fig. 5.8. The aim is to produce head-turning responses to sound, since these are more reliable than subtle activity changes. False-positive head-turn responses can easily be produced, by intrusion into the baby's visual field (Fig. 5.9), shadows, a draught created by shaking a noise-making toy, or even perfume or aftershave. The distractor is in the best position to recognize these artefacts.

The distractor

The skill of the distractor is crucial. The baby's visual attention is built up by means of interesting toys, amusing facial expressions, talking or any other available means. This stimulation is then abruptly reduced, creating a sudden 'sensory vacuum'. The baby looks surprised at the sudden cessation of entertainment, and waits tensely for its restoration. This tension reaches a plateau, and the tester must then present the sound stimulus, before the baby begins to look around for new interests (Fig. 5.10). When the baby turns to look for the sound source, he/she is immediately rewarded with brief praise. The tester then turns away and measures the level of sound at which the baby responded, while the distractor regains the baby's attention.

If the baby does not turn, the tester raises the intensity of the sound stimulus in gradual steps, until the baby responds. If the baby loses interest, the distractor must regain their attention. If there is no response to a loud sound, the tester touches the baby's cheek to ascertain their responsiveness to other stimuli and confirm that the baby is able to turn his/her head normally. The responses to visual stimuli must also be checked. If the baby turns to touch or to visual stimuli but not to sound, hearing is likely to be impaired.

One common problem in distraction testing is

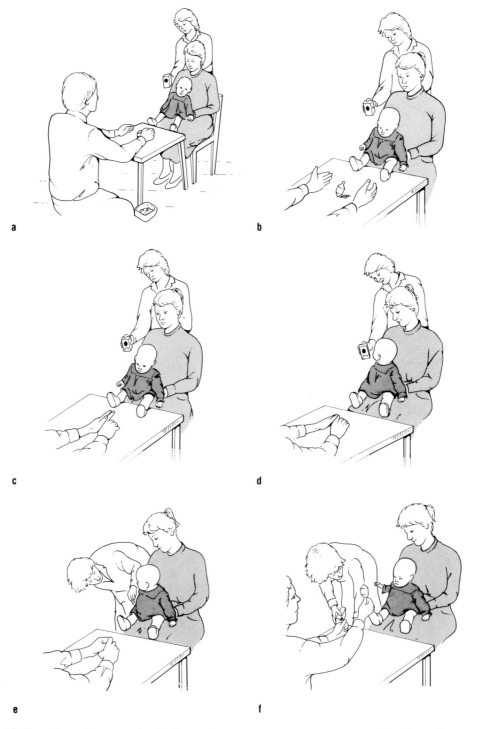

Fig. 5.8 Distraction testing: **a**, test situation; **b**, attention capture; **c**, fine manipulation of attention; **d**, head turn response; **e**, response reward by assistant; **f**, attention recaptured by distraction. From McCormick (1988).

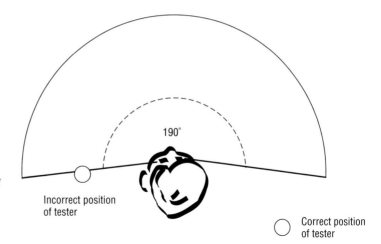

Fig. 5.9 Visual fields. Because they extend beyond 180°, it is easy to produce false-positive turning responses due to vision rather than hearing.

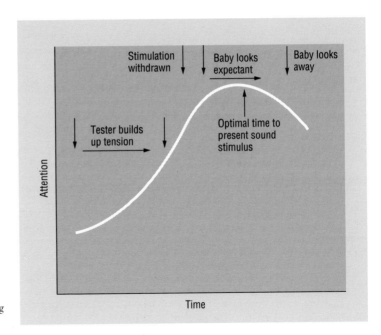

Fig. 5.10 Distraction testing: timing is crucial. After Taylor (1964).

that the baby becomes too interested in the distractor's face and therefore does not respond to the sound stimulus. To avoid this, the distractor should avoid making prolonged eye contact with the baby. When the moment is chosen to reduce the level of visual stimulus, the toy used to control the baby's attention is placed on the table and the distractor covers it with his/her hands,

making just enough finger movements to prevent the baby's gaze from shifting to his/her face. The baby will then be more likely to turn and seek the source of the sound stimulus.

Visual alertness

Some babies turn frequently to seek novel visual

stimuli. This is particularly a problem with babies who are older than 9 or 10 months. To control for this possible source of wrong results, 'no-sound trials' should be used. The distractor and tester go through the routine of making a test sound, except that no sound is actually made. If the baby repeatedly turns during no-sound trials, their responses to sound stimuli must be deemed unreliable.

Unilateral hearing loss

It is customary to present test sounds on each side, but this type of testing does not yield reliable estimates of hearing in the individual ears unless one is occluded; this is seldom tolerated by young children. Incorrect localization is very suggestive of an asymmetric hearing loss, but gives no indication of its severity in the worse ear. The value of distraction tests is that they indicate the level of functional hearing and, in a hearing-impaired child, may show which is the better ear.

Frequency and intensity

The aim of the distraction test is to establish whether the infant responds to high-frequency (4 kHz and upwards) and low-frequency (500 Hz) sounds on each side. It is also useful to use-mid-frequency (2 kHz) sounds as occasionally the hearing may be defective only in this range. If the infant is responsive and the history does not suggest any hearing loss, the intensity of the test sounds should be at minimal levels, i.e. 30–35 dBA. When responses are not easily obtained, louder sounds may be used to gain the baby's interest. The intensity is then progressively reduced until responses become inconsistent or cease.

Visual reinforcement

Some audiology rooms are equipped with loudspeakers through which a variety of electronically controlled signals can be played, in a sophisticated version of distraction testing. The child can be rewarded for turning to localize the sound source by a variety of visual stimuli, such as lights, toys or moving puppets. Visual-reinforcement audiometry is useful for children over the age of 10 months.

Co-operative testing

Distraction testing becomes more difficult after the age of 15 months but few children can carry out audiometric tests with headphones before the age of 3 or 4. The co-operative tests described here are occasionally possible in children as young as 18 months, although others are unable to perform these tasks reliably until the age of 2.5 or even 3. Children's ability to cope with these tests itself gives useful insight into their overall development and maturity.

The tests fall into two groups: those that make use of the child's ability to discriminate speech, and those that demand a response to other sounds. If possible, one test of each type should be performed. The history and preliminary distraction tests indicate whether a major hearing loss is likely. Errors are commonly made because the tester begins with the assumption that the child can hear his/her instructions and test sounds. To hearing-impaired children, the tasks required of them are meaningless, but they try to co-operate, making full use of any visual and situational clues, and may well succeed in misleading the tester. The only safe approach is to begin with a 'null hypothesis' that the child has no hearing. The estimate of their hearing threshold is then progressively revised as evidence is collected from the history and examination.

Unilateral or asymmetric hearing loss

At this age, it is difficult to assess the hearing in each ear separately. This does not usually matter; the immediate aim is to determine the *functional* hearing level. However, any suspicion of asymmetric responses should be followed up until definitive tests are possible.

Disabled children

Even if children are physically disabled, they can respond by eye-pointing or by any motor response which is under their command. Satisfactory results may also be obtained with children who have learning difficulties, provided that the mental age is about 2.5 years or more.

Test procedures

Often it is possible to exclude serious hearing loss very quickly by three simple tests. Firstly, choose a suitable moment when the child is looking elsewhere and say in a very quiet voice 'please shut the door', 'where's my teddy gone?' or some similar remark to which the child might respond readily. Secondly, make a quiet 'sss' sound and observe the response. Thirdly, make a sound when the child is looking elsewhere, to check localization. Visual clues and responses must be avoided.

Speech discrimination tests

The choice of words and the structure of the test depend on the child's vocabulary and behaviour. Toys are useful to gain attention and overcome shyness in the less mature child, but the child may become too involved in play to co-operate with the test and pictures may then be more suitable.

The child should preferably be seated at a table (Fig. 5.11) but, if the child prefers, he/she can sit on their mother's lap or on the floor, or even under the table! Each object or picture is shown in turn. The parent is asked to indicate if an unfamiliar item is presented. Neither tester nor parent should ask the child to name the items him/herself, but it is important to find out the child's word for each object. Often, the child will start to name them him/herself, but for the purposes of the hearing test it does not matter if the child remains silent throughout. The tester then says, 'Show me the ...' Once the child understands the task, the tester reduces voice intensity

a

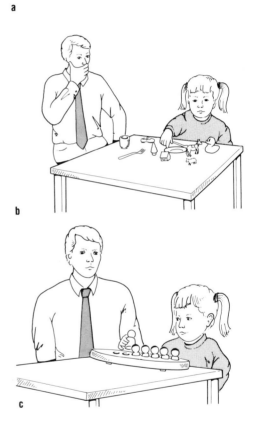

b

c

Fig. 5.11 The McCormick toy discrimination test: a, examples of test items; b, obtaining responses from the side; c, position for presenting the 'go' and 's' stimuli. From McCormick (1988).

and covers his/her mouth with a hand or card, so that the child cannot lip-read.

In a quiet room, with the tester and the child separated by a small table, the child should be able to correctly identify the toys or pictures with the tester's voice at minimal intensity, around 30–40 dBA.

Clues to hearing loss. Certain behaviour patterns provide useful preliminary clues to the presence of a hearing loss. The child may keep looking at the tester's face with a puzzled expression, instantly replaced by enlightenment when the word is repeated at higher intensity. The child may ignore the tester and play when he/she cannot hear the tester or become tearful and retreat to the parent. The child may make a few errors when the items are not sufficiently familiar but this can usually be distinguished from errors due to hearing difficulty.

The child with a hearing loss may be very alert to visual clues, and the tester must be careful not to glance at the item he/she is about to name. When the voice intensity is raised, the child often repeats the word after the tester, and yet does not respond by selecting the correct item. It can sometimes be established that the difficulty lies with the hearing, rather than with the child's understanding of the task, by asking for items using mime instead of words. The normally intelligent but hearing-impaired child will respond instantly to such signals.

Performance tests

In these tests, the child is asked to make a specific response each time he/she hears a sound. They may be the only way of assessing a child who does not understand English or who has impaired language comprehension. The sound stimulus may be warble tones or narrow-band noise, produced by a free-field audiometer, or speech sounds of known frequency composition such as 'go' (low frequency) and 's' (high frequency). The 'g' of 'go' is omitted at low intensities. The tester must be behind the child to avoid visual clues. The response may involve placing a brick in a basket, a marble in a pot, or any other simple response which the child's play and the tester's ingenuity may suggest.

The child is gently guided through the response required, using as stimulus either a loud 'Go' or the loudest tone on the audiometer, at a frequency of 1 kHz. When it is certain that the child is hearing this loud sound, he/she is given generous encouragement for each correct response, however tentative. As the child gains confidence, the tester gives less and less assistance until the child has mastered the game. The tester then reduces the intensity of the sound stimulus by small increments, usually of 10 dB, until a point is reached where the child will no longer respond.

The aim is to obtain a reliable response at 35 dBA at each frequency but, if it can be shown unequivocally that the child hears 35 dBA at all frequencies, it can be assumed that the child has adequate hearing to acquire speech. It is common to find children with conductive hearing loss who respond hesitantly to the 35 dBA sound, but only become confident at 45 dBA. This behaviour is characteristic of a modest conductive hearing loss, which may nevertheless be clinically significant. A child who gives unreliable responses to auditory stimuli, but responds reliably when visual stimuli such as flashing lights on the warbler are added, is probably hard of hearing.

Pure-tone audiometry

PTA using headphones is the standard audiometric technique for children of 5 years and upwards, but a PTA may sometimes be obtained in children under the age of 3 years. With preschool children a PTA should only be attempted when some information has been obtained by the methods described above and one has established some rapport with the child. Usually, the child, using headphones, is asked to make a similar response to that in the sound-field test.

The PTA is performed according to a standardized procedure. Start with an easily audible tone, e.g. 50 dBHL at 1 kHz; the signal intensity is reduced by 10 dB until the child fails to respond and is then increased by 5 dB until the threshold is 'bracketed'. As attention span may be short, it is sometimes preferable to obtain readings at only three frequencies initially (500 Hz, 1 kHz and 4 kHz) and then to test the opposite side.

Pitfalls

PTA is subject to the same potential errors as free-field audiometry, particularly a rhythmic presentation of signals and unintentional visual or facial clues by the tester or some other person in the room. Excessively anxious children sometimes will not admit to hearing a sound until it is very loud, and bizarre and improbable audiograms may then be obtained. It is important to cross-check such findings using the child's responses to formal or informal speech tests.

Air and bone conduction

Sound is normally transmitted most efficiently to the middle ear and cochlea by air conduction but, if there is middle-ear dysfunction, sound transmission to the cochlea via bone may be more efficient. This is the basis for the classic tuning-fork tests of Rinne and Weber, but these are difficult to perform and interpret in preschool children.

When there is a conductive hearing loss, bone conduction thresholds are significantly better than air conduction and there is said to be an air–bone gap (Fig. 5.12). Bone conduction is tested by placing a bone vibrator on the mastoid process, behind the pinna. When this is done, sound is transmitted with almost equal efficiency via bone to the test ear and to the opposite ear. The result of a bone conduction test is therefore the threshold of the better ear, not necessarily the side under test.

Masking

With air conduction tests via headphones, transmission of sounds to the ear opposite the one being tested is less efficient and the intensity falls by 40–50 dB. However, if the ear under test is severely deaf but the opposite ear is normal, the latter will start to hear the tone at 40–50 dBHL

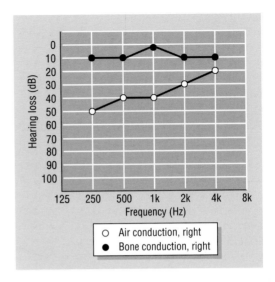

Fig. 5.12 Audiogram showing the air–bone gap in conductive hearing loss.

and the subject will respond. The technique of masking is used to overcome these problems. Details of masking techniques should be obtained from standard audiological texts.

The vibrator used in bone conduction testing may produce sufficient vibration to elicit a tactile response, particularly with low frequencies. This may lead to the incorrect diagnosis of an air–bone gap in children with a severe sensorineural hearing loss (Fig. 5.13). Another problem is that, because of anatomical variations, bone conduction thresholds vary between subjects by 10–15 dB, so that, if the bone conduction is better than the air conduction threshold by this amount, it does not necessarily indicate an air–bone gap.

Speech tests — 5 years and upwards

In the older child and adult, speech audiometry is an accurate and sophisticated technique. Speech tests using standard word lists or sentences can be used as a primary diagnostic aid, and also as a means of assessing the effectiveness of amplification in children using hearing-aids. Speech tests are essential to confirm the results obtained

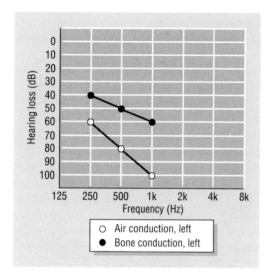

Fig. 5.13 Audiogram showing a spurious air—bone gap, caused by tactile response to the bone conduction test.

by PTA and may identify children with functional hearing loss.

Electrical response audiometry

A few milliseconds after a sound reaches the ear, action potentials are propagated from the cochlea, along the auditory pathways to the brainstem and cortex. It is possible to detect these potentials and use them to find a patient's threshold of hearing. They may also add information about the site of the lesion. These 'objective' methods are invaluable techniques which can be of great help in solving difficult problems.

Brainstem-evoked response (BSER)

The BSER is recorded from three surface electrodes (usually scalp, mastoid and forehead). It represents the transmission of the auditory signal from the cochlea to the brainstem. The BSER can be recorded with the child awake (if very relaxed), asleep or under anaesthetic. The complex waveform is demonstrated by computer analysis of the electroencephalogram (EEG) as a number of peaks, which correspond to different levels in the auditory pathway and are numbered by Roman numerals I to VII (Fig. 5.14a).

BSER is particularly useful in children who are autistic, blind or severely learning-disabled, but should never be a substitute for behavioural assessment. In the child with multiple impairments, it may be convenient to record the BSER using portable equipment, while the child is having an anaesthetic for other reasons such as a brain scan, or for middle-ear surgery in cases where there is thought to be a mixed sensorineural and conductive loss. BSER tests performed for other reasons, for example to test the integrity of the neural pathways in the neonatal intensive care unit, are not designed to provide information about hearing thresholds and are not a substitute for an audiological assessment.

The responses change and mature in the early weeks of life, or after a severe neurological illness. Low-frequency hearing impairment or residual low-frequency hearing can be missed. Experience, caution and common sense are vital in interpreting the results — the test is not totally 'objective'.

Evoked otoacoustic emissions (EOAE) (Fig. 5.14b)

A sound stimulus produces an acoustic emission from the cochlea, which is commonly, though incorrectly, called a 'cochlear echo'. This can be detected by a small microphone placed within the ear canal, analysed and displayed. Any hearing defect, even a minor conductive defect, abolishes the emission and this is therefore a very sensitive test, both for screening and for diagnosis. It is also useful for localization of the lesion responsible for the hearing defect. The EOAE is a simple test and takes less than 5 minutes, but the child needs to be calm and still. The method is not yet able to establish the degree of hearing loss or to provide reliable frequency-specific information.

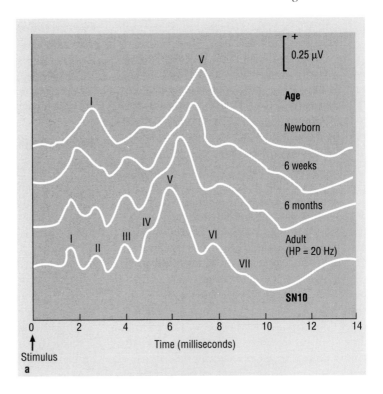

Fig. 5.14 a, The components of the waveform obtained by brainstem-evoked response (BSER) audiometry. Waveform amplitude decreases as sound intensity is reduced and wave 5 is traced to threshold. **b,** The ILO288 auditory screener: the otoacoustic emission display, using a portable computer. Courtesy of Otodynamics Ltd., Hatfield.

Electrocochleography (ECoG)

A needle electrode is inserted through the tympanic membrane, on to the promontory of the middle ear, and the action potentials produced by the cochlea are recorded. The stimulus is normally a train of clicks. A general anaesthetic is needed in children for this technique. As it is an invasive test, it is rarely used.

Impedance

The measurement of impedance gives an objective assessment of the mobility of the tympanic membrane and ossicular chain. The middle ear presents some resistance to vibratory motion, in response to a sound stimulus. Some of the acoustical energy is accepted by the middle ear and the remainder is reflected back into the external canal. The ratio of acceptance to reflection is dependent on the middle-ear resistance, which in turn is affected by the presence of fluid or other abnormalities. An ear which absorbs a large amount of sound energy has low impedance. The inverse of this measure is compliance.

The measurement is made via a probe inserted in the external ear canal to form an airtight cavity

(Fig. 5.15). Under normal conditions, compliance is maximal when the pressures on either side of the ear drum are equal. Thus, if the pressure in the middle ear is below atmospheric, compliance will be greatest when external canal pressure is correspondingly reduced (Fig. 5.16).

Early detection of hearing defects

Early detection of sensorineural hearing loss is important. Parents need to be able to communicate with their baby and they wish to know as soon as possible if there is any serious impairment. Early amplification and auditory training may improve the quality of speech and language development. Many authorities believe that for optimal results intervention should begin within the first 3 months of life, although the evidence for this is not conclusive. Very early diagnosis of hearing loss facilitates investigation for the cause of the defect, particularly with regard to serology for congenital infections (p. 163).

Many hearing defects are first suspected by parents, but some are missed, either because they are of lesser severity or are predominantly high frequency, or because the parents are not sufficiently familiar with normal child behaviour and

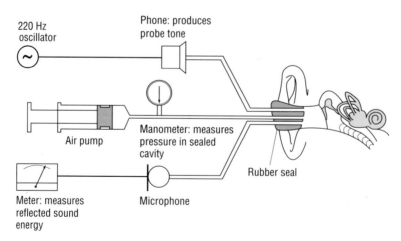

Fig. 5.15 Measurement of acoustic impedance. A probe tip with three apertures is sealed in the external meatus with a rubber cuff. An oscillator and phone deliver the 'probe' tone into the meatus and a microphone monitors the sound level. An air pump is used to place varying loads on the tympanic membrane. From Fria (1981).

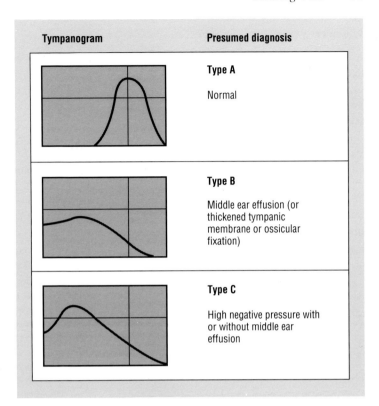

Tympanogram	Presumed diagnosis
	Type A Normal
	Type B Middle ear effusion (or thickened tympanic membrane or ossicular fixation)
	Type C High negative pressure with or without middle ear effusion

Fig. 5.16 Impedance measurement. Interpretation of the three commonest tympanogram curves.

development. Unlike blind children, the deaf infant looks normal and behaves in most respects just like a hearing child. Some cases of late diagnosis can be traced to the parent's inability to face the dawning awareness that their baby does not hear normally; they may actively avoid having the baby's hearing checked.

Screening

For all these reasons, screening for hearing loss has been thought desirable. The traditional way of doing this in the UK has been by distraction testing at 6–9 months, usually carried out by health visitors. The test itself is satisfactory and reliable, but the level of continued training and supervision required to maintain high standards has been seriously underestimated in the past. Opinions differ as to the value of screening for secretory otitis (glue ear, p. 220), but it is generally held that a single screening test is not appropriate for a condition which is fluctuant and may present at any time in childhood.

Neonatal screening

One attractive alternative is to screen all newborn infants, but the costs and logistics of testing all newborns have so far been prohibitive. Selective screening of high risk infants is more promising, using BSER and/or OAE. Suitable selection criteria are: more than 72 hours in the neonatal intensive care unit; family history of a possibly genetic hearing loss in childhood; consanguinity; dysmorphic syndromes; suspected maternal intrauterine infection. By testing all such infants (5–10% of births) between 40 and 60% of all congenitally hearing impaired infants can be detected.

Vigilance

All staff dealing with young children should maintain a high level of vigilance about hearing loss, and parents should be educated about the ways in which they can recognize defects themselves, using a check-list or fact-sheet (Fig. 5.17). A quick response to parental concerns and rapid, easy access to the audiology service are essential. Children with other major developmental impairments, or who have suffered meningitis, severe neurological illnesses or head injuries, should be referred for audiological assessment as soon as is practical.

The School Entrant Test

All school entrants undergo a screening test of hearing, known as the 'Sweep Test'. This is a simplified PTA performed at a fixed intensity, usually 20–25 dBHL, although sometimes the level is fixed at 30 dB to reduce false positives caused by inattention or background noise. Children who fail have a complete audiogram carried out and, if necessary, are then referred for detailed assessment in the audiology clinic. A failure rate of between 5 and 10% is expected in school audiometric testing; about half of these children have normal hearing on retest. Of the remainder, most have secretory otitis media, and some authorities have suggested that impedance measurements might be more efficient than audiometry for screening schoolchildren.

Although bilateral sensorineural hearing loss has usually been detected by school age, new cases are still found, at least in inner city areas

---

HEARING TESTS FOR BABIES

YOU CAN CHECK YOUR BABY'S HEARING BY WATCHING EVERYDAY BEHAVIOUR.

* Do not expect your baby always to respond in the same way. Sometimes he/she may take no notice of loud sounds, because something else interesting is going on. The exact age when a baby learns to do something new varies a lot.

* As the baby gets older he/she learns more about sounds such as speech and ordinary noises at home. He/she cannot tell where a noise is coming from until about 6 or 7 months of age.

* Do not try to test the baby's hearing yourself! If you get worried, ask for a proper hearing test at the clinic!

First two months of life:
* sudden loud noises (a hand clap or a door banging) make him jump or blink.
* shows interest in noises like a vacuum cleaner.

Two to six months:
* listens to your voice even if s/he cannot see you.
* interested in noises like parent entering room; food being prepared; bath running; dog barking; radio, TV.
* may wake up if parent creeps into room.

Seven to twelve months:
* looks to see where quiet sounds are coming from.
* likes to "talk" to you.
* says "ma", "ba", "da".
* may begin to understand his name, "no", "bye-bye".

Second year
* understands simple words or instructions when you talk to him/her
* beginning to say some words

No test is perfect. Even if your baby "passes", ask for a repeat test if you are worried about your child's hearing at any time.

Fig. 5.17 Fact sheet for parents: this is inserted in the Personal Child Health Record.

among the socially deprived, and in recent immigrants. Severe unilateral hearing loss is also detected, often for the first time, since free-field audiometry rarely identifies this. Although treatment is rarely possible or necessary, the child's teacher must be made aware of this disability (see Fig. 12.5).

References and further reading

Fria, T.J. (1981) Assessment of hearing. *Pediatric Clinics of North America*, **28** (4), 757–75.

McCormick, B. (1993) *Paediatric Audiology, 0–5 years*. Whurr, London.

McCormick, B. (1988) *Screening for Hearing Impairment in Young Children*. Croom Helm, London.

Newby, H.A. (1979) *Audiology*, (4th edn). Prentice Hall, New Jersey.

Nolan, M. and Tucker, I.G. (1981) *The Hearing-impaired Child and the Family*. Human Horizons Series. Souvenir Press, London.

Taylor, I.G. (1964) *The Neurological Mechanisms of Hearing and Speech in Children*. Manchester University Press, Manchester.

Whetnall, E. and Fry, D.B. (1964) *The Deaf Child*. Heinemann Medical, London.

CHAPTER 6

Assessment of Visual Function

The paediatrician does not need a detailed knowledge of ophthalmology, but should understand the principles underlying the diagnosis of the commoner visual defects in childhood and the limitations of standard methods of ophthalmic examination.

Serious visual disorders are rare but, because they are often caused by obvious abnormalities of the globe and are accompanied by abnormal visual behaviour, recognition does not usually present great difficulties. In contrast, minor visual impairments, in particular squints, amblyopia and refractive errors, are not always obvious even to the most observant parent, and a deliberate search for these is often needed. Nevertheless, they are among the commonest defects found in otherwise normal children while up to 50% of disabled children may have some visual defect.

Early development of vision

Kittens temporarily deprived of vision do not develop normal visual acuity (VA) since the cortical neurons responsible for vision do not acquire the ability to discriminate and process the stimuli which reach them from the retina. For this system to develop normally, adequate visual stimuli must be available during the 'critical period' of neuronal maturation. The critical period is brief and well defined in the kitten, but is more difficult to determine in humans. The immediate practical application of these discoveries is in the management of cataract and squint, as discussed below.

Visual acuity

This is a measure of the ability to separate visual stimuli, i.e. to distinguish the details and shapes of objects. This ability is dependent on the cerebral cortex as well as the eyes, and VA can therefore only be assessed accurately if the subject is able to give a response to what he/she sees, although electrophysiological methods can provide an estimate of VA without the subject's direct co-operation.

The Snellen letter chart is the criterion against which all other VA measures are standardized. It is used at a distance of 6 m to give a measure of distant vision. Similar charts with reduced type are used to assess near vision. The VA for distant vision is expressed as a pseudofraction, e.g. 6/60 means that the subject can see at 6 m a letter that can be seen by the normal person at 60 m. Thus 6/6 is normal vision, 6/5 better-than-average vision; 6/18 a moderate loss of acuity and 6/60 very poor vision. If the test is done at 3 m (p. 98), the equivalent values are 3/3, 3/2.5, 3/9 and 3/30. Testing at 3 m results in a slight loss of optical precision, but this is of no practical importance and it has the advantages of retaining rapport with the child more easily and also of being more practical in the crowded conditions of many clinics and schools. Near vision is expressed either as a Snellen pseudofraction or by type size (N5 = normal VA). VAs should always be stated both with and without spectacle corrections.

Exact measures of VA are not meaningful in infants, since VA depends not only on the clarity of the retinal image but also on the brain's interpretation of what is seen. The infant's preference for interesting stimuli (p. 31) can, however, be used to give some estimate of their vision in terms of the Snellen chart (Fig. 6.1). In the first week of life, black and white stripes of 3.5 mm width can be perceived, corresponding to a VA of 3/60. There is rapid development of visual discrimination, and adult levels of acuity are probably approached by the age of 6 months. Binocular

Fig. 6.1 The acuity card procedure. The child sits in front of the screen with as little to distract him/her as possible and cards with varying grating size are placed in the central panel. The child is observed through a minute central peep-hole as to whether their fixation is drawn to the side with the grating. From Taylor (1991).

vision is thought to be present by the sixth week of life and is well established by 4 months. The 'sensitive period' for binocular vision development is probably the first 6 months; if it is not present by then, the child is unlikely ever to develop normal binocular function. Colour discrimination is probably established by 3 months.

Refraction and refractive error

The eye is an optical system in which rays of light are brought to a focus on the retina. A sharp image is obtained, whatever the distance of the object being viewed, by changes in the curvature and therefore the power of the lens. The accommodation reflex enables near objects to be viewed; to do this the eyes converge and the curvature of the lens is increased. For distance vision, the reverse occurs. In the first weeks of life, the infant is capable of adjusting accommodation within a range of about 75 cm from an object, although control is very imprecise. The baby can focus briefly at distances greater than 75 cm, but cannot maintain this. Fairly accurate accommodation is achieved by 3 or 4 months; this process of maturation is delayed in neurologically impaired infants.

The power of a lens is measured in dioptres:

$$\text{Dioptre} = \frac{1}{\text{Focal length in metres}}$$

Convex lenses are recorded as plus and concave as minus. By convention, the refractive error of an eye is stated in terms of the lens needed to correct it (Fig. 6.2).

A significant difference between the refractive error of the two eyes is known as *anisometropia*. In this situation the differing power of the two lenses produces images of different sizes. The brain can correct for this difference to a limited degree but a difference in refraction of 2.5 dioptres results in a 5% difference in image size, beyond which fusion becomes difficult and one image may then be suppressed, causing amblyopia (see below).

Few eyes are perfect optical systems (Fig. 6.3). Even mild and apparently asymptomatic hypermetropia, anisometropia and astigmatism may predispose to squint and amblyopia, but there is no exact degree of refractive error which should be regarded as pathological. Refraction changes with age. Premature infants may be mildly myopic, whereas many full-term babies are mildly hypermetropic. There is a decline in the prevalence of astigmatism after the first year.

Measurement of refractive error

In young children who cannot co-operate by fixating a distant target, the amount of accommodation is constantly changing and therefore the refractive power of the eye can be measured only when this reflex has been paralysed (cycloplegia). Atropine or cyclopentolate is used for this purpose; these agents also dilate the pupil (mydriasis). Refraction is measured objectively using a retinoscope. Considerable practice is required to obtain reliable results.

In older children and adults, the refractive power of the lens can be assessed by determining, with the co-operation of the subject, the power of the spectacle lens which gives the clearest vision of a distant or near target, usually a Snellen chart. This is called subjective refraction. Subjective

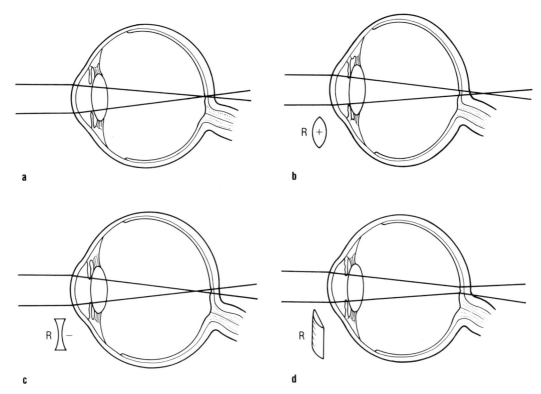

a

b   R (+)

c   R](-

d   R

Fig. 6.2 a, An eye with normal refraction is said to be *emmetropic.* Parallel light rays from a distant object are brought to a focus on the retina without any increase in the curvature of the lens. The light rays from a near object are divergent. The curvature of the lens, and therefore the refractive power, is increased by the accommodation reflex in order to focus the image on the retina. **b,** The long-sighted or *hypermetropic* eye is usually smaller than normal. There is no difficulty in viewing distant objects. Children with hypermetropia seldom complain directly of problems with near vision but the increased accommodative effort needed to maintain a focused image predisposes to convergent squint. A convex lens is needed to correct hypermetropia. **c,** The short-sighted or *myopic* eye is usually larger than normal. There is no problem with near vision but light rays from distant objects are brought to a focus in front of the retina and the image is therefore blurred. A concave lens is used to correct myopia. **d,** The lens of the eye may not have the same refraction in all meridians, resulting in a distorted image. This is known as *astigmatism.* The lens to correct it is cylindrical rather than spherical in section. From Robb (1981).

refraction provides a measure of VA; in other words, it defines how much the subject can see. In contrast, objective refraction by retinoscopy describes the eye as an optical system and determines whether spectacles would produce a sharper retinal image; it provides no information about VA. An eye could have normal refraction and yet be blind.

In clinics and schools, where ophthalmic re-ports are often not immediately available, the type of refractive error may usefully be deduced by examination of the child's glasses. An object is viewed through the lens, and the glasses are moved from side to side. If the lens is convex (hypermetropia, aphakia) the object appears to move in the opposite direction to the movement of the spectacles, but it seems to move in the same direction if the lens is concave (myopia).

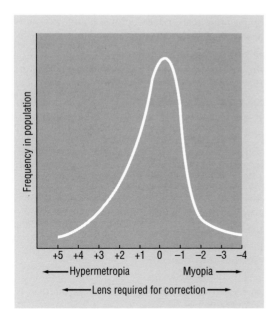

Fig. 6.3 Measurements of refraction in a population form an approximately normal distribution curve.

When the spectacles are rotated, changes in refractive power between the meridians of each lens are immediately obvious, giving a 'scissoring' effect, and the child may be assumed to have astigmatism.

Squint — strabismus, heterotropia

This is a condition in which the visual axis of one eye (the squinting eye) is not directed to the object being looked at by the other eye (the fixing eye). The *visual axis* is the line from the fovea to the point of fixation. A *microsquint* (microtropia) is a squint of very small angle which is not detectable by observation alone. A *concomitant* squint is one in which the angle is the same in all directions of gaze, and whichever eye is fixing; it is by far the commonest type in children.

A *paralytic* (incomitant) squint is one in which the angle alters with different positions of gaze and with a change of fixation between the eyes. It results from paralysis of one or more of the extraocular muscles or from damage to the cranial

nerves supplying them. An important example is Duane's retraction syndrome, which is easily mistaken for a sixth-nerve palsy. In its usual form, there is failure of abduction and widening of the palpebral fissure, with protrusion of the globe on attempted abduction; attempted adduction is accompanied by retraction of the globe and narrowing of the palpebral fissure. A *uniocular* squint is one in which one eye is habitually the squinting eye; an *alternating* squint is one in which each eye squints alternately.

The direction of the squint may be convergent (esotropia) or divergent (exotropia), or vertical (hyper- or hypotropia). Exotropia is less common than esotropia. There may be divergence on depression and convergence on elevation (the A phenomenon) or the reverse (the V phenomenon). A *latent* squint (heterophoria) is one in which an underlying tendency to squint is controlled by fusional mechanisms except under conditions of fatigue or illness. The cerebral fusion mechanism can be disrupted by rapidly covering the eyes alternately (the cover–uncover test), and the latent squint may then become manifest.

A *pseudosquint* is the illusory appearance of a convergent squint (Fig. 6.4). It occurs when a wide nasal bridge or broad epicanthic fold hides part of the sclera.

Binocular single vision (BSV) is the fusion into a single perception of the slightly disparate images from the two eyes. In addition to achieving single vision, this synthesis gives perception of depth or stereoscopic vision. BSV will not develop unless there are reasonably clear and similar images in the two eyes, functioning cerebral fusion mechanisms and precise co-ordination of eye movements.

Causes of squint

Defective cerebral fusion

There is little direct evidence about this but it may be the explanation for the high prevalence of squint in children with learning disability or cerebral palsy. Squints seem to occur more commonly in children who are clumsy, poor readers,

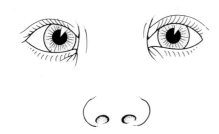

Fig. 6.4 Pseudosquint.

etc., although it should not be assumed to be the cause of these problems.

Defective visual stimulation

BSV is needed to maintain alignment of the eyes. The brain is unable to control the alignment of an eye that does not receive a clear image. Squint is therefore commonly seen in infants with cataract, and in congenital eye defects, due to poor visual stimulation in the critical period. Refractive errors which produce blurred or unequal images may also cause squint.

Refractive error

Hypermetropia is commonly associated with squint because the child has to accommodate excessively to obtain a clear image of near objects. The excessive accommodation is reflexly associated with excessive convergence activity, which may lead to a convergent squint. This may often be treated simply by the appropriate convex spectacle lens. Much less commonly, myopia may be associated with a divergent squint, particularly when looking at distant objects.

Genetic factors

There may be a hereditary element in the aetiology of squint.

Management of squint

Any child with a suspected squint should be seen by an orthoptist and/or ophthalmologist. Squint is most commonly detected first by a parent or relative, but delays in referral are common, due to the widespread myths that squints are normal in the first 6 months of life and that treatment is impossible or unnecessary until the child is older. In the neonate, the eyes may be mildly divergent, and in the first weeks a number of transient disturbances of eye movement may be seen which in older children would be considered abnormal. However, a persistent uniocular squint is abnormal at any age and should be investigated for two reasons: firstly, treatable defects (cataract, retinoblastoma) can cause squint and, secondly, the prevention (as opposed to the treatment) of amblyopia probably depends on early diagnosis.

Treatment depends on the cause. Sometimes correction of the refractive error is all that is needed. Exercises may be used for older co-operative children. Surgical correction is often necessary, although in many cases the main benefit is cosmetic. Sometimes a child with severe cerebral palsy makes considerable progress after squint surgery, for reasons which are not clear.

Eye movements

The physiology and development of eye movements are complex and not fully understood. Several neural systems with different localizations in the brain (supranuclear systems) are responsible for ocular movements but the final common pathway is via the brainstem nuclei and cranial nerves — the nuclear and infranuclear parts of the pathway.

The pursuit system enables the eyes to track a moving object smoothly and accurately. The neonate can only do this if the target is moved very slowly. The saccadic system involves a rapid shift of gaze from one object to another, for example from the end of one line of print to the beginning of the next. The fast component of nystagmus is a saccadic movement. Young infants have slower and less accurate saccadic movements, and these mature by the end of the first year. Saccades are the way in which fixation is changed. An infant who makes frequent, accurate, normal-velocity saccades will be perceived by an observer to have good vision whereas, if saccadic movements are defective, as in congenital oculomotor apraxia (p. 228), vision may erroneously be regarded as impaired. The vestibulo-ocular reflexes enable the visual image on the retina to remain stationary while the head and body are moving.

Nystagmus

Nystagmus is an involuntary rhythmic oscillation of the eyes. Both the physiology and the clinical assessment are difficult to interpret and in some cases defy explanation. The exact pattern of movement varies; there may be an obvious difference between the fast and slow phases or the to-and-fro movements may seem symmetrical.

Physiological nystagmus can be elicited by rotation or by optokinetic stimuli. Vestibular nystagmus results from acquired lesions of the vestibular system, such as head injury, vestibular neuronitis or benign paroxysmal vertigo. Its amplitude is greater when looking in the direction of the fast component. Recovery with disappearance of the nystagmus is usual within 1 month.

Gaze-paretic nystagmus is associated with a wide variety of lesions of the nervous system and may occur at any age (see also p. 227). It is not usually present when looking straight ahead, but occurs when the individual tries to fixate a target in the periphery of gaze. The neural mechanisms responsible for maintaining gaze are unable to do so; the eyes then drift towards the midline, and are relocated with saccadic movements (see above), which are the fast phase of nystagmus.

Sensory-deprivation nystagmus is the result of severe visual defects involving the anterior visual pathways (i.e. not the visual radiation or cortex) in the early years of life. It is unlikely to occur in people who lose their sight after mid-childhood. There are two main patterns. Wandering eye movements are slow, large in amplitude and variable in direction. They are associated with very severe visual impairment. Nystagmus with apparently symmetrical oscillation, almost always in the horizontal plane, occurs in idiopathic congenital nystagmus (p. 227) and in many conditions in which VA is reduced, notably albinism and achromatopsia (pp. 227 and 229). Isolated congenital nystagmus is most often noticed at about 6 weeks but may be present at birth; when associated with other disorders, the onset typically is at about 3 months.

Amblyopia

An amblyopic eye can be defined as one which, even after correction of any refractive error with a spectacle lens, shows a defect in VA which cannot be explained by structural disease of the eye. It can only develop in a child under the age of about 7 years, and is due to defective development of vision during the critical period of rapid brain maturation. It is not yet clear either what is the peak age for development of amblyopia, or how early the predisposing factors need to be recognized if treatment is to result in the development of normal VA and BSV.

The severity of amblyopia ranges from one line on the Snellen chart (i.e. the best vision attainable with optimal spectacle correction is 6/9) to near-blindness. An amblyopic eye frequently has better vision for single letters than for a line of adjacent letters. This is known as the crowding phenomenon and has important implications for vision tests in young children (p. 98).

Amblyopia may result from the following factors.

1 Structural lesions that obscure vision, such as corneal opacity, cataract (p. 226) or ptosis (see below).

2 A blurred image due to refractive error, particularly where there is a marked degree of anisometropia and/or astigmatism. Uncorrected refractive error can cause unilateral or bilateral amblyopia. Astigmatism may cause amblyopia which is more severe in one axis than in the other — meridional amblyopia.

3 An image displaced by squint away from the fovea (much the most sensitive part of the retina). Amblyopia does not usually occur with alternating

squints, because each eye in turn receives normal retinal stimulation.

Significance of amblyopia

Unilateral amblyopia has the following effects: in severe cases the child is effectively one-eyed and loss of vision in the good eye would let him/her with a significant visual impairment; depth vision will never be perfect so performance in ball games and in tasks requiring good depth vision (e.g. connecting electronic components) will be impaired; and some careers, such as the armed forces, flying and crane operating, may be closed to the adult. Untreated bilateral amblyopia can impair VA and functional vision.

Treatment of amblyopia

The aim is to restore VA in the amblyopic eye. Any refractive error is corrected. Various methods are used to blur or obscure the vision in the good eye, in order to stimulate use of the amblyopic eye. Some children, particularly if they have other disabilities, may find the temporary impairment of vision very disturbing and the potential gains may not always justify this. The long-term results of treatment are sometimes disappointing and the initial gains in vision may be lost in later years.

Ptosis

Unilateral or (less frequently) bilateral ptosis is a common isolated anomaly. Much more rarely, ptosis is associated with other disorders, e.g. Horner's syndrome, Marcus Gunn phenomenon ('jaw winking'), muscle diseases and a variety of dysmorphic syndromes. If the eyelid occludes the pupil, amblyopia may result, but otherwise correction is needed only for cosmetic reasons.

Prevalence of visual defects

Minor anomalies of visual function are among the commonest defects found in children; up to 10% of schoolchildren have some visual defect. Be-tween 4 and 7% of 5 year olds have a squint and between 3 and 5% have amblyopia. Squint is more common in infants born preterm. The prevalence of refractive errors is difficult to measure for reasons discussed above. Myopia is rare in the first few years but becomes increasingly common in the school years.

Published figures for the prevalence of eye defects among disabled children vary between 20 and 50%. Every child with a disability should first be examined by an orthoptist, and should then have a refraction and fundoscopy by an ophthalmologist.

Assessment

A complete assessment of a child with a visual defect includes relevant medical history, the parents' observations, systematic inspection of the eyes, examination of eye movements and visual fields and measurement of VA.

Information from parents

Most congenital disorders of vision present either as an anomaly obvious to inspection or as abnormal visual behaviour, both of which are likely to be noted first by the parent. Most parents are certain that their baby can see from a very early age, and in infancy normal visual behaviour provides better evidence of functionally adequate vision than any test readily available to the paediatrician. Even when the child is old enough to co-operate with VA testing, the information obtained from observations of the child's spontaneous activity and play is indispensable. The question, 'Have you any worries about the child's eyesight?' should be asked as part of any developmental assessment. Some further useful questions and observations are suggested in Table 6.1.

A complete developmental assessment is mandatory in any infant whose parents suspect a significant visual impairment because:
• abnormal visual behaviour is sometimes a manifestation of learning disability or autism rather than an ophthalmic disease;

Table 6.1 Useful questions and observations

General questions
Do you think the child can see? Why/why not?
Does the child recognize you/strangers?
Does the child look at toys or pictures?
Does the child keep watching you as you walk away?
Does the child reach for objects/take them?
Does the child hold objects close to their eyes?
Does the child feel for objects?
Does the child pick up tiny things, e.g. pieces of fluff, biscuit crumbs?
Does the child look at windows/bright lights?
Does the child look at their hands/and feet ('hand/foot regard')?
Do you think their vision has got better/worse recently?
Does the child bump into things?
Does the child go up close to objects, e.g. toys, TV?
Does the child complain of difficulty with vision?
Have you ever noticed a squint (cast, turn, lazy eye), or unusual eye movements?

Observations of behaviour specific to visual impairment
Eccentric fixation (adopted to optimize vision, e.g. to dampen nystagmus)
Eye poking or pressing (retinal disease)
Gazing above object of interest (central scotomata, e.g. colobomata, optic nerve disorders)
Head turned but eyes rotated to look straight ahead (hemianopia)
Light gazing (cortical vision defects)

- eye defects are commonly associated with other impairments;
- visual impairment affects other aspects of development. The development of the visually impaired infant is discussed in Chapter 13.

Squint is also most commonly detected first by a parent or relative but, with the exception of severe myopia, refractive errors are not usually clinically apparent unless they cause a squint. In early childhood, the majority of refractive errors cause only a minor impairment of VA which is not readily detected even by the standard preschool tests (see below).

Qualitative assessment of vision in infancy

It is not always easy to determine whether a baby can see normally. A blink response to a bright light can be detected from 28 to 30 weeks gestational age; a flashgun can be used if there is no response to a torch. Head-turning to a more diffuse light source is usually present by 36 weeks' gestational age. Following movements to a red ball or a light can be demonstrated in full-term infants and in some premature babies, but it is important to move the target slowly (p. 90). Eye closure in response to threat (e.g. a finger moved rapidly towards the eye) occurs from about 4 months of age but misleading reactions may occur due to air flow if the whole hand is used. Smiling in response to silent gestures or facial expressions and visually directed reaching are also useful, although indirect, indicators of visual function.

Rotational tests make use of the vestibulo-ocular reflexes. The baby is held up at arm's length and the examiner spins around on his/her own axis. This induces a tonic deviation of the eyes opposite to the direction of movement (if the baby is moving towards his/her — the baby's — right, the eyes deviate to his/her left), followed by a fast phase in the opposite direction. Nystagmus occurs in the opposite direction when rotation ceases, but this is inhibited quickly by visual fixation if the baby can see — within 1 second if the baby is more than 3 months old. The inhibition of postrotation nystagmus is a valuable way of detecting severely reduced visual function and also gives information about eye movements. Demonstration of optokinetic nystagmus requires a drum or tape; its physiology is not fully understood but like rotational tests it can give useful information about visual function and eye movements. The Catford drum was designed in an attempt to simplify such tests but does not in fact make use of optokinetic nystagmus. Neither technique has proved to be reliable in the assessment of VA.

Systematic examination

The eyelid, cornea, iris and anterior chamber of each eye are inspected and compared. It is easy to overlook differences in the size of the eye or cornea, or variations in pigmentation. An eye which is too small (microphthalmic) often has poor vision. Minor differences in pupil size are common in infancy but, in the absence of other anomalies, are usually of no significance.

Pupil reactions are present from 31 weeks' gestational age. A careful examination of the pupil with a lens (an otoscope without speculum is convenient) should be made before concluding that pupil reactions to light are absent. When there is a little vision in one eye, changing accommodation may produce alteration in size of the other pupil, which can be mistaken for a light response.

Ophthalmoscopy can be difficult. Young infants are more likely to open their eyes when sitting upright. No attempt should be made to forcibly hold the eyes open, but their attention should be distracted by an assistant so that they do not look directly into the ophthalmoscope. Children old enough to co-operate can be asked to look at a target such as a small picture fixed on the wall or ceiling of the consulting-room. For the detection of opacities such as cataract, the ophthalmoscope is set on +1 to +3 and the pupil is viewed from a distance of about 30 cm. Opacities show clearly against the red reflex from the retina. Adequate fundoscopy is difficult without dilating the pupils and it may only be possible to obtain a fleeting glimpse of the optic disc. This often appears somewhat pale in early infancy.

Tests for squint

Squint and other abnormalities of eye movement can be detected by the methods described here. It is advisable to spend a few sessions in an orthoptist's clinic in order to acquire some practical expertise, as there are several pitfalls for the inexperienced.
1 Young children turn the head as well as the eyes when tracking a moving object. If the examiner attempts to eliminate the head movements to simplify the assessment by physically restraining the head, the child will probably concentrate on trying to break free and will not look at the target object.
2 When a hand or other object is used to cover one eye during the cover test, children may perceive this either as a threat or as something interesting, and will move their head back so that they can inspect it, unless they are allowed to do this before the test begins.

Corneal reflections. A bright torch producing a narrow beam is held at 30 cm from the child. If the eyes are straight, the reflection in the two corneas will be symmetrical. This is best judged by comparing the positions of the reflexes in relation to the pupils (Fig. 6.5).

A head tilt. This is often adopted by the child to compensate for a squint and may be the presenting feature.

Eye movements. These are examined by moving an interesting small target within the child's visual field. The target should be a small toy that can sustain interest by squeaking, moving or flashing.

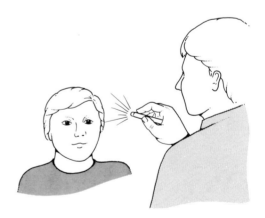

Fig. 6.5 Checking corneal reflections. A bright torch producing a narrow beam is held at 30 cm from the child. If the eyes are straight, the reflections in the two corneas will be symmetrical. This is best judged by comparing the positions of the reflexes in relation to the pupils.

It is often easier to make the target appear in different positions of gaze, thus inducing refixation movements, than to try to elicit following movements. Both horizontal and vertical movements are examined. The target must not be too close to the eyes, nor should it be moved too far laterally, as both errors are liable to evoke jerking movements of the eyes. These are commonly recorded as 'nystagmoid jerks' and wrongly interpreted as minimal nystagmus.

Cover tests. The correct technique for these is illustrated in Figs 6.6–6.8. If the child objects or struggles when one eye is covered but not the other, he/she is probably dependent on vision from one eye only. In the absence of obvious eye disease, this behaviour is very suggestive of amblyopia.

Stereo tests. The presence of BSV or 'stereo' vision indicates that both eyes are healthy and are functioning as a pair. Young children can be tested using the Titmus 'fly' test. This is a picture of a large and somewhat repulsive fly which is seen in three dimensions (3-D) when stereo spectacles are worn. A positive result is indicated by the child reaching out to grasp the fly's wings, or by a look of horror! For older co-operative children, more sophisticated tests of stereo vision are used by orthoptists, for example, the Lang test, the Randot and the Frisby.

Visual fields

Although newborns may respond to peripheral visual stimuli, the 'visual world' is small. There is rapid enlargement of the lateral visual fields during the first 6 months. In children too young to co-operate, visual fields can be examined by introducing an object into the child's visual field from behind, although only extensive defects can be detected in this way. Some learning-disabled and autistic children often behave as though they have field defects, but they usually turn out to be a behavioural feature associated with variable attention. From about 3 years of age upwards, con-

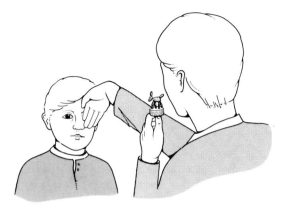

Fig. 6.6 The cover tests. These should be performed with a near and a distant target.

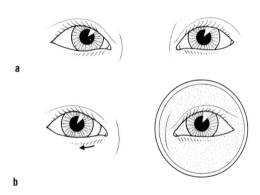

Fig. 6.7 The cover test. a, Is there a convergent squint in the right eye? b, When the left eye is covered, the right eye moves outwards to assume fixation. Diagnosis: right manifest convergent squint.

frontation testing can be used. In hemiplegia, the suspected field defect would be homonymous hemianopia, which can be detected with both eyes open together. When a bitemporal defect is suspected (as in craniopharyngioma), the eyes must be tested separately.

Very young children can rarely manage the classic method by which the examiner introduces a target progressively into the visual field. They often do not admit to seeing the target until it is in front of the nose, resulting in a spurious diagnosis of tunnel vision. The most successful method is

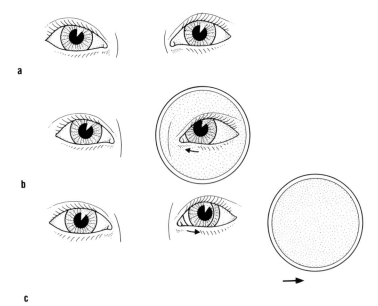

a

b

c

Fig. 6.8 The cover–uncover test for latent squint. **a**, No squint is apparent. **b**, Left eye covered: unable to maintain fixation, it deviates medially behind the cover. **c**, The outwards recovery movement to resume fixation is observed as the cover is removed. Diagnosis: left latent convergent squint. Note that this test may need to be repeated several times on each eye.

to ask the child to point at whichever finger is moving. Older children can count the number of fingers displayed.

Measurement of visual acuity

Measurement of VA by clinical techniques presents great difficulties under the age of about $2\frac{1}{2}$ years and, although many ingenious methods have been devised, none can compare in precision with the Snellen. Three groups of tests can be distinguished (Table 6.2).

1 The simplest tests are those that attempt to establish the size of the smallest object visible to the child — the 'minimum observable'. Tests of this type can be performed even with very young or disabled children. If presented under carefully controlled conditions, they can provide an objective, though approximate, measure of VA in children with visual or intellectual impairment; however, they are not sensitive enough to be useful in detection of minor VA defects such as those caused by mild refractive errors. Attempts have been made to calculate the Snellen equivalent of 'minimum observable' tests but the visual dis-

crimination and separation of objects is a much more complex function than their detection; it is easy to overestimate functional vision if Snellen equivalents are extrapolated from these tests. Furthermore, movement of the target object considerably enhances its visibility.

2 Precise estimates of VA as previously defined can only be obtained by tests that measure the ability to separate visual stimuli — the 'minimum separable'. These tests require a greater degree of subject participation.

3 The presence of normal visual function and the severity of impairment in the mentally or visually impaired can often be determined best by qualitative methods which make no pretence of giving an accurate VA measure.

Testing the eyes separately. Whichever method is used, each eye should be tested separately if the child's co-operation can be secured. This may be possible in babies up to 8 or 9 months old, but is less readily tolerated thereafter until the child is over 2 years old. The eye not being tested is covered with the parent's hand or an elasticated or adhesive patch. Spectacle frames with a black-

Table 6.2 Classification of vision tests

Minimum observable
Hundreds and thousands
Silver sweets
Smarties
Cubes
Stycar graded balls

Minimum separable
Snellen charts
Sonksen−Silver test
Stycar letter tests
Stycar toy test
Sheridan−Gardiner letter tests
Illiterate E test
Silhouettes
'Ladybird' pictures
Stycar panda test (for visually impaired children)
Forced-choice preferential looking − acuity card
   procedure

Qualitative tests
Play observations
Person recognition
Object recognition, e.g. toys of graded sizes
Pictures: lifesize, miniature, stylized
Responses to TV
Observe effects of distance, lighting, contrast, colour

ened lens, or a crumpled tissue held in front of the eye by the parent are also effective. The child's own hand is not sufficient; he/she will peep through their fingers, particularly if the vision is defective in the eye being tested. Most 'normal' children can co-operate with vision testing with both eyes open at about the age of 3 or soon after; but have difficulty in coping with one eye covered until they reach the age of 4. If the eyes cannot be tested separately, a useful estimate of vision can be obtained but a serious uniocular defect could still be missed.

Near and distant vision. In the 'normal' population, only 0.5% of children with normal distance vision have a near-vision defect. In routine vision checks, therefore, it is usual to test distance vision

only. Assessment of near vision is important in visually impaired children, for the accurate prescription of vision aids and teaching equipment, and may be much easier to achieve in children with other developmental disabilities, because of poorly sustained attention for distant targets.

Minimum observable tests

Stycar graded balls tests

These are normally performed at a distance of 3 m from the child. The white balls can be mounted on a matt black stick held up against a black background, or rolled on a black cloth. Visualization of even the smallest ball (3 mm in diameter) does not require perfect vision; subjects old enough to co-operate can frequently locate a target of this size even when able to read only the top line (6/60) of the Snellen chart. The information obtained by these tests is limited and they are now rarely used.

Near vision

Small round sweets about 1 mm in diameter (hundreds and thousands), saccharine tablets (2 mm), cake decoration balls (3 mm) and Smarties (15 mm) are useful in assessing the near vision of children with visual or developmental impairments. Snellen equivalents are of little significance in this situation. Infants with high degrees of hypermetropia can perform this task without difficulty, but they may squint while fixating the object. If the eyes are tested separately, amblyopia may be recognized. The following points are important when performing these tests:
• only one sweet should be used, not a handful;
• the sweet should be stationary, not moving;
• it should be placed in front of the child without any sound cues such as rattling the sweets together;
• the pass−fail criterion is precise fixation of the object from at least 25 cm distance;
• searching or roving eye movements, peering, feeling for the object or poorly sustained gaze are

suspect and an indication for more detailed examination;
• in order to assess the accuracy and precision of fixation, the examiner must be in front of the child and just below their eye-level.

Minimum separable tests

The Acuity Card Procedure

This was described on p. 87. It is currently the best available clinical procedure for assessment of VA in infancy.

Stycar miniature toys test

In this test the child is required to distinguish between a toy knife, fork and spoon at a distance of 3 m. Most children who can do this test reliably will be able to perform other more accurate tests. It is occasionally useful in assessing children with learning difficulties.

Letter-matching tests

These require the child to recognize differences between letters (or other shapes), but the ability to name the letters is not necessary (32% of 'normal' 5 year olds and 9% of 6 year olds cannot name letters). The child is first taught the task, using a training card and booklet, or plastic letters. When the examiner is sure that the child understands the concept of matching, the test chart is displayed at a distance of either 3 or 6 m. Young children perform better with the shorter distance (charts are available for either distance).

The Stycar and the Sheridan–Gardiner tests use single letters 'optotypes', but a full line of letters is preferable, because amblyopia (see above) is associated with the 'crowding phenomenon', in which VA for single letters is often much better than that for a line of letters. (The child with amblyopia may be able to identify the first and last letters in a row more easily than those in the middle.) This means that the visual loss in an amblyopic eye can be seriously underestimated if

only single letters are used. Single-letter tests were introduced in the belief that they would be easier for the child than rows of letters; but once the child has understood the concept of matching he/she can usually cope with either task equally well, and there is therefore little advantage in the use of single-letter systems.

The standard Snellen chart is confusing to young children because of the many rows of letters. The Sonksen–Silver Acuity System (SSAS) uses single rows of letters and is easier for the child to cope with; it is designed to be used at 3 m distance. Other methods that take account of the crowding problem and are acceptable for young children include the Cambridge Crowding Cards and the Glasgow Acuity Cards (McGraw and Winn, 1995). Another useful approach is the use of coloured pictures chosen on an essentially empirical basis as in the Sonksen Picture Test. Shape-matching tests and the illiterate E test have little advantage either optically or in simplicity from the developmental point of view.

Functional tests

Observations of visually directed behaviour and the child's response to play activities are an important part of assessment; for examples, see Table 6.2.

Specialized techniques of ophthalmic investigation

Electrophysiological techniques

These are useful in the investigation of some visual disorders, particularly the inherited retinal degenerations, cerebral storage disorders and demyelinating disease. The electroretinogram (ERG) is derived from the superficial or outer layers of the retina and may therefore be normal even when there is obvious optic atrophy; a normal result does not imply that the child can see. Conversely, the ERG may be grossly abnormal in children with retinitis pigmentosa long before the defect is clinically apparent. Corneal electrodes are necessary to record the ERG from each eye separately, but many of the conditions in which the test is useful affect both eyes and in this situation the ERG from both eyes together can be recorded, using a single electrode on the bridge of the nose, obviating the need for anaesthesia.

The visual evoked response (VER) represents the electroencephalographic (EEG) activity generated when nerve impulses travel from the eye to the cortex, and is used to assess the integrity of the visual pathways. It is obtained by computer analysis of the EEG activity evoked by visual stimulation, using a flashing light or chequerboard pattern. The VER is a valuable complementary investigation to the ERG although, in cases of suspected cortical blindness with nonprogressive learning disability, results are often equivocal and their main value is in ruling out other disorders. Binocular testing can be used to assess the presence or absence of binocular visual function. Chequer-board stimuli provide a useful estimate of VA.

Computerized tomography/magnetic resonance imaging (CT/MRI) scanning

These investigations are useful where structural lesions of the ocular pathways or occipital cortex are suspected.

VA assessment in the visually impaired child

This presents considerable difficulties and exact measures may not be possible for some years; similar problems occur in children with severe learning disabilities. The 'visual world' of normal infants is limited and they pay attention only to their immediate close surroundings, for reasons which are probably more related to psychological development than to optical factors. Their visual world expands rapidly so that, by 8 or 9 months, interesting visual stimuli will hold their attention at a distance of 3 or even 6 m. In the visually or mentally impaired child, the visual world expands more slowly, and it is often impossible to obtain any response to tests at more than 60 or 90 cm from the infant.

Functional observations (see Table 6.2) and tests provide the most relevant information, but limitations in the child's responses are sometimes due to impaired intellectual or language development rather than poor vision. Visual impairment so reduces children's experience of objects, faces and pictures that they may show little interest in them, and therefore estimates of VA made prior to any intervention or training may be unduly pessimistic (an analogous situation occurs with the newly diagnosed deaf child). Conversely, children's familiarity with their own possessions may deceive their parents into overestimating their VA, and their responses should be checked with unfamiliar examples of the same objects.

Further essential information is obtained by an objective refraction and electrophysiological methods may also be useful, but none are a substitute for functional assessment. Furthermore, if the assessment is performed in the presence of the parents and the teacher, it provides an invaluable demonstration of the child's disability, and helps them to construct a mental picture of the child's visual experiences and perceptions (see also pp. 231−5).

Colour vision

Impaired colour vision usually affects red−green discrimination and is much commoner in boys (8%) than girls (0.5−1%). Blue−yellow colourblindness affects about one in 30 000. Although colour-coded educational materials are widely used, in practice impaired red−green discrimination does not often seem to result in serious classroom difficulties. It may be important for older pupils to be aware of their disability, which may affect their choice of career. If a colour vision defect threatens a desired career, expert advice should be obtained.

The Ishihara plates are the standard method for testing for red−green colour defects. Most 5 year olds can perform this test if the tester has

enough time and patience. The City University
test is useful for older children, but too difficult
for 5 year olds. The Farnsworth–Munsell 100-
hue test is the most accurate colour vision test,
but needs a mental age of at least 7–8 years.

Early detection of visual defects

Serious congenital visual impairment is rare
(p. 224). Most cases are detected in one of four
ways: at the routine newborn examination; as a
result of high-risk screening (e.g. retinopathy of
prematurity, or a known history of inherited eye
disease in the family); by parents' or relatives'
own observations of abnormal eyes or visual behaviour; or following examination of an infant
with one or more other major impairments. However, some parents may be aware that their baby
does not appear to see, but imagine that this is
normal in the first few weeks of life.

The association between refractive error, squint
and amblyopia, together with the high prevalence
of these defects, may eventually justify refraction
of all infants, using retinoscopy or an automatic
refraction device, followed by the provision of
spectacles for those with refractive error. This
seems to reduce the incidence of squint and
amblyopia later in childhood; but further research
is needed before this becomes a routine
procedure.

One solution to the problem of screening for
minor visual defects is to employ a community
orthoptist, who spends much of their time visiting
community clinics and nurseries. Although orthoptic techniques do not provide a direct measure
of VA in this age-group, they do establish whether
the eyes are healthy and are working together as a
pair. Ease of access to the community orthoptist
facilitates the prompt referral and investigation of
any child suspected of having a visual defect.

References and further reading

Friendly, D.S. (1993) Development of vision in infants and
   young children. *Pediatric Clinics of North America*, **40**,
   693–703.
McGraw, P.V. and Winn, B. (1995) Measurement of letter
   acuity in preschool children. *Ophthalmic Physiology and
   Optics*, **15**, suppl. 1, S11–S17.
Menacker, S.J. (1993) Visual function in children with
   developmental disabilities. *Pediatric Clinics of North
   America*, **40**, 659–74.
Robb, R.M. (1981) *Ophthalmology for the Pediatric Practi-
   tioner*. Little, Brown, Boston.
Sonksen, P.M. (1993) The assessment of vision in the
   preschool child. *Archives of Disease in Childhood*, **68**,
   513–16.
Taylor, D.S. (ed). (1991). *Paediatric Ophthalmology*.
   Blackwell Scientific Publications, Oxford.

CHAPTER 7

Coping with Disability

Talking to parents

To the parents, a consultation about their child's suspected disability is a major event. Although the details may later be forgotten, the overall impression will remain for many years, perhaps for a lifetime. The consultation is not merely a diagnostic assessment. It should be the first stage in the therapeutic process of helping the family to cope with a disability which may affect their entire lifestyle. This is a task which cannot be rushed; far more parental unhappiness and dissatisfaction with their medical advisers can be traced to difficulties in communication or to lack of information than to clinical ignorance or diagnostic incompetence.

There is abundant evidence that parents wish to be informed as soon as there is any suspicion that their child is abnormal (Table 7.1). Adequate information must be provided as soon as possible and in language appropriate to their educational background, so that they know what problems may face them. Stock phrases which carry a wealth of meaning to doctors are meaningless to the parents, e.g. 'invasive investigation', 'conservative management', 'progressive lesion', etc. Scientific terms mean very little to those who have never studied biology, and words like 'chronological' and 'environment' are not part of the everyday vocabulary of ordinary people. The words 'acute' and 'chronic' are easily misunderstood. Unpleasant facts must not be disguised in medical jargon, although this is often done by the doctor to spare the parents and him/herself from the pain caused by everyday words which the doctor knows will have a more devastating impact.

It is often tempting to defer an explanation of the most distressing aspects of the diagnosis (such as progressive deterioration and early death, or the fact that a disorder is inherited) until the parents have recovered from the shock of hearing that their child has a disability. The need to explain these additional facts at a subsequent interview will make some parents very angry and lose faith in the doctor, because they wonder what further information is being withheld from them. Deliberate withholding of the facts is quite different from genuine uncertainty, which must be acknowledged.

Talking to parents is a skill which can be learnt and improved (Table 7.2). Parents do not remember all the information they are given. Even when relaxed, they may retain less than a third — and even this may be inaccurate. If upset by bad news, they may well 'switch off' and absorb nothing further except the fact that their child is abnormal. If they feel inhibited about

Table 7.1 News-breaking: what parents want

When a child is thought to have any significant disability (or other medical problem), parents want to be told:

1 As soon as possible. They consider that they have a right to share in any information the professionals may have

2 Together: both parents if possible, otherwise one parent accompanied by another person, e.g. grandparent, sister. If it is impossible to wait until both parents are available together, tell one but arrange to meet both together as soon as possible. Some parents would like to be accompanied by another professional, e.g. health visitor

3 In privacy, with adequate time (tell parents how much time can be allocated) and without interruptions (e.g. hand radiopager to someone else)

4 In a warm, friendly and caring style but without excessive emotion on the part of the professional

5 Honestly, with facts set out clearly and areas of uncertainty defined and explained

Table 7.2 Practical guidelines for news-breaking

1 Before starting the meeting with the parents, check that the room you will use is free and private and ask permission for any colleagues to be present (e.g. junior staff, therapists). Have a box of tissues to hand

2 Avoid jargon as much as possible; define the jargon words that the parents will need to know

3 Do not give a lecture; allow parents to take the lead in asking for information

4 Don't worry about pauses in the conversation

5 Give the parents an opportunity to talk about their feelings; quote experiences of other parents as a way of helping them to express their thoughts

6 Remember that it is the parents' problem; they must deal with it in their way, not that prescribed by the professional. Don't say 'I know how you feel' — you don't!

7 Convey confidence that the parents can and will cope, however devastated they feel. Don't even hint that they might not want to look after the child. Show personal acceptance of the child by looking at him/her and speaking to him/her if appropriate; ask if you can hold the child

8 Answer their questions if possible; if not, explain why. Be careful when dealing with questions of life expectancy (p. 113)

9 Explain what will happen next, e.g. visits from peripatetic teacher, further tests. If local policy includes a key worker, case manager or named person, explain how the system works

10 Offer specific services (therapy, teaching, contact with other parents, details of voluntary organization) but make clear that the timing of these is in the parents' control

11 Explain that they will receive a written report, so they do not need to remember everything you say

12 Arrange a follow-up meeting or discussion, preferably face to face, but by phone if not practical; or offer a home visit. Suggest that for the next meeting they write down their questions in advance

13 Remind parents that the child must not miss out on routine care, e.g. immunizations, etc.

---

asking questions, misunderstandings *will* persist. Rather than delivering a lecture, the doctor should involve the parents in the conversation from the beginning, for example, 'What do you think about your child yourselves?' Their comprehension of a problem can be checked by asking how they would themselves explain the child's disability to an enquirer such as a grandparent. Further feedback on the success of communication can often be obtained from the health visitor, GP or social worker; this is invaluable in correcting misconceptions and in improving one's own skills. Most parents appreciate a written report (Table 7.3) and some like to tape-record the consultation. It is remarkable that parents are the people who are usually given the least information about the doctor's opinion even though they have the most personal interest!

Three levels of diagnosis

Parents are easily confused by the terminology used to describe disabilities and developmental disorders (see pp. 2–4 for definitions of these terms). The exposition of the child's problem should focus on three levels of diagnosis: the type of disability, the cause and the effects.

What kind of disability?

There is seldom much difficulty in answering this question when there is an obvious major disability, for example cerebral palsy or autism, although there may be a period of doubt if the child is very young when first seen. The diagnosis of developmental disorders such as language impairment is often more difficult. The term 'developmental delay' (p. 147) is legitimate while there is a genuine doubt, but it must not be used as a euphemism for more specific terms such as learning disability or language disorder. Words like 'slow' or 'delayed' may be used in the initial stages of a discussion but, unless they are subsequently clarified, there is the risk of implying to the parents that the child will 'catch up' and it must be made clear that this cannot be guaranteed.

The point at which words like 'disability' or 'retardation' are introduced needs delicate judgement. The parents can be told that these words

Table 7.3 Written reports for parents

The written report:

Can be addressed to the parents with a copy to the general practitioner or vice versa

Must be written in clear English

Should describe the history, examination, investigations and conclusions with reasons. Predictions should be carefully phrased, with any uncertainties explained

Should set out what actions have been agreed and who is to undertake them

Should specify who is to receive copies of the letter

Can be circulated to others; either obtain parents' permission in advance to send copies to other agencies, e.g. education, or send them a spare copy which they can pass on, e.g. to the child's teacher, if they so wish

Must *not* omit important items of information or opinion which are then sent to colleagues separately; parents may request access to the child's notes, will find out that they have been deceived and will not trust professionals again

May acknowledge parents' grief, anger, etc.

Can be difficult to write; if the opinion is that, for example, the child's problem is related to parental management, spend time thinking how this can be stated in a constructive fashion

Must *not* be used as a means of conveying information that was too painful to discuss face to face; if important facts were not reviewed, make a new appointment

Note Readability can be measured; the score is related to the number of syllables per word and the number of words per sentence. Therefore, use short words, short sentences, short paragraphs and no long convoluted clauses. Jargon words *should* be used, because parents need to know them, but they should be defined. Take into account parents' educational background.

Make use of the word processor to store frequently used paragraphs such as those giving items of local information.

the parents that, although the child's *impairment* may not be cured by any available intervention, it is within their power to modify the extent of the child's *handicap*.

The starting-point for discussion has to be the parents' own perceptions of the child's abilities and problems. The extent of their anxiety and their own explanations for the child's slow development must be considered. Nothing will be gained by urging them to accept the diagnosis before they are ready. Many parents recognize that their child is 'developmentally delayed' but feel that he/she should be given every opportunity to progress before the child is 'labelled' as disabled. They should be assisted in arranging whatever intervention is most appropriate and encouraged to observe their child carefully, aided perhaps by a developmental chart (pp. 12 and 58) or by observing other children of the same age at a nursery or playgroup. If the child makes rapid progress, everyone is pleased; if the child turns out to be disabled, no time has been wasted and the parents have had time to recognize the problems for themselves.

When the parents do not appreciate that their child has, for instance, a general learning disability, there is something to be said for an approach which introduces potentially alarming terms in a graded way. Thus one might start by asking the parents whether they think their child is keeping up with other children of the same age as far as the child's development is concerned.

Then one can comment that the child is, indeed, slow in development which indicates that he/she is a slow learner — in other words that the child has learning difficulties. This phrase is both a description and an educational term — a more modern version of the older idea of backwardness. The progression subsequently to using terms such as learning disability, developmental or mental retardation or mental handicap provides a less stark introduction of the notion of disability. It is also a way of introducing the full range of terms which parents might be exposed to subsequently. These points can then be reiterated in the written report.

might apply to their child unless the child's current slow rate of development accelerates, but that it is impossible to predict what effect the child's future experiences may have on the child's ultimate level of function. This can be presented as an advantage, because it implies (correctly) to

What is the cause?

It is important for parents to understand the distinction between the type of disability and the underlying cause, even when no exact diagnosis can be determined. They may be helped by an outline of the main causes of disability which are relevant to their child and should be told which of these might merit further investigation.

Parents are usually grateful for an exact diagnosis, even if it has serious implications for the child's future progress. People brought up in the Western tradition feel more secure when there is a rational explanation for their experiences. Without a specific diagnosis, parents may continue to wonder whether the child's disability might be attributable to something they did or failed to do, or to some negligent act by the obstetrician or midwife; and they question whether there might be a miracle cure, if only the exact diagnosis could be established. Not surprisingly, therefore, parents may be very upset and angry if a diagnosis made previously turns out to be incorrect and their child's disability reverts to the 'cause unknown' category. For this reason, it is important to ensure that diagnosis is as accurate as possible. There is a particular temptation to overdiagnose dysmorphic syndromes, especially those for which no definitive test exists.

The possibility of overlooking a specific disease process should not be allowed to dominate clinical judgement. It may be difficult to decide whether, when and how much investigation is justified, but there are few situations where a delay of a few months in establishing a diagnosis will have any adverse effect and it allows time for the parents to come to terms with the disability before investigation is undertaken. One possible exception to this is where the mother is already pregnant again and there is a possibility that the child's diagnosis might have genetic implications.

What are the functional effects of the disability?

Parents want to know whether the child is likely to walk and talk. They usually enquire about prospects for education in mainstream school, and for an independent adult existence. Some may be particularly worried about epilepsy, either because of a family history or because of general background knowledge about the association between brain lesions and epilepsy. Others have anxieties about adolescence and sexuality, although these concerns are perhaps less severe than they were a decade ago, because of wider public knowledge about disability. Boys may be seen as potentially aggressive or even as future rapists, a fear that is often disguised as a general anxiety about 'growing up'. Parents commonly worry about girls becoming promiscuous or pregnant, or catching acquired immune deficiency syndrome (AIDS).

It is seldom easy to give a prognosis in childhood disability, but one way of dealing with uncertainty is to suggest some limits — the best and the worse that might happen. These limits should be broad in the early years and will become narrower as one watches the child's progress. For example, with learning disability of moderate degree, one could suggest that the limits might lie somewhere between non-skilled labour on the open market with community support, and a need for sheltered workshop accommodation and regular supervision. In their concern that parents should not be given false hopes, many professionals tend to give an unduly gloomy picture of the child's future prospects. Many disabled children (with the exception of those with profound learning disability accompanied by cerebral palsy) make more progress than the professionals predicted; parents often say that, although they want to be told the truth, they also need to be given hope for the future.

The problem of uncertainty

Months or even years may elapse before a definite diagnosis and prognosis can be established. This period of uncertainty is difficult both for parents and for the professionals who advise them. In chronic disorders, it is impossible to overemphasize the importance of continuity of care by one person.

The bereavement reaction

The response of parents to the diagnosis of a serious disability in their child has many parallels with the reaction to bereavement. The main difference is that the child's disability is a permanent source of sorrow, whereas death marks a crisis point beyond which readjustment can begin (Fig. 7.1). Although it is convenient to describe the bereavement reaction as if it occurred in a sequence of definable stages, human emotions are not so tidy and elements of several stages can often be discerned at any particular time.

Shock

When told that their child is disabled most parents experience a sense of shock, panic and disbelief, although this may be concealed behind a mask of reasonableness and acceptance. The reaction is usually more severe when the disability is caused by a sudden unanticipated catastrophe, such as birth asphyxia or a road accident, or in cases where the parents have not suspected or acknowledged that their child is not developing normally. Conversely, it is not uncommon for parents to realize the extent and nature of the child's disability long before any professional will believe them, and they may actually greet the diagnosis with a smile of relief. This response may be puzzling if it is not correctly interpreted. In some cases many months elapse before the professionals can be certain that the child really has a problem. This process can be called an evolutionary diagnosis. A common mistake in this situation is to assume that the parents have been able to keep up with the experts' thoughts on the diagnosis; it is vital to keep the parents' informed and to ensure that, sooner or later, they are given a definitive opinion.

It is common and natural for parents to feel revulsion for the abnormal child, particularly if there are obvious external deformities such as cleft lip or eye anomalies. Revulsion is a mixed emotion, often tinged with guilt and simultaneous protective feelings aroused by the child's helplessness.

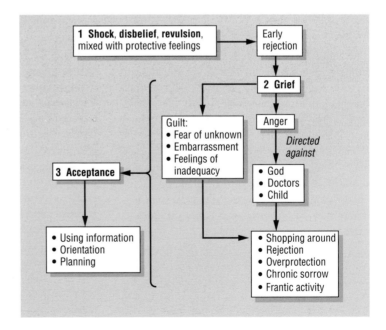

Fig. 7.1 Parental reactions.

Grief

An intense grief reaction occurs immediately after diagnosis or recognition of disability. This initiates a period of mourning, which may be regarded as grieving the loss of the perfect child who has now been replaced by one who is disabled. The sadness caused by disability never quite disappears, but the intensity of the grief diminishes with time as the parents adjust to the child's problems. The period of mourning is likely to be prolonged or suspended if the parents do not know the extent and details of the problem which confronts them.

Grief may be projected inwards, resulting in feelings of guilt, despair and isolation, or outwards, when it is manifest as anger. Some people do not complete the process of mourning and instead develop a variety of maladaptive behaviour patterns, which may limit their own happiness and inhibit their child's development.

In some cases, the parental grief reaction may be so intense that the professionals caring for the child may worry about suicide risks or the possibility that the parent may seriously injure the child, but in reality such tragedies seem to be very rare.

Guilt

The notion that a damaged child is a punishment for past sins might be thought rather archaic, but it is a widespread and deep-seated reaction. Parents often ask themselves, 'Whose fault is this?' There may be anxieties about psychiatric or neurological disorders in the family tree (even though they may not be genetically relevant), guilt about smoking, drug usage, alcohol, previous termination of pregnancy, or deliberate delay in childbearing for social and financial reasons. There may be questions about survival and life expectancy that cause further guilt feelings. 'Whose fault?' is a question of particular significance in some ethnic or cultural minority groups where any defects in the child may be regarded as being caused by some defect in the wife or her family. Nevertheless, guilt is not universal and parents become irritated when well-meaning counsellors repeatedly return to this issue.

Anger

A sense of frustrated anger and bitterness is a normal part of the bereavement response. The anger may be directed against God or against the child who has caused them so much sorrow. Anger may be very intense in a middle-class couple whose careful planning of their life and reproduction has been disorganized, or where there has been ambivalence about the pregnancy in the first place; in contrast, the philosophical attitude to life taught by some religions may virtually eliminate anger and bitterness.

Anger is frequently directed at doctors or other professionals, because of medical errors, or because the child's survival is or has been an achievement of modern medical care. Failure of antenatal screening procedures to detect the presence of a disabling condition also upsets parents, many of whom have come to believe that medical science can guarantee that they will have a perfect baby. Other common genuine grievances are that the child is seen merely as an interesting case (p. 150); that little interest is shown in minor intercurrent problems, such as infections, because the child is 'too handicapped to be worth the trouble'; that detailed diagnosis is offered but no treatment plan is made; and that too little help is available for major behaviour problems.

Parents may also feel angry if there has been an unreasonable delay in diagnosis, either because of a reluctance to tell them the truth or because of genuine medical difficulty. This anger has nothing to do with lost treatment opportunities and only rarely is it associated with the failure to offer genetic counselling prior to another pregnancy — although clearly these may be potent sources of justified anger in some situations. The explanation for the parents' anger in most cases is probably that the extent of the loss they feel — the loss of the normal child which will be associated with the diagnosis of a disability — is greater as the child gets older, because the parents and the child have a longer shared history.

The problem of litigation

Many parents suspect that their child's disability is the result of mismanagement during pregnancy or labour; less often, they may blame immunization reactions, illnesses or accidents, anaesthetics, medications, etc. In some cases, it is easy to deal with these concerns and parents will accept the assurances of the paediatrician about the true cause of the child's problems. If these matters are not dealt with, the parents will continue to worry about them. Whether or not they embark on litigation, the relationship between the parents and the professional team is likely to suffer, to the detriment of the child's care.

When responding to these concerns, it is essential first to review the relevant history and then to explain whether the medical evidence supports the parents' view. If it seems that they may be justified in attributing the child's disability to medical error, the parents should be offered the opportunity of meeting the relevant staff — most often this will be the consultant obstetrician. If after this they wish to take the matter further, they may need to take legal advice.

Their decision may be influenced by many factors, but perhaps the commonest reason given by parents is the wish to find out 'what really happened'.

From the professionals' point of view, litigation is a distressing problem, even if the staff caring for the child are not directly involved. They may feel that it is their institution that is under attack; and the parents often feel embarrassed about the situation. It is important for all concerned to continue the professional relationship so that the care of the child and family does not suffer.

Second opinions — the 'shopping around' syndrome

Some parents collect endless opinions about their disabled child. The motives for their behaviour need careful analysis. Sometimes the reason is genuinely that the initial counselling or diagnosis was inadequate; questions that could have been answered were ignored or sidestepped. There are many parents who accept the facts of the disability but want specific advice on what they themselves can do to help the child; they may, for instance, be dissatisfied with the available educational facilities.

In some cases, however, people who shop around are very distressed, disturbed and difficult to help. They may still be angry or suffering from guilt feelings, usually with an overlay of chronic sorrow and depression; this is sometimes associated with organic symptoms but, not surprisingly, fails to respond to antidepressants. The paediatrician should not regard these parents as an irritating nuisance or as a challenge to prove his/her superiority over those previously consulted. A detailed assessment of the child's abilities is usually superfluous in such cases. It will have been done before — many times! A careful life history of parents and child and an attempt to define the source of their confusion and despair are more likely to be profitable.

One feature of the 'shopping around' syndrome is that a certain person or place is idealized and seen as a potential miracle-worker. From the parents' perspective, if the goal seems inaccessible, due to distance, cost or the reluctance of a family doctor to refer the child, it merely becomes more desirable. However, a pilgrimage of a religious nature is not necessarily a manifestation of this syndrome. It may indicate the parents' acceptance that the child is disabled because it is the will of God. A pilgrimage, for example to Lourdes, may be invaluable and should be encouraged.

Many parents feel that their child's potential for learning and progress is not being fully exploited. In their eagerness to persuade the professionals that this is so, they may exaggerate the child's skills. In most cases, it is possible to establish agreement between parents and professionals as to how the child is functioning. We have, however, seen a few parents who appear to live in a fantasy world as regards the child's abilities; for instance, they may produce poems or pictures supposedly created by a child who appears unable to understand even the most basic of concepts. As far as we could ascertain, these parents had no other evidence of mental illness.

Overprotection and rejection

These two apparently opposite attitudes are not mutually exclusive; indeed, traces of both can be identified in the majority of parents of disabled children in Western society. Parents feel that they have a duty to care for their disabled child, reinforced by professional counselling, which is almost invariably directed towards home-based care and barely admits of any alternatives such as fostering or institutional placement. Parents are under constant pressure to prove that they can cope and can live up to the expectations of society. It is not surprising that some parents devote excessive care and zeal to their disabled child while others reject the child resentfully.

Overprotective parents often have sound reasons for their behaviour. Some children with severe disability are very difficult to handle or feed, or there may be anxiety about medical emergencies such as fits. The parents may learn by bitter experience that it is not possible to leave the child with a babysitter. Unfortunately, over-protection can easily become a maladaptive response that inhibits the development of independence. The parents' fear of what the child will be like when adult encourages them to keep the child as a baby for as long as possible; one mother explained, 'Everyone loves a handicapped child but nobody loves a handicapped man.'

The disabled child may provide a purpose for living, without which the parents would be lost. One or other parent, commonly the father, often becomes an enthusiastic and vociferous member of voluntary societies and charities. In a few cases this seems to serve the purpose of releasing the parent from the chore of caring for the child, because he/she is so busy with charitable work.

A very useful service can be performed by the Child Development Team in helping the parents to maintain an appropriate level of involvement with that child, by showing that other people can handle the child and by introducing the idea of respite care (p. 123). Because they are professionals, they will often earn the parents' confidence sooner than relatives or friends can.

Acceptance

Acceptance has been defined as 'the death of an imaginary perfect child and the redirection of parental love to the newly perceived child as he/she is in reality'. It may take many years and the pace should not be forced to fit the professionals' notion of acceptance. Good preschool services provide adequate help for the child while allowing parental understanding to evolve at a natural speed.

For many parents, the care of a disabled child does become rewarding; they are able to make some sense of the experience, and perhaps to offer sympathy and guidance to new parents of children in similar circumstances. An opportunity to meet such parents and disabled people who have a positive attitude to disability does much to bring back a sense of proportion to those suffering the first shock of diagnosis.

The effects of disability on families and individuals

The concept of coping

Coping is the attempt to resolve stress (Fig. 7.2). It can be considered under three headings.

Problem-focused coping

This is indicated by attempts to remove the source of stress or minimize its impact. For parents, this will include attempts to find a cure for their child's condition. If these become frantic, the attempt to cope is maladaptive because it creates more difficulties or interferes with other areas of coping; but, in origin, it is a logical way of dealing with the stressor.

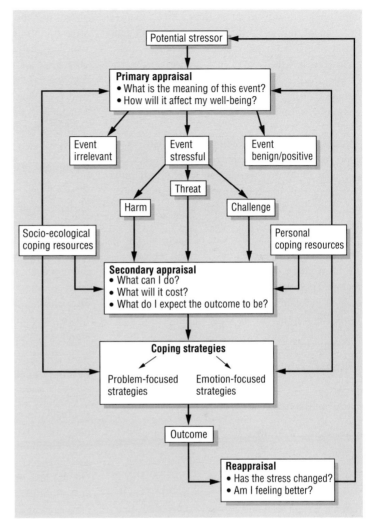

Fig. 7.2 The process model of stress and coping. *Coping* is 'the process of managing demands (external or internal) that are appraised as taxing or exceeding the resources of the person'. Coping is a *process*, an interaction between an individual and the environment. It is viewed in terms of *management* rather than mastery — not every problem can be solved. *Appraisal* is the way experiences are perceived and represented in the mind of the individual, i.e. it is concerned with subjective assessment rather than an objective or 'professional' view. An experience or situation which appears stressful to the child development team may not appear so to the parents. Coping involves *mobilization of effort*. It needs *resources*. From Beresford (1994).

Emotion-focused coping

This includes the ways in which parents try to help themselves feel less distressed or adjust to the demands of a situation. Contacting parents of similarly disabled children is a very practical and constructive measure. Not allowing oneself to think about the future might be seen as mal-adaptive, even though the short-term gains in terms of emotional comfort are clear. The grief reaction to the loss of an anticipated normal child is an example of the way in which an emotional adjustment might be made with an eventual goal of emotional acceptance, even though it involves unpleasant emotions in the shorter term.

Cognitive reframing

This involves thinking about the problem or stressor in ways which enable a greater degree of mental comfort or which help other ways of coping. Thus one parent was helped to feel closer to his son when it was pointed out that much of his son's behaviour was an effort to deal with the impairments of autism, rather than a direct manifestation of autism itself. Some parents feel relieved when they realize that it is not just their child who has the stigma of handicap; ordinary people are handicapped by an inability to communicate with a child who has a language comprehension impairment.

These various ways in which people endeavour to cope with stressful circumstances or events do not just apply to parents but to children and teenagers as well. Children with a disability cope too. It is important not to fall into the trap of assuming that a severe disability is the most stressful. Mild disabilities can be more stressful for children than severe ones. A small amount of ataxia, dyslexia or learning disability may mean that children are constantly having to explain the reasons for their difficulties to others. Alternatively, their problem in keeping up with other children may be perceived as motivational rather than arising out of an impairment, so that they are criticized by their teachers for laziness.

Family differences in reactions to disability

Parents do not necessarily recognize or acknowledge the existence of disability at the same speed. These differences are not abnormal in themselves but are a potential source of conflict and disharmony, which may be exacerbated if both parents are not seen and counselled together. In a mutually supportive marriage, the relationship can be strengthened following the diagnosis, but unstable relationships often collapse under the strain. Other members of the family may take much longer to accept the situation. In particular, grandparents cause much distress by their often prolonged insistence that the child is normal, forcing parents continually to emphasize the child's deficiencies in discussions with them.

Having a disabled child is a painful and a stressful experience, but people undergo many other stressful experiences during their lives, such as illness, death of a spouse, bankruptcy or redundancy. There are wide variations in the ability of individuals and families to cope with stressful events. Table 7.4 summarizes factors which are liable to increase stress for families and also some of the protective mechanisms which may increase their ability to cope with stress. An understanding of these factors is helpful when considering the different ways in which services might be needed and utilized by families.

Problems of the siblings

The siblings of a disabled child reflect their parents' emotions but also have some problems unique to themselves. They may feel neglected and ignored, and may display neurotic or antisocial symptoms. Their own social life may be disrupted and often they are embarrassed to bring friends home. The disabled person's future care after the parents' death is an additional worry. Lastly, as teenagers, they may become anxious about the genetic risks to their own offspring.

Feelings of the disabled person

All but the most profoundly disabled children gradually develop some insight into the fact that they are different. This process often begins in early childhood, accelerating in adolescence as social expectations begin to demand the development of sexualized relationships based on physical attraction. Successful adaptation to the personal predicament of being disabled is dependent on the attitudes of family, professional staff and society in general. Misdirected kindness and failure to treat disabled people as responsible and sensitive individuals in their own right encourage them to lapse into unnecessary dependence, adoption of the 'sick role' and manipulative behaviour. They may retreat into fantasy or become selfish or self-centred. These undesirable characteristics are not an inevitable part of being disabled; modern attitudes may produce more positive personality characteristics in adult life.

Even people with a severe or profound general learning disability are capable of forming attachments to other individuals, places, pets and special

Table 7.4 Stress and coping

Factors which increase stress	Protective factors
Behaviour problems in the child	Happy stable relationship with partner
Hyperactivity in the child	Family cohesion: shared family activities and values
Very severe learning disability: little perceived response from the child	Accessible supportive extended family
Many life events, especially recently: illness, hospitalization, death in the family, redundancy, bankruptcy, homelessness, etc.	Strong religious/moral/spiritual beliefs in the family
Marital disharmony	Parents feel in control of events
Financial difficulties	Ability to formulate and solve problems
Poor housing: stress relates more to perception of housing than to any absolute measure of housing quality	Ability to utilize support in the social network
Inadequate transport: no car, poor public transport	Friends who are themselves parents of disabled children
Tendency to passive acceptance of situation	Appropriate level and timing of professional supporting services
Too little professional support: too many demands made on parents to undertake therapy, etc.	Ability to be assertive without being aggressive
Too much professional support	
Critical grandparents	

objects or routines. Breaking these attachments, for instance by the death of a relative or carer, may have unpredictable and sometimes bewildering effects. Challenging behaviour, eating disturbances or bizarre 'funny turns' may occur. Sensitive handling of bereavements and changes in the life of the disabled child may avoid these problems.

Abuse of disabled children

The severely disabled child or adult is very vulnerable to abuse of all kinds. Physical abuse is well known to occur in institutions for the adult disabled but is less common in childhood. Sexual abuse has been recognized increasingly in recent years. Children and teenagers who have serious difficulties in communicating are at particular risk. Since diagnosis of sexual abuse, in the absence of unequivocal signs such as pregnancy

or sexually transmitted disease, depends very much on disclosure by the child, it can be extremely difficult to establish that abuse has occurred. Cases rarely present early and abuse may have continued for many years before discovery. Challenging behaviours and psychological problems may be the first or only clue. Sexual relations with a minor are illegal, but the law is more complex where people with learning disabilities over the age of 16 are concerned. As with non-disabled children, any suspicion of sexual abuse needs to be reported to the social services department; the evidence must be reviewed carefully before any action is taken; and the investigation must be conducted according to the standard guidelines. The procedures and their consequences (a brother or father leaving home, for instance) can be confusing and frightening in their own right.

Further crises

Parents who have apparently come to terms with their child's disability may show a renewal of the grief reaction at crisis points, including: the child's failure to walk and talk at the usual time; realization that the child will not be able to attend normal school; the need for residential care if the family breaks up; times when behaviour or management problems become intolerable; realization that the child is never going to walk unaided; the time of transfer from junior to secondary school; the problems of early adolescence; and the time of school-leaving.

An unexpected crisis is sometimes caused by the use of a new and unexpected word; for example, an apparently well-adjusted family may use the terms 'learning-disabled', 'retarded' and 'backward' in connection with their child without any distress; but become very disturbed at the use of the words 'mentally handicapped'. For this reason, it is essential to discuss all the relevant words with parents at the time of initial diagnosis, preferably in writing.

Residential care

Requests for residential care of a disabled child may be made during the acute early grief reaction, when they may be seen as evidence of rejection, or later, after the stage of acceptance has been reached. Thirty years ago, recommendation for institutional care was a common reaction of professionals faced with any disabled baby, but it is usually better, both for the progress of the child and the psychological health of the family, that he/she should become an accepted part of a family unit, even if only for a few years. The decision to place the child in some form of residential care is usually then made after much thought, and for good reason, such as the needs of other normal children in the family.

The pendulum has swung too far in favour of keeping disabled children at home at all costs. For many families, a residential school will be the right answer and every possible help should be given in finding a suitable placement. Modern units are run on compact family lines and have little in common with the old style of purely custodial care in large hospital wards.

Professional reactions to disability

Health professionals are not immune from the reactions described above. Feelings of sorrow, revulsion, therapeutic inadequacy and anger are natural responses of sympathetic people to the tragedy of childhood disability. Difficulties in communication may arise when these feelings are deliberately stifled in the cause of 'professionalism' instead of using them to empathize with the parents; or when the professional is unable to distinguish between their own private reactions and those of the parents.

It is much easier to work with some families than others. There are parents who are expert at finding their way through the complex systems of the health, education and social services; usually they are people who are confident of their ability to control their own lives in other respects and to get what they want, even in adversity. They cooperate with treatment and therapy, keep appointments and record treatments, fits or behaviour problems when requested to do so. Other families are perceived as difficult; they may be aggressive or demanding, want everything explained in detail, fail to keep appointments, have fixed ideas about the cause or the management of the child's disability, adopt unorthodox treatment systems, or seem unable to express their concerns clearly when offered the opportunity to do so. The truly professional team aims to offer the same standard of care and service for these families as for the 'easy' ones and recognizes that sometimes the 'difficult' families are those who are rising to the challenge presented by their child's disability. A liaison child psychiatrist may be able to help the team to deal more effectively with parents who are perceived as difficult.

Thinking about death and survival

In cases of very severe disability, it is natural for the parents to wonder if the child will survive. They may well hope that he/she will not, but be afraid to express this view to professionals and perhaps even to themselves. Lack of opportunity to examine these feelings intensifies the guilt which they cause. Clues to their existence include questions such as, 'What happens to babies like this?' and 'How long do children like this usually live?'

These questions may be dealt with on several levels. They may be a genuine request for information. Life expectancy for children with severe learning disabilities is discussed on p. 171. If these are used for counselling parents, it is essential to make clear that they are averages, not predictions for the individual child. It can be disastrous to give parents specific predictions such as 'children like this die before they are 6 months old', because so often they turn out to be wrong. As the predicted date approaches and then passes, the parents become bewildered, upset and angry. They may have planned their lives on the basis that they will only be looking after the child for a certain period of time and this may lead to major career changes or family upheavals. Specific predictions should only be offered when the prognosis is very well established, for example classic Werdnig–Hoffmann disease (p. 292), and even then parents must be warned about the variations that occur.

Alternatively, such questions may indicate the parents' need to think about their own feelings and reactions if the child were to become seriously ill or to die. They may want to develop a plan of action in case the child's condition should deteriorate and will be anxious to know how the medical staff would react. The views of parents on the prolongation of the child's life in the event of life-threatening illness vary enormously, change with time and can seldom be predicted on the basis of social class, ethnic origin or religion. It is important to find out what the parents feel about these issues, while at the same time ensuring that they

do not shoulder the ultimate responsibility for making decisions. It is often useful to discuss the issues and negotiate a policy when the child is well.

Life-threatening medical problems in the severely disabled should, if possible, be managed by the same doctor who has previously been responsible for the child's general care. If the doctor knows the family well, he/she is more likely correctly to gauge their feelings as to the appropriate management. The ethical issues surrounding the maintenance of life in severe disability cannot be avoided, but it is not desirable to have rigid rules derived from one's own personal beliefs. The medical responsibility is to determine what course of action is most acceptable in terms of the family's personal beliefs and then to share the burden of that decision. It may sometimes be right for the doctor to continue active treatment of the child who has, in the doctor's view, no useful future. However, a doctor should not succumb to pressure to discontinue treatment, or actively to hasten death, against the dictates of his/her conscience. When confronted with such difficult situations, the views of medical and nursing colleagues, therapists and perhaps the chaplain may be helpful. All such consultations, and the reasons for the decisions reached, should be carefully documented in the child's notes.

Acute illness in the severely disabled child

Staff who do not often deal with the death of a severely disabled person sometimes imagine that the issue is simply a question of whether or not the child should be resuscitated in the event of cardiac arrest. In reality, this problem rarely arises; the questions which do need to be considered are set out in Table 7.5. Each professional and parent will have their own views on the answers to these questions. A middle-of-the-road approach is usually best as a starting-point for discussions with parents or staff; they can be told that this is a policy which many people feel comfortable with, but that no policy can be right for every child on every occasion.

Table 7.5 Issues about death and dying that worry parents and staff

CARDIAC OR RESPIRATORY ARREST

If it occurs at home, what should the parent do?
　　Advice on simple first aid may be appreciated. Do the parents want a suction device
　　at home? Should they call an ambulance? or the GP or community nurse?

If in hospital or a residential unit, what should the staff do?
　　Suction and oxygen only? Cardiac massage if needed plus stimulant and
　　antiarrhythmia drugs? Should the child be ventilated for: (a) a short period of
　　stabilization only; or (b) for as long as is needed?
　　*Note: Often it is best to follow the usual routines of resuscitation up to and including (a) if
　　they are in doubt; this allows time for senior staff to discuss the situation with parents,
　　without any commitment to long-term ventilation*

CHRONIC FEEDING PROBLEMS

Would a Haberman feeder help? Should the child be tube-fed? If so, does this apply to
liquids only? or also to feeds? Is it a short-term measure to overcome a period of illness
or a long-term measure? Should a gastrostomy be made?
　　*Note: Without tube-feeding many profoundly disabled children would die; many children
　　with degenerative disease, e.g. Batten's disease, would die much sooner*

ACUTE ILLNESS

Should the child receive antibiotics/antiasthma drugs for acute infections or
respiratory symptoms?
　　*Note: Many people imagine that antibiotics are essential to save the life of any disabled child
　　with chest infection. In fact, most children, even if profoundly disabled, recover from most
　　'chest infections' without antibiotics, possibly because many are viral and/or asthmatic in
　　nature. Asthma is as common in the disabled as in the normal population*

Should intravenous fluids be used if the child is dehydrated?

TERMINAL CARE

Should the child be given any medication to ease distress, e.g. analgesics, sedatives?
　　*Note: There should be no hesitation in using strong analgesics or opiates for terminal care,
　　particularly if the child is distressed or agitated, as may happen in the terminal stages of
　　neurodegenerative diseases*

Should other drugs or treatments be withdrawn?

Guiding principles to be considered by parents and staff
1 What is this child's quality of life?
2 What would this child say if he/she could speak for him/herself?

It is often difficult to decide when a child is terminally ill, even in neurodegenerative conditions with a relentless downhill course. This uncertainty may deprive the child of adequate symptom relief, because of professional concerns about the distinction between medical care and euthanasia. Children in fact tolerate the standard doses of narcotics very well and benefit from them. A 'cocktail' given by syringe pump (Table 7.6) is invaluable when oral treatment is inappropriate.

Table 7.6 Useful medications for terminal care of a disabled child

For distress and restlessness: morphia, oral or im
• Give 100 μg/kg if under 1 year of age, 200 μg/kg if aged 5–12 years
• Watch for constipation and delayed gastric emptying
NB. Provided the dose is carefully monitored, there is no need to withhold narcotics for fear of depressing respiration; this unjustified fear often deprives children of valuable symptom relief

For excessive salivation and secretions:
• Use hyoscine patches behind the ear, half a patch if under age 4

For neurodegenerative diseases with intractable fits, salivation and restlessness, particularly if complicated by impaired gastric emptying:
• Use a subcutaneous infusion driven by syringe pump, with diamorphine 15–20 mg: hyoscine 600–800 μg, midazolam 20 mg
• For a child weighing 10–20 kg, these are dissolved in 48 ml of normal saline and the mixture is run initially at 1–5 ml/hour. The dose of each ingredient can be varied independently of the others each time the mixture is made up

Death of a disabled child

When a disabled child dies in hospital, the parents should, of course, be permitted all the time and privacy they desire, and should be encouraged to touch and hold the child. It is important to respect the religious beliefs of the family and to ensure that, as far as possible, the appropriate measures are taken. The death certificate should be completed after explaining to the parents what are to be entered as the main and contributing causes of death. Most hospitals have procedures to ensure that medical records and appointments officers and the GP are informed of a death, but the doctor should accept responsibility to remember others who ought to be told; in particular social workers, educational psychologists, peripatetic teachers and staff at the child's day nursery or school must be notified promptly. Parents sometimes appreciate help in managing other problems, such as funeral arrangements, donation of tissues or organs for research (and occasionally for transplant), what to tell siblings or how to organize a memorial fund for the child.

Staff who have known the child well often wish to attend the funeral. This should be permitted if at all possible, although it is wise to ensure that the family would welcome their presence, particularly with families from ethnic minorities. The family mourning which follows the death may be complicated by relief, and by guilt at feeling relieved; but professionals and relatives should avoid the trap of assuming that the family will *necessarily* be relieved that 'it is all over'. An opportunity should be offered for a further discussion with the doctor or other professionals after the funeral, and in some cases contact may need to be continued for a long time.

References and further reading

Beresford, B.A. (1994) Resources and strategies: how parents cope with the care of a disabled child. *Journal of Child Psychology and Psychiatry*, 35(1), 171–211.
Bicknell, J. (1983) The psychopathology of handicap. *British Journal of Medical Psychology*, 56, 167–78.
Fletcher, C.M. (1973) *Communication in Medicine.* Nuffield Provincial Hospitals Trust, London.
Leonard, A. (1994) *Right from the Start. Looking at Diagnosis and Disclosure – Parents Describe how they found out about their Child's Disability.* SCOPE, London.
Sloper, P. and Turner, S. (1993) Determinants of parental satisfaction with disclosure of disability. *Developmental Medicine and Child Neurology*, 35(9), 816–25.

CHAPTER 8
Services for Disabled Children

Evolution of Child Development Centres

In 1968 the Sheldon Working Party recommended the creation of comprehensive Child Assessment Centres, but gradually the term Child Development Centre (CDC) came to be the usual designation for such units. The CDC may be sited on a hospital campus or in the community. Hospital sites have advantages of efficient use of professional time and easy access to facilities such as the pharmacy, radiology and laboratory services, but community-based units are often more accessible to families and less intimidating.

As it became increasingly obvious that the parents of a disabled child need more than therapy, the role of the CDC expanded. Parents want a 'single front door', so that they do not have to navigate their way through the complexities of different provider agencies (i.e. health, social services and education together with voluntary groups). The modern CDC aims to co-ordinate the many services needed by the child, in order to reduce the burden of frequent visits to a variety of different specialists and experts.

Many children have more than one impairment, and in such a broad field no profession has a monopoly of wisdom in assessment or remediation, so multidisciplinary teamwork is essential. Mutual professional respect, flexibility in allocating tasks, familiarity with each other's abilities and interests and adequate time for discussion are essential ingredients for success. In order to emphasize these points, the term '*inter-disciplinary*' is now often preferred.

The District Handicap Team

The Court Report (1976) on paediatric services suggested that the professionals involved in the care of disabled children should function as District Handicap Teams, but it is now clear that each child requires a unique combination of professional expertise which cannot always be met by the 'core team' members, and the number of disabled children in each District is in any case too large for the core team to have a personal knowledge of each child's current status and needs.

The term 'Child Development Team' is a convenient, though loose, designation for those professionals who elect to work together to provide services for disabled children, but the complexities of management hierarchies currently present insuperable obstacles to the creation of a single team with sufficient autonomy and resources to function as a unit.

However, a strategic planning group is needed to negotiate and carry through the arrangements that need to be made both for individual children and for new service initiatives, such as respite care provision. The term 'Special Needs Planning Group' is in keeping with current thought.

Changing ideas about services for disabled children

There have been major changes in the relationship between the parents of disabled children and the professionals who claim expertise in their care (Table 8.1). They reflect the move away from a professional-led service, towards a more consumer-orientated society, in which the consumers (the parents) select which of a variety of services they want, decide when and how they want to use them and are not afraid to complain if the quality of the service is not acceptable. The philosophy of normalization has also influenced attitudes to disability. Normalization is 'the use of

Table 8.1 Different ways of providing services for disabled children. After Appleton and Minchom (1991)

THE EXPERT MODEL

The professionals give information; they inform the parents of the results of the assessment; they assess and treat the child:

- according to their own perceptions
- with minimal negotiation of goals with parents or other carers
- in a place of their choosing

The expert model is outmoded; it does not allow for the differences between families, nor does it consider the need to relate professional goals to family needs and priorities

THE TRANSPLANT MODEL

The professionals provide the expertise and teach the parents to carry out particular tasks. In this model it is implicitly assumed that:

- parents know their own child better than anyone else can
- parents are motivated to help their child
- parents have the personal resources to carry out what is required of them
- the professionals will be in charge of the management plan
- the professionals have the ability to communicate the necessary skills to the parents

The transplant model maintains the dependent role of the family in relation to professional services. It does not address the problem of multiple professional inputs

THE CONSUMER RIGHTS MODEL

This model emphasizes the parents as consumers and assumes that:

- parents have the right to select services and interventions that they feel are appropriate
- parents will need information in order to make these choices
- parents have the expertise to judge for themselves what is needed in the light of their life situation

It follows that:

- service packages would need to be tailored to individual family needs
- sometimes the family and the professionals would have different perceptions of the services needed; if this happened the parents' views would be respected
- negotiation about service provision would be essential
- parents would be part of the management structure of special needs services

The danger of this model is (in theory, at least) that it neglects the child's needs in favour of those of the whole family

THE SOCIAL NETWORK MODEL

This model emphasizes the child as a member of a social network and assumes that:

- environmental factors interact with biological disadvantage in complex ways
- under most circumstances, the child's social network is a more powerful factor in influencing development than any professional service
- families may rate factors causing social disadvantage (poor housing, unemployment) as more important than developmental problems
- parents will draw on their social networks for information, ideas and support, as much as, or more than, their professional advisers
- families previously labelled as 'difficult' or 'non-compliant' would be regarded as having different priorities
- professional skills would be used to assist the family to set, adjust and achieve its priorities for the child

THE EMPOWERMENT MODEL

This combines features of the consumer rights model and social network model. It emphasizes the empowerment of parents, i.e. the aim is to facilitate the parents' ability to make and carry out decisions and actions which they consider to be right for them. It emphasizes the strengths of the family rather than its weaknesses. It retains the professional role and responsibility to consider the needs of the child and to help parents to consider how these can be met. It has implications for the ways in which services are provided and monitored

---

measures which are as normal as possible for the cultural background of the person in question, to establish and maintain personal behaviours and characteristics which also are culturally as normal as possible'.

New insights into the concept of stress (p. 109) present fresh challenges and it is now obvious that no single service model or package can be appropriate for all families at all times; indeed, perhaps it is surprising that professionals ever thought otherwise.

The challenge now is to match the needs of the child as perceived by individual experts (in education, therapy, etc.) to the priorities of the family, so that both parents and professionals are working towards the same goals at the same time. In the USA, one approach has been the introduction of the Individual Family Service Plan or IFSP. This is negotiated with the parents and aims to set out the goals of the family (both for the child and for other family members), the ways in which services will be provided, the extent of family involvement in teaching and therapy, the additional resources required, etc. In line with this philosophy, we now take it for granted that parents will attend most case conferences and case discussions about their child. Honest negotiation depends on a full, frank exchange of information. Parents tell us that they like to hear the professionals' deliberations. Disagreements do not worry them; indeed, it is helpful for them to hear how the 'experts' reach their conclusions.

Key workers and care managers

Parents need someone to take an overview of their child's needs in the context of the whole family and help them to make use of specialist expertise. The idea of a key worker or named person was introduced some years ago to fulfil this need, but has not been universally successful, for several reasons. Firstly, the key worker was usually the professional most involved with the child at that time, for example the physiotherapist, and therefore the perspective on the child's needs was that of one particular discipline and tended to be too narrow. Secondly, the child's needs and

the family's priorities change over time, but few teams had a mechanism for changing the key worker. Thirdly, since the key worker was also a service provider, the family were reluctant to complain about the service they received, or to ask for it to be withdrawn even if it was no longer a priority from their point of view.

An alternative approach is that of care management (this concept evolved from, but is not identical with, *case* management). The care manager is not primarily responsible for providing a service (i.e. teaching, therapy, etc.) to the child, but rather for deciding with the family what services are needed, helping them to arrange them and monitoring their provision and effectiveness. The care manager might be a doctor, psychologist, therapist or social worker. To be effective he or she must be able to cross service boundaries and negotiate with any of the agencies involved with the child's care. Inevitably, care management adds to the cost of service provision for the disabled child, but it may at the same time increase parent satisfaction and achieve the best possible match between the demands of the parents and the needs of the child, within the constraints of available resources.

The Children Act 1989

This updated the legislation on a wide variety of issues related to child care. The main provisions which are relevant to the care of children with disabilities are summarized in Table 8.2.

Services needed by parents of disabled children

Information

An important function of the CDC is to provide an information resource (Table 8.3).

Follow-up consultations

The need for regular attendance at the CDC should be kept under review. Some parents may prefer to request appointments only when new

Table 8.2 The Children Act 1989. From HMSO (1991)

The Act covers a variety of matters relating to children, including child protection, adoption and fostering, residential care, disability, etc. The main provisions relevant to disabled children are summarized below.

1 *Child protection.* A Child Assessment Order can be made on the application of a Social Services Department (SSD) or other authorized person (e.g. National Society for the Prevention of Cruelty to Children (NSPCC)) when the Court is satisfied that the child may be suffering harm, needs an assessment and is unlikely to receive one without the order. Seven days are allowed. Arrangements should be made in advance of the application. (Staff of the Child Development Team CDT may be asked to arrange such an assessment. Since expert opinions on the quality of child care may be requested, staff should ensure that all necessary expertise is available, often including child psychiatry.)

Emergency Protection Orders (EPOs) provide immediate short-term protection, for up to 8 days. (CDT staff may be asked for advice on the needs of the disabled child and his/her capacity to understand what is happening, when he/she is the subject of an EPO.)

2 *Children in need.* A child is defined as being in need if
(a) he/she is unlikely to achieve a reasonable standard of health or development without provision of services by a local authority;
(b) his/her health or development is likely to be significantly impaired without provision of such services; or
(c) he/she is disabled. 'Disabled' means blind, deaf or dumb or suffers from mental disorder of any kind or is handicapped by illness, injury or congenital deformity. Such a person now qualifies for services both before and after the age of 18.

3 *General duty of SSD for children in need.* To provide services to promote their welfare and so far as is possible to promote the upbringing of such children by their families.

4 *Register of children with disabilities.* The SSD must keep a register, but parents are not obliged to register and services are not dependent on registration. (CDT staff may be asked to collaborate in the development of registers to avoid duplication of effort, and also to encourage parents to register their disabled children.)

5 *Care management.* The SSD has the overall responsibility to ensure that the child's services are co-ordinated.

6 *Partnership with families.* Families including the children should participate in making decisions about the services needed and how they are provided. There is also a duty to ensure that parents are fully informed about voluntary organizations which might be able to help them.

7 *Services for families.* SSDs together with education and health authorities should provide domiciliary services (e.g. Portage, health visiting). Family centres should be provided to support families with complex needs. Befriending schemes to support parents under stress should be encouraged. (CDTs may be involved with these activities both clinically and as a resource for educating and assisting the SSD and volunteer staff involved.) Foster parents for disabled children may need training and support.

8 *Notification of SSD by Education Authority.* When the Education Authority proposes to carry out a formal assessment, it must notify the SSD.

9 *Education Supervision Orders (ESOs).* The Education Authority may apply for an ESO as a means of dealing with non-attendance. (Non-attendance in the case of disabled children usually has complex causes, e.g. dissatisfaction with the curriculum or school environment or the wish to undertake unorthodox intensive programmes. CDT staff may be asked for advice on such cases. Negotiated solutions are better than confrontation; the ESO is a last resort.)

10 *Accommodation.* SSDs have a duty to promote contact with family and friends if the child is in residential accommodation. If a child is not visited regularly, the SSD may appoint an independent visitor. A disabled child resident in health authority accommodation for more than 3 months must be notified to the SSD. SSDs have a duty to safeguard the disabled child's welfare in independent schools. For *respite care* criteria of good practice are specific (see p. 123).

11 *Transition to adulthood.* SSDs are required to collaborate with Education Authorities to assess the needs of school-leavers. Co-operation between these agencies and health workers (both specialist and primary care) is emphasized.

Table 8.3 The Child Development Centre (CDC) as an information resource

Developmental charts, such as the Parent Involvement Project

Growth charts (including special charts for Down's, Turner's syndromes)

Books and videos on child development and disability, alternative medicine, education

Parent workshops, seminars, coffee mornings

Information about voluntary organizations and how to contact them. Encourage parents to join and support these groups; they stimulate research, keep parents and professionals informed of advances and act as a pressure group for better facilities in the future
    Caution: warn parents that some parent literature can be slanted towards the severe end of the spectrum in respect of many disorders; ensure that they have the opportunity to discuss it with professionals

Opportunity to contact other parents who have had similar experiences
    Caution: try to match severity and prognosis when introducing parents to each other, or else warn them of any obvious differences between their children

Information about toy libraries, horse-riding, music, art, dance and drama therapy, adventure playgrounds, swimming lessons, whirlpool baths, holidays, incontinence advisers, etc.

Parents tell us that they want this information — *they* will decide whether it is relevant to them, they do not want the professionals to make this decision for them

problems arise. They may wish to keep in touch with some more accessible person, for example their GP, school doctor or health visitor.

Telephone consultations and community nursing visits should be used where possible. These can maintain regular contact with the family, without requiring them to travel all the way to the hospital simply to report that a child has no new problems or is having no convulsions.

Using child psychiatry and psychology services

Developmental and behavioural problems, unusual parental reactions to stress and problems in coping may best be dealt with by a child psychiatrist or psychologist. This does not necessarily need a direct referral; for example, a liaison child psychiatrist can meet with the professionals who have raised the concern and determine whether a referral is needed and, if so, how it should be arranged. A successful consultation is more likely if the parents understand what kind of help is being offered. A personal

introduction or an initial joint consultation may be invaluable.

Supporting children of parents with learning disabilities

CDT staff may be asked to assess the development, health and quality of care of a child whose parents themselves have learning disabilities. Often there will then be a commitment to monitor the child's progress and ensure that appropriate services are mobilized, usually in collaboration with social services and education (Table 8.4).

Child health surveillance

The primary care programme of routine child health surveillance is designed for *all* children (Hall, 1996). Primary care staff readily assume that the routine care for disabled children is being provided by the specialist team, but often this is not so. For instance, checks on height, weight, testicular descent, etc. are frequently neglected. This is unfortunate, because growth

Table 8.4 Children of parents with learning disabilities

Low intellectual ability is associated with low earning power and poverty; these factors may themselves affect child development

Parenting skills are less likely to be competent if the mother's intelligence quotient (IQ) is less than 55

Above this level, IQ is less relevant than social competence, ability to plan, etc.

If one parent has learning disability, there is a 15% risk that the child will also have learning disability; if both parents are affected the figure is closer to 40%

This means that any developmental delay which is identified may have both genetic and environmental components

There is probably an increased risk of child abuse when parents have learning disability

Parents with learning disability can improve their parenting abilities but need carefully planned teaching programmes

Parents with learning disability do not generalize their learnt skills, i.e. they have to be taught how to deal with each new situation rather than extrapolating from previous experience. This means that support needs to be prolonged indefinitely

Assessments of parenting ability and child development should ideally be carried out jointly with a child psychiatrist

disorders are often associated with other impairments (for instance, in the Russell–Silver and Prader–Willi syndromes) and may even be the first clue to the correct diagnosis. Iron deficiency in disabled toddlers is probably at least as common as in their normal peers. Health education on matters such as accident prevention, nutrition, dental care and immunization (see below) are no less important because the child is disabled.

Dental care

Preventive dental care is important. Parents should register the child with a general dental practitioner if possible, or alternatively should be referred to a specialist service. As with all children, health education on dental hygiene and diet, particularly with respect to sugary drinks and foods, is the first priority; advice should be obtained from the dentist about the use of fluoride. Cavities and periodontal disease are more likely to occur in the disabled child because of the difficulty in maintaining oral hygiene, often compounded by the use of medicines containing sugar. In addition, abnormalities of tooth structure and other orthodontic problems occur in many dysmorphic syndromes. Dentistry for the disabled

is 'special' not because of any particular technical problems, but because of the need for quiet surroundings, an unhurried approach and the availability of sedation or anaesthesia.

Immunization

There is no reason to withhold diphtheria, pertussis, tetanus and polio immunization from disabled infants. Mumps, measles and rubella (MMR) and *Haemophilus influenzae* type b (Hib) immunizations should also be given; the risk of contracting these diseases and of developing complications is just as high for disabled children as for any others. If the child has epilepsy or has ever had febrile fits, antipyretics should be advised. Occasionally rectal diazepam may be provided as well (p. 345). In the case of MMR, the parents should be told that the risk of a febrile fit occurring with the vaccine is much less than that with natural measles. There are very few genuine contraindications to immunization. The Department of Health handbook should be consulted in cases of doubt and if necessary the District Immunization Co-ordinator will offer advice or see the child.

The clinical genetics service

In addition to the obvious role of the geneticist in counselling parents about the risks of recurrence of a particular condition, other useful services are offered.

- Expertise in the recognition of unusual syndromes.
- Up-to-date knowledge of the subtypes, variant forms and associated problems of genetic conditions.
- Access to the latest advances in prenatal diagnosis.
- Talking to parents about the recurrence risks of conditions that are usually *not* inherited and what they can do to minimize the risks of other disabling conditions.
- Long-term follow-up of people with genetic conditions which have many possible complications but do not fit naturally into any one medical service (e.g. neurofibromatosis). This not only offers continuity of care to the individual but allows the continued accumulation of knowledge about unusual genetic disorders.

The majority of parents who have a child with moderate or severe disability of any kind will appreciate a consultation with the geneticist.

Respite care

Respite care is among the most highly valued of the services which can be offered for disabled children. A multiagency management group with parent representation helps to ensure that standards are maintained (Table 8.5). An occasional break from caring for a disabled child may help to preserve the parents' health and the stability of their marriage, and allows them to spend more time with their normal children. Some societies and charities offer special holidays for disabled children. Day nursery facilities provide valuable experiences for the child as well as relief for the parents.

Many parents find it very hard to start using respite care. They may feel guilty about 'abandoning' the child; they often say that the family misses the child while he/she is away; they may be unable to relax and frequently telephone several times each day, until they have used the service many times and begin to have more confidence in it. Parents must be reminded that this is an accepted and legitimate use of resources. If the child is very severely disabled, they may be happier using a hospital respite bed initially; the availability of nursing and medical expertise around the clock enables them to relax in the knowledge that the child will be safe if he/she has a convulsion or other urgent problem.

Some children react adversely to the separations involved in short-term respite care. Their distress may present as restlessness (searching for familiar people or possessions), agitation, withdrawal or regression. Staff and parents sometimes fail to identify these signs. They are really acute separation reactions and have much in common with the well-recognized responses of normal children to hospitalization without their parents. The management principles are similar: help the child to become familiar with the place or family before staying there, allow the child to take something familiar, possibly a parent to stay with him/her for the first occasion, and so on. For children who continue to be troubled by respite separation, foster families who visit frequently enough to get to know the child well first, or relief care in the child's own home, may be desirable alternatives.

Financial help

Statutory allowances are payable for children who are disabled. These are not means-tested and parents should be encouraged to take advantage of them. Details can be obtained from social services offices and the parents should be offered a benefits review. These allowances are awarded on the basis of the level of disability; whether or not the family has particular financial problems is irrelevant. The social worker can advise about the Family Fund and some similar local charities which may be able to help parents with special needs that cannot be met by any statutory provision.

Table 8.5 Respite and short-term care: what parents want

A choice of options between residential units, family-based schemes and relief in their own homes

Local services, wherever possible, close to home and school

Care compatible with the child's age, ability and medical/nursing needs, and with family background and culture

Flexible rota care (for example, 1 week in 6)

Occasional 'emergency' respite

A warm, friendly atmosphere

Continuity of care by familiar staff or families

Sufficient activities for the child to avoid boredom

Competence in feeding and handling, particularly for children with complex needs

Maintenance of the child's normal routine

The confidence that the child is not at risk of being neglected or abused

Short-term care should be part of a wider programme of support for family needs

Long-term care

Occasionally, parents may be so devastated by the discovery that their child is disabled that they feel unable ever to care for him/her at home. More often, long-term care becomes imperative because of parental illness, marital breakdown or death of a parent, or the child's care needs or behaviour may place intolerable demands on the family. One solution in this situation is adoption or long-term fostering. Several organizations now specialize in finding adoptive parents for 'hard-to-place' children. Detailed counselling and adequate family support are essential. There is often anxiety about the adoption of children whose natural parents are psychotic, psychopathic or alcoholic. Although all these disorders have a genetic component, a good environment in childhood has some protective effect, and adoption therefore seems particularly desirable for such children.

Only a small number of families are willing and able to foster or adopt a severely disabled child; furthermore, arrangements can seldom be made quickly, so that at times of crisis other solutions may be required. Many children are therefore cared for in small children's homes which provide a family atmosphere. Neither the funding nor the number of places in these units is adequate to meet the demand and long delays may be experienced in placing a child. For the adolescent and young adult, various forms of hostel and sheltered accommodation are being developed and these should eventually cater for most disabled people. Those for whom nursing care will always be needed should be accommodated in small units offering skilled management combined with privacy and dignity.

The disabled teenager

Teenagers with disabilities that affect mobility or communication often have social difficulties in developing independence. Many of the voluntary societies provide clubs and holiday activities which can boost self-confidence and morale. Social skills training is helpful to shy, awkward teenagers with learning disabilities or communication disorders; for example, through role-play exercises, they may practise buying something in a shop or entering a room full of people. This is done in small groups and a video system provides immediate feedback as social competence improves.

The sexual needs of disabled teenagers and adults are now recognized, although the potential for sexual fulfilment is often difficult to evaluate. Several groups, notably SPOD (Sexual Problems of the Disabled), have devoted much attention to this problem in recent years. Physical disabilities may directly affect sexual function, as in spina bifida, or may inhibit sexual activity by making the person totally dependent on others as, for example, in severe athetosis. In mild learning disabilities, the main problems are likely to be social rather than biological, for example, the development of stable relationships, the control of fertility and the avoidance of exploitation. In individuals with severe learning disabilities, sexual relationships are unlikely, but other problems may need attention (p. 144).

Caring for the carers

Staff who work with disabled children tend to be caring sympathetic people with high professional standards, and staff morale is important. Team meetings, social occasions and study opportunities are vital. The liaison child psychiatrist can often contribute by supporting staff who are dealing with distressing problems. Child care staff who work in day nurseries and children's hostels or homes should not be forgotten; they are poorly paid and carry a heavy responsibility for the care of often very difficult and demanding children.

Outcome measures

Since severely disabled children make progress only very slowly and are very rarely 'cured', it is difficult to use conventional types of outcome measure to determine the value, success and quality of the services provided by a Child Development Team. Improvements in muscle power, mobility or ability to communicate occur over a long time span and cannot be used as indicators of the effectiveness of therapy.

The principles of tertiary prevention form another frame for evaluating interventions or a service. Minimizing secondary handicaps or, preferably, preventing their occurrence can be measured. Doing so may avoid such activity being viewed disparagingly as 'damage limitation'. Policy statements are useful (Table 8.6) but wider measures of success need to incorporate estimates of parental satisfaction, adaptation and coping ability.

Therapy and psychology services

Therapists may work with the family at the CDC or in the home or day nursery. When the child starts school, much of the therapy provision will be offered there, although for some children, particularly those who are placed in mainstream schools, therapy may still be provided at the CDC. This is sometimes preferred because it avoids disrupting the child's school day and avoids the embarrassment for the child of being singled out for special provision. Therapists may integrate their programme of activities and therapy with that of the Portage adviser.

'Unorthodox' or alternative medicine

Homeopathy, osteopathy, acupuncture, aromatherapy, etc. have a powerful attraction for many parents. A trial of 'alternative' medicine is often seen as evidence that parents have not yet accepted their child's disability — but there may be other explanations. The proponents of alternative medicine often show an enthusiasm and an understanding of the family's total situation which is sometimes lacking among professional staff. There may be strong cultural pressures to try a traditional form of medicine. Visits to other establishments provide new opportunities to meet other parents who are facing similar problems. The fact that a particular treatment is not available on the National Health Service and has to be obtained privately is also, for some people, clear evidence of its superiority.

Some parents feel that they should investigate

Table 8.6 Special Needs children. The Child Development Team use this check-list as an audit tool, to determine whether each child has received all the services, information and help available for Special Needs children. Alternatively, it can be given to the parents

---

Do the parents know the correct name for the child's condition? If no exact diagnosis has been made, do they know what tests have been done and what the results mean?

Have they received a written report?

Do they know what sort of therapy or teaching the child is receiving and how they can help?

Do they know if there are other methods of treating the child's condition? and, if there are, why they are not being used for their child?

Have they had advice about the genetic aspects of the child's condition (i.e. whether it might be inherited or affect other children)?

Has the child had: a hearing test; an eye check; a dental check; a hip X-ray; all his/her immunizations; measurements to make sure s/he is growing normally?

Do they want: more information about the child's condition; a meeting with another parent whose child has the same problem; the name and phone number of the organization for children with this condition?

Do they know about: day care (day nurseries, etc.); respite care (short breaks)?

Do they know about preschool educational help (home teachers, etc.); their rights under the Education Act?

Do they know about: benefits; the Family Fund?

If the child takes any medication, do they know what, why and how much? Do they have a medication card and is it up to date?

Have they been given all the equipment and aids the child needs, when they need them?

---

new 'unscientific' ideas, for fear of overlooking something that may later turn out to be valuable. They will not be impressed by talk of controlled trials or of the implausible nature of the claims made for these treatments. They should be given whatever factual information or advice they request, together with a balanced opinion. If they do explore an unorthodox or alternative system, they should be encouraged to remain in touch with the paediatric team. Certain systems arouse such anger in some doctors and therapists that parents who adopt them may be banned from their CDC! This is inexcusable; it is the parents' right to try whatever form of medicine they choose, particularly when dealing with disabilities which are so obviously incurable by orthodox means.

There is little evidence of harm from alternative medicine. Two exceptions are, firstly, the use of homeopathic whooping cough vaccine, which is ineffective, and, secondly, toxic effects from massive doses of vitamins. Intensive treatment methods may appear to the outsider to have devastating effects on family life, but are unlikely to cause physical harm to the child provided they are properly supervised.

The Doman–Delacato method

This was devised at the Institute for the Achievement of Human Potential in Philadelphia, USA. It includes a variety of manoeuvres which are not supported by modern neurophysiology. The individualized programme which is prepared for each child may occupy most of the child's waking hours. For its execution, the parents have to gather a circle of helpers. Parents who have felt impotent to help their child are made to feel that his/her recovery and future are in their hands. In the early stages, some improvement may be seen, but there is no evidence that more orthodox approaches (physiotherapy, education, etc.) are any less effective, particularly if applied with similar intensity, and the Institute has not published its long-term results in any scientifically acceptable format.

Vitamin, trace element and mineral supplements

Massive vitamin supplementation has been used for the treatment of learning disabilities, but there is no evidence of its efficacy (except in a few extremely rare inherited metabolic disorders). Hair analysis to obtain a 'profile' of mineral deficiencies has also had a vogue, but the mineral content of hair bears little relationship to total body composition; furthermore, there is little evidence that mineral imbalances contribute significantly to disability. The Feingold diet and other dietary approaches to 'hyperactivity' and learning problems are described on p. 332.

Education

After the family, school is the biggest influence in the life of a disabled child. All children, however disabled, have a right to receive education from the age of 5. Many local authorities now make provision for disabled children to start school at 3, or even earlier in some cases.

Preschool teaching services

Nearly all disabled children are capable of learning, even though the pace may be slower than that of other children. Some parents appreciate a detailed programme of activities, and these should make use of behavioural principles (Chapter 9) to teach increasingly complex skills in a series of small steps. The Portage system is one example of a planned programme and is currently very popular. It is named after the town of Portage in North America, where it originated. A home adviser visits the family, usually on a weekly basis,

and works through an assessment schedule with the family, to establish a preliminary baseline. The adviser and the parents then together select realistic goals to work for and devise teaching strategies. The parents record teaching times and progress and review these with the adviser each week. The Portage model does require a high level of parent participation and for this reason is not universally applicable. A modified version is available for severely physically disabled children (Fig. 8.1), but as yet Portage is not ideal for those with profound learning difficulties, in whom the rate of progress is so slow.

Education authorities employ peripatetic teachers for children with vision and hearing defects, and some also offer a service for children with learning disabilities. This arrangement provides continuity of teaching when the child goes to school.

Early school placement

Early school placement has many advantages. All the necessary services are available under one roof, and a co-ordinated programme of management is easily arranged. Children are weaned away from excessive dependence on their parents and given valuable social experiences. The atmosphere of the school is a more normalizing influence than a CDC and encourages the parents to see disability as an educational and social problem rather than a medical one. Many special schools run coffee mornings and other social events. Parents are kept informed about their child's progress by means of a notebook which travels to and from home with him/her.

Special schools

The education services in the UK have a distinguished record in providing special schools, with their high staff-to-pupil ratio, therapy services and specialized equipment. Decisions about special school placements are the responsibility of the education authority, but the paediatrician is often in the best position to know when

Item	Behaviour	Date achieved
90	Can hold upright kneeling position when placed	/ /
91	Pulls self to kneeling upright	/ /
92	From upright kneeling places one foot forwards into 'half kneeling'	/ /
93	Pulls self to standing position	/ /

a

Adult behaviour (9–12 months)
Help the child to move in and out of positions, such as sitting to kneeling, kneeling to standing, pulling to standing

b

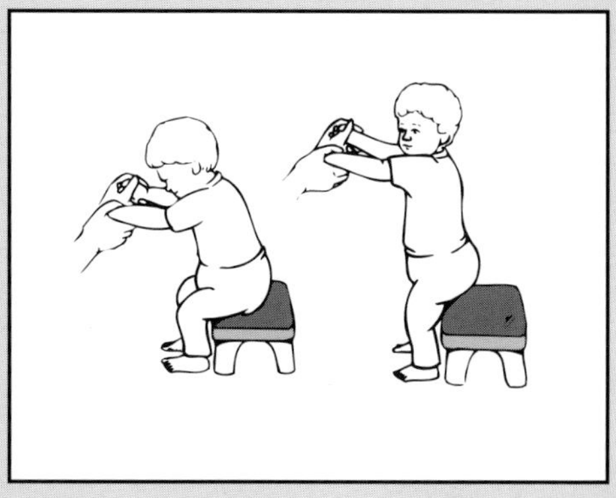

c

Fig. 8.1 The *Guide to Early Movement Skills* (GEMS) is a Portage-based programme for promoting motor development. It consists of: **a,** a checklist of skills; **b,** guidance on what the carer can do to help; and **c,** illustrations of activities. Illustrations reproduced from the *Guide to Early Movement Skills* © Mollie White, Chris Bungay and Helen Gabriel, 1994, (adapted and developed from the Portage Early Education Programme © CESA 5 and NFER-NELSON 1987) by permission of the publishers NFER-NELSON Publishing Company Ltd. All rights reserved.

and how to introduce the parents to the idea that some form of special educational provision might be needed. Health professionals have no authority to make decisions about school placement and it is usually unwise to discuss particular schools by name until the education authority has completed the statutory assessment. However, the parents may like to visit some local special schools by private arrangement with the headteacher. Parents may have fantasies about special schools which are far more alarming (or optimistic) than the reality.

Placement in a special school has always been a potential source of conflict between parents and professionals. Some parents feel that special schools stigmatize the child; that the child will learn 'bad habits' from other disabled children; and that he/she would have more chance of learning social skills in a mainstream school. These misgivings are by no means unjustified and should be acknowledged. The merits of special schools should also be explained: the expertise of teachers trained in special education, the advantages of small classes, and avoiding the depressing effects on children of being unable to keep up with their peers in a normal class or play with them outside the classroom.

The curriculum needs of children with severe learning disabilities differ from those of mainstream children; goals might include skills such as personal care, hygiene and safety, development of acceptable social behaviour, and short journeys in a familiar neighbourhood. For those with mild learning disabilities, the curriculum may be similar to that in mainstream schools, but the pace is slower and some important skills such as shopping and travel may need special attention. It may reassure parents to know that special school placements are regularly reviewed and that there is no bar to transferring to a mainstream school. There will probably always be a need for both options and parents say that what they want is the right and the opportunity to choose.

In the past, parents often felt that formal intelligence quotient (IQ) test results were 'unfair'. Most educational psychologists now incorporate informal observations, teachers' reports and parental information into their assessment, using tests where necessary to explore particular aspects of psychological functioning. It is essential that the parents feel that the psychologist has obtained a true picture of the child. Only then can discussion proceed to the interpretation of the findings and the future management.

Boarding-schools

There are a number of schools which cater for unusual combinations of disabilities. Many of these are in the independent sector. Because the number of children who need such specialized provision is small, it is often not economical to provide for them at local level and therefore boarding is often necessary. Such schools tend to be housed in pleasant surroundings, and attract charismatic headteachers and enthusiastic committed staff, with a high level of expertise. Parents may ask the education authority to meet the costs (which are often extremenly high). Although the education authority may agree to such placements if there are compelling educational grounds (i.e. the child's needs cannot be met locally), they will not normally do so for purely social reasons, such as the parents' inability to cope with the child's needs at home. In such situations, it will be necessary to negotiate with the social services and the health authority to find other sources of funding. Such problems highlight the need for a special needs planning team (p. 116).

The Warnock Report (1978), the 1981 and 1993 Education Acts and the 1988 Education Reform Act

The Warnock Report reviewed the educational needs of disabled children. Among its most significant recommendations were:

1 the concept of 'handicap' should be replaced by that of 'special educational needs';

2 the statutory designation of handicapped children by a single 'label' should be abolished;

3 parents should have more say in the education of their children;

4 the report took a balanced view on the question of integrating disabled children into normal schools, recognizing that for some this is desirable and possible, but for others integration could be detrimental both to the disabled child and the normal classmates.

The Education Act (1981) implemented the recommendations of Warnock. The sharp distinction between handicapped and non-handicapped children was abolished. It recognized that any child who is experiencing difficulties in school may need special help and this may be true of 20% of children at some point in their school career. The Act defined a child with special needs as one who has 'significantly greater difficulty in learning than the majority of children of his age or has a disability which prevents or hinders him from making use of the educational facilities generally provided for children of his age'. The local education authority must make this special educational provision available. Furthermore, they must do so in an ordinary school provided that: the parents agree; it is in the best interests of the child and the education of other children will not be adversely affected; and resources are thereby used efficiently. The authority must also identify and assess children who may need special help, must review them annually and must reassess them between 14 and 15 years of age. In addition, it is expected that most of these children will have access to the National Curriculum (Education Reform Act 1988).

Most children with severe disabilities are known to a paediatrician long before they are of school age. The health authority must notify the education authority that the child may need special education when the child reaches the age of 2, or as soon as the doctor forms the view that the child may have special needs. The parents should be consulted before this is done, and careful judgement is sometimes needed over the timing. Most parents welcome early notification to the education authority, even before the age of 2 years, especially when this results in the provision of educational services (see above). On the rare occasions when parents refuse to permit notification, it is usually best to review the matter in 3–6 months' time rather than ignore the parents' wishes, unless there is unequivocal evidence that the child's needs are being seriously neglected.

Children are initially assessed informally but those who have more complex or severe problems may need a more detailed multidisciplinary assessment. Section 5 of the 1981 Act describes the assessment procedures. The local authority must notify parents of their intention to assess the child. Appropriate professional advice and opinions must be submitted in written form, in language intelligible to the layman. The paediatrician's contribution is perhaps the most likely to contain difficult professional terms and it is good practice to discuss a draft with the parents. The child's strengths, weaknesses and needs for special resources or equipment are summarized.

Having collected this information, the authority may decide that the child's problem is complicated or severe, and will then make a 'Statement of Special Educational Need' (Section 7 of the Act). This includes summaries of professional opinions (but not the records on which they are based); the educational provision proposed, and the views of the parents, who must themselves receive a copy of the complete statement. This document forms the foundation of record-keeping, review and reassessment. At all stages of this procedure, parents have statutory rights to be consulted and informed, and they have a right of appeal, ultimately to the Secretary of State.

The 1993 Education Act updated this legislation and included a Code of Practice on identification and assessment of Special Educational Needs.

Integration

Integration must be seen as a powerful way of increasing society's awareness and acceptance of disability and this alone may justify the extra effort and cost involved. However, integration can cause problems. Children may be physically present in a normal class, but are not necessarily integrated socially, something which becomes an increasing problem at secondary school level. Alternatively, the disabled child may become a classroom 'pet' with possibly detrimental effects on emotional development. As the child gets older, he/she is at increasing risk of being bullied, rejected or ignored, at least by some of the children. Communication and social skills are probably more important to successful integration than physical abilities.

Successful integration depends both on the physical environment of the school and the enthusiasm and skill of the head and the teachers. Often a classroom helper is needed to support the child through the daily routine of school life. This tends to make the child 'different' and adds to the cost of integration. It is important to support the staff, explain the implications of the disability and share the inevitably increased responsibility for the child's safety and progress.

Leaving school

The statutory reassessment of all children who have a Statement of Special Educational Need, in the early teens, provides an opportunity and stimulus to plan for the future (Education Acts, Disabled Persons Act 1986). The parents should be informed about the facilities available when the child reaches school-leaving age, which may include an adult training centre (social education centre), a special class in a local college, and a variety of special hostels, communities and vocational training schemes. The care of the disabled adult is improving but services are still inadequate.

The psychological problems of the adolescent with severe disability have been sadly neglected by paediatricians, child psychiatrists and adult psychiatrists, who all feel that these people are somebody else's responsibility. The school doctor may be in the best position to provide medical advice when needed, but adequate consultant support is essential. Ideally the Child Development Team (or care manager) should ensure that there is continuity of care through the school years and arrange a formal hand-over to an adult-orientated Community Team, preferably before school-leaving age.

References and further reading

Appleton, P.E. and Minchom, P.M. (1991) Models of parent partnership and child development centres. *Child: Care, Health and Development*, **17**.

Audit Commission. (1994) *Seen but not heard: Coordinating Community Child Health and Social Services for Children in Need*. HMSO, London.

Beauchamp, T.L. and Childress, J.F. (1989) *Principles of Biomedical Ethics*. Oxford University Press, New York.

Chiswick, M.L. (1990) Withdrawal of life support in babies: deceptive signals. *Archives of Disease in Childhood*, **65**, 1096−7.

Cottrell, D.J. and Summers, K. (1990) Communicating an evolutionary diagnosis of disability to parents. *Child: Care, Health and Development*, **16**, 211−18.

Department for Education (1994) *Code of Practice (for the Implementation of the 1993 Education Act)*. HMSO, London.

Hall, D.M.B. (1996) *Health For All Children — A Programme For Promoting Child Health*. Oxford University Press, Oxford.

Heine, R.G., Reddihough, D.S. and Catto-Smith, A.G. (1995) Gastro-oesophageal reflux and feeding problems after gastrostomy in children with severe neurological impairment. *Developmental Medicine and Child Neurology*, **37**(4), 320−9.

HMSO (1991) *The Children Act 1989 − Guidance and Regulations. Vol. 6: Children with Disabilities*. HMSO, London.

Hobbs, C.J., Hanks, H.G.I. and Wynne, J.M. (1993) *Child Abuse and Neglect: a Clinician's Handbook*. Churchill Livingstone, Edinburgh.

Infectious Diseases and Immunization Committee, Canadian Paediatric Society. (1990) Cytomegalovirus infection in day-care centres: risks to pregnant women. *Canadian Medical Association Journal*, **142**(6), 547−9.

Leslie, S.C. (1993) Child protection — The Children's Act 1989. *Current Paediatrics*, **3**(3), 168−70.

Robards, M.F. (1993) *Running a Team for Disabled Children and their Families*. Clinics in Developmental Medicine, No. 130. Mackeith Press, London.

Westcott, H. (1991) The abuse of disabled children: a review of the literature. *Child: Care, Health and Development*, **17**, 243−58.

Wilson, R. (1993) Bereavement care — the role of the paediatrician. *Current Paediatrics*, **3**(2), 86−91.

CHAPTER 9

Behaviour Problems and their Management

Behaviour problems or 'challenging behaviours' (so called because they often present a challenge to the carer rather than a problem to the child) and skill deficiencies are common among disabled children, particularly those with severe learning difficulties. Behaviour problems may arise because of a deficit, for example in communication; they often represent an attempt by the child to find a solution to something that is a problem for them.

The following account is intended only to outline the scope of behavioural psychology and illustrate some practical applications in the field of childhood disability. The principles described here are also valuable in the management of non-disabled children and those with school problems (see Chapter 16). Several excellent reviews and manuals are recommended for more detailed study.

Behavioural psychology

In behavioural psychology, the term 'behaviour' includes all the observable abilities and activities of a living organism — movement, eating, speaking, and so on. For the behaviourist, the starting-point is the behaviour actually observed; diagnoses such as learning disability or 'developmental delay' and speculation about either the neurological basis or the long-forgotten origins of the behaviour is much less relevant. The goal is to identify specific areas of behaviour or behaviour deficit which might be amenable to useful change or improvement.

Behaviour therapy originated in the USA as a result of basic research, first in animal psychology and later on human subjects. In the past 25 years it has developed into a powerful and effective tool for changing the behaviour of both normal and disabled people of all ages. In recent years, 'cog-nitive behaviour therapy' has been introduced. This employs ways of helping children to change their thoughts and assumptions about the world, themselves and their responses when dealing with their problems.

There are five steps in managing a behavioural problem. It will be apparent that these steps reflect the general principles of the scientific method and, indeed, of good clinical practice. Each problem is treated as an experiment with a definite end result. Behaviour therapy is a method of approaching problems; it does not provide a series of prescriptions for specific behaviour disorders.

Stage 1: is there a problem?

Sometimes a parent or carer may ask for advice about a particular behaviour because they worry that it might become a problem in the future, or have some other serious significance. Reassurance may be all that is needed. For children with severe learning disability, some forms of play or social behaviour that would be unusual for someone of the same age with normal intellect might be explained as being appropriate for a child's mental age.

Stage 2: assessing the situation

Three categories of behavioural problems are recognized (Fig. 9.1). It may also be helpful to characterize the behaviour in terms of its function for the individual (Table 9.1). A detailed analysis is essential. For episodic behaviours, the ABC approach is useful.

• *Antecedents*. What happens before the behaviour in question? What situations seem to be associated with its occurrence?

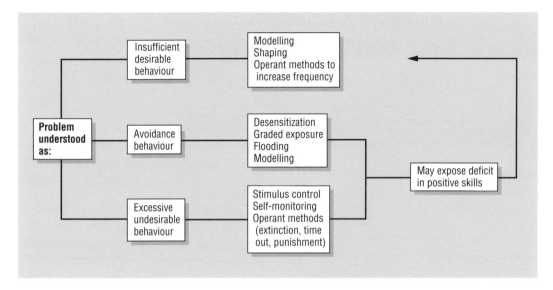

Fig. 9.1 Basic techniques in behaviour modification with children.

- *Behaviour.* What exactly does the person do or fail to do? How often and when? What emotional responses are observed?
- *Consequences.* What happens as a result of the behaviour?

Often it is helpful to ask the parents to keep a diary which will clarify these points. This provides a baseline measure of the frequency with which the problem occurs, so that the effectiveness of intervention can be assessed. If possible, the child should be involved in part of the discussion. It is also necessary to decide what change in the behaviour would constitute an acceptable solution.

In addition, some background information will be useful.

- The person's life history in recent years; change of home or caregiver, loss or bereavement.
- Problems in the person's life; frequent changes of routine, cancelled events, illnesses.
- Other evidence of psychological or psychiatric disturbance.
- Stress in the caregivers; support and relief available; disagreements between caregivers.
- Personal beliefs of caregivers regarding: their duty to the child; the child's life expectancy; the

cause of the behaviour problem; the likely response if intervention is attempted.

- Other individual factors which might affect the rate of response to treatment. For example, slow learners are slow to learn.
- Exclude physical disease. There is often concern about possible physical causes for a change in behaviour. Misery, agitation or distress may be related to pain (e.g. middle-ear disease, toothache, abdominal pain due to constipation, urinary infection or even calculi, headaches and migraine, hip subluxation). Behaviour changes might be caused by iron deficiency, drugs (particularly anticonvulsants), subtle deterioration in a neurological disorder (e.g. malfunction of a shunt system), hearing loss or subclinical seizures. Progressive visual impairment should be excluded, particularly in deaf children (pp. 211 and 213). Parents and carers will expect and appreciate a careful paediatric assessment to exclude these problems.
- Consider the possibility of mental illness (depression, obsessive compulsive disorder); disabled children and teenagers are at least as likely to develop these as normal people.

Table 9.1 Behaviours that cause concern. After Clements (1992)

COMMON	LESS COMMON
Physical aggression (includes biting, kicking, etc.)	Running away
	Excessive eating or drinking
Destructiveness	Eating inedible objects (pica)
Excessive noise (shouting, screeching)	Verbal abuse (swearing at carers)
Self-mutilation, self-injurious behaviour (SIB)	Spitting
	Soiling and smearing
Non-compliance	
Sleep problems	
Eating problems (distress, refusal, spasms, regurgitation, vomiting)	

CLASSIFICATION BY FUNCTION

Getting out of a situation
Getting out of requests or demands that are being made or are about to be made
A way of keeping people at a distance and thereby avoiding situations
Relief of high tension, arousal or excitement

Obtaining a desired outcome
Getting a response from other people (often a specific response is sought — not just 'attention-seeking')
Obtaining an object, item of food or drink, etc.
Sensory stimulation (touch, movement, sounds, etc.)

Response to provocation
Response to denial or withdrawal of something that previously was available
Reaction to teasing, irritations, discomfort, etc.

Stage 3: setting up a hypothesis

There may be many possible explanations for the persistence of an unwanted behaviour or the failure to develop desired behaviours. The range of possible hypotheses as to how environmental factors precipitate or maintain a behaviour may include aspects of the caregivers' attitudes and social situation; it is a mistake to focus exclusively on the child. It is important to ensure that the child is capable of doing what is desired; there is

no point in setting targets that are unattainable because of physical or learning disability.

Selection of the most plausible hypothesis is based on the information gained by interview, direct observation, experience with previous similar cases and a knowledge of child development. Sometimes, the discussion with parents or caregivers which is needed to develop the hypothesis will itself be therapeutic; it may give them the insights which are needed and may even resolve the problem.

Stage 4: testing the hypothesis

The intervention programme is designed in such a way that results can be measured. If the hypothesis was correct, improvement should follow intervention.

Stage 5: evaluating the results

The outcome of the programme is assessed to decide whether the object was achieved, whether the improvement was permanent and whether it could have been achieved with greater economy of effort. If implementation was successful but no change in behaviour resulted, then the hypothesis will need revision.

Behaviour therapy — some general points

1 Behaviour therapy does not provide a single prescription for a particular type of behaviour disorder.
2 The skills which are taught to children with learning disabilities do not always generalize from one situation to another. For example, toilet-training may be taught successfully in school, but the child may still be incontinent at home and has to be taught the necessary steps there as well.
3 Some parents are incapable of applying a behavioural programme, because of limited intellect, emotional and ethical objections, or serious disagreements between themselves.
4 Many adults are uneasy about manipulating a child's behaviour in this way, feeling that the

child should be 'good' without such 'artificial' methods. Token systems are often confused with bribery, although bribery is correctly defined as a 'reward offered to a person to induce him to act contrary to what is just and right'. All parents use behaviour modification techniques; the skill of a professional lies in using them effectively. It usually helps to explain that material reinforcers should virtually always be coupled with praise and that praise on its own is sometimes enough.

5 Complaints about a child's behaviour may mask more fundamental problems. For example, a sleep disturbance is sometimes used as a marital weapon by a husband or wife. Parents may quietly sabotage behaviour modification programmes designed to eliminate hyperactivity or other undesirable behaviours, for various reasons. They may have reached a point where they can no longer tolerate the burdens of caring for a disabled child, and want the behaviour to continue so that the child has to be taken into residential care; or the constant demands of the child may have become their main reason for living. Family problems are often revealed when a serious attempt is made to tackle a behaviour disorder and some form of family therapy or counselling may then be indicated.

6 There is a shortage of clinical psychologists trained in behavioural modification techniques. Although professional time is indeed expensive, anything which keeps children with learning disabilities out of residential care is likely to be cost-effective as well as humane.

How to help

Parents and caregivers may need support and encouragement; often their task is tiring and offers little reward. Child care staff are underpaid and often poorly trained in the management of the very demanding children they care for. Listening to and sharing their concerns is in itself valuable. Sometimes, a straightforward medical assessment to exclude an organic problem may suffice to reassure parents or carers. Information may also be useful; for example, assessing the risk

that a particular management approach already used by parents or staff might be ineffective or hazardous. Practical advice can be offered: for example, changes in staff routines or improved security to prevent a child rushing out into the street. Only when these measures have been considered should specific behavioural methods be invoked, as described below.

It is important to remember also that the staff caring for these children are vulnerable to considerable social, legal and media pressures and constraints with regard to the methods they are permitted to use. Any suggestions made regarding behavioural treatments must be compatible with current local guidelines, some of which make effective intervention very difficult.

Increasing wanted behaviour

Reinforcement

A reinforcer is any consequence of a behaviour which increases the likelihood that the behaviour will be repeated. Reinforcers may be an item of food or drink, attention, a cuddle, praise or tokens that may be exchanged for desired items. In the case of disabled children, reinforcers may be bizarre; for example, being allowed to twiddle a piece of silver paper might be reinforcing to an autistic child. The fact that a child seems to like something very much suggests that it might be a reinforcer (see Stage 3 above) but it must then be shown to actually increase the frequency of the behaviour in question (Stage 4). If it does not, it is not a reinforcer.

Not everything which appears rewarding will actually act as a reinforcer. Praise, for instance, which ordinarily is an excellent reinforcer, can embarrass a child or dissuade him/her from repeating the behaviour.

Reinforcement is used to increase wanted behaviour. The way in which the reward is delivered is crucial. The interval between the behaviour and the reinforcement must be as short as is practical. In the early stages, it should be provided every time the behaviour occurs, although later it can be provided intermittently. Intermittent re-inforcement tends to be more effective in promoting behaviours which endure. In the case of reinforcers which may satiate the child very rapidly, such as food, the quantity must also be carefully defined.

Shaping, prompting, chaining and modelling

These techniques are of particular value in building up complex skills, for example dressing or feeding. Having defined the desired behaviour, it is broken down into very small steps. Reinforcement is given for completion of each step. In shaping, the child has first to produce an approximation to the required skill before he/she receives their reinforcer. Prompting means that the child is guided, verbally or manually, to produce the required behaviour, which is then immediately rewarded; this is quicker than waiting for the child to perform spontaneously. If the skill consists of multiple small steps, each of which has to be acquired in sequence, the operation is known as chaining. It is usual to start with the last step, and work backwards ('backward chaining'). In modelling, the child learns by imitating the behaviour of other children or adults.

Example. G was an 8-year-old boy with a mental age of around 18 months. He made no effort to feed himself. The therapist held a spoon loaded with ice-cream against his lips, his hand was placed around the handle, and the spoon guided into his mouth. On each successive day, his hand was placed on the spoon at a greater distance from his mouth, until he was able to complete the entire sequence of movements himself. There were two reinforcers here — the ice-cream itself and the praise which accompanied each success.

A similar approach is used to bring about gradual changes in undesirable behaviour patterns and replace them with more acceptable ones. 'Scene-setting' is a useful addition to these techniques; a routine sequence of events is established and the child learns to recognize this routine as a cue that

a specific series of responses is expected. An example is described in the section on sleep disturbance (p. 139).

Tokens

A token may be used as a reinforcer. When sufficient tokens have been accumulated, they are exchanged for a reward. The star chart (commonly used in the treatment of enuresis) and the award of house points by schoolteachers provide familiar examples. Sometimes the token itself may be desirable, for example, Batman transfers or coloured beads. The reward may be tangible (a visit to the swimming-bath) or may be limited to the praise and approval of adults or peers.

Tokens have numerous uses in encouraging desired behaviour. With a little more ingenuity, they can also be useful in eliminating undesirable behaviour, for example by giving a token for *not* producing the behaviour during a specified time period. They can be woven into more elaborate schemes of earning and fining, called token economies.

If this method is to succeed, the child and parents must be quite clear as to what behaviour is required in order to earn a token and both parties must adhere to the agreement. They must decide in advance whether tokens are to be deducted for bad behaviour. The reward must not appear massive and unattainable (like a bicycle); it should be modest but desirable, quickly attained and within realistic reach in relation to the child's capabilities. It is better to arrange for the reward to be earned when a certain number of tokens have been collected rather than if they are collected by a certain time, since with the former method there is no prospect of ultimate failure to discourage the child. Tokens can be exchanged for a variety of rewards during the course of one programme. This flexibility helps to maintain enthusiasm for long enough to consolidate the 'cure' before the system is finally phased out.

Example. P was a mildly learning-disabled 12-year-old. His parents complained of his outbursts of temper, usually in the evening, and his refusal to get up in the morning. A token system was designed in which he earned stars on a chart for arriving at breakfast on time, and for each evening in which he had no tantrums. It was linked to his pocket money so that with good behaviour he could rent a video once a week.

Eliminating unwanted behaviour

Undesirable or intolerable behaviour is often the biggest problem faced by parents of a disabled child and may be thought to be an inevitable consequence of brain injury or global learning disability. However, although behaviour problems are certainly commoner in disabled children, there is no evidence that any particular pattern of behaviour is associated with any specific disorder (with the exception of disinhibition due to frontal lobe damage).

Probably several factors contribute to the reported high prevalence of behaviour disorder in children with disabilities.

1 By definition, these children are slow to acquire skills which would help them solve problems. They therefore adopt immature and primitive methods; for example, a child with no speech will have tantrums both from angry frustration and because they may well achieve the desired goal.
2 Regular contact with medical services provides an opportunity for reporting these problems, which is not so readily available to parents of normal children.
3 Parents may be less optimistic that behaviour problems will resolve spontaneously if the child has learning disabilities.
4 Many parents lack confidence in managing a child who is disabled and their feelings of inadequacy are easily increased by the well-meaning help offered by numerous and highly competent professionals. Some people feel unable to apply even the most gentle discipline in managing their disabled child, feeling that this bad behaviour is beyond the child's control. As a result they may tolerate appalling problems for months or years before seeking help.

5 There is sometimes a particular reluctance to discipline children who have fits, because of a fear that a tantrum may lead on to a fit.
6 The child's inability to generate their own ideas and activities often results in unwanted behaviour when the parents cannot give him/her unlimited attention.

In many cases the undesirable behaviour only occurs in specified situations, most often at home. Parents often feel distressed by this apparent discrimination and should be reminded that most people reserve their worst behaviour for situations in which they feel safe. In addition, the fact that the child can behave well in other situations is good evidence that the behaviour disorder is not an inevitable consequence of the neurological impairment.

Bad behaviours develop and become established because they solve a problem for the child or are effective in getting what the child wants or needs; in other words they are reinforced, usually unwittingly, by the response of someone or something in their environment. For children with learning disabilities, adult attention is often a potent reinforcer and it does not necessarily matter whether the attention is of a pleasant or punitive nature. Parental compliance with the child's demands is an additional reward for undesirable behaviour; as emphasized previously, anything that perpetuates a behaviour is a reinforcer.

The prevention of behaviour disorder in the disabled child has not received as much study as its treatment. Parents should be warned at an early stage that even very disabled children are quite capable of developing manipulative behaviour patterns if permitted to do so. Advice should be readily available so that any problems can be dealt with before they become entrenched.

Restructuring the environment

If the unwanted behaviour only occurs in certain circumstances, it is likely to be dependent on some preceding event or on some aspect of the surrounding environment. It is often possible to either remove the stimulus, alter it or change the situation so that the problem either resolves or becomes more manageable.

Example. An 8-year-old girl with profound learning disability, who was at boarding-school, persistently got out of bed every night and wandered in the corridor. She did no damage and always returned happily to bed, but the staff were afraid that sooner or later some accident might happen. They felt that they could cope with the problem if they could be alerted as soon as she was out of bed. This was easily accomplished by the construction of a simple alarm system.

Example. A 10-year-old boy with cerebral palsy and learning disability loved to turn all the taps on in the bathroom, causing frequent floods. A stopcock that could only be operated with a quarter turn of a screwdriver was inserted into the plumbing and solved the problem. However, he then became bored and more demanding and other avenues of help for the family had to be mobilized.

Extinction

If an unwanted behaviour is maintained by regular reinforcement, it can be eliminated by discontinuing that reinforcement. The predictable consequence is an initial increase in the unwanted behaviour which had previously been effective in securing the reinforcer. When the child realizes that the rewards are no longer forthcoming, there is a rapid decline in the frequency of the behaviour. Before embarking on a programme based on extinction, one must be certain that, firstly, the responsible adults are aware of and can tolerate the expected initial increased severity and frequency and, secondly, the increase will not be dangerous to the child. If these conditions are not met, other approaches must be used.

Example. A 5-year-old mildly disabled boy reacted to any instruction or reprimand from his teacher by banging his head with his hands. As he had arrested hydrocephalus, the teacher always gave in at once, fearing that he might injure himself.

She was advised that this would not occur and that she should not respond to his head banging. After the predicted initial increase, it rapidly disappeared.

Time out

This means the removal of the child from the social reinforcement which maintains the behaviour. Often the reinforcement is found, on careful analysis, to be social attention, sometimes of an apparently unpleasant kind (e.g. scolding or even a smack). Properly used, time out is a highly effective way of eliminating undesirable behaviour. It is often used by parents but is rejected as ineffective because they have neglected one or more of the important principles.

- A short period of time out (up to 5 minutes) is as effective and probably more effective than a longer period.
- The child may be removed from the room, for example to the hall or bedroom; it is essential to first establish that the suggested place is safe, and also that it really does lack social stimulation for the child.
- Sometimes, the parent leaving the room or the child facing a corner may be just as effective.
- The adult must plan how to take the child back without fuss if he/she does not stay in the time-out situation.
- When released from time out, the child does not have to repent or apologize.

Example. A child with severe learning disabilities frequently bit carers, gripping the forearm firmly with his teeth. This elicited a predictable reaction, which clearly reinforced his habit. Staff were shown how to pinch the child's nose and press the arm firmly against his mouth so that he had to let go in order to take a breath. They were told to give no verbal reaction and to avert their gaze, so as to remove the social reinforcement which had maintained the habit. The frequency of the behaviour rapidly declined.

Restraint

Firm physical restraint, for example with the arms held firmly by the sides, is an effective way of managing some problem behaviours. It not only breaks the cycle of frustration and anger for the child but also gives the parent or carer an opportunity to regain control of their own emotions. The adult should either hold the child from behind or avert their gaze so that there is no eye contact. Periods of restraint need only last for a matter of seconds. This method can be combined with a shout of 'no' in tones of controlled anger.

It is surprising how some parents and teachers are afraid to apply this technique, often reporting that a child 'is much stronger than I am'. Possibly there is a fear that restraint may damage the child in some way, either physically or psychologically, but there is no justification for this anxiety. More understandable is the concern among care staff that any form of physical restraint might be construed as an assault, with the risk of disciplinary proceedings or even criminal charges. Restraint is a useful technique which can safely be recommended to parents. Care staff may also use it but must be warned to take account of accepted current guidelines formulated by employers and professional organizations.

Restitution

This means that the child has to make amends for inappropriate behaviour by a directly relevant action, such as cleaning up food which the child has deliberately spilt. If necessary, the child is guided through their task by the adult. Sometimes this is extended so that the child has to perform the act of restitution several times or carry out several related tasks.

Reinforcement of desirable behaviour

Differential reinforcement of other behaviour (DRO), which is incompatible with the problem behaviour, may be used instead of or as well as methods to reduce unwanted behaviour. For example, the problem of a girl who bangs her head with her fists could be approached by reinforcement for keeping her hands by her sides. Development of desirable activity such as play or communication is often the only permanent solution to behaviour problems in children with severe learning disabilities. Understanding the function of the problem behaviour is important; if all therapeutic efforts are directed towards removal of an unwanted behaviour without encouraging an alternative repertoire of skills, new and equally undesirable behaviour problems will inevitably emerge.

Treatment of life-threatening behaviour disorder

Occasionally severely learning-disabled people develop potentially lethal habits, such as severe self-mutilation (p. 143) or persistent rumination and vomiting (p. 273). In cases where other methods have been ineffective, intensely aversive stimuli, such as electric shock, the smell of ammonia or the taste of lemon juice, have been used. It is wise, for ethical reasons, to obtain a second opinion before using these techniques.

Phobias

Phobias in children are usually treated by gradually increasing exposure to whatever is causing the irrational fear. An alternative approach is flooding — immediate and total immersion in the feared situation. This is rarely used for children.

Cognitive therapy

In essence, this means helping children to change the way they think. Children, like adults, can fall into ways of thinking that are maladaptive — thinking and saying to themselves that they are useless, incompetent or friendless. These negative thoughts can be replaced by positive ones. The child might be taught to say or think to himself 'I can do this if I try' or 'Stop and think'. Cognitive therapy is unlikely to be effective or practical for children with a mental age of less than about ten years.

Summary

When applying the techniques described above, some general points should be remembered.

- Ensure that everything has been done to make communication as good as possible. Many undesirable behaviours serve a communicative function and arise because the child cannot understand what is required of him/her or cannot use verbal techniques such as negotiation.
- Establish house rules; ensure that the child knows what is compulsory, when he/she has a choice, and how he/she can signal that choice.
- Decide how and when stimulating activities or situations desired by the child are to be made available or withdrawn.
- Divide the day into time periods to facilitate the recording of increased, decreased or non-occurrence of the target behaviour. The length of each time period depends on the frequency of the behaviour. Change the time periods as the frequency of the behaviour changes. Celebrate successful periods with the child!
- Do not reinforce unacceptable behaviours.
- Anxiety can be a problem in the severely disabled child. Try to reduce this by explaining what is happening and by graded exposure if a particular phobia is involved.

Common challenging behaviours and management problems

Sleep disturbances

Sleep disturbances are divided into *dyssomnias*, or primary sleep disorders, and *parasomnias*, episodic disturbances occurring during sleep. The latter are considered on p. 357.

Primary sleep disturbances are among the commonest of all behaviour problems. In normal children, the prognosis for spontaneous improvement is good, but in children with learning disabilities resolution may take many years.

Waking at night is in itself quite normal, but most children settle themselves to sleep again without waking the rest of the household. Problems arise when the child refuses to go to bed, insists on falling asleep in the parent's arms, wakes repeatedly and demands attention each time, transfers to the parent's bed or wakes very early in the morning. Prolonged sleep disturbance is exhausting to the parents and sometimes makes the child irritable; possibly it is one cause of 'hyperactivity', since fatigue may reduce attention span.

Sleep disturbances have many causes, most of which are environmental. The natural anxieties of parents responsible for the care of a young child are magnified when he/she is disabled. They often unwittingly perpetuate and reinforce undesirable bedtime behaviour and night waking, by responding patiently and caringly to the child's every demand.

Contributory factors may include:

- lack of bedtime routine;
- a more pervasive lack of routine throughout the day;
- too many daytime naps;
- going to bed unreasonably early (often because the child is very demanding when he/she gets home from school);
- overexcitement due to games or TV;
- fear of the dark;
- fear of sexual abuse;
- anxiety or depression;
- enlarged adenoids and tonsils causing sleep apnoea and drowsiness (pp. 221–2);
- being allowed to sleep in late because of late nights;
- drugs such as methylphenidate, anticonvulsants, theophyllines, paradoxical effects of sedatives.

Restructuring the environment may help; for example, making a stable-door or fitting a stair-gate may reduce the hazards of a child getting out of bed at night. Putting the mattress on the floor may eliminate anxiety about a restless child falling out of bed. Some parents report that an elasticated body-belt (available from Segufix-Bandagen das Humane System, see Appendix) is useful for children who climb out of their cots or beds.

Behavioural methods can be used to tackle sleep disturbances even in children with severe learning disabilities, but this is a challenging and time-consuming task. Better bedtime habits can be achieved by 'scene-setting'; for example, a regular quiet period before bed in which the child has a game, a story or a cuddle. For children who refuse to settle until their parents go to bed, 'graded change' is used to achieve an earlier bedtime, since it is usually easier to adjust the bedtime by small increments than by several hours in a single step. A star chart can be used to reinforce desirable behaviour such as staying in his/her own bed all night. Extinction, by leaving the child to cry, is effective, if carried out ruthlessly, but is seldom acceptable to parents; all positive reinforcements such as cuddles or drinks during episodes of night waking must be eliminated.

Sedative medication such as trimeprazine (Vallergan) 2−4 mg/kg, 1−2 hours before bedtime, may help, but although it induces sleep it seldom rectifies the total pattern of sleep disturbance. It can be used for long periods without side-effects but, as there have been isolated reports of cardiorespiratory collapse, it is sensible to start with a smaller dose, advise the parent to observe the child for a few hours when the first dose is given, and avoid the use of sedatives for children under 1 year of age unless under close supervision.

Zopiclone (3.75 mg) is a non-benzodiazepine hypnotic which is as yet unlicensed for children but shows promise when a brief course of a hypnotic is needed, as may be the case following a traumatic stress.

Pica

This is the ingestion of substances not normally considered edible. The name is derived from the scientific name of the magpie, a bird noted for its habit of collecting useless material. Sucking and mouthing of inedible objects is a normal developmental stage, but pica is not merely a prolongation of this phase; it is a specific maladaptive behaviour pattern which is commoner in, but not confined to, children with severe learning disabilities. It develops as a response to an unstimulating environment and may also occur in autism.

Virtually any substance may be ingested, but there is particular concern about lead-containing materials, such as old paint and some imported toys (now banned), and also over fibrous materials like hair or cloth, which can cause intestinal obstruction. Children with pica often have elevated blood lead levels but it is not usually possible to trace any particular behaviour disturbance to this and, except for cases which present with encephalopathy, the lead intoxication is not the cause of the child's learning problems (see also p. 167). Iron deficiency is also common; it has been suggested that this is the stimulus which prompts the child to eat mineral substances in search of iron, but more probably the iron deficiency is only the result of the distorted eating habit. There is, however, some evidence that iron deficiency can cause irritability and mood changes, which could initiate behaviour problems, and an improvement in mood sometimes results from iron therapy before any rise in haemoglobin is detectable.

Pica will usually respond to changes in the environment, for example provision of stimulating play opportunities, the development of a method of communication and the differential reinforcement of more appropriate activities. The blood lead and haemoglobin levels should be checked and a course of oral iron therapy may be beneficial. Occasionally, other measures may be needed.

Example. A 14-year-old boy with profound learning disabilities habitually ate cloth and other fabrics. All attempts to eliminate this behaviour failed and he required two laparotomies for intestinal obstruction. Arm restraints limited his activity and distressed him. He was supplied with a fencer's wire gauze face mask, which covered his mouth but did not limit his vision or breathing. This was well tolerated and prevented further pica.

Nocturnal enuresis (bed-wetting)

This is an extremely common problem among both normal and disabled children. The acquisition of continence is governed to some extent by neurological factors and by mental age, but enuresis can be often be treated successfully even in children with severe learning disabilities. It is inevitably more difficult if the child lacks motivation. As in normal children, a distinction is made between primary enuresis, in which the child has never been dry, and secondary enuresis, meaning that the child has become enuretic again after achieving night-time continence. The assessment of bladder function and organic causes of incontinence are discussed on p. 288.

Management may include the following.

• Deal with any general anxieties about use of the toilet; for example, the toilet may be too high for a girl to sit down comfortably. This can be remedied by resting the feet on a box. The child may be cold or afraid of the dark.

• A star chart system (see above) combined with appropriate praise and encouragement. This may be effective in its own right, but in any case provides a baseline measurement of the frequency of wetting.

• The enuresis alarm (buzzer and pad) method works well provided that the child is woken by the alarm and has to get out of bed to disconnect it. Bedside models and a body-worn version are available. Extra loud buzzers and vibrating devices can be obtained for heavy sleepers and for hearing-impaired children. Allow up to 3 months for treatment.

• An intensive behavioural programme called 'dry bed training' can produce excellent results rapidly, but is demanding on the time and energies of both parents and professionals. Success is more likely if the programme is supervised and supported by a professional. The full programme has several components, including the buzzer, hourly toileting during the first night, and aversive procedures such as helping to change the bed and 'practice toileting' if the child wets the bed.

• Desmopressin (1-deamino-8-D-arginine-vasopressin, DDAVP), an analogue of antidiuretic hormone) is safe and useful, particularly for short-term use. It is administered as a nasal spray (and in tablet form). There is a high relapse rate as soon as it is discontinued. When given as a nasal spray the drug is absorbed through the nasal mucosa; if it reaches the pharynx or is swallowed, it will be inactivated. It is therefore important that the child should be standing rather than lying and that he/she should avoid sniffing while the spray is activated. It is contraindicated in children with cystic fibrosis.

• Imipramine should rarely be used because it has only modest effectiveness, a high relapse rate and serious toxicity if accidentally ingested by younger siblings.

• Other methods, including regular lifting, bladder training, psychotherapy and family therapy, have also been tried but their effectiveness is unproven.

• Parents will appreciate practical advice, particularly if the enuresis is resistant to treatment, as often happens in children with severe learning disabilities. An incontinence laundry service is invaluable. Parents or social services may be able to obtain absorbent blankets which keep the rest of the bed dry (available from S.R. Holbrook Ltd, see Appendix), water-resistant barrier creams to protect the skin; deodorizing sprays; and fabric cleaners.

Daytime wetting

Like nocturnal enuresis, this seldom has a detectable organic cause (see p. 288 for further discussion). In most cases of daytime wetting among children with learning disabilities, the history suggests that, because of 'immaturity', signals from the full bladder do not impress themselves on the child's consciousness until it is too late to reach the toilet. Sometimes the adult attention gained while the child is cleaned and changed reinforces the pattern.

The history should be reviewed to ensure that

organic disorders are not being overlooked. A diary record of the child's wetting and toileting should be kept for a few days. This problem often responds to a token system, in which rewards are earned for appropriate use of the toilet and/or remaining dry for a specified period. This may be combined with a graded programme of regular toileting under supervision, perhaps starting hourly or half-hourly, according to the initial frequency of wetting, and the interval then being gradually lengthened. The body-worn version of the enuresis alarm can be worn during the day. The alarm can be an audible signal, for the carers, or vibrating, if the child can respond him/herself.

Faecal soiling

Soiling in the disabled child is often associated with chronic constipation to which poor diet, lack of independent mobility, low tone in abdominal muscles and, occasionally, anal fissures may contribute. An improved bowel habit can often be achieved with a stool softener such as lactulose, combined with a laxative such as Senokot, given at night. Increased dietary fibre and use of a bulking agent may also help. If necessary a glycerine or Dulcolax suppository is given in the morning to initiate regular toileting. In some cases, use of an enema may be unavoidable, in order to reduce gross faecal loading, before retraining can have any chance of success. At the same time, reinforcement (e.g. using a token system) is introduced. Tokens are awarded for sitting on the toilet and/or opening the bowels in the toilet rather than for having clean pants since, if the latter is made the main goal, faecal retention may unwittingly be encouraged. Treatment must be prolonged for weeks or months even after regular defaecation is established, to allow chronic distension of the colon and rectum to return to normal.

Faecal smearing is a less common complaint. It may occur as an activity akin to finger painting in children with severe learning disabilities, particularly when inadequately stimulated and poorly supervised; or in children with milder impair-ments, when it may be more suggestive of some emotional or environmental disturbance. A few children find anal stimulation ('anal masturbation') highly pleasurable. Whatever the circumstances, the furore created by these activities is often reinforcing to the child. Approaches to management might include a manipulation of the situation in which it occurs, for example, a change of toilet routine or use of clothing which the child cannot remove him/herself so that he/she does not have access to soiled nappy or pants. Any positive reinforcement which seems likely to perpetuate the habit, such as the attention involved in cleaning up the mess, is identified and eliminated as far as possible, and methods such as 'time out' or restitution may be used.

Chronic or recurrent diarrhoea in the disabled child may be due to overflow of rectal contents associated with severe constipation ('spurious diarrhoea'), toddler diarrhoea, drugs (overdosage of lactulose, antibiotics, etc.) or, very rarely, some underlying disorder. Diarrhoea often occurs in mucopolysaccharidoses (MPS) and, in association with behavioural problems and language impairment, may be an early feature of MPS type III (Sanfilippo's syndrome). Toddler diarrhoea and MPS diarrhoea may respond to loperamide.

Aggressive behaviour in the nursery or playgroup

Children may be aggressive because they consider it a sensible way to solve an interpersonal problem (whether or not they know of any other way) or because they are too angry or upset to deploy more considered tactics such as negotiation. A complaint that a small child hits, pokes or bites other children in the absence of provocation should therefore lead to questions about the child: does the child know of other methods of resolving disputes and can he/she learn these? Not surprisingly, therefore, learning disability, language problems and impaired hearing may be associated with aggressive behaviour. A few children with secretory otitis media have sufficiently impaired hearing to misinterpret what is said to them and react to what they wrongly perceive as hostile overtures from peers.

It is important to enquire about home life. Do the parents habitually resolve their difficulties with the child or each other by aggressive coercion or violence, so that the child has learned the wrong lessons? If not the parents, what about older siblings? Some children are upset and angry because of insecurities or injustices in their home life. There are a few small children who have a malicious interest in causing pain to others. Patterson's classical study in a playgroup demonstrated that aggressive, coercive behaviours between young children are rapidly learned and that tearfulness provokes aggressive attacks by others. The appropriate first lines of management are close supervision, prompt intervention for safety's sake, and tuition in alternative, civilized ways of managing disagreement. Practical advice may include the following.

• Intervene immediately at any outburst of aggressive behaviour.

• Place the child in a situation where he/she can be observed but is isolated from social interaction, for 5 minutes. When the child is receptive, describe and demonstrate to him/her more appropriate ways of behaving, along the lines of 'What we do here is . . .'. Often this calls for the basic skills of sharing, turn-taking, asking nicely and doing simple deals ('If you let me . . . then I'll let you . . .').

Self-injurious behaviour (SIB) (also known as self-mutilation)

Mild forms of SIB, such as head-banging, may occur in normal children but they are usually transient and need no specialized management. In children with learning disabilities, SIB may be serious and even life-threatening and poses a most distressing problem to those who care for them. It takes many forms: head-banging, self-biting, eye-poking, etc. It is particularly common and intractable in autism, the Lesch–Nyhan syndrome (p. 368) and the Cornelia de Lange syndrome.

The aetiology is not understood. Parents often feel it has begun as a response to pain, and this is occasionally evident in a non-communicating child with recent onset of SIB. In long-standing cases, however, there is seldom any evidence for this. The child may gain some pleasurable sensation or relief from the activity in spite of its apparently painful consequences. Sometimes there is a strong social element, since the SIB appears to produce a reward or act as a means of avoidance. Most often, however, the behaviour seems to be 'driven' — as if there is some inner compulsion to self-mutilate even though this is distressing. Biochemical mechanisms have been suggested, including dopamine receptor deficiency, dysfunction of the limbic system and endorphin theories.

Many approaches have been designed to treat SIB, but none is universally effective. Advice from a psychiatrist or psychologist with experience in the management of the problem should be obtained as soon as possible; once the problem becomes entrenched, it will be very difficult to deal with and may make the child all but unmanageable. Treatment approaches have included the following.

• A detailed functional or ABC analysis to ascertain whether the behaviour has an identifiable relationship with environmental situations, events or changes (p. 131). Behavioural measures may include: restructuring of the child's daily routine to include more stimulating activities; extinction (when the behaviour is maintained by attention, but only if the predicted initial increase in frequency will not be dangerous); 'punishment' by means of restraint and a shout; improved communication skills to alleviate the child's sense of frustration; slowing the social approaches of carers for children who find social contact unsettling.

• Medication may help. Fluphenazine, haloperidol, naltrexone and many other drugs have been tried.

• Restraints such as elbow splints or helmets may be used as a short-term measure and may break the habit, but they are not always a satisfactory long-term measure, because they limit the child's play and mobility and often simply result in the child discovering another means of SIB which circumvents the restraints.

• An orthodontist can make a dental appliance to protect the lips and tongue if the mouth is being damaged by the SIB.

• Massage has been reported to have a dramatic effect in some cases and raises the possibility that SIB may sometimes be a response to emotional and/or sensory deprivation.

• Rarely, more extreme aversive measures are needed (p. 138). There are both ethical and practical difficulties in these cases, and an intensive behavioural programme in a specialized unit may be the only solution.

Puberty and sexuality

Sexuality in disabled people has until recently been a taboo subject, but now the need of disabled young people to receive sex education and to have the opportunity to develop close relationships is increasingly recognized, both by individuals and in law. Legislation now requires school governors to consider the sex education policy within their school, and schools for children with learning disabilities are responding by developing appropriate teaching methods for their pupils. It is vital that parents should be involved in this process, since they may have more difficulty in accepting the sexuality of their disabled children.

Onset of puberty

Most children with learning disabilities will develop secondary sexual characteristics and experience the onset of puberty at much the same time as their peers. In some conditions, however, for example Prader–Willi syndrome, the onset of puberty may be delayed. It is said to be earlier in blind children.

Precocious puberty

This is an uncommon but well-recognized sequel of brain abnormalities and may occur in association with cerebral palsy, hydrocephalus and trau-matic brain injury. The problems associated with early puberty depend on the level of disability. Children who have mild learning disability but are otherwise functioning normally may be particularly vulnerable to exploitation. Precocious puberty results in a reduction in adult height, although the significance of this for the severely disabled child may be minimal. The early onset of menstruation brings forward by several years the problems of managing menstrual hygiene, which many parents of disabled children anticipate with considerable anxiety.

In a child with established cerebral abnormality and with no other abnormal findings in the history or examination, there is rarely any need to undertake extensive investigation for other causes of precocious puberty, but it may be sensible to do an ultrasound scan of the liver, adrenals and ovaries to exclude neoplasms in these organs. The advice of a paediatric endocrinologist should be obtained if it is felt that more extensive investigation is needed.

In some children the progression of puberty is very slow and the signs may even temporarily regress. A period of observation may therefore be warranted before embarking on treatment. Before using drug treatment, it is important to consider what one is trying to achieve. Although the manifestations of puberty can be postponed, and in particular the onset of regular periods, treatment is unlikely to influence the final adult height. If the child is too disabled to be troubled by the psychological aspects of early puberty, and the parents feel that they can cope with the child's periods, it may be sensible to avoid drug treatment altogether.

The most widely used drug is medroxyprogesterone acetate, which is a strong antigonadotrophic progestogen. It has mild glucocorticoid activity, which is only significant in high dosage. Cyproterone acetate (an antiandrogenic steroid) and a gonadotrophin-releasing hormone (GnRH) analogue which binds to GnRH receptor sites have also been used, although the latter has to be given by injection and is very expensive. An increase in dosage of cyproterone may be needed if the child is taking enzyme-inducing anticonvulsants. If any of these drugs is needed, careful monitoring is important and a decision should be made about the criteria for discontinuing therapy.

Management of menstruation

The girl will need to be taught, by demonstration, how to use pads or tampons, where to keep them and how to dispose of them. She will also need to be taught about privacy; she must not lift up her dress and tell the world about her period! Premenstrual tension undoubtedly does occur in girls with learning disabilities. Even if they cannot always articulate their tension, it is indicated by a change in mood or behaviour. Dysmenorrhoea is as common as in any other adolescent and can be managed in the same way, with aspirin or naproxen.

Hormonal therapy for dysmenorrhoea is occasionally needed, although complete suppression of menstruation is requested by parents surprisingly infrequently. Contraception may be considered if parents are anxious about pregnancy, but adequate preparation for coping with sexuality and protection from exploitation are usually more relevant. Sterilization and hysterectomy are both drastic measures which should only rarely be necessary. Since the girl cannot give consent herself, it is wise to obtain legal advice before considering this course of action.

We have found that a sympathetic family-planning doctor, who is willing to see teenagers with learning disabilities in a quiet time at the end of a clinic, is often the best person to advise on these topics.

Inappropriate sexual behaviour

The commonest problems are lack of normal social inhibitions and ignorance of social conventions, rather than a pathologically increased sex drive. Masturbation in public places may cause concern. This can usually be dealt with by a simple behavioural programme in which the person is taught that this is done only in private. Some youngsters will masturbate for a long time without

discovering how to produce orgasm. Such prolonged activity often concerns staff or parents. Various methods such as pictures and slides have been used to teach this skill, but showing a learning-disabled teenager by demonstration cannot be recommended as it may expose the carer to charges of indecent assault.

Inappropriate touching is another common concern. Parents and staff must discourage this firmly. The child must learn what is and is not acceptable in terms of affectionate behaviour; otherwise they are likely to be exploited or to get into trouble with the law.

References and further reading

Bambrick, M. and Craft, A. (1991) The sexuality of people with severe learning difficulties — myths and realities, issues and challenges. *Current Paediatrics*, 2(1), 25–8.

Clayden, G.S. and Agnarsson, U. (1991) Constipation. *Current Paediatrics*, 1(1), 8–12.

Clements, J. (1992) Teenagers with severe learning difficulties — management of challenging behaviour. *Current Paediatrics*, 2(1), 18–21.

Ferber, R. and Kryger, M. (1995) *Principles and Practice of Sleep Medicine in the Child*. W.B. Saunders, Philadelphia.

Fernandes, E. (1991) The unstable bladder in children. *The Journal of Pediatrics*, 118(6), 831–7.

Fraser, W.I. and Rao, J.M. (1991) Recent studies of mentally handicapped young people's behaviour. *Journal of Child Psychology and Psychiatry*, 32, 79–108.

Griffiths, M. (1991) Teenagers with severe learning difficulties — skill building for adulthood. *Current Paediatrics*, 2(1), 22–4.

Griffiths, P., Meldrum, C. and McWilliam, R. (1992) Dry-bed training in the treatment of nocturnal enuresis in childhood: a research report. *Journal of Child Psychology and Psychiatry*, 23, 485–95.

Hill, P. (1982) Behaviour modification with children. *British Journal of Hospital Medicine*, 27, 51–8.

Hill, P. and Berger, M. (1992) Behaviour therapy with children: basic terms and concepts. *Current Paediatrics*, 2(1), 14–17.

Hyman, S.L., Fisher, W., Mercugliano, M. and Cataldo, M.F. (1990) Children with self-injurious behaviour. *Paediatrics*, 85, 437–41.

King, B.H. (1993) Self-injury by people with mental retardation: a compulsive behaviour hypothesis. *American Journal of Mental Retardation*, 98, 93–112.

McAuley, R. (1992) Counselling parents in child behaviour

therapy. *Archives of Disease in Childhood*, **67**, 536–42.

St James-Roberts, I., Harris, G. and Messer, D. (1993) *Infant Crying, Feeding and Sleeping: Development, Problems and Treatments* (Developing Body and Mind Series).

Harvester Wheatsheaf, London.

Stores, G. (1992) Sleep studies in children with a mental handicap. *Journal of Child Psychology and Psychiatry*, **33**, 1303–17.

CHAPTER 10
Learning Disability

The term 'mental retardation' is still widely used, but a number of articulate people with limited intelligence have stated that they find the term pejorative, preferring the phrase 'learning disability', which we have adopted in this book. There is no completely satisfactory definition of learning disability, although the ICD-10 (World Health Organization, 1992) description comes close: 'a condition of arrested or incomplete development of the mind, which is especially characterized by impairment of skills manifested during the developmental period, contributing to the overall level of intelligence, i.e. cognitive, motor and social abilities'. Traditionally learning disability is divided into gradations of intellectual disability. The medical classification (exemplified by ICD-10 and DSM-IV) (American Psychiatric Association, 1994) uses four categories. In the United Kingdom, the educational system and the Mental Health Acts use two. In the medical classification, the four levels of mental retardation are:

- mild (intelligence quotient, IQ 50−69. In adults, a mental age of 9−11 years inclusive);
- moderate (IQ 35−49. In adults, a mental age of 6−8 years inclusive);
- severe (IQ 20−34. In adults, a mental age of 3−5 years inclusive);
- profound (IQ below 20. In adults, a mental age of below 3 years).

These categories do not represent any fundamental differences either in type of pathology or in functional terms; they rely on standard deviations in IQ test scores. The two-category educational system is easier to use and enables some useful distinctions to be made, although the changing terminology is confusing.

Until 1971 children who had an IQ below 50 were designated 'severely subnormal'. They were generally considered to be ineducable, and were the responsibility of the health services. The Education Act of 1971 transferred responsibility for the education of all children to the local education authority, and this was a major step forward in improving educational facilities for children with severe learning disability. In this Act, the terms educationally subnormal (mild) (ESN-M) and educationally subnormal (severe) (ESN-S) were used to describe children with IQs in the approximate ranges 50−75 and under 50, respectively. Separate schools cater for children in each of the two groups, although many factors other than IQ are considered in selecting the most appropriate school for a child. The Education Act (1981) recognized the increasing reluctance to 'label' disabled children and encouraged the trend towards integration of the less severely impaired into normal school.

In the mid-1980s, the terms ESN(M) and ESN(S) became less popular and parents and professionals began to speak of 'people with learning difficulties'. The terminology has recently changed again and the currently accepted phrase is 'people with learning disabilities', although this can cause confusion because this term has been widely used, particularly in North America, to describe specific learning problems such as dyslexia (see Chapter 16).

Other terms are sometimes used. 'Psychomotor retardation' implies that both motor and intellectual development are affected, but is best avoided as it has a specific meaning within psychiatry, referring to the slowing of thought and action in severe depressive illness. 'Developmental delay' may be a legitimate label when there is genuine uncertainty about the significance of an unusual pattern of development, but it carries the implication that the child will eventually catch up and may therefore have the effect (intended or otherwise) of misleading the parents.

In this book, therefore, the terminology used is as follows. *Global (or general) learning disability* refers to an overall reduction of intellectual capacity, and replaces the terms 'ESN' and 'learning difficulty', 'global' may be omitted and the adjectives mild, moderate, severe or profound may be added. The abbreviations 'MLD' (mild learning disability) and 'SLD' (severe learning disability) are often used. *Specific learning disability* denotes a deficit in one or more abilities, not primarily attributable to a global reduction of intelligence. This terminology enables health and education to share the same terms, so that parents are less likely to become confused; it also recognizes that sometimes the distinction is not absolute and that a person with global difficulties may also have some particular and specific impairments of learning.

Although there is, of course, no absolute distinction between those with MLD (IQ 50–70) and those with SLD (IQ < 50), there are some generalizations which may be useful.

1 Children with SLD frequently show some evidence, either in the history or on clinical examination, of some form of brain pathology. This is much less common among those with MLD.

2 Because SLD is usually due to organic pathology, it is likely that the child will have other physical impairments.

3 Children with SLD generally have little success in academic tasks. If reading and writing are achieved at all, this will be at a very simple level.

4 As adults, those with SLD are unlikely to be able to lead independent lives, whereas people with MLD have their principal area of difficulty in learning academic skills and frequently make a good adjustment to the adult world of work, within which they enter practical, non-academic occupations.

5 MLD is more common in the lower socioeconomic groupings whereas SLD is more evenly distributed across all social classes.

6 MLD is most commonly due to a combination of genetic and environmental factors rather than an organic disorder.

Epidemiology

The prevalence of SLD is approximately 3.7 per 1000 children. Because education is universal and compulsory, virtually all such children are identified and therefore this figure is reasonably accurate. Case-finding is less complete among adults.

Figures for the prevalence of MLD are necessarily less precise. If MLD is defined on the basis of IQ alone, then 3% of the population have an IQ more than two standard deviations below the mean, but this is a purely statistical definition and neglects the important factors of social competence, educational management and family support — which together ultimately determine whether the person will need special education at school and supporting services in adult life. For these same reasons, case-finding is incomplete at all ages. Because of the relationship between MLD and social class, prevalence figures are dependent on the social class structure of the population under study.

Presentation of learning disability

The age at which learning disability presents is dependent upon the severity, the presence of recognizable specific disorders, the alertness of the parents and the quality of the paediatric services.

1 *Presentation at birth.* Recognizable malformation patterns, such as Down's syndrome, are usually diagnosed at birth.

2 *First year of life.* Recognition of learning disability is often possible in the first year of life. Slow motor development is sometimes the most obvious feature and may be associated with hypotonia or 'floppiness' (p. 254), although some babies with SLD have little or no motor delay. Children with severe cerebral palsy often have SLD as well, but it is usually the motor disorder which first brings them to medical attention.

The mother may detect that 'turn-taking' behaviour and play are absent or deficient, and in some cases unresponsiveness leads to a suspicion of deafness or blindness. The baby is often described as 'too good'; he/she is quite content to sleep or gaze vacantly at their hands.

3 *Second and third years of life.* The child may present at this age with delays in one or more areas, most commonly in speech development. This is invariably associated with impairment of language comprehension, which is not always immediately obvious (Chapter 11). There may also be delay in walking, but this is rarely the presenting feature. Some cases present because of disturbing social behaviour, such as head-banging, casting of objects, excessive mouthing, temper tantrums, aimless hyperactivity or destructiveness.

In a few cases, there is clear evidence, from a retrospective history and from previous development assessments, that early development was within normal limits. The child begins to use single words and may even begin to join words. Gradually their language and general development slow to a halt and may even regress. In a proportion of these, there is also increasing social impairment and the terms 'disintegrative disorder' or 'late-onset autism' may be applied (pp. 191–5); however, in other cases social skills are retained and the ultimate picture is of a sociable child with a learning disability. This sequence of events inevitably suggests a progressive disorder, and usually neurological investigation is necessary, but only rarely is a truly progressive disorder identified.

This uncommon but well-recognized sequence of events should be distinguished from the common and frustrating observation made by parents of a child with learning disabilities, that the child seems to learn and use a word, but then forgets it and refuses to use it again in spite of coaxing and prompting.

4 *Fourth and fifth years of life.* Children with MLD may be detected during assessment for speech delay, but some cases may not be recognized until they begin to fail in school. Indeed, if their behaviour and social skills are satisfactory, children may survive 2 or more years of schooling before their disability is recognized, particularly if they have an inexperienced teacher.

Causes of learning disability

A biological cause is rarely found in children with IQs in the 50–70 range; nevertheless, mild/moderate learning disability can be caused by many syndromes and disorders. A careful search for a biological cause of MLD is particularly indicated when the child's parents are highly intelligent, but the possibility of an organic cause should always be considered, however low the parents' IQ may be, since their own low ability may be the result of a specific disorder. It is also important to look for interactional effects between biological disadvantage (low birth weight, syndromes, etc.), sensory impairments (particularly secretory otitis media) and an impoverished environment.

Among the SLD group, chromosome disorders account for 20–25% and, of these, 80–90% have Down's syndrome. Another 20–25% have identifiable disorders or syndromes; only a small minority of these have progressive metabolic or degenerative diseases. SLD in association with severe cerebral palsy, microcephaly or infantile spasms accounts for about 10–20% and postnatal cerebral insults (meningitis, trauma, etc.) for perhaps 10%. There are many cases in which defects of growth or dysmorphic features clearly indicate that the neurological impairment originated in the prenatal period, even though no recognized syndrome or exact cause can be identified (Table 10.1).

In this chapter, only the most common disorders and those with complex features are described — details of other disorders are given in the Glossary.

Dysmorphic syndromes

The word 'syndrome' means 'to run together'; 'dysmorphic' means 'abnormally formed'. Thus a dysmorphic syndrome refers to a collection of abnormalities of bodily structure which are found to cluster together more often than would be expected by chance. The cause may be a chromosome disorder, a defective single gene, exposure to an adverse intrauterine event, such as an

Table 10.1 Classification of the causes of learning disability

Prenatal
Chromosome disorders
    Autosomes, e.g. Down's syndrome
    Sex chromosomes, e.g. XYY, XXY, XO, FraX, etc.
Single-gene defects
    Dominant inheritance, e.g. neurocutaneous syndromes:
      tuberose sclerosis, neurofibromatosis
    Recessive inheritance, e.g. disorders of metabolism:
      amino acids, carbohydrates, lysosomal storage
      diseases, etc.
Dysmorphic syndromes of uncertain and variable
    inheritance
Intrauterine infections: toxoplasmosis, cytomegalovirus,
    rubella
Intrauterine insults: placental insufficiency (?), alcohol,
    other teratogenic agents, hypothyroidism

Perinatal
Severe asphyxia (usually associated with cerebral palsy)
Complications of extreme prematurity
Meningitis
Kernicterus
Hypoglycaemia
Hydrocephalus

Postnatal
CNS infection (meningitis/encephalitis)
Non-accidental injury
Accidental trauma
Severe convulsions
Lead poisoning
Reye's syndrome
Environmental: severe deprivation, malnutrition

CNS, central nervous system.

infection or toxin, or a biochemical disorder. Although most of the latter do not affect a child's physical appearance, a minority may do so. In many cases, it is reasonable to surmise that a syndrome is genetically determined and may be caused by a single gene even though it has not yet been identified; in others, the evidence does not support a genetic basis and there must be some other cause.

Around 2000 syndromes have already been identified. Details are kept on computerized databases of many children with collections of anomalies that do not yet constitute a definite syndrome, but may do so in the future. A clinical geneticist is likely to have more expertise in syndrome identification than most paediatricians, and rapid advances in molecular genetics permit increasing sophistication in diagnosis and may affect prognosis, management and genetic counselling. The nomenclature used for dysmorphic syndromes is summarized in Table 10.2. Individual conditions are described in the Glossary.

There are some general principles in the management of a child with a dysmorphic syndrome.
1 Parents greatly resent the child being regarded purely as an 'interesting case', to be demonstrated to colleagues and students.
2 Excessive preoccupation with the unusual medical aspects of the child's condition may divert attention from their care and service needs, which are probably the same as those of any other child with a similar level of disability. This is particularly a danger if the child attends a distant specialist centre because of some complex problem such as congenital heart disease.
3 It is advisable to gather a dossier of literature about the syndrome and to ensure that all the known complications and associations have been checked and, if necessary, repeatedly monitored as the child grows. Parents should participate in this task. In the long run, it will not prove a kindness to conceal the possible complications of their child's disorder. They will seek information in any case, from libraries (often with outdated reference books), voluntary organizations or the Internet.
4 The diagnosis should be reviewed from time to time. Advances in genetics may reveal that the child has a different subtype of the condition or that the diagnosis or genetic counselling previously offered is now incorrect.
5 Caution is advisable in the diagnosis of syndromes in cases where the features are borderline or equivocal. Parents are often very relieved to have a definite diagnosis but, if subsequently it becomes clear that the diagnosis was wrong, they

Table 10.2 Terminology for description of dysmorphic diseases

Term	Meaning
Malformation	A primary structural defect
Deformation	Alteration in shape or structure of a previously normal part
Anomalad	A malformation together with its consequential structural change
Malformation syndromes	Recognized patterns of malformation presumed to have a common aetiology
Association	A pattern of malformations occurring together more often than expected by chance but not definitely regarded as a syndrome

will often be distressed and will feel very let down.

6 Certain behaviour patterns seem to be associated with some syndromes (e.g. Williams, Noonan's, fragile-X) and are important both for diagnosis and management; nevertheless, there is a wide diversity. Prediction that a particular child will exhibit these features is unwise.

7 When the diagnosis of a dysmorphic syndrome is first suspected, it will usually be necessary to mention the possibility of genetic implications for the parents and for other family members, but the distressing and sometimes devastating effects of receiving such information must be remembered when planning how to handle further diagnostic tests and enquiries.

8 Professionals should encourage the parents to join the relevant support group or organization. This will give them access to information, offer opportunities to share experiences with other parents and help them contribute to the advance of knowledge about their child's disorder. The professionals should encourage the parents to be 'experts', and should not feel threatened by this!

Chromosome disorders

Down's syndrome

This is the commonest and most familiar of all dysmorphic syndromes. It is also known as mongolism, but this term is now regarded as obsolete and offensive by many parents. It occurs in all races. The incidence is around one in 660 of all live births. The risk of Down's syndrome is also related to maternal age; it rises from less than one in 1000 in young mothers, to one in 800 in the early 30s and greater than one in 100 in the over-40s. Paternal age is probably much less significant, although this point is still undecided. Although the risk of having a Down's syndrome baby is higher for older women, a large majority of women have had their babies before they are 30, and therefore most Down's syndrome babies are born to mothers in this age-group. (For this reason a significant reduction in the overall incidence of Down's syndrome will never be achieved by a screening programme that concentrates on the over-35s.)

Down's syndrome is usually caused by an additional chromosome 21, i.e. trisomy 21, which is caused by non-disjunction during meiosis; this is related to maternal age. In 20–25% of cases the extra chromosome comes from the father. It is not known exactly why an extra chromosome should have such a remarkable effect, but one particular region of the chromosome 21 seems to be responsible for many of the features observed. A minority of cases (about 3–4%) are caused by translocations, with about equal occurrence of D/G and G/G translocation. Nearly half of the former but less than 10% of the latter arise from a balanced translocation carrier parent. Translocation is unrelated to maternal age; it accounts for a higher proportion of cases in young mothers, although even in these the figure is only about 6%. Mosaicism accounts for 2–6% of cases, and a few other rare chromosomal variants also occur.

When one parent is a translocation carrier, the risk of recurrence in subsequent pregnancies is high. Mothers who have had a baby with trisomy

21 have approximately twice the risk of Down's syndrome occurring in a subsequent pregnancy, compared with other women of the same age. Although the risk is still small except for the over-35s, most couples accept the offer of amniocentesis for chromosome analysis in subsequent pregnancies.

The so-called 'triple test', involving measurement of α-fetoprotein, unconjugated oestriol and human chorionic gonadotrophin is said to be capable of identifying about half of all fetuses with Down's syndrome, but the place of this screening test in antenatal care is still controversial because of technical and ethical problems (Fletcher *et al.*, 1995). The same applies to antenatal detection of chromosome disorders by ultrasound.

Clinical features. The diagnosis is usually easy in the full-term baby, although it is readily overlooked in sick premature infants. The main features are shown in Table 10.3. Cardiac defects are important in Down's syndrome, since they are the main factor that determines life expectancy. Some of these (notably atrioventricular canal defects) are not always clinically obvious in the early months of life. Cyanosis, cardiomegaly and murmurs may be trivial or absent. An electrocardiogram (ECG) is often helpful since it may reveal left-axis deviation (vertical axis), which is always abnormal. The parents should not be told that the heart is normal until careful clinical evaluation, ECG, chest X-ray and an echocardiogram have been performed. Echocardiography in infancy is technically demanding and there should be no hesitation in repeating the study if there is any reason for concern. The unexpected discovery of heart disease, later in the first or second year, often causes intense parental bitterness and distress at a time when they are just getting over the shock of the original diagnosis.

Large left-to-right shunts in Down's syndrome seem to progress to pulmonary hypertension more quickly than in normal children, and severe cyanosis and shunt reversal may be seen very

Table 10.3 Features of Down's syndrome

Hypotonia

Small stature (some may benefit from growth hormone therapy)

Small nose and low nasal bridge
Chronic rhinitis
Middle-ear disease
Large adenoids and tonsils with tendency to snore and develop sleep apnoea

Conjunctivitis
Blepharitis
Blocked tear duct
Brushfield spots (speckled iris)
Lens opacities
Refractive error (hypermetropia most common)

Simian palmar crease
Distal axial triradius
Small middle phalanx of fifth finger
Clinodactyly
Wide gap between first and second toes

Orthopaedic problems
   Atlantoaxial subluxation (see text)
   Scoliosis
   Hip dysplasia
   Patellofemoral dysplasia

Cardiac defects
   AV canal defect
   VSD
   PDA
   ASD
   Aberrant subclavian artery

Hyperkeratotic skin
Fine soft hair
Erythematous papular eruptions
Alopecia and vitiligo
Cutis marmorata (mottled skin when cold)

Male hypogonadism
Cryptorchidism
Low fertility

Bowel disorders
   Duodenal atresia
   Malabsorption
   Constipation
   Hirschsprung's disease

Continued

Table 10.3 (*continued*)

High incidence of
  Leukaemia
  Thyroid disorders (mainly hypothyroidism)
  Alzheimer's disease in adult life
  Bacterial pneumonias
  Bacterial tracheitis

Slightly raised incidence of epilepsy

AV, atrioventricular; VSD, ventricular septal defect; PDA, patent ductus arteriosus; ASD, atrial septal defect.

early. All children with heart defects should be assessed by a paediatric cardiologist. Sometimes a decision may be made not to operate on an operable lesion, particularly if the risks are very high and the child is thriving; but the decision must be made with the parents' full agreement. Parents should not be left with the impression that the child has been refused surgery simply because he/she has Down's syndrome.

Eye defects and conductive hearing loss due to 'glue ear' are both very common in Down's syndrome. These sensory impairments, which may be of small significance to the normal child, are undoubtedly important when superimposed on other disabilities. An eye examination and regular vision and hearing checks are essential.

Behaviour. Traditionally, Down's syndrome children are said to be often musical and of a placid and friendly personality, but this is a crude generalization which is by no means constant and behaviour problems are certainly not unknown. Possibly the early recognition and understanding of their disability aids their parents in management so that, in contrast with other disabling conditions, slow development does not lead to excessive parental pressure and anxiety. Social impairment, hyperactivity and autism are very rare in Down's syndrome, but do occur occasionally.

Development. Down's syndrome children all have learning disabilities, but the degree is variable (Table 10.4). Intelligent parents tend to have more intelligent Down's syndrome children. Environmental factors undoubtedly influence ultimate intelligence. In the first few years, development is often more rapid than parents expected and may even approach the normal range. Learning problems become more evident after the age of 3 or 4 years. Educational placement should be decided on the basis of the child's abilities, not the diagnosis. Some Down's syndrome children enjoy integration into mainstream schooling, although most will eventually require some form of more specialized provision.

Puberty and adult life. Most females start to menstruate at the normal time. Females are potentially fertile but there is no known case of a male fathering a child. Precocious puberty occurs only rarely. Adults with Down's syndrome always have learning problems but their potential ability may be greater than has been realized in the past, and they benefit from modern attitudes to disability. Some have excelled in sporting activities and the arts. Life expectancy is reduced by congenital heart disease and an increased risk of infections; those who escape these problems may live to middle age but there is a very high incidence of presenile dementia due to Alzheimer's disease.

Management. Parents should be told of the diagnosis as soon as it is suspected (p. 102).

Table 10.4 Milestones in Down's syndrome (compiled from several authors)

	Mean (months)	Range (months)
Sitting	13	6–30
Standing	22	9–48
Walking	30	12–60
Single words	34	12–72

Reading: achieved by 40%
Maximum reading age: accuracy = 10–12 years;
  comprehension = 8 years

Confirmation by chromosome culture is desirable; apart from the need to recognize translocation cases, it eliminates any doubts in the parents' and professionals' minds and this may help the parents to accept the situation more easily. In neonatal surgical emergencies, rapid diagnosis is possible using bone-marrow cells and allows informed decision-making, but Down's syndrome is not normally a reason to withhold necessary treatment.

The parents should be told of the likely development of a Down's syndrome child, as they may have unnecessarily pessimistic expectations. An introduction to local services and to the parent support group should be offered (see Chapters 7 and 8). A plan should be made for necessary medical supervision, including vision and hearing checks, growth monitoring, a full immunization programme and routine child health checks. Parents should be informed about particular problems with Down's syndrome children, notably the risks of infection, hypothyroidism (see below), middle-ear disorders and refractive errors.

Parents usually value specialist medical support for the first year or two but as they become more confident they realize that the child can be treated normally in many respects, and they may decide that regular visits to a paediatric clinic are no longer necessary. They should keep a copy of the Down's syndrome growth chart.

There is an increased incidence of thyroid disorders in children with Down's syndrome. Congenital hypothyroidism is about 28 times more common than in the population as a whole. Compensated hypothyroidism (i.e. raised thyroid-stimulating hormone (TSH) with normal thyroxine (T_4), is also common, but is not usually associated with raised autoantibodies, has no obvious clinical significance and may resolve spontaneously. Hypothyroidism needing treatment is relatively rare. Hyperthyroidism also occurs, but again is often asymptomatic and may not need treatment. Not surprisingly, therefore, there is as yet no consensus on the need for or frequency of screening for thyroid disorders in children with Down's syndrome. A test at school entry and one on transfer to secondary school

are desirable; some authorities suggest testing every 3 years. Parents and primary care staff should be alert to the possibility of thyroid disorders, remembering that the features of hypothyroidism are similar to those of Down's syndrome.

In recent years, some people with Down's syndrome have been offered cosmetic surgery, involving major craniofacial reconstruction, with the aim of making less obvious the features of the condition. There is perhaps a danger that the procedure may be done mainly for the satisfaction of the carers, since there is little evidence of any real benefit to the person with Down's syndrome. Partial glossectomy has also been undertaken to reduce the bulk of the tongue and to improve speech and facial appearance. The tongue is not larger in Down's syndrome than in other children, but protrudes because of hypotonia. There may be some minor cosmetic benefit but so far there is little evidence of any functional improvement in speech.

Screening, by cervical spine X-rays, for atlanto-axial instability has also been proposed, particularly for teenage Down's syndrome people who are active in sports like trampolining and diving, but there is little evidence that screening is beneficial. In most of the rare cases where a Down's syndrome person has suffered spinal cord compression, the onset has been insidious rather than following sporting injury. It therefore seems sensible to warn parents and carers about the possibly increased hazards of these sports, advise them to report any unexplained change in gait or sphincter function immediately and investigate any such case without delay.

Sex chromosome disorders

The features of the commoner sex chromosome disorders (Turner's, Klinefelter's, XYY and XXX syndromes) are summarized in the Glossary. Longitudinal studies of children found to have sex chromosome defects in a programme of universal neonatal screening reveal that some of these are compatible with essentially normal intelligence, development and behaviour, and therefore the fact that a child has a sex chromosome disorder does not necessarily mean that this is the cause of their problems.

Fragile-X syndrome

It has been known since the nineteenth century that moderate to severe learning disabilities are more common in males than in females and that the disability may run through several generations. Some, though not all, of the excess male cases are accounted for by the fragile-X syndrome (also called fragile-X mental retardation 1, shortened to FMR-1), which is probably the commonest cause of global learning disability after Down's syndrome. The total population prevalence is estimated at one in 1360 males. For every four affected males there is one who inherits the gene without being affected (normal transmitting male). The disorder also produces learning disability in one in 2000 females, but there are twice that number of females who carry the gene but are asymptomatic. It accounts for perhaps 6% of global SLD in boys. Some studies report a similar prevalence in boys with less severe learning disabilities.

The condition derives its name from a constriction site at the end of the long arm of the X chromosome (position Xq27.3). The site is revealed only when the chromosomes are cultured in a folate-deficient medium. The gene was characterized in 1991 and is of unusual interest; it consists of multiple replications of the base sequence cytosine−guanine−guanine (CGG), which is the fragile-X gene. The number of repeats correlates with the degree of clinical involvement. This gene is regarded as a pre-mutation and may expand further during female meiosis. When the number of repeats becomes excessive, the gene is silenced, preventing production of the FMR-1 protein, whose precise function is not yet known. Although the syndrome behaves rather like a sex-linked disorder, there are some atypical features, and in some cases the clinical manifestations only appear after trans-mission through an intermediate and asymptomatic generation. The gene is partially expressed phenotypically in some female carriers (see Table 10.5) and yet in some women who are undoubted carriers the gene cannot be detected.

The chromosome culture techniques required to demonstrate the fragile site are difficult and this may explain the discrepant estimates of the prevalence, but it is now possible to use deoxyribonucleic acid (DNA) technology to identify the fragile site directly. In cases where there are no features suggestive of other chromosomal disorders, this may be a more economic investigation

Table 10.5 Physical features of fragile-X (Martin−Bell) syndrome

---

Affected males

Physical features
  Long face and slightly increased head circumference
  Macrognathia
  Large protuberant ears
  Flattened nasal bridge
  Abnormal dermatoglyphics (deep vertical anterior plantar crease)
  Macro-orchidism (present from birth but only diagnostically useful after puberty)
  Infantile hypotonia
  Connective-tissue dysplasia (joint laxity and soft velvety skin)
  Aortic dilatation and mitral valve prolapse
  Recurrent otitis media
  Failure to thrive in infancy
  Tonic−clonic or partial epilepsy, temporal spikes on EEG
  MRI scan abnormalities (especially cerebellum)

Psychological and behavioural features — see text

Carrier females

May be similar cognitive profiles and physical features though less marked
Increased prevalence of depression and psychotic disturbance

Note All these features vary widely in degree of expression EEG, electroencephalogram; MRI, magnetic resonance imaging.

and should be undertaken in all cases of un-explained global learning disabilities, speech–language impairment or autism in boys; it may also be worth considering in girls with these problems. More wide-ranging screening pro-grammes may eventually be considered.

Management is primarily that of the associated learning and behavioural problems but there has been some interest in the use of folate; it is said that this reduces hyperactivity and improves concentration.

Fragile-X variants. A group of fragile-X syndrome variants has recently been discovered. These conditions have a similar hypochromic fragile site on cytogenetic analysis. However, the molecular abnormality is elsewhere in the distal portion of the X chromosome's long arm.

A common fragile site is located at Xq27.2 and has been called *FraX-D* to distinguish it from fragile-X syndrome (*FraX-A*). This site is a potential source of misdiagnosis in female carriers, prenatal testing and occasional males with very low levels of fragile site expression. Its general population prevalence is unknown, but it is not thought to be associated with learning disability.

Some families show a fragile site at Xq27.3, and yet have no detectable expansion in the FMR-1 gene and there is an absence of the Martin–Bell phenotype, even though they may have mild mental impairment. The fragile site in these families is distal to the FMR-1 gene, in the proximal portion of Xq28. It is folate-sensitive and has been named *FraX-E*. Cytogenetically it is virtually indistinguishable from FraX-A. The molecular abnormality in FraX-E does not appear to undergo transgenerational amplifi-cation. Intellectual retardation is usually mild. Individuals with this fragile site possess GCC repeat amplifications.

A third fragile site, *FraX-F*, exists in Xq27–q28. It lies distal to FraX-A and FraX-E. The site is folate-insensitive and manifests on standard chromosomal culture. Its exact frequency and its relationship to learning disability and behavioural problems have yet to be clarified.

It is therefore necessary to undertake cyto-genetic as well as DNA analysis to ensure that a variant is not being missed.

Behavioural characteristics. These are often far more striking than physical features and can give the clue to diagnosis.

Intellectual impairment is very variable and is often in the mild to moderate learning disability range. Verbal intelligence characteristically exceeds performance abilities in both affected males and non-retarded female carriers. The rate of intellectual development diminishes with age, particularly after puberty. Simultaneous information-processing abilities exceed sequen-tial information-processing skills. Increasing demands on the latter probably explain the observed intellectual slowing.

Speech and language development is almost always retarded, with dysfluent conversation, incomplete sentences, echolalia (repetition of words or phrases just heard), palilalia (multiple repetitions of the same phrase or word with increasing speed and diminishing volume) and verbal perseveration. There is often a jocular quality to speech with narrative, compulsive utterances and up-and-down swings of pitch ('litany-like'). 'Cluttering' refers to the fast and fluctuating rate of talking with repetitions, garbled and disorganized speech, poor topic maintenance and tangential comments.

Social impairments can be part of typical autism but more often present as a characteristic profile in non-autistic individuals. Social anxiety (rather than social indifference) coexists with an aversion to eye contact, usually in a socially responsive and affectionate individual. Self-injury occurs, notably hand-biting and scratching, provoked by frus-tration and excitement. Sometimes poor imitative and symbolic play, with stereotyped repetitive behaviours, is seen, e.g. hand-flapping. Most individuals with fragile-X syndrome do not have autism but many display communicatory and ritualistic problems which are also seen in autistic disorders.

Attention and concentration difficulties are often

associated and may be disproportionate to the degree of learning difficulty. Inattentiveness and fidgetiness may occur without overt overactivity. Hyperactivity may be the presenting feature in non-retarded boys with fragile-X. Frank over-activity usually diminishes with age but there is evidence that poor concentration, restlessness and fidgetiness persist, interfering with the develop-ment of social relationships and academic progress.

Single-gene defects — inherited metabolic and storage disorders

The term '*inherited metabolic disorder*' (IMD) includes disorders of amino acid, carbohydrate and uric acid metabolism, a variety of storage disorders due to lysosomal enzyme defects and peroxisomal and mitochondrial disorders.

Metabolic disorders are a rare cause of learning disability. The best known, phenylketonuria, is usually detected by neonatal screening, and many of the others present early in life with symptoms which demand urgent investigation, for example coma, hypotonia, convulsions, unusual odour, vomiting, episodic ketosis, megaloblastic anaemia or gross developmental delay. The number of individual disorders now recognized is so large and the manifestations so variable, that some clinicians 'screen' for IMDs (p. 169) in the inves-tigation of unexplained learning disability.

Lysosomal storage diseases (LSDs) result from a deficiency in one or more acid hydrolase enzymes in the lysosome, which is a membrane-bound organelle found in all cells. Excessive quantities of substrate accumulate, causing cell expansion, disturbed function and eventually cell death. The clinical effects depend on the concentrations and the functions of the various substrates in different body tissues. At least 40 different conditions are known. They are all very rare, and even collectively they occur with a frequency of no more than one in 5000 births. The exact figure depends on the ethnic composition of the population, since two of the commonest diseases are more prevalent in Jews. In spite of their rarity, they are important for several reasons: they provide valuable insights into the physiology of nerve cells; they have gen-etic and prognostic implications; and in some conditions new methods of treatment are being developed. The inheritance of LSDs is autosomal recessive, with the exceptions of Fabry's and Hunter's diseases, which are transmitted as sex-linked recessives.

Details of some LSDs are provided in the Glossary. It is, however, more helpful for the clinician to know when to suspect these disorders and initiate investigation (Table 10.6). None of the features listed here is invariable. The recog-nition of LSDs in their classic and advanced form is seldom difficult, although only laboratory studies can determine the specific metabolic defect. The problem facing the paediatrician, who sees predominantly learning disability of non-progressive type, is to recognize the early or atypical case, without overloading laboratory services with requests for complex and expensive tests. Particular difficulties arise in those rare cases in which deterioration is so slow that the

Table 10.6 Features suggestive of lysosomal storage diseases

Neurodevelopmental features
Severe failure to thrive in infancy
Microcephaly
Macrocephaly
Hepatosplenomegaly
Gait disturbance — ataxia, spasticity, neuropathy
Abnormal eye movements
Cherry-red spot at macula
Optic atrophy
Fits (rare)
Deafness

Dysmorphic features
Short stature
Coarse facies
Corneal clouding
Large tongue
Airway obstruction
Limitation of joint movements
X-ray abnormalities of vertebrae, hands, etc.
Scoliosis

child continues to acquire new skills and dys-morphic features are lacking, so that the child is thought to have a static disorder. Indeed, LSDs have occasionally been diagnosed in adults whose disability has apparently remained static for many years.

Diagnosis

A urine screening test for mucopolysaccharides (MPS) may be justified in all cases of unexplained learning disability (p. 169), but will not detect conditions which masquerade as MPS (see Glossary). Assays of many specific enzymes are now available and have largely replaced biopsy of the brain, rectum or appendix as the most direct way to diagnose the LSDs. Other useful inves-tigations include blood film, bone-marrow exam-ination (for white-cell inclusions), radiological survey, acid phosphatase, electroencephalogram (EEG) and electroretinogram (ERG).

Management

Accurate diagnosis and genetic counselling are essential. Antenatal diagnosis is possible in some cases. In most cases management is supportive. Since the rate of progression of these disorders is variable, the child's care should be based on their current status rather than their expected deteri-oration. Specific treatment with enzyme replace-ment has, in general, been disappointing, except in one form of Gaucher's disease, but recent work with bone-marrow transplantation may offer new approaches. This is a rapidly changing field and advice must be obtained from a centre with special expertise in the subject.

Other degenerative disorders

These are all very rare and account for a tiny minority of children with learning disability. Some present early and progress rapidly so that early investigation is inevitable, but in others pro-gression may be so slow that the possibility of a degenerative condition is overlooked for months

or years. In addition, mental deterioration may occur in many other disorders but be over-shadowed by spasticity, ataxia or weakness (Chapter 14).

Abnormal size or shape of the head

Large heads

The commonest cause of a large head is normal variation. By definition, 2% of the population have a head circumference above the 98th centile. Familial factors account for some of the variation and the parents' and siblings' heads should be measured and compared with the normal. (The normal adult head circumference range (mean ± 1 SD) in males is 55 cm ± 1.46 and in females is 54.27 cm ± 1.14).

Some children have large heads at birth, an excessive rate of head growth and even some suture separation. Computerized tomography (CT) scan shows a ventricle size at the upper limit of normal but no other pathology, and their development and progress are normal. Siblings and one or other parent (usually the father) may also have large heads. The condition has been called benign familial megalencephaly but it should be regarded as a normal variant, not a disease. It should not be confused with true megalencephaly (see Glossary).

Pathological causes of cranial enlargement (Table 10.7) can be divided into those with hydro-cephalus and those in which this is usually absent or a minor additional feature. Although hydro-cephalus is commoner than all the other con-ditions put together, the word must not be used as a synonym for a large head.

Hydranencephaly

Hydranencephaly means massive enlargement of the ventricles with little or no remnant of cerebral cortex, and variable head enlargement. The head transilluminates (but this should not be done in the presence of the parents). In the early weeks of life it is surprisingly easy to overlook the diagnosis

Table 10.7 Causes of cranial enlargement

Normal and familial variations
Hydrocephalus
Hydranencephaly
Subdural haematoma
Neurocutaneous syndromes (especially neurofibromatosis)
Alexander's disease
Canavan's disease
Miscellaneous storage diseases
Sotos' syndrome
Gorlin's syndrome
Achondroplasia
Megalencephaly
Thickened skull (rickets, haemolytic anaemias, bone
    dysplasias)
Tumours

Table 10.8 Classification of hydrocephalus

*Obstruction within the ventricular system (non-communicating
    or obstructive)*
Malformations of the aqueduct of Sylvius (stenosis, atresia,
    forking, etc.)
X-linked aqueduct stenosis (may be associated with
    abnormal thumbs)
Obstruction by mass lesions
Obstruction by inflammation: bacterial meningitis (also?
    mumps); haemorrhage; congenital infections
Obstructions of the fourth ventricle outlet foramina:
    inflammation; Dandy–Walker syndrome

Obstruction outside the ventricular system (communicating)
Adhesions in basal cisterns or subarachnoid space:
    infection, subarachnoid haemorrhage
Developmental abnormality or acquired obstruction of
    arachnoid villi
Arnold–Chiari malformation (may also be associated with
    aqueduct lesion)

Excess production of CSF
Choroid plexus papilloma

if the head is not grossly enlarged. Survival beyond a few months is unusual, although not unknown.

Hydrocephalus

Hydrocephalus is a condition in which an imbalance between production and reabsorption of cerebrospinal fluid (CSF) leads to ventricular enlargement. The ventricles can also become enlarged due to atrophy or loss of brain substance, but this situation can usually be distinguished from true hydrocephalus by the clinical and radiological findings.

Hydrocephalus may be caused by an obstruction within the ventricular system, around the exit foramina in the posterior fossa, in the CSF spaces surrounding the brain, or at the sites of reabsorption, which are mainly but not exclusively the arachnoid (Pacchionian) granulations along the superior sagittal sinus. The main causes are summarized in Table 10.8. The terms obstructive, internal, external and communication hydrocephalus are no longer popular because they lack precision. The commonest cause of hydrocephalus in children is the Arnold–Chiari malformation in association with neural tube defects (Chapter 15). Extraventricular obstruction

and aqueduct stenosis are the two other common causes.

Progressive enlargement of the head is the usual presenting feature. The head circumference is noted to be crossing the centile lines. If the head was initially small, severe hydrocephalus can exist long before the head circumference reaches the 98th centile. Indeed, hydrocephalus can develop even when the head circumference is, by definition, in the microcephalic range. Other features include irritability, failure to thrive, developmental delay, a large tense fontanelle, hyperreflexia in the legs, squint and the 'sunset' sign with loss of upward gaze. A rim of sclera may be seen above the cornea in normal babies at times, but 'sunsetting' in hydrocephalus is usually more dramatic and persistent. There may be other evidence of oculomotor or visual disturbance.

Papilloedema is rarely seen. The cry is sometimes harsh and high-pitched; rarely, stridor occurs. The skull may have a 'crackpot' sound on percussion. Any or all of these signs may be absent, depending on the intracranial pressure and the rate of ventricular enlargement.

Investigations and management. Skull X-ray may be of some help and ultrasound is invaluable if the fontanelle is still open. The definitive study is a CT or MRI scan. It is important to investigate any child with a suspiciously large head, instead of causing months of worry by repeated head measurements. Treatment is discussed in detail in Chapter 16. The insertion of a CSF shunting system is associated with more complications than any other routine operation in paediatric surgery, and is not undertaken unless essential. The presence of ventricular enlargement does not automatically mean that treatment is needed; for example, premature babies who have had intra-ventricular haemorrhage may have large ventricles without evidence of raised pressure. Ventricular enlargement may be the result of brain atrophy. In some children with evidence of impaired CSF reabsorption, stabilization may occur spontaneously. Marked asymptomatic hydrocephalus is occasionally discovered in older children or adults and has evidently arrested without treatment.

Hydrocephalus may also present at any time in later infancy or childhood, with features of acute raised intracranial pressure, with more insidious disturbances of gait or intellect, or with optic atrophy. A clinical diagnosis of 'arrested hydrocephalus' should not, however, be suggested to the parents of children with minor developmental disorders simply on the basis of a large head circumference.

Sequelae and prognosis. Whether or not they are treated surgically, children with hydrocephalus often have one or more disabilities. There is often some spasticity and ataxia, particularly affecting the lower limbs; the legs are believed to be more affected than the arms because of the greater vulnerability of their nerve fibres to stretching by the enlarged lateral ventricles.

Squint, optic atrophy and varying degrees of visual loss are common. The IQ is very variable. There is often mild to moderate learning disability, and the verbal ability tends to be better than performance. There may be difficulties with visual perception and scanning, and with tasks needing fine co-ordination. In some children there is a tendency for verbal fluency to exceed content, providing a tendency to inconsequential facile chatter (the 'cocktail party' syndrome), although this may also be seen in other forms of learning disability.

Shunt surgery decreases mortality and removes the risk of a grotesquely ugly enlarged head. The gains in IQ and other motor function are less dramatic. Ultimate IQ does not correlate with the extent of the ventricular enlargement or with the thickness of the cerebral cortical mantle. The outcome is probably determined by the disorder causing the hydrocephalus rather than the hydrocephalus *per se*. This certainly appears to be true in the case of posthaemorrhagic hydrocephalus in premature infants, where it seems that the extent of ventricular dilatation is not the main determinant of the outcome, but rather the extent of cerebral tissue damage.

Genetic aspects. It is generally believed that isolated hydrocephalus is not genetically related to neural tube defects. Hydrocephalus has many causes, the majority of which are not inherited. Some cases of aqueduct stenosis are inherited as a sex-linked recessive and many of these infants have flexed fingers and adducted thumbs. There are several syndromes in which hydrocephalus occurs, including FG, hydrolethalus, and Walker–Warburg or hydrocephalus, agyria, retinal dysplasia, with or without encephalocele (HARD ± E) syndromes.

Small heads

Microcephaly is sometimes defined as a head circumference more than two standard deviations below the mean — roughly equivalent to the 2nd centile. This is unsatisfactory because, by definition, 2% of the population have head measurements below this figure, and many of them are normal in every respect. Although the probability of neurological and intellectual deficit increases rapidly with decreasing head size below the -3 standard deviation level, no single measurement can define microcephaly; the term implies not only that the head and brain are smaller than the 'norm' but also that brain structure or function is abnormal.

There is probably a genetic element in the determination of head size. It is important to measure the head circumference of parents and siblings as well as that of the patient. Some families are known where extremely small head size is transmitted as either a dominant or a recessive condition, but the subjects are normal in all other respects including intelligence. Not surprisingly, small children are more likely to have small heads; but, even when head size is adjusted for height and weight, it still remains a weak predictor of intelligence or abnormality. It follows from these observations that, when a young child is found on routine measurements to have a small head circumference but is otherwise normal, it may be very difficult to offer the parents anything other than statistical predictions about the risk of learning difficulties in the future. Conversely, when a child presenting with learning problems is found to have a small head, this should not too readily be accepted as an 'explanation' of the child's difficulties.

The main causes of microcephaly are classified in Table 10.9. The importance of ascertaining the head circumference at birth is obvious. Serial measurements are essential in the follow-up of children who have suffered severe cerebral insults. A head circumference which is falling away from the centile lines is an ominous sign in these circumstances. Decline in the rate of head growth is observed in some other serious conditions, but it may also occur as an isolated finding and children followed for several years may show little or no evidence of any developmental problems. A small head which is growing parallel to the centile lines gives less cause for concern. There may also be some faltering in

Table 10.9 Causes of microcephaly

Primary: present at birth
Microcephaly with recessive inheritance
Abnormal neuronal development, cause(s) unknown
   Lissencephaly (agyria)
   Macrogyria
   Polymicrogyria, etc.
Craniosynostosis of all sutures
Numerous chromosomal defects and other dysmorphic
   syndromes
Severe intrauterine growth retardation*
Insults to previously normal brain*
   Fetal alcohol syndrome
   Intrauterine infections
   Radiation
   Maternal phenylketonuria
   Vascular disturbances (particularly in monozygotic
    twinning)

*Secondary: head circumference normal at birth**
(Insult occurs or abnormality becomes manifest in infancy
   or early childhood)
Severe anoxia or asphyxia
Meningitis, encephalitis, encephalopathy
Non-accidental injury (shaking)
Inherited metabolic disorders
Lysosomal storage diseases
Vascular accidents
Rett's syndrome
Angelman's syndrome

---

* Some authors classify all insults (pre- or postnatal) to a normal brain as secondary microcephaly.

head growth in any child who is failing to thrive, followed by catch-up growth on recovery.

Investigation. A careful examination for other anomalies may help in recognition of a specific syndrome. Chromosome studies, maternal phenylalanine levels and tests for congenital infections may be indicated. A CT scan may reveal malformations which may occasionally be relevant in genetic counselling. Calcification caused by congenital infections may be revealed on a CT scan long before it is visible on plain X-ray. Magnetic resonance imaging (MRI) scanning is more likely than CT to reveal abnormalities of brain development and neuronal migration and is probably the imaging method of choice.

Development and prognosis. This is very variable, since microcephaly is not itself a diagnosis. In general, the probability and severity of disability correlate with the head circumference only with the more extreme degrees of microcephaly. There may be spastic quadriplegia, visual or auditory defects, seizures and behaviour problems. In some children with microcephaly, early development seems reasonably normal, motor development proceeds steadily and several years elapse before the extent of the intellectual handicap is apparent. In others, intellectual development is severely affected and yet the child has little or no motor disorder.

Genetic aspects. Most cases of microcephaly are caused by pre- or postnatal insults or form part of a dysmorphic syndrome. Among the remainder, with unexplained and often severe microcephaly, a significant proportion is recessively inherited. It is no longer thought that these can be identified purely on the basis of physical appearance.

Craniosynostosis (craniostenosis)

Growth of the skull vault usually occurs along the sutures. In craniosynostosis, one or more of the sutures are inactive, the normal interdigitations are reduced, the suture line becomes obliterated, with bony thickening, and the bones become fused prematurely. The brain is unable to expand in the plane of the closed sutures and the head therefore develops an abnormal shape. Isolated sagittal craniosynostosis results in a boat-shaped head (scaphocephaly) early in infancy. This can be confused with the flattening of the head often seen in infants who were premature. There are usually no associated anomalies and intellect is normal. Surgical treatment is undertaken for purely cosmetic reasons and the results are good if the operation is performed within the first 3 months.

In coronal craniosynostosis, the head is broad

and the anteroposterior diameter is reduced (acrocephaly). In addition, there may be underdevelopment of the maxilla (Crouzon's syndrome) or limb defects such as syndactyly (Apert's syndrome). Plagiocephaly (asymmetry of the head) may result from asymmetric craniosynostosis, although it is more commonly a simple postural anomaly that corrects itself with time.

Children with craniosynostosis may have a number of associated problems, including airway obstruction, middle-ear disease, proptosis, squint, complex eye movement disorders, craniovertebral anomalies, feeding problems, failure to thrive and psychomotor retardation. A significant proportion of these children also have hydrocephalus or develop it after surgery. The manifestations may be subtle and careful follow-up is essential.

In all these conditions the shape of the head is obviously abnormal. The only situation in which a normal-shaped head can occur with craniosynostosis is when all the sutures are involved — total craniosynostosis. In this very rare condition, skull X-ray shows a gross excess of digital markings due to the chronically raised intracranial pressure. The distinction between total craniosynostosis and primary microcephaly causes some unnecessary anxiety; the presence of any suture on the skull X-ray of a baby with microcephaly rules out the diagnosis of total craniosynostosis.

Management. A baby with suspected craniosynostosis should ideally be referred to a specialist craniofacial centre, rather than a general neurosurgical service, even if skull X-ray findings are equivocal. The sutures can be opened by removing a strip of bone and periosteum — craniectomy. The French surgeon Tessier pioneered techniques for the reconstruction of the more complex craniofacial malformations. As with other complex problems requiring treatment at an often distant specialist centre, local supervision of the child's care and support of the family are also vital.

Genetic aspects. Craniosynostosis, uncomplicated by other malformations, is usually sporadic but cases of both dominant and recessive inheritance have been reported. In familial cases the patterns and severity of suture involvement may not be the same in all family members.

Congenital infections

The three infections which are of particular interest as a cause of disability, cytomegalovirus (CMV), rubella and toxoplasmosis, have a number of features in common. The organisms normally cause only trivial or subclinical illness in the adult but, when a primary or first infection occurs in a susceptible (non-immune) woman during pregnancy, they may cause severe fetal damage. Only a proportion of primary maternal infections result in fetal infections, and only a proportion of fetal infections are symptomatic.

Recently congenital infection with human immunodeficiency virus (HIV), the cause of acquired immune deficiency syndrome (AIDS), has become a significant cause of disability in childhood. Childhood AIDS is already widespread in other parts of the world and over the next decade it will become an increasing problem in Europe. Other congenital infections include herpes simplex, chickenpox, parvovirus B19, listeriosis, syphilis and lymphocytic choriomeningitis. Occasionally a child with clinical and CT scan findings suggestive of congenital infection shows no serological evidence of any of these conditions. In a few cases, recurrence in a sibling suggests that some recessive genetic disorder might provide an identical clinical picture.

There has been much concern that young female child-care staff and nurses may be at risk of having congenitally infected infants themselves as a result of acquiring CMV in the course of their work, but in reality the risks are very small (Table 10.10).

Interpretation of laboratory data

The classical clinical features of congenital infection with CMV, rubella, toxoplasmosis and HIV are well known (see Glossary). Diagnosis may not be so easy when these features are absent. The older the child is when first seen, the more difficult it is to interpret laboratory data. The following points should be considered.

1 The first antibody to appear in response to infection is immunoglobulin M (IgM). This has a high molecular weight and therefore does not cross the placenta. It appears within 7–10 days after the infection has been acquired, reaches a plateau and then slowly declines over 4–8 months.

2 Measurement of total IgM in the infant is of little value in the diagnosis of congenital infection. It is essential to assay IgM specific to the suspected infection. This is technically difficult and some methods are more reliable than others. Accurate results can be obtained with the enzyme-linked immunosorbent assay (ELISA) technique. The test is specific (i.e. unlikely to give false-positive results) but is not always a reliable means of diagnosing congenital infection for the reason set out in the next paragraph.

3 If specific IgM antibody is detected in the blood of the newborn infant, it is probable that the baby is infected. Cord-blood tests are less reliable because contamination with maternal blood may give rise to false-positive results. However, if congenital infection occurs in the first 18 weeks, there may be little antibody response, or the baby's IgM may have fallen to undetectable levels by the time he/she is born.

4 IgG antibody appears slightly later than IgM, and production continues indefinitely, although the titres decline from the immediate postinfection peak to lower levels. IgG has a lower molecular weight and therefore crosses the placenta from mother to fetus.

5 The finding of IgG antibody in the infant's blood may indicate either fetal infection or passive transplacental transfer from the mother.

6 If the infant is congenitally infected, IgG will persist and the level may rise further in the early months of life.

7 If the infant is not infected, any IgG antibody found in their blood must come only from the mother and the level will decline in the early months of life. The fact that transplacental transfer of IgG antibody has occurred is not proof that

Table 10.10 Cytomegalovirus (CMV), human immunodeficiency virus (HIV) and hepatitis B — the risks of infection in day nurseries, hospitals, etc.: information and advice to carers

---

CMV

The infection is very common but the risks are very small

The virus is present in saliva, urine and other body fluids

Any child may be shedding virus, not just those who have disability related to CMV — although in the latter the child may shed virus for a longer period of time

Transmission requires intimate contact, e.g. kissing child, child putting fingers in mother's mouth. Sexual transmission is also common

No need to exclude infected children from day nurseries

Risk of CMV infection is not significantly greater in child-care staff than in other young women

HIV

The virus is less infectious than hepatitis B

It is spread by sexual intercourse, blood products, contaminated equipment such as needles

It is *not* spread by normal social contact, droplets, the sucking of toys, shared facilities such as toilets, eating utensils, or by living in the same house, or by normal care routines

There is a tiny risk of infection through open sores, weeping eczema, etc.

The risk of infection by being bitten by an infected child is remote

Infected but otherwise normal children should attend day nursery/school

Infected disabled children who are not continent and those who bite need individual assessment but should usually be able to attend day facilities

Swimming in a chlorinated pool is not a hazard

Mouth-to-mouth resuscitation should make use of a special mask or double-ended airway if possible, but resuscitation should not be withheld if these are not available, as the risk of infection is infinitesimal

'Blood-brother' games (sharing blood), ear-piercing with unsterilized equipment and tattooing are potential causes of infection

Risk of an individual being infected as a result of a needlestick injury is remote

Hepatitis B

Transmitted through breaks in skin or mucous membrane (scratches, needles, tattoos, etc.), blood products, biting, sexual intercourse, via the eyes, or from mother at time of birth. Causes acute or chronic liver disease. Can survive in the environment for weeks

Units for care of disabled are regarded as high-risk areas

Infectivity *much higher* than HIV (Public Health Laboratory Service (PHLS) Hepatitis Subcommittee, 1992)

Precautions for staff working with young children who may have these infections

No indication for antibody-screening of staff or of children using day care facilities

Screening not feasible, therefore assume that *any* child might be carrying one of these viruses

No CMV or AIDS vaccine available yet, but hepatitis B vaccine is available, effective and safe: *all staff must be vaccinated and must have postvaccination antibody measurement*

If child is aggressive or bites (p. 137), plan ahead and take advice from psychologist if needed

Good hygiene is crucial

  Regular hand-washing after changing child, etc.

  Avoid allowing child to kiss or dribble on adult's face

  Separate changing and other surfaces and regularly clean all surfaces

  Cover cuts or abrasions with plasters; gloves for open skin lesions on hands

  Follow recommended policy of the organization concerned regarding waste disposal, blood spillages and surface cleaning

Report all accidents at once

Table 10.11 Drugs with teratogenic effects

Definite teratogens
Thalidomide
Cytotoxic drugs
Radiation
Vitamin A (excess)

Probable teratogens
Alcohol
Phenytoin
Trimethadione
Warfarin
Lithium
Quinine
Sodium valproate

Possible teratogens
Sex hormones
Barbiturates and primidone
Chloroquine
Operating-theatre environment (?nitrous oxide)

the mother has had a primary infection during pregnancy. She may simply have a high antibody level from a previous infection. The finding of specific IgM in her blood at term suggests that she may have had a primary infection during pregnancy, but sensitive assays may detect very low levels of maternal IgM for months or even years after the infection occurred. On the other hand, if the infection occurred in the first trimester, IgM may be undetectable by the end of pregnancy, even with very sensitive tests. Thus both false-positive and false-negative results can occur.

8 The presence of IgG or IgM antibodies in the infant, after the first few weeks of life, may reflect acquired rather than congenital infection.

For all these reasons, diagnosis of congenital infection is difficult unless the infant has the classical clinical features. In most cases, specific IgM measurement and, often, repeat testing on both mother and infant are necessary to confirm or eliminate the diagnosis of congenital infection. It is essential to liaise with the laboratory whenever a congenital infection is suspected. Full details of both mother and infant must be provided. Parents must be told that they may have to wait some time for a definitive answer. Other investigations may help, for example a CT scan, and an eye examination to look for retinopathy.

Other prenatal causes

The fetal alcohol syndrome, hypothyroidism and a variety of other dysmorphic syndromes are described in the Appendix.

Drugs

Parents often worry about drug ingestion in early pregnancy as a cause of their child's disability. Table 10.11 lists those drugs known or suspected to have definite adverse effects in pregnancy. If other drugs have been taken, it may be advisable to check with the manufacturers or a hospital pharmacy to ensure that no new associations have come to light, but in general parents should be reassured that standard medications are unlikely to have done the fetus any harm.

Substance abuse

Mothers who abuse drugs are at particular risk of having infants with a variety of impairments and disabilities. Morphia and heroin abuse do not seem to produce a consistent pattern of abnormalities, but benzodiazepines may lead to a pattern rather similar to that seen in the fetal alcohol syndrome. Cocaine causes lesions in the renal and gastrointestinal tracts, attributed to vascular occlusions, and areas of brain infarction have also been described. In addition to the direct teratogenic effects of these drugs, there are other hazards. The mother may also abuse alcohol; her nutritional state may be poor; she may have episodes of coma leading to fetal hypoxia; she often receives poor antenatal care; there is a high risk of hepatitis B and HIV infection; both mother and baby may become severely ill with withdrawal symptoms. The social situation is often unstable and is complicated further by the presence of a drug-abusing partner, poverty and distrust of statutory agencies.

Perinatal insults

Perinatal disorders which may cause brain injury include asphyxia, meningitis, symptomatic hypoglycaemia and metabolic disorders. Intrapartum asphyxia can cause cerebral palsy with or without learning disability, and is an important cause of profound multiple disability; but it is very rare for intrapartum asphyxia to result in learning disability *without* cerebral palsy. Children with learning disabilities often have a history of abnormal pregnancy or birth, but it is likely that these abnormalities are caused by, rather than the cause of, the brain dysfunction. The high rate of minor and major congenital anomalies affecting organs outside the nervous system provides further evidence that the learning disability often originates in the early months of fetal life (pp. 60 and 316). Similarly, disability is sometimes attributed to breech delivery, but the breech position often occurs because of pre-existing abnormality and is common in, for example, Prader–Willi syndrome, Cornelia de Lange syndrome, fetal alcohol syndrome, and many other syndromes.

There is no doubt that prolonged symptomatic hypoglycaemia can cause brain injury. The hazards of asymptomatic hypoglycaemia are less clear. There is no single statistical value which defines hypoglycaemia in all babies, but levels below 2.6 mmol/l may be associated with reversible neurological dysfunction; it is possible that this may progress to irreversible damage if sufficiently prolonged, even though no dramatic symptoms are observed.

Whatever the perinatal insult may have been, it is important to consider carefully whether it was of sufficient severity to cause the observed impairments. This is not merely an academic point: failure to appreciate the prenatal origins of a disabling condition can result in an inappropriate decision about referral for genetic counselling. Furthermore, the implication that better obstetric care might have prevented the disability causes much unwarranted bitterness and may have medicolegal implications.

The effects of extreme prematurity on intellectual development are difficult to assess. Except for those children with obvious extensive brain damage, in whom cerebral palsy is usually a prominent feature, the outcome in survivors is generally satisfactory with most very-low-birth-weight (VLBW) babies (birth weight below 1.25 kg) being able to attend mainstream primary schools, although nearly one in three will have scholastic difficulties in several subjects. Any reduction in intelligence may partly be attributed to the social or obstetric factors which caused the prematurity, although birth weight is itself a powerful, probably the most powerful, determinant of outcome; the smallest babies tend to have lower scores on tests of intelligence, concentration and motor co-ordination, even after excluding those with demonstrable brain injury. Babies who suffered intrauterine growth retardation tend to do less well than those who were normally grown for gestational age, even if they subsequently show catch-up growth. Hypoglycaemia, apnoeic spells, neonatal fits and suboptimal nutrition in the early weeks of life may be contributory causes of learning disability in this group of children.

Neonatal ultrasound scans in low-birth-weight infants have some predictive value. Normal scans are rarely associated with major impairments, but there is a high incidence of subtle motor problems, high-tone hearing loss and minor cognitive deficits. In particular, simultaneous information-processing seems to be more difficult for these children than sequential processing. Uncomplicated periventricular haemorrhage has a similarly satisfactory outcome, but both minor and major impairments are much more likely if the scan shows ventricular dilatation, hydrocephalus or cerebral atrophy.

Postnatal disorders

Examples of the disorders which may cause learning disability are given in Table 10.1 (see above).

Often there are other defects as well, such as cerebral palsy, cortical blindness and secondary microcephaly. When a cerebral insult occurs after the neonatal period, it is usually possible to determine that previous development was normal and that the insult is the sole cause of any residual disability. However, parents often attribute the child's disability to a postnatal event such as immunization, a minor illness or a convulsion. Careful probing will reveal whether or not there was in fact any change or regression in development after the incident.

Two possible postnatal causes of learning disability merit further discussion here. Febrile fits are described in Chapter 17.

Pertussis immunization

Some children suffer severe convulsions and permanent brain damage following pertussis immunization. However, a severe encephalopathy with fits may also occur in babies who have not been immunized. Since immunization is a common event, it is statistically inevitable that some cases of encephalopathy will coincide with a recent immunization; it cannot be assumed that the events are necessarily related.

The National Childhood Encephalopathy Study showed that encephalopathic illness is commonest at precisely the peak age for immunization and that pertussis immunization could, at worst, only account for a minority of cases. The risk of permanent severe brain damage was estimated at one case per 300 000 immunizations (with wide confidence limits). Some authorities now doubt that neurological damage is ever caused by pertussis vaccine; certainly it is extremely rare. The new acellular vaccines have been shown to have fewer minor side-effects but their efficacy is uncertain and it would be extremely difficult to demonstrate their superiority over the safe and effective vaccines currently in use.

Pertussis immunization should certainly not be accepted as the cause of a child's neurological impairment unless there is a close temporal relationship between the procedure and a severe neurological illness. Even in these circumstances, the apparent association may be spurious and the possibility of another diagnosis, such as a metabolic disorder, should be remembered.

There is no reason to think that children with other neurological disorders are at increased risk of encephalopathy from pertussis vaccine and they should be offered immunization in the normal way. Only in the case of an unexplained and uncharacterized neurological illness should the vaccine be temporarily withheld, to ensure that the parents do not assume a causal connection rather than because of any real risk.

Lead poisoning

This deserves detailed consideration because it is the cause of much public and parental concern. Lead poisoning may present as a severe encephalopathy with convulsions and cerebral oedema. There is a significant risk of permanent neurological damage. Children with acute encephalopathy have usually had a heavy exposure to sources such as old paint or batteries. A detailed account will be found in standard paediatric texts.

Chronic lead poisoning is more difficult to recognize and its significance as a cause of hyperactivity and other neurological impairments is controversial. Pica accounts for significant lead consumption in some children (p. 140). The whole population is continually exposed to low levels of lead from many sources, including food, water, air and dust, and much of this occurs naturally. There is undoubtedly a contribution from petrol engines and industrial emissions, both directly through the air and indirectly through soil, food and water, but it is uncertain how much total lead intake or blood lead levels would fall if these sources of pollution were to be removed.

There is a correlation between increasing lead levels in blood and other tissues and poorer performance on measures of intellect, academic achievement, concentration and behaviour. The differences between children with low and high lead levels, although statistically significant, are small. In terms of intelligence, for instance, the difference is less than 5 IQ points. As with all epidemiological studies, there is no proof of a cause-and-effect relationship and there are several possible explanations for the results. For example, it is possible that increased lead ingestion occurs as a result of some other factor which is also responsible for the neurological impairment, so that the elevated lead level is merely a marker for another adverse factor.

At present, the official recommendation in the UK is that efforts should be made to identify and reduce sources of lead exposure if a child's lead level exceeds $25\,\mu g/100\,ml$. Few clinicians would consider active treatment unless the level was much higher than this. At present, it is unwise to attribute minor intellectual impairment or behaviour problems to marginally elevated lead levels. Screening is not recommended. Nevertheless, lead has no known beneficial effects and, in view of the damage which lead pollution *may* be causing, it is desirable to reduce lead contamination in the environment.

Environmental causes

Environmental causes of learning disability, including 'subcultural deprivation' and malnutrition, are discussed in Chapter 2.

What to tell the parents

Terminology

Many parents do not understand that the various terms used to describe learning disabilities (p. 147) have essentially the same meaning. Although recent terminology represents a shift in society's perceptions of disability and for that reason is to be welcomed, there is a danger that parents will fail to understand its significance and will not make the link with the older terminology of 'mental handicap'. They may then be devastated when some less enlightened professional or relative describes their child as 'mentally handicapped' or even 'subnormal'. It is important to spend time helping parents to navigate their way through this maze of changing terminology and its significance. For parents from other cultures, it may be necessary in some cases to explain that mental handicap is not the same as mental illness, since some languages do not recognize this distinction.

Some parents may read or see television programmes about specific language impairment, dysphasia, autism, hyperactivity or dyspraxia and may consider these labels appropriate to their child. In the past such parents were often suspected of searching for a more socially acceptable label, but this is rarely the primary motivation. More often, they have been led to believe, by voluntary societies or the popular press, that such conditions are more likely to respond to specific medical treatment, expert therapy or specialized teaching than is 'simple' global learning disability. The fact that the precise 'medical' cause of learning disability is often uncertain causes much distress and is perhaps the reason why so many parents continue to seek a label that is more meaningful to them. This problem is further discussed on pp. 1–2.

Investigation

Many parents find it hard to accept that, in spite of advances in medical technology, it is often not possible to identify the precise cause even in children with profound learning disability. They should be warned of this fact *before* investigation is undertaken. The nature of each test should be briefly explained, since many people have only heard of blood tests for anaemia and blood grouping.

Intensive investigation of a child with learning disability can rarely be justified by the hope of finding a treatable disorder, but an exact diagnosis is nevertheless useful to the parents for several reasons. The recognition of a specific syndrome may alert one to search for associated impairments recorded by previous observers, and allows more accurate genetic advice to be given. Furthermore, for the parents an explanation of the cause of the child's disability is very important.

There are no 'routine' investigations for learning disability. The history and physical examination occasionally suggest a specific diagnosis or line of investigation. If the child has dysmorphic features the advice of a clinical geneticist may be invaluable. Most children with biochemical disorders look physically normal, but there are exceptions — for example, Menkes' syndrome, homocystinuria, and some LSDs. Developmental regression or the presence of additional findings such as profound hypotonia (p. 254), deafness, retinopathy, coarse facial features, intractable epilepsy, hepatosplenomegaly or other unexplained physical signs would usually be an indication for a full paediatric neurology work-up, best carried out at a tertiary centre.

There are, however, many children with learning disabilities who exhibit none of these characteristics. This is particularly true for those in the mild or moderate range of disability. Many of these children present with speech and language delay and are often managed entirely in community clinics. It would not be feasible to refer them all for extensive investigation. In this situation the clinician has a dilemma. The parents may expect investigations to be performed, and there is always a fear that one might miss a diagnosis which, even if not treatable, might have important genetic implications. On the other hand, experience shows that the yield of even the most extensive investigation protocol is negligible in the absence of the features mentioned above.

A chromosome study and a fragile-X test are probably the two most valuable tests in this situation. These can be justified on the grounds that chromosome disorders, particularly fragile-X, can be associated with relatively mild learning disability and dysmorphic features are not reliably present. Chromosome analysis is expensive but the fragile-X DNA test is now a low-cost routine procedure and should be requested without hesitation for girls as well as boys.

Parents often request or even demand a scan. A CT or MRI scan may be worthwhile if the learning disability is profound, the size or shape of the head is abnormal, the disability is progress-ive or the child also has cerebral palsy or epilepsy. In cases of mild or moderate learning disability without any of these features, the yield of a scan is extremely small and it is doubtful whether the benefits justify the cost, the need for anaesthesia and, for CT, the not inconsiderable radiation dosage involved.

An EEG is not routine but it should be done when one suspects hypsarrhythmia, non-convulsive status, Angelman's syndrome or infantile neuronal ceroid lipofuscinosis. In these conditions the findings are often specific and virtually diagnostic. In most other situations, the EEG will be normal or show non-specific findings. It will not predict whether or not the child is likely to develop epilepsy or reveal anything about the child's intellect, as parents so often imagine. Visual evoked response (VER) and ERG may be useful in some cases (p. 231).

Parents are surprised and sometimes disbelieving that scans and EEGs can be normal even when the child so obviously has a serious impairment of brain function. The analogy of a defective TV set can be helpful; when one looks inside the set the components may all look normal and yet there may be a defect at microscopic level in one of the circuit boards. The parents need to understand that existing scanners cannot look at the cellular level of function in the brain, only at the crude anatomy.

The value of routine biochemical tests is uncertain. Blood calcium levels and a creatine phosphokinase (CPK) estimation may be worthwhile because pseudohypoparathyroidism and Duchenne muscular dystrophy (which may present with developmental and speech delay) are easily missed. Similarly, a urine MPS estimation is justifiable because, although most MPS diseases produce coarsening of the facial features, which provides a helpful clue to the diagnosis, the early signs of Sanfilippo's syndrome are similar to those seen in the large numbers of children with non-specific speech and language delay accompanied by middle-ear and upper-airway disease. The possibility of hypothyroidism should be remembered, but this is unlikely to cause learning difficulties in the absence of other diagnostic clues. Tests for congenital infection (the so-called 'TORCH screen' for toxoplasmosis, rubella, cytomegalovirus and herpes) are difficult to interpret (p. 163) and are best done in consultation with the laboratory. Phenylalanine should be measured in the mother's blood in cases of unexplained microcephaly.

Some clinicians also routinely undertake some or all of the following: urine amino and organic acid studies, blood ammonia, uric acid (Lesch–Nyhan syndrome, molybdenum cofactor deficiency), very-long-chain fatty acids (peroxisomal disorders), cholesterol (abetalipoproteinaemia) and specific enzymes for lysosomal and mitochondrial disorders. The presence of a prominent movement disorder raises other possibilities (p. 253).

Clinicians working in this field need guidance on the role, value and health economics of intensive investigation in children with apparently non-specific and non-progressive learning disability. At present, the policy for investigation, if it exists at all, seems to be based mainly on personal idiosyncrasies.

Genetic aspects

If single-gene disorders, common dysmorphic syndromes and chromosomal abnormalities are excluded, recurrence risks for learning disabilities are usually based on empirical evidence. The presence of identical anomalies in two or more siblings born to normal parents may be suggestive of recessive inheritance, even if no exact diagnosis can be made. Learning disability with multiple congenital anomalies occurring as a sporadic case has a low risk of recurrence, about 1 in 30 to 1 in 50, but it is essential to exclude the many rare single-gene malformation syndromes. Learning disability associated with cerebral palsy has similarly a low risk of recurrence, except in some diplegias (p. 253), as do those cases with idiopathic epilepsy or severe hypotonia.

In pure learning disability without significant anomalies, microcephaly or severe epilepsy, recurrence risks depend on the sex of the disabled child. When the proband is a boy, the risk is about 1 in 20, if fragile-X is excluded and there is no pedigree suggestive of X-linkage (p. 155). If the proband is a girl the risk is about 1 in 30.

Other checks

It is vital to ensure that all children with learning disabilities have a competent audiological assessment and an eye examination. In the case of recognized syndromes, an active search should be made for the other impairments known to be associated with the disorder. In particular, cardiac defects are easily missed. The usual programme of child surveillance, including growth monitoring and immunization, should not be neglected.

Prognosis

Parents will often want to discuss the prognosis for walking and talking. Unless the child's learning disability is profound and is associated with cerebral palsy or extreme hypotonia, or the child has a progressive disorder, the parents should be given an optimistic opinion on this point, although the age at which the child may walk is often very difficult to predict. The majority of learning-disabled children also acquire some speech but, as this may be slow, other approaches to communication should be discussed (p. 201). Most parents are also concerned about daily care needs, support services and the prospects for the child's education and future independence; these topics are discussed in Chapters 7 and 8.

The diagnosis of learning disability may raise alarming fears about the future. These perceptions may be derived from a variety of sources such as childhood memories, the popular press or uninformed prejudice. In recent years, however, society has become more open and more accepting about severely disabled persons and parents are more likely to have some understanding of disability, so that these fears are less prevalent than they used to be. Nevertheless, learning-disabled boys may still be perceived as potential violent and aggressive rapists and girls as becoming promiscuous or pregnant. The management of menstruation may also cause concern (p. 145). These fears should not be ignored, but parents can be told that sexually aggressive behaviour in boys is seldom a major problem. Promiscuity and unwanted pregnancy are no greater a problem than in normal girls and are easier to avoid because the learning-disabled teenager is more likely to be under regular close supervision.

A common anxiety for parents is that their child will be permanently dependent upon them and this will raise fears for their future care if he/she outlives them. The level of intelligence, if this can be measured accurately, provides a guide. Those with an IQ in the MLD range (50−70) will be able to undertake unskilled or semiskilled labour, although they will suffer from the fluctuations of the employment market more than those better qualified. Given sufficient schooling, the vast majority will be able to live independently unless they also have problems with language, mobility or neurological and psychiatric disorder. Only a very small proportion of adults with an IQ in the 35−50 range will acquire useful literacy and numeracy skills and all of them will need supervision at work. It is very unlikely that a child with an IQ in this range will eventually live independently. An adult with an IQ below 35 is highly likely to have associated neurological or communication problems and will need close supervision or care tailored for high-dependency needs.

Older parents, and grandparents, who have memories of long-stay mental hospitals, may be appalled at the thought of the child spending their life in such a place. They should be told that the education and care of learning-disabled adults is improving steadily, and a more normal existence in small units or hostel accommodation can be anticipated. There are now plans to accommodate even the most profoundly disabled people in this way. Some parents will also wish to make financial provision for the child's future and should consult one of the voluntary organizations for information about savings schemes and other financial manoeuvres.

Life expectancy

Questions about life expectancy need careful handling because they may conceal several concerns (p. 113). Although accurate data are scarce, the life expectancy of people with severe learning disabilities is probably reduced, for several reasons. In some cases the underlying condition is progressive, leading to increasing physical and intellectual impairment. The ability to adopt healthy lifestyles and access medical care may be reduced. The most important factors for prediction of life expectancy are: (i) severity of intellectual impairment; (ii) degree of immobility; and (iii) swallowing and chewing difficulties. Epilepsy and scoliosis do not appear to have much additional effect, perhaps because the other factors have such a profound impact on survival in people with multiple impairments.

For children who are essentially immobile and have little or no hand function, and have profound intellectual impairment and feeding problems, median survival is probably to the late teens or early 20s. The figure is probably similar whether or not they have been diagnosed as having cerebral palsy. For mobile children with learning disabilities and for children with cerebral palsy of lesser severity, survival is much longer, probably at least into the 30s or 40s and in some cases beyond this.

Management

Once the diagnosis has been established and all reasonable investigations have been completed, the management of children with learning disabilities, from the purely medical point of view, is largely supportive. It is important to explain and discuss the young person's limitations, in language they can understand. The books by Hollins are useful for this purpose.

Liaison with education services, parental support and the management of behavioural difficulties are discussed in Chapters 7, 8 and 9 and that of epilepsy in Chapter 17.

References and further reading

Aicardi, J. (1992) *Diseases of the Nervous System in Childhood.* Clinics in Developmental Medicine, No. 120. Mackeith Press, London.

American Psychiatric Association (1987) *Diagnostic and Statistical Manual of Mental Disorders*, (3rd edn, revised). American Psychiatric Association, Washington, DC.

Carr, J. (1988) Six weeks to twenty-one years old: a longitudinal study of children with Down's syndrome and their families. *Journal of Psychology and Psychiatry*, **29**, 407–31.

Cuckle, H. (1994) A rational screening policy for Down's syndrome. *European Journal of Public Health*, **4**, 77–8.

European Collaborative Study. (1990) Neurological signs in young children with human immunodeficiency virus infection. *Pediatric Infectious Disease Journal*, **9**, 402–6.

Fletcher, J., Hicks, N.R., Kay, J.D.S. and Boyd, P.A. (1995) Using decision analysis to compare policies for antenatal screening for Down's syndrome. *BMJ*, **311**, 351–7.

Gable, R.A. and Warren, S.F. (1993) *Strategies for Teaching Students with Mild to Severe Mental Retardation.* Jessica Kingsley Publishers, London.

Gath, A. and Gumley, D. (1987) Retarded children and their siblings. *Journal of Child Psychology and Psychiatry*, **28**, 715–30.

Gath, A. (1988) Mentally handicapped people as parents. *Journal of Child Psychology and Psychiatry*, **29**, 739–44.

Gooskens, R.H.J.M., Willemse, J., Bijsma, J.B. and Hanlo, P.W. (1988) Megalencephaly: definition and classification. *Brain Development*, **10**, 1–7.

Hagerman, R.J. (1992) Fragile X syndrome: advances and controversy. *Journal of Child Psychology and Psychiatry*, **33**, 1127–39.

Hawdon, J.M. and Aynsey-Green, A. (1994) Hypoglycaemia in the newborn. *Current Paediatrics*, **4**(3), 168–73.

Hollins, S., Sinason, V., Hutchinson, D. and Webb, B. (1993) *A New Home in the Community.* Sovereign Series Books, St George's Mental Health Library, London.

Hollins, S., Sinason, V., Hutchinson, D. and Webb, B. (1993) *Bob Tells All.* Sovereign Series Books, St George's Mental Health Library, London.

Hollins, S., Sinason, V., Hutchinson, D. and Webb, B. (1993) *Jenny Speaks Out.* Sovereign Series Books, St George's Mental Health Library, London.

Hollins, S., Sinason, V., Hutchinson, D. and Webb, B. (1993) *Peter's New Home.* Sovereign Series Books, St

George's Mental Health Library, London.

Hutton, J.L., Cooke, T. and Pharaoh, P.O.D. (1994) Life expectancy in children with cerebral palsy. *BMJ*, **309**, 431–5.

Jones, K.J.L. (1988) *Smith's Recognisable Patterns of Human Malformation.* W.B. Saunders, Philadelphia.

Land, J. (1994) Diagnosis of developmental delay: the metabolic biochemist's approach. *Current Paediatrics*, **4**(4), 216–21.

Lissauer, T., Ghaus, K. and Rivers, R. (1994) Maternal drug abuse — effects on the child. *Current Paediatrics*, **4**(4), 235–9.

Lunt, P.W. (1994) Diagnosis of developmental delay: the geneticist's approach. *Current Paediatrics*, **4**(4), 222–7.

Minns, R.A. (1991) *Problems of Intracranial Pressure in Childhood.* Clinics in Developmental Medicine, No. 113/114. Mackeith Press, London.

Paneth, N., Rudelli, R., Kazam, E. and Monte, W. (1994) *Brain Damage in the Preterm Infant.* Clinics in Developmental Medicine, No. 131. Mackeith Press, London.

Public Health Laboratory Service (PHLS) Hepatitis Subcommittee (1992) Exposure to hepatitis B virus: guidance on post-exposure prophylaxis. *Communicable Disease Report*, **2** (review no. 9), R97–101.

Public Health Laboratory Service (PHLS) Working Party (1990) TORCH syndrome and TORCH screening. *Lancet*, **335**, 1559.

Ratcliffe, S.G., Masera, N., Pan, H. and McKie, M. (1994) Head circumference and IQ of children with sex chromosome abnormalities. *Developmental Medicine and Child Neurology*, **36**(6), 533–44.

Tymchuk, A.J. (1992) Predicting adequacy of parenting by people with mental retardation. *Child Abuse and Neglect*, **16**, 165–78.

Van Baar, A. and De Graaf, B.M.T. (1994) Cognitive development at preschool-age of infants of drug-dependent mothers. *Developmental Medicine and Child Neurology*, **36**(12), 1063–75.

Von Knorring, A. (1991) Children of Alcoholics. *Journal of Child Psychology and Psychiatry*, **32**, 411–21.

Wentz, K.R. and Marcuse, E.K. (1991) Diphtheria–tetanus–pertussis vaccine and serious neurological illness: an updated review of the epidemiological evidence. *Pediatrics*, **87**(3), 287–97.

World Health Organization (1992) *ICD-10: The ICD-10 Classification of Mental and Behavioural Disorders: Clinical Descriptions and Diagnostic Guidelines.* World Health Organization, Geneva.

CHAPTER 11

Communication Disorders

Abnormalities of speech and language development are the commonest single reason for referral to a child development centre (CDC), with a peak age of presentation between the second and third birthdays. In many of these children, intellect and hearing are normal, and unclear or inadequate speech is the only problem, but failure to develop speech may also be the presenting feature of other serious disorders, such as learning disability, hearing loss or autism. Because such a premium is placed on communicative competence, even apparently well-informed parents sometimes focus on the lack of speech and fail to recognize the significance of delays in other aspects of their child's development.

In addition to those children in whom failure to develop speech is the predominant and presenting complaint, there are many others with established major disabilities such as cerebral palsy, mental retardation or severe deafness, which cause major difficulties in communication; indeed, the parents often regard this as the child's greatest problem.

The term 'communication disorder' is defined in varying ways and is not itself a diagnosis. In this chapter, it is used as an umbrella term for a group of conditions and disorders characterized by impaired production and, in some cases, comprehension of spoken language. Some but not all of these children also have difficulties with communication in a broader sense, including body language, gesture and empathy with the feelings of others. Note, however, that some authors restrict the use of the term 'communication disorder' to children who have these more wide-ranging difficulties. Isolated reading deficits (p. 319) are not normally regarded as communication disorders.

Central to the concept of a communication disorder is the realization that profound impairments of language can coexist with normal or superior ability in other areas of intellectual function. The diagnosis does not indicate any single underlying pathology. The justification for grouping these conditions together is fourfold. Firstly, they all require a similar approach to assessment. Secondly, they often blend into each other. Thirdly, there may well be more than one cause (e.g. pseudobulbar palsy and global learning disability) for the final communicative problem. Fourthly, although the details of management may differ widely, the principles are common to all of them; it is crucial to describe the mechanisms or deficits rather than taking delayed speech as a diagnosis in its own right or seeing it as a symptom of a single underlying condition.

Problems of terminology

There is no completely satisfactory classification of communication disorders. Although the literature gives the impression that there are a number of clearly definable entities, in reality there are many children whose problems vary widely in severity and do not fit comfortably into any one category; they may have partial or attenuated forms of the entities described, may represent extreme deviations of a normal distribution, or may move from one category to another as they mature.

Children with communication disorders have attracted the interest of several disciplines, each with its own conceptual framework and jargon. Thus paediatric neurologists seek lesions within the brain and talk of 'dysphasia' and 'dyspraxia'; psychologists postulate the existence of auditory processing systems; linguists describe the child's speech in terms of phonology, prosody, syntax, semantics and pragmatics; teachers and speech and language therapists try to identify clinically useful patterns and treatment needs.

Delay, disorder and impairment

After excluding children with an obvious cause for their communication problems (for example, deafness, cleft palate, cerebral palsy or severe learning disability), there remains a group of children whose rate of language acquisition is outside 'normal limits' (see Chapter 2) and cannot be explained by any identifiable neurological lesion or environmental disadvantage. A 'developmental' origin is usually inferred; this seems to be short-hand for the assumption that the biological and environmental processes required for language development have gone wrong in some ill-defined way.

The term 'delay' has been widely used in cases where a young child's language appears to be developing along normal lines and yet at a rate slower than expected by the parents or predicted by other evidence of intellectual normality. Implicit in the term is an assumption that the child will 'catch up'. This is true for some children, but others may have difficulties throughout childhood and, indeed, these may be lifelong. There is currently no reliable way of predicting the outcome in the first few years of life. Parents should not be encouraged to believe that the term 'delay' implies any guarantees regarding the progress to be expected.

Paula Menyuk in 1964 was probably the first to make a formal distinction between 'language delay', in which the child's language is similar to that of a normal younger child, and 'language disorder', in which qualitative abnormalities are present. This distinction has been the subject of much controversy and research. It now seems clear that there is no absolute difference between the two and therefore the single term 'specific language impairment' (SLI) is now favoured to describe children with unexplained language difficulties. This has the merit of avoiding the 'delay or disorder' controversy and implies no assumptions about aetiology. The term 'delay', instead of having the status of a diagnostic label, is reserved for the unresolved problem of a young child who is slow to talk for reasons that have yet to be established.

Separate categories or a continuum of impairment?

Early accounts of children with communication disorders of obscure origin focused on those with very severe difficulties and various diagnostic categories were coined. For example, many of these children were unable to speak at all and were labelled 'aphasic', or had no comprehension of speech or non-speech sounds ('auditory agnosia'). With the increasing sophistication of parents and primary care professionals, however, more and more children referred for assessment are found to have similar but much less severe impairments of language development, sometimes coexisting in one child and evolving over a period of time. It now seems that these early reports represented the extreme end of a spectrum of dysfunction.

The concept of a continuum of language competence now looks more attractive than relying solely on a categorical approach. At one end of the scale are highly verbal and articulate children who talk early and master their native language rapidly and without effort. At the other extreme are those with considerable difficulty in learning one or more aspects of language. In some of these, pathological processes may be inferred or demonstrated and specific diagnostic 'labels' may be warranted. Examples include auditory agnosia and acquired receptive aphasia. In the middle are a large number of children for whom 'labels' seem to work less well.

Similarly, although classical autism is rare, a larger number of children are described as having 'mild autism' or 'some autistic features'. The central feature of autism is now thought to be an impairment of reciprocal or empathic social interaction, possibly based on an inability to find other people interesting and uniquely important in human activities. A more helpful concept is that there is a continuum of severity, extending from classical autism through Asperger's syndrome and linking with normal variation in this area of development. (This is not the same as 'sociability', which is an aspect of temperament governing the extent to which a child seeks the company of others.)

To complicate matters further, not only is each child different in the extent of their language and social deficits, but they differ also in intellectual and motor abilities and in temperamental styles. Slow or arrested development in these areas will have implications for language development. In children with complex communication disorders it is often necessary to assess and specify not just language functioning but level of intelligence, social interactive skills, motor development, other cognitive features (such as rigidity of thought) and sociability according to temperament. In some children, hearing defects may also contribute to the overall problem, and yet are not in themselves of sufficient severity to account for the whole picture.

Multiaxial description

For complex communication disorders we favour the use of a multiaxial descriptive profile for each child (Fig. 11.1), so that a statement can be made about the severity of the child's difficulties on each of three dimensions of language, social interaction and (non-verbal) intelligence. A further subdivision can usefully be made according to whether the language impairment involves primarily production (expressive language) or also comprehension (receptive ability). It is often helpful also to specify the degree of rigidity of thought or routine-dependence since this is not uncommon in severe SLI.

Although we relate such a profile where possible to one of the recognized categorical 'syndromes' (such as autism), it is made clear to parents and other professionals that each child is unique and that therefore to some extent a categorical diagnosis is an artificial exercise. Some parents welcome a multiaxial approach as being more practical and acceptable than a single label. Nevertheless, many parents also value 'shorthand' terms like 'autism' or 'Asperger's syndrome', when explaining their child's problems to relatives, friends and teachers. It is wise also to retain categorical terms when writing official reports for other agencies.

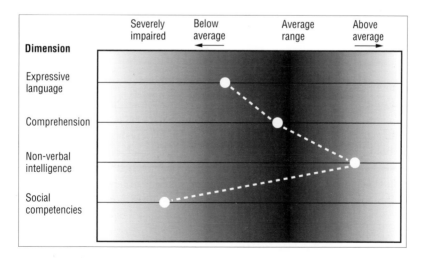

Fig. 11.1 A diagrammatic representation of four axes used for explaining communication problems to parents. The example suggests a child with modest language impairment, at least normal intelligence, but severely reduced social competence.

Comorbidity with psychiatric disorder

Many children with communication disorders also have emotional, temperamental and behavioural difficulties, and child psychiatrists may approach their problems with priorities different from those of the speech therapist. The association with psychological problems may partly be due to the children's difficulty in expressing themselves and in understanding their parents' explanations and instructions. This is probably not the complete explanation; sometimes there seems to be a common cause for both psychological and language difficulties, as in the tendency for hyperactivity and language impairments to associate. Furthermore, parents or teachers are more likely to rate the behaviour of a child with communication difficulties in negative terms (shy, difficult, un-co-operative, etc.), so that these become the priority for referral.

Behavioural and psychological problems often persist, sometimes into the teens, and are often accompanied by low self-esteem and school failure. Conversely, previously unsuspected speech and language impairment may present in later childhood at child psychiatry clinics because of emotional or behavioural problems.

Practical approach to assessment of communication disorders

The aim of assessment is to clarify the nature, cause, prognosis and management of the child's communication disorder, not to impress other professionals with a mixture of sophisticated neurological and linguistic terminology. Recognition of the classical patterns of communication disorder is crucial and, because of the problem of associated difficulties in other areas of personal and physical functioning, a full appraisal of the child is mandatory.

As a general rule, parents and other professionals welcome a statement, in plain English, and in writing (p. 103), along the following lines.
1 The nature of the child's communicative impairments, how they are related to each other, and how they are changing over time.

2 The extent to which they are explainable by general developmental delay.
3 The presence of a particular type, pattern or syndrome of communication disorder.
4 The underlying cause. Can it be treated medically? Is it inherited?
5 What is likely to happen in the future.
6 How the child can be helped.

Patterns of communication disorder

Although each child with a communication disorder is unique, four patterns of impairment can be identified.
1 A group of disorders in which the primary problem is in producing speech, because of either mechanical (anatomical) defects or impaired neuromuscular control of the speech apparatus.
2 Under the heading of SLI, all disorders characterized by problems of language comprehension and/or production for which there is no identifiable explanation.
3 A subgroup with a history of an onset and deterioration. These are rare and are considered in less detail.
4 A group in whom language impairment is accompanied by problems with social interaction.

Pattern 1: disorders affecting speech production

Neurological causes of dysarthria

The term 'dysarthria' denotes defective articulation, attributable to disordered function of the articulatory organs. It should be distinguished from 'functional' disorders of sound production, i.e. those in which no anatomical or neurological abnormality can be demonstrated ('phonological' disorders, p. 183).

The cerebral palsies

Children with pyramidal or extrapyramidal lesions often have pseudobulbar palsy (p. 350), which causes varying degrees of dysarthria, or, in the most severely affected, anarthria. There may also be dysphasia, but this can be difficult or impossible to assess. In addition, many childen with cerebral palsy have learning difficulties, hearing loss or visual impairment, which adds to their difficulties with communication.

Spasticity of speech musculature is associated with slow laboured speech, difficulty with precise tongue movements, and tongue thrusting. In athetosis the speech is jerky and poorly articulated due to impaired control of the speech and respiratory musculature, and high-frequency deafness is a common additional problem. Similarly, there is often severe speech delay in cases of ataxia, and the intonation pattern is often abnormal.

Rare causes

Other rare causes of dysarthria include congenital pseudobulbar palsy, the opercular syndrome and Moebius syndrome (see Glossary).

Structural causes of impaired speech production

Cleft lip and palate

Within the cleft lip and palate group of defects, there is a wide spectrum of severity, ranging from minor deformities such as notching of the lip or bifid uvula to complete unilateral or bilateral clefts of lip, alveolus and palate (Fig. 11.2). The incidence is approximately 1 in 600 live births. There are genetic, embryological and epidemiological differences between cleft lip, with or without cleft palate, and isolated cleft palate. Cleft lip, with or without cleft palate, is more common in boys than girls and in Caucasians than blacks. Isolated cleft palate occurs in 0.5/1000 births, is commoner in girls and has no racial predilection. Median clefts of the lip are rare (less than 1%) but should not be confused with severe bilateral

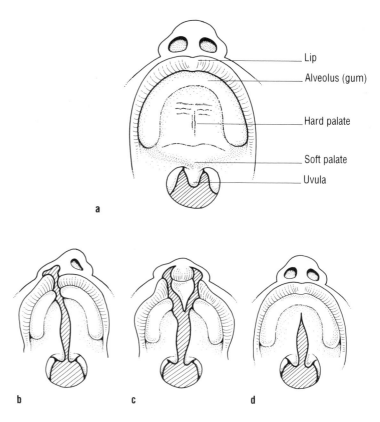

Fig. 11.2 **a,** Anatomy of the normal palate. **b,** Right unilateral cleft lip and palate. **c,** Bilateral cleft lip and palate. **d,** Cleft palate. From Watson and Pigott (1991).

clefts, since the former are usually associated with other severe cerebral or facial malformations.

Syndromes. Over 250 syndromes including clefts of lip or palate have been described. Some of these are chromosomal or have a single-gene inheritance, while others are sporadic or show no clear-cut pattern of inheritance. The more common syndromes include the velocardiofacial syndrome; Van der Woude's syndrome; Pierre Robin anomaly and Stickler syndrome; fetal alcohol syndrome; facioauriculovertebral anomalad; Treacher–Collins syndrome.

Associated anomalies. The lowest frequency of associated anomalies is found with cleft lip and the highest with isolated cleft palate. Earlier studies found that less than 10% of children with clefts had identifiable syndromes, but more recently up to a half have been reported to have at least one other anomaly. The commonest additional findings are microcephaly, short stature, learning difficulties, other craniofacial malformations and eye defects, but any organ or system can be affected. In many children the clustering of anomalies does not represent any identifiable syndrome.

In those cases of cleft lip or palate which do not form part of a specific syndrome, inheritance is probably multifactorial, with a number of genes interacting with unknown factors in the environment. However, some families are known where isolated cleft lip, with or without cleft palate, is inherited as a dominant trait, with variable penetrance and expression. For genetic counselling, it is essential to rule out the numerous syndromes mentioned above. Empirical risk figures are available for cases where the cleft does not form part of any known syndrome. Recurrence risks increase with the severity of the cleft.

Management. Cleft lip is obvious at birth; isolated cleft palate should be detected in the routine neonatal examination, but submucous cleft is easily overlooked (see below). Inspection for other anomalies is essential, followed if necessary by appropriate investigations. Management of clefts is undertaken by a multidisciplinary team, including the plastic surgeon, orthodontist, speech and language therapist, oral surgeon, dentist, ear, nose and throat (ENT) surgeon and audiologist. An early visit by the specialists who will treat the baby, and photographs of previous patients before and after surgery, help the parents through the initial shock of recognition. Primary repair of the lip may be undertaken in the neonatal period but is most commonly performed at about 3 months of age, and the palate between 6 and 18 months. Complications of surgery include breakdown of the repair, hypertrophic scars, stenosis of the nostril, palatal fistula and palatal incompetence.

Advice on feeding techniques may be needed, as babies with clefts may be slow to feed, particularly if they have other anomalies. Many ingenious devices have been used such as the Haberman feeder (available from Arthrodax Surgical Ltd, see Appendix), invented by the mother of a baby with Pierre Robin syndrome. The Rosti feeder is cheaper and is currently popular. These feeders are pleasant to use and significantly reduce the time taken to feed the baby (Fig. 11.3).

Regular supervision by a speech and language therapist should begin as soon as possible. Further surgery may be needed to improve the appearance and function of lip or palate. Dental problems are common. Advice on hygiene and diet are vital, fluoride should be introduced early and regular dental supervision must be maintained. Orthodontic treatment is often needed when the secondary teeth have erupted. Secretory otitis media affects up to 90% of these children, and regular hearing and ENT checks should be arranged. Adenotonsillectomy should be performed only after consultation with the plastic surgeon, since this operation may compromise palatal function. Growth should be monitored, since there is an increased incidence of both growth hormone deficiency and unexplained short stature.

Speech and language therapy. The palate and the posterior and lateral walls of the pharynx together form the 'velopharyngeal sphincter', which controls the flow of air through the nose. Because

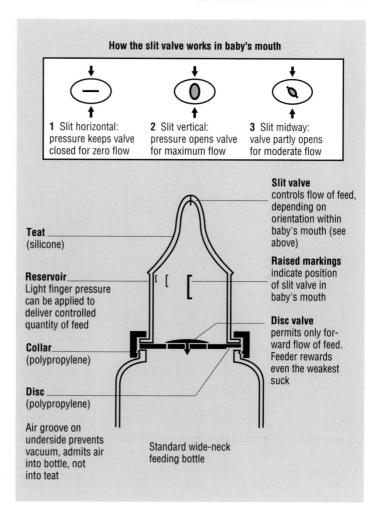

How the slit valve works in baby's mouth

1 Slit horizontal: pressure keeps valve closed for zero flow

2 Slit vertical: pressure opens valve for maximum flow

3 Slit midway: valve partly opens for moderate flow

Slit valve controls flow of feed, depending on orientation within baby's mouth (see above)

Teat (silicone)

Raised markings indicate position of slit valve in baby's mouth

Reservoir Light finger pressure can be applied to deliver controlled quantity of feed

Disc valve permits only forward flow of feed. Feeder rewards even the weakest suck

Collar (polypropylene)

Disc (polypropylene)

Air groove on underside prevents vacuum, admits air into bottle, not into teat

Standard wide-neck feeding bottle

Fig. 11.3 The Haberman feeder was invented by the mother of a baby with Pierre Robin syndrome. It can be used to give expressed breast milk. Courtesy of M. Haberman.

palatal structure, function and musculature are abnormal in cleft palate, there is an uncontrollable escape of air through the nose, making the speech hypernasal. Articulation of many consonants is defective and there may also be delay in expressive language development.

Prolonged speech and language therapy may be needed to improve these defects, even after a successful surgical repair. If significant palatal incompetence persists after 6 months' therapy, full reassessment is indicated. The child with persistent nasal escape after primary closure of

the palate may benefit from various surgical procedures, such as pharyngoplasty, in which the posterior wall of the pharynx is built forwards to improve the function of the sphincter.

'Congenital palatal incompetence' ('cleft palate speech without cleft palate'). This may result from neurological disorders or from anatomical defects, such as velopharyngeal disproportion, in which the pharynx is large in proportion to the palate. Occasionally the speech problem only becomes apparent when adenoidectomy unmasks an

imbalance between the depth of the pharynx and the length of the palate.

The most common defect is the submucous cleft, which is easily overlooked. It is recognized by the triad of bifid uvula, notched or absent posterior nasal spine and translucent central area of the soft palate. Slow feeding with nasal regurgitation in infancy may be the first clue. Any child with this complaint or with persistent hypernasal speech should be referred to the cleft palate team for assessment, whether or not the child has any visible abnormality of the palate. Barium-coated videofluoroscopy and nasopharyngoscopy may help to establish the diagnosis. There is a high incidence of persistent middle-ear disease with submucous clefts and also, as with overt clefts, associated anomalies are common. It may therefore be difficult in some cases to decide whether a child's speech and language problems are directly attributable to the submucous cleft.

Nasal obstruction

Chronic enlargement of the adenoids and obstruction of the nasal airway causes defective articulation, particularly of the nasal sounds 'n', 'm' and 'ng'. The child sounds as if he/she has 'a cold in the nose' (hyporhinophonia). It is commonly associated with a history of recurrent upper respiratory infections and 'tonsillitis' but adenotonsillectomy does not necessarily lead to either dramatic or permanent improvement. A similar picture may occur in cleft lip and palate patients who have a deviated nasal septum.

Macroglossia (enlargement of the tongue)

This is usually associated with conditions that cause learning disabilities (Hunter's, Down's, Beckwith's syndromes; hypothyroidism). Probably the size of the tongue plays little part in the child's speech problems in most cases (see p. 154). Cosmetic surgery to reduce the size of the tongue is occasionally undertaken, although the value of the procedure and sometimes its ethical justification are open to question.

Tongue-tie

This is widely believed by the layman to be a cause of late talking and defective articulation, but it should only be diagnosed if the frenulum is so tight that the tongue cannot be protruded to the outer margin of the lower lip, in which case there will be a history of feeding difficulties in infancy. If in doubt, the cleft palate team has the skills to assess the child properly and ensure that surgery is undertaken only if indicated.

Malocclusion of the jaws

This is commonly but inconstantly related to articulatory problems. If the lower jaw is underdeveloped or there is anterior malocclusion (open anterior bite), the tongue may be thrust out during speech, causing interdental sigmatism or 'lisping' (e.g. 'thing a thong of thickthpenth'). When the mandible protrudes, the lower incisors lie anterior to the uppers and this may cause lateralization of 's' sounds, making the 's' sound like the Welsh 'll' in Llandudno. Either of these articulatory patterns may also occur without any apparent anatomical cause.

Malocclusion and jaw abnormalities may be isolated, and sometimes familial, or may be part of a dysmorphic syndrome. The orthodontist and plastic surgeon will advise on the probability of spontaneous improvement with growth, and may be able to improve appearance and articulation when necessary. Associated disabilities should be carefully considered before recommending treatment. Improving the articulation of speech will not necessarily increase language competence and usage if the child has defective language abilities or has severe global learning disability.

Tracheostomy

This is sometimes necessary in the care of small premature infants and the child may be dependent on it for months or even years. The standard tube does not allow any air to flow across the vocal cords and therefore the child is unable to cry or vocalize, but in some cases a fenestrated tube may be used, which does permit part of the airstream to flow through the larynx.

Children with long-term tracheostomy learn to understand language at a level commensurate with their overall developmental stage, and sometimes they may acquire some manual signs as a means of communication. When, finally, the tracheostomy is closed, they do not usually pass through the babbling stage, but rapidly learn to vocalize and catch up with their peers in expressive language ability.

Dysphonia

This term implies a difficulty in voice production and most often refers to a hoarse voice. Voice quality may vary with changes in volume and pitch or in different situations. Vocal abuse in excitable, chattering overactive children is a common cause. Other psychological factors may contribute in some cases. Any child with unexplained persistent voice disorder should undergo a laryngoscopy. Inspection of the vocal cords often reveals chronic inflammatory changes or, more rarely, nodules or papillomata. Recurrent laryngeal nerve palsy is a very rare cause of dysphonia in children.

Dysfluency

This means an incoordination between respiratory and articulatory function, causing prolongation of word sounds, arrest or blocking of speech, or repetitions of one or more words or sounds. Dysfluency is so common between the ages of 2 and 4 that it may be regarded as normal non-fluency or physiological stuttering. It is possible, though by no means proven, that undue parental concern over this phase may generate anxiety in the child, leading to a persistent stammer in later childhood. Even if true, this explanation could clearly account for only part of the problem of stammering; but, if parents are worried about stammering in a child of this age-group, they should be offered an interview with a speech and language therapist, not for treatment but to alleviate anxiety. This is particularly important when there is a family history of stammer.

Although ~3% of children stammer at some time during childhood, persistent stammer or stutter affects only ~1% of school-age children. The literature on the aetiology and treatment of the condition is vast and confusing. These cases are rarely seen by paediatricians and are quite rightly referred directly to speech and language therapists, since even meticulous history and neurological examination contribute little or nothing to further management. Unless there is something very atypical about the dysfluency, one can be confident that it is not an indicator of any sinister neurological disease; nor is it a consequence of emotional or functional disorders, although it may promote social anxiety, which subsequently exacerbates the problem in a vicious spiral.

is this right, in place?

Elective mutism

This condition is sometimes referred to as selective mutism, which may be a better term. The child does not talk in certain selected situations, most commonly in school, but talks normally at other times, typically at home. Unlike most developmental disorders, in which boys outnumber girls, in elective mutism girls equal or even outnumber boys. About 7 children per 1000 do not speak in school at the age of 5, but often this is a transient problem and persistent elective mutism probably occurs in about 1 child per 1000.

Shyness, of which psychological inhibition of speech is a component, is evident in the earliest years of life as an inherited trait but, even when severe, is often not considered abnormal by parents until the child goes to school. It is not always easy to distinguish between normal shyness and pathological mutism, although there are theoretical grounds for thinking that the two differ. Most cases of elective mutism present soon after school entry, although sometimes many months elapse before the teacher realizes that the child consistently avoids speaking. Speech may be the only area of concern, but some children also avoid all other social contact and activity and their school work may be poor. Sulkiness, negativism, poor adaptability to change and problems of bowel and bladder control are not infrequent accompaniments.

The disorder is undoubtedly emotional in origin, although there is likely to be an interaction with developmental vulnerabilities. In some cases of recent onset, a stressor may be identifiable and it is wise to consider the possibility of sexual abuse. There is no specific pattern of family disturbance, although an increased incidence of parental neurosis and depression is reported. There are probably predisposing temperamental character-istics in the child and, in a significant proportion of cases, a speech or language abnormality con-tributes to the child's reluctance to talk. The intelligence quotient (IQ) tends to be in the low-normal or mild learning difficulties range.

To establish the diagnosis it is necessary to confirm that the child is capable of functionally adequate speech and play. This may require a home visit or obtaining a tape- or video-recording made by the parents. Alternatively, they can be asked to play with the child in an observation room with a one-way mirror.

Management

The most successful treatment uses a graded approach to bridging the situations in which the child does and does not speak, based on behav-ioural principles. Starting with the situation in which the child will speak, new elements are introduced so that the range of circumstances in which speech is used is increased. Simultaneously, the child is praised for progression through a series of graded tasks such as blowing (a whistle or balloon), making other mouth noises, whisper-ing, reading aloud and eventually talking to familiar people in strange surroundings or less well-known people in familiar surroundings, care-fully calibrating the degree of unfamiliarity. This is often a protracted procedure requiring the guidance of a psychologist.

To this may be added desensitization to particu-larly alarming situations, positive reinforcement of every attempt to communicate, and identifi-cation and removal of factors, such as peer interest in and sympathy with mutism, which reinforce its persistence.

Pattern 2: specific language impairments (SLI)

Whereas it is common for children to have more difficulties with expression than with comprehen-sion, the reverse situation is theoretically improb-able; children are not likely to use meaningfully a language structure that they do not comprehend. A language profile in which expressive language appears to be superior to receptive ability may be found when formal test results are distorted by a child's inattention and lack of concentration, or if the child produces whole phrases learned by imitation (delayed echolalia), which give the im-pression of greater linguistic competence than he/she really has. An instance of the latter is the 'cocktail party chatter' of children with Williams syndrome. This pattern can also occur in those rare cases where a child has suddenly or rapidly become severely deaf, for example after meningitis.

Whenever a child is found to have serious difficulties with the comprehension of spoken language, the hearing must be checked with par-ticular care before accepting a diagnosis of SLI. Children with severe deafness are usually ident-ified in the first year of life, but those with a high-frequency or progressive hearing loss are easily overlooked until they present with impaired language development. The diagnosis may some-times be unexpectedly difficult to confirm.

Prevalence and definition of SLI

There is no agreement as to the prevalence of these conditions, since there are considerable difficulties in defining exactly what is meant by SLI. Between 3 and 8% of children perform below the 3rd centile on formal tests of language (depending on the test, the age and the standard-ization sample used), but this does not necessarily mean that they need intervention or special edu-cation or that children whose language scores are above this level have normal language development.

It is preferable to describe language abilities in terms of standard deviations (SDs) from the mean (see Fig. 3.2a) since descriptive criteria such as less than 30 words at 24 months are only useful at the specified age. Some speech and language therapists would regard an expressive language score of 1 or 1.5 SDs below the mean as being abnormal and requiring referral and intervention. Others would follow an approach that is more conventional in medicine and specify a score of at least 2 SDs below the mean as the criterion for diagnosing SLI.

A diagnosis of SLI implies a discrepancy between the language abilities and non-verbal IQ, but there is no general agreement on how wide the difference should be. The child's failure to acquire language may be a reflection of globally low intellectual ability, but there is sometimes a wide discrepancy between the child's language and non-verbal ability. Arguably, therefore, the diagnoses of SLI and intellectual impairment should not be incompatible, and yet some authors specify that SLI can only be diagnosed if the non-verbal IQ is no more than 1 SD below the mean.

Similarly, most authors distinguish between purely expressive deficits and expressive/comprehension deficits, but the magnitude of the difference required for this distinction to be meaningful is currently a matter for individual judgement.

Subtypes of specific language impairment

'Simple' expressive language delay

It is quite common for a child to present with a delay in expressive speech and language development associated with normal comprehension, for which no cause is demonstrable. A family history of delayed speech milestones in a few other relatives will sometimes be obtained. Nearly all such children acquire functional speech before the age of 4, but the extent to which their vocabulary and fluency of speech catch up to normal standards varies and cannot be predicted with accuracy.

Various patterns of expressive SLI are recognized, although they are not usually clearly demarcated and the pattern may change as the child matures. The severity is very variable; the child may have minor articulatory difficulties or be so severely affected that he/she is essentially mute ('expressive aphasia' in old terminology). More sophisticated methods of assessment reveal that many children thought to have a 'pure' expressive SLI also have some problems with comprehension, although of much less severity.

Classification is confused by the mixing of terms derived from linguistics with 'neurological' labels. There is some evidence for a hierarchy of severity; children with isolated phonological problems tend to do best, followed by those with syntactic deficits. Semantic and pragmatic difficulties have a less favourable outlook. Comprehension deficits, which probably reflect other cognitive abilities more closely, are the least likely to resolve completely.

Phonological—syntactic deficit

This term is increasingly used by linguists and psychologists to denote a deficit in the child's ability to produce accurately the sounds of their native language and to manipulate the grammatical structures required, e.g. 'that bush single-desker' (that bus is a single-decker), even though their musculoskeletal speech apparatus is intact. The problem is characterized by a history of slow speech development from the start, slow progress in language development, and a male preponderance. There is often a family history of early speech problems.

Articulatory dyspraxia

Whereas the term 'phonologic—syntactic deficit' is a purely linguistic description of the child's difficulties, 'dyspraxia' implies a theory about the underlying neurological lesion or disorder. The relationships between articulatory dyspraxia and phonological—syntactic deficit and the value, if any, of the distinction are yet to be clarified.

Articulatory dyspraxia is defined as a difficulty in carrying out the rapid, discrete and highly accurate patterned movements of the speech musculature required to produce fluent speech, in the absence of any other demonstrable abnormality of neurological function. In other words, it is regarded as a deficit in the motor 'programme' which controls the movements of the speech apparatus in producing the desired words.

Characteristically, the phonological errors made by the child are inconsistent; they become more prominent as the sound combinations become more complicated and the utterances get longer. The sentences are often short or 'telegrammatic' and this observation is usually interpreted as the child's response to the difficulty in articulating, so that he/she concentrates on the words that are essential to get their meaning across to the listener. This may be too simple an explanation, because some children may also have difficulties in the formulation of sentences. In the more severe cases, difficulties in communication may persist for years and the child may also experience problems with spelling.

A history can sometimes be obtained of sucking and chewing difficulties in infancy. Careful examination may reveal that the child cannot carry out rapid repetitive movements or accurate placing of their tongue and facial musculature. (These findings could also be interpreted as evidence of subtle neurological dysfunction in the co-ordinating mechanisms or neuronal pathways, i.e. dysarthria, whereas the concept of dyspraxia implies that it is the motor programme which is faulty.) Similarly, some children have evidence of dyspraxia affecting other motor abilities (the so-called 'clumsy child', p. 324), sometimes to the extent that communication by signing is also difficult; but the significance of this finding is uncertain. Subtle comprehension deficits may be found in some children.

Lexical–syntactic deficit

This refers to a particular difficulty in accessing the mental word store (lexicon = mental dictionary or word store), i.e. a word-finding difficulty. The child has the word in their vocabulary but cannot retrieve it when it is required. A variety of manoeuvres may be used to disguise the problem, e.g. 'Well ... we went to this kind of er place and then we put on these ... things and then we played this sort of ... er ... game' (an account of an away football match). Intelligent children can conceal their problem by using alternative phrases (paraphasias), which can be quite complex and give a false impression of fluency, e.g. 'It's a machine ... which you work when you want to tell the car that it's time to go round a swerve in the road' (when the steering-wheel of a toy car was pointed to and its name plus an explanation of its function asked for).

Word-finding difficulties can exist independently or as a feature of phonological–syntactic deficit. Mild forms are not uncommon in the general population.

Semantic–pragmatic deficit

Children with SLI of semantic–pragmatic (for definitions of semantics and pragmatics see p. 30) type may begin to talk at a later than average age, but, when they do speak, their sound production, vocabulary and grammar are, or become, satisfactory. Their problem lies at a higher level of language function; language content and use are abnormal, much of what they say is irrelevant to the situation and they may play with words without understanding their meaning. Parents say, 'You can't have a proper conversation with him/her', 'He/she gets hold of the wrong end of the stick', 'He/she keeps going off at a tangent'. Their semantic capabilities are poor and their grasp of the link between language and meaning is erratic; for example, their use and creation of conceptual categories is idiosyncratic. The ability to sustain a consistent thread of meaning through a narrative or conversation is impaired.

They often have problems with social attention and this may account for the apparent discrepancy sometimes found between expression and comprehension on formal language testing. They may be able to name spontaneously a series of pictures, and yet fail to identify them when asked to do so, because they do not engage socially with the tester to the extent normally taken for granted in a testing situation. Alternatively, they may perform well on a standard test of comprehension, but become confused when confronted with running conversation. When uncertain what is expected of them they may relapse into echolalia, at an age when most children have outgrown this response, divert attention or even withdraw from the situation.

The following 'conversation' (see Fletcher, 1987) is typical of a child with a semantic−pragmatic deficit. C is the child, T is the therapist; the activity is hammering wooden pegs into a peg board.

    C. He kicked me.
    T. Who kicked you?
    C. No. I don't want them.
    T. Are you going home tomorrow?
    C. No.
    T. Are you going home to Mummy?
    C. Yes, no Mummy, want to see Daddy; no Daddy; no sister.
    T. Have you got a little girl?
    C. Yes I can't have it. You can't have it. Yes I can. It's trapped. It's no sticks. Hers pushed off.
    T. What happened last night?
    C. Happened last night.

One striking feature is their inability to understand the rules of conversation and social behaviour and the way in which the communicative use of language takes the immediate social situation into account (which is what 'pragmatics' means). Subtleties of language such as sarcasm are lost on them and they may ignore the conventions of school life, such as sitting quietly in the classroom when the teacher is talking. Their use of gesture and non-verbal cues is restricted so that they can appear insensitive, blunt or rude to others.

These children can be regarded as having some impairment of social interaction, and the 'semantic−pragmatic' category of SLI merges into those of the autistic disorders and Asperger's syndrome (Fig. 11.4). Indeed, the narrowing of thinking and constrained creativity typical of such conditions are sometimes evident in children with semantic−pragmatic deficits, even when their

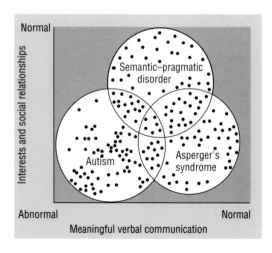

Fig. 11.4 Two-dimensional model of the autistic continuum. From Bishop (1989).

interpersonal relationships are quite warm and flexible. However, a preoccupation with routines or a single-minded obsession with unusual topics such as plumbing or bones can be a source of stress for their parents. They may be constantly pestered about them or faced with tantrums if they attempt to divert the child to other more productive interests.

Overlap between categories

The above categories quite often overlap or replace each other in development and are not mutually exclusive in any one child. One consistent feature among children with SLI is that they master the more subtle points of grammar (e.g. 'they are running' instead of 'they running') at a later stage than normal, and their use of these grammatical forms is more limited. They continue to produce ungrammatical and immature sentences even when trying to convey quite complex messages. There are often marked discrepancies ('asynchronies') in the rate at which they master different aspects of language, for example their mastery of vocabulary may outstrip their skill in reproducing sounds accurately (phonology), or their ability to convey complex ideas may be hampered by their problems with the mastery of grammar.

Another finding is that they produce a number of linguistic errors which occur far less frequently in the speech of 'normal' children, as in the following examples (Fletcher, 1987).

1 'One is in the fishfinger' (a child trying to describe a picture showing plates of food); here the child displays his inability to arrange the words in an appropriate fashion.

2 'To see if I need any trouble with my speaking' (a child talking about a visit to his speech and language therapist); here the child is confusing two messages, 'if I need any help' and 'if I have any trouble'.

3 'She's sitting on a table' (describing a picture of a child sitting on a chair); this child had difficulty in finding the word he wanted.

Comprehension deficit

Some children with delayed expressive language development have in addition an underlying impairment of comprehension greater than any associated intellectual impairment would predict. Testing by a speech and language therapist in early childhood reveals the level of functioning to be low but, when speech develops, it usually displays qualitative abnormalities of grammar, word selection or semantics as described above. It is unusual, though by no means unknown, for a child with marked comprehension deficits to have a normal or high non-verbal IQ. An overall score in, or close to, the mild learning disability range, with a wide scatter of subtest scores, is a common finding. Dissociation between comprehension and non-verbal IQ is seen most clearly in the child with a severe hearing loss, which must always be ruled out with extra care in this situation.

Congenital auditory imperception (auditory agnosia)

This is the most severe form of receptive SLI and the one type on which most authors agree. The child's responses to sound are variable and unpredictable from early infancy, and there is little or no evidence that the child can understand even simple everyday sounds such as the bath-water being run or, when a little older, a packet of crisps

being rustled. Nevertheless, the parents may well assert that their child can hear, even in the face of contrary professional opinion.

In the first year of life, clinical audiological assessment may result in a diagnosis of hearing loss, but electrical response testing (p. 80) reveals normal responses to pure tones. In older subjects, pure-tone audiometry is usually normal but the ability to identify sounds against a background of noise may be impaired. The responses to testing can be variable, a finding which may be incorrectly interpreted as lack of co-operation, poor testing technique or intermittent secretory otitis media. It is assumed that the condition is caused by some neurological impairment in the central auditory connections.

Congenital auditory imperception must be distinguished from severe global learning disability and autism, by determining whether the child has normal non-verbal intellectual capabilities on the one hand, and attachment formation and symbolic play on the other. The history of a problem dating back to infancy and the lack of a history of deterioration distinguishes this condition from Landau−Kleffner syndrome (see below).

In its pure form congenital auditory imperception is a very rare condition and the prognosis for acquisition of spoken language is poor. However, we have seen a number of parents who report that their child was thought to be deaf in infancy, but by the time the child presents with impaired language acquisition it is clear that he/she has begun to respond appropriately to sounds and often to some familiar words. Later still, the child may have deficits of the type described above. These observations suggest that, as with other forms of SLI, there may be a spectrum of severity. Milder forms of congenital auditory imperception may resolve as the child gets older.

Predicting outcome in children with specific language impairments

Because of the wide range in the rate and route of language acquisition among normal children (p. 35), it is difficult to offer parents a prognosis for improvement and progress, or for the child's chances of coping in mainstream school. Not surprisingly, the difficulty is greater in very young children. Parents' concerns regarding the future of a child of 18 to 24 months who is saying very few words should be taken seriously, particularly if the child is generally silent and does not babble or vocalize, or shows any difficulty in understanding. Severe problems with swallowing or chewing, persistent dribbling, facial immobility or other neurological deficits are other warning signs. Nevertheless, at this age it is seldom possible to be certain whether the problem will turn out to be persistent.

The link between language impairment at age 3 and later school failure, demonstrated in several large studies in the early 1980s, is the main reason why delayed language acquisition has attracted so much professional attention. It is now clear that much of the association is explained by the globally low intelligence that often accompanies delayed language acquisition. Among children diagnosed as having SLI at age 4, the most important predictive factor is the non-verbal intelligence. If children with low non-verbal IQ are excluded, the probability of good developmental progress is high. Language problems are more likely to persist in children who cannot give even a simple account of a story sequence. It does not seem to matter if their pronunciation or grammar is poor; what counts is the ability to convey an orderly sequence of ideas.

Not surprisingly, a history of continuing progress over recent months is a good sign; conversely, the outlook for a child whose language has not progressed at all for many months is much more guarded. If the child's language impairments have resolved by $5\frac{1}{2}$, the risk of subsequent reading difficulties is relatively small, although increased in comparison with children whose language development was normal. Persisting SLI at this age may be followed by a number of learning problems, including poor reading comprehension; rather surprisingly, reading and spelling accuracy are somewhat less affected (see also p. 319).

When a history is obtained that other family members also had significant delay or difficulties with language acquisition, it is important to determine their subsequent progress. If this was satisfactory, a positive family history can in general be regarded as a good prognostic sign.

Causes of specific language impairments

Normal variation

As with other psychometric measures, there is a wide degree of variation in the rate and eventual level of language acquisition. There is now overwhelming evidence for biological 'programming' of language acquisition. This is a robust mechanism, which functions even when the quality of input is less than optimal. It is to be expected that some children will have less effective 'programming' for language acquisition than others and that some will be more vulnerable than others to adverse environment and to sensory impairments such as mild hearing loss.

Chromosomal influences

SLI is more common in boys than in girls. Although differences in child-rearing practices may be partly responsible for sex differences, biological factors certainly play a large part. The two interact. For instance, in an experimental setting, a boy baby dressed as a girl elicits more speech from those introduced to him than if he is dressed as a boy. The X and Y chromosomes affect maturation and development, and children with XYY, XXY, XXYY and various mosaic patterns all have a higher than expected prevalence of language impairment.

In the syndromes of X-linked retardation (including fragile-X), a variety of communication disorders have been reported, ranging from minor dyspraxias to autism with severe learning difficulties. Typically these children have a singsong, repetitive, 'litanic' (or 'litany-like') intonation with a tendency to superficial and tangential comments, often repeated several times in rapid sequence. See p. 155 for further details.

Genetic factors

There is a strong genetic influence on language development and a positive family history for speech and language disorders can often be obtained in children with SLI. It is only in recent years that there has been a high level of awareness of communication problems and parents may have forgotten, or may never have known, that they had some delay in learning to talk. The parents should be asked to check with their own parents, uncles or aunts to determine whether they, or other family members, were ever thought to be late in talking. A few families have been described with an SLI that is undoubtedly dominantly inherited.

Dysmorphic syndromes

Some dysmorphic syndromes are associated with SLI and this ranges in severity from minor problems to severe dysphasia. Examples include ectodermal dysplasia, Noonan's syndrome, Floating Harbour syndrome, Williams' and Angelman's syndrome (see Glossary). In these the mechanism is unknown but it is assumed that development of the language areas of the brain is particularly affected as a result of the underlying defect.

Relationship between brain lesions and dysphasia

The impact of focal brain injury on language acquisition and functions is important not only for those children who suffer the effects of such lesions, but also because of the insights they offer into language impairments in general.

It has been known since 1863 that lesions in the third frontal convolution (Broca's area) result in a difficulty in the production of articulate speech — expressive aphasia or Broca's aphasia (Fig. 11.5). Subsequently, Wernicke showed that more posterior lesions produce fluent, grammatically correct speech which is empty of content and often contains word substitutions, mispronunciations and strings of meaningless sounds.

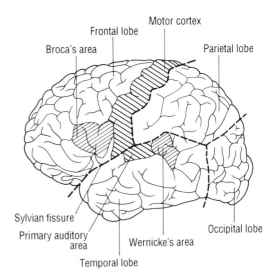

Fig. 11.5 Side-view of left cerebral hemisphere. From Bishop and Mogford (1988).

These patients are said to have Wernicke's or fluent aphasia.

Although these two categories of aphasia are still accepted, the situation is much more complicated than was originally thought, and their relevance to children who are still acquiring language is still being debated (Table 11.1). Focal brain injury may occur on a vascular basis; it may be associated with infective processes, trauma or neoplasms; and it may be produced surgically in the treatment of epilepsy. Cases in which there is only one clearly definable lesion are rare; more often, damage is bilateral or diffuse and conclusions drawn on the basis of such cases must be treated with caution.

The patterns of deficit and recovery which result from demonstrable brain lesions are clearly different in many respects from those seen in children with so-called 'developmental' language impairment, and it no longer seems justified to postulate focal brain damage as the likely cause of these conditions.

Table 11.1 Brain lesions and aphasia

---

1 In the vast majority of cases, aphasia is related to lesions of the left hemisphere rather than the right

2 Although aphasia in a left-handed person is usually the result of a left hemisphere lesion, a right hemisphere lesion is more likely to cause aphasia in a left hander than in a right hander. Aphasia as a result of a right hemisphere lesion in a strongly right-handed person is called crossed aphasia and is very rare in childhood

3 The left hemisphere is 'dominant' for language but the right hemisphere is not 'minor' (p. 317)

4 Damage to the language areas of the left hemisphere in the first year of life results in the development of language representation in the right hemisphere. Aphasia does not occur; thus in children with congenital hemiplegia but no other neurological deficit, there is no difference in verbal skills between those with left and right hemisphere lesions

5 Damage to the language areas of the left hemisphere in childhood produces aphasia, but this has some different characteristics from that seen in adults. Initially, there is extreme reluctance to speak and the child may seem mute or reticent. As they recover they pass through a phase of dysarthria and telegrammatic speech, and some children also show features similar to those seen in adult fluent aphasia, although these seldom last more than a few months. The extent of their difficulties can be underestimated because of the reticence, which is mistakenly attributed to shyness

6 The outcome in children who become aphasic under the age of 10 may be somewhat better than for older children or adults, but they do not recover completely. There are persisting problems with writing and with verbal comprehension, although these may be detected only by appropriate objective assessment procedures

---

Impaired processing

Children with SLI differ from normally developing controls in the speed at which they process rapidly changing acoustic signals, as when listening to speech, and this may be the physiological basis for language impairment. Another hypothesis is that the impairment in language reflects a more extensive difficulty in the use and manipulation of symbols. It is suggested that these children do not perform so well on tasks involving symbolic play and mental imagery. The question is still unresolved.

Secretory otitis media

Another area of controversy is the relationship between secretory otitis media ('glue ear') and impaired language acquisition. This condition may be relevant in some cases but is unlikely to be the only or main cause of SLI (p. 220).

Inadequate input

Recent advances in the understanding of normal language acquisition (Chapter 3) have prompted the suggestion that children with SLI may have been exposed to a communicative environment that is in some way suboptimal. The hypothesis is not generally supported. In general it seems that, although the parents of these children do inevitably interact with them at a less sophisticated language level than they would with normally speaking siblings, this is the result of the SLI rather than the cause. Furthermore, the normally hearing child of deaf parents learns the elements of communication at home and rapidly acquires normal spoken language, provided that family life is otherwise normal and the child is exposed to normally speaking people for a minimum of 5–10 hours per week.

Severe deprivation

Language development is in general a fairly robust

function and most children learn to talk even if their exposure to language is not optimal, but some children may be more vulnerable than others to adverse circumstances, because of temperamental factors or inherited predisposition to language problems. In some families, children do suffer very severe deprivation of linguistic experience, usually but not always in association with other forms of neglect, deprivation or abuse. However, children who have been rescued from such situations and placed in a more normal environment acquire language rapidly and do not show the characteristic features of SLI.

Children who are passed from one incompetent child-minder to another, or to a series of au-pairs, each of whom speaks a different language, or who at home are discouraged from any conversation or vocalization, may be delayed in language development. It is not always easy to identify this situation if the parent presents a plausible story. Usually such children will begin to communicate when they are placed in a more normal environment but in some cases improvement may not be apparent for many months.

A picture superficially similar to that of autism may be seen in children subjected to repeated abuse and neglect, or who have suffered separation or bereavement — the child is remote, self-absorbed, mute, does not play and may soil.

Exposure to two languages

Bilingualism alone is not enough to explain severe language delay or SLI and most children cope well with two languages, distinguishing between them at a surprisingly early stage. Inappropriate and misguided use of the two languages may sometimes cause some difficulties. For example, some immigrant parents make a policy decision that their children must learn English as their first language and should not be exposed to their parents' mother tongue until they are older. As the mother who cares for the children all day speaks little English, and the father can spend little time with them, learning opportunities are limited, and the children may appear to be delayed

in the acquisition of both languages. Nevertheless, the speed with which language is acquired when appropriate opportunities are made available excludes any fundamental language disorder.

Spurious factors

Large families, twins and sex differences in language acquisition should not be accepted as 'explanations' of slow language development until other possibilities have been excluded.

Pattern 3: children who stop talking

Loss of speech in a child who has previously been talking is a rare but dramatic and frightening complaint and, unless there is an obvious explanation such as acquired or progressive hearing loss, head injury or meningitis, the child will require full neurological evaluation. Diagnoses to be considered may include neoplasms, degenerative diseases, congenital infections, minor epileptic status, metabolic conditions (Wilson's disease, Sanfilippo's disease, glutaric aciduria, metachromatic leucodystrophy), Rett's syndrome and vascular lesions (sickle-cell anaemia). Psycho-social problems should be excluded.

'Disintegrative' processes

With the exception of a transient disturbance of speech and listening due to secretory otitis media, none of these conditions are common. In our experience the commonest 'cause' of progressive deterioration of speech is in association with the onset of an autistic or semantic—pragmatic behaviour pattern in a child who has previously apparently been developing normally, a so-called disintegrative process (see p. 195). In these cases, the child not only loses the ability to speak and comprehend but also to interact socially.

Acquired receptive aphasia

Much less commonly, the deterioration is confined to language functions and is accompanied in many cases by the onset of seizures — the so-called acquired receptive aphasia (epilepsy aphasia syndrome, Landau−Kleffner syndrome). In this condition, typically the onset is between the ages of 3 and 9. There is no obvious neurological illness, but the child may develop generalized or partial seizures, which often are not particularly severe or frequent. The loss of language skills may be sudden or insidious and is sometimes so complete that deafness is strongly suspected. The course of the condition is variable; in some there is fluctuation in association with seizures; there may be no recovery at all, or some improvement, although usually slow and incomplete. The prognosis seems to improve with increasing age of onset.

Imaging studies are rarely helpful. The electroencephalogram (EEG) shows asymmetrical paroxysmal activity, particularly over the postcentral region. The changes in the EEG over time do not correlate with clinical improvement. The underlying pathology is unknown. Therapy is of uncertain value. Steroids and adrenocorticotrophic hormone (ACTH) have been tried. Anticonvulsant drugs do not dramatically affect the aphasia, although some benefit is occasionally reported. Lamotrigine in particular may be helpful. Some children have benefited from neurosurgery (subpial resection).

Links to other conditions

The relationships between the variants of this disorder, those conditions in which the child never seems to establish language adequately (for example, congenital auditory imperception), and those in which an autistic behaviour pattern appears in a previously normal child, are uncertain. EEG abnormalities have also been observed in the latter group. It seems possible that all can sometimes be a reflection of the same underlying pathological process or deviant brain development.

Other conditions causing loss of speech

A sleep EEG is crucial in the diagnosis of the strange condition of electrical status in sleep with continuous $2−2.5\,Hz$ spike−wave discharges. These children have usually had some fits in the past and then present at an average age of 8 years with a deterioration in language and a fall in IQ.

Pattern 4: Impaired language and social interaction — the pervasive developmental disorders (autism and autistic disorders, Asperger's syndrome)

The term 'early infantile autism' was coined by Kanner in 1943. In the past, some authorities regarded autism as a form of childhood psychosis or childhood schizophrenia but this is no longer accepted. True childhood schizophrenia is recognized as a distinct entity with the characteristic psychopathology of hallucinations, delusions and disrupted thought and motivation, with an onset in late childhood or the early teens. There is often a family history of schizophrenia. In autism, the clinical picture does not resemble schizophrenia, the onset is earlier and there is no evidence of a family history of any particular psychopathology or personality type, but an increased rate of developmental language abnormalities among relatives.

Earlier findings of an excess of autistic children in middle-class families have not been confirmed, but there is an unexplained increase in incidence in the children of first-generation immigrant families to Europe from non-European countries. There is absolutely no support for the outdated notion that the parents of an autistic child tend to be cold, aloof and unloving. Nor is there any evidence for the often quoted belief that middle-class parents find autism a more 'socially acceptable' diagnosis than mental handicap, although they may mistakenly believe that autism has a better prognosis.

Definitions

Current use of the term autism refers to a disorder within the broader group of pervasive developmental disorders (PDDs). These are characterized by impairment of reciprocal social interactive skills, evident in all social situations (hence 'pervasive', which is a rather misleading term). Autism is the prototype PDD but, as narrowly defined, is not the commonest. Traditionally, four key features are considered essential to the diagnosis of typical autism (Table 11.2). Classical or 'nuclear' autism, so defined and in association with near-normal intelligence (Kanner's syndrome), is rare, occurring in 3–5 children per 10 000. It is outnumbered by the clinical picture of 'autistic traits', 'autistic features' or, in International Classification of Diseases (ICD) terms, 'atypical autism'. In these children the social and language impairments are evident, but the cognitive rigidity, exemplified by 'preservation of sameness' and routine-boundness, is not present.

There are a number of children whose social disabilities do not fit precisely into any disorder category. The degree of impairment of social reciprocity, which is often taken to be the central feature of autism, can vary and be located on a spectrum or continuum of severity (Table 11.3). Some children will move along this spectrum as they mature and develop some empathic and pragmatic skills.

Prevalence

Around 30 children per 10 000 show atypical autism, having impaired social interaction of the autistic type but without the full picture of routines required for the diagnosis in ICD terms. Many of these children have other impairments as well, affecting language, responses to sensory stimuli, motor co-ordination and gait, and, most importantly, intellectual deficits. The latter are often severe; two-thirds of children with atypical autism have a non-verbal IQ below 50; one-fifth have an IQ between 50 and 69; and the remainder are in the borderline to normal range of intelligence.

Table 11.2 The four essential features of autism. From World Health Organization (1992)

---

1 Impaired and abnormal social development which has a number of special characteristics and is out of keeping with the child's intellectual level

2 Delayed and deviant language development which has certain defined features and is out of keeping with the child's intellectual level

3 Insistence on sameness as shown by stereotyped play patterns, restricted and repetitive behaviours, rigid and abnormal preoccupations, or resistance to imposed change

4 Onset before the age of 3 years

The more severe the intellectual disability, the more likely it is that some autistic behavioural features will be observed. The IQ affects the sex ratio; among children with high IQ, boys substantially outnumber girls but among the severely mentally handicapped the sex ratio is more nearly equal.

There are also some children who have social impairments without significant intellectual deficits and with little expressive language impairment. These are variously known as mild autistics or Asperger's syndrome (see below). There is also an overlap between this category and that of semantic–pragmatic disorder (see Fig. 11.4).

The 'classical' autistic child

In classical autism (as in Table 11.2), boys outnumber girls by about 4 : 1. In many cases parents recognize even in the early weeks of life that normal 'turn-taking' behaviour is difficult or impossible to elicit, and they may be unable to obtain normal eye contact. In retrospect, parents often say that 'they were not really there' as far as their baby was concerned. There may be a history of 'delayed visual maturation' (p. 231) or a story of abnormal visual fixations (e.g. on light-bulbs).

Infancy. The baby is unable or unwilling to respond to the parents' 'baby talk' by vocalization or facial expression. As the child gets older, he/she seems

Table 11.3 The autistic continuum. After Wing (1988)

THE TRIAD OF SOCIAL IMPAIRMENTS IN AUTISM

Impairment of social recognition
(Most severe)
• Aloofness and indifference; ignore or actively avoid social contact with others, particularly with peer group. May make approaches to get what they want then become aloof once need is gratified. May enjoy physical contact (cuddling, tickling or chasing), but no interest in the social aspect of the interaction
• No spontaneous contact, but accept approaches amiably. May be used for passive roles by classmates (e.g. babies in a game of mothers and fathers). Wander off at the end of the game unless redirected by peers
• Make odd social approaches. No interest in or feeling for the feelings of others. Pursue their own favourite topics even in the face of active discouragement or disinterest. Those with no speech make intrusive and embarrassing physical contacts
• Adults who were impaired as children may show poverty of grasp of the rules of social interaction and lack of perceptiveness. May have learnt social behaviour as intellectual exercise rather than intuition
(Least severe)

Impairment of social communication
(Most severe)
• No desire to communicate with others
• Needs expressed but no other form of communication
• Factual comments made, but not as part of social exchange and often irrelevant to the context
• Talk, but no reciprocal conversation: repetitive questions or lengthy monologues. Take no account of the responses of the listener
(Least severe)

Impairment of social imagination and understanding
(Most severe)
• No copying or pretend play
• Copying of other people's actions but without understanding of their meaning or purpose. May copy other children's play actions (e.g. bathing a doll) but no spontaneous pretend play. May automatically copy other people's gestures (cf. echolalia)
• Repetitive stereotyped enacting of a role (e.g. of a TV character or animal) but without variation or insight
• Older more able people may recognize that something goes on in other people's minds but no idea of how to guess at what this may be
• An intellectual but not empathic recognition of other people's feelings
(Least severe)

REPETITIVE ACTIVITY IN AUTISM
(Most severe)
• No spontaneous activity; adopt the same bodily posture, often in same room or chair. Small bodily movements such as tooth-grinding or fist-clenching
• Simple bodily stereotypies; rocking, finger-flicking, pacing or fascination with simple sensory stimuli
• Complex bodily movements; fascination with one piece of music; repetitive manipulation of objects; attachment to objects such as pebbles, bits of plastic or empty packets
• Insistence on carrying out particular sequences of actions; rituals at bedtime, same routes to familiar places, repeated models or drawings which do not vary
• Verbal or intellectual forms; facts on sterile subjects, such as timetables, genealogy, etc. Peculiar intensity of pursuit of these interests
(Least severe)

to be aloof and remote because he/she does not make eye contact or demand cuddles or comfort. The child is described as 'living in a world of their own'. The child makes little or no distinction between familiar and unfamiliar adults, or between people and inanimate objects, and does not resist separation. In other words, normal attachment behaviour does not appear. The child may be regarded as abnormally quiet and 'good', being content with their own company for long periods. When the child does vocalize, only a very limited range of sounds is used; he/she may screech and scream intermittently for no apparent reason.

By the first birthday, when most children begin to understand some words, the autistic child is still unresponsive to the parents' speech and shows little or no interest in communication (see also p. 38). This impairment of verbal comprehension is very slow to resolve and, in more severely affected cases, may be permanent. Deafness may be suspected — indeed, the autistic child is sometimes referred first to an audiology clinic; but the parents can often report occasional unexpected but appropriate responses to sounds such as doorbells or sweet papers, and these help to rule out this diagnosis. Deafness and autism sometimes coexist and, since clinical hearing tests may be extremely difficult, electrical response audiometry is often necessary to clarify this.

Language development. Speech is usually very delayed and in about half of all cases never develops. In the more intelligent autistic child, the stage of labelling, using mainly single nouns, may be only slightly delayed, but fails to progress at the normal rate to the formation of spontaneous two- and three-word sentences. There is often immediate echolalia of the terminal sounds of questions which the child cannot understand and this may persist for many years, whereas in normal children the common developmental phase of echolalia usually disappears by the third birthday. Learned phrases are often used as answers to simple questions (delayed echolalia), or as requests; for example, the child may say 'Do you want a biscuit?' meaning that he/she wants a biscuit.

The child has great difficulty in mastering the grammatical rules of sentence construction and transformation, so the use of pronouns, tenses, etc. is frequently bizarre. The intonation pattern is odd and the delivery is stilted and mechanical. 'Yes' and 'No' are used incorrectly or not at all.

Although these rules may eventually be mastered in adolescence, the more subtle aspects of language, such as metaphor or sarcasm, may continue to bewilder the child and they will tend to express themselves in a stilted, wooden way. They find it hard to read the subtle non-verbal signals which are part of normal communication, lacking the empathy to understand other people's feelings and reactions. Similarly, they will show deficits in the social use of language (pragmatics) and appear rude and brusque in the way they communicate.

The language impairment of autism includes all modalities of symbolic thought and communication, so that, in addition to these syntactical and pragmatic deficits, there are semantic difficulties. Young autistic children do not use symbols in play; ordinary imaginative play is absent and they do not attribute human motives and feelings to inanimate objects. The ability to extract meaning from experience is impaired and this is associated with a general cognitive difficulty, so that it is hard to deduce a general concept from a particular example and the children are bewildered by exceptions to the rules they have learnt. Only by clinging to their self-imposed rules system can they make sense of a bewildering world and they therefore become very distressed by apparently trivial changes. The use of an unfamiliar synonym for a familiar object (for example, bucket for pail, dish for plate) may precipitate an extreme reaction, such as uncontrollable crying or screaming. Changes in clothing, furniture, routes to the shops and so on may elicit similar responses.

Rituals, obsessions and stereotypies. These are typical of autism and may be regarded in part as a natural outcome of these difficulties. By retreating into restricted, repetitive and predictable cycles of activity, autistic children protect themselves against any emergence of new stimuli which they cannot decode and do not understand. The complexity of the rituals bears some relationship to intelligence, although even the most intelligent autistic children have a constrained imagination and show a relative lack of creativity. Any assumption that social withdrawal in autistic children indicates a retreat into a rich, fertile inner mental world of their own is mistaken.

Elaborate activities related to maps, routes, timetables, mechanical objects or astronomical matters are usually confined to the more intelligent autistic children, whereas such rituals as twiddling and twirling of silver paper, picking up fragments of wool or paper, spinning toys or fiddling with light switches are suggestive of severe retardation if they persist beyond early childhood. These obsessions tend to perpetuate the child's handicap since they exclude any more productive activities. They can sometimes be reduced by behavioural techniques.

Social behaviour. Autistic children show a characteristic aloofness and a lack of interest in or curiosity about other people. They have a marked lack of empathy, which prevents them from sharing emotions with other people, and are solitary, impersonal and apparently preoccupied with their own inner world. In contemporary formulations they lack a 'theory of mind' so do not make the automatic assumption that other people have minds independent from their own. They thus lack curiosity about other people, seeing them merely as extensions of themselves or as part of the natural world. Only when other people thwart them or otherwise impinge upon them do they react, sometimes angrily or fearfully. Such a lack of interest and insensitivity to others is radically different from the usual human condition and is striking in its extreme abnormality. Various mannerisms, such as tiptoe-walking and hand-flapping, are commonly seen and add to the impression of 'oddness'.

Other problems. Children with autism commonly have a number of other behavioural or emotional difficulties, such as tantrums, aggressive behaviour

to other children, self-injurious behaviour (hand-biting, head-banging, etc.) and irrational fears. These are not crucial to the diagnosis but represent major problems for carers, siblings and teachers. They require treatment on their own merits.

Childhood-onset autism and disintegrative disorder

Some autistic children seem to have developed normally in all aspects, including language until the age of 18−36 months, and then gradually use fewer and fewer words, becoming mute and withdrawn. At the same time, comprehension, social interaction and play deteriorate. In retrospect, the parents may remember vague concerns about some aspect of the baby's early development, but more often they have not noticed any abnormality until the second or third year. Confirmation of normal development and communicative ability in infancy can sometimes be obtained when experienced child health professionals have made detailed records at routine health checks.

The rate of the deterioration is very variable but usually takes place over a period of weeks. It may be so dramatic that urgent neurological investigation is undertaken, although usually no cause is found. The investigations which may be considered in this situation include: sleep and waking EEG for absence status; computerized tomography (CT) to exclude space-occupying lesions; magnetic resonance imaging (MRI) for demyelinating and metabolic disorders; very-long-chain fatty acids for adrenoleucodystrophy; copper or ceruloplasmin for Wilson's disease; Venereal Disease Reference Laboratory (VDRL) test; human immunodeficiency virus (HIV); aryl sulphatase for metachromatic leucodystrophy; mucopolysaccharides (MPS) for Sanfilippos.

Causes and associated factors

Rarely, typical autistic behaviour may follow proven viral encephalitis, particularly herpes simplex. A disintegrative picture may also be seen in some children with severe visual impairment (p. 232). In many cases, however, the deterioration is so insidious as to be recognized only in retrospect, and in these children investigation is usually unrewarding. The associated loss of all attempts to communicate or play distinguishes these cases from the syndrome of acquired receptive aphasia (see above). The onset may seem to coincide with a family upheaval, such as birth of a sibling or move of house, but such life events are commonplace in the lives of young families and cannot be the sole cause. The initial referral is sometimes to an audiology or ENT clinic. Since glue ear is so common in childhood, it is not surprising that this condition is sometimes identified and treated in the mistaken belief that it is the cause of the child's problems.

These cases overlap with those described as having a 'disintegrative disorder', a term originally used for children whose deterioration began at a slightly later age. However, there is as yet no evidence that the underlying pathology of autism varies according to age of onset, although the general prognosis appears to be worse for later-onset cases.

Psychometric assessment in autism

Psychometric testing of an autistic child is often extremely difficult but results obtained by a psychologist experienced with autism have a surprisingly good correlation with future progress. Low scores tend to be persistent and must not be unreasonably attributed to the child's apparent disinterest or poor motivation during assessment. Sometimes the parents' ability to understand and interpret their autistic child's bizarre behaviour, together with the preservation of 'islands' of skilled behaviour, such as the ability to solve jigsaw puzzles, lead to their overestimating the child's abilities. In general 'verbal' IQ is a better prognostic indicator than non-verbal ('performance') IQ, but it is usually the latter which is higher. In the mentally handicapped autistic child there is no hidden intelligence needing only the right key for its release, but unfortunately many parents

acquire from the popular press the notion that autism is in some way a more hopeful diagnosis than mental handicap.

Adolescence and adult life

Most autistic children remain severely handicapped, totally unable to live an independent existence. An IQ below 50 and failure to develop useful speech by the age of 5 are conventional predictors of a very poor outcome, and there is a high incidence of epilepsy, which often begins at adolescence. When the non-verbal IQ is above 70, the outlook for adult life is more hopeful and epilepsy is less frequent.

At adolescence, many autistic children show a variety of increasing behavioural disturbances, including unprovoked aggression, self-injurious behaviour, inappropriate sexual activity, depressive mood and intense anxiety. Very occasionally there may be evidence of frank deterioration. A combination of behavioural methods and drugs may be needed to control these problems. Whenever possible, a psychiatrist specializing in learning disability, or a child and adolescent psychiatrist with a special interest in autism, should care for the autistic teenager.

At school-leaving age these unfortunate individuals leave the educational system, with its network of psychologists, devoted teachers and residential facilities. The lucky ones may manage simple work, join a specialized community or go to a modern residential hostel. Many will stay with ageing parents, attending social education centres (Adult Training Centres) on a daily basis. A few will need residential hospital care.

Causes of autism

Controversy exists as to whether autism is largely a single condition with a genetic cause or a behavioural syndrome which may arise in association with many types of pathology, such as congenital rubella, tuberose sclerosis, etc. In most individuals, however, no other condition can be identified, except in cases where 'autistic' features are seen in association with severe or profound learning disability.

There have been a number of hypotheses about the basic neurological deficit in autism. Imaging techniques have produced some contradictory findings. There have been various reports of abnormal brain morphology, but little consistency among these. Reports of cerebellar abnormalities are a case in point. There is no abnormality on brain imaging which can be used as a reliable diagnostic feature.

It is often claimed that fragile-X is a cause of autism, but the social abnormalities of most children with fragile-X are not quite the same (p. 155). They display gaze avoidance instead of an inability to use gaze contact socially, and they have curious prosodic qualities to their speech. Nevertheless, the fragile-X deoxyribonucleic acid (DNA) test is cheap and should be done routinely.

Asperger's syndrome

The terms 'autistic psychopathy', 'atypical child', 'schizoid personality' and 'Asperger's syndrome' have all been used to describe children with a condition that might well be regarded as mild autism. Asperger's syndrome is the currently preferred designation for this condition which appears to be a behavioural symptom complex rather than a single biological entity. There are many similarities between Asperger's syndrome and autism but also some distinctions. Although there is some variation in the use of the term, a growing consensus holds that, in Asperger's syndrome, early speech development is not delayed and the extreme aloofness of the autistic child is not seen.

Children with Asperger's syndrome are likely to be referred at a slightly later age than the typical autistic child. Boys substantially outnumber girls. By the above convention, speech development is not delayed but is pedantic in content and expression is stilted. There is a tendency to lapse into lengthy dissertations on sterile subjects. These children lack empathy, are solitary and emotionally detached, unable to enjoy reciprocal games or group activities with peers. There is often an odd loping gait. Although they may be superficially imaginative and creative, they are liable to become obsessed with one particular system of ideas, which may dominate their activities and thoughts for months or years at a time.

If they are fortunate, their eccentricities are affectionately tolerated by their peers but more often they are the cause of merciless teasing. In the teens they continue to have difficulties with relationships and cannot handle complex language structures or abstract concepts. Although the picture has much in common with so-called schizoid personality, affected adults are more prone to depression rather than to schizophrenia. The clinical picture is of a personality type rather than an illness or disorder. There may be a close relative with a similar personality.

Recognition of the condition and the distinction from classical autism is worthwhile since, although the personality cannot be altered, secondary educational and behavioural problems may be alleviated by adequate counselling and psychological guidance where appropriate; furthermore the child and family can be spared intensive psychotherapy, which is of no value in Asperger's syndrome.

Rett's syndrome

In 1966 Rett described a syndrome of autistic-like behaviour, beginning at the end of the first year of life and occurring only in girls (Hagberg, 1993). Subsequently it has become clear that this condition is not excessively rare and affects perhaps one child in every 10 000 female births. The main features are summarized in Table 11.4. Although the behaviour pattern differs from classic autism in that the children may show more eye contact and even be superficially friendly in some cases, Rett's syndrome should be considered in any girl with an onset of an autistic behaviour pattern in the first 2 years of life. A very few cases of apparent Rett's syndrome have been described in boys, but whether these actually represent the same condition is unclear.

The underlying metabolic or degenerative defect

Table 11.4 Rett's syndrome

Normal prenatal and perinatal period; not dysmorphic
Normal development for the first 7–18 months of life
Stagnation of development, followed by deterioration of
    behaviour, speech and mental status, resulting in severe
    mental handicap
Intent but blank expression
Loss of purposeful use of the hands
Wringing, patting or clapping movements of the hands
Grimacing, tooth-grinding and other stereotypies
Decline in rate of head growth, becoming microcephalic
Episodes of panic, air-swallowing and hyperventilation
Deterioration of gait; becoming ataxic and eventually non-
    ambulant in the teens
Cold, red, clammy feet
Hypotonia progressing to rigidity
Scoliosis
Epilepsy

Investigations
Imaging: unhelpful — mild generalized atrophy
EEG: flat waking record with occasional spikes or spike —
    waves; strikingly abnormal sleep record with repetitive
    slow spike–wave activity

EEG, electroencephalogram.

is not known. The inheritance is also uncertain; the condition does not seem to be familial and it has been suggested that it may be caused by a mutation of a dominant gene on the X chromosome which is lethal in male fetuses.

Management of communication disorders

Assessment and investigation

Children with speech and language problems are often assessed and managed by a speech and language therapist. It is usual to arrange for audiological testing in all such cases, but a paediatric evaluation is not always necessary. Multidisciplinary assessment and supervision at a Child Development Centre (CDC) is advisable for children likely to have long-term problems, for example where complex communication disorders or acquired conditions are suspected; or where the child's management involves several other disciplines outside the CDC (for example, in cases with craniofacial malformations).

Neurological examination and investigation

This is essential if there are other movement disorders, muscle weakness, or difficulties with oral function, such as excessive dribbling, expressionless face or problems with chewing and swallowing. In any boy who is also clumsy, weak or late to walk, Duchenne dystrophy should be excluded (p. 290). An EEG should be done when there are severe receptive language problems. A chromosome study is justifiable to exclude fragile-X and other sex chromosome anomalies. Further investigations are probably only worthwhile when there are other neurological deficits, e.g. learning disability or epilepsy, or a history of deterioration.

Education

Parents often request assessment at a CDC because of uncertainties or conflicts about education. It is important that both the parents and the education authorities appreciate the rapidity and extent of the changes that can take place in a child's communicative ability in the year or two before starting school. An educational plan which seemed reasonable at age 4 may well be irrelevant by 5. Flexibility and frequent review are essential.

Two educational issues which often worry parents are the use of augmented communication, such as a manual sign system, and the quantity of speech and language therapy available. The first of these points is discussed on p. 201. The role of speech therapy, which is considered further below, depends on the age of the child and the nature of the problem, but in many cases the therapist's role is to act as an adviser and consultant to the parents and other staff, rather than to treat the child him/herself. Parents should be advised that the number of hours of speech therapy may be less important than the skill of the therapist in communicating their knowledge to others who work with the child all day.

School placement. The options for school placement may include mainstream school, with or without a support worker; a specialized language unit, usually attached to a mainstream school; a school for children with learning difficulties; a boarding-school for children with severe communication disorders; a school for autistic children (day or residential). The staff of a CDC should not normally recommend one particular school, unless the assessment is done jointly with education colleagues; but they can offer some general advice.

Integration. Although integration is desirable for children with disabilities (p. 126), children with communication disorders can easily become excluded from their peer group, and true integration is often difficult to achieve and sustain. Parents should be advised to look at all the options on offer, and not to make up their minds on the basis of the 'label' attached to the school, but rather on the atmosphere, the curriculum, the extent to which augmented communication is used and the attitude of the staff. What works well in a primary school with a single class teacher, a single classroom base and good supervision can go badly wrong in a large secondary school with multiple teachers, different classrooms and a greater degree of pupil autonomy.

In all but the most severe cases, language deficits appear to resolve by the early teens, but careful testing may still reveal some problems. Often there is difficulty in following complex, rapidly delivered verbal information and this can result in underachievement and frustration in school (see also p. 323).

Counselling

Teenagers with communication disorders may benefit from counselling on a variety of matters. It may be necessary to use visual methods to communicate with them, such as cartoons, pictures, diagrams or dolls. Social skills groups, with role-play and similar exercises to build social discrimination and social skills, can enhance self-esteem as well as providing the skills for greater social independence.

Explanation to parents

Parents must be told that there is no medical treatment for communication disorders other than the control of epilepsy and behavioural disturbances with drugs, when needed, and the appropriate management of hearing loss. In spite of advances in our knowledge of normal language development, little is known about the causes of language delay or disorder. Many laymen find it hard to believe the extent of our ignorance about the neurological basis of language development, and 'shop around' for someone who will give them definite answers. Particular problems occur in the use of the terms language disorder, dyspraxia and dysphasia, because the lack of standard terminology confuses discussions between doctors and educationists. Parents must be guided away from the search for a label and instead must concentrate on finding the most appropriate educational provision.

In many cases, the process of assessment and the discussion which accompanies it are themselves reassuring and therapeutic. Simple measures to encourage language development can be demonstrated to the parents, and strategies which are suspected to be disadvantageous (Chapter 3) can be corrected. Genetic advice may be requested: most severe communication disorders are sporadic and have a low recurrence risk, with the exception of those few cases of autism associated with a specific mental handicap syndrome.

Speech and language therapy

There is little information about the most economic and effective way of using the speech and language therapist's skills. In preschool children, it seems unlikely that any intervention occurring for $\frac{1}{2}$ or 1 hour per week will have much effect on language development. Only when the children are old enough to practise what they have learnt from the therapist are they likely to benefit from sessional therapy; in practice this applies mainly to children of school age with articulation or rhythm disorders. There is a little evidence that more intensive intervention, either by regular parental instruction, guided by a therapist, or by attendance at a 'language group', can accelerate language in the preschool child. Over 20 schemes have been devised for the acceleration of language development, but few have been evaluated against each other or against adequate controls (Table 11.5).

Nurseries and schools

Placement in a day nursery is often recommended for children with language delay and certainly many parents believe that this is beneficial, but it is uncertain how much these apparent gains are translated into any long-term advantage. Nursery staff vary widely in commitment, enthusiasm and training, and in practice can seldom devote as much time to each individual child as a parent. Speech therapists probably use their time more effectively by training nursery staff rather than treatment of individual children.

More specialized provision is needed for some children. 'Language units', which have both teachers and speech therapists on the staff, usually cater for a small number of children who have exceptional difficulties in learning language. For children with severe communication disorders, highly specialized teaching, perhaps using an alternative means of communication (see below), may be essential. Such cases are rare and there are only a few schools in the country which cater for them, so boarding is often necessary.

Management of autism

Where possible, management of the autistic child should be shared with a modern department of child psychiatry. In the absence of any evidence that family pathology is responsible for autism, child or family psychotherapy is unlikely to have any significant impact on the child's problems. Behavioural techniques are sometimes effective

Table 11.5 Intervention for children with speech and language problems: the diversity of approaches. After Law (1994)

Approaches relevant to all language impaired children
The Hanen early language parent programme
The Derbyshire language scheme
Living language (a language syllabus for special schools)
Teaching talking (a set of procedures designed to enable mainstream teachers to support and work with children with speech and language difficulties)
Functional learning, family work, language and communication: (an integrated therapeutic approach)
Non-directive therapy

Approaches relevant to children with specific language impairment
Psycholinguistic approaches
Combined cognitive, linguistic and interactional strategies
Augmentative communication (see text)

Approaches relevant to children with speech impairments
Nuffield dyspraxia programme
Metaphon

in modifying undesirable behaviour and in teaching new skills, but are very demanding on parental and professional time. Each new step has to be taught, since autistic children are unable to generalize or extend ideas for themselves. The educational gains from individualized structured teaching are modest but worthwhile. Bright autistic children are best educated in a school catering for their special needs. Teaching techniques and skills relevant to autism are used in schools catering for sociable children with severe learning disability and therefore less intelligent autistic children do not necessarily need to be educated in a separate establishment. Those with severe behaviour problems are very disruptive both to the school and to their family and either regular respite care or a boarding placement is desirable for such children.

In cases where the diagnosis of 'autism' is borderline or in dispute, it is more important to select the most appropriate educational environment than to engage in fruitless debates about diagnostic labels.

Magic cures

The parents of children with complex communication disorders, particularly autism, are presented on a virtually annual basis with new approaches to treatment, many offering cure, from a range of sources outside the medical mainstream. Recent years have seen exclusion diets, evening primrose oil, holding therapy, 'magic ear', auditory integration therapy, options approach and facilitated communication. Just a few children do seem to have improved on some of these but it is difficult to know exactly what the crucial component was. The vast majority of children exposed to such interventions have not made substantial improvements. The paediatrician is placed in a difficult position. Some such treatments are extremely expensive or arduous, and a blanket approach of benign approval is not always justified. Often the best attitude is one of polite curiosity coupled with the question, 'How will you know if it doesn't work?' or 'If it isn't working as much as you hoped, how will you know when to stop?'

Augmentative and alternative means of communication

The development of spoken language may be very slow in children with severe cerebral palsy or learning disability, particularly when complicated by additional impairments, such as hearing loss or visual defects. To complicate matters further, the children's environment is often impoverished because their need for communication is not recognized and they are deprived of ordinary 'baby talk'; this is particularly true in cerebral palsy, where there is a danger that all therapeutic energies are directed to their physical disability. Some of these children eventually develop some speech, but only after several years of frustration, because they can understand but cannot respond. The more severely disabled may never learn to speak and verbal comprehension remains very limited. Without a means of communication they may become severely disturbed, frustrated adults who are likely to need institutional care.

Many ingenious systems are now available to bypass the need for speech in communication. The term 'alternative and augmented communication' (AAC) is used to describe these systems. AAC can take many forms, ranging from eye-pointing, body language, gesture and signing, to the use of a book, communication board or sophisticated electronic aid.

The introduction of AAC should be considered in any disabled child in whom language acquisition is severely delayed. Careful explanation to the parents is essential and several objections are commonly encountered. Firstly, the parents invariably fear that the child will become lazy so that he/she will not make any further effort to speak. In fact, experience shows unequivocally that these systems encourage language development, reduce frustration and may produce remarkable improvement in personality. Furthermore, no other means of communication is as versatile or rapid as speech. Even the most effective communication aids are very slow compared with speech and the child will abandon other methods as soon as he can make himself understood with speech. Secondly, the parents may point out that the child can understand their speech even if he/she cannot reply and therefore it is a waste of effort for them to learn the augmented system to communicate with the child. They should be told that the acquisition of the new system is like that of speech: children must gain experience in understanding the system before they themselves can use it to respond.

Parents often become despondent after a brief trial, reporting that the child sees the system only as a game or a tedious academic exercise. Children who have been passive and unable to control their environment in any way need time to learn that their communication system can be useful and produce rewards in a normal everyday setting. Parents and teachers may feel that a child is 'too young' or not developmentally 'ready' to use an alternative means of communication, but it is wise to give him/her the benefit of the doubt. To ensure that parents understand the child's needs, a speech and language therapist should be involved in the management of any severely disabled child as soon as the diagnosis is made.

Assessment

The selection of the most appropriate system is difficult and these children should be referred to a Communication Aids Centre with experience of such problems. Many parents seem to communicate almost intuitively with their handicapped child and can interpret their apparently meaningless efforts with confidence. The analysis of the means by which they do this is the first step in the selection and introduction of an AAC system. A multidisciplinary assessment is needed to construct a profile of the child's needs, abilities and weaknesses (Table 11.6). Unfortunately, many schools concentrate on only one method of AAC, but it is important to select and use the method that is most appropriate for the individual child.

A new skill

Parents will expect their specialist advisers to understand the subtleties of communication with an AAC user (Table 11.7). This is a skill and needs practice.

> Given that communication devices do not provide a direct substitute for natural speech, and are limited or different in terms of communication rate, vocabulary access and communication modes, it can be expected that communication via these systems has many unique characteristics and limitations ... Given the constraints in augmentative modes, it is also quite probable that interactions between aid users and others are accomplished in a different manner than interaction between two speaking partners. Both the user and the communication partner must make adaptations to this unique medium. Non-speaking people communicate not only with words, sentences and linguistic content, but with a variety of non-verbal means: physical

distances and postures, gestures, vocalisations, attentiveness, appearance and silence — that is, what they don't say.
> (Kraat, 1985)

The listener must be aware of, and respond to, all these different ways of communicating. A user might gesture or sign, use a communication board and an electronic communication aid all in one utterance. The communication situation will dictate the structure of utterances. For example, a more informal style may be used with parents and friends than would be used with a teacher.

Methods of communication

Object and picture boards

These are simple and cheap. A few common objects, or pictures of them, are attached to a large board; the child is taught to point at these to indicate their wants. Any means of pointing may be used, for example, a head pointer or the direction of gaze.

Symbols

Bliss symbols (Fig. 11.6) can be used on cards, boards, cloth badges sewn on clothing, or electronic systems. Some children master several hundred symbols. Because the word is indicated below each picture, no specialized knowledge is required by the person conversing with the child. The system is ideal for non-speaking children with cerebral palsy but is also useful for some children with moderate or severe learning difficulties. The Rebus method has many similarities to Bliss but has some advantages, being linked more closely to the teaching of reading. Makaton symbols may also be used (see below).

Makaton vocabulary

The Makaton vocabulary is a collection of approximately 350 words, which are grouped in eight stages and are believed by the system's

Table 11.6 Augmentative and alternative means of communication (AAC): the need for multidisciplinary assessment

Paediatrician/audiologist/ophthalmologist
What is the underlying diagnosis? And the prognosis?
Does the child have any hearing loss?
How much can the child see?

Speech and language therapist
Does the child show any wish to communicate?
Who will the child be communicating with? Where?
Does the child respond differentially to different stimuli? e.g. auditory, visual, tactile
Can the parents interpret the child's needs? If so, how? e.g. by his cry, eye-pointing, gesture or vocalization
Can the child confidently indicate any particular need? If so, describe how
Offered a choice, can the child indicate their selection? If so, how?
How much do the parents use spoken language to communicate with the child? How much does the child understand?
If the child can vocalize, how wide a variety of sounds can he/she make?
If the child uses words, is he/she frustrated because of not being understood? Is there a wide discrepancy between their
    expressive and receptive abilities?
Can the child: call for attention? greet? interrupt? initiate and terminate communication?
Do adults tend to interrupt and anticipate what the child is trying to say?

Psychologist and teacher
What are the child's non-verbal abilities?
Does the child understand the concept of cause and effect?
What strategies can the child use to solve problems?
Are there any particular or specific learning deficits?
Can the child use any form of gestural or verbal communication to indicate answers to questions?

Written communication
Does the child understand the concept of writing left to right? Can s/he form letters? Is this conscious or automatic?
What is the speed of writing? Is fatigue a limiting factor?

Physiotherapist, occupational therapist, engineer and/or physicist
What movements are under the child's control? Hands, eyes, feet, head, etc.
Is the child able to perform better in one position than another? Can their posture be adjusted to improve this?
Is the child frustrated by spasticity, athetosis, ataxia, etc.?
Are the child's responses very delayed? How long does it take him/her to initiate a movement?

Social worker and interpreter
Do the parents understand what is meant by AAC?
Do they appreciate its scope and limitations? Are they expecting a miracle?
Do they realize what the effects of AAC on their family will be?

Management
How will the equipment and training process be funded? Purchase or loan?
Who will be responsible for maintenance and replacements?
Who will ensure continuation after leaving school?
Will the equipment be needed at school and at home?

Table 11.7 Listening to non-speakers. From Kraat (1985), courtesy of ACE Centre, Oxford

Access

1 All charts should contain a brief description of how the chart is accessed. It is important to take time to read this and so prevent drastic communication breakdowns

2 If you are uncertain about the child's means of access, ask him/her to find a particular symbol, and explain why you are asking (depending on the age and experience of the child)

3 Many users are not able to point to individual symbols and may use encoded systems with hand- or eye-pointing

4 It is useful to ascertain how the child indicates 'yes' or 'no'. If the child has no reliable means of indicating 'yes'/'no', try to discover (by asking familiar adults) how he/she expresses pleasure and discomfort

5 Utterances may be very short and telegrammatic, which is quite acceptable for conversation. Key words may be given first and then elaborated. Initial letters only may be given as clues to names or places

Listener strategies

1 If the child using an augmentative communication system has some speech, it is likely to be used as one of the modes of communication and should be treated as such

2 The listener must be aware of how to maintain and develop a conversation
  (a) Signalling and turn-taking in conversation, allowing the child a turn
  (b) Noticing the child's efforts to attract attention and responding to them
  (c) Allowing the non-speaking child to initiate and control a communicative interaction
  (d) Non-continuously asking 'yes/no' questions

3 Social structures within communication that the listener should be aware of, and try to promote, include:
  (a) commenting on the environment, e.g. 'look big dog'
  (b) requesting information, objects, etc., e.g. 'Where is teacher?'
  (c) transferring personal information, e.g. 'I go home Saturday'
  (d) greetings, e.g., 'Hello'
  (e) protesting/rejecting information or actions, e.g. 'I not like PE'

4 It is also important to remember:
  (a) not to ask more than one question at a time
  (b) not to ask negative questions, e.g. 'You didn't go to a party, did you?'
  (c) not to guess wildly if you do not understand — rather ask structured questions, e.g. 'Who is this about?' 'What is he doing?', 'What is it?'
  (d) to give the child time to reply

5 If you do not understand a remark, ask:
  (a) if it can be said another way
  (b) structured questions (as shown in 4c)
  (c) for a clue
  (d) if there are sufficient symbols/words/pictures to express the utterance
  (e) questions to establish if it is all one topic
As a very last resort you should leave it and try again later, having given the non-speaking person the choice of continuing or abandoning the topic

6 Due to misinterpretation by either speaker or listener, communication can break down. Some strategies to enable communication to continue include:
  (a) repetition of a previously used utterance, possibly in a slightly different way
  (b) confirmation of an utterance at the listener's request
  (c) specification of a vague utterance
  (d) elaboration of an utterance in response to a question from the listener
  (e) not being embarrassed about asking the child to repeat and explain something he/she has said

Continued

Table 11.7 (*continued*)

7 It is not usually necessary to point to symbols when talking to the child, nor is it necessary to talk slowly or 'talk down'. As a rough guideline, talk to the non-speaking person as you would to anyone of their age. However, if talking to a young child or a relatively new symbol-user, then pointing to the symbols allows him/her to see that their system of communication can be used by others, and also reinforces their knowledge of symbols. You can easily simplify your speech if necessary without causing offence.

This can also prompt conversation between peers as the non-symbol-user can learn the system as well

8 When listening to an augmentative communication-user:

(a) verbalize each symbol as it is pointed to and, when an utterance has been completed, repeat and expand the utterance, e.g. 'Mummy — come — school' ... 'Mummy is coming to school'. In this way the child can check that you have understood their message and is, at the same time, provided with a correct model

(b) for fairly fluent users, it may be more appropriate to wait until the end of each phrase before repeating and expanding each phrase

(c) for sophisticated users, it may be more natural simply to keep quiet, absorb what the child has said and answer appropriately

originators to be those most needed by disabled and handicapped children. The most widely used form of Makaton utilizes manual signs borrowed from the British Sign Language for the Deaf (BSL, p. 218), but physically disabled children may lack both the manual dexterity and the perceptual ability to make the signs and the vocabulary can also be used in the form of symbols. Makaton is easy to learn (Fig. 11.7), but its grammar and vocabulary are limited, and it has been criticized on the grounds that it may constrain progress in more able children. The parents should be better at signing than their child is.

Paget–Gorman Sign System (PGSS)

PGSS is an invented language. The signs each represent a word, and word endings and inflections may be added. PGSS may provide a better basis for language teaching, particularly in children with severe communication disorders, but it takes time and effort to master. Complex hand and finger positions are used, presenting difficulties for children with movement disorders. It is used in only a small number of schools and may be of limited value in adult life.

Communication aid technology

Modern computer technology now offers a wide variety of devices to overcome difficulties in communication (Fig. 11.8). The child can access the system by means of a joystick, by using movements of the head, feet or eyes, or even by breath control. Voice recognition techniques are likely to offer further advances in the next few years. Keyboards range from a simple pressure plate, through a 'concept' keyboard which can be programmed according to the child's fine motor competence, to a full-function keyboard. A keyguard is often useful for children with excessive unwanted movements of the upper limbs. It consists of a sheet of metal or perspex through which finger holes have been punched, corresponding to the layout of the keyboard.

The output from the communication aid can be symbols or words displayed on a screen or typed on paper; or it can be in the form of speech, which can either be prerecorded or synthesized. A range of software packages are available to simplify input, correction and calculation. Character scanning and recognition systems are now available and are of particular value for people

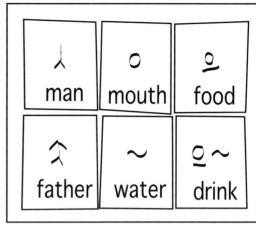

a

b

Fig. 11.6 **a,** A Bliss board in use. **b,** Bliss symbols.

Sweets   **Cold**

Ice cream

Fork

Fig. 11.7 Examples of signs from the Makaton vocabulary.

with visual defects (p. 233). Computer systems also offer disabled adults opportunities for environmental control; for example, they can switch on the television or use the telephone.

Communication aids are rightly perceived as an important advance and increase the quality of life for many disabled people, but there is a danger that parents may perceive them as

a

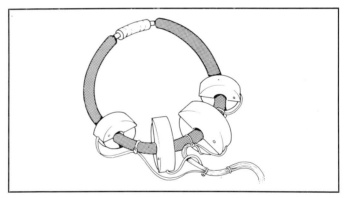

b

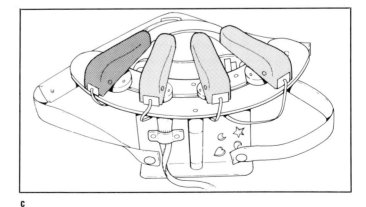

Fig. 11.8 Devices to overcome difficulties in communication. a, The ORAC is a portable speech communication aid with both digital and synthetic speech. Courtesy of MARDIS. b, Necklace and c, chin switches which can be used to control keyboards or powered wheelchairs. After McCarthy (1992).

c

miraculous. The limiting factor is usually the child's intellectual level rather than their physical incapacity; technology cannot overcome a lack of social awareness or interest in communication. It is essential that assessment is carried out by an experienced team with access to a range of aids and that parents, teachers and therapists are clear how to use the aid and what progress can be expected; otherwise disappointment is inevitable and an expensive piece of equipment will be wasted.

Reading

There is no point in teaching reading as a purely mechanical skill, but when used appropriately reading can help language development. The layout of text on the page, the use of various methods of emphasis and, of course, relevant illustrations can all be useful if carefully planned. In the Moor House scheme, for example, different colours are used to indicate different parts of speech — red indicates nouns, blue verbs and so on.

References and further reading

Asendorpf, J.B. (1993) Abnormal shyness in childness. *Journal of Child Psychology and Psychiatry*, **34**(7), 1069–82.

Bishop, D.V.M. (1989) Autism, Asperger's syndrome and semantic–pragmatic disorder — where are the boundaries? *British Journal of Disorders of Communication*, **24**, 107–21.

Bishop, D.V.M. (1992) The underlying nature of specific language impairment. *Journal of Child Psychology and Psychiatry*, **33**, 3–66.

Bishop, D. and Mogford, K. (eds) (1988) *Language Development in Exceptional Circumstances*. Churchill Livingstone, Edinburgh.

Bishop, D.V.M., North, T. and Donlan, C. (1995) Genetic basis of specific language impairment: evidence from a twin study. *Developmental Medicine and Child Neurology*, **37**(1), 56–71.

Chalmers, D., Stewart, I., Silva, P. and Mulvena, A. (1989) *Otitis Media with Effusion in Children — the Dunedin Study*. Clinics in Developmental Medicine, No. 108. Mackeith Press, London.

Connolly, K. (1992) The cost of ignorance. *Developmental Medicine and Child Neurology*, **32**(11), 943–9.

De Negri, M. (1994) Electrical status in childhood: neurophysiological impairment and therapeutic management. *Developmental Medicine and Child Neurology*, **36**(2), 183–6.

Fletcher, P. (1987) Aspects of language development in the preschool years. In *Language Development and Disorders*, Clinics in Developmental Medicine, No. 101/102, (ed. W. Yule and N. Rutter), pp. 70–89. Mackeith Press, London.

Gillberg, C. and Coleman, M. (1992) *The Biology of the Autistic Syndromes*. (2nd edn). Clinics in Developmental Medicine, No. 126. Mackeith Press, London.

Gillberg, C. (1990) Autism and pervasive developmental disorder. *Journal of Child Psychology and Psychiatry*, **31**, 99–120.

Gillberg, I.C. and Gillberg, C. (1989) Asperger syndrome — some epidemiological considerations. *Journal of Child Psychology and Psychiatry*, **30**, 631–8.

Green, J. (1990) Is Asperger's a syndrome? *Developmental Medicine and Child Neurology*, **32**, 743–7.

Hagberg, B. (1993) *Rett Syndrome — Clinical and Biological Aspects*. Clinics in Developmental Medicine, No. 127. Mackeith Press, London.

Happé, F. and Frith, U. (1991) How useful is the 'PDD' label? *Journal of Child Psychology and Psychiatry*, **32**, 1167–8.

Haynes, C. and Naidoo, S. (1991) *Children with specific Speech and Language Impairment*. Clinics in Developmental Medicine, No. 119. Mackeith Press, London.

Jolleff, N., McConachie, H., Winyard, S., Jones, S., Wisbeach, A. and Clayton, C. (1992) Communication aids for children: procedures and problems. *Developmental Medicine and Child Neurology*, **34**(8), 719–30.

Kraat, A. (1985) *Communication Interaction between Aided and Natural Speakers*. International Project on Communication Aids for the Speech-impaired. Oxford.

Kurita, H. (1985) Infantile autism with speech loss before the age of thirty months. *Journal of the Academy of Child Psychiatry*, **24**(2), 191–6.

Law, J. (1992) *Early Identification of Language Impairment in Children*. Chapman and Hall, London.

Law, J. (ed) (1994) *'Before School', a Handbook of Approaches to Intervention with Preschool Language Impaired Children*. AFASIC, London.

McCarthy, G.T. (ed) (1992) *Physical Disability in Children. An Interdisciplinary Approach to Management*. Churchill Livingstone, Edinburgh.

Pinker, S. (1994) *The Language Instinct*. Allen Lane, Penguin Press, London.

Shprintzen, R.J., Siegel-Sadowitz, V.L., Amato, J. and Goldberg, R.B. (1985) Anomalies associated with cleft lip, cleft palate, or both. *American Journal of Medical Genetics*, **20**, 585–95.

Sommerlad, B.C. (1994) Management of cleft lip and palate. *Current Paediatrics*, **4**(3), 189–95.

Watson, J.D. and Pigott, R.W. (1991) Management of cleft lip and palate. *Hospital Update*, April 1991, 306–12.

Whitehurst, G.J. and Fischel, J.E. (1994) Early developmental language delay: what, if anything, should the clinician do about it? *Journal of Child Psychology and Psychiatry*, **35**(4), 613–48.

Wing, L. (1988) The continuum of autistic characteristics. In *Diagnosis and Assessment in Autism*, (ed. E. Schopler and G.B. Mesibov), pp. 91–110. Plenum Press, New York.

Yule, W. and Rutter, M. (1987) *Language Development and Disorders*. Clinics in Developmental Medicine, No. 101/102. Mackeith Press, London.

World Health Organization (1992) *ICD-10: The ICD-10 Classification of Mental and Behavioural Disorders: Clinical Descriptions and Diagnostic Guidelines*. World Health Organization, Geneva.

CHAPTER 12
Hearing Loss

Definitions

The terms 'hearing-impaired' or 'hard of hearing' are commonly used in preference to 'deaf', which many laymen take to mean total deafness. A hearing loss which is present before speech has been acquired is described as 'prelingual'. In 'conductive hearing loss' the lesion is in the external auditory meatus, tympanic membrane or middle-ear cavity. In 'sensorineural hearing loss' the lesion is in the cochlea and/or the neural pathways to the auditory cortex. Most cases of conductive hearing loss in paediatric practice are acquired and are caused by secretory otitis media, whereas most sensorineural deafness is of congenital origin. Both types may be unilateral or bilateral.

There is no universally accepted classification of hearing impairment on the basis of severity. A hearing loss of 21−40 dB in the better ear is generally regarded as mild, although the effects may not be mild. Between 41 and 70 dB, a hearing loss is moderate, from 71 to 95 dB it is severe, and if greater than 95 dB it is profound. The severity of the hearing loss is only one of the factors which determines the child's use and understanding of spoken language; intelligence, motivation, parental support and education all play a part. The type and location of damage to the auditory pathways are also important, since children with identical hearing losses as determined by pure-tone audiometry show substantial variation in their ability to discriminate the complex sounds of speech.

Education authorities distinguish between partial hearing loss and deafness and make separate provision for these two groups (p. 217). For the reasons outlined above, the distinction is based not on the severity of the hearing loss, but on an assessment of the child's educational needs.

Congenital bilateral sensorineural hearing loss

Epidemiology

The 1977 European Economic Community (EEC) survey (Martin and Moore, 1979) found that approximately one per 1000 children had a hearing loss of 50 dB or more in the better ear at the age of 8 years, and one-third of these had a hearing loss greater than 100 dB. There was a very slight preponderance of affected boys. Recent evidence suggests that these figures may be an underestimate and the true figure may be closer to 1.3−1.5 per 1000. More complete ascertainment of cases, particularly among profoundly and multiply disabled children, and possibly a small real increase, due to increasing survival of very premature infants and of severely brain-injured babies and children, probably account for the change. There is less information about mild and unilateral hearing loss, but perhaps 1−2 per 1000 children have a mild bilateral defect (21−40 dB) and the same number have a significant unilateral loss. Thus up to 5 children per 1000 may have a sensorineural hearing defect. About 30% of hearing-impaired children have other impairments (Table 12.1).

Causes

These are summarized in Table 12.2. There are over 200 syndromes associated with deafness. The more common ones are described in the Glossary. Until a few years ago, congenital rubella was the commonest identifiable cause but it has now been overtaken by cytomegalovirus (CMV). Acquired hearing loss due to meningitis, head injury or, occasionally, a severe conductive loss due to middle-ear disease make up another 10%.

Table 12.1 Associated impairments of hearing-impaired children

Impairment	Percentage of total
Learning disabilities	4.8
Learning disabilities and visual	0.6
Learning disabilities and other	2.5
Visual	4.8
Visual and other	2.0
Neurological dysfunction (cerebral palsy, etc.)	3.5
Behaviour disorder	1.5
Disorders of other systems (cardiac, renal, etc.)	10.3
Subtotal	30
No other impairment	70
Total	100

Table 12.2 Causes of hearing loss in childhood (see Glossary for further details)

Prenatal causes
Genetic hearing loss with:
- no other abnormalities
- abnormal external ears (e.g. Treacher−Collins, Goldenhaar's, Melnick−Fraser syndromes
- eye disease (e.g. Usher's, Alstrom's, Refsum's, Cockayne's syndromes)
- musculoskeletal disease (e.g. otopalatodigital, Klippel−Feil, Crouzon's, DIDMOAD syndromes)
- skin, nail or hair disorder (e.g. Waardenburg syndrome)
- renal disease (e.g. Alport's syndrome)
- neurological disease
- metabolic and endocrine disorders (e.g. Pendred's syndrome)
- miscellaneous abnormalities (e.g. Jervell Lange Nielsen syndrome)

Sporadic malformations of inner or middle ear
Intrauterine viral infections

Perinatal causes
Prematurity
Hypoxic−ischaemic (neonatal) encephalopathy (p. 252)
Persistent fetal circulation
Kernicterus (hyperbilirubinaemia)
Meningitis
Aminoglycoside antibiotics

Postnatal causes
Middle-ear disease
Meningitis
Other childhood fevers
Trauma
Ototoxic drugs

DIDMOAD, diabetes insipidus, diabetes mellitus, optic atrophy, deafness.

There is no doubt that perinatal events are potential causes of hearing loss, but their importance is uncertain. The cause is completely unknown in about half of all cases, but this group includes a substantial number of inherited disorders.

In the absence of other defects, the distinction between genetically determined and non-genetic hearing loss may be impossible if the family history is negative or incomplete, and therefore the exact prevalence of the genetic types is not known. Probably 40−50% of all cases of congenital hearing loss are genetically determined, and of these the recessive forms account for 70−85%. Many different subgroups are recognized, distinguished by the mode of inheritance, age of onset and severity and frequency pattern of the hearing loss. Usually the hearing loss is static, but progressive deterioration occurs in a few cases (p. 219). Genetic sensorineural hearing loss is nearly always bilateral, although families are known where some members have a unilateral loss. In 70% of cases the hearing loss is the only defect; in the remaining 30% it is part of a 'syndrome'.

Perinatal causes

Perinatal events, singly or in combination, undoubtedly account for some cases of hearing defects, but their significance is often overestimated and the alternative possibility of genetic hearing loss must always be considered.

Prematurity. Estimates of the risk of sensorineural hearing loss in premature infants vary widely, although there is no doubt that the incidence is increased. The exact reasons are unclear; fears that incubator noise and aminoglycoside antibiotics might damage the hearing have not been realized.

Hypoxia and asphyxia. Sensorineural hearing loss may occur in children who have spastic quadriplegic cerebral palsy resulting from severe perinatal hypoxia and asphyxia (p. 252), although the association is surprisingly uncommon. A high-frequency loss may be found in children with athetoid cerebral palsy caused by hypoxia. It is very rare for asphyxial encephalopathy to cause hearing loss in the absence of any other neurological impairment.

Jaundice. The healthy full-term neonate may tolerate bilirubin levels of over 340 µmol/l without any immediate or long-term sequelae, but sick or premature babies are susceptible to bilirubin damage at much lower levels. Full details of the neonatal period must be obtained; a parental report of jaundice is not sufficient. Hearing loss can be attributed with more confidence to hyperbilirubinaemia when features of kernicterus have been noted in the neonatal period, but this is rare in developed countries. One-fifth of children with athetoid cerebral palsy caused by kernicterus have a hearing loss.

Development of hearing-impaired children

The major impact of congenital sensorineural hearing loss is on language acquisition. Hearing-impaired children use their vision to acquire social and non-verbal communicative skills and are less likely to develop bizarre behaviour and mannerisms than the visually impaired child, although behaviour problems may emerge if their hearing loss remains unrecognized. Unless they have other impairments, the development of cognitive and performance skills usually progresses normally, except that language deficiency limits their ability to solve problems in which verbal strategies are useful.

Although only moderate in audiological terms, a 50 dB hearing loss may cause both a marked delay in language development and defective speech. Even mild losses of less than 30 dB may be significant in some cases. When the hearing loss exceeds 70 dB, spontaneous acquisition of language is unlikely. Even with optimal amplification, by means of a hearing-aid, and expert teaching, many children with sensorineural hearing loss have immense difficulty in acquiring spoken language. This is because the ear has a reduced ability to discriminate sounds, no matter how loud they may be. Figure 12.1 illustrates how an increase in intensity of speech beyond a certain point is of no further help to the subject and he/she is unable to correctly identify 100% of words at any intensity.

A further problem is the phenomenon of recruitment, which occurs with cochlear lesions. This is an abnormally rapid increase in the sensation of loudness, once the subject's hearing threshold is passed. Thus, many people with sensorineural hearing loss experience increasing distortion and discomfort when using a powerful hearing-aid. Recruitment and distortion are difficult to measure, particularly in children, but explain in part why the results of amplification are sometimes disappointing.

Children with a severe prelingual hearing loss have little or no experience of sound until amplification is provided. They do not associate sound with meaning and have never learned to attend to auditory stimuli, nor can they modulate and control their voice patterns. The concept of a word as a group of sounds with a specific meaning, which is acquired effortlessly by the normal infant, must be specifically taught to hearing-impaired children. As they learn to listen, their hearing loss may show apparent improvement and they respond to quieter sounds; for this reason the initial assessment of their hearing loss may be unduly pessimistic. Some children learn to make full use of the minimal acoustic information audible to them and, by supplementing this with clues from lip-reading, facial expression and the social situation, make excellent progress in listen-

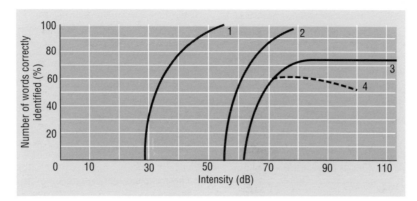

Fig. 12.1 Speech intelligibility with various hearing defects. **1,** Normal hearing: 100% of words heard correctly at 50 dB. **2,** Conductive hearing loss: 100% of words heard correctly at 80 dB. **3,** Sensorineural hearing loss: some words not heard correctly at any intensity. **4,** Sensorineural loss with recruitment: increasing intensity may make speech less intelligible. After Huizing and Reyntjes (1952).

ing and speaking. Unfortunately, in many cases, their speech remains unintelligible to strangers; they use only single-word utterances, and are unable to understand normal conversation, even with hearing-aids.

Severe retardation in reading is common. The written work of hearing-impaired children reflects their impoverished linguistic experience. Sentences tend to be short and contain numerous syntactic errors, which follow a distinct pattern (Table 12.3). There is some evidence of recent improvements in these outcomes, perhaps associated with more enlightened educational approaches, neonatal diagnosis with introduction of a hearing-aid within the first few months of life, and the rapid improvements in hearing-aid technology. Cochlear implants offer hope for further progress in language acquisition for the most severely deaf children.

Management

Diagnosis and investigation

Every child with a congenital sensorineural hearing loss should have a full physical examination. Physical anomalies may provide the clue to a specific diagnosis of a syndrome with genetic implications (Table 12.4). External ear anomalies, for example malformations of the pinna or cutaneous pits, are often associated with a hearing loss, which may be conductive, sensorineural or mixed (e.g. Treacher–Collins, Goldenhaar and Melnick–Fraser syndromes). The external ear canal may be narrow or atretic, making otoscopy impossible.

There is no single investigation protocol applicable to children with hearing loss, but the following should be considered: tests for rubella and CMV (p. 163); thyroid studies (Pendred's syndrome); electrocardiogram (ECG) to exclude Jervell–Lange–Nielsen syndrome; urine examination for red cells (Alport's syndrome); urine for mucopolysaccharides; electroretinogram (Usher's syndrome); chromosomes; assessment of close relatives — physical examination (for anomalies, for example in suspected Waardenburg's syndrome) and audiograms. An ophthalmic assessment is essential, both to identify possible clues to the underlying cause, such as a retinopathy, and to ensure that the child has no impairment of visual acuity.

Referral to tertiary centres may sometimes be needed for specialized imaging techniques, or for

Table 12.3 Examples of common syntactic errors, made by deaf students. After Martin (1978), based on original work of Quigley

The cat under the table.
John sick. The girl a ball.
Jim have sick.

Tom has pushing the wagon.
The boy was pushed the girl.

Beth made candy no.
Beth threw the ball and Jean catch it.
Joe bought ate the apple.

For to play baseball is fun.
John goes to fishing.
John goes to fish
Bill liked to played baseball.
Jim wanted go.

I helped the boy's mother was sick.
John saw the boy who the boy kicked the ball.

Who a boy gave you a ball?

Who the baby did love?
Who TV watched.

I amn't tired. Bill willn't go.

John chased the girl and he scared.
[John chased the girl. He scared the girl.]

The dog chased the girl had on a red dress.
[The dog chased the girl. The girl had a red dress on.]

what?

otological and plastic surgery assessments. The techniques of hypocycloidal polytomography and high-resolution computed tomography may be helpful when middle-ear malformations are suspected, and can also establish the structural integrity of the cochlea and semicircular canals. In some cases malformation of the inner ear can be visualized and this may help to clarify the nature of the hearing deficit. Reconstruction of an atretic ear canal or of ossicular anomalies may be possible. Plastic surgical repair of the pinna may be undertaken for cosmetic reasons, or a prosthesis may be used.

Table 12.4 Paediatric examination and investigation of the child with a hearing loss: findings which may suggest a specific cause or syndrome

Examination

External ear
  Atresia of canal
  Preauricular pits or nodules
  Low-set ears
  Small malformed ears

Eyes
  Heterochromia (different colour) of iris
  Hypertelorism
  Vision defect
  Optic atrophy
  Retinopathy
  Cataract
  Corneal clouding

Musculoskeletal
  Abnormal length or spacing of digits
  Short neck
  Craniosynostosis
  Cleft palate
  Kyphoscoliosis

Skin and hair
  White forelock
  Vitiligo

Miscellaneous
  Congenital heart disease
  Ataxia
  Neuropathy
  Goitre
  Hepatosplenomegaly
  Short stature
  Developmental delay
  Microcephaly
  Branchial cyst

Investigation
Family history
Audiograms of other close relatives
Physical examination of close relatives

Laboratory-tests to be considered
Serology and virus culture (congenital infections)
Chromosomes

Continued

Table 12.4 (*continued*)

Thyroid studies (perchlorate test)
ERG (for Usher's syndrome)
Skull X-rays and/or CT scan (for calcification, cerebral and inner ear anomalies)
Middle ear
ECG (for Q–T interval)
Mucopolysaccharides, amino acids

ERG, electroretinogram; CT, computerized tomography; ECG, electrocardiogram.

Counselling and support

Approximately 90% of deaf children are born to hearing parents. For them, diagnosis of congenital hearing impairment can evoke the same parental reactions as any other disability. They must be told where the lesion is, preferably with the aid of a model or diagram, and why a surgical cure for sensorineural deafness is not possible. Many parents are puzzled by the word 'deaf', particularly in cases of high-tone hearing loss, since their observations confirm that the child has some hearing. A simple explanation of the audiogram helps to clarify this. The possible causes should be discussed. A consultation with a clinical geneticist is often appreciated. It should be remembered that in unexplained congenital hearing loss the risk of having a further affected child may be as high as one in 10.

Most parents are distressed at the thought of their child using a hearing-aid, fearing that the child will be stigmatized or ridiculed, that he/she will refuse to wear it, or that the aid will be damaged or lost. It is also essential to explain why an aid is not the complete answer to sensorineural hearing loss, for reasons explained above. Particular care is required in the counselling of hearing-impaired parents. Many members of the deaf community are proud of their traditions and culture, and may prefer their hearing-impaired child to learn to communicate by signing. There is no reason at present to regard this as detrimental

to the child and some evidence that it may be beneficial.

As with other childhood disabilities, social services support and advice may be appreciated. The hearing-impaired child should receive the usual routine checks and health visitor input via the Child Health Surveillance programme. Particular attention should be paid to child protection; parents need to be aware that children with communication problems are particularly vulnerable to various forms of abuse and sexual exploitation.

Hearing-aids

A hearing-aid is a device to amplify sound. It may be worn behind the ear or in a pocket or harness on the body (Fig. 12.2). Some aids have special features, such as selective amplification of high or low frequencies and circuits to reduce sudden peaks of intense noise. Most aids provided for schoolchildren can be used with the 'loop' wiring system, which transmits the teacher's voice, thus bypassing background noise interference. Radio transmission systems are valued for their increased clarity and range and reduced noise interference. Powerful hearing-aids can produce a very high output of over 130 dB, and fears have been expressed that acoustic trauma might cause further damage to the hearing, but there is no evidence that this is so.

The earphone of the hearing-aid is attached to an ear mould, which is made from an impression of the child's ear taken with a rapid-hardening material (Figure 12.3). The ear mould must be a good fit; otherwise amplified sound escapes from the ear canal, is picked up by the microphone of the aid and is amplified yet further. The resulting loud whistle is known as acoustic feedback, and prevents the child from making full use of the gain available in the instrument. While children are growing rapidly, new moulds may be needed every few months. The efficient provision of these presents difficult organizational problems and in many areas children are repeatedly deprived of

a

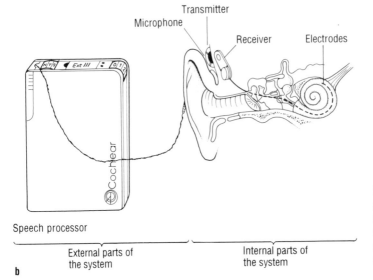

Transmitter

Microphone

Receiver   Electrodes

Ext III

Cochlear

Speech processor

External parts of
the system

Internal parts of
the system

b

Fig. 12.2 Hearing-aids. **a,** Parent
and child using radio-operated
hearing aid. Courtesy of Sennheiser
UK; **b,** a cochlear implant. Courtesy
of the Nottingham Paediatric
Cochlear Implant Programme.

adequate amplification while they wait for new
moulds to be delivered. Other problems associated with ear moulds include occlusion by wax
and chronic otitis externa. Bone-conduction aids
may be used if there is atresia of the ear canal or
chronic discharge. Implantable bone-conduction
aids may be the solution in such cases.

Cochlear implants. In essence a cochlear implant is
an expensive and sophisticated hearing-aid, which
can bypass the inner-ear hair-cell system and
stimulate the ganglion cells of the eighth nerve
directly. The implant consists of two parts — a
speech processor, which extracts and transmits
data about the incoming speech pattern, and the
receiver (the actual implant), which stimulates the
nerve via electrodes placed either adjacent to the
round window or inserted into the lumen of the

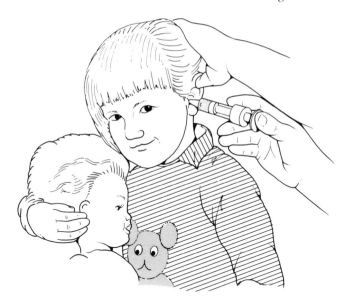

Fig. 12.3 Taking an impression of the ear. A rapid hardening material is injected gently into the meatus using a syringe.

cochlea. Cochlear implants are indicated for children with profound hearing loss and an intact eighth nerve. Experience is still limited but some children who, prior to implantation, did not respond to environmental sounds are now able to discriminate simple speech without lip-reading. The technique requires not only surgical skill but also an experienced rehabilitation team.

Education

The peripatetic teacher of the deaf (more recently known as the adviser to the hearing-impaired) is employed by the local education authority and is responsible for introducing the child to the use of the aid and teaching the parents about its management and maintenance. Later, he or she advises on school placement, liaises with the school and provides continuing supervision if the child is placed in a normal school. A speech therapist specializing in hearing impairment may also be involved in the child's teaching programme.

About 70% of hearing-impaired children (excluding those with multiple disabilities) attend mainstream schools. The remainder attend either partially hearing units (PHU), which are often attached to mainstream schools, or schools for the deaf. The distinction between the two is not sharply defined. The children attending at PHU must be able to make good use of their residual hearing whereas, in schools for the deaf, more intensive and individual methods are needed to help children acquire language and there may be a more extensive use of sign language. Educational needs rather than the audiogram determine school placement, but as a generalization children with a hearing loss greater than 90 dB are likely to need the type of education provided in a school for the deaf.

Controversy about the education of hearing-impaired children can be traced back 200 years. Some educators favour an oralist approach, arguing that deaf children must eventually live and communicate in a world of hearing people and must therefore learn to speak. Within the oralist tradition there are two variants: natural auralism, which assumes that deaf children will acquire spoken language 'naturally' through normal conversational exchange; and structured oralism, involving a more carefully planned input of syntax and vocabulary.

With adequate amplification, lip-reading and

the use of touch and vibration sense, many children do progress well. Lip-reading is limited by the fact that many consonant sounds look identical. The system of 'cued' speech was designed to overcome this problem. Hand signs displayed at chin level are used to differentiate similar-appearing consonants. A more recent development is the use of electronic analysers, which convert voice patterns to visual displays, thus enabling children to compare their articulation and voice patterns with those of their teacher. The 'tactual vocoder' offers another solution; it transforms the sounds of speech into tactile stimuli.

In spite of all these innovations, many children still have a severe communication impairment, resulting in emotional and behavioural problems. For this reason, more educators now favour the use of manual communication methods such as British Sign Language (BSL) and finger-spelling. In the past, oralists have argued that sign language is limited in its capacity to transmit and manipulate ideas, but this argument has been overturned by the discovery that sign languages in many countries are rich and complex in their vocabulary and linguistic capabilities. BSL is a highly versatile system developed over many years by the deaf themselves. Each sign represents a word, a phrase or a sentence (Fig. 12.4). Finger-spelling is used to spell out words for which there is no BSL sign.

BSL has its own grammar and word order, which differ from those of spoken English.

The use of sign language in early childhood encourages language development rather than inhibiting it. Advocates of the 'manual–visual' approach may recommend the acquisition of BSL as a first language, to which spoken English can be added later as a 'second language'. Others suggest that, for severely hearing-impaired children, a 'total communication' approach should be used. The teacher speaks in everyday English (using spoken English word order) and supports the meaning of each word or phrase with the appropriate sign ('sign-supported English'). Alternatively, BSL can be used in modified form, with signs added for verb endings and plurals ('signed English').

The education of mentally or visually impaired children who also have a severe hearing loss presents exceptional problems and for these some form of manual system is invaluable. The end result of a purely oral approach in such cases is usually a non-communicating, severely disturbed adult.

Psychological assessment of hearing-impaired children

Items selected from standard tests such as the Wechsler intelligence scale for children (WISC), Merrill–Palmer or Stanford–Binet can be used

Baby: slightly rock the arms

Exams: take 'thoughts' from head down on to paper on desk

Queen (or **King**)

Apple: jerk hand slightly forward and down as if biting a crisp apple

Fig. 12.4 British sign language for the deaf. Four examples to show the logical derivation of signs.

to assess non-verbal abilities, although they are not standardized for use with deaf children. The Leiter scale and the Hiskey–Nebraska and Snijders–Oomen tests are specifically designed for non-verbal presentation, and are very useful for assessing children with any form of communication disorder. Raven's progressive matrices may also be used, although this test may tend to underestimate the abilities of very deaf children. Vocabulary and language tests may be employed to measure progress. A picture vocabulary test can be presented with or without lip-reading and hearing-aids, and with the aid of mime or sign language. Discrepancies in the child's performance with and without these forms of assistance will sometimes dramatically demonstrate to parents or teachers the differences between a purely oral approach and total communication.

Deaf children often experience delays in social and psychological development. In early childhood, interactions between deaf children and their parents are often characterized by an over-controlling and intrusive quality. In a similar fashion peer relationships are frequently impaired and preschool deaf children show difficulty in situations involving more than one other person. These difficulties can be partially attributed to the parents' emotional response and partially to delayed language development, but they also reflect the practical difficulty of interacting in a purely visual medium, that of dividing attention within one channel of communication. These difficulties extend into middle and late childhood, with evidence of social immaturity and poorly developed interpersonal problem-solving skills. The risk of deaf children developing emotional behavioural difficulties is approximately 1.5–2 times higher than for comparable hearing children. This reflects a combination of language delay, intrafamilial difficulties, social and psychological delays and, for a small proportion, brain abnormalities. The fact that deaf children of deaf parents are far less susceptible to both social and psychological delays and difficulties suggests that communication difficulties and family responses are the two most important variables.

Acquired and progressive sensorineural hearing loss

Acute bacterial meningitis may cause severe hearing loss. It probably occurs very early in the course of the illness and, unlike the other complications of meningitis, is not necessarily preventable by early diagnosis. Other causes of acquired hearing loss include tuberculous meningitis, viral infections including measles, trauma, non-accidental injury and ototoxic drugs.

Acute bacterial meningitis is an indication for audiological assessment. This is urgent, for two reasons. Firstly, progressive sclerosis of the cochlea may occur after meningitis, making cochlear implantation increasingly difficult if this should be needed. Secondly, the child who has already had some experience of language before losing their hearing has a tremendous advantage over the congenitally hearing-impaired child, but this will be squandered if expert help is not supplied rapidly.

At least 9% of all cases of congenital sensorineural hearing loss in childhood are progressive. Some forms of genetic deafness (both isolated and syndromic) are progressive and may present as acquired defects. Deterioration is also seen in hearing loss caused by rubella, CMV and (rarely) bacterial meningitis. Acoustic neuromas are very rare in childhood (p. 369).

Unilateral hearing loss

Mumps is the most common cause of the total unilateral hearing loss which is occasionally found during routine hearing testing of school entrants. There may be a history of otological symptoms or vertigo during an attack of mumps. Other childhood fevers, inherited disorders, CMV and middle-ear disease may cause unilateral hearing loss. These children should all be seen by an otologist, but further investigation is rarely necessary.

Unilateral hearing loss is responsible for poorer speech recognition in noisy surroundings and causes great difficulties in sound localization.

It represents a significant social impairment at meetings and parties.

Children who are deaf in the right ear perform less well on psychological and school achievement tests than those with left-sided impairment, indicating that the defect does have some impact on learning processes.

Children with unilateral hearing loss seldom benefit from the use of a hearing-aid but they should, wherever possible, sit with their better ear towards the teacher, who should be aware of their disability (Fig. 12.5). An annual check of the hearing in the normal ear is a sensible precaution.

Conductive hearing loss

Congenital forms

There may be a conductive component in the hearing loss associated with ear malformations, for example in Treacher–Collins syndrome. Congenital anomalies of the ossicles may also occur in isolation. Otosclerosis is rarely seen in paediatric practice.

Acquired conductive hearing loss

Secretory otitis media (SOM) ('glue ear', otitis media with effusion)

SOM is among the commonest of all defects in young children. There is a middle-ear effusion behind an intact drum, without evidence of acute infection. The effusion varies in viscosity from watery to an almost solid rubbery consistency. The viscosity does not correlate closely either with duration of the condition or with severity of the hearing loss. The fluid contains leucocytes, dead bacteria and a number of mucoproteins, which are secreted by the middle-ear epithelium. Postulated causes include upper respiratory infections, allergy, inadequate antibiotic therapy of acute otitis media and Eustachian tube dysfunction. It is particularly associated with cleft palate, submucous clefts, Down's, Turner's and craniostenosis syndromes, and primary ciliary dyskinesia.

The main symptom is hearing loss; this may vary from negligible to 50–55 dB, with an average of 28 dB. All frequencies may be affected but most commonly the hearing loss is more severe

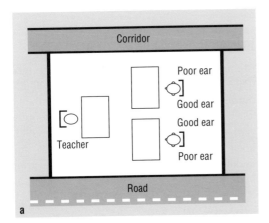

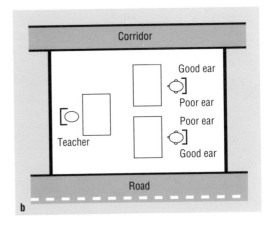

Fig. 12.5 **a**, A good seating arrangement for a child with unilateral hearing loss: the child faces the teacher and has the good ear towards the teacher. The poor ear is directed towards the noisier area (corridors or roads). **b**, A poor arrangement. From Children's Hearing Assessment Centre (1992).

in the lower frequencies. Mild pain may occur, perhaps indicated by the young child rubbing or poking their ear. SOM is often found in children who snore, mouth-breathe and have chronic catarrh.

The otoscopic signs are very variable (Fig. 12.6). The drum may look almost normal except for loss of the usual grey translucent sheen; there may be hyperaemia, or the colour may be obviously abnormal, varying from golden to slate blue. The presence of the cone-shaped light reflex is not a reliable indicator of normality. Bubbles or fluid levels may occasionally be seen. Retraction is a difficult but useful physical sign. The pneumatic otoscope (Fig. 12.7) demonstrates reduced mobility. Impedance measurement is invaluable as a confirmatory investigation (p. 82).

The commonest pattern is an isolated attack in association with an upper respiratory infection, followed by recovery within 6−8 weeks. Some children have recurrent episodes but recover completely after each episode. In a minority, the SOM persists for months or even years. Serious middle-ear complications such as cholesteatoma are recognized but are very rare.

Clinical importance. SOM is often found in children with delayed language development, behaviour problems or school failure. The condition is very common and it must not be assumed

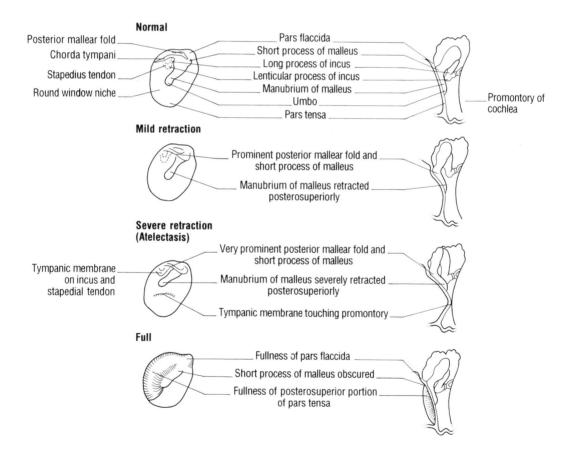

Fig. 12.6 Various positions of tympanic membrane as visualized by the otoscope and a lateral section through the tympanic membrane — middle ear. From Bluestone (1981).

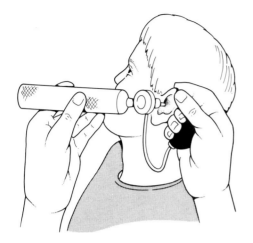

Fig. 12.7 Otoscope with pneumatic speculum.

that it is necessarily the cause of the child's disability. The impact of SOM on language acquisition is still controversial. The best current assessment is that for most children SOM is little more than a transient nuisance, but for a small minority it is a serious and disabling impairment. The identification of this latter group involves the following considerations.

1 Whether the SOM is transient or long-standing. The parents may know how long the child has been hard of hearing. A history of repeated ear infections may help. In the absence of these clues, it is advisable to see the child again after 6−8 weeks to see if the condition has resolved.

2 The severity of the hearing loss. This may fluctuate from day to day.

3 Other impairments. There may be some interaction between SOM and learning disability or a genetic predisposition to specific language impairment.

An intelligent outgoing child, in an articulate communicative family, will probably cope better with a hearing impairment than a self-sufficient, quiet child who lives with a depressed single parent.

4 Ear, nose and throat (ENT) problems. SOM is often associated with symptoms of airway obstruction — snoring, mouth-breathing, difficulty in chewing and swallowing, and constant nasal discharge. In some cases intermittent respiratory obstruction caused by large tonsils and adenoids leads to sleep disturbance, with repeated episodes of sleep apnoea and tiredness and irritability during the day. Blood oxygen saturation may fall and carbon dioxide levels may rise during sleep and occasionally may even cause pulmonary hypertension and right heart failure. This problem is readily identified by monitoring oxygen saturation overnight. Symptoms of adenoidal hypertrophy and airway obstruction in the child with SOM would bias one towards earlier intervention.

Management. A broad-spectrum antibiotic such as cotrimoxazole may be tried, although its value is uncertain. Decongestants do not help and have undesirable side-effects. Short courses of steroids (inhaled beclomethasone or oral prednisolone) may help, although further trials are needed. Surgical treatment consists of drainage of the ear by myringotomy and suction, and ventilation tubes (grommets) may be inserted. Adenoidectomy should be done if there are symptoms of airway obstruction and may improve outcome in children who require grommets more than once. SOM is not an indication for tonsillectomy.

Surgery is effective in the short term, but the frequency of both spontaneous remissions and relapses makes long-term results very hard to assess. The operation is not free of complications and continuing discharge and infections may be troublesome. Ears which have been treated with grommets show evidence of scarring and sometimes calcification (tympanosclerosis) and this has a slight but measurable effect on hearing thresholds. Nevertheless, for children who have a functionally significant hearing loss at a time when they should be acquiring language rapidly, the short-term benefits of surgery outweigh the long-term minor disadvantages. Hearing must always be retested after surgery, to confirm improvement; the possibility of a coexisting sensorineural loss must not be overlooked.

An additional consideration is the question of

swimming. There is no evidence either that water is likely to enter the ears while swimming, or that it would be harmful even if it did do so. However, if the surgeon is concerned about this, cotton wool plugs with vaseline (or an ear mould) and a tight-fitting bathing hat can be used. Diving is forbidden.

A small minority of children with SOM suffer repeated attacks in spite of surgical treatment and have a substantial hearing loss for a large percentage of their early childhood. These may benefit from a hearing-aid and extra educational support. Children suffering a combination of environmental language deprivation and mild deafness due to SOM need special attention. Parents and nursery nurses should make a specific effort to teach them to sit still and listen.

Other types of conductive hearing loss

Chronically discharging ears, perforation of the tympanic membrane and cholesteatoma formation are now relatively rare in developed countries. The conductive hearing loss may be severe enough to be of educational significance and the child may benefit from surgery or a hearing-aid of the bone-conducting type.

The production of wax varies widely among children and is partly determined by genetic factors. Wax only causes a hearing loss when it totally occludes the auditory meatus. Contrary to popular myth, middle-ear disease can and often does coexist with impacted wax, and it is essential to remove the wax and retest the hearing before accepting that wax is the sole cause of the hearing loss.

References and further reading

Bluestone, C.D. (1981) Recent advances in the pathogenesis, diagnosis and management of otitis media. In *Symposium on Pediatric Otolaryngology. Pediatric Clinics of North America*, **28**(4), 727–55.

The Children's Hearing Assessment Centre (1992) *Unilateral Hearing Loss. A Guide for Parents and Teachers*. CHAC, Nottingham.

Davis, A. and Wood, S. (1992) The epidemiology of childhood hearing impairment: factors relevant to planning of services. *British Journal of Audiology*, **26**, 77–90.

Fonseca, S.J. and Patton, M.A. (1992) Clinical assessment of deafness. *Current Paediatrics*, **2**(4), 229–32.

Hindley, P. (1992) Psychological and psychiatric problems of deaf children. *Current Paediatrics*, **2**(4), 233–6.

Huizing, H.C. and Reyntjes, J.A. (1952) Articulation curves. *Laryngoscope*, **62**, 521–7.

Laurenzi, C. (1993) The bionic ear and the mythology of paediatric implants. *British Journal of Audiology*, **27**, 1–5.

Martin, F.N. (1978) *Pediatric Audiology*. Prentice Hall, New Jersey.

Martin, J.A.M. and Moore, W.J. (1979) *Childhood Deafness in the European Community*. Commission of the European Communities, (EUR 6413), Brussels–Luxembourg.

Maw, A.R. (1994) Management of chronic glue ear. *Current Paediatrics*, **4**(3), 129–33.

McCormick, B. (1993) *Paediatric Audiology, 0–5 years*. Whurr, London.

Murdoch, H. and Russell-Eggott, I. (1990) Visual screening in a school for hearing-impaired children. *Child: Care, Health and Development*, **16**, 253–61.

Reardon, W. (1992) Genetic deafness. *Journal of Medical Genetics*, **29**, 521–6.

Sacks, O. (1989) *Seeing voices*. Picador Books, London.

Wood, D. (1992) Total communication in the education of deaf children. *Developmental Medicine and Child Neurology*, **34**(3), 266–9.

CHAPTER 13
Visual Impairment

The paediatrician does not need a detailed knowledge of eye disorders but should be able to: recognize the signs of important eye diseases, particularly those that may need urgent treatment; detect associated malformations and disorders; assess the impact of the child's visual impairment and other disabilities on development; ensure that adequate arrangements are made for the child's general paediatric care and education.

Blindness and partial sight cannot be defined solely on criteria of visual acuity (VA). Visual field defects, colour vision disturbances and visual experience prior to the onset of the visual impairment must all be considered. Bright children whose defective vision is their only disability will do much better than those who have learning difficulties or another impairment such as a hearing loss.

A blind child can be defined as one who will require education by methods not involving sight and, if of adequate intelligence, will need to learn Braille. Similarly a blind adult is one who is unable to do any work for which sight is essential. In practice this usually means that VA is around 3/60 or less but a person whose visual field is severely constricted may be effectively blind with a better VA than this. A partially sighted child is one with a significant visual impairment who can nevertheless make substantial use of their residual vision. This corresponds to a VA of between 6/18 and 6/60 in most cases, depending on the other factors mentioned above. See Table 13.1.

Epidemiology

In Western countries, serious eye defects in children are rare, occurring in 3–4 children per 10 000 births. About 2000 children in the UK are registered blind and 2500 partially sighted. In poor developing communities, where conditions such as measles, vitamin A deficiency, ophthalmia neonatorum and other infections are

Table 13.1 World Health Organization terminology for visual impairment. From Fielder, Best and Bax (1993)

Category of vision	Degree of impairment	Best corrected visual acuity	Alternative definition
Normal vision	None	$\geqslant 6/7.5$	—
	Slight	<	Near-normal
Low vision	Moderate	< 6/18	Moderate low vision
	Severe	< 6/48	Severe low vision. Counting fingers at 6 m or less
Blindness	Profound	< 3/60	Profound low vision or moderate blindness. Counting fingers at < 3 m
	Near-total	< 1/60	Severe or near-total blindness. Counting fingers at 1 m or less or hand movements at 5 m or less
	Total	No light perception (NPL)	Total blindness (including absence of the eye)

important causes of eye disease, the prevalence may be three or four times higher.

Routine epidemiological data for the UK are obtained from three sources: notification of congenital malformations during the first week of life; registration on form BD8, which is completed by a consultant ophthalmologist in respect of every blind and partially sighted child, providing national data on causes and prevalence of visual impairment; and educational data. Cortical visual impairment associated with multiple impairments is substantially under-reported, as shown in recent surveys by the Office of Population Censuses and Surveys (OPCS) and the Royal National Institute for the Blind (RNIB).

The OPCS survey estimated that there are 21 000 visually impaired children (aged 0−15) in the UK; of these, 6000 are 'multiply handicapped visually impaired' (MHVI). The RNIB's survey of children between 3 and 19 years was based on the records of education authorities. This produced an estimate roughly half that of the OPCS, but the methods were not comparable. The number of children registered as visually handicapped is larger than the number attending special schools for the partially sighted or blind. This is because some attend normal school and many others have an additional impairment which is of greater educational significance than the visual defect, so that some other type of school is more appropriate.

Additional impairments are common in blind and partially sighted children; many of the conditions responsible for eye damage also cause learning difficulties or cerebral palsy. Over half the children in the RNIB survey had at least one other disability. About 10% had impairment of both vision and hearing. Emotional and behaviour disorders occur in up to two-thirds of children at some stage of their lives. Tedious repetitive speech, withdrawal, aggression and 'blindisms' such as head-banging, rocking or eye-poking (p. 232) are examples of the problems encountered. These figures are more meaningful when considered in the context of a single health district (Table 13.2).

Table 13.2 Visual impairment in children in West Sussex*. From Fielder, Best and Bax (1993)

Total population 0−15 years	152 000
Total visually impaired	99
Blind (vision 3/60 or worse)	18
Blind one eye, low vision (6/24−6/60) other eye	24
Low vision both eyes	57
Multiple disabilities	60
Cerebral palsy or severe motor deficit	31
Epilepsy	12
Deafness	9
Additional structural malformation	10

* Data compiled from special needs register and validated by Dr Ann Abra, Consultant Community Paediatrician.

Of the 99 visually impaired children, 46 were unable to perform formal tests of visual acuity. An ocular diagnosis was recorded in 73 children, and 20 had evidence of visual pathway damage.

If cortical visual impairment is excluded, genetic disorders account for at least half of all congenital visual impairment. Cataracts, retinal dystrophies and albinism are the most common conditions. Optic atrophy and optic nerve hypoplasia are also important causes and may be sporadic or genetically determined. No more than 10% of cases result from non-genetic disorders such as microphthalmos, congenital infections and glaucoma. Retinopathy of prematurity (retrolental fibroplasia) accounts for about 12%, a smaller proportion than was the case 25 years ago, although there has been a recent increase.

Eye disorders

A classification based on the presenting problem is suggested (Table 13.3).

Group 1 — eyes look abnormal to simple inspection

Cataract and corneal opacities

Cataracts range in size from tiny opacities to total obstruction of vision. The pupil is described by

Table 13.3 A classification of the commoner paediatric eye disorders

Group 1 — obvious external abnormality of the eyes	Group 2 — mass behind the lens	Group 3 — eyes look normal but visual behaviour is abnormal
Cataract	Retrolental fibroplasia	Refractive error
Corneal opacity	Retinoblastoma	Retinal degenerations
Microphthalmos	Toxocara	Optic atrophy
Cryptophthalmos	Norrie's disease	Optic nerve hypoplasia
Glaucoma		Coloboma
Anterior chamber cleavage syndrome		Congenital infections
		Cortical blindness
Albinism		Delayed visual maturation
Nystagmus		
Oculomotor apraxia		
Aniridia		

the parent as hazy or milky but this appearance may only be easily visible in certain lighting conditions. Early and reliable detection is best accomplished by looking at the pupil through an ophthalmoscope held about 0.2 m away from the child with the lens set on +1 to +3.

In about one-third of cases, cataracts are inherited as isolated defects, and the inheritance may be dominant, recessive or sex-linked. Examination of other family members may be helpful. The causes are summarized in Table 13.4.

Sometimes vision can be improved by dilating the pupil with atropine but, when the vision is seriously impaired, current opinion is that surgical treatment should be attempted in the first months of life whenever possible, because irreversible amblyopia (p. 91) develops very rapidly in untreated cases. Urgent referral to an ophthalmologist is therefore recommended whenever cataract is suspected in infancy. After surgery, the aphakia (absence of lens) leaves the child severely hypermetropic, and this may be corrected by spectacles, contact lenses or intraocular lenses. Advances in lens technology are mainly responsible for the improved results of early surgery.

Corneal opacities are less common than cataracts. Various inherited anomalies of the cornea may occur. Cystinosis and some mucopolysacchar-

Table 13.4 Some important causes of cataract

Inherited: recessive, dominant, sex-linked forms
Idiopathic
Congenital infections
  Rubella
  Cytomegalovirus
  Toxoplasmosis
Chromosome disorders, e.g.
  Down's syndrome
Metabolic disorders, e.g.
  Galactosaemia
  Galactokinase deficiency
  Hypoparathyroidism
  Lowe's syndrome
Dysmorphic syndromes e.g.
  Hallermann–Streiff
  Marinesco–Sjogren
  Myotonic dystrophy
Miscellaneous, e.g.
  Post-inflammatory
  Post-traumatic
  Association with lens dislocation
  Glaucoma
  Retinopathy of prematurity
  Persistent hyperplastic primary vitreous

idoses cause corneal clouding but other features are usually apparent. Corneal scarring due to gonococcal ophthalmia neonatorum, trachoma or vitamin A deficiency is now rare in Western countries but is a major cause of blindness worldwide.

Microphthalmia

Microphthalmia ('small eye') may be associated with other developmental defects such as coloboma, or with intrauterine infections. It is occasionally recessively inherited. The eye is hypermetropic.

Cryptophthalmos

In cryptophthalmos ('hidden eye'), palpebral fissures are absent; there are often defects of the anterior part of the eye. There may be associated abnormalities of the ear, genitalia, kidney, etc.

Glaucoma

Infantile glaucoma (buphthalmos) is rare, but rapid diagnosis and referral are important, since it is one of the few paediatric eye disorders where effective treatment is possible. It may be unilateral or bilateral. It presents in the first year of life, with any of the following: large eye, corneal clouding, excessive tears (epiphora) without stickiness (in contrast to the more common condition of blocked nasolacrimal duct) and photophobia. The eye may be intensely painful, causing misery and perhaps vomiting. The corneal diameter is usually greater than 12 mm (normal < 11 mm). Buphthalmos may be an isolated anomaly or a secondary phenomenon associated with a variety of other eye diseases, including neurofibromatosis, homocystinuria, Marfan's, Lowe's and Rieger's syndromes and congenital rubella.

Albinism

This is a disorder of the melanin pigmentation system caused by defective conversion of tyrosine to melanin. There are oculocutaneous and ocular forms. The overall incidence is around 1 in

10 000. In the oculocutaneous forms, there are decreased pigmentation of hair and skin, pale iris and a red reflex from the eye due to transillumination through the iris. The child usually has poor VA, which is worse for distant than for near vision, variable refractive error, nystagmus, squint and photophobia. Binocular vision does not usually develop. There is an increased risk of skin tumours.

Two main types and several rare variants are known. Among the latter is the Hermensky–Pudlak syndrome, in which albinism is combined with a bruising tendency. The inheritance is autosomal recessive. Ocular albinism is less common and the abnormality is confined to the eyes. Inheritance is as X-linked recessive.

There is no specific treatment for albinism. A hat, and high-factor-number sun barrier cream should be used, as sunburn can occur after very brief exposure. Regular eye checks are important to detect refractive error. Tinted spectacles and magnifiers may be needed. Distance vision is often below the legal standard for driving. Refractive errors are common and should be corrected. The visual and cosmetic problems combine to make this a distressing disorder, particularly for members of black communities and for those who live in very sunny countries. There is an active support group and parents should be encouraged to join this.

Congenital nystagmus

Congenital nystagmus begins within the first few months of life. It is sometimes familial and may be inherited as a dominant, recessive or X-linked disorder. Typically it is horizontal in all positions of gaze. VA may be impaired but often is surprisingly good. Near vision is often better than distant vision. The subject does not have any sensation of apparent movement (oscillopsia). There may be associated head-nodding movements. Since many other disorders, notably albinism and achromatopsia, can produce identical eye movements, all cases must be reviewed by an ophthalmologist; congenital nystagmus is a diagnosis of exclusion unless there is a well-defined family history.

Unusual disorders of eye movement

Coarse bobbing movements of the eyes, fluttering and an overshoot on lateral gaze, followed by several very-large-amplitude jerks ('ocular dysmetria') are occasionally seen in children with severe brain damage, and are thought to indicate disruption of the pathways controlling eye movement. Occasionally such movements are mistaken for minor seizures.

In oculomotor apraxia the child has difficulty in initiating saccadic movements of the eyes (p. 90) and learns to overcome this problem by a jerk of the head. It can be an isolated disorder or may occur in association with brain damage or storage diseases. In the first 6 months of life, the infant may be thought to be blind because of the inability to fixate or follow objects away from the midline. When the head thrust appears, usually around 6 months, the diagnosis becomes more obvious.

Group 2 — mass behind the lens

In these conditions, the ease with which the mass can be seen is variable; presenting features may be the mass itself, abnormal vision or squint.

Retinopathy of prematurity (retrolental fibroplasia)

A few years ago this was among the commonest causes of childhood blindness. In the 1970s there was a substantial decline in the incidence, but with the increasing survival of extremely low-birth-weight babies the incidence is rising again. Although the development of this condition is probably related in some way to the oxygen sensitivity of retinal vessels in the premature infant, there are other factors which are not yet fully understood and the condition is not entirely preventable. The role of vitamin E is still uncertain.

Four stages of severity are recognized. The early acute changes sometimes regress and dis-

appear. In those children who develop a disabling cicatricial retinopathy, proliferation of blood vessels and fibrous tissue are the main features. In the most severe cases, the eye is small and a mass of whitish tissue can be seen behind the lens. Retinal detachment and glaucoma may complicate the picture. As this is now primarily a disorder affecting sick premature infants weighing under 1000 g, additional impairments such as spastic diplegia and learning difficulties are common. Cryotherapy may in some cases control the progression of cicatricial retinopathy and early detection by screening of high-risk infants is therefore important. The examination is difficult and must be done by an ophthalmologist.

Retinoblastoma

This may present with squint or retrolental mass. About 25% of cases are familial with dominant inheritance and these may be bilateral. Deletion of chromosome 13 has been described in association with retinoblastoma. Radiotherapy may be successful but enucleation is often needed.

Group 3 — child's visual behaviour is abnormal but the eyes appear normal to external inspection

Refractive error

Every child whose vision is suspect must have a refraction, since refractive errors such as high myopia are easily overlooked in the search for more exotic disorders. There is an increased frequency of myopia in premature infants, particularly those with retrolental fibroplasia, and also in those with albinism, Down's syndrome, muscular dystrophy and myotonic dystrophy.

Myopia occurring as an isolated disorder may either present in infancy ('congenital' myopia) or later in childhood (acquired myopia). The latter is uncommon before the age of 3, but the incidence increases steadily through the school years. Acquired myopia is more common in academically successful children. Very severe myopia is occasionally complicated by retinal detachment. There is no evidence to support the old belief that children with high myopia need to 'rest their eyes'.

Refractive errors are also found in association with dislocation of the lens, for example in Marfan's syndrome and homocystinuria.

Retinal disorders

This is a mixed group of disorders, some of which are very rare. The commonest is Leber's congenital amaurosis, a recessive disorder which presents early in infancy with a severe visual deficit. The appearance of the retina is unremarkable in the early stages, but the electroretinogram is attenuated or absent. There may be associated renal lesions and hearing impairment; cerebral defects and cardiomyopathy also occur. The diagnosis should be considered in any visually impaired infant with normal appearance of the eyes on fundoscopy, with or without other neurological impairments. It is sometimes mistaken for cortical blindness, a serious error because of the genetic implications.

Other retinal dystrophies include achromatopsia (congenital cone dysfunction), Joubert's syndrome and Zellweger's syndrome (see Glossary). Achromatopsia is often associated with a fast small-amplitude nystagmus, photophobia with onset at around the first birthday and vision that is better in very dim light. Precise diagnosis of retinal dystrophies can be difficult at first presentation and an initial diagnosis of Leber's amaurosis may need revision.

Retinitis pigmentosa (RP) is a degenerative disorder affecting the rods first and the cones in later stages. Pigment is deposited in clusters which resemble a bone corpuscle. It is unusual for it to present before adolescence. The first complaint is usually poor vision in dim illumination; the child may have difficulty in going down stairs in the evening. There is increasing constriction of the visual fields, with preservation of a central tunnel of vision (the visual field is really cone-shaped and increases in diameter with increasing distance from the eye). There are several types; it can be inherited as a dominant, recessive or sex-linked trait.

Rarely, RP is associated with a variety of other abnormalities (e.g. Usher's syndrome, Laurence–Moon–Biedl syndrome, juvenile neuronal ceroid lipofuscinosis, Refsum's disease, abetalipoproteinaemia).

Optic atrophy

This condition is recognized by the abnormal pallor of the nerve head, which is of normal size and contour. The normal disc is quite pale in infants and diagnosis may be difficult. The electroretinogram (ERG) is normal unless there is associated retinal disease (which may not always be apparent on clinical examination). There may be a fall in amplitude and an increase in the latency of the cortical visual evoked response (VER).

Optic atrophy may occur as an isolated disorder, with dominant inheritance, and begins insidiously in childhood. Leber's optic atrophy (not to be confused with Leber's amaurosis) is a distinct entity, in which there is sudden loss of vision with signs of optic neuritis occurring in the second or third decades. Other important causes of optic atrophy include papilloedema with secondary optic atrophy, craniopharyngioma, optic nerve glioma and hypertensive encephalopathy. It is essential to eliminate these possibilities when there is no obvious cause for the optic atrophy.

Optic atrophy may also occur in association with hydrocephalus, cerebral palsy, Behr's syndrome, diabetes insipidus/diabetes mellitus/optic atrophy/deafness (DIDMOAD) syndrome, microcephaly, non-accidental injury, cerebral storage disorders, hereditary ataxias and demyelinating diseases. It is doubtful whether optic atrophy in the absence of other evidence of cerebral damage should ever be attributed to perinatal hypoxia, and the diagnosis of isolated 'congenital' optic atrophy is of dubious validity.

Optic nerve hypoplasia

Distinguished from optic atrophy by the small size of the disc, this may be unilateral or bilateral. It is frequently associated with absence of the septum pellucidum and varying degrees of hypopituitarism. The combination is called septo-optic dysplasia and should be considered in cases of blindness with short stature. Intelligence is usually normal. The condition is nearly always sporadic. Many other structural central nervous system (CNS) anomalies have been observed in combination with optic nerve hypoplasia.

Coloboma

This is a congenital defect affecting the eyelid, iris, retina or optic nerve. It may be an isolated defect or be found in association with other anomalies, including CHARGE association, Warburg syndrome and various chromosome anomalies (see Glossary).

Congenital infections

Details of the eye defects associated with congenital infections are given in the Glossary.

Cortical visual impairment (CVI)

This is probably the commonest cause of permanent severe visual impairment in childhood in the Western world (p. 225). Most often the infant is first seen because of obvious, severe developmental delay, and assessment reveals that the child's visual behaviour is also abnormal. Sometimes, however, the parents become concerned about the child's vision before they realize that he/she has other problems as well.

Recognition. Children with CVI behave as if they have some vision and they do not 'look blind'. If they can walk there may be enough vision for navigation. They have an apparently short visual attention span. A characteristic feature is that the parents and teachers report apparent fluctuations in visual competence. These seem to be highly sensitive to environment, lighting, colour of the background and contrast. Colour perception is sometimes surprisingly good and these children are attracted to bright colours, especially yellow and red. Many children with CVI like to view objects at close range and some also turn their heads to one side when viewing objects, presumably in order to use peripheral visual fields. It is often difficult or impossible to determine the level of visual function in terms of VA.

Other features which may be observed, but are poorly understood, include tunnel vision, probably due to occipital infarcts, vision that is better either for moving or for stationary objects, and photophobia. Self-stimulation behaviours characteristic of ocular blindness, such as eye-pressing, are not usually found in children with CVI; however, gazing at lights and flicking the fingers in front of the eyes are common features of CVI.

Causes. Most commonly, the aetiology is either hypoxic−ischaemic encephalopathy or the complications of prematurity. Congenital brain malformations, meningitis and shunt failure in hydrocephalus, leading to occlusion of the posterior cerebral arteries and infarction of the occipital cortex, account for some cases. Occasionally cortical blindness may occur as a more discrete entity following a severe cerebral insult such as trauma, anoxia or hypoglycaemia. In some cases, there is near-total destruction of the occipital cortex and yet the child seems to show an orientating response to light or movement. This and other observations suggest that there may also be subcortical pathways for vision.

Examination. Ophthalmic examination reveals normal light reflexes, clear media and healthy fundi. Refractive error must be excluded. Optic atrophy may occur, probably as a result of nerve pathway degeneration secondary to damage to the visual cortex and optic radiation. This probably only happens with congenital or perinatal injury. There may be poorly sustained nystagmus of the gaze-paretic type (p. 91) and irregular jerky eye movements, but children with CVI do not have the roving eye movements or sustained nystagmus typical of visual sensory deprivation. Nor do they necessarily manifest the severe impairment of pursuit and tracking movements observed in children with congenital ocular blindness, although many children with CVI also have cerebral palsy, which can affect all aspects of motor control, including eye movements and head posture.

Investigations. These are directed towards determining the cause and excluding other conditions. In CVI, the ERG is normal; the VER may be, but is not always, abnormal. Computerized tomography (CT) or magnetic resonance imaging (MRI) scan may show abnormalities in the optic pathways and the region of the occipital cortex.

Implications. The associated learning and motor difficulties are likely to be the limiting factor in the child's progress. Therapy and education must be planned accordingly. Those working with the child will benefit from some knowledge of the problems of 'normal' blind children, but will soon discover that CVI calls for different educational approaches. Many, though not all, children with CVI show significant improvement over a period of many years, but most will still have significant visual disability. Even the most fortunate are likely to have visuoperceptual problems.

Delayed visual maturation (DVM)

This is probably the commonest single cause of failure to see in the first few months of life. The child presents when it is realized that he/she is not showing interest in visual stimuli such as faces, lights or moving toys. Paediatric and ophthalmic examination reveals no obvious defect to account for the poor vision. Subsequently, the vision improves without any medical intervention.

Four groups of children with DVM are now recognized. In group 1, there are no other findings, and the vision improves, often very rapidly, and typically between 10 and 20 weeks of age. The ERG is always normal and the pattern and flash VERs are within normal limits when compared with age-matched controls. Most of these babies do well, but some may have mild developmental problems and there is an increased incidence of squint and nystagmus.

In group 2, DVM is probably a manifestation of a more extensive developmental problem, particularly moderate or severe learning difficulties, and recovery is slower and less dramatic. Autistic features have subsequently been observed in a few of these children.

In group 3, DVM is associated with recognized ocular disease such as infantile nystagmus or albinism. The visual impairment is greater than expected from the underlying pathology. Vision gradually improves and in some cases the improvement in visual function is accompanied by the onset of nystagmus.

Group 4 consists of those cases where the child has severe bilateral eye disease, but nevertheless shows some improvement in visual function in spite of the fact that the underlying pathology has not changed.

The cause of DVM is unknown. In some cases it may simply represent unusually slow maturation of a particular pathway or system. Delayed myelination seems insufficient to explain the findings. A dissociation in development, or differential damage, between the occipital cortical system and the postulated subcortical system (see above) may account for the observations made on group 3 infants.

DVM is a diagnosis made firstly by exclusion of more serious disease and secondly by prolonged follow-up. Unless it is obvious that the vision is already rapidly improving when the baby is first seen in a paediatric clinic, a full ophthalmic examination is essential and in some cases detailed neurological investigation may also be required.

Development of the baby with visual impairment

It is frequently the mother who first recognizes visual impairment in her baby when she fails to elicit eye contact. The importance of vision in helping to establish a close relationship between mother and child was discussed in Chapter 3. The mother may feel rejected by the baby's inability to respond to her approach, as well as being frankly repelled if the eyes are physically unattractive. The baby may smile at 6−8 weeks in response to the mother's voice, but this is unpredictable, and only gross physical stimuli such as tickling reliably elicit a smile.

Between $2\frac{1}{2}$ and 6 months sighted children learn to discriminate their mother's face from unfamiliar faces. Visually impaired babies have to learn a similar discrimination by voice and by tactile exploration of the face. However, their auditory and tactile senses are sufficiently developed for them to protest at being held by a stranger not very much later than sighted children.

Visually impaired babies will 'freeze' when they hear a sound and, at 2 months, there may be a reflex movement of the eyes towards the sound. This reflex movement does not reward them with an interesting spectacle and therefore disappears, so that by 5−6 months there is no movement of the eyes towards a sound. Because they cannot watch their hands, they do not learn to bring them together in the midline and the hands are frequently held immobile at shoulder level. Skilled use of finger−thumb opposition is often delayed and instead raking movements of all four fingers are used to search for objects.

The concepts of object and person permanence are very difficult for visually impaired babies to grasp. They have to master the association between voice and person, and between sound and sound-maker. Reaching for a sound source begins in the last quarter of the first year, some 4−5 months later than the visually directed reach of a sighted child. Reaching is followed by an increased urge to mobility in pursuit of sound. Person permanence may be demonstrated by extension of the arms towards the mother upon hearing her voice, creeping towards her, or by using the word 'Mama'. The delay in achieving all these milestones may lead to an incorrect label of mental retardation and further rejection by the mother.

The acquisition of social competence is also more challenging for the blind child and it is perhaps not surprising that some are regarded as showing 'autistic features'. In some cases, children who have very severe visual impairment show developmental arrest or regression, with behavioural disintegration, in the second or third year of life (see p. 106). This has been described most commonly in Norrie's disease and Leber's amaurosis (Cass, Sonksen and McConachie, 1994) but may occur in a variety of other conditions. The explanation is not known but associated neurological abnormalities interacting with environmental stresses have been postulated.

The early language development of a visually impaired baby experiencing normal care may not be markedly different from that of a sighted child, although vocalization and babble are often diminished. However, some children with minimal or no perception of light show an unusual pattern of development; they produce word combinations several months before they show evidence of comprehending simple requests.

The inability to explore and master the environment and the need to make a tactile search of new objects often delay the acquisition of vocabulary and of the more complex forms that involve the relationships of two concepts. The stage of echolalia may be prolonged and the child may echo whole sentences without understanding their meaning. The use of 'I' is delayed, since the child takes longer to become aware of him/herself as a person separate from others. Later, language skills may become as sophisticated as those of a sighted person. Concepts of colour, width, depth, speed, etc. may present difficulties for a very long time, but eventually they seem to develop meaning even for children with severe visual impairment.

These children frequently develop mannerisms such as eye-poking, eye-rubbing, and rocking; these mannerisms are sometimes known as 'blindisms'. They should be regarded as a means by which a child who is struggling to overcome the enormous problems of congenital visual impairment can, through self-stimulation, achieve a satisfying level of arousal. Children with retinal disorders can use crude retinal stimulation by eyeball pressure to produce 'visual' sensations. Rocking induces kinaesthetic stimulation. Either may be used by the children to increase arousal or to soothe themselves when upset. The quality of the child's environment and the other sensory channels through which the child can access it are important, since the blindisms may be the child's way of compensating for deficiencies in sensory input.

Developmental scales (e.g. Reynell–Zinkin) provide data on the developmental milestones of visually impaired infants. The range of 'normal' development of infants with visual impairment is even wider than that of normal infants, when the range of visual disability is taken into account; it follows that the early recognition of associated learning difficulty is problematic. Neither blindisms nor the patterns of delayed development outlined above should in themselves be regarded as evidence of associated learning disability.

Early intervention programmes can improve development, increase parental confidence, and minimize the emergence of blindisms and other behaviour problems. The outcome for visually impaired children is often better than one might expect, even for those who have multiple impairments or maladaptive behaviours in early childhood.

Management

Referrals from a primary care team of an infant thought to have serious visual impairment should be regarded as an emergency, since the parents will be desperately worried. A busy ophthalmic outpatient department is not the ideal place for parents to learn that their child is blind or partially sighted.

Often the paediatrician will be in the best position to receive such referrals; having met the parents he/she can arrange appropriate ophthalmic assessment. The principles of caring for families of a disabled child are equally applicable to visual impairment as to any other disability and the care, counselling and support of the family

should, where possible, be based in a Child Development Centre, with referral to and utilization of specialist services as appropriate. This policy also ensures that other impairments can be detected and managed promptly and appropriately.

A subgroup of the Child Development Team should form a special team for the visually impaired, collaborating with the ophthalmologist, orthoptist and teacher of the visually impaired, to ensure that parents of these children receive the best advice available (Table 13.5). Since visual impairment is uncommon, the specialized help of a regional centre may be required if there is any doubt about a child's developmental progress or educational needs.

Accurate diagnosis is essential. Individual congenital vision defects are rare and may only be identified by an ophthalmologist with a special interest in paediatrics. Regular ophthalmic checks are important to detect any new pathology and in particular to ensure that refractive error is identified and corrected. Consultation with a clinical geneticist is often advisable. The genetic basis of many eye disorders is now known or will be determined within the next few years and recent advances open up new possibilities for more precise classification and antenatal diagnosis.

Every child with visual impairment must have an audiological assessment as soon as possible. Clinical testing by the distraction method is possible but is often difficult and objective tests such as brainstem evoked response (BSER) may be helpful.

Education

Because visual impairment is rare in childhood, it is difficult for the education authority to provide viable local units. Residential units serving a wide area were for many years seen as the only answer to this problem. Residential schooling for very young children is now less popular. Instead, a peripatetic advisory teacher for the visually impaired, provided by either the local authority or the RNIB advises the parents on methods of helping the preschool child at home. Some

Table 13.5 Early intervention — advice for parents. From Hunt (unpublished data)

Developmental stage	Features	Implications for intervention
Attachment	Lack of eye-to-eye regard and smiling to face. 'Stills' when listening — does not extend arms to be lifted. Seen as unresponsive	Baby reported as 'good baby'. Left to lie without human contact. Worker can act as ambassador for the baby, interpreting the baby's behaviour and needs to the parents. Plenty of physical contact is desirable
Midline handplay	Midline handplay gives knowledge of their position in space — a prerequisite to reaching out. Blind child often has 'dead hands' remaining in fetal position	Aid baby to identify hands, e.g. stirrup bells on each wrist, or bring hands together around squeaky toy. Encourage 'clap hands' lap-play
Reaching on sound cue	Sighted baby 'visually insatiable' — reaches and obtains objects at 4 months, extending knowledge and becoming active agent on world. Blind baby rarely reaches to sound before 9 months, limiting world to body. Beginnings of 'blindisms'	Make sounds meaningful. Bring baby to source of sound. Aid reaching to sound. Stop rocking and eye-poking at onset
Feeding and chewing	Resistance to spoon, new flavours and chewing without introduction that sight and imitation brings	Introduce new flavours early. 'Teach' chewing by reward-producing foods (crisps, crackers)
Creeping and crawling	Directed mobility unlikely before reach on sound cue established. Bottom-shuffling and crawling backwards common	Incentive for mobility lacking. 'Lure' creep or roll to accessible known sound (parent's voice, favourite sound toy). Bells, etc. on shoes/socks encourage mobility
Speech and language	Without vision, lacks shared frames of reference via pointing, imitation or preverbal gestural communication. Sounds produced lack communicative function. Echolalia may start and persist	Imitate and reward sound production. Keep up 'running commentary' around infant about what the baby's doing and ongoing events to co-ordinate sounds with meaning. Play with familiar household objects and action rhymes important

severely visually impaired children may be able to attend and enjoy a normal nursery or nursery school. With modern equipment, many can make good use of their residual vision and, provided the class teacher is appropriately advised and supported (Table 13.6), some will progress well in ordinary school.

Prior to school entry, the child may be seen by a specialist educational psychologist for assessment. Several psychometric scales and tests are available for the visually impaired, including the Reynell–Zinkin, Callier–Azusa and Columbia Mental Maturity Scales and the Williams Test. Prolonged observation in a nursery or assessment unit is often the most effective way to decide about a child's future school placement. The child's intellect, their ability to make use of their residual vision, the wishes of the family, and the child's long-term prognosis determine whether he/she should be placed in normal school, partially sighted unit or school for the blind.

Recent improvements in this area of education

Table 13.6 Integration of visually impaired child into mainstream school — advice for teachers

---

Good lighting conditions — even illumination without glare

Permit use of low-vision aids and/or tape-recorders

Adequate type size in books

Should be allowed to approach wall display materials

Use of felt-tip pens for writing

Writing on shiny blackboards is hard to read

Needs extra time to inspect objects, books, etc.

May have difficulty judging distances, stairs, ball games, etc.

Consider visual and acoustic impact on visually impaired when making structural or decorative changes in the school

---

include better optical aids, such as magnifiers, binoculars and telescopes; closed-circuit television; touch-sensitive computer screens; other 'high-tech' communication aids, which can convert print into synthetic speech or Braille (see also p. 205); reading material prepared in very large type (although this is often less useful than a magnifier); and well-designed desks at a comfortable angle. Lighting is important, although the precise requirements may vary from child to child; some will benefit from clear bright lighting whereas others, for instance those with albinism, may have problems with glare if the light is too bright or direct. Braille, of course, remains an essential method of reading for the most severely impaired, provided that their intelligence is in or near the normal range. Tape-recorders and teaching machines are also widely used. Tactile photocopying is a recent innovation which allows students to feel the contours of diagrams, maps, etc.

Mobility training is an essential part of the curriculum. As the child matures, he/she learns to travel outside the school, first under supervision and then on their own. The long cane is widely used, and has yet to be displaced by more sophisticated electronic or ultrasound devices. The length for the cane is chosen so that the tip just touches the ground one pace ahead of the user.

Education of the visually impaired in the UK has had to adapt to changing needs and opinions. There has been an increase in the survival of children with very severe brain damage associated with cortical blindness, and an increasing trend towards integration of the less severely impaired into normal school. Special schools have to provide services for multihandicapped visually impaired children; the expertise needed to teach, and provide equipment for, visually impaired children of normal intellect must be provided within mainstream schools.

Employment for the visually impaired schoolleaver, particularly in times of high unemployment, presents great problems. Some will overcome their disability and succeed in a variety of occupations, and a small minority will take on the traditional occupations of the blind such as piano-tuning. Unfortunately many will be virtually unemployable on the open market. Details of facilities for the adult blind and of equipment for use in the home (writing aids, kitchen devices, telephone modifications, etc.) are obtainable from the voluntary organizations representing the visually impaired.

The deaf–blind child

A deaf–blind child can be defined in the following terms: 'a child who has both auditory and visual impairments, such that one sense cannot compensate for the other, to the extent that the child cannot be catered for in special education programmes either for the hearing-impaired or for the visually impaired'. This devastating combination of impairments was until recently seen most commonly in congenital rubella syndrome. Other causes include Usher's syndrome, Refsum's disease, congenital malformation syndromes, perinatal brain injury and acquired deafness in a blind child.

The rarity of the combination makes management difficult since few education authorities have enough cases to justify provision of a specialist unit. In addition, these children may also suffer from learning difficulties, cerebral palsy or epilepsy. Deaf–blind children are inevitably delayed in their development and it must not automatically be assumed that they also have learning difficulties. Formal psychometric assessment may be difficult or impossible and careful prolonged observation is essential when planning the child's education. Various developmental scales can be adapted for use with these children, such as the Portage programme (p. 126), the Behaviour Assessment Battery, the Reynell–Zinkin scales, etc. The Callier-Azusa observational scales for deaf–blind children (University of Texas) may be helpful in some situations.

Early management combines elements of the care outlined previously for both deaf and blind children. Predictable daily routines of daily management, the development of the senses of touch and smell, and the encouragement of movement and mobility are vital. A white stick with red bands may be used to denote deaf–blindness but most deaf–blind children and young people need to be escorted unless they are in safe familiar surroundings.

Communication is the greatest problem. Paget–Gorman or British Sign Language for the deaf may be used; the latter is now thought to be more suitable by many teachers. The children use touch to 'read' the signs and the teacher helps them to make the signs themselves by positioning their hands. The manual alphabet is used as soon as the child can master it. Real objects and tactile pictures may also help the child to convey meaning.

Although this combination of impairments presents the parents with enormous problems, improved teaching methods and new technology give more hope for future development and communication. The parents should be encouraged to contact the relevant voluntary society for information, assistance, books and videos.

References and further reading

Cass, H.D., Sonksen, P.M. and McConachie, H.R. (1994) Developmental setback in severe visual impairment. *Archives of Disease in Childhood*, **70**(3), 192–6.

DHSS. (1988) *Causes of Blindness and Partial Sight among Children Aged Under 16, Newly Registered as Blind and Partially Sighted Between 1985 and 1987*. Statistical Bulletin, No. 3/9/88. HMSO, London.

Eken, P., De Vries, L.S., Van Der Graaf, Y., Meiners, L.C. and Van Nieuwenhuizen, O. (1995) Haemorrhagic-ischaemic lesions of the neonatal brain: correlation between cerebral visual impairment, neurodevelopmental outcome and MRI in infancy. *Developmental Medicine and Child Neurology*, **37**(1), 41–55.

Fielder, A.R., Best, A.B. and Bax, M.C.O. (1993) *The management of Visual Impairment in Childhood*. Clinics in Developmental Medicine, No. 128. Mackeith Press, London.

Jan, J.E., Good, W.V., Freeman, R.D. and Esperzel, H. (1994) Eye-poking. *Developmental Medicine and Child Neurology*, **36**(4), 321–5.

Jan, J.E., Groenveld, M. and Anderson, D.P. (1993) Photophobia and cortical visual impairment. *Developmental Medicine and Child Neurology*, **35**(6), 473–7.

Martyn, L.J., Pileggi, A.J. and Baird, H.W. (1985) *Optic Fundus Signs of Developmental and Neurological Disorders in Children: A Manual for Clinicians*. Clinics in Developmental Medicine, No. 89. Mackeith Press, London.

McConachie, H.R. and Moore, V. (1994) Early expressive language of severely visually impaired children, *Developmental Medicine and Child Neurology*, **36**(3), 230–40.

Moller, M.A. (1993) Working with visually impaired children and their families. *Pediatric Clinics of North America*, **40**, 881–90.

Pebenito, R. and Cracco, J.B. (1988) Congenital ocular motor apraxia. *Clinical Pediatrics*, 27–31.

Pike, M.G., Holmstrom, G., De Vries, L.S., Pennock, J.M., Drew, K.J., Sonksen, P.M. and Dubowitz, L.M.S. (1994) Patterns of visual impairment associated with lesion of the preterm infant brain. *Developmental Medicine and Child Neurology*, **36**(10), 849–62.

Potter, W.S. (1993) Pediatric cataracts. *Pediatric Clinics of North America*, **40**, 841–53.

Robinson, R. and O'Keefe, M. (1993) Follow-up study on premature infants with and without retinopathy of prematurity. *British Journal of Ophthalmology*, **77**, 91–4.

Stoll, C., Alembik, Y., Doff, B. and Roth, M.P. (1992) Epidemiology of congenital eye malformations in 131 760 consecutive births. *Ophthalmic Pediatrics and Genetics*, **13**, 179–86.

Youngson-Reilly, S., Tobin, M.J. and Fielder A.R. (1994) Patterns of professional involvement with parents of visually impaired children. *Developmental Medicine and Child Neurology*, **36**(5), 449–58.

CHAPTER 14
Cerebral Palsy

Terminology

Cerebral palsy (CP) is not a single or specific condition and it would be more accurate to speak of the 'cerebral palsies' (Table 14.1). CP is defined as 'a persistent but not necessarily unchanging disorder of posture and/or movement, due to a non-progressive lesion of the brain, acquired during the stage of rapid brain development'. The term cerebral palsy is the cause of much confusion.

1 The definition includes an enormous range of problems, from a minimal hemiplegia which has negligible effects on the child's life, to severe quadriplegia associated with profound learning disabilities.

2 The layman's term for any child with CP is 'a spastic' but in fact the spastic type is only one form of CP. Many young children with CP have variable muscle tone and do not necessarily feel stiff or 'spastic' when handled.

3 To most laymen and many doctors, cerebral palsy is synonymous with 'brain damage at birth', but often this is not the cause.

4 By definition, the term CP refers only to the motor deficit. CP, however severe, is not incompatible with a normal intellect, but nevertheless learning disabilities are common in these children.

5 Children in whom the main motor problem is hypotonia or non-progressive ataxia often have severe learning disabilities. Some authorities label these as having CP, while others regard the learning disability as the main problem and the motor delay as secondary.

6 When the effects of a progressive brain lesion, such as hydrocephalus or a tumour, are arrested or reversed by treatment, the child may be left with a non-progressive neurological deficit and such cases are often grouped with the CPs.

7 The period of most rapid brain development is the first 2 or 3 years of life, but there is no exact age at which the above definition ceases to be applicable.

8 Although the definition of CP excludes older children with acquired brain damage and those with progressive disease, their service needs have much in common with those of CP children. Staff caring for them sometimes use the term 'CP' for any child with permanent neurological deficits.

9 Terms such as hemiplegia are often regarded as a diagnosis whereas in fact they are only a description.

Classification

Conceptual disagreements and interobserver variability in clinical assessment bedevil the classification of CP. The following simple approach emphasizes, firstly, the nature of the cerebral lesion and, secondly, the presenting features and functional problems of the child.

1 *Unilateral, focal damage to an otherwise normal brain.* The physical signs and the functional motor problems are mainly confined to the limbs and trunk on the affected side and the child's early motor development, although obviously characterized by asymmetry, passes through an essentially normal sequence.

2 *Bilateral, widespread or generalized damage to a previously normal brain or abnormal development of the brain,* indicated by bilateral motor abnormalities. These children are further divided into two groups.

　(a) Children with increased tone (hypertonia) or variable tone. In contrast to the first group, these children tend to have severe disturbances of early motor development. Their motor progress is often slow and associated impairments

237

Table 14.1 Cerebral palsy

Term	Meaning
Types of abnormal tone and movement disorder	
Hypotonia	Diminished tone (atonia = absence of tone)
Hypertonia	Increased tone: may be of spastic or rigid type
Spasticity	Increased muscle tone, weakness, brisk reflexes, extensor plantars. Two types, phasic and tonic (see text)
Rigidity	Increased tone throughout the range of movement, often associated with dyskinesia
Dyskinesia	Involuntary movements and changes in muscle tone, which usually involve the whole of the body, although there may be some asymmetry. All motor activities including speech are affected. Includes athetosis, chorea and dystonia
Athetosis	Unstable, constantly changing tone, usually with patterns involving the whole body; small random movements at rest; writhing movements of limbs; on approach to an object there is extension and fanning of the fingers and extension of the wrist
Chorea	Quick jerky movements of the limbs
Dystonia	Slow writhing movements of trunk and/or proximal limb muscles with distorted postures; may affect isolated muscle groups
Ataxia	Early hypotonia, very delayed walking. Gait is broad-based, marked incoordination, tremor and titubation of the head
Dysequilibrium	Lack of awareness of body's spatial relationships; tendency to fall from standing position; lack of compensatory and protective reflexes
Distribution of movement disorder	
Hemiplegia*	Involvement of the face, arm and leg, on one side of the body
Diplegia	Involvement of all four limbs but legs affected substantially more than the arms. Diplegia may be symmetric or asymmetric
Quadriplegia (tetraplegia)	Implies approximately equal involvement of legs, arms, head and trunk; may be symmetric or asymmetric
Paraplegia	Involvement of the legs only. Pure paraplegia is suggestive of a spinal lesion rather than cerebral palsy
Double hemiplegia	Differs from quadriplegia in less trunk and head involvement, less dominated by persistent stereotyped patterns. Pseudobulbar palsy (involvement of speech and swallowing musculature) due to bilateral upper motor neuron lesions
Monoplegia	Involvement of one limb only; rare

*Strictly speaking, the suffix -plegia refers to complete weakness or paralysis, whereas -paresis implies partial weakness; however, the terms are used interchangeably.

Table 14.2 Neurology of increased muscle tone (see Brown and Minns, 1989)

SPASTICITY
Defined as 'an abnormally increased contraction of a muscle in response to stretch'

Phasic spasticity
- Increased tendon reflexes
- Clonus
- Clasp-knife phenomenon — when the muscle is suddenly and rapidly stretched from position of full extension there is a short-lived increase in tone, which then dies away. The phenomenon is velocity-dependent, i.e. it is not seen if the muscle is stretched slowly
- Loss of skilled fine movements, more marked in distal than in proximal muscles
- Spasticity is more marked in antigravity muscles, i.e. arm flexors and leg extensors
- Lengthening reaction or extensibility is not reduced, i.e. there is no restriction in the range of movement

Tonic spasticity
- Resistance to stretch is not velocity-dependent
- Extensibility of the muscle is reduced
- There is marked reciprocal inhibition of the antagonist muscle, producing clinically apparent weakness, e.g. spasticity of the hamstrings is associated with weakness of the quadriceps
- If the tonic spasticity is removed (e.g. by cutting the tendon), the inhibition is removed and the antagonist may become overactive
- Proximal muscles are affected more than distal
- Flexor muscle groups are predominantly affected
- Proximal muscle groups show tonic spasticity with bilateral lesions, i.e. tonic spasticity not prominent in pure hemiplegia
- Muscle growth in length is impaired, with reduced range of joint movement

RIGIDITY
Defined as 'an involuntary sustained contraction of a muscle which is not dependent on muscle spindle activity (i.e. not stretch-dependent)'. It is associated with lesions of the basal ganglia and extrapyramidal system.
- There is constant resistance at varying lengths of muscle and not just when the muscle is stretched from its shortest position (lead-pipe rigidity)
- The dominant pattern may be either extensor or (less often) flexor rigidity
- Abnormal reflex patterns involving sudden changes of tone and posture are prominent (e.g. tonic labyrinthine, tonic neck; see p. 246)
- Positional and sensory stimuli, anxiety, etc. may provoke changes in pattern and symmetry of muscle tone; hence the term 'dystonia'
- If very severe, all movement may be inhibited
- Growth of muscles is not impaired; provided there is no associated spasticity, apparent deformities disappear and a full range of movement is possible when the rigidity is eliminated, e.g. asleep or under anaesthetic
- Continuous undamped changes of tone produce dyskinesias

are more common and more severe. This group includes: (i) spastic diplegia; and (ii) children with 'total body involvement' or 'four-limb CP' (athetosis, the spastic and rigid quadriplegias and double hemiplegia).

(b) Children with decreased tone in infancy (hypotonia), either in isolation or accompanied by ataxia.

Neurology of hypertonia

The variable responses of children with CP to drugs, surgery and therapy and the differences in the extent to which deformity occurs are at least partly due to the fact that there are several causes of hypertonia (Table 14.2), which may coexist in the same child and evolve at different rates.

Epidemiology

The number of cases of CP is described as the birth prevalence, i.e. the number of cases of CP per 1000 live births. Most estimates in developed countries are around 2 to 2.5 per 1000 births. Between 25 and 40% of cases are found in the 6−7% of children who weighed under 2500 g at birth. Between 8 and 20% are attributed to 'birth asphyxia' and 10% are caused by postnatal events. About 30% of CP children have hemiplegia, 20% have diplegia and the remainder have total body involvement.

In recent years there has been little change in the prevalence of CP among children weighing over 2500 g at birth but the prevalence has risen among those who were of low birth weight. Among graduates of neonatal intensive care units, both hemiplegia and diplegia occur and there are many children with severe total body involvement. The pattern of diplegia in these infants is different from that seen in classic spastic diplegia, which has become less common. Pure athetosis has become rare since the virtual disappearance of kernicterus due to rhesus disease.

Hemiplegia (Fig. 14.1)

Hemiplegia may be congenital or acquired. Professionals tend to regard hemiplegia as a relatively minor problem, but it is not minor to the parents and the significance of a disability which looks rather trivial in a 9-month-old baby should not be underestimated.

Congenital hemiplegia

Early development

Most commonly, congenital hemiplegia is first suspected between 3 and 6 months when the parents observe asymmetry of hand function, but there is often a delay before they are sufficiently certain to seek advice. The affected hand shows a relative poverty of movement and is frequently tightly fisted. Asymmetry of lower limb movement may not be so apparent at this stage, although there may be a slight difference in reciprocal kicking, observed most easily while the baby is being changed or is in the bath. The hemiplegic leg extends when the baby is pulled to sitting. Quite commonly, there will be only minimal signs in the leg at this stage.

By the first birthday the hemiplegia is more obvious. In mild or doubtful cases the classical neurological signs of increased tone and reflexes may be confirmed by asymmetry of the parachute response and the placing reaction. Sitting and crawling are not very much delayed, but the mean age of walking is some 2−3 months later than the normal. Some hemiplegic children are also bottom-shufflers (p. 49) and these walk several months later than normal bottom-shufflers.

When the child begins to walk, the toddler's frequent falls and natural broad-based gait may rather obscure the abnormality in the hemiplegic leg, but a limp, spasticity and weakness gradually become more obvious, and this may create a mistaken impression of deterioration.

Upper limb function

The functional disability in the arm and hand may be categorized as follows:
1 independent use of the hemiplegic hand;
2 used as an active assistant to the normal hand;
3 limited use, mainly for stabilization and fixation;
4 no functional use.

The repertoire of hand skills in the normal baby is limited and the disability caused by a hemiplegic hand may not be very apparent, but it becomes more evident in the second and third years (although in fact use of the upper limb is probably increasing over this period), and the relative dwarfing of both arm and leg become more obvious. The child's attempts to utilize their abnormal movement patterns to maximize function results in many different postures and strategies of hand used. Distal weakness and loss of skilled movement are typical of a pyramidal tract lesion; but some children have a tendency to hyperextend

a

b

c

d

e

f

Fig. 14.1 Hemiplegia. **a,** Hand function: note flexion of wrist and extension of the fingers with attempted grasp — compare the normal left side. **b,** Flexion and spasm of right hand while concentrating on a difficult motor task. **c,** This boy has a right hemiplegia — note the posturing of the right hand and the associated spasm of the left hand while running. **d,** Difficulty in transferring his weight to the right side in a balance task. **e,** There is muscle spasm of the whole right side of the trunk — it is not only the limbs which are affected. There is relative underdevelopment of the right leg. **f,** When walking there is diminished hip extension and hyperextension of the knee. He holds the right hand firmly in the left to prevent it taking up embarrassing unwanted postures. **g,** Marked dwarfing of the hand and forearm (acquired left hemiplegia — stroke in infancy due to sickle-cell disease). Acknowledgements to the children and to Christine Bungay for the photos.

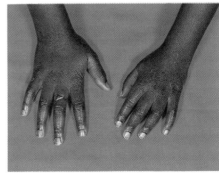

g

the wrist and fingers on approach to an object, indicative of extrapyramidal involvement.

Associated reactions are common in hemiplegia. When the child makes a movement with the normal limb, the hemiplegic limb makes unwanted postural changes. This can be demonstrated by asking the child to run or to undertake an activity needing intense concentration. Some cortical sensory loss also occurs and may be as important a cause of disability as the motor deficit.

Acquired hemiplegia

The sudden occurrence of hemiplegia in infancy or childhood is well recognized. Some cases present with convulsions followed by hemiplegia, others with sudden paralysis. This clinical picture, which was previously called the 'acute infantile hemiplegia syndrome', has many causes and full neurological investigation is essential. Language may be lost temporarily if the dominant hemisphere is involved, but permanent aphasia is rare (see p. 189).

Atypical hemiplegia

Some of the children who acquire a label of 'hemiplegia' have a variety of impairments, of which hemiplegia is only one, and not necessarily the most important. For example, the child may also have learning disabilities, ataxia and a disproportionate delay in speech development. Children with moderate or severe learning difficulties sometimes have mild unilateral pyramidal tract signs, with minimal movement disability. Although technically accurate, a label of hemiplegia in such cases is irrelevant to the child's main problems and is misleading to other professionals.

There are also children who have pyramidal signs on the apparently 'normal' side, and in these the designation of double hemiplegia is more appropriate. In such cases the cause is more likely to be a diffuse or bilateral lesion than a single area of focal damage, and pseudobulbar

palsy is much more likely to be found in such cases.

Other impairments in children with hemiplegia

Speech and language development may be a few months delayed compared with the norm, but this is rarely a major problem. The mean intelligence quotient (IQ) of children with hemiplegia is about 15–20 points lower than that of the normal population, but individual children may have average or above-average intelligence. Right hemiplegia is slightly commoner than left. The pattern of psychological deficits in relation to the side and the age of onset of the lesion (pp. 189 and 317) are of academic interest but they are not sufficiently reliable to be clinically useful. Serious defects of hearing and vision are rarely associated with hemiplegia. Various forms of visual field and attention deficits occur and it is important for the teacher to be aware of the child's difficulty in responding to stimuli from the impaired visual field.

The risk of epilepsy is related to the severity of the neurological deficit, and is probably higher with acquired than with congenital hemiplegia. The electroencephalogram (EEG) is often abnormal, particularly over the damaged hemisphere, but does not predict whether or when the child might have a fit, and there is no value in prescribing 'prophylactic' anticonvulsants. However, a few children develop severe epilepsy, often focal in onset with secondary generalization, and this may be difficult to control (Chapter 17). Parents have told us that they would prefer to know about the increased risk of epilepsy so that they can be educated about the appropriate first aid.

Causes of hemiplegia

In premature infants, hemiplegia may result from haemorrhage into the ventricles and white matter, with associated ischaemia. In the full-term infant, there is sometimes a history of abnormalities of pregnancy, such as hypertension. Occasionally there is evidence of hypoxic–ischaemic encephalopathy (HIE), although such cases often have more widespread evidence of brain dysfunction. In many cases, it is impossible to establish the precise cause. Computerized tomography (CT) scanning often shows evidence of infarction of all or part of one cerebral hemisphere, with shrinkage due to atrophy and compensatory mild enlargement of the lateral ventricle. A porencephalic cyst or a malformation may be demonstrated. Occlusion of the middle cerebral artery, or one of its branches, probably explains many of the pathological features. Both the reason for and the time of its occurrence are usually obscure, but sometimes scans of the fetus, or of the neonate immediately after birth, show that a cerebral infarct must have occurred *in utero*. Thrombosis, embolism, haemorrhage, trauma to the mother's abdomen, intrapartum arterial damage and neonatal polycythaemia have all been implicated. Neonatal fits, either unilateral or bilateral, are sometimes blamed, but are more likely to be the effect rather than the cause of the lesion.

Differential diagnosis of hemiplegia

The pattern described as preferred head-turning is probably an extreme variation of the normal asymmetry which can be detected in most babies. It is probable that the asymmetry determines the position in which the baby lies and sleeps rather than vice versa. There is asymmetry of the skull (plagiocephaly) and the head is persistently turned to one or the other side, occasionally to the extent that a sternomastoid 'tumour' is suspected. In most cases the baby looks to the right. The fist on the occiput side is closed and movement in that limb is diminished (Fig. 14.2). There may in addition be a mild postural scoliosis with some moulding of the chest. When the child begins to walk, the gait is asymmetrical and the right thigh rotates externally more than the left (see p. 49). All these signs gradually disappear.

Other causes of asymmetry of limb appearance and/or function include unilateral tiptoe gait, congenital dislocation of the hip, Erb's palsy, occult spinal dysraphism, poliomyelitis; isolated

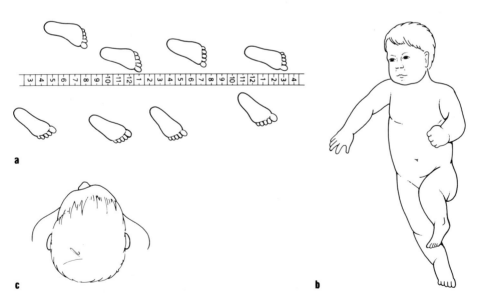

Fig. 14.2 Preferred head-turning of hemiplegia, **a,** Asymmetry of gait — footprints show line of march. From Robson (1968). **b,** Asymmetry of posture at 6 months. Child turns more readily to sounds on right. **c,** Prominent right brow when seen from above.

defomities, such as bowing of the tibia, Poland's anomaly, Sprengel's shoulder; hemimegalencephaly and hemihypertrophy. The latter may be associated with aniridia, Russell–Silver syndrome and Beckwith's syndrome. Provided one is aware of their existence, none of these should cause any diagnostic difficulty.

Cerebral palsies with bilateral signs: hypertonia

Movement patterns in CP change continually over the first few years of life. It is extremely difficult to predict how the child will progress or what type of movement disorder will be dominant. The situation is further complicated by the lack of any universally agreed description of the abnormal movement patterns. For these reasons, the early evolution of the spastic and dyskinetic CPs will be considered together and the distinctive features of each type in the older child will then be described.

Early evolution

In the first few months of life, the diagnosis of CP is easily missed. Subtle signs can be observed, although their interpretation can be extremely difficult. There is usually some poverty of spontaneous movement and such movement patterns as are present are limited and stereotyped. Any behaviour with a motor component may be affected and visual following, facial expression and 'turn-taking' behaviour in response to social stimuli are often reduced. Motor milestones are delayed. Tone is variable; it is sometimes diminished and there may be marked head lag, but the tendon reflexes are nevertheless brisk and sustained ankle clonus may be present. Some infants may show marked increase in tone from a very early stage, and extensor hypertonus affecting trunk and neck muscles is an important sign. Monitoring of the head circumference may reveal a fall-off in growth, indicating secondary microcephaly due to diminished growth of a brain severely damaged by anoxia, infection or other insults (see also p. 161). There is often failure to thrive, which may be attributed both to brain damage and also to diminished food intake caused by impaired sucking and swallowing.

The physical signs gradually become more obvious during the second half of the first year. There are three main features:
1 abnormalities of tone;
2 delays in appearance of the normal postural reactions and therefore in motor milestones;
3 persistent abnormal patterns of movement.

Tone

In some babies, tone is increased in all positions. More often, tone is dependent on the posture and position of the baby. There may be gross head lag when the baby is pulled to sitting, but when held in ventral suspension extensor tone increases — sometimes to the extent that an erroneous diagnosis of advanced motor development is made.

There are also babies whose tone is persistently low. When held in vertical suspension the head and limbs hang limply, forming an inverted U.

Delays in motor development

These are usually apparent by 6 months of age. There is a poverty of normal spontaneous movement and such movements as are present are slow in initiation and execution and stereotyped in pattern. The normal postural mechanisms do not appear at the usual time and marked head lag and delays in rolling over and in sitting are usually found. The parachute reactions develop slowly between 6 and 24 months; in the most severe cases they may never be more than fragmentary. Appearance of the foot-placing reaction may also be delayed.

In the vertical position, the ability to weight-bear which is seen in the normal infant is impaired. Some evidence of a normal supporting reaction is seen by 12–15 months of age in infants whose predominant problem will be increased tone. In these babies there is often slight flexion of the hips and knees, equinus at the ankles and scissoring. The placing response is not easily demonstrated. In infants whose tone is very variable, the supporting reaction may appear even later, at 18–27 months. These infants are more likely to be hypotonic when held vertically. Equinus is often less prominent and there is no scissoring, but the placing reaction is easily elicited.

Persistent abnormal patterns of movement

In CP a single movement can set off a complete stereotyped total-body pattern (Fig. 14.3); the baby cannot make isolated discrete movements. The abnormal reflex patterns of movement are not merely due to retention of primitive reflexes. Although similar stereotyped patterns of movement are observed in the normal infant, they are never obligatory. These unwanted reflexes often become less powerful as the child matures but in the most severely affected cases obligatory abnormal patterns persist throughout life.

The findings on examination are therefore much influenced by the position in which the child is examined. Assessing movement only in the traditional medical examination position, supine on a couch, will not give a complete picture. Tone will be affected by flexing the head and by keeping the head in the midline position; these manoeuvres simplify the examination of the child with CP.

Spastic diplegia

Little in 1862 identified the association with abnormalities of pregnancy and delivery, and in particular with prematurity. A century later, the precise causes of classic spastic diplegia are still unclear. The typical picture may be seen in children who, though born early, apparently had an uneventful stay in the neonatal intensive care unit. Ultrasound scans performed on the first day of life sometimes reveal mature brain lesions which must have developed several weeks before the baby was born. A rather different pattern of diplegia has been seen in recent years in babies who have been of very low birth weight and have undergone prolonged intensive care. There are various syndromes associated with spastic diplegia

and the disorder can be inherited (e.g. Sjögren–Larsson, Kjellin syndromes).

In the first 2 or 3 years of life many of these children show abnormalities of tone and reflex patterns, dystonia and delayed appearance of postural reflexes, or abnormal postural mechanisms, as described above. They are frequently irritable and difficult to handle. This so-called dystonic phase merges into one in which spasticity alone is the most striking feature and abnormal reflex patterns become less apparent. The more rapidly this process happens, the better the prognosis.

In some cases, usually those with very severe cerebral damage, profound hypotonia persists for many years. The history, upper motor neuron signs and associated learning disabilities reveal the correct diagnosis. Such cases are sometimes called atonic diplegia or quadriplegia. They may be explained on the basis of a dissociation between tonic and phasic spasticity. There are also children with mainly proximal tonic spasticity. They walk with fairly plantigrade feet, but have flexion at the hip and knee and a waddling gait.

Some very premature infants who develop diplegia show a different pattern. There is external rotation of the thighs, slight knee flexion, and eversion of the feet, but adduction of the thighs is usually not a problem. In spite of learning to crawl they are slow to walk.

Upper limb involvement

The extent and symmetry of upper limb involvement are variable but the term 'diplegia' should be reserved for cases with minor or moderate upper limb involvement, i.e. reasonable bilateral hand function. Increase in tone and reflexes, and dyskinesia, may be noted. Even in cases where these signs are minimal, careful observation of play and manipulation often reveals exaggerated grasp and release, and slowness of finger movements.

If there is no evidence of upper limb involvement, the term 'paraplegia' is preferred. Although a pure paraplegia of cerebral origin can occur, it is rare. Other diagnoses, such as a spinal lesion or hereditary spastic paraplegia (Table 14.3) should

a

b

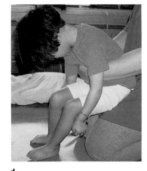

c

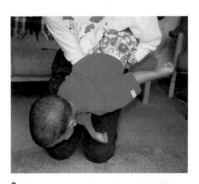

d

e

f

g

h

be excluded, particularly if there are no other indicators of brain involvement (impaired intellect or speech, epilepsy, etc.).

Early mobility

Some children with mild diplegia may shuffle or roll; others progress by 'seal-walking'. Children with mild diplegia on average sit 2 months, stand 5 months and walk 10 months later than the normal. In more severe cases, progress often seems very slow in the first 2 years but then continues steadily, reaching a plateau around the age of 7−8 years. The probability of eventual independent walking and crutch-walking can be predicted by the age of 3 years (Fig. 14.4).

The stance and gait of a child with diplegia are determined by the degree of spasticity and weakness in the lower limbs (Fig. 14.5). There is usually some undergrowth of the pelvis and legs, and muscle bulk is diminished. The trunk extensor muscles are weak and unable to maintain the child in the upright position. This can be demonstrated by asking the child to bend forward

Table 14.3 Spastic syndromes of spinal origin can be mistaken for cerebral palsy

---

Familial spastic paraplegia (FSP)
A relatively common condition, often misdiagnosed as spastic diplegia

(a) Pure form − can be inherited as autosomal recessive or dominant. Mean age of onset of recessive form is 11 years, of dominant form is 20 years, but can start at any age
• Features: mild delay in walking (in some cases); stiffness of legs; difficulty in walking long distances; tendency to fall
• Weakness minimal in the early stages but spasticity is marked
• Diagnosis may be difficult because onset is insidious and progression very slow; upper limb signs, wasting of hand muscles and sensory loss may occur late
• Orthopaedic surgery may be helpful

(b) Complicated forms − FSP may be associated with features suggestive of peroneal muscular atrophy, ataxic syndromes, optic atrophy, skin disorders and learning disabilities of varying severity. Variable age of onset; usually recessive

Miscellaneous
• Vascular and traumatic lesions, perinatally acquired
• Hypoxic ischaemic encephalopathy may involve the spinal cord as well as the brain
• Postnatally acquired cord lesions (see Table 15.7).

Fig. 14.3 (*Facing page*) Children with cerebral palsy (CP) have persistent abnormal patterns of movement and delay in achieving normal motor skills. The persistent patterns include the asymmetric tonic neck reflex (ATNR), the symmetric tonic neck reflex (STNR), the tonic labyrinthine reflex (TLR), and extensor thrust. a, The ATNR is derived from proprioceptive receptors in the neck. Turning the head to the right is associated with increased extensor tone on the face side and increased flexor tone on the occiput side. The ATNR is seen in transient form in normal babies but in CP it is obligate, i.e. it can be imposed and the child cannot break free from the posture. This pattern restricts purposeful movement and increases the risk of scoliosis and hip dislocation (compare Figs 14.8 and 14.10 which show the same child). b, c and d, The respective contributions of the STNR and TLR vary and depend on posture and movement. The STNR is also derived from neck proprioceptors. When the neck is extended, the arms extend and the legs flex. Neck flexion has the opposite effect. The TLR is derived from stimuli in the labyrinths which monitor the position of the head in space. The effect is to increase extensor tone in supine and flexor tone in prone.

Extensor thrust (not illustrated): if the child is held by the axillae and lowered smartly to the floor, there is progressive extension of the lower limbs and trunk, with adduction and internal rotation of the legs ('extensor thrust').

The normal saving reactions are slow to appear: e, when the child is moved briskly towards the floor, the arms show no forward-saving response and the hands remain partially closed; f, when tilted sideways, there is no corresponding sideways propping reaction of the left hand and arm.

Small children can easily be held in the upright position but the motor disorder prevents independent standing or walking. g, The child is not weight bearing, shows abnormal posturing, and attempts to walk produce a 'dancing' pattern of ineffective movement. h, This child shows a different pattern, of adduction and internal rotation of the legs; the ATNR is prominent (compare with Figs 14.3 and 14.10).

Acknowledgements to the children and to Christine Bungay for the photos.

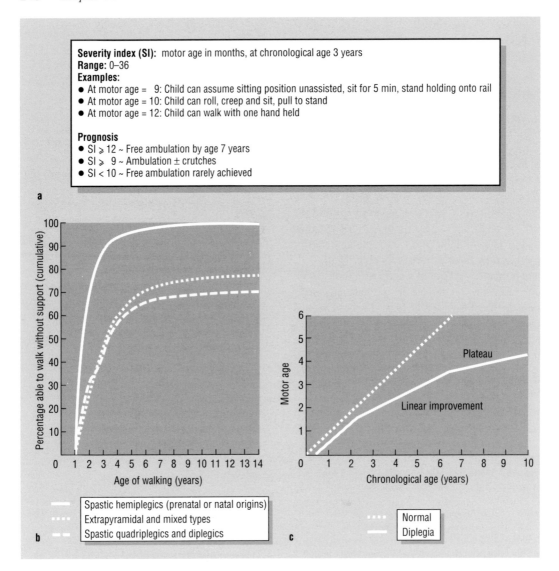

Severity index (SI): motor age in months, at chronological age 3 years
Range: 0–36
Examples:
● At motor age = 9: Child can assume sitting position unassisted, sit for 5 min, stand holding onto rail
● At motor age = 10: Child can roll, creep and sit, pull to stand
● At motor age = 12: Child can walk with one hand held

Prognosis
● SI ⩾ 12 ~ Free ambulation by age 7 years
● SI ⩾ 9 ~ Ambulation ± crutches
● SI < 10 ~ Free ambulation rarely achieved

a

Spastic hemiplegics (prenatal or natal origins)
Extrapyramidal and mixed types
Spastic quadriplegics and diplegics

b

Normal
Diplegia

c

Fig. 14.4 Prognosis for walking. a, Prognosis for ambulation in spastic diplegia (Beals). b, Percentage of cerebral-palsied patients able to walk, according to age ($n = 289$ cerebral-palsy patients). c, Spastic diplegia: probability of significant improvement in motor performance declines after age 7. After Bleck (1987).

and then straighten up — the latter movement will be difficult or impossible. Often there is a tiptoe gait with the body weight on the inside of the foot, scissoring due to adduction and inwards rotation of the thighs, thoracic kyphosis and lumbar lordosis.

Associated impairments

Learning disability tends to be more severe in proportion to the degree of upper limb involvement. However, most children with classic diplegia can benefit from mainstream education

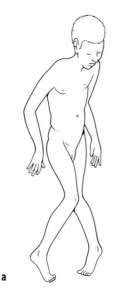

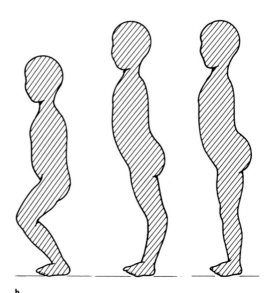

Fig. 14.5 a, A child with spastic diplegia. The typical patternis shown: hip flexion contracture; hip internal rotation with femoral anteversion; hip abductor spasm and contracture; knee flexor or extensor spasticity may predominant or may be equal; equinus at ankles; pes valgus. **b,** Three gait patterns in spastic diplegia. From left to right: flexed hips and flexed knees; flexed hips and hyperextended knees; flexed hips and balanced hamstring and quadriceps function. Almost all have hip internal rotation during stance and swing phases. Some have increased pelvic rotation, which depends upon the amount and the extent of spasticity in the hip musculature and the degree of weakness of hip extension. From Bleck, 1987.

and should be able to lead productive and independent lives. There may be some difficulties with articulation but the speech is usually sufficiently clear for the child to communicate without difficulty (although children with CP are, of course, not immune from other developmental speech and language problems (Chapter 11)). Epilepsy is rarely a major problem. Sensorineural hearing loss is also unusual, although it may occur when diplegia is associated with a syndrome, for example in congenital rubella. Cortical vision defects may lead to visual perceptual problems.

Total body involvement (four-limb cerebral palsy)

Severe involvement of all four limbs occurs in quadriplegia and double hemiplegia. There are some children with bilateral motor signs in the distribution typical of hemiplegia, but with preservation of trunk balance and head control, who may best be categorized as having double hemiplegia. Those who have severe involvement of trunk and head muscles and of all limbs, together with persistent reflex patterns, are described as having quadriplegia. The distinction is not always clear and is not accepted by all authorities.

Many of the children with severe four-limb involvement have multiple impairments. There is often a pseudobulbar palsy, causing difficulties with chewing, swallowing and dribbling, in addition to speech impairment. There is a high risk of deformity, particularly in those with asymmetric involvement. Dislocation of the hip and scoliosis are common.

Dyskinetic cerebral palsies

The term dyskinesia includes athetosis, chorea and dystonia. In athetosis, there are frequent and unpredictable fluctuations of tone, so that rigid hypertonia and hypotonia may both be found in the same patient within moments of each other. In pure athetosis, when the child is at rest the basic postural tone is low, but there are small, random muscle movements. More extreme unwanted movement patterns may be initiated by any attempts at voluntary movement or speech, or by discomfort, postural changes or anxiety. The head turns, the face grimaces, and the arms, trunk and legs execute bizarre writhing movements, which are usually bilateral. There is often some asymmetry, but true hemiathetosis is rare. All the abnormal movements disappear in sleep.

In the early years, head control is poor and postural reflexes are very slow to appear. The child learns to position his/her head to make use of these abnormal patterns and bring them under some degree of voluntary control. The child may use the asymmetric tonic neck reflex (ATNR) pattern to turn towards and grasp an object, but the grasp is weak and objects are released too early and without voluntary control. There is often a back-handed grasp with hyperextension of the fingers (Fig. 14.6).

Athetoid movements in the upper limbs may appear between 1 and 3 years or even later on occasions. Their early appearance is indicative of less severe athetosis, since the more severe cases have little or no useful hand function in the first 2 years. A degree of ataxia is often superimposed on the athetosis.

Young children with athetosis may be able to sit on the floor with externally rotated, extended and abducted legs, but they cannot sit alone in a chair; they either collapse forward with total flexion or fall backwards in total extension. It may take years to achieve standing and walking and in some cases these abilities are never acquired. People with athetosis walk with hyperextended hips and knees and an exaggerated high-stepping gait; they lean backwards, extending the shoulder

Fig. 14.6 An infant with early signs of athetosis. Note the hyperextension and fanning of the fingers as the left hand approaches the object, the fisting of the right hand and the relative freedom to play produced by the side-lying position.

girdle and trunk, to reinforce extensor tone and prevent a sudden collapse into flexion.

Independent walking and improvement in speech may be achieved as late as the early teens. Those who are most severely afflicted will require a powered wheelchair and alternative or augmented means of communication (p. 201). Adults with severe athetosis face particular problems of independence and social contact since the bizarre involuntary movements, together with incomprehensible speech, frequently lead the general public to regard them as mentally retarded or mentally ill. Later in life, they may suffer from degenerative joint disease, particularly affecting the cervical spine, because of the constant abnormal movements.

Other impairments associated with athetosis

Learning difficulties of variable degree are common but intelligence is preserved more often in the face of severe physical disability than in other kinds of CP, and the head circumference is more often normal. This probably reflects the fact that this type of CP is associated with relatively localized damage to the basal ganglia, which seem to be particularly vulnerable to acute, severe hypoxia. Epilepsy is relatively rare. Dysarthria and severe delays in speech development are common and some children remain virtually anarthric. High-frequency deafness is very common in children with athetosis due to kernicterus, but occurs in perhaps one-tenth of those caused by asphyxia. In cases due to kernicterus, loss of upward gaze and dental enamel hypoplasia are also seen. The vestibulo-ocular reflex is preserved and this enables the child to maintain a stable visual axis even when the head is moved. The ocular avoiding reaction is common and annoying, resulting in the head and eyes being averted from the object of gaze. Probably the child takes in the requisite visual information instantaneously, but he/she certainly cannot maintain gaze and this is embarrassing socially.

Subluxation of joints may occur because of the continual movements, but for the same reason fixed deformities are rare. Orthopaedic surgery is rarely helpful and the results are unpredictable. Furthermore, postoperative immobilization in plaster is hazardous and there is a serious risk of sores developing from friction due to the constant movements.

Four-limb spastic/rigid quadriplegias

Sometimes a four-limb spastic/rigid CP can occur without other impairments, but often it is associated with severe to profound learning difficulties, pseudobulbar palsy, cortical visual impairment, epilepsy, hearing loss (although this is relatively uncommon) and orthopaedic deformities. Often the skull circumference is small, reflecting severe impairment of brain growth. Feeding is time-consuming and tube-feeding or gastrostomy may be necessary (p. 271). The epilepsy is often impossible to control, although from the child's point of view it often seems that the fits cause little or no distress.

The management of such children is technically difficult and emotionally demanding for the professionals as well as for the parents. The child needs almost constant attention and yet, because of the profound disability, gives little or no response to the carers and may not even recognize

the difference between familiar and unfamiliar family members or staff. This is distressing to the parents and may weaken their resolve to continue caring for the child. Teachers need to set very simple and limited goals because progress is so slow.

Causes of four-limb cerebral palsies

CP is a descriptive label and not a diagnosis. CP may result from lesions occurring in pregnancy and is not always preventable by better obstetric care (Table 14.4). Postnatal brain injury is discussed on p. 298.

Prenatal and perinatal causes

Low birth weight. Very-low-birth-weight infants are at risk of germinal matrix haemorrhage and intraventricular haemorrhage (IVH), but this finding in itself does not have a bad prognosis. When the infant is a few weeks old, ultrasound may reveal cavitating periventricular leucomalacia, which is associated with spastic diplegia and often with cortical vision defects; or a single cyst (porencephaly), which may be associated with hemiplegia. Posthaemorrhagic ventricular dilatation may be associated with cortical atrophy, obstruction to cerebrospinal fluid (CSF) pathways, or both. It is an adverse prognostic sign, but this may be because of the accompanying cortical damage rather than the ventricular dilatation itself. Normal ultrasound scans throughout the neonatal period indicate that the infant has a low risk of developing any serious motor or intellectual impairment. The finding of mature lesions in the brains of preterm infants within hours of birth confirms that in some cases CP has an antenatal origin rather than resulting from the complications of prematurity.

Intrapartum asphyxia. In the full-term infant, this is an important cause of CP. Sometimes the event responsible for the asphyxia is obvious, for example in cases of massive placental abruption; but often there is no apparent reason and the

Table 14.4 Cerebral palsy (CP) can be caused by antenatal factors — the evidence

---

Epidemiological evidence
There is an association between CP and the following antenatal factors
- Maternal mental retardation
- Baby very small for dates
- Placenta small (under 325 g)
- Sudden onset of reduced fetal movements before start of labour
- Breech presentation (association with hypotonic/immobile infant, e.g. Prader–Willi syndrome)
- Other malformations which can be dated to early in pregnancy

Specific evidence in individual cases
- Prenatal demonstration of brain lesions by ultrasound
- Presence of cystic lesions in brain established on ultrasound soon after birth
- Brain malformations associated with abnormal neuronal proliferation/migration dated to early pregnancy (e.g schizencephaly, holoprosencephaly, lissencephaly)
- Association of hypoxic–ischaemic lesions with history of maternal cardiovascular collapse in pregnancy
- High prevalence of CP in identical twins, particularly when one has died *in utero* (believed to be related to shared circulation)
- Neuropathology: established lesions, with neuronal death and gliosis in infants who were apnoeic at birth, suggests that apnoea may be sign of pre-existing brain damage rather than cause of brain damage
- Other identifiable causes, e.g. congenital rubella

---

pathophysiology of asphyxia is not yet fully understood. Abnormal fetal heart records, depressed Apgar scores, impaired feeding and abnormal muscle tone may all result from antenatal brain damage and are not diagnostic of intrapartum asphyxia. The best marker of significant asphyxia is now thought to be the syndrome known as hypoxic–ischaemic encephalopathy (HIE). CP is unlikely to have been caused by birth asphyxia if there is no history of moderate or severe HIE.

The infant with HIE is usually (though not always) slow to establish respiration at birth. In mild (stage 1) HIE, the infant is only irritable and jittery, seizures do not occur, and recovery takes only a few days. In moderate (stage 2) or severe (stage 3) HIE, responsiveness is impaired. Convulsions begin after a variable period, but usually within the first 24 hours, and continue for several days, in spite of anticonvulsants. The baby cannot feed; eye movements are abnormal; and often there is also renal dysfunction with oliguria or polyuria and rising blood urea and creatinine.

Mild HIE has an excellent prognosis but the moderate and severe stages are associated with a significant mortality and a high morbidity in the survivors. The precise nature of the child's impairments varies, as do the pathological findings. As a generalization, an episode of acute severe hypoxia is usually followed by a dyskinetic CP with reasonable preservation of intellect, whereas chronic hypoxia or repeated hypoxic episodes are more likely to be followed by spastic quadriplegia and severe learning disability. It is extremely unusual for HIE to cause learning problems or deafness without any evidence of CP. However, occasionally children with middle cerebral artery occlusion (which may be, but is not always, associated with asphyxia) show a pattern of very mild hemiplegia which improves to the point of being almost undetectable, but nevertheless have marked learning problems, sometimes accompanied by behavioural problems and fits.

Although the term HIE is widely used, it would be better to call the syndrome neonatal encephalopathy, since asphyxia is not the only cause of neonatal fits. For example, investigations may reveal evidence of intracranial bleeding or infarction, which can occur independent of asphyxia. Other diagnoses, such as malformations and metabolic disorders, should be considered.

Other perinatal causes of CP. Traumatic injury during delivery is rare in modern obstetrics, but forceps delivery is often thought by parents to be the cause of their child's CP. Other perinatal causes include meningitis, viral encephalitis, metabolic illnesses, prolonged severe hypoglycaemia and kernicterus. Kernicterus is caused by the deposition of bilirubin in the basal ganglia. It most commonly occurs between 2 and 5 days of age and is characterized by apathy and hypotonia, interspersed with spasms and episodes of opisthotonos. In full-term babies, kernicterus very rarely occurs with bilirubin levels below 329 μmol/l, but sick premature infants may suffer damage at lower levels. The commonest cause of severe hyperbilirubinaemia used to be rhesus incompatibility, but ABO incompatibility and hereditary disorders such as glucose-6-phosphate dehydrogenase (G6PD) deficiency are now more important.

Diagnosis and investigations

To establish a diagnosis of CP, the cause, nature and evolution of the movement disorder must be considered (Table 14.5). Many conditions can masquerade as CP. For example, four-limb spasticity can result from tumours around the skull base or high cervical cord and lower limb spasticity from spinal cord lesions or hereditary spastic paraplegia. A mixed picture of upper and lower motor neuron lesions may be seen in metachromatic leucodystrophy. In dyskinetic or athetoid cases, dopa-responsive dystonia and organic acidaemias such as glutaric aciduria should be considered. Investigation may help to exclude these and other unusual conditions. Magnetic resonance (MR) scans may show evidence of hypoxic or vascular lesions but it is rarely possible to specify the precise cause of these or to determine when they occurred. Occasionally they reveal unsuspected tumours, or anomalies such as neuronal migration disorders, which clearly indicate an antenatal cause for the child's CP.

Hypotonic and ataxic cerebral palsies

These present different problems of diagnosis and management from those seen in spastic and dyskinetic CPs.

Ataxic cerebral palsy

In the neonatal period these babies may come to attention because they are floppy and inactive. Motor and speech development are slow and hypotonia is usually persistent; indeed, ataxia and hypotonia are difficult to distinguish in infancy. It may be difficult to decide whether the child

Table 14.5 Children with movement disorder — questions to consider

Does the child have delayed milestones, a movement disorder or a normal variant?
- Normal variants: e.g. tiptoe-walkers: preferred head-turning: bottom-shufflers
- *Caution*: there is a range of normal tone; some normal infants may feel quite floppy; others feel stiff. Premature infants may show definite abnormal motor signs in the first 2 years of life which later resolve
- Parents can understand and appreciate the concept of delay and disorder

What sort of movement disorder?
- Spastic/rigid/dyskinetic/hypotonic/ataxic

At what level in the nervous system is the lesion(s) likely to be?
- Brain: often other evidence, such as abnormal size of head, fits, intellectual deficits
- Spinal cord: suggested by sensory loss, sphincter disturbance (patulous anus, dribbling of urine) or discrepancy between motor deficit in arms and legs
- Anterior horn cell, nerve or muscle: low tone, weakness, hypoactive reflexes, absence of signs of brain disorder
- *Caution*: may be lesions at more than one level

Is the movement disorder part of a syndrome?
- *Caution*: movement disorders, particularly hypertonia, may be associated with dysmorphic syndromes but do not necessarily evolve in the same way as CP caused by perinatal brain injury
- *Caution*: unusual associations, such as eye disease or deafness with diplegia, may indicate a specific genetic syndrome

Is the child's movement disorder: (1) static and dating from infancy; (2) acquired but now static; (3) progressive?
- In CP the movement disorder evolves and changes; disability may get worse with contractures, immobility, illness or puberty: but 'progressive CP' by definition cannot exist
- Disorders that are very slowly progressive can mimic CP
- To parents the word 'progressive' means getting better; to neurologists it means getting worse

Is there any aetiological explanation for the movement disorder?
- Is there positive evidence for a perinatal cause?
- Is there any evidence for antenatal brain injury or malformation?
- If not, have other conditions/causes been considered?

CP, cerebral palsy.

shows simple motor delay, with the normal toddler phase of a broad-based unsteady gait prolonged because of global slow development, or whether the term 'ataxic cerebral palsy' is applicable. In general, however, the hypotonic child begins to show improvement when he/she is encouraged to be upright against gravity, whereas the ataxic child shows more obvious impairments of balance and trunk control when upright.

Walking may be achieved as late as the third or fourth year or even later, and ataxic children may show a persistent fear of falling, so that they walk with hands held for many months or even years, before they will risk independent walking. There may be exaggerated balancing movements with the arms outstretched. In some cases disequilibrium is the dominant motor problem (p. 334), whereas in others tremor and dysmetria are more obvious. Nystagmus, however, is unusual. Delay in speech development is common, but may be related to the learning difficulties which are often associated with ataxic CP; typical cerebellar dysarthria is rarely observed in these children.

The prognosis for ataxic CP depends more on the extent of any associated learning disability than on the cerebellar disorder itself, but there is a tendency for motor function to improve slowly.

Causes

Many cases are of prenatal origin and are probably due to abnormal development of the cerebellum and its connections. Genetic factors are important in ataxic CP, particularly when associated with severe learning disabilities and also in those with marked disequilibrium ('disequilibrium syndrome'). Some children have cerebellar hypoplasia or agenesis and there are also a number of dysmorphic syndromes in which ataxia may be an important feature (e.g. Joubert's, Angelman's, Behr's, Marinesco–Sjögren).

Congenital cytomegalovirus infection occasionally causes a pattern of multiple impairments including ataxia. Perinatal brain injury only rarely results in a pure ataxic syndrome and it is doubt-

ful whether asphyxia and HIE ever do so. Congenital hypothyroidism and fetal alcohol syndrome may be associated with non-progressive ataxia. A mixed ataxic–spastic diplegia is the commonest motor impairment associated with hyrocephalus (p. 159).

Acquired ataxia may be the end result of meningitis, encephalitis, encephalopathy or trauma. There is a long list of other causes, including tumours, ataxia telangiectasia, spinocerebellar degenerations, etc. A full neurological evaluation will often be needed to distinguish these from non-progressive ataxic CP. Whatever the cause, an active rehabilitation programme is essential.

Hypotonic cerebral palsy

This category of CP is difficult to define and it may be better to avoid the term altogether. Hypotonia is a clinical sign with many causes. It may present in the neonatal period as a 'floppy baby' or at any time in infancy, when hypotonia is often associated with a presenting complaint of generally delayed milestones. It is convenient to divide the causes of hypotonia into normal variation (see p. 49), central causes and peripheral causes.

Hypotonia of central origin

Many babies with perinatal brain injury pass through a period of hypotonia before spasticity or dyskinesia become apparent. The brisk tendon reflexes, variations in tone and presence of an obligatory ATNR usually indicate the origin of the hypotonia.

Conditions associated with severe learning difficulties are the other major central cause of hypotonia. There is no difficulty in recognizing the child with a dysmorphic syndrome, but children of normal appearance may cause confusion. Unlike the primarily brain-injured group described above, these infants are usually hypotonic in all positions. There is often an increased range of passive movement. Tendon reflexes should not be relied on as a means of distinguishing central from peripheral hypotonia. The ATNR may be elicited more easily than normal up to the age of 8 or 9 months, but one rarely sees the abnormal total-movement patterns which occur in severe spastic or dyskinetic CP. There is usually plenty of spontaneous limb movement and weakness is not an important feature.

These children show extreme motor delay rather than the persistent abnormalities of posture or movement which are the hallmark of CP, and are better described as having 'learning disabilities with hypotonia and motor delay'. The diagnosis depends on recognition of the associated delayed intellectual, communicative and social development.

Causes. The differential diagnosis and investigation are essentially as described for learning disabilities (Chapter 10). Infants who are systemically unwell, or who have been undernourished and socially deprived, may sometimes be surprisingly hypotonic, but usually respond quickly to treatment or to improved nutrition and handling. The Prader–Willi syndrome which can be associated with profound hypotonia is easily overlooked in infancy (see Glossary).

Hypotonia of peripheral origin

This is caused by disorders of the anterior horn cell, peripheral nerve (lower motor neuron), muscle end-plate and muscle. Werdnig–Hoffmann disease (p. 292) is by far the commonest. Infants with peripheral hypotonia are weak; they are unable to support their limbs against gravity or withdraw from a painful stimulus. The ATNR cannot be elicited. In Werdnig–Hoffmann disease, tendon reflexes are absent, and social responsiveness and intellectual development are usually unimpaired. This condition can usually be recognized clinically and, if it can be excluded, the statistical probability in the hypotonic child is strongly in favour of a central cause, since the many forms of learning disability and associated syndromes are much commoner than congenital

myopathies or neuropathies. Very rarely, confusion can occur in conditions where the pathological process involves both the peripheral nervous system and the brain.

Mild ligamentous laxity (joint hypermobility)

This is very common and may run in families. It may be normal, or may occur in association with other causes of hypotonia, but it is an unsatisfactory 'explanation' for slow motor development. Extreme degrees of joint laxity may occur in uncommon disorders of connective tissue (Larsen, Ehlers–Danlos and Marfan syndromes) and occasionally as an isolated phenomenon. These children are not necessarily hypotonic or weak, but they have a markedly increased range of passive movement, which can be mistaken for hypotonia, and they may have delayed motor development.

Management of cerebral palsy — general principles

Children with CP require multidisciplinary assessment and care. Parents often focus on the motor disorder and must be reminded that communication, social adaptation and cognitive development are just as important. Every child with CP should have hearing and vision checks as soon as possible after diagnosis (Chapters 5 and 6).

Early management

Neonatal intensive care sometimes results in the survival of a disabled infant who otherwise would have died. The parents may have serious reservations about the wisdom of having saved the baby's life and may find it very hard to love and care for the baby. The care and support given by staff and by other parents during these difficult weeks have a considerable effect on the parents' ability to cope with any subsequent disability. The initial follow-up care of a potentially disabled infant should ideally be the responsibility of the paediatrician who cared for the child in hospital. It must not be delegated to a succession of inexperienced junior staff. If the child's long-term follow-up is to be handed over to another doctor or team, the timing is important. The parents should not be left with the feeling that the neonatal specialist is abandoning them because the baby is disabled.

It is often difficult to know when first to raise the possibility of neurological impairment, but most parents say that they want to be told as soon as there is any suspicion — even if this turns out to be wrong. Parents in Western society are well aware that brain damage can occur in high-risk babies and it is futile to pretend that all is well when a child is showing obvious signs of cerebral damage. When there is real doubt, the physiotherapist can counsel the parents on various aspects of handling and management and is able to support them during this period of great anxiety.

Early recognition by developmental surveillance

Specialist follow-up of babies who have suffered severe asphyxia or the complications of prematurity is the commonest way in which the more severe cases of CP are diagnosed. In the absence of such a history, early recognition of CP by routine developmental checks is much more difficult. There is wide variation in normal milestones, and a number of infants show unusual patterns of movement, such as hypotonia, irritability, persisting primitive reflex patterns, and hypertonia with dystonic posturing and scissoring, and yet are eventually perfectly normal. Parents are often the first to recognize hemiplegia or spastic diplegia in cases where no neonatal risk factors are apparent.

The role of the therapists

The occupational therapist advises on equipment such as wheelchairs, seating and bathing equipment, and on play materials and activities, whereas the physiotherapist is expert in handling and

mobilization of the child. The speech therapist deals with feeding and communication problems.

The aims of therapy are to enable disabled children to make maximum use of the movements under their control, to prevent deformity, and to encourage learning, play, communication and social development, in spite of their difficulties. Therapy must be planned with specific goals in mind — for example, prevention of deformity, attainment of a good sitting posture or independent walking. Both short-term and long-term goals should be set. Positioning and mobilization in general follow the normal sequence of development, i.e. sitting, crawling, standing, walking. It is quite unnecessary to insist that the child passes through each stage in turn; for example, it may be desirable to provide a means of mobility for a child who cannot even sit on his/her own. The goals specified for movement skills must be appropriate to the child's overall cognitive level of function.

Physiotherapy and occupational therapy techniques

The therapist is responsible for educating the parents about movement disorders, and supervising the child's total physical management and mobilization; he/she is an essential participant in planning for orthopaedic surgery and in postoperative rehabilitation. Frequently the therapist becomes a family's main confidant and adviser.

Many therapy systems have been devised (Table 14.6). The therapist aims to draw on the most appropriate techniques and methods for each child, rather than fitting the child into a single favourite system. It is doubtful whether any of these techniques can significantly change the functioning of the damaged brain, and few therapists would now claim to cure CP.

The techniques of neurodevelopmental therapy are valuable in handling and positioning, even though they do not 'cure' the underlying motor disorder. Conductive education has attracted a great deal of attention recently. For some children this approach offers a more motivating routine and many parents are convinced that it is more

Table 14.6 Approaches to therapy for children with cerebral palsy (CP)

Bobath neurodevelopmental therapy
Widely used approach to understanding and treatment of
CP. Original programme emphasized analysis of tonic
reflexes and need to pass through a developmental
sequence of movement (rolling, sitting, etc.). Therapy
involves reduction of abnormal and unwanted movements
by means of reflex inhibiting patterns and facilitation of
normal postural and balance reactions. Parents must learn
handling techniques and apply them throughout each day
(see Finnie, 1991)

Conductive education
Devised by Peto (pronounced pett-oo) in Budapest. An
educational system aimed at helping children to function
adequately without aids, in the best way for that child —
'orthofunction'. All the child's needs are met by one
person — the conductor. Emphasizes enjoyment,
motivation and participation. Organization and approach
rather than therapeutic content make it unique. Also used
in Hungary for children with spina bifida

Vojta (pronounced voyter)
Treatment programme elicits patterns of reflex movement
by pressure on trigger zones that induce creeping, turning,
lying, etc. Patterns of movement thus produced are
believed to be stored in the brain for future use

Kabat
Proprioceptive neuromuscular facilitation. The method
aims to increase the power of movement by manual
resistance and by giving the child the kinaesthetic
sensation of movement

Rood
Attempts to reduce spasticity by tactile stimulation

Doman–Delacato (based on the work of T. Fay)
Uses passive imposed exercises designed to reproduce the
evolutionary progression of movement — from fish,
through amphibian and reptile and finally to primate.
Other measures designed to raise cognitive ability.
Stresses frequent and prolonged exercises (patterning),
which take many hours each day, requiring zeal, dedication
and commitment on the part of family and friends

Ayres
Sensory integration therapy. Originally promoted for
learning disabilities but sometimes used in CP

Portage
An educational programme which can be adapted for use
with CP children

Sports
Horse-riding and skiing are valuable for children with CP.
Swimming and whirlpool baths are also enjoyed and help
to produce muscle relaxation

effective than anything they have tried previously,
even though objective evaluation has so far failed
to confirm any superiority over other methods.
The reasons why conductive education has become so popular are complex but include inadequate therapy input, lack of continuity of therapy
and teaching, and difficulty in understanding the
principles and aims of the Bobath method.

Sitting and standing

Young children with abnormal reflex patterns do
not easily adapt their body posture to normal
cuddling or nursing. When distressed or angry,
they may go into extensor spasm associated with

spasm of hip adductors, a movement which often
seems to be the only one under voluntary control
and therefore their only means of protest. This
behaviour is minimized by correct handling (Fig.
14.7), but is harder to control when the child is
placed in a chair, and seating must take account
of the abnormal movement patterns. Prone-lying
over a wedge and side-lying are useful alternatives
to the supine position (Fig. 14.8). Regular changes
of position are desirable to reduce the risks of
deformity and contracture. Often there will be
some positions in which function improves. For
example, hand function may be better in the side-
lying position.

Devices such as the standing-frame and prone-

a

b

c

d

Fig. 14.7 Good handling helps. Child with severe four limb mixed cerebral palsy with marked dystonic features. **a,** Seated on the floor — inadequate support and postural control — unable to use hands or communicate; **b,** when carried in the conventional way the child has no stability and feels insecure; **c,** stabilized on the floor — is now able to maintain eye contact and communicate with parent; **d,** stabilized in sitting posture — the hands are free for play and support and the head control and posture are improved. Acknowledgements to the subjects and to Christine Bungay for the photos.

board (Fig. 14.8) are a useful intermediate stage in mobilization, giving the child experience of the upright posture. Many children who cannot tolerate the prone position will be happy on a prone-board and in this position tone may improve. These devices are valuable in preventing deformity, and have the additional advantage of freeing the hands for play activities. Provided the child is placed in a symmetrical posture, early standing may be beneficial; early weight-bearing probably improves the development of the acetabulum and reduces the risk of dislocation. In the school-age child, a good stable seat, with the feet firmly on the floor or if necessary on a box, and a table at the correct height and angle are vital (Fig. 14.8).

The seating clinic

In a multidisciplinary seating clinic, a range of equipment is available for trial and special seats can be made for those who need them. The child is assessed in the lying, sitting and standing positions, without any additional supports, and then in their current seat or chair. The aims are to facilitate function, prevent or arrest deformity, avoid tissue damage (particularly in children with sensory loss) and ensure that the child is comfortable. An understanding of the biomechanical forces involved can lead to more rational prescription of chairs and ancillary equipment, such as pads, cushions, knee blocks and straps.

Table 14.7 Classification of walking ability

Community walker
Can get about the whole community with or without walking aids (e.g. crutches)

Household walker
Can move about the household, but a wheelchair is required outside the home

Physiological walker
Can walk only in a physical therapy department (or at home) with parallel bars or with assistance of another person. A wheelchair is required in all other locations

Non-walker
Needs a wheelchair for all activities. The wheelchair-dependent person can be further classified as:
1 Independent — able to get in and out of the chair without help
2 Assisted transfer ability — needs help from one person to get in and out of the chair
3 Dependent — unable to do assisted transfers and must be lifted in and out of the chair

Mobility

For parents, the ability to walk seems to be the passport to normal life. Prognostic indicators were given in Figure 14.4. It is helpful to discuss with them what exactly is meant by walking and independent mobility (Table 14.7). Most parents will appreciate that the child might learn to walk but still need a wheelchair for maximum independence.

The physiotherapist may provide a variety of aids for the child who is beginning to walk. Boots may help to maintain plantigrade feet in the spastic child, and give a stable base for the ataxic. Modern boots look smart and are more socially acceptable than the old-fashioned surgical boots. They are expensive and their value should be reviewed every time a new pair is requested. Lightweight orthoses can be worn inside the boot to help maintain the feet in good position. It is important to ensure that the boot and splint are really holding the foot in the intended position;

rotation commonly occurs inside the boot but is not immediately obvious unless carefully checked.

Callipers are no longer used routinely for children with cerebral palsy, since they are heavy and do not usually improve the gait sufficiently to justify their weight and inconvenience. Nevertheless, for some children they are worth a trial. Crutches, tripods, walking-frames, swivel-walkers and sticks all have their uses. A lightweight helmet may reduce the amount of trauma to the head if the child falls frequently, for example in ataxic CP.

Pushchairs, electric buggies and wheelchairs must be selected with the same care as one would prescribe a drug (Figs 14.8 and 14.9). Children are often given chairs that are the wrong size or inadequately modified for optimum posture and prevention of deformity. Powered chairs can be operated by some children less than 3 years old. Individually designed switches may be needed by some severely disabled children. Outdoor chairs with a range of several miles and even kerb-climbing ability are available and the disability allowance may be used for the purchase of such items, or local charities may be persuaded to donate them.

The child who has not achieved useful independent walking by the early teens is unlikely to do so thereafter. Too often, weekly sessions of physiotherapy continue up to school-leaving age without any clear objective. The doctor, therapist, child and family must together consider whether management should rather be directed towards achieving maximum wheelchair independence, perhaps using a powered wheelchair. Physiotherapy should continue, in order to maintain function, into adult life; but the aims must be specified.

Activities of daily living

The occupational therapist guides the parents in the choice of toys in order to develop co-ordination and control of hand and finger movements, and gives advice on activities of daily living, modifications to eating utensils, techniques of dressing and equipment for bathing, for

a

b

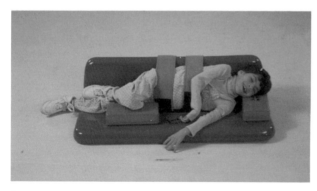

c

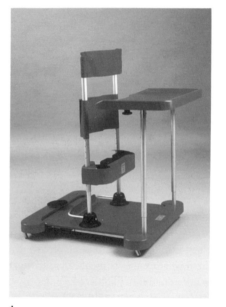

d

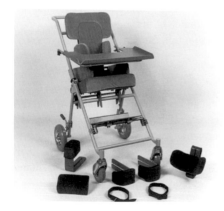

e

f

g

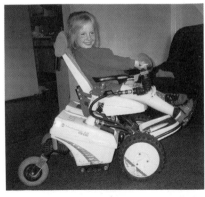

h

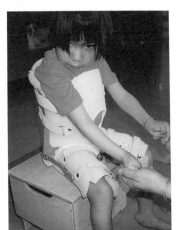

i

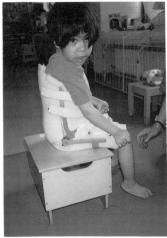

j

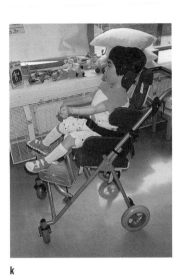

k

Fig. 14.8 (*Facing page and above*) Examples of special equipment to help with the needs of daily living and aids to mobility. Regular changes of position are important to prevent deformity and to determine which positions facilitate the use of hands and communication **skills.** a, Seating. b, Prone lying. c, Side lying. d, Standing frame. e, Buggy with postural support. f, Prone standing board. g, Corner seat. h, Electric mobility — at a price! i, j, and

k, Child with severe four limb cerebral palsy, showing improved postural control and functional benefits of orthosis (compare with pictures of same child in Fig. 14.10). a, b, c, d and g courtesy of Camp Ltd., Winchester; e, courtesy of Radcliffe Rehabilitation Services, Brackley; f, courtesy of Taylor Therapy, Pleck; h, i, j and k, courtesy of the subjects and Christine Bungay.

example a bath seat or hoist. He/she also collaborates with the speech therapist in the assessment of children with complex communication needs.

Communication

Perhaps the greatest advance in the care of people with CP over the past 20 years has been the realization that communication is an even more important part of normal life than independent mobility. Early assessment of communication skills and potential should be undertaken by the speech therapist; often at the same time he/she will review the child's oral function with regard to feeding, as there is inevitably a link between oropharyngeal function and speech. The evaluation and remediation of communication problems is discussed in Chapter 11.

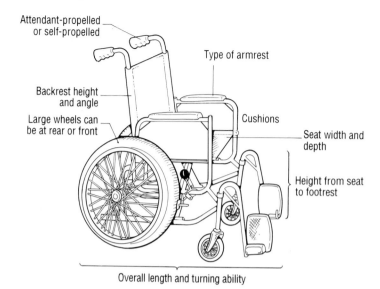

Attendant-propelled or self-propelled

Type of armrest

Backrest height and angle

Large wheels can be at rear or front

Cushions

Seat width and depth

Height from seat to footrest

Overall length and turning ability

Fig. 14.9 Points in the selection of a wheelchair.

Table 14.8 Orthopaedic surgery in cerebral palsy (CP)

1 Surgery is most likely to be useful in spastic CP and is liable to have unpredictable results in dyskinetic CP

2 Functional improvement is more likely to follow surgery to the lower limb than to the upper limb. Surgery done for purely cosmetic reasons (e.g. to make the foot 'look more normal' at rest) may not always be accompanied by functional improvement

3 The functional goal of each procedure should be clearly defined

4 Surgery should not be undertaken without the availability of a planned intensive physiotherapy programme to obtain maximum benefit

5 Surgery does not accelerate neurological maturation but may change its course

6 Orthopaedic procedures often cause a temporary setback in the development of the child with CP. It may take up to a year for the full benefits to be realized

7 Postoperative analgesia must be adequate, whatever the age and level of disability; there is no excuse for leaving children in pain after surgery

8 The family must be carefully briefed about the proposed operation and their role in postoperative rehabilitation (Table 14.9). Information leaflets and/or a letter from the surgeon may avoid misunderstandings, disappointment and even litigation

The role of orthopaedic surgery

The best results are obtained if all CP children are seen regularly at a combined paediatric/orthopaedic clinic, where expertise can be shared and developed. Such clinics are time-consuming, since only 10 or 12 patients can be seen in one session. Nevertheless, they are probably cost-effective, because they result in satisfied parents and (in many clinics) fewer but better-planned operations. The input of a physiotherapist who knows the child well is fundamental to the success of these clinics.

Because CP is so variable in its manifestations and in the changes over time, the results of surgery are hard to assess. Table 14.8 summarizes some general points about orthopaedic surgery, and Table 14.9 offers a check-list of information needed by parents.

Orthopaedic aspects of hemiplegia

Asymmetry of leg length is common in hemiplegia but the leg length discrepancy rarely exceeds 1.5 cm. There is a compensatory postural lumbar scoliosis but this is unlikely to progress. The limp is not caused by the difference in leg length and a shoe raise is rarely helpful.

a

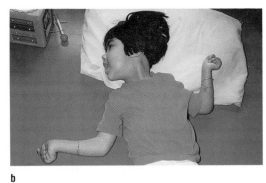

b

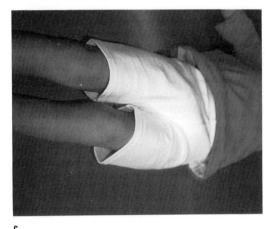

c

d

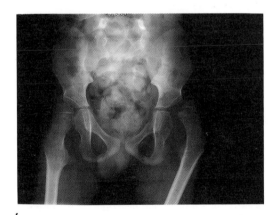

This hip is at risk
of dislocation

e

f

Fig. 14.10 The origins of deformity — the so-called 'windswept' posture. **a,** Child with four limb involvement — note asymmetry of lower limbs and **b,** strong asymmetric tonic neck reflex. **c,** The posture results in pelvic obliquity, with the right leg abducted and the left leg adducted. **d,** Postural control gives improved position of the pelvis and lower limbs (see also Fig. 14.3 which shows the same child). **e,** Diagram to show how the left hip is at increased risk of dislocation. **f,** X-ray of child with windswept hip. Acknowledgements to the child and to Christine Bungay for photos **a** to **d** and to Dr Alan Sprigg for **f**.

Table 14.9 Checklist: information needed by parents prior to surgery

What is the operation intended to achieve?
What will it not achieve?
What exactly is to be done?
What are the possible hazards of the operation?
What adverse effects might result?
Will the operation need to be repeated in the future?
What would happen if the child does not have the operation?
How urgent is it?
Will the child have adequate pain relief after the operation?
What sort of plaster will the child have, will it need changing and how long will it be needed?
Will any orthoses be needed?
Will the child be able to sit or weight-bear?
If not, what help can be given? (e.g. special pushchair)
Can the child go back to school in plaster and would any special transport arrangements be needed?
What and when should the child, and the nursery/school staff, be told about the operation?
Can the child visit the ward before the admission date?
Can the parent stay with the child?
Will the child be in a children's ward?

Table 14.10 Assessment of child with hemiplegia and equinus gait

1 The child should first be examined supine on a mat. In this position the effect of gravity on muscle tone is eliminated. Tone is graded as normal, increased or decreased

2 The child with moderate or severe hemiplegia will lie with the hip on the affected side partially flexed and medially rotated, the knee flexed and the foot plantar flexed and inverted. It may be difficult to overcome the increased tone when trying to fully flex the knee and hip. The child is then asked to lift his/her bottom clear of the mat

3 In mild hemiplegia, both buttocks and thighs are easily lifted clear, with the knees remaining flexed. In moderate and severe cases, the affected leg extends

4 The child is then asked to stand. In mild cases, the child usually gets to stand through half-kneeling. If severely affected, the child pivots and extends the affected leg

5 Next, the child is observed walking. The step length is noted and the cadence can be assessed by listening. The leg may be used purely as a prop, or may weight bear effectively. The child is asked to walk backwards; this requires active extension of the hip and enables the power of this movement to be assessed

6 The child is then asked to stand on the affected leg; the ability to weight bear is assessed and the posture and balance reactions are observed

7 Lastly, the child is asked to sit and the range of dorsiflexion is assessed. The foot must be held in the inverted position, to avoid movement at the subtalar and midtarsal joints. Steady pressure should be applied to overcome spasticity, otherwise the degree of fixed deformity will be overestimated

Equinus deformity, due to tightness of the Achilles tendon with limited dorsiflexion, is the commonest and most obvious orthopaedic problem in hemiplegia. Weight-bearing in equinus results in the body weight being concentrated on the metatarsal heads, which may cause pain. The ankle is unstable and prone to injury in this position. Unilateral equinus creates relative lengthening of the limb and pelvic obliquity. The child has to increase knee and hip flexion or circumduct the whole leg, so that the foot can clear the ground when walking. However, up to 5° of equinus may be useful in that it compensates for leg length discrepancy.

Careful assessment is important (Table 14.10). Some children with mild or moderate hemiplegia may have normal or even low tone at rest; when they walk the tone increases and they tend to walk on their toes. It may be possible to overcome the equinus deformity by passive dorsiflexion. If the tendon is weakened by a lengthening operation in this situation, the child may instead develop a crouching gait. If, however, the child has a mod-erate to severe hemiplegia, with raised tone at rest, and a fixed deformity (i.e. the foot cannot be dorsiflexed passively to the neutral position), surgery is more likely to improve the gait.

Physiotherapy may help to delay Achilles tendon tightness, but can seldom prevent it entirely. The parents should learn the techniques since they must be applied frequently if they are to be effective. Firm boots and moulded plastic splints (ankle–foot orthoses or AFOs) may also help to slow the development of equinus deformity. If the child has increased tone but little or no fixed deformity, the gait can sometimes be improved by the use of a cast. This may defer the need for surgery by 6−9 months. The cast is sometimes reapplied several times, usually at 5- to 10-day intervals, and dorsiflexion is increased each time. Sometimes a greater increase in the range of dorsiflexion can be obtained if the child is given a brief general anaesthetic.

Fixed deformity will usually need surgical treatment eventually, although there is seldom any real urgency about this; the equinus gait does no permanent harm. It is useful to delay surgical treatment as long as possible; parents should be warned that there is a high recurrence rate when Achilles tendon lengthening is undertaken in early childhood.

Other orthopaedic problems associated with hemiplegia include varus, valgus and cavus foot deformities, metatarsus adductus, hallux valgus, bunions, flexion of the toes, knee flexion and hyperextension deformities, hip flexion and internal rotation.

Upper limb surgery. Assessment of the upper limb with a view to surgery should be shared with the physiotherapist and occupational therapist. The main points can be summarized as follows.

1 Pronator contracture is common and the limitation of supination makes certain tasks, such as catching a ball, very difficult. Occasionally it is associated with posterior dislocation of the radial head. Elbow flexion deformity is also found in many children with hemiplegia. Surgery may be considered if the deformity exceeds 30−40°.

2 The power of the wrist, finger and thumb extensors and flexors is assessed with the wrist held flexed and extended. When there is severe flexion deformity of the wrist and fingers and the flexors and extensors have negligible voluntary movement, little functional improvement can be expected from surgical procedures, although the cosmetic appearance may be improved in various ways.

3 Where some activity can be demonstrated in wrist flexors and extensors but extension is very weak, and sensory impairment is not severe, tendon transfer from flexor to extensor groups may be considered.

4 The common 'thumb in palm' deformity has been variously treated by correction of the thumb adductor contracture and by procedures involving the extensor pollicis tendons.

Upper limb surgery in children is seldom considered before the age of 8 or 9 years. Operations for cosmetic indications should be performed only if the patient is enthusiastic about the possible improvement in appearance. Before performing an operation for functional improvement, one must ask: what will the patient be able to do after surgery which he/she cannot do now?

Surgery in diplegia

Improvement of gait is the usual aim of surgery in children with diplegia and this is often accomplished between the ages of 4 and 8 years. Three patterns of gait are recognized in these children (see Fig. 14.5).

Gait analysis. Ambulant children with diplegia often undergo a series of surgical procedures, each of which alters the gait without necessarily leading to either functional or cosmetic improvement. The technique of gait analysis is intended to facilitate a more rational approach, by monitoring simultaneously the forces and range of movement at each joint in the lower limb, the electromyogram (EMG) and the energy costs of walking. The child may then undergo several orthopaedic procedures either at the same time or within a few weeks of each other, followed by an intensive rehabilitation programme. It is claimed (though not proven) that this integrated approach produces better results, with less time in hospital or in plaster, than the more cautious stepwise approach.

Deformity at the hip. Adductor spasticity is obvious when the child walks. There is close proximation of the knees and thighs and, in more severe cases, scissoring is observed, with one limb crossing over the other. Adductor spasticity and contracture may be relieved by a variety of procedures. Division of the adductors and the gracilis muscle, sometimes combined with anterior obturator neurectomy, has been widely used, but may result in overweakening of these muscles. Adductor longus tenotomy with gracilis myotomy is a less extensive procedure. Where there is doubt, the likely effects of surgery can be mimicked by myoneural block of the adductor muscles. Many children with classic diplegia also have marked internal rotation at the hips, caused by spastic muscles, and excessive femoral anteversion (twisting forwards of the head and neck of femur). Derotation femoral osteotomy is used to correct this.

Hip flexion deformity is associated with spasticity in the iliopsoas muscle. The iliopsoas can be lengthened surgically, but complete division of the tendon is only done when there is no prospect of the child walking.

Deformity at the knee. Knee flexion deformity is usually due to spastic and/or contracted hamstring muscles and is often accompanied by hip flexion deformity. It can also be caused or exacerbated by excessive surgical lengthening of the Achilles tendon. The crouched gait results in an increase in the energy requirement of walking and imposes enormous pressures on the joint surfaces, which lead to early degenerative arthritis.

Tightness of the hamstrings is assessed with the child supine on the examination couch. The hip is flexed to 90° and the knee is extended to the point of resistance. If the knee cannot be completely extended when the thighs are extended on the table, there is probably also contracture of the posterior knee joint capsule. Surgery for tight hamstrings is often undertaken at the same time as correction of hip and ankle deformities.

Foot and ankle. Children with diplegia often have an equinus gait when they start to walk, but this is usually dynamic, i.e. it is more prominent on walking and is not accompanied by fixed deformity. It may sometimes be a means of compensating for hamstring contracture. Valgus deformity is more common than pes varus in children with diplegia. The deformity may improve in early childhood. Boots, supports and orthoses are not very effective. Some children benefit from an arthrodesis or a tendon transfer.

Orthopaedic considerations in total body involvement

Deformities are particularly prominent in children with severe four-limb involvement. A number of factors contribute (Table 14.11).

Subluxation and dislocation of the hip joint. There are three patterns which place the hip at risk of subluxation and dislocation.
1 *The windswept hip* (Fig. 14.10) describes a combination of adduction and internal rotation of one hip together with abduction and external rotation of the other.
2 *Bilateral or unilateral adduction* is usually caused by hypertonia.
3 *Bilateral hip abduction and external rotation with knee flexion* can result in anterior dislocation of the hip. This may occur in profoundly hypotonic children with severe learning disabilities who lie in this position for long periods, and in children who have had adductor surgery for hypertonia. In the latter group, the risk factor for this complication is probably unstable tone or dyskinesia.
Subluxation means that at least part of the femoral head is congruent with the acetabulum; in dislocation congruence is totally lost. It is important to prevent subluxation and dislocation of the hips (Table 14.12), which interferes with perineal hygiene, causes difficulties with seating and may be associated with pelvic obliquity and scoliosis. It may eventually lead to pain. (Parents think of dislocation as an acute and agonizingly painful event; they should be told that the dislocation occurs gradually with remodelling of the acetabulum. Any pain that does occur comes later, with muscle spasm and degenerative processes in the opposing bony surfaces.)

Most authorities consider that these problems are sufficiently troublesome to justify determined efforts to prevent dislocation. On the other hand,

Table 14.11 Causes of deformity in children with cerebral palsy (CP). After Brown and Minns (1989)

---

1 Hypertonus. Tonic spasticity is associated with muscle imbalance across a joint (p. 239). Contractures do not occur in pure dystonic rigidity

2 Lower motor neuron lesions. Muscle imbalance may occur because of the unopposed pull of normal muscles against the paralysed muscles

3 Impaired growth of limbs. This is often attributed to disuse but may be due, at least in part, to impaired central nervous control of the limb. Possibly trophic factors are involved

4 Reduced muscle growth. Muscle growth keeps pace with skeletal growth by an increase in the number of sarcomeres (muscle cells). If the muscle is in a constantly shortened state it will adapt to this by reducing the number of sarcomeres. Such changes can occur in a matter of weeks, explaining how a deformity can become fixed very rapidly. *Splinting a muscle in a stretched position for at least 6 hours out of 24 (i.e. overnight) may be sufficient to bring about the desired growth in sarcomere numbers*

5 Muscles become stiff with disuse and the viscous resistance is reduced by stretching and movement (thixotropy). This suggests a mechanism whereby passive stretching may reduce disuse atrophy

6 Exaggeration of normal asymmetry. Most normal babies show a preferred direction of head turn. Exaggeration of this normal neurological asymmetry may account for the increasing windswept deformity in children with severe CP

7 Compensation for other deformities; for example, lordosis caused by hip flexion contracture

8 Soft-tissue fibrosis. This may be congenital as in muscle diseases or ischaemic damage

9 Iatrogenic; for example, overlengthening of the Achilles tendon leading to crouch gait

10 Sitting posture; for example, W-sitting in the hypotonic child may increase femoral anteversion

---

there are some who take the opposite view, particularly in the most profoundly disabled children, for the following reasons.

1 Many profoundly disabled children do *not* seem to experience severe pain with dislocation.

2 It is often difficult to know whether a child or teenager with severe CP is suffering pain from the hip or has some other cause of distress and discomfort.

3 Such pain as they do have may be transient and responds to simple analgesics together with careful handling and positioning.

4 It is usually possible to seat the child or find satisfactory ways of making the child comfortable.

5 Surgery inevitably carries a degree of risk in these immobile and often underweight children and it is not invariably successful in preventing dislocation. If reoperation is needed this can be technically difficult.

6 The development of pain, which surgery is designed to prevent, may not be a problem until later in life, but many of these children will have a limited life expectancy.

7 If the surgeon does have to operate on a painful dislocated hip in the older child, teenager or young adult, surgical options are available; they include reconstructive operations, hip arthrodesis, hip replacement and proximal femoral resection. These are indeed all major and difficult procedures, but they are not very often necessary.

Knee, foot and ankle. Contractures at the knee may need correction if they interfere with positioning in bed or if they prevent assisted transfers from the wheelchair. Severe equinus may prevent placement in a standing-frame and make wheelchair life more difficult. However, many foot and ankle deformities in the profoundly disabled are best left alone and it is sometimes more sensible to use very soft flexible shoes such as trainers or to provide soft sheepskin slippers, rather than embark on quite extensive surgery.

Scoliosis. In children with severe CP this has a bad prognosis with a high probability of progressive deterioration. Good seating may help to make the child more comfortable and plastic body jackets may slow the rate of progression but often the curve becomes worse in spite of these measures. Electrical stimulation of the spinal muscles has been used but is not widely available. Surgery remains the most effective method of treatment,

Table 14.12 Dislocation of the hips in cerebral palsy (CP). From D. Scrutton (unpublished data)

- *High risk*: four limb CP. Risk factors: windswept hips, adduction, abduction with external rotation and knee flexion, non-ambulant
- *Low risk*: early walking diplegia
- *Very low risk*: hemiplegia
- In children with CP, the *mean age of dislocation* is said to be around 6 or 7 years though it can occur at any age; however, subluxation usually starts much younger
- In previously normal children who had been walking prior to an acquired brain injury, the hip rarely dislocates, though it can do so with alarming speed in the early stages of recovery
- The hip joint is capable of substantial remodelling in the first 4 years of life but becomes less able to do so with increasing age. This suggests that prevention of dislocation by good positioning, and surgery when needed, are more likely to be successful in early life

Monitoring

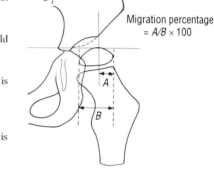

X-ray of left hip

Migration percentage
= A/B × 100

- An X-ray of the hips should be taken *when bilateral CP is first diagnosed*. This should be repeated at age 30 months and thereafter at 6 or 12 monthly intervals depending on the findings
- *A standard position is vital* so that comparisons can be made. The child should be X-rayed supine, in neutral ab/adduction and the patellae facing vertically. The pelvis should not be rotated transversely or vertically. The therapist may need to accompany the child to ensure this is achieved
- *The migration percentage* (see figure) in the normal child may slowly increase; the mean MP under 5 years of age is approximately 5%
- An MP of > 33% ('subluxed') at age 30 months means that the hip is at high risk; > 50% means that there is a high chance of rapid progression to dislocation
- *Acetabular obliquity* appears when the MP is > 20%, and rarely before the age of 30 months

What to do
- *Regular physiotherapy and good seating* may help to reduce the risk and rate of dislocation but is not always effective
- *Soft tissue surgery* alone may prevent further subluxation, particularly in children under the age of four; but does not obviate the need for good seating subsequently
- *Children with dystonic patterns* may develop severe abduction deformity after adductor surgery
- *Myoneural block* of the adductor muscles can be used to predict the likely effect of surgery
- The adductors are weakened by *myotomy*, sometimes combined with anterior obturator neurectomy (the need for this is controversial)
- For *windswept hips*, initial surgery should be only on the adducted side. Operating on the abducted hip may lead to extreme abduction. Nevertheless, the other hip may need an adductor tenotomy later
- For *bilateral adduction*, even if very asymmetric, surgery should be bilateral
- A hip spica, broomstick plaster or orthosis will be needed after surgery, followed by long-term postural control
- Many severely affected children will eventually need further and more extensive procedures, such as pelvic osteotomy and/or femoral osteotomy, to prevent dislocation

If surgery is undertaken, it must be made clear to the parents that the aim is to prevent dislocation, rather than to increase the probability of walking, and that the prevention of dislocation is a worthwhile goal in a profoundly disabled child

- *Surgery in older children and teenagers* is undertaken when there are extreme difficulties in nursing care or secondary deformity is impairing quality of life. Dislocation can cause pain but this is unusual. Proximal femoral resection involves removing the head, neck and upper end of the shaft of the femur. 3–6 weeks postoperative traction are needed. Heterotopic bone formation may impair the result

---

MP, migration percentage.

but these operations are extensive, with a significant mortality and considerable morbidity.

Severe scoliosis makes seating and nursing care more difficult; it is cosmetically unattractive; it may eventually affect cardiorespiratory function; and it may cause pain and discomfort. However, surveys of severely disabled adults suggest that those with scoliosis do not differ significantly from those without, in terms of pain, discomfort, seating problems or chest disease. Scoliosis surgery in this situation raises difficult ethical as well as technical questions.

Drug treatment of cerebral palsy

Spasticity (but not rigidity) can be reduced by baclofen. This drug acts mainly at spinal level and is valuable where severe spasticity is causing painful spasms or serious functional problems in mobility or dressing. It may be particularly useful in the postoperative period after orthopaedic surgery. Young children require a small dose initially, perhaps 1.25 to 2.5 mg twice daily. The dosage is monitored by clinical response and is gradually increased as necessary, up to a maximum dose of 60 mg daily in three divided doses. The dose can be manipulated by the parents and physiotherapist. Side-effects include nausea and mild drowsiness, which are usually transient, and excessive hypotonia. Baclofen can safely be given to children with epilepsy. No serious long-term problems have emerged but it is advisable to withdraw therapy occasionally to determine whether the child is still obtaining benefit from it. It should be withdrawn over several days as abrupt discontinuation has been associated with fits and hallucinations.

Diazepam is also used in severe spasticity but it tends to cause an unacceptable degree of drowsiness before adequate muscle relaxation is achieved. Clonazepam is useful for myoclonic epilepsies in CP and muscle relaxation may be an added bonus, but hypersalivation and bronchial secretions may be troublesome. Dantrolene sodium also reduces spasticity but is not recommended for children because of its hepatotoxicity.

Other approaches to treatment

Stereotactic brain surgery has been undertaken in a few centres but the long-term results are disappointing and unpredictable. Cerebellar stimulation similarly has not been very successful. Section of the posterior nerve roots (posterior rhizotomy) can reduce lower limb spasticity and improve function. The technique requires careful preoperative selection and intraoperative EMG monitoring. Spasticity in individual muscles can be reduced by injection of botulinus toxin. Doses up to a total of 120 μg/kg (spaced over several injections) have been used. Mild botulism may occur and parents must be informed about the features to watch for. This technique can reduce the action of a muscle group for a period of many months, thus delaying the need for surgery. The intrathecal infusion of baclofen by implantable pump may offer another means of reducing spasticity, although there is an ever-present risk of infection.

Psychological assessment

For children who have adequate speech and hand function, psychological assessment presents no particular difficulty, but for the severely disabled child, with little or no speech and poor control of the hands, the task may be very daunting. Much can be learned from the parents' observations (Table 14.13) and the child's attempts at social interaction. An instrument such as the Vineland Scale, which uses parental observations, can take this process a stage further but a number of items are irrelevant for children with a motor disorder. The child may be very slow to initiate a movement or sound when asked a question, and it is important to distinguish delayed responses from intellectual impairment.

Sometimes, standardized test batteries can be used. So long as some form of yes/no response can be elicited from the child (even if it is only an eye movement or grunt), useful information can be obtained. The Columbia Mental Maturity Scale and the British Ability Scales are particularly well suited to simple yes/no and pointing

Table 14.13 Using parental knowledge of the child

GROSS MOTOR SKILLS

Can the child sit alone, stand, move purposefully (some profoundly disabled children move or pivot when placed on the floor but without any obvious goal)?

FINE MOTOR SKILLS

Ask and observe how much control the child has over the hands. If this is very limited, is it because of motor impairment or because the child lacks motivation and organization to undertake complex movements? If the child has enough control to place their hand on, or strike, a target, then the child should be able to access a computer system (provided he/she has had the opportunity)

The aim is to determine the level of motivation to function in spite of the movement disorder

COMPREHENSION OF SPEECH

Does the child hear? How much does the child understand (Chapters 3 and 4)? Is it limited to everyday sounds, simple instructions and information, stories, etc. (this information is useful even if the child has visual impairment)?

Impaired comprehension of speech, not due to hearing impairment, can be due to specific language impairment, but is more often accompanied by other learning disabilities

EVERYDAY UNDERSTANDING

Does the child identify familiar people and places? Is the child selective about TV programmes and videos? Which ones does he/she like? Does he/she show evidence of understanding what is going on? Does he/she laugh at appropriate places? (This is useful even if the child has impaired hearing)

The child's ability to learn about the world through his/her eyes gives some idea of his/her learning potential in the non-verbal area of function

---

responses. A speech therapist can use identical methods to assess verbal comprehension. Picture vocabulary tests and the Test for Reception of Grammar (TROG) can also be used.

Children with CP may have a variety of learning problems. Visual—spatial concepts seem to present particular difficulties. This has often been attributed to their lack of mobility, preventing them from exploring the world and understanding the concepts of movement, gravity and perspective; but children with movement disorders of equal functional severity due to muscle disease do not have such problems and it is more likely that the difficulties are a direct consequence of their brain abnormality.

Computers play an increasingly important role, both in assessment and in teaching children with CP. The child's ability to understand and make use of appropriate software and switches helps parents and teachers to estimate the child's level of conceptual thinking and to plan the educational programme accordingly.

Education

Many children with hemiplegia or diplegia can be integrated into mainstream school. However, apart from the increased incidence of learning problems, children with CP in normal schools have a number of practical difficulties, particularly with sporting and handicraft activities. For example, they are likely to be slow in dressing after games and swimming. Integration may be possible even for children with severe motor disability, provided that the layout and design of the school are suitable and the staff are enthusiastic. On the other hand, specialist schools for physically disabled children can concentrate on one site the necessary teaching expertise, communication and mobility aids and therapy support.

Some educationists (notably those who favour the conductive education system (see Table 14.6) believe that children with CP should use a minimum of equipment, seating supports and microtechnology, in order to encourage initiative and self-reliance and reduce dependence on mechanical aids. Others argue that stable, secure seating and appropriate technical aids free the children from the mechanical tasks of maintaining their posture and communicating their ideas, so that their learning potential can be developed more easily. These viewpoints are often regarded as mutually incompatible; like most professional arguments, this one is detrimental to the child. A well-planned curriculum can integrate the advantages of both approaches.

Common problems in the care of children with cerebral palsy

Feeding problems

Defining the problem

The causes of feeding problems in children with CP and the common presenting complaints are summarized in Table 14.14.

Adequacy of intake

A dietitian should review the daily intake with the parents and determine whether this meets the child's nutritional needs.

Functional assessment of chewing and swallowing

A speech therapist should review the child's ability to chew and swallow. The therapist will observe whether the child has persistent primitive reflex patterns (rooting reflex, bite reflex, tongue thrust); whether he/she is able to form a bolus with food; how readily he/she can transfer food to the posterior part of the mouth into the pharynx; and how well he/she can swallow. These points should be reviewed both for liquids and for solids of varying consistency. The therapist will determine how much the ability to feed and swallow is affected by positioning and seating and will assess the extent to which the primitive reflex patterns can be inhibited by various manoeuvres. This assessment may be purely clinical or may be supported by radiological studies, which have contributed a great deal to our knowledge of feeding problems in CP.

Videofluoroscopy

This allows study of the three stages of swallowing. The *oral* stage includes the movements between lips and posterior pharynx. This stage is

Table 14.14 Causes and presentation of feeding problems in severely disabled children

Presenting complaints
- Time-consuming, tedious and frustrating feeding for carers and child
- Distress during, just before or just after meals (may be manifested by spasms)
- Poor weight gain and nutritional status
- Vomiting or regurgitation — unpleasant, makes child unattractive and smelly
- Respiratory symptoms due to aspiration of food or liquids into the lungs

Causes
- Movement disorder resulting in poor seating posture and head control while eating
- Motor dysfunction of the tongue, palate, jaws and pharynx
- Impaired motivation to eat
- Child is unable to control his/her own eating; cannot forage for or demand food when hungry or refuse when satiated
- Child is signalling an aversive response, remembering previous experiences of choking or forced feeding (often the cause of extensor spasms)
- Gastro-oesophageal reflux causing regurgitation, vomiting, dysphagia, haematemesis or pain
- Psychogenic vomiting due to stress, boredom, anxiety or as means of protest
- Drugs such as clonazepam may cause hypersalivation; other drugs may cause nausea
- Attention-seeking behaviour is very rarely the correct explanation

under voluntary control, although this may be severely affected in children with neurological disorder. In the *pharyngeal* stage the swallow reflex is initiated and food passes over the closed larynx to the open oesophagus. In the *oesophageal* stage food passes onwards down to the stomach. The latter two stages are not under voluntary control. For a successful videofluoroscopy of the oropharynx, children need to be accompanied by familiar adults and should use their own eating and drinking utensils. Both liquid and semisolid barium is used. Lateral views are taken as the barium is taken into the mouth and swallowed, using videorecording. The radiologist examines in turn the tongue, palate, pharynx, epiglottis, cricopharyngeus and oesophagus. Particular attention is paid to the occurrence of aspiration, nasal regurgitation, failure to clear the oral cavity or pharynx and oesophageal spasm.

Assessment of gastro-oesophageal reflux

Reflux should be considered if the child has repeated vomiting, particularly when accompanied by some haematemesis; if the child has obvious pain or 'spasms' associated with meals; if there is evidence of aspiration into the lungs; and in dysphagia which may be due to oesophagitis or stricture. Investigations include a barium study of the upper gastrointestinal tract; endoscopy, plus or minus biopsy; and a 24-hour pH study (the 'gold standard' test for reflux). Alternatively, a treatment trial can be undertaken.

Seating

A physiotherapist and/or occupational therapist may need to review the child's seating. Carers find it easier to feed the child by dropping food into the back of the throat, with the child in the semireclining position, but it is really very difficult to swallow in this position and a more upright posture will often be more satisfactory.

Management

It is essential to define the problem, decide on the nature and severity of any dysfunction demonstrated, and agree on the aims of intervention with parents and carers. For example, other family members may be putting pressure on the parents to carry out a particular regime of feeding or care, and explanations and advice to them may make life easier for the family. Therapists may worry about children who have not mastered lumpy foods, in the belief that this is detrimental to development of oral and speech skills, but there is no evidence for this and these children will probably always be happier taking purées. Removing this pressure from parents may in itself help to resolve the situation.

For children who have great difficulty in eating and chewing, changes in the consistency of foodstuffs may improve feeding behaviour and reduce reflux. Simple changes of routine, for example telling the child when a mealtime is about to begin, and setting time limits on how long one should persist, may take the tension out of the problem. Desensitization of overactive mouth reflexes is popular with some therapists, although it is of uncertain value.

If feeding is very stressful or if aspiration is causing frequent respiratory distress and infection, the child may have a better quality of life and be happier if wholly or partly fed by tube or gastrostomy. Opinions differ on the significance of aspiration of gastric contents into the lungs when this is not accompanied by distress or any evidence of respiratory problems. It has yet to be shown in the latter group that the discontinuation of oral feeds is justified by improved quality or length of the child's life.

Tube feeding

Plastic tubes have been superseded by the 'Silk^{TM}' tube, which is prelubricated and, because it is made of polyurethane, is much softer. It is inserted using a reusable guidewire and can be left *in situ* for long periods without the need for frequent changes. Oral feeding with a small amount of favourite foods can be continued for pleasure and to maintain mouth hygiene. The parents and carers can relax during the oral feeding, knowing that the child's nutritional requirements can be topped up by means of the tube. However, long-term tube feeding has several disadvantages. Some children find the tube uncomfortable and it may increase salivation, bronchial hypersecretion, retching and heaving. It is unsightly. Some children deliberately or accidentally remove the tube repeatedly, causing further stress to the carers. A tube can cause soreness and erosion of the nose, pharynx and oesophagus and increase gastro-oesophageal reflux. In these circumstances, it may be wise to consider the creation of a gastrostomy.

There is an ethical concern regarding the prolongation of life by tube or gastrostomy feeding in a profoundly disabled individual; but many will take the view that the *quality* of the child's life is the important issue.

Treatment of reflux

If significant reflux is suspected or demonstrated, 6 weeks' intensive medical treatment should include some or all of the following:
1 a surface-active agent such as Gaviscon;
2 an H_2 antagonist (cimetidine or ranitidine) given in full standard dosage for the child's weight;
3 omeprazole is an alternative to the H_2 antagonists but has not yet been widely evaluated in this situation;
4 an agent to improve gastrointestinal motility — metoclopramide, cisapride or domperidone; however, note that cimetidine and omeprazole may interact with anticonvulsants (p. 351).

If the child does not improve, an antireflux operation (a Nissan or Thal fundoplication) may be contemplated. This will usually prevent reflux and therefore often improves quality of life quite substantially. It is nevertheless a major procedure with several complications, including the inability to vomit or to bring up wind. In carefully selected patients, however, antireflux surgery can dramatically improve the quality of life for the child and also for the family.

Management of regurgitation and rumination without reflux

Regurgitation without significant reflux may respond to small frequent feeds, and thickening of the feeds with cereal or Nestargel. Medications should be reviewed in case they are causing nausea. Drugs which reduce spasticity (p. 269) may make feeding easier. Rumination, the deliberate regurgitation of stomach contents for pleasure, may occur in children with severe learning disabilities, with or without cerebral palsy. It can be reduced by giving less fluid with meals, giving small, more frequent meals, and provision of other activities at times when rumination is

likely to occur. The contribution of psychological factors in regurgitation and vomiting is often underestimated.

Gastrostomy

A gastrostomy is an alternative to prolonged tube feeding. This can be created either by an open operation or by an endoscopic technique (percutaneous endoscopic gastrostomy (PEG)), which causes less patient discomfort and reduced scarring. If the child has gastro-oesophageal reflux, gastrostomy may make it worse, but it is not necessary to do an antireflux operation at the same time as the gastrostomy unless the reflux is severe and symptomatic.

Management of gastrostomies. The dietitian will advise on suitable feeds for gastrostomy feeding. Support and advice will be needed from a paediatric community nurse. Gastrostomy feeding may have unexpected effects; for instance, it may result in increased fluid intake, exacerbating problems of incontinence. Since the day is no longer fully occupied by feeding the child, other activities become possible for the child and family. Relationships may be put under new strain because of a change in lifestyle. Teenagers may enter puberty as a result of the greatly improved nutrition although, even when children are fed by gastrostomy to the calculated requirement, growth may be suboptimal (others, however, become obese). These findings suggest that the brain's control over growth is not mediated solely by food intake.

Complications. Localized infection and peritonitis can occur as a result of leakage. In this situation, a return to nasogastric feeding, nasojejunal feeding or the surgical creation of a feeding jejunostomy may be considered.

Dribbling

Difficulty in swallowing, poor head control and weakness of the jaw and facial muscles contribute to this intractable problem, which is distressing both for the child and their parents. Devices to support the chin and behavioural training (to promote regular swallowing) have not been very successful, but recently some progress has been made with orthodontic appliances. Transplantation of the salivary ducts to the posterior part of the pharynx has in the past been associated with dryness of the mouth and dental and gum disorders; but recent improvements in technique seem to have reduced the incidence of these problems.

Temporary relief for special occasions may be obtained with atropine tablets (0.6 mg) or scopolamine patches (250 µg under 12, 500 µg over 12 years). Benzhexol has also been used. Soreness of the chin and neck can be prevented by silicone barrier cream, and 1% hydrocortisone is effective in treating areas of inflammation caused by constant soaking in saliva.

Constipation

Constipation is almost universal in children with four-limb CP. It can cause pain and muscle spasm, particularly if a fissure is present. Many parents are convinced that seizure control deteriorates when the child is constipated. Contributing causes include small food and fluid intake, highly refined foods with little bulk, weakness and spasticity of abdominal muscles, and associated learning disability, reducing motivation to acquire continence. A stool-softener such as lactulose is often useful, in doses of 5–30 ml/day. Docusate given for 2–3 weeks softens hard stools and sodium picosulphate can be used to eliminate the softened stool. Senokot is unlikely to be effective in the presence of massive hard stool until these preliminary measures have taken effect. In some cases, a microenema or regular manual removal may turn out to be the easiest solution.

Urinary incontinence

This is discussed in Chapter 15.

The miserable child

Possible causes of misery include inability to change position when uncomfortable, a feeling of insecurity due to absent postural mechanisms, discomfort due to extensor spasms or reflux oesophagitis and painful subluxation or dislocation of the hip, as well as ordinary paediatric problems such as otitis media, urinary tract infection, asthma, migraine and functional abdominal pain. True depressive illness may occur in disabled teenagers as it does in normal ones and can be very difficult to recognize.

Cold hands and feet are associated with poor circulation and diminished activity. In very cold weather, children with severe CP may develop peripheral cyanosis and even oedema, which may take several days to resolve. Chilblains, however, do not seem to be any more common than in non-CP children.

Another common problem is that the children get bored very quickly, because they cannot entertain themselves. Intensive programmes may condition them to expect constant attention and to resent it when this cannot be provided.

Life expectancy

There is a considerable increase in mortality rates of children and teenagers who have severe four-limb involvement, profound learning difficulties and problems with chewing and swallowing (p. 171). There may be a modest reduction of life expectancy in those with less severe disability but there are no reliable data.

The adult with severe cerebral palsy

The school doctor, teaching staff, social services, careers officer and parents should review the future needs and prospects of the disabled teenager. A planned handover to adult services is very important for continuity of care. A combined clinic with a consultant in rehabilitation medicine is one way of achieving this. The GP must also be updated on the role he or she can play.

At the end of their school career children with CP may attend colleges and special centres. Those with straightforward hemiplegia or classic diplegia have a reasonable prospect of obtaining work. Only a few of those with severe four-limb involvement will be able to progress to higher education or to compete for work in the open market; in most cases the multiplicity of impairments makes this impossible. Voluntary organizations, notably SCOPE (formerly the Spastics Society), have shown how the imaginative design and construction of living accommodation and the use of environmental control systems can give the adult disabled more satisfying lives, with an acceptable degree of independence. Advances in powered wheelchair design, legislation about wheelchair access to public buildings and modified control systems in cars together allow a greater degree of mobility than ever before. Nevertheless, much remains to be done and parents should be encouraged to give their support to one of the voluntary organizations active in this field.

References and further reading

Armstrong, R.W. (1992) Intrathecal Baclofen and spasticity: what do we know and what do we need to know? *Developmental Medicine and Child Neurology*, **34**(8), 739–45.

Bax, M. and Nelson, K.B. (1993) Birth asphyxia: a statement. *Developmental Medicine and Child Neurology*, **35**(11), 1022–34.

Blasco, P.A. and Allaire, J.H. (1992) Participants of the consortium on drooling. Drooling in the developmentally disabled: management practices and recommendations. *Developmental Medicine and Child Neurology*, **34**(10), 849–62.

Bleck, E.E. (1987) *Orthopaedic management in Cerebral Palsy*. Clinics in Developmental Medicine, Vol. 99/100.

Bobath, K. (1980) *A Neurophysiological Basis for the Treatment of Cerebral Palsy*. Clinics in Developmental Medicine, No. 75. Mackeith Press, London.

Brown, J.K. and Minns, R.A. (1989) Mechanisms of deformity in children with cerebral palsy. *Seminars in Orthopaedics*, **4**(4), 236–55.

Campos de Paz, A., Burnett, S.M. and Braga, L.W. (1994) Walking prognosis in cerebral palsy: a 22-year retrospective study. *Developmental Medicine and Child Neurology*, **36**(2), 130–4.

Clay, M.M. (1989) *Quadruplets and Higher Multiple Births*. Clinics in Developmental Medicine. No. 107. Mackeith Press, London.

Cornell, M.S. (1995) The hip in cerebral palsy. *Developmental Medicine and Child Neurology*, **37**(1), 3–18.

Cosgrove, A.P., Corry, I.S. and Graham, H.K. (1994) Botulinum toxin in the management of the lower limb in cerebral palsy. *Developmental Medicine and Child Neurology*, **36**(5), 386–96.

De Negri, M. and Rolando, S. (1990) Child ataxias: a developmental perspective. Brain Development, **12**, 195–201.

Dubowitz, V. (1995) *Muscle Disorders in Childhood*. W.B. Saunders, Philadelphia.

Finnie, N. (1991) *Handling the Young Cerebral Palsied Child at Home*. Butterworth Heinemann, Oxford.

Gage, J.R. (1991) *Gait Analysis in Cerebral Palsy*. Clinics in Developmental Medicine. No. 121. Mackeith Press, London.

Goldberg, M.J. (1991) Measuring outcomes in cerebral palsy. *Journal of Paediatric Orthopaedics*, **11**, 682–5.

Goldmann, A. (1993) 'Pain management'. *Archives of Disease in Childhood*, **68**, 423–5.

Gordon, N. (1993) Hereditary spastic paraplegia — a diagnostic reminder. *Developmental Medicine and Child Neurology*, **35**(5), 452–5.

Govaert, P. (1993) *Cranial Haemorrhage in the Term Newborn Infant*. Clinics in Developmental Medicine, No. 129. Mackeith Press, London.

Haskell, S.H. and Barrett, E.K. (1993) *The Education of Children with Physical and Neurological Disabilities*, (3rd edn). Chapman and Hall, London.

HMSO (1993) *Evaluation of Conductive Education for Children with Cerebral Palsy*. Final Report, Parts I and II. HMSO, London.

Hughes, I. and Newton, R. (1992) Genetic aspects of cerebral palsy. *Developmental Medicine and Child Neurology*, **34**(1), 80–6.

Iivanainen, M. and Kaakkola, S. (1993) Dopa-responsive dystonia of childhood. *Developmental Medicine and Child Neurology*, **35**(4), 362–7.

Kalen, V., Conkin, M.M. and Sherman, F.C. (1992) Untreated scoliosis in severe cerebral palsy. *Journal of Paediatric Orthopaedics*, **12**, 337–40.

Levitt, S. (1995) *Treatment of Cerebral Palsy and Motor Delay*. Blackwell Science, Oxford.

Lewis, D.W., Fontana, C., Mehallick, L.K. and Evervett, Y. (1994) Transdermal Scopolamine for reduction of drooling in developmentally delayed children. *Developmental Medicine and Child Neurology*, **36**(6), 484–6.

Lonstein, J.E. (1995) The spine in cerebral palsy. *Current Orthopaedics*, **9**(3), 164–77.

Mandelstam, M. (1992) *How to get Equipment for Disability*,

(2nd edn). Jessica Kingsley, London.

McLaughlin, J.F., Bjornson, K.F., Astley, S.J., Hays, R.M., Hoffinger, S.A., Armantrout, E.A. and Roberts, T.S. (1994) The role of selective dorsal rhizotomy in cerebral palsy: critical evaluation of a prospective clinical series. *Developmental Medicine and Child Neurology*, **36**(9), 755–69.

Reilly, S. (1993) Feeding problems in children with cerebral palsy. *Current Paediatrics*, **3**(4), 209–13.

Robson, P. (1968) Persistant head turning in the early months: some effects in the early years. *Developmental Medicine and Child Neurology*, **10**, 82–92.

Scrutton, D. (1984) *Management of the Motor Disorders of Children with Cerebral Palsy*. Clinics in Developmental Medicine, No. 90. Mackeith Press, London.

Spitz, L., Roth, K., Kiely, E.M., Brereton, R.J., Drake, D.P. and Milla, P.J. (1993) Operation for gastro-oesophageal reflux associated with severe mental retardation. *Archives of Disease in Childhood*, **68**, 347–51.

Stanley, F. and Alberman, E. (1984) *The Epidemiology of the Cerebral Palsies*. Clinics in Developmental Medicine, No. 87. Mackeith Press, London.

Thomas, A.P., Bax, M.C.O. and Smyth, D.P.L. (1989) *The Health and Social Needs of Young Adults with Physical Disabilities*. Clinics in Developmental Medicine, No. 106. Mackeith Press, London.

Trahan, J. and Marcoux, S. (1994) Factors associated with the inability of children with cerebral palsy to walk at six years: a retrospective study. *Developmental Medicine and Child Neurology*, **36**(9), 787–95.

CHAPTER 15

Neural Tube Defects
and Other Motor Disorders

After cerebral palsy, neural tube defects, Duchenne muscular dystrophy and acquired brain injury are the most common motor problems seen in a Child Development Centre.

Neural tube defects

The group of conditions known as neural tube defects are the commonest malformation of the central nervous system. They result from a failure of the neural folds to close, a process which is normally complete within 28 days of conception. The classification of neural tube defects is illustrated in Fig. 15.1 The clinical problems of spina bifida occulta are quite distinct from those of the cystica form and are described separately (p. 289). Anencephaly is a lethal malformation and is not discussed here. Encephaloceles are described in the Glossary.

Spina bifida cystica

In this condition there is absence of the vertebral arches with widening of the spinal canal together with defects in the skin and soft tissues overlying the spine. The lesion may occur at the thoracolumbar junction (45%), in the lumbar (20%) or lumbosacral area (20%), over the sacrum (10%) or in the cervical region. Thoracic lesions are much less common and multiple defects occur in 1% or less of all cases.

About 80% of infants with spina bifida cystica

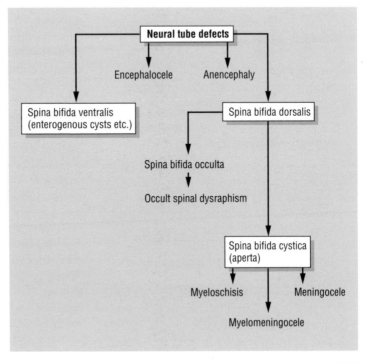

Fig. 15.1 Classification of neural tube defects.

have myelomeningocele. There is an extensive midline defect with neural tissue lying exposed on the surface, covered only by a meningeal sac, which usually ruptures during delivery. If left untreated the membrane may epithelialize and enclose the myelomeningocele. There are often extensive anomalies of the spinal cord, such as hydromyelia or syringomyelia. In some cases there is a long exposed area of spinal cord with an open or 'filleted' appearance, more accurately described as myeloschisis. Most of the children with myelomeningocele or myeloschisis will have extensive neurological deficits. In a meningocele, the sac is formed by meninges with or without skin cover, but there is no involvement of the neural tissue. The lesion is usually less extensive than in myelomeningocele and rarely involves more than three vertebrae. There should be little or no neurological deficit.

The majority of children with myelomeningocele also have the Arnold–Chiari malformation. This consists of prolongation of the cerebellar vermis and displacement of the fourth ventricle and medulla into the upper cervical canal. There is usually enlargement of the ventricles; the cerebrospinal fluid (CSF) pathways may be interrupted by deformities of the aqueduct at the level of the fourth ventricle or around the brainstem. Other malformations are often found in the cerebral cortex. Spina bifida is associated with an increased risk of other anomalies (see below).

Epidemiology, aetiology and genetics

Neural tube defects are commoner in females than males. It is estimated that 40% of fetuses with spina bifida and 80% with anencephaly may be aborted. There are regional and international geographic variations in incidence, ranging from 1 per 300 births in parts of Northern Ireland to 1 per 1000 or fewer in some European countries and in the USA.

The incidence has fallen over the past decade but the figures are difficult to interpret, because the fall may be due to several factors, including antenatal screening and termination of affected fetuses, changing socio-economic conditions, and preventive measures such as periconceptional vitamins (see below). There is a social class gradient, with highest rates in the lowest socio-economic groups, but this becomes less apparent as the incidence declines in a particular community. People emigrating from high-prevalence areas continue to be at increased risk, although this is not necessarily true for subsequent generations.

The cause of neural tube defects is unknown. Genetic factors contribute but the inheritance does not follow simple Mendelian patterns and is assumed to be linked with a strong environmental contribution. The nature of this is uncertain, but various foodstuffs and toxins have been suspected (p. 287).

Preliminary management

A preliminary assessment should be undertaken so that the parent can be given at least some idea of the likely prognosis. When a baby is born with spina bifida, both parents must be told, as soon as possible. It is usually better for the parents to see and hold the child, since their fantasies about the malformation are often worse than the reality. Often transfer to a regional centre is desirable for detailed assessment. The lesion should be covered to reduce evaporation heat loss. The infant is nursed prone. The GP should be informed.

Assessment. A general examination is carried out to exclude other major organ malformations, although these are uncommon. Occasionally, however spina bifida may form part of a single-gene syndrome, which may be important for genetic reasons (trisomy 18, Kousseff's syndrome). The presence and extent of hydrocephalus, cranial nerve palsies and other defects are noted. The most important task is to assess the level at which normal spinal cord function ceases (Fig. 15.2). Muscle power is assessed as follows: 0 = no contraction; 1 = flicker of contraction; 2 = active movement with gravity eliminated; 3 = active movement against gravity; 4 = active movement against gravity and resistance; 5 = normal power.

Lower limb dermatomes

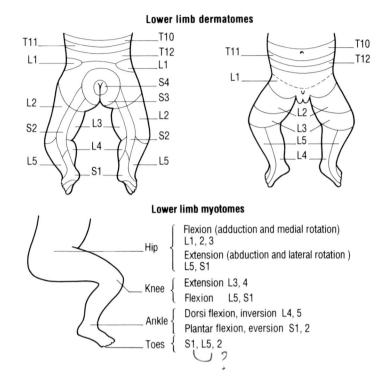

Lower limb myotomes

Hip { Flexion (adduction and medial rotation) L1, 2, 3 / Extension (abduction and lateral rotation) L5, S1

Knee { Extension L3, 4 / Flexion   L5, S1

Ankle { Dorsi flexion, inversion L4, 5 / Plantar flexion, eversion S1, 2

Toes { S1, L5, 2

Fig. 15.2 Neonatal assessment — dermatomes and myotomes. From Brocklehurst *et al.* (1976).

There may be varying combinations of upper and lower motor neuron lesions (Table 15.1). It is important to exclude movements caused by reflex withdrawal from painful stimuli; these are mediated through peripheral nerves and spinal cord and do not imply the presence of intact pathways between brain and spinal cord. Anal tone is assessed. The anal reflex is tested by stroking the perianal skin with an orange-stick.

In the neonate, the best single predictor of neurological deficit is the sensory level. This can sometimes be determined by response to pinprick, starting at S_5 (see Fig. 15.2) and moving proximally over the dermatomes when the baby is asleep or drowsy. The level is often higher than that of the motor deficit, but does not correspond reliably with the visible extent of the lesion.

The Arnold–Chiari malformation can produce a bulbar palsy in the neonatal period, even if there is a functioning shunt. This can be recognized by deterioration in the feeding pattern, nasal regur-

gitation, change in the cry and stridor. If a policy of active treatment is being followed, urgent neurosurgical advice should be obtained.

Selection for treatment

Without treatment there is a high death rate. Thirty years ago, only 20% of babies survived to the age of 2. With early closure of the back lesion, treatment of hydrocephalus by shunting and aggressive supportive care, the survival is better; nevertheless, in a cohort born 20 years ago, one-fifth died before the first birthday and another fifth before they reached adult life. The majority of the survivors are physically disabled and incontinent and one-third have moderate or severe learning disabilities.

Because the quality of life is so poor for many of these young people, many centres now try to select for active treatment only those infants who are likely to have reasonable neurological

Table 15.1 Classification of lesions

Type 1
One-third of children. Complete loss of spinal cord function below an identifiable level. There is sensory loss and absence of reflexes. Muscle deformities result from the muscle imbalance

Type 2
Two-thirds of children. There is some reflex activity in the isolated distal segment of the spinal cord, below the lesion

Group A
Below the lesion is a segment of absent function (flaccidity, no sensation, no reflexes) and, below this, isolated cord function with reflex activity and spasticity, sometimes manifest by toe clonus

Group B
As in A but there is little or no flaccid segment

Group C
Incomplete cord lesions. Spastic paraplegia, some voluntary movements and sensation are preserved. In a few patients there is marked asymmetry between the two sides

Table 15.2 Spina bifida: adverse prognostic signs used in selection for treatment

Clinical features
There is no lower limb movement under normal upper motor neuron control (i.e. there is a paraplegia from L_1 downwards)
There is clinically established hydrocephalus at birth (enlarged skull circumference)
There is an associated lumbar kyphosis or severe scoliosis
There are serious congenital malformations in other systems
The general neurological state of the infant is poor (from birth trauma or anoxia)

Radiological features
Spine
  Eversion of pedicles
  Kyphosis
  Hemivertebrae
  Double ribs
  Absent ribs
Skull
  Craniolacunae
  Shallow posterior fossa
  Eversion of petrous temporal bones
  Enlargement of foramen magnum

function; these are characterized by the absence of significant sensory deficits and of the adverse prognostic signs listed in Table 15.2. These signs are predictive of severe morbidity rather than mortality. Active treatment includes early closure of the back lesion, and insertion of a shunt, where necessary, to control the hydrocephalus. The decision to withhold such treatment must be made with and understood by the parents. They can still change their minds; the back lesion can be closed several months later without any apparent worsening of the prognosis for survival or function.

If a decision is made to manage the baby conservatively, many parents will opt for home management, supported by their family doctor and community nurse. Parents who have made this choice are more likely to view the experience positively than those who have never taken their baby home. Because of antenatal screening and the policy of selection which is now followed in many centres, there is a decline in the number of children afflicted with the severe problems of total paraplegia and there are now relatively more cases with only mild or moderate disability.

Treatment

Spina bifida is a complex problem, and is best managed in centres which can accumulate and share experience. Combined clinics facilitate clinical decision-making and reduce the amount of time and money spent by the family in visiting hospital.

Hydrocephalus

Computerized tomography (CT) scan or ultrasound is useful to demonstrate ventricular size and cortical thickness. A head circumference more than 2 cm above the 90th centile and a cerebral mantle thickness of less than 1 cm are both associated with low intellect in most, but not all, survivors; around 20% of such cases may achieve an intelligence quotient (IQ) of 80 or more. However, cortical thickness of less than 5 mm is rarely associated with normal intellect.

Medical treatments are of only transient benefit. Surgical treatment involves the insertion of a shunt system consisting of a ventricular catheter, a valve which opens at a preset CSF pressure (usually $50-70$ mm H_2O) and has a non-return action, and a distal catheter. The CSF drains to the peritoneal cavity. Many other routes have been used in the past, notably to the right atrium, but the ventriculoperitoneal shunt is now the established favourite. There is a wide variety of shunt systems but the technical details are mainly of interest to the neurosurgeon. A reservoir may be included in the system to allow access to the CSF for diagnostic taps or for treatment. Routine manual pumping of the valve is no longer recommended.

The parents need to know where the shunt has been placed, what complications to expect and how to recognize them, where to seek help in emergency, and where the child's ultrasound or CT scans are kept (or they can have copies themselves).

Complications of shunt surgery are very common. Over half of all patients require at least one revision and up to a quarter have one or more infections. Malfunction and infection are the main problems. The shunt may become disconnected or obstructed at either the proximal or the distal end. Although an X-ray may help in the recognition of shunt disconnection, the components may not all be radio-opaque and therefore misleading conclusions can easily be drawn. Similarly, pumping the valve in an attempt to deduce the presence and site of the malfunction is very unreliable.

Shunt malfunction may present as a sudden catastrophic loss of consciousness or more usually with variable and often non-specific features of raised intracranial pressure, including drowsiness, vomiting, headache, squint, ataxia or deterioration in performance or personality. Other childhood illnesses may have very similar symptoms and whenever there is any doubt the child must be admitted for observation. Migraine, viral illnesses and minor head trauma may cause particular difficulty. Hypertensive encephalopathy must always be excluded.

When the onset of symptoms and signs of raised intracranial pressure are accompanied by obvious enlargement of the ventricles on the CT scan, there is no diagnostic difficulty and the shunt is replaced as soon as possible. In a few children, however, identical symptoms and signs occur in association with normal or near-normal ventricular volume. This situation has been called the 'slit-ventricle syndrome'. In some of these children the symptoms are intermittent and there is slight ventricular enlargement only when the child is symptomatic; in others, there are life-threatening acute signs and yet the ventricles are not enlarged and isotope studies show that the shunt is working. It is thought that in the hydrocephalic child with small ventricles the normal intracranial pressure waves are not buffered by a shift of CSF, so that rapid intracranial pressure changes can occur. Some of these children may benefit from subtemporal decompression. In some children, CSF drainage may reduce the pressure to too low a level, evidenced by a very sunken fontanelle, with general misery and malaise. This is most likely to occur shortly after shunt revision.

In older children with chronic raised intracranial pressure, there may be papilloedema or optic atrophy, a 'crackpot' sound on percussing the skull, and evidence of suture spreading on skull X-ray. CT scan, isotope studies and pressure readings may be useful in difficult cases. Infections of the shunt may cause either ventriculitis, with signs similar to those of meningitis, or septicaemia, with fever, anaemia and splenomegaly. Infection is usually caused by *Staphylococcus albus* (*epidermidis*). Often the main manifestation is intermittent shunt malfunction with mild fever. There may be a localized collection of fluid around the tip of the peritoneal catheter. CSF from the shunt reservoir and blood cultures often remain sterile. Antibiotics are given under the guidance of the microbiologist and neurosurgeon. Shunt revision is usually needed.

Convulsions occur in about 30% of children with treated hydrocephalus. Repeated revisions probably increase the risk. Electroencephalogram (EEG) abnormalities around the catheter site suggest that focal scarring may give rise to an epileptic focus.

Less common complications include: (i) shunt nephritis, which may cause symptoms suggestive of infection, but is sometimes only recognized by the finding of haematuria and proteinuria; (ii) pulmonary emboli and pulmonary hypertension (nephritis and emboli were associated with shunts into the vena cava or atrium and are therefore now rare); (iii) subdural haematoma, probably caused by rapid decompression of the ventricles by the shunt, with rupture of the bridging veins between brain and skull; (iv) skin necrosis over the valve and catheter; (v) perforation of blood-vessels or other organs by the catheter; (vi) cranio-synostosis — premature fusion of one or more sutures; (vii) trapped ventricle — i.e. a ventricle which is unable to drain and acts as a space-occupying lesion.

Hydrocephalus may arrest spontaneously, pre-sumably because a balance is achieved between production and absorption of CSF. The shunt is usually left in place at least until the child is beyond 5 years of age. Measures of head circum-ference over a long period and isotope studies may help to decide when arrest has occurred.

Orthopaedic management

When intensive management of spina bifida was first introduced, the goals of orthopaedic surgery were independent mobility and normal function. Results were often poor, repeated operations were needed and intellectual deficits limited the ef-fectiveness of the surgery. Most surgeons now adopt a more conservative approach.

An early orthopaedic assessment is essential. Foot deformities, fixed flexion deformities of knee or hip, and hip dislocation may all improve with regular stretching and splintage without surgery. By the second birthday the child's intellectual and motor limitations can be assessed. Realistic goals should be set which can be achieved by a minimum of surgery. Where the neurological deficit is mild, the child may need only short callipers, splints or special footwear.

Early in childhood, a variety of means may be employed to give the child experience of inde-pendent mobility (see pp. 258–60). Once the child shows a desire to get on his/her feet, long callipers may be supplied. An upright weight-bearing posture has obvious psychological benefits, reduces the risks of osteoporosis and decubitus ulcers, and may also improve kidney and bladder function.

For carefully selected patients, the reciprocat-ing gait orthosis (Fig. 15.3) may assist their efforts to walk. The ideal user has a lesion at the twelfth thoracic (T_{12}) or first lumbar level (L_1), good power-to-weight ratio, and no major contractures or deformities. Parents are sometimes keen to raise funds for the purchase of these expensive items, which are only rarely likely to be useful. Tactful discussion and an orthoptic assessment will be needed to help them come to an informed decision. Even if the child seems to be suitable, he/she may prefer whenever possible to use the swing-through gait, which increases walking speed, so that the child can keep up with their peers.

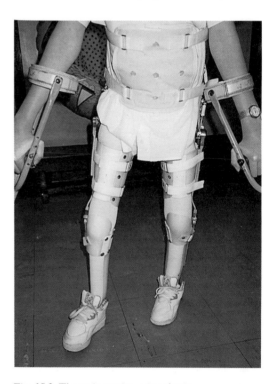

Fig. 15.3 The reciprocating gait orthosis.

A child who cannot stand alone at the age of 6 is unlikely ever to walk without help. If the lesion is at or above the level of L_1 it is almost inevitable that the child will eventually use a wheelchair as the preferred means of mobility. Because of the effort, energy costs and embarrassment of walking with long callipers, it is better to support the child, and encourage him/her to develop their intellectual and upper limb skills, than to waste time in pursuit of unattainable goals. Development of independence in daily living, participation in wheelchair sports and social opportunities are more important.

Operative procedures

In carefully selected cases iliopsoas transfer is performed for dislocation of the hip, but sometimes this is best left alone and flexion or adduction deformity treated by simple tenotomy.

At the knee, release of flexion deformity is useful, as fixed flexion makes fitting of callipers difficult. Hamstring transfer may help, but the loss of active flexion can result in a stiff, straight knee, which can be a nuisance when sitting. Osteotomy for correction of deformity is best deferred until maturity. Surgery may be indicated to prevent or release contractures that would interfere with the wearing of long callipers.

About 85% of children with myelomeningocele have some type of foot deformity, such as talipes, congenital vertical talus and valgus deformity at the ankle. If the child will be able to stand or walk, the aim is to produce a plantigrade foot on which the child can weight-bear without developing pressure sores. This may be achieved by soft-tissue releases in many cases.

The spinal deformities associated with myelomeningocele are complex and need careful follow-up. The aim of management is to achieve a spine of normal height and a level pelvis, with the ultimate aim of comfortable stable sitting and minimal cosmetic disability. Kyphosis may be associated with poor sitting and breakdown of the overlying soft tissues. Progressive scoliosis may be managed initially by an orthosis and custom-made seating. Orthoses do not prevent progression of the curve although they promote a better sitting posture. Most children with progressive scoliosis will eventually need spinal surgery, which is often successful but nevertheless has a significant morbidity and mortality.

Tethering of the spinal cord, attributed to adhesions at the site of the closure of the original lesion, should be considered when there is increasing spinal deformity, or if the child has pain, increasing spasticity or deterioration in function of the bladder or lower limbs.

Complications of paraplegia

Pressure sores usually occur in anaesthetic skin overlying a bony prominence and subjected to repeated pressure or friction. Inadequate footwear, together with uneven weight-bearing due to deformity, may cause severe sores on the sole or toes. A full-thickness sore on the heel is a very serious problem and may be almost impossible to cure. Prolonged sitting, particularly in wet nappies, may cause ischial tuberosity sores, which may only heal with a prolonged period lying prone. Prevention of pressure sores requires constant vigilance, by parents and by the child as soon as he/she is old enough. Regular inspection of feet (including use of a mirror to see the soles) and of the buttocks is vital. The child must be moved regularly, and must learn to change position in bed or wheelchair. Callipers, the edges of plaster casts and friction of heels on bed sheets are potential causes of sores. The latter can be prevented by use of a fleece. Cold injury can be avoided by use of fleece-lined boots. Playing in snow is hazardous. Scalds from radiators or hot-water bottles are also easily acquired. If pressure sores do occur, carefully planned management and surgical advice are important.

Pathological fractures are liable to occur in spina bifida children. Osteoporosis due to disuse, lack of pain and immobilization in plaster contribute, together with metabolic bone disease in children with advanced renal problems. The history of injury is often trivial or absent and the signs are often suggestive of infection — fever, redness and high white blood cell count. At first, X-ray changes may be minimal, although new bone formation is visible within 4 or 5 days. Healing is rapid but may be associated with increased deformity. The minimum treatment needed to maintain alignment is recommended.

Bladder and urinary tract

In the normal bladder, continence is maintained by the tone of the pelvic floor muscles which keep the bladder neck elevated. These muscles are supplied by pudendal and perineal nerves (S_{2-4}). The exact role of the internal sphincter is uncertain. The external sphincter is regarded as a second line of defence. During micturition the sphincters relax, the bladder neck descends and the detrusor muscle contracts to empty the bladder (Fig. 15.4). The neurological control of the bladder is complex and incompletely understood. There is a sympathetic component from $T_{10}-L_2$ which is responsible for contraction of the proximal sphincter region and for inhibition of detrusor contraction; some sympathetic fibres also arise from S_{2-4}. The importance of the sympathetic innervation is still uncertain. The parasympathetic fibres from S_{2-4} initiate contraction of the detrusor. Bladder sensation is mediated through sensory fibres that accompany both the autonomic and the somatic nerves. The centre responsible for the co-ordination of bladder function is in the pons, although other higher areas of the brain must also be involved. Reflex activity of the bladder is organized in the conus medullaris.

Examination. The term 'neuropathic bladder' describes abnormal bladder function caused by spinal cord lesions. The exact level of the lesion is not important in determining the nature of the bladder dysfunction; the key factors are, firstly, whether or not the cord lesion is complete and, secondly, whether the conus is intact. Signs suggesting an intact conus are presence of the anocutaneous and glans–bulbar reflexes and preservation of sensation in the second to fourth sacral segments, particularly the pain and temperature modalities.

In the absence of these positive signs, the child is unlikely to achieve continence. It is also important to ascertain if the bladder is palpable; to observe the baby passing urine, to see if there is a good stream; and to determine whether urine is passed while crying.

Investigation. Renal ultrasound is a simple non-invasive investigation which can be repeated as often as necessary. Renal function must be assessed by standard means. A DMSA scan is useful as a

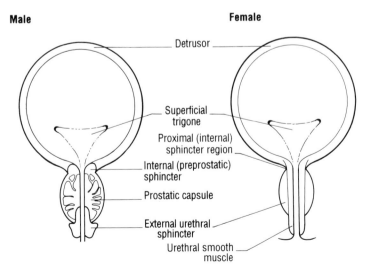

Male   **Female**

Detrusor

Superficial trigone

Proximal (internal) sphincter region

Internal (preprostatic) sphincter

Prostatic capsule

External urethral sphincter

Urethral smooth muscle

Fig. 15.4 Functional anatomy of the bladder.

measure of functioning renal tissue. Creatinine clearance may also be useful, particularly during the adolescent growth spurt.

The Videourodynamic study (VDU) is now a standard investigation for all children with spina bifida. The VDU consists of two parts: a pressure study (cystometrogram), which gives information about the changes in pressure and volume within the bladder, while it is filling and emptying; and a cystourethrogram, which reveals the changing shape and size of the bladder and the urethra. The two components are displayed side by side. The combined study is intended to answer the following questions.

1 What is the shape, size and capacity of the bladder?
2 What is the residual urine volume?
3 Is there any reflux from the bladder up the ureters (vesicoureteric reflux (VUR))?
4 How do the detrusor muscle, the sphincter and the bladder neck behave during bladder filling and emptying?

Classification of bladder problems in children with spinal lesions is complex. The bladder contractility is the most important consideration (Table 15.3). If unstable high-pressure contractions occur, urine may be forced through the sphincter or up the ureters. Dysfunction of the distal urethral sphincter (detrusor sphincter dyssynergia (DSD)) is very common. The sphincter contracts instead of relaxing when the detrusor contracts, thus obstructing the flow of urine and raising the bladder pressure; in some cases this causes reflux. Alternatively, the sphincter may be incompetent, resulting in incontinence. DSD and reflux may be present at birth but are not always apparent in the first few years of life. This means that a single evaluation is not sufficient; renal function must be monitored throughout life.

Management. The aims of management are:
1 to prevent and control infection;
2 to protect the upper urinary tracts;
3 to achieve continence.

Prophylactic antibiotics (trimethoprim or nitrofurantoin) should be given as a single daily dose

Table 15.3 The classification of bladder function in spinal lesions

Acontractile
• The detrusor muscle does not contract
• The sphincter is weak and coughing, crying or straining provokes incontinence
• The sphincter does not relax sufficiently and there is some resistance to urine flow
• The upper urinary tract is rarely at risk
• Continence may be established by artificial urinary sphincter (AUS)

Contractile
• The detrusor muscle contracts strongly but because of DSD there is outflow obstruction and therefore a significant residual volume
• The hyperreflexic bladder has diminished storage capacity
• Renal dysfunction may occur if there is reflux
• Sphincterotomy may be necessary to reduce outflow obstruction
• Bladder capacity can be increased surgically (cystoplasty)
• An AUS may be implanted to achieve continence

Intermediate type
• The commonest type of bladder dysfunction in spinal lesions
• There are continuous but weak and ineffective contractions of the detrusor and DSD
• The effective storage capacity is much reduced and there is continuous incontinence
• Upper urinary tract damage is common and sphincterotomy, cystoplasty and AUS may be needed

at night, for children who have reflux or recurrent infections, and perhaps also for infants and very young children, in whom adequate assessment of the state of the urinary tract and the risk of infection is difficult. Symptomatic infections should always be treated, but positive cultures without symptoms do not always merit antibiotics. Adequate fluid intake and bladder drainage are essential (see below).

Bladder emptying can be achieved by expression, straining, clean intermittent catheterization or continuous catheterization. Expression can be used if the bladder is acontractile, but it is difficult and many children dislike it after the age of 2 or 3 years. Clean intermittent catheterization (CIC) is used initially by parents, but from the age of about 6 years the child may learn self-catheterization. A lubricated plastic catheter is used. It is inserted, using clean but non-sterile technique, with the aid of a mirror for girls, usually every 3–4 hours. Each catheter may be used for 1 week. Complications include infection and bleeding, and patients need access to expert advice if they have any concerns; a specialist nurse is the ideal person to teach and supervise CIC. Continuous catheterization may be used for children who have serious upper tract dilatation and as a permanent solution for severely disabled wheelchair-bound older girls.

Detrusor hyperreflexia often contributes to the child's incontinence and this can sometimes be helped by anticholinergic drugs; oxybutinin (2.5 mg b.d.–5 mg t.d.s.) is currently the drug of choice. Continence can sometimes be improved by the adrenergic agonist ephedrine, which acts on the sphincter mechanism.

For boys, penile appliances may be useful. They are difficult to fit in very young children because of leakage, and sores or ulceration can occur, but they may be very useful for adolescents and young adults. There are no satisfactory urinary appliances for girls.

There have been major advances in the urological surgery of neuropathic bladder in the last few years. It is important that children enjoy the full benefits of such expertise and this means that follow-up of all such children should be in a combined paediatric–urological clinic, so that monitoring, investigations and treatment can be co-ordinated. As they get older these children may develop chronic renal failure and hypertension; it is therefore essential that their follow-up is lifelong.

Obstruction to the urinary outflow tract may be useful to maintain continence and can be overcome by CIC or continuous catheterization. The alternative is to divide the sphincter surgically, resulting in incontinence. This may be necessary to protect the upper urinary tracts from damage due to inadequate bladder drainage. The capacity

of the bladder can be increased using a piece of bowel (augmentation cystoplasty) or the bladder can be replaced with a new one constructed from intestine (substitution cystoplasty). Complications include poor emptying, infection and, later in life, carcinoma. One important problem with these procedures is mucus production by the bowel mucosa, which may be associated with obstruction, infection or calculus formation. It is treated with bladder washouts. The new bladder may be drained using a catheter via the patient's own urethra, a ureter brought to the surface of the abdominal wall, or an interposed appendix fashioned to provide a continent microstoma (Metrofanoff procedure).

The artificial urinary sphincter (AUS) offers the possibility of achieving continence for some of these children. The Brantley Scott is currently the most successful. It consists of three components connected by tubing: an inflatable cuff, which encircles the urethra; a reservoir placed in the iliac fossa; and a pump, which is placed in the scrotum or the labium majorus, so that the patient can control it. Pump failure, infection and erosion of the cuff through the urethra are occasional complications. This expensive device may be useful in those few patients with good manual dexterity and intellectual capabilities.

Diversion procedures (i.e. bringing the urine to the surface of the abdominal wall via a conduit and stoma) are now used less commonly than they were 10 years ago, but may occasionally be necessary. Undiversion refers to procedures which convert a conduit system to a continent bladder or bladder substitute, using small or large bowel, and drained via a continent microstoma.

Many of the surgical techniques are still relatively new and the long-term complications such as metabolic changes in the growing child and the risks of malignancy cannot yet be assessed.

Bowel problems

In children with spina bifida these receive less attention than problems affecting the urinary tract, but they add significantly to the total disability.

Toilet training should be commenced when the child can co-operate, with the child sitting on a comfortable potty or potty-chair.

Children with high spinal lesions tend to have absence of sensation but an intact reflex arc which can maintain sphincter tone; those with low lesions may have some sensation but the reflexes are absent. The anocutaneous reflex should be elicited to determine whether the reflex arc is intact. Anorectal manometry can be performed, although its value as a routine investigation is doubtful.

If there is no reflex, it is likely that there will be incontinence due to a lax sphincter. Abdominal pressure, straining or manual evacuation may be needed to help defecation. Bulking agents may help (p. 274). If there is a reflex, a bisacodyl suppository, stimulation with a finger or a micro-enema may initiate defecation. Stool-softeners and bowel stimulants are also useful if the bowel is overloaded with hard stools. Twice-weekly colonic washouts via an interposed appendicular microstoma also have a place in some individuals (the 'ACE' procedure). Colonic catheters, behavioural methods and biofeedback training have also been used to help children improve their bowel control.

Sexual problems

There is an increased incidence of cryptorchidism and of precocious puberty in children with spina bifida and hydrocephalus. Loneliness and social isolation are important issues for the teenager and young adult with spina bifida. Sexual dysfunction is commoner in those with high lesions, but some degree of sexual fulfilment seems to be possible even in those with more extensive deficits. Girls with spina bifida are fertile and contraceptive advice should be offered where appropriate. The risk of a woman with spina bifida having an affected child herself is about 3%.

General problems

Families with spina bifida children have the same problems and need the same support services as those with other handicaps, but because of the medical complexities of the disorder the children are likely to spend much more time at hospital, both in clinics and as inpatients. The financial burdens of frequent travel, often to a regional centre, should not be forgotten, but travel to a single centre is likely to be less burdensome than attendance at various separate local clinics.

Prevention

Genetic advice. All parents who have had a child with a neural tube defect should be offered genetic counselling. Recurrent risks are shown in Table 15.4. If the affected child had spina bifida, then about two-thirds of the recurrence risk is for spina bifida, one-third for anencephaly; and vice versa. The occasional occurrence of a recessive disorder such as Meckel's syndrome should be remembered.

Antenatal diagnosis. Screening by assay of α-fetoprotein (AFP) in maternal blood is widely available. Borderline or elevated levels are checked by AFP measurement in amniotic fluid, which is

Table 15.4 Estimated recurrence risks for spina bifida or anencephaly or both

Family history	Estimated risk
One sib affected	1 in 20
Parents and sib affected, two sibs affected	1 in 8
Three sibs affected	1 in 5
One sib and second-degree relative affected	1 in 11
One sib and third-degree relative affected	1 in 14

very reliable, although some babies with mild or moderate lesions will be missed. If available, ultrasound examination of the fetal head and back is performed. (Parents do not usually understand that the latter is a more skilled and complex procedure than routine ultrasound measurement of the fetal head and, having seen the technique on TV programmes, they wonder why their baby's lesion was 'missed'.)

Primary prevention. Folic acid supplements before and around the time of conception reduce the risk of a neural tube defect in babies born to mothers who already have one affected baby. Women taking sodium valproate while pregnant have an increased risk of having a baby with spina bifida and must be screened with particular vigilance.

Other problems of urinary continence

Night-time wetting (nocturnal enuresis) is discussed on p. 141.

Excessive drinking

Excessive drinking, often of water or juice, is a common cause of parental concern among otherwise normal children and those with mild learning disabilities. Polyuria and polydipsia due to organic disorders such as diabetes mellitus, diabetes insipidus and renal disease are usually easy to exclude, because the excessive drinking occurs only in the daytime and thirst rarely wakes the child from sleep. A urine analysis and an early-morning urine osmolality may be sufficient to eliminate these possibilities. Sometimes banning orange squash from the home is sufficient. Otherwise, eventually the habit seems to resolve without treatment in most cases.

Frequency of micturition

This may be associated with urinary tract infection, polyuria or neurological disorders of bladder control, but often it is simply a habit. The child

becomes anxious about wetting and empties the bladder at every opportunity. In some cases the pattern of toileting visits becomes quite obsessive and very disabling. Simple behavioural approaches may help; a regular programme of visits to the toilet is worked out, starting with very short intervals and gradually lengthening them. Alternatively, the child is taught to 'count crocodiles' during urination. At the start of a stream of urine, the count (1 crocodile, 2 crocodiles ...) starts and then stops at the end of the stream. As the child aims for higher counts, conservation of larger volumes of urine is encouraged. Psychological or psychiatric advice may be needed for more severe cases.

Daytime urinary incontinence

This is an important problem in children who are apparently neurologically normal. These children may be divided into two groups. Firstly, there are children who pass urine at inappropriate times and places, but without any evidence of abnormalities in the process of micturition. These usually respond to a training programme. Infection and polyuria should be excluded, but are rarely found. The second group, in whom girls predominate, are 'dysfunctional voiders' and have bladder instability. This disorder is characterized by involuntary and uninhibited detrusor contractions. The wetting is accompanied by urgency and frequency, or these complaints may occur on their own. The child may seem to have little awareness of micturition until it is too late; or there may be an attempt to suppress bladder emptying by pressure with a hand on the perineum, or by squatting with the heel against the perineum. However, the child is sometimes dry, at least for short periods; continual leakage of urine so that the child is never dry is more suggestive of an ectopic ureter. Some children void urine during laughter ('giggle' micturition), the mechanism for which appears to be central and thus differs from stress incontinence in adults.

The cause or causes of unstable bladder are not understood. Constipation, reflux and urinary infections are sometimes associated but the nature of the link is not clear, although these problems should be sought and treated if found. The condition must be distinguished from true neurogenic bladder, which can occur not only with classic spina bifida but also with occult defects and occasionally with other spinal cord lesions. Hinman's syndrome is an uncommon condition in which the features are suggestive of neurogenic bladder but no neurological lesion can be demonstrated.

If the child has a good stream and no other complaints it is unlikely that there is an obstructive lesion. The residual urine volume in the bladder should be measured after micturition, by ultrasound, and the kidneys should be scanned, looking for a duplex collecting system. Other investigations, including tests of renal function, calcium, osmolality and further imaging, including micturating cystourethrography and urodynamic studies, may be required. Counselling, behavioural training, anticholinergic medication and biofeedback are variously useful in treatment. This is a condition for which an enthusiastic specialist team is desirable; unfortunately, few children have ready access to such a service.

Daytime wetting in the disabled child

This may reflect severe learning and communication difficulties, or it may be associated with immobility and the generally passive attitude that immobility engenders. Problems of continence are often observed in children with cerebral palsy or head injury, although it can be difficult to separate psychosocial causes from the effects of injury to the brain centres and spinal pathways controlling micturition. Nevertheless, daytime wetting, urgency, frequency and various other symptoms are sometimes attributable to hyperreflexic detrusor contractions and to detrusor–sphincter dyssynergia. These children may benefit from urodynamic investigation and some may be helped by oxybutinin or a variety of other treatment methods.

Primary urological disorders

These include distressing conditions such as bladder exstrophy and cloacal abnormalities. They may occur alone or in association with other impairments. The families of children with these disorders may suffer all the problems found with other handicapping conditions and need the same support. In particular, they may value the help of a community nurse with training in the management of incontinence.

Spina bifida occulta

Minor degrees of spina bifida occulta affecting the lower lumbar and sacral vertebrae (usually L_5 or S_1) are extremely common and, in the absence of any other features, are unlikely to be of clinical or genetic significance.

Occult spinal dysraphism

A number of developmental defects may affect the spinal cord, causing slowly progressive damage. These include diastematomyelia (a cartilaginous or bony spur in the spinal canal), intraspinal dermoid, lipoma or haemangioma. With these there is always spina bifida occulta and often the X-ray also shows widening of the spinal canal. There is usually a cutaneous lesion over the lower spine, a tuft of hair, a lipoma or naevus, or a dermal sinus (not to be confused with a dimple).

Asymmetric wasting or weakness of one or both legs, foot and hip deformities and bladder dysfunction may present in infancy or may appear and progress insidiously. If the cutaneous features mentioned above are found, a CT or magnetic resonance imaging (MRI) scan will usually be indicated. If treatment is deferred until the neurological or bladder signs are obvious, the results of surgery are disappointing. These lesions are genetically related to spina bifida cystica and the genetic advice should be the same.

Other disorders of movement

Duchenne muscular dystrophy

This is the best known of the inherited disorders of muscle and the commonest in childhood. It is transmitted by an X-linked gene and is therefore, with very rare exceptions, confined to males. The incidence is of the order of one per 3000 male births. The onset is insidious. First symptoms are most often noted between 2 and 4 years but the delay before diagnosis is often as long as 3 years. An abnormal gait, frequent falls and difficulties on steps are the commonest complaints. About half of these children are late in walking, although muscular dystrophy accounts for less than 1% of all late-walking males.

The waddling gait is associated with a lumbar lordosis and toe-walking. The child is never able to run or hop normally. Even small steps present problems. Gowers' manoeuvre (p. 61) is an indication of proximal muscle weakness and is not diagnostic of muscular dystrophy. Examination shows the typical firm enlargement of the calf muscles (pseudohypertrophy) (Fig. 15.5) which is often noted by parents and the child may complain of painful muscles when tired. Tendon reflexes are usually absent, with the exception of the ankle jerk, which may be brisk.

Associated problems include a mild reduction of intellect. The cause of this is unknown. The IQ distribution curve in Duchenne muscular dystrophy is normally shaped but the mean is shifted downwards by about 15 points. There is no deterioration in mental capacity as the disease advances. In some of these children with mild global developmental delay, a speech problem may be the presenting feature. Cardiac involvement is common but there is rarely clinical evidence of this in the early stages. Later, there may be a persistent tachycardia, but congestive heart failure is rare.

Once the diagnosis has been considered there is no difficulty in confirming or excluding it, for the creatine phosphokinase (CPK) is massively elevated, usually to 50 or 100 times normal, even

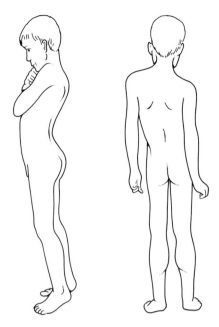

Fig. 15.5 Enlarged calf muscles in a child with Duchenne muscular dystrophy.

before symptoms appear. Confirmation of such a serious diagnosis by biopsy is highly desirable.

Management

Genetic advice. The early diagnosis of muscular dystrophy may avoid the birth of further affected siblings. It is essential that a CPK estimation be arranged for any boy with features compatible with this diagnosis. Neonatal screening and screening of all boys not walking at 18 months have been advocated by some authorities, but the number of cases prevented each year would be very small, and these approaches have not been widely accepted.

The disease is inherited as an X-linked recessive and is caused by a mutation on the gene at the region designated Xp21, which is responsible for the production of a muscle protein, dystrophin. This protein is severely deficient or undetectable in the muscles of boys with Duchenne muscular dystrophy. Some cases are due to new mutations rather than a transmitted gene, so it cannot be assumed that the mother is necessarily a carrier unless another member of the family is also affected. All families with a Duchenne child should be referred for genetic advice, so that they can benefit from the rapid advances in deoxyribonucleic acid (DNA) technology.

The Becker form of muscular dystrophy. This occurs in one per 9000 male births, i.e. one-third the incidence of the Duchenne variety. The gene is at the same locus as in Duchenne dystrophy; dystrophin is not absent as in Duchenne dystrophy, but the amount of dystrophin is reduced and varies among muscle fibres. The clinical onset is later (between 4 and 25 years) and the progression is much slower, with loss of walking ability occurring in the late teens or in adult life. There is an overlap between Duchenne and Becker types, so that in a few cases distinction may be difficult even in a specialist clinic. As a general rule, most boys with Duchenne dystrophy lose the ability to walk by the age of 12, whereas nearly all boys with Becker dystrophy are still ambulant at the age of 16.

Physiotherapy and orthopaedic aspects. As with cerebral palsy, children with muscular dystrophy should be reviewed regularly in a combined clinic with the physiotherapist and orthopaedic surgeon. While the child is ambulant, contractures and deformities are not a major problem, although some tightness may develop in hip flexors and the Achilles tendon. The physiotherapist must instruct the parents in passive exercises through a full range of movement. The child should spend some time lying prone, for example to watch TV. Ankle–foot orthoses (AFOs) may help to delay the progression of the foot and ankle deformities which develop as the child gets weaker; they may be worn as night splints and also in the shoes during the day, if they are tolerated.

Loss of ability to walk occurs between the ages of 7 and 13. Immobilization even for short periods may cause permanent loss of ambulation. Walking may be prolonged by the use of leg callipers, preceded when necessary by the release of contractures at hip, knee and ankle (although in many cases these can be avoided by early physiotherapy and night splinting). Advance planning, rapid mobilization and intensive postoperative physiotherapy are essential for success. This method may offer the boy, on average, another 18 to 24 months walking, and may slow the progression of scoliosis and contractures, but not all families can cope with the commitment required and some doubt that the benefits justify the effort involved.

The child eventually will inevitably become wheelchair-dependent and it is important to plan for this in advance, with appropriate modifications to the home and school, for which the advice of an occupational therapist will be needed. Hoists, stair-lifts, ramps or bathroom aids and adaptations may be needed. Wheelchair sports and the use of adapted tricycles may help the transition to wheelchair life.

Once the boy stops walking, there is a high risk of rapidly progressive contractures and deformities. The control of obesity is an important challenge and must be addressed before the boy is grossly overweight. Scoliosis is another important problem and can sometimes be prevented or at least controlled by a moulded spinal jacket. This needs to be checked regularly with a scoliosis film taken with the jacket in position. Scoliosis surgery using the Luque technique (or modifications of it) is now commonly undertaken. Early mobilization is possible and, although it is a major procedure, boys who have undergone this operation consider that it improves their quality of life. Boots and correctly placed footrests on the wheelchair keep the feet at 90°.

Recently, there has been interest in the hypoventilation and carbon dioxide retention which occur during sleep, late in the course of the disease, resulting in impaired mental alertness. Various forms of ventilator support overnight have been tried to overcome this problem.

Prednisolone and myoblast transplantation have been tested but clearly are not the solution; and there have been many other 'treatments' including allopurinol, verapamil and other drugs.

Most boys with muscular dystrophy die of respiratory failure or infection in their late teens or early 20s. Parents worry about what they should tell their sons, but most probably know or guess the prognosis and see evidence of the relentless progression of the disease in their friends, particularly if they attend a special school. The ability to face the future and talk about it within the family makes life easier and happier.

The spinal muscular atrophies

This is a group of hereditary conditions in which progressive muscular atrophy and weakness occur in association with chronic degeneration of the anterior horn cells. Heart muscle is not involved and intellect is preserved. Traditionally three main types have been recognized, although there is some debate about the genetic and clinical validity of these divisions. The recent mapping of the gene for spinal muscular atrophy to chromosome 5q should clarify the situation and facilitate antenatal diagnosis for parents who have had an affected child.

Severe (Werdnig–Hoffman disease)

The onset may be *in utero* with diminished fetal movements or may be in the early months of life. Sometimes it may begin quite acutely. There are severe generalized hypotonia and paralysis; any movement is confined to ankles, forearms and hands. Tendon jerks are absent. Sucking and crying are weak, but the facial expression is often normal. Mild contractures may occur, particularly at the shoulders. Many children with this condition die before the first birthday and survival to the age of 2 is exceptional.

Parents need to know the likely prognosis, even though this is very distressing. They should be helped to plan how they want to care for the child; many wish to avoid hospitalization, even in the terminal stages, and with good community nursing support and appropriate medication (p. 113), this should usually be possible.

Intermediate

Usually these children learn to sit, but cannot take weight on the legs and do not learn to stand or walk. There is usually fasciculation and atrophy of the tongue, and the parents may notice a tremor in the hands. This group presents the most difficult management problems. Respiratory insufficiency, flexion contractures and severe scoliosis are common. The length of survival depends mainly on the degree of respiratory muscle involvement, but many people with this condition survive to adult life.

Mild (Kugelberg–Welander)

Walking is achieved usually without undue delay, but mild proximal muscle weakness is noted. These children are easily mistaken for early cases of Duchenne muscular dystrophy. A tremor of the outstretched hands is commonly seen. The weakness is usually static and ambulation is not lost.

Diagnosis

The clinical picture of Werdnig–Hoffman disease is characteristic, although very rarely it can be mimicked by other muscle diseases. The CPK may be raised in the intermediate and mild types, but is usually normal. The definitive tests are electromyogram (EMG), nerve conduction and muscle biopsy (see below).

Genetic counselling

With the exception of a few cases of the mild type which may have dominant inheritance, spinal muscular atrophy is transmitted as an autosomal recessive. Within a family, cases are usually, but not always, of similar severity. Prenatal diagnosis by genetic linkage is possible in suitably informative families, with a 5% risk of error.

Management

There is no specific treatment for any of the

forms of spinal muscular atrophy. In the severe form, early death cannot be prevented by any supportive measures. In the intermediate type, regular orthopaedic supervision is essential, as with Duchenne muscular dystrophy. A spinal jacket should be supplied before scoliosis has become apparent, and if necessary further measures such as spinal bracing or a plaster jacket may be used. Careful monitoring of the spinal curve and early surgical evaluation are essential.

Some children may be able to use callipers if the hips are supported by a pelvic band. Walking may then be achieved with crutches or a rollator but, even if this is not possible, the children enjoy the upright posture, and it probably helps to prevent deformity. A good time to introduce callipers is at school entry at 3 or 4 years of age. Most of these children should start at a school for the physically disabled, where regular and intensive physiotherapy supervision is available. Intelligence is not affected and there is no intrinsic reason why they should not attend normal school, but adequate physiotherapy and medical support are essential for successful integration. A powered buggy or wheelchair should be considered before the child starts school and can be successful as young as 3 years or even 2 in some cases. It offers greater mobility and independence, and is often a vital part of an educational programme.

Other movement disorders

Many other conditions affect movement and can cause disability, including congenital myopathies, neuropathies, poliomyelitis, achondroplasia and osteogenesis imperfecta. Precise diagnosis may require attendance at a distant specialist centre; however, the child's management, therapy and support services are usually provided locally and must not be neglected. Details of these conditions can be found in standard paediatric neurology texts.

Congenital limb deficiencies

The limbs develop between the fourth and eighth week of gestation. Agents which cause limb de-

ficiencies must exert their effects within this period. The best-known teratogenic agent is thalidomide, which caused an epidemic of limb defects between 1959 and 1962. With this exception, congenital limb deficiencies occur at a rate of 4–8 per 10 000 births. There have been many classifications of limb defects; one simple approach is summarized in Table 15.5 and illustrated in Fig. 15.6.

Management. As these defects are so rare and vary so much in their functional effects, it is essential to obtain advice from one of the centres which specialize in this field. There are 28 disablement services centres in Britain, but many of these deal primarily with adults and have little paediatric experience. The baby should be assessed by a paediatrician, an orthopaedic surgeon, orthotist, occupational therapist and physiotherapist. The parents should be given an explanation of the problem, a preliminary plan of management and an introduction to the relevant parent organization, as soon as possible. In the UK, the voluntary organizations REACH and STEPS can advise on availability of expertise and also provide valuable support. Parents need to be advised as soon as possible about the following.

• A known cause can rarely be identified. It is reasonable to enquire about drugs and X-rays in pregnancy but these are very rarely the cause and the parents should not be led to believe that a cause will be found.

• Nothing that the parents did, took or omitted to do was responsible.

• As these defects are very uncommon and are difficult for the radiologist to identify, they are rarely detected on antenatal ultrasound scans.

• The presence or absence of associated defects and whether or not these form part of any syndrome.

All infants with limb defects must have a complete general examination, and a genetics opinion may be helpful, since some (particularly radial defects) may be part of a recognizable syndrome with genetic implications, and there is a high incidence of other anomalies, such as congenital heart disease, renal disorders, cleft palate,

Table 15.5 Upper and lower limb anomalies

UPPER LIMB

Transverse types

Forearm deficiency — absence of hand and a variable part of the forearm. Rudimentary digital buds. Almost always
    unilateral. Left affected more often than right. The commonest type of congenital limb defect; not associated with defects
    elsewhere

Partial or complete absence of hand — rudimentary digital buds. Unilateral or bilateral

Above- or through-elbow deficiency — rare. Usually no digit buds; often more than one limb affected

Complete absence of both arms (amelia)

Longitudinal types

Partial or complete absence of radius. Hand deviates to the radial side of the wrist. Thumb often rudimentary or absent.
    Upper part of humerus is often deficient if radius virtually absent. Check for platelet defects if thumbs well preserved in
    children with bilateral radial deficiency

Ulnar deficiency. Clinically identified by absence of third, fourth and fifth fingers. A reduced radius may be fused to
    humerus (radiohumeral synostosis), with usually only one or two digits. Upper part of humerus preserved

Flipper hand. No humerus or radius, may have an ulna. Defect as associated with thalidomide. Usually not more than three
    fingers remain

Miscellaneous

Lobster-claw deformity — bifid hand. Feet may also be affected and there may be distal tibial hypoplasia

Ring constriction of digits — deep sulcus giving appearance of encircling band. Often multiple

LOWER LIMB

Longitudinal types

Absence of the tibia with loss of, or duplication of, first and second toes

Absence of fibula with shortened and anteriorly curved tibia, skin dimple at apex of curve. Small everted foot with loss of
    fifth and sometimes fourth and fifth toes

Proximal femoral deficiency

Transverse types

Absence of all or part of the foot

Through knee and above knee. May be associated with congenital dislocation of hip or proximal femoral deficiency, or
    fibular or ulnar defects in other limb(s).

Absence of lower limb: either both legs absent but pelvis intact, or absence of hemipelvis

---

oesophageal atresia, anal stenosis and vertebral defects (see VATER association in the Glossary, p. 372). Radial aplasia may be associated with thrombocytopenia (TAR syndrome). Vision and hearing should routinely be checked as in any disabled child.

Children with limb defects will require careful and prolonged follow-up by a paediatrician, paediatric orthopaedic surgeon and orthotist. The paediatrician has much to contribute to this situation; the family will need long-term support and counselling, co-ordination of referrals and in-terpretation of the opinions given by many other specialists, and advice about school and independence. The skills of other specialists may be needed.

The timing and planning of surgical procedures requires expert judgement. Management depends entirely on the distribution of the defects and on the function of the remaining parts. Only general principles can be given here. Digits, however rudimentary, should never be amputated since the child may learn to make use of them. Children without arms should be encouraged to use their

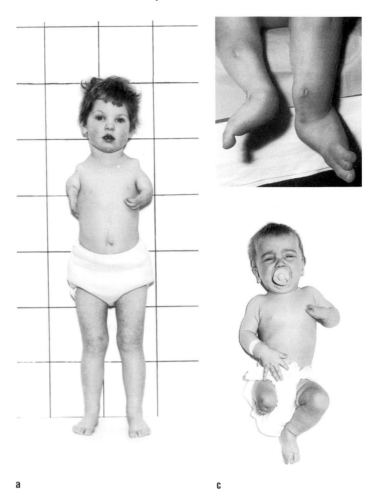

Fig. 15.6 Examples of congenital limb defects. **a,** An infant with the thalidomide phenotype, showing prominent acromioclavicular joints due to shoulder joint deficiency. Persistence of third, fourth and fifth digits and shortened ulnar and humeral remnants. **b,** Deficiency of fourth and fifth toes and fibular aplasia. **c,** Defects of the fourth and fifth digit ray with hypoplasia or aplasia of the ulna and fibula are sometimes combined with proximal femoral deficiencies and transverse deficiencies at any level; asymmetry is common. Courtesy of Dr C. Newman (Queen Mary's Hospital, Rochampton, SW15).

a   c

feet, mouth and chin for function. The combined experience of therapists and other parents will often suggest ingenious adaptations of toys, feeding equipment, clothing, toileting and personal hygiene equipment, etc. (Fig. 15.7). Helmets should be supplied for armless babies when they start to walk, as they cannot save themselves when they fall.

Babies with upper limb deficiencies can be assessed for a prosthesis when they can sit, at around 6−8 months (Fig. 15.8). Initially this is mainly for cosmetic reasons, although it may also help the baby to accept the use of the apparatus as part of normal life. A functional prosthesis can be used at about 2 years, but the more sophisticated powered devices are seldom useful until the child is older. The body-operated split hook (Fig. 15.8) is preferred by many children to the more sophisticated devices, even though it looks primitive. In spite of dramatic advances in bioengineering, an upper limb prosthesis is still a poor substitute for even a rudimentary limb that has sensation. Children may only use their prosthesis under pressure from adults and may function better without it, or may elect to use it only for certain specific activities.

Children with severe lower limb defects have problems in acquiring sitting balance. A 'bucket'

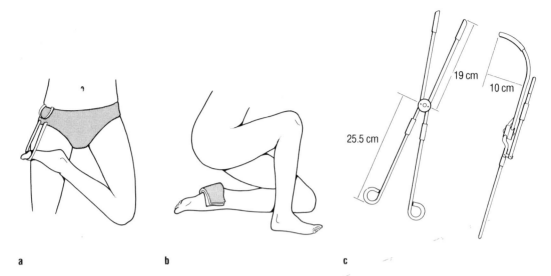

a   b   c

Fig. 15.7 There are many ingenious solutions to the problems of daily living. **a,** Loop placed to help with pulling trousers and pants down. **b,** The heel method of wiping after use of toilet. **c,** A folding toilet appliance made by The Bioengineering Centre, Rochampton. From Hardy (1992).

a   b   c

Fig. 15.8 Equipment for children with limb defects: **a,** 'bucket' trolley; **b,** artificial limb in use; **c,** detail view of limb. Courtesy of 11. Steeper, Rochampton Limb Fitting Unit.

seat may help to overcome this (Fig. 15.8). Later, various forms of swivel-walker or a cart may be used until the child is old enough to walk using an orthotic appliance.

Arthrogryposis

Arthrogryposis means curved or crooked joint and denotes the presence of congenital contractures (Fig. 15.9). Usually isolated contractures, such as talipes, are excluded and the term is reserved for those children with multiple contractures. Arthrogryposis is merely a description, not a diagnostic entity. Over 150 causes and associated conditions have been identified; the feature they have in common is fetal immobility. They fall into four groups (Table 15.6).

In some children all four limbs are involved, whereas in others the legs are predominantly affected. It is rare for the arms alone to have contractures. The 'typical' case is characterized by severe and predominantly distal muscle weakness, with hypotonia and absence of reflexes; no skin creases; dimpling of skin over affected joints; and abnormal dermatoglyphics. The contractures are variable but most often result in internally rotated shoulders, extended elbows, flexed wrists, fixed flexion or extension of the knees and talipes equinovarus. Hip deformity may be accompanied by dislocation. Involvement of the jaw and tongue may result in feeding and articulation difficulties and also has important anaesthetic implications.

Management. From the parents' point of view this is a most distressing condition and it may be helpful to introduce them to a child with similar problems who has been effectively habilitated. There is an excellent support group for parents in the UK. Diagnostic evaluation should be undertaken by a paediatric neurologist and a geneticist and will usually include an EMG, nerve conduction studies, a CT scan and often a chromosome study.

Arthrogryposis is an uncommon condition and advice should be obtained from a specialist team with a special interest in the condition. This team will include an orthopaedic surgeon, orthotist and occupational therapist. Since feeding and speech problems may also occur, the advice of a dietitian and speech therapist may also be needed. The first phase in management is passive stretching under the supervision of a physiotherapist, and this may be continued for 6 to 12 months, as long as progress is being made. Serial plastering may further improve the position. A plan for surgical

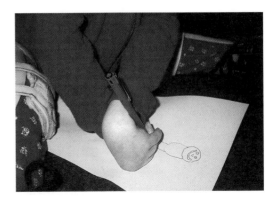

Fig. 15.9 A child with arthrogryopsis. Unorthodox grip but effective use of pen.

Table 15.6 Causes of arthrogryposis

Cerebral causes (often lethal)
Cerebral dysgenesis
Chromosome disorders
Dysmorphic syndromes

Spinal cord defects
Anterior horn cell degeneration (commonest cause in
    infants who survive — the 'typical' case) (previously
    called amyoplasia by some authors)
Werdnig−Hoffmann disease of prenatal onset
Sacral agenesis

Neuromuscular diseases
Congenital myopathies and neuropathies
Myotonic dystrophy

Miscellaneous
Oligohydramnios
Skin disorders

---

correction is made and may involve extensive surgery, particularly to the lower limbs. In some cases, it is better to accept the deformities and mobilize the child in lightweight prostheses, aided by crutches.

Surgery for the upper limbs is rarely undertaken in young children, because the children will often discover a variety of ingenious ways of using whatever function they have. The occupational therapist may be able to help with adapted spoons, dressing and toileting devices, and equipment such as mouth sticks, roller-mounted pencils, arm supports, etc. for use in the classroom. A computer with appropriate keyboard or switches and software will often be needed. Only when the child's ability to use their arms can be fully assessed should surgery be contemplated.

Poliomyelitis

This is now exceptionally rare in the Western world, but occasionally a child who acquired polio in Africa or Asia seeks treatment in the UK. The book by Huckstep (1975) provides an excellent overview of the orthopaedic, orthotic and physiotherapy treatments for this condition.

Acquired quadriplegia and paraplegia

Traumatic injury to the spinal cord in children under the age of 16 years accounts for less than 10% of all spinal injuries. In younger children, injuries tend to be more severe, often affect the cervical or upper thoracic cord, and may not be accompanied by bony injury (spinal cord injury without radiographic abnormality (SCIWORA) syndrome). Delayed neurological deterioration up to 4 days after injury and recurrent injury before healing is complete are important preventable factors. The best indicator of outcome is the neurological status on admission. Other causes of spinal cord lesions are listed in Table 15.7.

High cervical lesions often result in impaired respiratory effort and permanent ventilator assistance may be needed. This can be provided at home, although this, of course, requires an immense effort of organization and care. Upper limb function may also be very limited and the child is dependent on others for every need.

In the early stages after acute spinal injury, the lower limbs are often flaccid, but gradually spasticity develops and may become extreme. This may give rise to functional problems and uncomfortable spasms, which are often precipitated by urinary infections. Baclofen is helpful in the reduction of spasticity and spasm (p. 269).

Long-term goals for mobility depend on the

Table 15.7 Causes of paraplegia in childhood

Poliomyelitis
Neural tube defects
Accidental trauma (perinatal or postnatal). (NB. Often with fracture or subluxation of vertebra, but spinal cord injury without radiological abnormality (SCIWORA) may occur. Trauma includes falls from heights, motor accidents, diving and sports injuries
Non-accidental injury (shaking)
Vascular lesions: idiopathic; iatrogenic (e.g. after surgery for scoliosis or coarctation of the aorta)
Compressive lesions
  Tumour (commonest: secondary neuroblastoma)
  Abscess
  Tuberculosis
  Angioma
  Cysts
Transverse myelitis
Foramen magnum and atlantoaxial anomalies

level of the lesion. If this is above T_8, the child is unlikely to achieve independent walking that will be useful in adult life, whereas if it is below T_{10} this may be possible using long leg callipers and crutches. Lesions of the cervical spine may be complicated by brachial plexus injury. Prevention of deformity is an important goal of management. In particular, contractures of hip flexors and of the Achilles tendon can develop rapidly. Scoliosis is common and a brace or jacket should be supplied before it develops. Callipers not only assist standing and mobilization but protect against trauma and fractures of the lower limbs.

After an acute lesion of the spinal cord, an indwelling urethral catheter is usually required, though in some circumstances a suprapubic catheter or intermittent catheterization may be preferred. Later an 'automatic bladder' develops. Reflex bladder contraction can often be initiated by stimulating the skin of the lower abdomen. Intermittent self-catheterization may be useful until the automatic bladder is established. Subsequent management has much in common with that of spina bifida.

Two additional problems affect people with spinal cord injury. The first is autonomic dysreflexia. This occurs with cervical and high thoracic lesions. The commonest cause is a distended

Table 15.8 Causes of acquired brain injury

TRAUMATIC HEAD INJURY

Mechanisms

Direct trauma to the head and brain, which may cause focal deficits, although often recovery is remarkably good

Acceleration–deceleration injuries — these are caused by shearing between the layers of white and grey matter, and can occur without any outwardly visible sign of injury

Neuronal disruption, caused by violent pressure changes within the neurons

Secondary effects of the injury such as hypoxia, hypotension, brain swelling and intracranial bleeding

Main causes

Road accidents (as pedestrian, cyclist or passenger)

Falls from a height (e.g. out of the windows of high-rise flats)

Non-accidental injuries, particularly shaking in infancy

INFECTION

Bacterial or tuberculous meningitis

Viral encephalitis (especially herpes simplex)

Mycoplasma encephalitis

Cerebral malaria

ENCEPHALOPATHY (acute brain dysfunction, often with brain swelling, not caused by any identifiable infection)

Causes

Reye's syndrome and similar conditions

Diabetic coma

Inherited metabolic disorders

Haemorrhagic shock–encephalopathy syndrome

ANOXIC INJURY

Near-miss cot death

Suffocation (deliberate, smoke)

Drowning

Choking (e.g. on sweets, toys)

Anaesthetic accidents

Airways obstruction (e.g. epiglottitis, foreign body)

Cardiorespiratory arrest from any cause

MISCELLANEOUS

Vascular accidents

Hypertensive encephalopathy

Haemorrhage

Arterial occlusion (stroke)

Status epilepticus

---

bladder, but other conditions which would normally be painful (urinary infection, anal fissure, constipation, etc.) may be responsible. Reflex sympathetic overactivity occurs and may lead to dangerous hypertension. Repeated attacks can occur. Immediate treatment is to remove the cause — most often, this means emptying the bladder. The problem can arise at any time after spinal injury or in congenital conditions including spina bifida, for example after spinal surgery.

The second is the development of a cystic dilatation or syrinx of the cord at the site of old injury, whatever the original cause may have been. This may be asymptomatic but can cause progression of the neurological deficit, including deterioration in bladder or bowel function, and in some situations may cause pain. The incidence has been estimated variously from 5 to 20% of spinal injury patients and the time scale varies from months to many years after the acute event. These patients should be kept under observation indefinitely and investigated if new features appear.

Acquired brain injury

Children who suffer acquired brain injury differ (Table 15.8) in a number of ways from those who are disabled from infancy; the pattern of deficits, the psychological and emotional sequelae and the tendency to slow but continuing improvement place different demands on the staff and parents caring for the child. Nevertheless, the majority of children with acquired brain injury will be cared for most appropriately by their local child development and child psychiatry services; a small minority may benefit from more intensive periods of rehabilitation. The problems of traumatic brain injury are summarized in Table 15.9.

Management

Because of the multiple problems experienced by the brain-injured child and the family, management should be the responsibility of a multidisciplinary team. Family support and close liaison

Table 15.9 Problems associated with acquired brain injury

Movement disorders
- Spasticity, rigidity, ataxia, tremor, contractures and deformities, dislocations of joints. Motor slowness in responses
- May need full range of interventions as in cerebral palsy (Chapter 14)

Emotional/psychological disorders
- Agitation, anxiety, distressed inconsolable crying during emergence from coma
- Reduced speed of information processing and slow responses
- Global reduction in IQ
- Specific deficits: difficulties with attention and concentration; memory defects (particularly for events subsequent to the injury — memory for events and knowledge gained prior to the injury are often surprisingly good
- Unstable mood, social and sexual disinhibition, outbursts of anger and 'aggression', lack of motivation
- Sadness, loss of friends in peer group, loneliness, survivor guilt, victims of bullying and teasing
- Overall increase in psychiatric/psychological problems after brain injury, but only disinhibition is specific to brain injury
- Problems with executive skills: planning, organization, self-evaluation and self-monitoring
- Insensitivity to others, self-centredness

Speech, language and communication together with feeding problems
- Pseudobulbar palsy, dysarthria, dysphasia, dyspraxia, dysphagia
- Associated problems with chewing, swallowing and dribbling (see Chapter 14 for management)

Epilepsy
- Early post-traumatic epilepsy, i.e. fits in first week after injury
- For late post-traumatic epilepsy (after first week), risk factors are early fits, intracranial bleeding, depressed fracture, familial predisposition to epilepsy
- Risk is 10–15% after severe head injury; EEG not useful for prognosis or prediction
- Fits may be complex partial seizures with varying manifestations, often secondary generalization
- Risk declines rapidly after first year
- Some children may need anticonvulsants but routine prophylactic anticonvulsants no longer recommended

Hearing defects
- Sensorineural deafness
- Conductive deafness due to disruption of the ossicular chain

Vision defects
- Local trauma to the eyes
- Squint and diplopia due to cranial nerve damage
- Field defects
- Tracking and scanning disorders
- Perceptual defects, including sensory inattention

Manifestations of hypothalamic and pituitary damage
- Diabetes insipidus, excessive appetite and weight gain, occasionally other hormonal deficiencies
- Unstable temperature and blood-pressure (in the most severely injured)
- Gynaecomastia (boys)
- Precocious puberty (see p. 144)
- Excessive eating

Loss of smell and/or taste

Other injuries
- Effects of fractures, dislocations, spinal injury, bladder and urinary tract damage, peripheral nerve injuries

Continued

Table 15.9 (*continued*)

Heterotopic calcification
- Deposition of bone in soft-tissue sites — rare in children, more common in teenagers
- Associated with local trauma but can also occur as a result of head injury or spinal cord injury
- Presents as hard mass, limited movement
- Bone becomes mature after about 18 months, can be excised if necessary but may recur
- Mechanism unknown

with the education service are of particular importance, since the needs of these children are complex and continually changing. For the parents, acquired brain injury is particularly devastating, since the child may look the same physically and yet the personality has changed.

Rehabilitation begins in the acute phase. The parents may value support by professionals, other parents and voluntary groups. They need information about the nature of the injury and the prognosis although, as explained above, it is often difficult to offer any detailed opinion at this early stage. Some parents may wish to use the 'coma arousal' approach of multimodal sensory stimulation. Good nursing and physiotherapy care includes the prevention of pressure sores and of deformities; adequate nutrition; bladder care; and an active approach to the treatment of other injuries. As the child begins to improve, it is important to encourage visiting by friends, to maintain social contact. Loneliness is one of the commonest complaints of children recovering from moderate head injuries.

This is followed by an intermediate phase, in which there is often a period of rapid progress. Many of the resources needed will be available in or through a child development centre, but need to be mobilized rapidly and in a co-ordinated fashion. During this phase, the child needs physical therapy, good seating and perhaps mobility aids and training; the child may benefit from communication aids and assistance in activities of daily living. A teacher and psychologist should develop a cognitive programme and work on strategies to overcome specific deficits and behavioural problems. Medication such as baclofen or anticonvulsants may be needed.

Liaison with the education authority is vital at this stage. Assessment of acutely brain-injured children must be seen as a priority and it must be prompt; otherwise it will be out of date before any recommendations are put into action. A change of school may be required, or additional support in the child's original school. A gradual return to school is more likely to be successful than an immediate return to full-time attendance. Information to school staff about the effects of the injury and the likely problems will be appreciated.

Social services should be contacted to review the need for modifications to the home. Family support should include not only the parents, but also grandparents and siblings. Parents may also need advice about litigation if the accident involved any possibility of negligence.

The intermediate phase is a time of alternating emotions. Periods of rapid progress suggest that the child may eventually be nearly normal again, but at other times the child's deficits and problems seem all too obvious. This phase merges into the late phase; gradually the parents learn what they can expect and how much recovery they can hope for and they begin to adjust their lives accordingly. The child will, however, still need follow-up to ensure that gains are maintained and that the family is receiving all possible help — particularly with regard to educational and psychological problems.

Prognosis

Staff dealing with brain-injured children and their parents will invariably be drawn into discussions about prognosis. Three factors should be considered: data about the injury itself and the neurological findings in the first few days or weeks after the injury; the age of the child; and the process of recovery.

The prognosis for children suffering traumatic head injury is based on depth and duration of coma and duration of post-traumatic amnesia (PTA), defined as the period in which the child is confused and disorientated, suffers retrograde amnesia and lacks the capacity to store and retrieve new information. Coma duration less than 20 minutes is mild; up to 6 hours is moderate; 6–48 hours is severe; over 48 hours is very severe. PTA over 2 weeks is also indicative of severe injury. However, even 'mild' injuries can be associated with organic changes in the brain, indicating that the so-called post-traumatic syndrome is not necessarily purely 'functional'.

Survivors after the most severe forms of brain injury are sometimes described as being in a 'persistent vegetative state' (PVS); they exhibit sleep–wake cycles and spend long periods with their eyes open, but show no meaningful activity or awareness of the environment. It is, however, very rare that this is truly persistent and unchanging; most children who initially present with 'PVS' eventually recover some degree of awareness of their surroundings. This is not necessarily a blessing, since they may also have some awareness of their predicament and helplessness, leading to depression or anger.

Prognosis in other forms of brain injury is less well studied. In encephalitis, adverse factors include coma, age under 1 year and the finding of herpes simplex or *Mycoplasma* as the causative agent. Cardiac arrest in children occurring outside the hospital has a very poor prognosis for recovery of neurological function. Detailed data are available from a study on drowning. Children admitted after drowning were likely to make a full recovery if they were breathing spontaneously on admission to hospital, or if the pupils were reactive on admission or became reactive within 6 hours. Fits for more than 24 hours predicted a poor outcome. Very prolonged immersion in water below 10°C is compatible with normal survival.

It is widely believed that very young children are likely to make a better recovery than older ones, because of the supposed greater plasticity of the brain. The extent of this is unfortunately limited and any advantages it may confer are outweighed by the difficulty in the acquisition of new knowledge commonly experienced by brain-injured children; the younger the child at the time of injury, the smaller the pre-existing knowledge base on which he/she has to build. Thus the younger child may have more global deficits and a poor prognosis.

Even after very severe injuries, it is unwise to offer any detailed prognosis in the first few months, because the child may initially make unexpectedly rapid progress after recovery from coma. The parents' hopes may then be raised excessively, particularly if motor functions improve, but problems with intellect, memory and attention may still be troublesome. Recovery continues for some years and significant changes may still be occurring up to 5 years after the injury occurred. During recovery, new neuronal connections are formed, but these may be misdirected and may not always improve function. It is also possible for new problems to be unmasked as the child's brain matures and new demands are placed on the child. In particular, difficulties with high-level language functions, abstract reasoning and planning and executive skills may become apparent during adolescence, many years after the injury.

Behaviour problems may also emerge as a direct or indirect consequence of brain injury. Disinhibition, both social and sexual, can cause great embarrassment and distress to family, friends and school. Changes in personality may also occur; these are often the most distressing of all the sequelae of brain injury from the family's point of view, because the child looks the same physically and yet is now a different person from the one they used to know.

Osteogenesis imperfecta (OI) ('brittle bone disease')

This affects at least 1 in every 20 000 births. It is caused by mutations that either reduce the synthesis of type I collagen or alter the structure of the molecules (Table 15.10).

Some infants have fractures at or even before birth and are diagnosed in the perinatal period, while others have so few fractures or other features that they are identified only because of a family history. Those with the mild variants may be identified when fractures occur as a result of trivial injury or even with no recognizable trauma. The parents may be unable to explain how the injury happened and in this situation child abuse may be considered (Smith, 1995). Children with OI have a variety of signs and symptoms (Table 15.11) but the predominant problem is the fragility of the bones, which results in frequent fractures. In severe cases a wheelchair life may be inevitable. The fracture rate usually declines markedly in the teens and adult life. The emphasis is on imaginative management and safe handling (Table 15.12 and Fig. 15.10). These children are generally of normal intelligence and can usually be educated in mainstream schools.

Table 15.10 Osteogenesis imperfecta. After Byers *et al.* (1991)

Type I
Normal stature, little or no deformity, blue sclerae, hearing loss in 50%, dentinogenesis imperfecta uncommon. Autosomal dominant

Type II
Lethal in perinatal period. Minimal calvarial mineralization. Beaded ribs. Marked bony deformities. Usually autosomal dominant, new mutation

Type III
Progressive deformity, usually with some deformity at birth. Very short stature. Sclerae variable. Dentinogenesis imperfecta and hearing loss common. Autosomal dominant or (less often) recessive

Type IV
Normal sclerae, mild to moderate deformity and shortness of stature. Dentinogenesis imperfecta common, hearing loss in some. Autosomal dominant

Table 15.11 Features of osteogenesis imperfecta. It is important to recognize that no patient has all the features and that some, undoubtedly affected on family history, have none of them

Clinical features
Fractures with minimal or no trauma
Blue or grey sclerae
Increased liability to bruising and nosebleeds
Increased joint laxity
Impaired growth
Deformity of long bones (particularly late after fractures)
Scoliosis (usually beginning in childhood)
Dentinogenesis imperfecta (fragile, discoloured teeth)
Excessive sweating, heat intolerance
Deformity of skull ('triangular' or 'tam-o'-shanter' shape)
Deafness (usually conductive) (onset in second, third and fourth decades)
Constipation
Hypertrophic callus formation (very rare)

Radiological findings
Fractures of all types, including asymptomatic rib and skull fractures
Fractures healing at normal rate
Osteopenia (in a minority)
Wormian bones in excess
Deformity of long bones

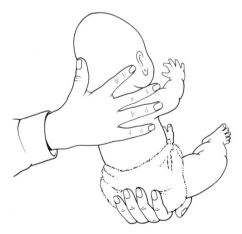

Fig. 15.10 One way of picking up an infant with osteogenesis imperfecta to minimize the risk of rib fractures. More severe cases may at first need to be picked up on a pillow or a Plastazote support. From quite an early age it is helpful for the parents to explain to the child in advance what they are about to do. Courtesy of the Brittle Bone Society (C.R. Paterson).

Table 15.12 Management of osteogenesis imperfecta

Advice about handling

Early consultation with specialist occupational therapist for advice on equipment and appliances

Ensure parents hold and lift baby correctly (see Fig. 15.10)

Speak to baby before moving and avoid startles, which may cause fractures

Experiment with different lying positions; try side-lying, wedges, bouncing cradles, cushions

Do not lift by the ankles when changing nappy

Devise safe play area when child is learning to sit

Keep prognosis for walking under review: consider early provision of manual or powered chair

Encourage activity as far as possible; swimming is valuable

Orthopaedics

Plan of care for fractures agreed with orthopaedic surgeon: direct admission to ward under named consultant, with written instructions held by parent; light splints, elasticated net, Robert–Jones bandage

Hospitalization and X-ray not always necessary. Analgesia: oral or rectal administration if possible, use DF118 orally or diclofenac rectally, then paracetamol. Stronger analgesics if these are not adequate

Surgical intervention: multiple osteotomies; medullary rods (can be expansible, i.e. grow with the child); pneumatic orthosis. For prevention and management of scoliosis: good positioning, jackets or surgery

---

References and further reading

Bannister, C.M. and Tew, B. (1992) *Current Concepts in Spina Bifida and Hydrocephalus.* Clinics in Developmental Medicine, No. 122. Mackeith Press, London.

Borzyskowski, M. and Mundy, A.R. (1990) *Neuropathic Bladder in Childhood.* Clinics in Developmental Medicine, No. 111. Mackeith Press, London.

Brocklehurst, G., Forrest, D., Sharrard, W.J.W and Start, G. (1976) *Spina Bifida for the Clinician.* Clinics in Developmental Medicine, No. 57. Mackeith Press, London.

Brown, D.C., Stirling, H.F. and Kelnar, C.J.H. (1994) Precocious puberty. *Current Paediatrics*, 4(3), 184–8.

Brown, J.K. and Minns, R.A. (1993) Non-accidental head injury, with particular reference to whiplash shaking injury and medico-legal aspects. *Developmental Medicine and Child Neurology*, 35(10), 849–69.

Byers, P.H., Wallis, G.A. and Willing, M.C. (1991) Osteogenesis imperfecta: translation of mutation to phenotype. *Journal of Medical Genetics*, 28, 433–42.

Cole, G.F. (1993) Rehabilitation after head injury. *Current Paediatrics*, 3(4), 230–4.

Delight, E. and Goodall, J. (1988) Babies with spina bifida treated without surgery: parents' views on home versus hospital care. *BMJ*, 297, 1230–3.

Epstein, F., Lapras, C. and Wisoff, J.H. (1988) 'Slit-ventricle syndrome': etiology and treatment. *Pediatric Neuroscience*, 14, 5–10.

Gibson, P.J. (1991) Occult spinal dysraphism. *Current Paediatrics*, 1(1), 42–5.

Hageman, G., Ippel, E.P.F., Beemer, F.A., De Pater, J.M., Lindhout, D. and Willemse, J. (1988) The diagnostic management of newborns with congenital contractures: a nosologic study of 75 cases. *American Journal of Genetics*, 30, 883–904.

Hardy, E. (1992) *Children with Multiple Limb Handicaps. A Guide to Independence.* REACH, The Association for Children with Artificial Arms, Chard.

Hill, A.E. (1993) Problems in relation to independent living: a retrospective study of physically disabled school-leavers. *Developmental Medicine and Child Neurology*, 35(12), 1111–15.

Hilton, T., Orr, R.D., Perkin, R.M. and Ashwal, S. (1993) End of life care in Duchenne muscular dystrophy. *Pediatric Neurology*, 9, 165–77.

Huckstep, R.L. (1975) *Poliomyelitis.* Churchill Livingstone, Edinburgh.

Hull, J. and Harkness, W. (1992) Common complications of cerebrospinal fluid shunts. *Current Paediatrics*, 2(2), 77–9.

Hunt, G.M. and Poulton, A. (1995) Open spina bifida: a complete cohort reviewed 25 years after closure. *Devel-*

opmental Medicine and Child Neurology, **37**(1), 19–29.

Iannaccone, S.T., Browne, R.H., Samaha, F.J. and Buncher, C.R. (1993) Prospective study of spinal muscular atrophy before age 6 years. DCN/SMA Group. *Pediatric Neurology*, **9**, 187–93.

McCarthy, G. (1991) Treating children with spina bifida. *BMJ*, **302**, 65–6.

McEnery, G., Borzyskowski, M., Cox, T.C.S. and Neville, B.G.R. (1992) The spinal cord in neurologically stable spina bifida; a clinical and MRI study. *Developmental Medicine and Child Neurology*, **34**(4), 342–8.

Millar, F., Moseley, C.F. and Koreska, J. (1992) Spinal fusion in Duchenne muscular dystrophy. *Developmental Medicine and Child Neurology*, **34**(9), 775–86.

Pang, D. and Pollack, I.F. (1989) Spinal cord injury without radiographic abnormality in children – the SCIWORA syndrome. *The Journal of Trauma*, **29**(5), 654–64.

Rautonen, J., Koskiniemi, M. and Vaheri, A. (1991) Prognosis factors in childhood acute encephalitis. *Pediatric Infectious Disease Journal*, **10**, 441–6.

Reardon, W., Newcombe, R., Fenton, I., Sibert, J. and Harper, P.S. (1993) The natural history of congenital myotonic dystrophy: mortality and long-term clinical aspects. *Archives of Disease in Childhood*, **68**, 177–81.

Robinson, R.O. (1990) Arthrogryposis multiplex congenita; feeding, language and other health problems. *Neuropediatrics*, **21**, 177–8.

Ruge, J.R., Sinson, G.P., McLone, D.G. and Cerullo, I.J. (1988) Pediatric spinal injury: the very young. *Journal of Neurosurgery*, **68**, 25–30.

Seller, M.J. (1994) Risks in spina bifida. *Developmental Medicine and Child Neurology*, **36**(11), 1021–5.

Sharples, P.M. and Eyre, J.A. (1993) Head injury in childhood: the most important cause of death and acquired handicap. *Current Paediatrics*, **3**(4), 225–9.

Smith, R. (1995) Osteogenesis imperfecta, non-accidental injury and temporary brittle bone disease. *Archives of Disease in Childhood*, **72**(2), 169–76.

Thomas, N.H. (1994) Duchenne muscular dystrophy: present and future therapy. *Current Paediatrics*, **4**, 203–7.

CHAPTER 16

Educational Underachievement

Every schoolteacher has experience of children who, in spite of apparently adequate intelligence, fail to make progress in one or more areas of learning. Since there is often no apparent reason for the child's failure, it is assumed that he/she must have some intrinsic deficit in cerebral or psychological function and a medical opinion is therefore requested. Problems with reading, writing, spelling and arithmetic are most commonly the cause of referral for expert advice, but this probably merely reflects the natural pre-occupations of parents and teachers. Undoubtedly, if society gave a higher priority to athletic, musical or creative skills, children would be referred for failure in these areas.

Assessment of educational underachievement

General considerations

Is the problem really underachievement?

Parents' or teachers' expectations are not always realistic. A stray comment from years ago may have led them to believe the child is more intelligent than is actually the case. A talent for one skill may be taken as an indicator of excellent general ability rather than an isolated competence. Conversely, the child's achievements may be adequate without being as high as parents wish.

Two pieces of information are vital: what the child is actually producing in the way of school work, and what his/her level of intelligence is. It is therefore desirable that responsibility for the identification and initial evaluation of a child who is failing academically at school should rest with the teaching staff and the educational psychologist. Paediatric consultation may subsequently be

requested to exclude organic disease or assess the relative importance of biological factors in the aetiology of the child's problems; before this is attempted, it is important for the paediatrician to verify that a problem of real educational underachievement has been identified.

A common reason for referral of children with educational underachievement is a conflict between parents and the school over the recognition, interpretation or management of the child's difficulties. Sometimes the paediatrician can act as mediator, and a brief conference at the school, involving parents, doctor, teacher and psychologist, can be invaluable in improving communication and mutual confidence between family and school.

Another reason for referral to a health rather than educational facility may be the parents' frustration about delays in responding to the child's problems. There are wide variations in the ages at which children are first suspected to have a learning disability, depending perhaps on the approach of the school, the availability of remedial teaching and the awareness of teachers. Too often, a child's lack of progress is attributed to developmental variations, laziness, lack of motivation or disinterested parents. The first years of schooling may slip by without any action being taken.

Educational underachievement usually has multiple causes

Most cases of educational underachievement are the result of a complex interaction between the ethos and teaching style of the school, the attitudes and support of the parents and difficulties intrinsic to the child. Simple explanations are seldom correct. Adverse factors tend to coexist — the dull child who lives in a poor environment and has unemployed parents is more likely to be attending a school where staff morale is low and there are chronic problems of indiscipline and underachievement.

Loss of skills

Parents often complain that the child is 'falling behind' but they usually mean only that the child is failing to make progress. In contrast, actual loss of previously acquired skills is an uncommon and sinister complaint, which should prompt full neurological and psychiatric review. Many rare conditions may present in this way. In such instances, the child's problems are usually global rather than specific to certain skills, and other features such as visual deterioration, fits or movement disorders may provide additional clues to the presence of progressive disease. However, neurological diseases are a very rare cause of educational underachievement.

It is essential to confirm that skills really have been lost. A fall in intelligence quotient (IQ) scores, even if quite substantial (20 points or more), often turns out to be due solely to testing variables rather than to organic disease, and in such cases corroborative evidence should be sought (school work, teachers' opinions, etc.).

Defining the terms

Children are often referred with a query as to whether they are 'dyslexic' or 'hyperactive'. It is essential to discover what is meant by these terms and to establish who is worried — is it the teacher, the parents, or both? The history should include a list of those things which the child cannot do; equally important is to list the skills that the child does have. Whatever the deficiencies may be, the existence of some well-developed skills is useful evidence against a major disorder of the nervous system. Occasionally, the complaint is that the child produces no work at all. This is more likely to have a motivational basis than a sinister organic cause.

Table 16.1 Causes of educational underachievement

Long-standing problem
Low intelligence which has been unrecognized
Inadequate or inappropriate teaching
Impairment of wider skills needed for learning (disorganization, hyperactivity, attention or memory deficit, low self-esteem)
Visual deficit
Hearing deficit (including monaural deafness)
Specific reading retardation/dyslexia
Other specific learning disabilities (dyscalculia, spelling disorder, etc.)
Unsupportive or antieducational family

Recent onset
Dementing process (extremely rare but very important)
Preoccupation with non-academic topics (parental divorce, bullying, etc.)
Depression
Fatigue (sleeplessness, sedative medication)
Rebellion against 'swot' label or high parental ambitions
Bad relationship with particular teacher
Unsuspected truancy or poor attendance because of chronic illness or anxiety (borderline school refusal)
Sexual abuse
Boredom (especially with gifted children)
Drug and solvent abuse during schoolday (especially in lunch-hour)
Subclinical epilepsy
Closed head injury

Evolution of the problem

The evolution of the current difficulties should be reviewed; many children who fail in school have a history of delayed language development, glue ear, early behavioural difficulties, or motor problems such as hypotonia or late walking. The paediatrician will be expected to comment on the relevance of these conditions for the current educational difficulties.

It is helpful to know the duration of the apparent underachievement. A long-standing problem indicates a different range of explanations than does one with a recent onset (Table 16.1).

Holt (1969, 1970) described how children who are struggling to master the intricacies of reading or arithmetic experience anxiety and tension if they are not succeeding. Fear of failure and humiliation leads them to adopt a variety of strategies, including distracting or disruptive behaviours, to conceal their lack of understanding from their peers and teacher. If the teacher fails to appreciate the significance of the children's increasingly bizarre mistakes, they become more and more confused as the complexity of work increases.

Separate interviews with the child and the parents

The effect of the child's shortcomings on his/her everyday life, self-esteem, family and relationships with peers should be assessed. Part of this is best conducted with the child alone at some stage during the assessment. Note that the child is most unlikely to even hint at the existence of major problems like sexual abuse or parental alcoholism to a stranger in a single interview. It may subsequently be necessary to pursue suspicions of serious family problems in collaboration with educational or social work colleagues.

The interview with the child may be difficult to carry out if the child is sensitive to academic failure and thus apprehensive that he/she might give the 'wrong' answer to an adult. It is wise to start by asking about non-threatening topics which are straightfoward to answer such as where the child lives or what he/she likes doing at weekends.

Questions about mood or school can be introduced later and eventually the interview should focus on determining the child's mental state and attitudes. Is the child happy, sad or frankly depressed? Would the child describe him/herself as a worrier? Does the child feel that he/she is good at anything? Is the child worried about their supposed disability and has he/she been teased or called cruel names (like 'spastic') because of their educational problems? Are there any particular children who are causing him anxiety, for example by bullying, blackmail or stealing? Does the child have friends whom he/she can name and whom the child plays with out of school? Does the child like going to school or would he/she rather stay at home in the morning? How does the child think their family feel about him/her? Does the child like the teacher and does the teacher like the child? Are there some activities that the child enjoys and looks forward to?

Issues emerging in the interview with the child should be checked in an interview with the parents on their own. They should also be asked for their views on these points, and on the child's temperament, relationships with peers and attitudes to learning. Their own expectations and attitudes to academic success should be discussed. Over-ambitious parents are sometimes blamed when their children are found to have low self-esteem, but often the children are unavoidably caught up in the lifestyle of a high-achieving family and are depressed because they cannot live up to their own high standards or those that they observe each day.

Often these children also have a variety of psychosomatic complaints, such as headaches or abdominal pains, for which they may concurrently be under investigation by other specialists and the child should be asked about them directly. The relationship of these physical complaints to the educational underachievement may not be immediately apparent or may even be concealed by the parents, so that they can ensure that the child is thoroughly checked for organic disease.

Depending on the circumstances, it may be necessary to consider other more serious possibilities, such as drug or alcohol misuse, pregnancy or physical or sexual abuse. The child may need to be asked about these directly since the parents may just not know. Rather similarly, parents may not know about the child's truancy, preoccupations or symptoms of depression. Problems at home may be important; while in class, the child may be preoccupied with concerns about an ill parent, impending family breakup or family poverty. The effects of any long-term medication such as anticonvulsants (p. 347) must be assessed by asking both child and parents about them.

Background history: individual development and family history

The obstetric history is not usually helpful or relevant (p. 252), although parents may be keen to attribute their child's problems to 'brain damage' at birth.

The family history is often revealing; one or more members may have had language, learning or activity/attentional difficulties in childhood (p. 5). Parents may not always remember their early problems at school and should be asked to check with their own parents if possible. Adults are also adept at concealing their own current difficulties, particularly with reading or maths, and may, for example, ensure that their spouse or business partner deals with accounting and paperwork. Uncovering such a history can be embarrassing and may even cause marital disharmony. The parents should be reminded that the child has probably inherited their strengths as well as their weaknesses!

The attitudes of the parents to the child's school work and progress are also extremely important. Indices of parental interest, such as the display of a child's work on the walls at home, discussions about homework and educational and cultural outings, all correlate with academic progress. Families who maintain customs and traditions and who eat and enjoy leisure together are more likely to have well-adjusted and academically successful children.

Until very recently, parents were commonly discouraged from helping their children to master essential skills such as reading, for fear of 'confusing' them. As a result, a valuable resource was wasted. Many schools now involve parents more extensively in the child's education.

Background history: school factors

It is convenient to assume that, if a child fails to learn, the problem must lie with the child, but the skill and personality of the teacher are equally important. Every parent knows how a child's demeanour, behaviour and progress can change dramatically when the child enters a new class with a new teacher. Children generally strive to please their teacher but, if their efforts do not seem to be appreciated and encouraged or, worse still, are met with ridicule, many simply stop trying.

The widespread belief of parents that some schools are better than others at promoting academic achievement has received experimental confirmation in many studies. The differences between classes may be at least as important as those between schools. School size and class size have less effect on educational outcome than many people imagine. Factors which have been found to correlate with higher attainment include the use of praise in the classroom, feedback to pupils about their behaviour and performance, the extent of pupil involvement in lessons, good working conditions, opportunities for children to take responsibility, and well-organized lessons.

Even in a very deprived locality, indices of educational success or failure can be influenced by the involvement and support of the entire school community, including the families of the children attending there. All of these factors are within the power of any school to modify and improve. Nevertheless, it is now realized that the concept of 'good' versus 'bad' schools is an oversimplification. Schools can be effective in one aspect of their corporate life (for example, in sport) and yet perform poorly in others. Similarly, they may be effective for some subgroups of pupils but inadequate or even damaging for others.

The attitudes of parents and child to the school and the teachers should be specifically asked about. With the parents' permission, it is worth writing to the child's headteacher, asking for a report on the child's academic and social progress, and requesting a record of attendance.

Physical examination

Physical examination is usually unrewarding. Defects of visual acuity or of hearing should be excluded. Although they are rarely, if ever, the sole or main cause of a learning disability, they may contribute. Unilateral hearing loss is often dismissed as trivial but has been shown to affect educational progress adversely. For children with reading problems, an orthoptic assessment may be justified (p. 321). Skin naevi, such as *café au lait* spots (p. 369), and minor dysmorphic features should be noted in view of their possible association with syndromes, learning problems and attentional deficits. If the child presents with loss of skills or with co-ordination problems, a detailed neurological examination is essential.

The height should be measured and in older children the stage of sexual maturation should be observed. Boys who are late to mature seem to have an excess of academic problems, although it is not clear whether this is a developmental phenomenon or whether it is related to the low self-esteem that may accompany late onset of the puberty growth spurt. If the latter is suspected, counselling and sometimes hormonal therapy to induce puberty may be justified. Unexplained short stature may also be the first clue to a syndrome associated with specific learning problems, such as Noonan's.

Discussion of findings with parents

Straightforward explanation is sometimes all that is needed. The parents can usually be reassured that there is no serious disease of the nervous system, that the child's problems are real and not imaginary or due to laziness or naughtiness, and that the clinical picture is familiar. Parents find it oddly comforting that the doctor has seen it before. They are often relieved to learn that constitutional factors are involved and that the problem is not immediately attributed to something they have done or failed to do.

Usually, however, further evaluation will be needed and in some cases a formal educational assessment may be needed (p. 7). If the child has not already been assessed by a psychologist, this should be arranged. Depending on the nature of the problem suspected, further management may be left entirely in the hands of the psychologist, although many parents will appreciate at

least one further paediatric consultation to review progress. Sometimes the most appropriate referral will be to the child psychiatrist, particularly if there are suspicions of depression, hyperactivity, abuse or a dysfunctional pattern of family relationships.

Psychological assessment

The child with educational underachievement is more likely to be assessed by an educational than by a clinical psychologist, although the latter may be involved if the child presents first to the paediatric team. In districts where each discipline respects the particular skills and interests of the other, there need be no difficulty in deciding who is the more appropriate professional to deal with each individual case. The following observations apply to both educational and clinical psychologists.

The respective roles of the paediatrician and psychologist in the evaluation of educational underachievement depend on the skills and working relationships of the individuals involved. In general, psychologists do not welcome referrals simply for psychometric assessment and function more effectively when invited to use their full range of skills. The psychologist's assessment will usually include an interview with parents and child, an IQ test, measures of attainments (reading, writing, arithmetic, etc.), other tests designed to explore the child's difficulties in more detail and consultation with teachers.

The nature of the intervention depends, of course, on the type of problem. In most cases, the aim is to support the child in their usual school whenever possible and to enable him/her to continue working within the National Curriculum. This may involve advice to teachers regarding the selection of teaching materials or behavioural approaches, the provision of remedial teaching time or referral to a specialist teaching unit. It may be necessary to offer therapy if serious emotional disorders are identified.

Other more practical interventions may also be suggested (p. 323). For older children with specific learning disabilities (see below), the educational psychologist may request that the child be allowed extra time for writing public examinations.

The role of IQ testing

The correlation between IQ and a given academic ability is always less than perfect, as an IQ is a single expression of a variety of intellectual competencies. For instance, if a child has an IQ of 120, it does not follow that the child's reading age should be 20% above the norm for their age. It will usually be somewhere in between the average for their age and 20% above, but occasional children will be reading at a level more than 20% above — overachievement is as common as underachievement and may confuse adult expectations.

It follows that, while some children of normal or above-average IQ have serious difficulties in school, others of very limited intelligence do surprisingly well, presumably because of such factors as good teaching, strong motivation and effective family support. Thus it is useful to assess the IQ of a child with a learning disability in order to assess how far low intelligence can account for their problems; but intelligence testing does not elucidate the other factors which may be responsible, nor does it help directly in remediation.

The role of child psychiatry

The advice of a child psychiatrist may be needed if the child is thought to have significant emotional or conduct problems in association with educational difficulties. A child psychiatrist may also contribute to the assessment by interviewing the child in depth. Many paediatricians will prefer to leave prescription of stimulant or other psychotropic drugs (p. 330) to their psychiatric colleagues, although with careful diagnosis and monitoring this should be within the scope of paediatric practice.

Several problems loosely thought of as psycho-logical can interfere with classroom learning. The mechanisms are various. There may be a lack of resources — a lack of cognitive skills such as attention and concentration, poor-quality teaching, or a poor relationship with a teacher — so that the child is not motivated to please. Some children, particularly those with dyspraxia, lack anticipatory organizational skills and never have the right books for a lesson. Their teachers become extremely irritated, compounding the situation. Alternatively, processes may actively interfere with classwork: bullying in the classroom (a common problem — see Table 16.2), books being stolen, intoxication with volatile substances during lessons, being repeatedly excluded. An interview with the child, including some direct questions about such topics, is important.

Any source of stress can give rise to anxious preoccupations, which distract the child's thoughts, or cause emotional upset, which impairs the motivation for learning. The source of such stress may be at school (persecution by other children or by teachers) or at home (parental divorce, sexual abuse). Extreme stress can produce remarkably intrusive memories of distressing events, as in post-traumatic stress disorder. A low level of self-esteem may either predispose to a maladaptive reaction to stress or follow a failure to deal with it. Children with poor self-esteem and little faith in their own abilities will have a fear of failure so that they are reluctant to produce work or, if they do so, then destroy it. They anticipate criticism which would confirm their own doubts about themselves.

Not all conditions associated with anxiety disrupt educational performance. Teenagers with mild obsessive–compulsive disorder or anorexia nervosa may actually overachieve as a result of exaggerated concerns they have about the quality of their work.

There are three specific topics which need particular consideration when the issue is general academic underachievement: depression, school attendance problems and chronic fatigue syndrome.

Table 16.2 Bullying

Key points
1 Bullying is common: up to 10% of children are victims
2 It takes several forms: physical attacks, verbal abuse, racial harassment
3 Victims tend to be passive and lacking in self-confidence, have low self-esteem and feel that they lack intelligence and attractiveness. They have few friends and are more likely to be obese or to be disabled — this is true for all forms of disability. Having a personal classroom 'helper' is a risk factor. A few victims are provocative and irritating and may have poor concentration or be hyperactive
4 Most bullying occurs in school
5 The bullying is known to teacher or parent in only half the cases
6 The presenting problem may be school refusal, anxiety, depression or a variety of psychosomatic symptoms
7 Bullying is a stable phenomenon — it is unwise to assume it will be 'just a passing phase'

Helping the victim and the parents
1 Ask the five Ws: *what* happens, *who* is involved, *where* does it happen, *when* does it happen, *why* does the victim think it happens?
2 Assure the child and parents that they have done the right thing in disclosing the bullying and that this must not be kept a secret
3 The parents should see the teacher or headteacher to explain what is happening
4 The school governors should be invited to consider the matter and adopt one of the programmes available to combat bullying
5 The child may need help to develop positive attributes and make new friends
6 Seek simple solutions (different route from school, other playground options); rehearse possible responses to verbal bullying; if necessary, consider referral for help in developing alternative strategies

Depression. This is a description of a mood state which may be primary or secondary to adverse circumstances. Miserable children will be preoccupied with the cause of their unhappiness and lack motivation, finding it difficult to discover the interest, energy and creativity to tackle school work. If the misery is extreme, idiopathic, or self-sustaining when situational adversities are removed, and is accompanied by such signs as lassitude, social withdrawal, sleep disturbance, poor concentration and pessimism, then a diagnosis of depression should be considered. Educational progress will be more seriously impaired than in situationally provoked misery, since there is an extension of dysfunction into cognitive areas and impairment of drive; the child is ill with his/her unhappiness. Misery can occur at any age but depression is rare before puberty. Treating depression simply by prescribing antidepressants is not especially likely to be effective and referral to a child and adolescent psychiatrist is indicated.

School attendance problems. These can contribute to or result from academic underachievement. It is necessary to ask directly about school attendance since information about this may not be volunteered or be too intermittent to attract attention in its own right. There are four main reasons for a child not being at school: illness, truancy, being kept at home by parents and an inability to attend school because of fear or anxiety. The latter may be rational (victim of bullying, etc.) or irrational and neurotic, in which case it is termed school refusal. This is thought to be a better term than school phobia because anxiety can arise from anticipated separation from a parent rather than a phobia of school itself. It is an indication for prompt return to school as it will not improve with time. Neurotic school refusal will need the attention of a child psychiatrist or psychologist.

Chronic fatigue syndrome (including myalgic encephalomyelitis). This may occasionally account for a child's failure to make progress in school. The definition, the aetiology and even the existence of this condition are still controversial. The diagnosis is made more commonly in adults than in children, although it may be underdiagnosed in paediatric practice. It may follow a clinically obvious viral illness but sometimes the onset seems to be insidious. The features are muscular fatigue, which follows even minor physical effort, muscle tenderness and cerebral dysfunction, manifested by impairment of memory and concentration, mood changes and anxiety. Any or all of these may become chronic and may take months or years to resolve. There are no generally available diagnostic laboratory tests, although investigations may help to rule out alternative diagnoses.

Management is difficult, but it is important to reduce excessive activity and exercise whilst maintaining an adequate range of physical activities, and to acknowledge that the symptoms are genuine rather than the result of laziness. Appropriate changes in school routines may need to be negotiated because it is important to try and maintain school attendance. The advice and support of a clinical psychologist or child psychiatrist may be useful but the parents should be assured that such a referral does not imply that the features are regarded as purely psychological. Sometimes graded exercise supervised by a physiotherapist can help the child to return to normal activity, particularly in cases where there does seem to be a strong secondary gain for the child as a result of the symptoms.

The concept of 'specific learning disability'

Origin of the term

When medical disorders, general backwardness and obvious emotional and family problems have been eliminated, there remains a large group of children who have unexplained difficulties in the acquisition of one or more basic skills such as reading, spelling, arithmetic or tasks like handwriting, which involve co-ordination and movement. These difficulties have fascinated researchers for a century or more and a variety of 'medical' labels have been attached to them. The term 'specific learning disability' was first used by Kirk in 1963 and seemed to have the merit of making no implicit assumptions about the nature of the child's difficulties; it merely recognized that the child had a problem.

A recent change in the terminology used for people with mental handicap has caused some further confusion in an already complex subject. These people are described as having 'learning disabilities' (p. 147), associated with an overall, general or global impairment of intelligence and social functioning. This concept is distinct from that of a specific learning disability.

The problem of definition

There have been many attempts to define 'specific learning disability'. There is general agreement that the concept relates to a discrepancy between the child's actual level of achievement and the level that might be expected, given their IQ and their social and educational environment, but a universally acceptable definition remains elusive.

The following definition, which has been widely used, illustrates a number of conceptual problems.

'Specific learning disability' means a disorder in one of the basic psychological processes involved in understanding or in using language, spoken or written, which may manifest itself in an impaired ability to listen, speak, write, spell, or to do mathematical calculations. The term includes such conditions as perceptual handicaps, brain injury, minimal brain dysfunction, dyslexia, and developmental aphasia. The term does not include children who have learning problems which are primarily the result of visual, hearing or motor handicaps, mental retardation, emotional disturbance or environmental, cultural or economic disadvantage. (USA: Education for All Handicapped Children Act, 1975)

This and other similar definitions raise many questions.

• There is little agreement as to what psychological processes are involved in learning and even less about the most appropriate methods of measuring them.

• The term 'disorder' seems to imply something more than limited performance in a particular psychological task and suggests that the learning process is deviant or abnormal, but the nature of this abnormality and the means of its recognition are not defined.

• The overall severity of learning problem that must be experienced by the child to meet the criterion is not specified. One possible definition is 'an achievement level 2 years behind that expected for the age'; but the significance of 2 years' delay might be very different at age 8 from the same gap at age 16. Alternatively, a discrepancy of one standard deviation between IQ levels and attainment scores (e.g. reading ability) can be taken as evidence of a learning disability.

• A discrepancy criterion is purely arbitrary; it has no scientific validity and often its main function is to regulate the number of children who require remedial teaching, in relation to available resources.

• How severe should the hearing or vision deficit be before attributing learning problems to them?

• How does one decide whether the learning problems of a child with such defects are attributable to them or to a 'specific learning disability'?

• Is it possible for a child with mild global learning difficulties also to have a specific learning disability?

• The most damaging aspect of this definition is the exclusion of children with socio-economic disadvantage; this makes it more difficult for poor children to obtain remedial help even though they have the greatest need. For this reason 'dyslexia' has in the past been contemptuously described by some educators as a 'middle-class disease'.

Prevalence

Since there are so many different definitions of learning disabilities, estimates of their prevalence vary widely. It is said that up to 20% of all children may at some time in their school career require some kind of additional help to deal with an educational problem. The most plausible estimates of the prevalence of specific learning disabilities lie between 4 and 10%.

The causes of specific learning disabilities

Not only is it difficult to define 'specific learning disability' but there is also disagreement over the extent to which individual disabilities (reading, arithmetic, etc.) overlap and coexist with each other and with behavioural, emotional and conduct disorders.

Four distinct views of the causes of specific learning disabilities can be identified.
1 A manifestation of organic brain damage or dysfunction.
2 A reflection of genetically or biologically determined variations in brain systems.
3 Aberrant psychological processing.
4 A response to emotional and environmental influences.
All four viewpoints are valid and are not mutually exclusive; there is a complex interaction between biological and environmental factors.

Organic brain disorders

There have been two general lines of reasoning. Firstly, behavioural and learning problems are observed in adults with documented brain damage; therefore, similar functional problems in children might also be attributable to areas of brain damage or dysfunction. Secondly, severe brain damage in infancy can cause severe handicap; therefore, minor brain damage might cause minor handicaps such as learning disabilities. Both assumptions are plausible but are not necessarily correct.

Effect of focal brain lesions

The Scottish ophthalmologist, Hinshelwood, was the first to write extensively on reading disorders. Word-blindness was first described in 1877, and the term 'dyslexia' was introduced some 9 years later. Hinshelwood and his contemporaries were impressed by the apparent similarity between the specific reading deficits seen in adults with localized brain lesions and the 'developmental' problems of children. More recently, Luria, a Russian neuropsychologist, showed that sharply demarcated brain lesions caused by war injuries could affect isolated aspects of reading, writing or calculation skills.

Since focal brain lesions can cause reading difficulties in adults, it is not surprising that a search for focal brain lesions in children with learning disabilities was initiated. Terms borrowed from adult 'lesion' neurology such as 'dyslexia', 'dyscalculia', 'dysgraphia', 'dysphasia' and 'dyspraxia' became firmly established in the literature of learning disabilities.

Diffuse brain damage or dysfunction

Two distinct theories have evolved, one involving damage, the other dysfunction. The first postulates that diffuse minimal brain damage is a mild form of severe brain damage, caused by similar insults of lesser degree. This idea was introduced in the 1950s, by Lilienfeld and Parkhurst and by Pasamanick and Knobloch. They suggested that, since severe cerebral insults are known to cause major impairments such as cerebral palsy, lesser impairments might well be caused by minor perinatal brain injuries. The term 'continuum of reproductive casualty' was introduced to indicate that perinatal brain damage might result in death, cerebral palsy or learning disabilities.

The difficulty with this approach is that the postulated diffuse damage could not be demonstrated objectively. Accordingly, the term 'minimal brain dysfunction' (MBD) came to be preferred, since this implied functional disturbance without the necessity to demonstrate anatomical abnormalities. This was conceptualized as a distinct entity involving an altered capacity for arousal, with impairment of attention control and stimulus filtering, possibly based on genetically determined neurotransmitter abnormalities. The name of Wender is particularly associated with this view.

In recent years the term 'MBD' has been commonly used, irrespective of its possible aetiology, to describe a childhood disorder 'characterised by deficits of attention and impulse control

associated with disorders of perception, motor function or cognition, in the absence of cerebral palsy or frank mental retardation'. No one doubts that there are children who have such problems in various combinations, but there are at least four reasons for questioning the concept of MBD as an entity.

Firstly, the number of symptoms suggestive of MBD in individual children forms a continuous distribution curve, from none to numerous; there is no 'hump' as one would expect if MBD were a separate entity. Secondly, although the overall incidence of psychological disorders is increased after proven brain injury, there is no clear-cut pattern of disorder, and therefore there is no reason to think that a definable pattern of disorder should follow unproven subclinical brain damage (see also p. 6). Thirdly, the notion of attention deficits or 'hyperactivity' as a unifying factor in MBD is not supported by detailed studies, as discussed below. Lastly, 'soft' neurological signs (p. 66) have been used as a clinical marker for identification of MBD but, although they are commoner in young children with learning difficulties than in those without, these differences largely disappear by the age of 10 years and the association between soft signs, hyperactivity and learning problems is weak, while that with perinatal disorder is weaker still. Most soft signs merely indicate a mild maturational delay in central nervous system (CNS) functioning.

The concept of MBD is now largely of historical interest. There are no common aetiological or diagnostic factors, no obvious clustering of the various symptoms into behavioural syndromes, and no universally effective method of treatment. It is more profitable to analyse each aspect of the child's problems and formulate the problems individually.

Modern imaging techniques

Techniques that permit structural or functional imaging of the brain have recently been applied to adults and, less extensively, to children with a variety of learning disabilities and associated problems of attention and concentration. With only a few rare exceptions, the findings do not support the notion of focal brain lesions as a cause of specific learning disabilities; but they do indicate some abnormalities of blood flow, glucose metabolism and electroencephalogram (EEG) patterns, whose significance is as yet unknown. The findings are compatible with localized cerebral dysfunction, but might equally well be a manifestation of failure to learn a skill which in other people would be localized in that area of the brain.

Genetic and developmental aspects

The preponderance of males, the existence of some individuals with a dramatic family history of a specific learning disability, and the association between learning problems of all kinds and sex chromosome disorders provide the most obvious evidence for a genetic factor. There is a substantial genetic influence not only on overall intelligence, but also on individual mental skills, abilities and deficits. This can be demonstrated in two ways: by examining the correlations between IQ subtest scores obtained by members of the same family; and by studies on some forms of learning disability which reveal a well-defined pattern of inheritance (pp. 188 and 320). Even in cases where the inheritance is less clear, there are often more family members with learning disabilities than would be expected by chance.

It is probable that in many cases specific learning disabilities are simply a reflection of genetic variation in the distribution of individual talents and deficits. In some families, however, learning disability may be a manifestation of a single gene defect or dysfunction.

Unusual patterns of brain development may also lead to learning disabilities, as well as to more generalized learning difficulties. Children of extremely low birth weight and those who suffered very severe intrauterine growth retardation or prolonged postnatal malnutrition tend to have some reduction of total IQ and often have co-ordination problems (p. 6). Cortical dys-

plasias have been found at post-mortem in a few adults with dyslexia. Heterotopias are found in people with neurofibromatosis, although their presence does not correlate with the severity of their learning difficulties. Children with more than three minor dysmorphic features have been found in some (but not all) studies to have an increased risk of various learning disabilities, whether or not these anomalies add up to a named dysmorphic syndrome (see p. 149).

In children with specific learning disabilities, the perinatal histories reveal more problems than in matched controls ('reduced optimality' is the term used to describe this finding), but this does not mean that the perinatal problems were the cause of the subsequent difficulties; it is equally likely that the reduced perinatal optimality reflects some pre-existing suboptimal fetal development or environment. Nor does an adverse perinatal event necessarily indicate actual brain injury.

Neuropsychological hypotheses

Neuropsychological models regard learning disabilities as a manifestation of inefficient regions or systems of the brain. Some are based on concepts of hemisphere specialization and plasticity (see also p. 189); others involve impairments in the processing of information.

Hemisphere dominance

In 1925, Orton, an American neurologist, proposed that the brain defects of learning-disabled children were functional rather than structural. This hypothesis was based on studies of cerebral hemisphere specialization and dominance. The idea was that the child, in learning to read or write, has to concentrate on left hemisphere images and suppress those in the right. If for some reason the left hemisphere is unable to establish this dominance over the right, confusion and delay result, a situation called strephosymbolia ('twisted signs'). Orton described six syndromes which he attributed to dominance failure: developmental dyslexia; developmental dysgraphia;

developmental word-deafness; developmental motor dysphasia; true childhood stuttering; and developmental dyspraxia.

Orton and his followers developed a system of remedial education based on his hypothesis. Although Orton himself did not in fact regard the production of hemisphere dominance as a primary goal, the assessment and development of dominance became a major preoccupation of many remedial educationalists. More recent evidence suggests that this is a misguided and naïve view.

Modern concepts of dominance. Dominance refers to the concept of lateralized specialization of hemisphere function; laterality describes the observed preference of an individual for use of one or other limbs, eye or ear. The 'dominant' hemisphere is the one responsible for speech and language, and this is usually the one controlling the preferred or more skilled hand. However, the situation is considerably more complicated than was realized at the time when Orton introduced his hypothesis (Table 16.3).

Clinical assessment of dominance. The clinical assessment of laterality is as difficult as its interpretation. Even for the simplest task, that of determining handedness, different results may be obtained by asking the subject which is their better hand, observing their preferred hand for writing, and administering a battery of specialized laterality tests. Similarly, footedness for hopping and for kicking may be different. Eye and ear preference is at least partly dependent on handedness, and also on peripheral defects such as refractive errors, amblyopia or mild middle-ear disease.

There are no simple, reliable correlations between dominance or laterality and learning disabilities that would be useful in diagnosis or remediation. Mixed laterality is irrelevant for clinical purposes. Further research is needed, but at present neither detailed assessment of laterality nor programmes aimed at changing it can be justified.

Table 16.3 Handedness and dominance: a complex problem (see Bishop, 1990)

1 Many left-handers have a left hemisphere localization of language, but in some it is localized to the right hemisphere or there is bilateral representation

2 Left-handedness occurs in about 10% of the population. It is often familial, but can be pathological, as when the left hemisphere is damaged. Thus left-handedness without a family history may be more significant than when the family history is positive

3 The Right Shift hypothesis proposes that a single gene, *rs*, determines the localization of language in the left hemisphere and that right-handedness is a secondary phenomenon. A single copy of the gene confers mild right-handedness, but there are disadvantages to having either two copies or no copies of the gene. This model predicts that:
• there will be an excess of poor readers in children who are very strongly left- or right-handed
• there will be more good readers among those who are **mildly right-handed**
• good readers will have good left-hand skills
• poor readers will have poor left-hand skills
These predictions turn out to be largely correct in practice, except that there is a small subgroup of bright 'dyslexics' who have reasonable left-hand skills

4 In children who sustain injury to the dominant hemisphere, temporary aphasia may occur, but the speed of recovery suggests that the other hemisphere already has a store of linguistic information; it does not have to relearn language from the beginning. This takeover of language functions occurs at the expense of other cognitive processes

5 The dominant hemisphere is only dominant for linguistic functions. Indeed, some aspects of language may be based in the right hemisphere, for example prosodics and emotional gesturing. The so-called minor hemisphere may be superior in spatial and complex visual functions and in some musical skills

6 Anatomical asymmetries in the size of the language areas of the temporal lobe and in the pyramidal tracts are detectable at birth and remain throughout life; but they do not always correlate with observed dominance or preference

7 Cerebral localization of a function may change with increasing fluency and competence in skill acquisition

Information-processing models

According to the information-processing approach, sensory inputs are transformed, rearranged, checked against stored memory, retrieved and used in a sequence of ordered stages, which can be represented in the form of a flow chart (Fig. 16.1). The schemes which result from this approach have the great merit of concentrating detailed attention on the child's difficulties and they are a rich source of hypotheses for remedial teaching and further research. However, remedial programmes designed to overcome deficiencies in the processing of information have yet to prove their worth.

Information-processing hypotheses are a product of the computer age, but it should be remembered that the brain does not work like a computer. Information-processing concepts may describe, even if incompletely, what happens when a task is being learned, but seem inadequate to account for the totality of psychological functions and skills. Newer computer models use neural network theory, which may more closely approximate the functions of the brain.

Miscellaneous hypotheses

Specific learning disabilities have been attributed to disturbances of vestibular function, defective perceptual or perceptuomotor functions, impaired integration of sensory and kinaesthetic information, problems of sequencing and short-term memory deficits. Some hypotheses involve the remediation of the supposedly defective system or function, others propose that instruction should be given through the intact systems. The existence and validity of many of the supposed neuropsychological processes are far from certain and comparisons between learning-disabled and 'normal' children reveal a considerable overlap in measures of perception, vigilance, memory, etc. between the two groups.

Emotional and environmental influences

Factors such as family strife, marital breakdown or death of a near relative sometimes account for a generally poor performance in school, accompanied perhaps by day-dreaming, school refusal or disruptive classroom behaviour. Conversely, learning disabilities may lead to emotional disturbances, including depression, social isolation and even school phobia. However, specific learning disabilities are not caused by emotional disturbance.

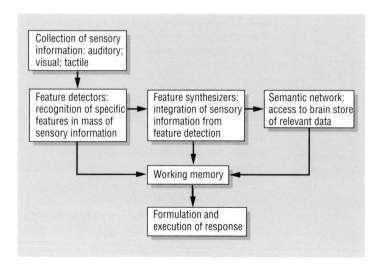

Fig. **16.1** A simple flow chart of human information-processing.

Types of learning disability

The *International Classification of Diseases* (10th revision) (ICD-10) refers to specific developmental disorders of scholastic skills and the American Psychiatric Association's *Diagnostic and Statistical Manual* (DSM-IV) describes learning disorders/academic skills disorders (World Health Organization, 1992 and American Psychiatric Association, 1994). Quite deliberately, neither system uses terms indicating aetiology. Within each category, various disorders are specified, both systems recognizing specific disorders of reading and arithmetic.

Reading disability

Learning to read

Reading is a highly complex skill whose acquisition is not yet fully understood. The representation of speech sounds by separate alphabetic symbols is a difficult concept for children to grasp, since speech is not perceived as a series of discrete segments. Reading may be taught using 'Look-and-Say' methods, in which children learn to recognize whole patterns rather than individual letters, or by phonic methods, which require children to sound out and blend the components of each word. To become competent readers children must acquire some skill in both techniques, and have to become familiar with the many words which do not conform to phonic rules. They then have to remember each word for long enough to absorb the meaning of a whole sentence. It is possible for children to be accurate readers and yet to have major problems in comprehending what they read.

It is difficult to define the point at which reading becomes 'automatic' but when this point is reached children can begin to enjoy reading as a pleasurable activity rather than a chore. Automatic reading of print, like the reading of music, can only be achieved by practice, but the amount of practice which can be supervised by a class teacher is very limited, and there is increasing evidence that parental help is invaluable.

Children who cannot read

Reading failure is the commonest learning disability seen in clinical practice, although this is probably because reading is fundamental to progress in nearly all other school subjects, and illiteracy is rightly perceived as a greater handicap than poor handwriting, poor spelling or difficulty with numbers. It is commoner in children of low IQ and of low social class, and in late-born children of large families.

Since reading skill is correlated with intelligence, most children who are poor readers are also delayed in other academic areas. These were described by Rutter as having general reading backwardness. In this group of poor readers, the sex ratio is approximately equal. There are also some children whose reading attainments are substantially below what would be expected on the basis of their intelligence; these are said to have specific reading disorder. Among this group, boys outnumber girls three to one.

Is specific reading disorder a single entity?

Specific reading disorder is a heterogeneous condition. Undoubtedly, there are some children in whom problems of attention, motivation, or family circumstances are the key factor, and others who have received inadequate or incompetent teaching. However, in many cases a strong family history of reading difficulties suggests that there is a hereditary or constitutional basis for the child's reading disorder.

In some children with specific reading disorder, the pattern of reading and spelling errors is so bizarre that some neurological disorder may be postulated. Critchley, a neurologist who did much to further the cause of people with severe reading problems, was convinced that 'dyslexia' was a clearly definable neurological entity and he described many cases in detail. Several authors have listed the features which might suggest such a diagnosis but these phenomena may also be regarded as symptoms of severe reading difficulties, rather than causes or key features which delineate a specific syndrome. Miles, for example, included difficulties with number sequences, and frequent letter reversals, in a list of 'typical' features.

The current view is that the terms '(developmental) dyslexia' and 'specific reading disorder' are equivalent. A predisposition to specific reading disorder runs in families. However, it is genetically heterogeneous, i.e. there are several variants, each of which may have a different genetic basis. In some cases there is suggestive evidence of dominant transmission and in up to a third of families with a clear family history of 'dyslexia' the condition may be linked to chromosome 15, although this is still an area of controversy. There is no simple clinical means of distinguishing the cases carried on chromosome 15 from those that are not, or of separating familial cases from the larger group of children with specific reading disorder.

Nature of the deficit in reading problems

As with other specific learning disabilities, the neurological basis of reading deficits is not known. Localized abnormalities of cortical architecture have been described in a few case reports, but it is not clear whether these are directly related to the functional deficit or are simply an incidental finding.

There have been many theories about the underlying deficit in children with specific reading disorders. Transient variable hearing loss due to middle-ear disease, eye-tracking defects, cross-modal integration failure (i.e. failure to integrate visual and auditory information), abnormal hemisphere dominance, failure to develop a fixing or dominant eye, impaired visual perception or, conversely, an excessively sensitive retinal fovea and a number of other hypotheses have been proposed in addition to those mentioned on p. 318. Unfortunately, much of the published research is invalidated by sample bias and the use of inappropriate controls.

Component skills and reading readiness

Reading can be broken down into a number of hypothetical component skills — for example,

distinguishing the print from the background, scanning from left to right, seeing the letters in sequence, matching the print pattern to stored word memories. There have been many attempts to predict a child's 'readiness for reading' by assessing these various functions and encouraging their maturation where appropriate, but in fact there seems to be little correlation between readiness for reading as measured in this way and the child's actual progress when he/she begins to read.

Subgroups of reading problems

It has been claimed that detailed assessment can identify some subgroups of 'dyslexics'. For instance, Boder divided dyslexics into dysphonetic (deficit in word analysis), dyseidetic (deficit in visual skills) and combined. Lyon described six subtypes and showed that different groups responded to remedial programmes in different ways. Rourke and others have described various subtypes and their neuropsychological correlates. In general, these attempts to delineate subgroups have not been very successful, because of a predominance of mixed types. In empirical studies there has been relatively more support for Boder's system.

Linguistic deficits and reading difficulties. The consensus now is that specific reading disorder most commonly originates from a linguistic problem rather than a deficiency of visuomotor or visuo-perceptual function. It has been known for some years that children with delay in speech and language acquisition often have difficulties in learning to read. To some extent, however, this is explained by the relationship between language delay and globally low intelligence; the link between specific speech and language impairment and reading problems is less clear-cut (see p. 186).

Spoken and written language have several features in common; in both, it is necessary to use a vocabulary of familiar words, to analyse sentence structure and to comprehend the message. However, readers must also comprehend the relation between the phonemes that they hear and the letters on the page. For example, there is no need for listeners to be aware that the words 'cat' and 'bat' each consist of three phonemes and differ only in the first, but this understanding is necessary for the reading of familiar and, more particularly, unfamiliar words.

Poor readers tend to be correct about the pronunciation of the first letter in a word but have increasing difficulty with subsequent letters. This is explained as a deficiency in phonological aware-ness. It is reflected in poor performance in syllable and phoneme counting games and in the detection of rhyme; the latter is of particular interest be-cause poor performance on rhyming games in 3 and 4 year olds is predictive of later reading problems.

Children with reading problems often have difficulties in at least four areas of linguistic function. These are: a deficiency in working memory capacity, which is specific to verbal memory processes; poor perception of words but not of other auditory stimuli; a difficulty in re-trieving from memory the sound structure of words, which to some extent reduces effective vocabulary size; and a deficiency in the application of their knowledge of syntax to the comprehension of sentences. Conversely, a fluent reader scanning an item on a familiar subject does not read every letter or word but concentrates on a search for meaning.

Visual defects. Some individuals with specific reading disorder appear to have severe difficulties in remembering and reproducing unfamiliar shapes and this may explain at least a part of their reading problem. Others may have problems in the fusion of retinal images. These are demon-strated by the Dunlop test, which requires the child to view two almost identical macular-size scenes through a synoptophore. The scenes are first fused, then the two are separated and the child attempts to diverge their eyes to maintain fusion. Children who have unstable responses appear to have increased difficulties in reading, which are improved when one eye is covered.

The significance of this work for diagnosis and remedial teaching is yet to be established. Although some reports have described substantial gains in reading ability with this treatment, the studies have been criticized on methodological grounds. Nevertheless, some children treated with this and other related techniques do make progress, which is occasionally dramatic. Further work is needed and it would be premature to offer these approaches as a routine aspect of care.

Developmental classification

For the paediatrician, a useful first step in classi-fication is to determine the stage at which the development of reading has become arrested. Some children have become frightened and con-fused about the whole process of reading; they do not understand the difference between letters and words or between the names of letters and the sounds they make; and the need to master both capitals and lower-case letters adds to their troubles. When such children are detected early, remedial help can be offered promptly; but, when they present at the age of 9 or 10, despair and low self-esteem make the teacher's task very much harder.

Problems may begin to emerge when the chil-dren have to move from simply visually memor-izing the appearance of short, simple words, to dealing with longer unfamiliar words. Their dif-ficulty with understanding the structure of words and the phonetic basis of spelling is revealed only when the 'look-and-say' approach becomes in-adequate for further progress. These children will often be able to identify a handful of common three- and four-letter words, although they may confuse words of similar structure; but as soon as they are confronted with an unfamiliar word they are quite unable to identify and blend the sounds of the individual letters.

The child may eventually learn to use the phonic approach to the analysis of words, but still have considerable difficulty in moving on to the stage of effortless fluent reading. This can only be achieved by further remedial help and prolonged practice. Lastly, there are some children who become fluent readers but continue to have problems with spelling, even into adult life (see below).

Management of reading disability

Learning disabilities are educational problems and their management should be based in school whenever possible. Regular visits to a paediatric centre are time-consuming and expensive for parents and they add to the child's disability a medical dimension which is seldom justified.

Children who are failing in school require expert, often individualized, tuition, whether their difficulties are due primarily to generally low intelligence or to a specific learning disability. Both parents and educators are increasingly reluctant to segregate children with problems in special schools. The need to distinguish between children who are 'intrinsically dull' and those who have 'specific learning disabilities' is less relevant if adequate remedial help is provided in main-stream school.

Many ingenious remedial schemes have been devised for learning-disabled children, but their relative effectiveness is not well established. Giving the children individual and sympathetic attention usually increases the teaching time provided for them, as well as having a powerful (and valuable) non-specific effect. This must be separated from the specific advantages of that particular teaching method.

Remediation of learning disabilities should be geared to the teaching of those specific skills which are deficient rather than to the development of hypothetical psychological processes. Specific training programmes such as those devised by Frostig, to improve visual perception, or by Ayres, to develop sensory integration, have proved to be no more effective (and possibly less effective) than the direct teaching of reading.

Parent involvement

Although short-term gains can be made with most classroom remedial reading programmes,

the long-term results have, in general, been disappointing. There is increasing evidence that the involvement of parents in reading practice at home is beneficial and, when the parents are keen to help, the technique of 'paired reading' provides a system of practising which avoids tension between parent and child.

Reading recovery

The problem of reading retardation is so serious and widespread that it seems important to devise better strategies within the education system, so that children who are not making progress are identified at an early stage (Hannon, 1995). The 'reading recovery scheme', devised in New Zealand by Marie Clay, is designed to select for remedial help those children who are the weakest readers in that particular school, before they and their families become anxious and defeated. A diagnostic reading survey is conducted when each child reaches the age of 6, after 1 year in school. The programme does not use arbitrary or fixed scores on standard reading tests as the criterion for entry to the remedial programme, and no attempt is made to separate those who have specific reading problems from those who are failing for other reasons.

Orthoptic treatment

The role of eye-patching, colour-filtering spectacles and so on is still uncertain, but they may prove to be of some value in certain cases. Many doctors know of at least one child who has benefited from such manoeuvres but they will also know a very much larger number of others who have not. How to select suitable referrals for such interventions is an unsolved problem since their advocates are not always self-critical and the practitioners are sometimes expensive.

Spelling, writing and arithmetic

In comparison with reading, the acquisition of these skills and disabilities affecting them have received much less attention.

Spelling problems

Spelling difficulties are known to be associated with specific reading disorder, and children with mild or moderate specific reading disorder often continue to have problems with spelling even after they have overcome their reading difficulty. Spelling problems can exist as a primary problem in their own right, often with a family history of pure spelling or mixed language problems, but are unlikely to be a reason for medical referral.

Writing problems ('dysgraphia')

Writing problems can be divided into three groups: motor problems, linguistic deficiencies and problems with content.

Motor problems. Firstly, writing may be impaired by anatomical defects (arthrogryposis, limb reduction defects) or by disorders of the pyramidal, extrapyramidal or cerebellar pathways. Writing difficulties are very rarely the presenting feature of such disorders; these children are usually already known to have some form of neurological abnormality. They may, however, be accompanied by various disturbances of visual perception and integration, and sometimes these may be as important as or more important than the motor difficulty.

Provided that the central executive motor 'programme' is intact, a child can overcome serious peripheral motor problems, as demonstrated for example by the ability of a child with phocomelia (p. 294) to write holding a pen between the toes. Much is made by some therapists of unusual pencil grips in the genesis of writing problems, but many adults hold their writing implements in a variety of unorthodox grips and yet can write without difficulty.

Writing problems are also commonly seen in children with 'clumsiness', attention deficit disorder and other learning problems. Some but not all of these are genuinely 'dyspraxic' (see below). Children with pure dyspraxia will be able to produce acceptable work using a typewriter or word-processor, or they can assemble words and sentences from prepared cards or plastic letters. If there are also problems with this task, it is likely that the difficulty is not purely a motor one.

Anxiety is another cause of poor writing. This may relate to any aspect of life at home or school and be associated with tension, an unnecessarily tight pencil grip and excessive pressure on the paper. Some children deliberately write very badly, in order to disguise their atrocious spelling; this must be distinguished from a true motor difficulty.

Linguistic deficiencies. In this group of children there are close parallels to problems of spoken language. The speed of writing may be slow, because the children have difficulty in recalling the structure of the words they require; they may avoid the use of words they cannot spell and have to think of alternative ways of expressing themselves. Spelling breaks down and words are written in a slavishly phonetic way or reflect local dialects. The structure of sentences and the use of grammar may also be defective. Spontaneous composition and writing to dictation are very poor.

In contrast to children whose problem is primarily motor, this group cannot easily read what they have written, but they can copy a sample of writing provided by the teacher quite neatly and accurately. Many have high-level language problems and find it difficult to formulate ideas in the form of sentences (pp. 183–4). If the children are able to dictate their ideas to the teacher more effectively than they can write them down, it is likely that the problem is specific to writing; if both modalities of communication cause difficulty, other causes should be sought.

Content problems. These children have problems with organizing their thoughts and ideas in addition to, or rather than, difficulties with getting ideas down on paper. They may have global learning problems and their poor writing output is merely a reflection of this; but in a minority it may reflect a more specific, though still wide-ranging, linguistic deficiency of the semantic–pragmatic type (p. 184).

Arithmetic problems ('dyscalculia')

Specific retardation in arithmetic may also occur, but these children are seldom referred for medical assessment unless they also have specific reading problems. While there are undoubtedly wide variations in the ability to handle mathematical concepts, the quality of teaching in this subject often leaves much to be desired, and this is an area where few parents feel competent to help, in contrast with the situation with reading.

A severe specific deficit in arithmetic as a manifestation of a focal brain lesion probably never occurs in childhood as an isolated phenomenon. Severe difficulties with arithmetic may be seen in children who have other evidence of brain damage, resulting for example from head injury, but other cognitive difficulties will also be evident.

Right hemisphere lesions have been associated with inability to understand concepts of quantity, and are accompanied by other characteristic features such as left limb incoordination, constructional dyspraxia and sensory inattention. Left hemisphere lesions produce an inability to deal with symbols and sequences of numbers, together with reading problems. When right–left confusion and finger agnosia are also present, the combination has been called the 'developmental Gerstmann syndrome'. However, as with all such deficits in childhood, the number of cases described is small and the possibility of more extensive and diffuse lesions can seldom be excluded, so that only tentative conclusions should be drawn from such attempts at localization. Furthermore, the value of such neurological speculation for remediation is questionable.

Management

The selection of remedial teaching programmes will usually be guided by specialist teachers or educational psychologists. It is important to recognize that some children have learning disabilities in several areas; for example, progress in arithmetic may be affected by a language impairment so that the child is easily confused by spoken instructions.

A speech and language therapist or teacher trained in the education of children with language impairment may contribute to remedial programmes for children with some forms of reading and writing difficulties. The occupational therapist may be able to offer useful suggestions for the child who finds writing difficult. Comfortable seating at the correct height, allowing the feet to be put firmly on the floor or on a footrest is the first essential, while non-slip desktop mats and thick pencils may also be helpful. For the more severely affected, whose output of imaginative work is severely restricted by inability to write or calculate quickly, a tape-recorder, word-processor or calculator may be invaluable. Schools are increasingly sympathetic to the use of such devices.

A few children with apparently specific arithmetical difficulties have a general learning disability masked by a relatively extensive vocabulary, the latter being due to upbringing in an articulate, literate family with resultant overachievement in this area. Psychological assessment will provide a broader picture. Others will have a poor technique for putting numbers down on paper so that columns of figures are unclear, even chaotic. Testing mathematical skills by asking for mental arithmetical calculations is therefore a necessary part of assessment.

Motor disability ('clumsiness')

Orton included developmental apraxia in his list of clinical syndromes associated with hemisphere imbalance, but the current interest in the subject was revived by Walton in 1962 and Gubbay in 1963 with publications on the 'clumsy child'. The 'clumsy child' is one who has difficulty in learning and performing motor tasks which their peers acquire without apparent effort.

The term 'clumsiness' is often used to describe those children who simply have an excess of natural exuberance (the 'bull in the china shop' syndrome) or have no concept of danger, or are restless, naughty and distractible in the classroom, but this is an inaccurate use of the term. If the term 'clumsiness' is to retain any useful meaning, it should be strictly reserved for motor problems. By analogy with the terminology used for reading problems, the term 'developmental disorder of motor function' has been used in ICD-10. The description used in the USA (in the draft of DSM-IV) is 'developmental co-ordination disorder' but this has not yet been widely adopted in Europe. The emphasis in this section is on higher-order co-ordination difficulties rather than on ataxia.

Presenting features of clumsiness

The presenting complaint may relate to gross motor functions, for example ungainly running, excessive falls or severe difficulties with sports and games; or the child's main problem may be in fine motor tasks, such as writing, cutting with scissors or dealing with buttons. Many parents believe their child to be suffering from 'the clumsy child syndrome', having read about it in a magazine or newspaper; but on closer questioning the child's problems turn out to be primarily in the domain of language development, reading or social skills. This concept of a clumsy child syndrome which includes numerous other learning disabilities is as unsatisfactory as that of 'minimal cerebral dysfunction'.

It is nevertheless true that 'clumsy' children do seem to have an excess of personality and socialization difficulties; they are often poor at sport and other physical tasks, and loneliness and depression are common during their teen years. It is an oversimplification to suggest that these children have no friends because their sporting skills are poor; many children with negligible athletic ability are gregarious and socially competent. Some clumsy children seem to have difficulties understanding the non-verbal communications of others and misread cues in social interactions.

It is more likely that social and motor difficulties have a tendency to occur together, rather than the one being the result of the other. Rourke described a group of children with rather similar features as having 'non-verbal learning disabilities'; and there are intriguing similarities between some clumsy children and those with Asperger's syndrome (p. 197).

A common problem among clumsy children is low self-esteem. This is generally assumed to be the result of repeated failure at tasks requiring motor co-ordination but it is sometimes so ingrained and intransigent as to raise the question of other aetiologies.

In adult life, clumsiness becomes less apparent but may be unmasked by appropriate testing or in stressful situations where physical activity cannot be avoided (for example, military training).

Subgroups of clumsy children

Tentatively, several subgroups of clumsy children may be recognized. Developmental dyspraxia implies a difficulty in organizing and executing a sequence of skilled purposeful movements, even though the peripheral neurological pathways appear to be intact and the individual component movements are well executed. A few of these children also have delayed speech development with dyspraxic features; this is not unexpected since speech is itself a complex movement (p. 176). Parents may find reassurance in the use of this impressive-sounding label, and in the fact that the problem is recognized, but they should be reminded that dyspraxia is simply a descriptive term and an imprecise one at that; it is not a diagnosis and is not indicative of any known neuropathology.

Other children may have little or no dyspraxia, but have excessive unwanted movements, such as tremor at rest or on action, or choreiform movements. Although it may be tempting to regard these as a minimal form of choreoathetoid cerebral palsy, the physical signs often resolve with maturation and this term should therefore be avoided. Alternatively, motor activity may be impaired by a true ataxia, for which there are various causes. There are yet other children who appear to be weak and to fatigue very easily, but investigation reveals no evidence of any neurological disorder. In these cases the problem often seems to be that the children cannot organize their movements to exert maximal strength, rather than a true weakness.

Mirror movements are common in young children. Movements carried out by one limb are duplicated involuntarily in the other. In pathological mirror movements the duplication is more extreme and can be disabling. This occurs in Klippel Feil syndrome and as an isolated finding.

Intelligence and achievement

In many children with co-ordination difficulties, intelligence and achievements in academic work are within the normal range, but these problems are more often found in children with learning difficulties. It might be anticipated that a standard IQ test would reveal a higher score on items that are dependent on language than on those that require visual and motor 'performance' skills, but such a discrepancy is not always found. Inspection of the results on the coding subtest of the Wechsler scales may reveal a low score because the child has to enter their responses in a series of small boxes under timed conditions and this penalizes motor incoordination.

Causes of clumsiness

Co-ordination problems, like reading difficulties, probably have many causes. Normal variation is probably sufficient explanation for many cases. Every class is likely to contain one child who is below the 3rd centile in height, and in the same way the child with the poorest co-ordination in a class may be designated clumsy. Temperamental variations, such as excessive timidity, and lack of opportunity to play and practise motor skills may also contribute.

In a minority of cases, the difficulties seem too severe for this explanation to be satisfactory. Children who were of very low birth weight or had severe intrauterine growth retardation, and those who suffered prolonged postnatal malnutrition, tend to be more clumsy than suitably matched controls, suggesting that brain maturation may have been impaired at a critical phase of development. The same is true of congenital hypothyroidism, even when treated promptly. Clumsy children rarely show any evidence of focal brain damage, although they should always be assessed carefully to exclude other neurological disorders.

The graduates of neonatal intensive care units have an increased incidence of cerebral palsy; those who escape this major disability are on average less well co-ordinated than matched controls. In addition to the relationship to very low birth weight, there is some correlation between the presence of abnormalities on cranial ultrasound in the neonatal period and the presence of motor difficulties.

Various test batteries have been devised for the assessment of children with learning disability, based on a particular theoretical view of learning, visuomotor development and clumsiness. They are often associated with remedial programmes, although these have in general been disappointing. For example, Ayres has proposed that, in clumsy children and, indeed, in other groups of learning-disabled children, there may be a defect in the neurological mechanism for the integration of sensory information. It was suggested that these children have impaired postrotation nystagmus and that this is evidence of impaired vestibular function. Unfortunately, remedial programmes ('sensory integration') designed to overcome this deficiency appear to have little impact on either the vestibular function or the academic progress of the child.

Other programmes have been based on the hypothesis that the main defect of clumsy children is in perception or in 'kinaesthetic feedback' (Laszlo); these approaches, although interesting from a research point of view, have not gained widespread acceptance.

Assessment

It is difficult to describe and measure the abilities and problems of clumsy children. The neurodevelopmental examination, which was designed to help the paediatrician assess learning-disabled children, lacks both a theoretical framework and any normative data (see Chapter 2). Descriptive tests, such as the Movement Assessment Battery for Children (which incorporates the Stott–Henderson Test of Motor Impairment), provide objective data on the ability to carry out specified tasks, without making any assumptions about the underlying processes.

Management

There is no clear guidance as to whether it is better to develop a child's strengths and interests or to try and overcome their deficiencies. This decision should be made for each individual. Physical education and the study of movement have a low priority in most schools and few teachers have any knowledge of remedial techniques in this field.

Occupational therapy (OT) is often recommended for clumsy children. The therapist's particular skill lies in his/her ability to separate everyday motor tasks, for example doing up buttons, into their component parts, which the clumsy child can learn at their own speed. Simple activities of this nature may have an additional spin-off effect in that the child's self-confidence and independence improve.

Any such programme has valuable placebo benefits (see above) and it is not always easy to assess the true value of OT in this situation. Every programme should have clearly defined goals and a limited duration, followed by review; otherwise there is a danger that it may continue for months or years without demonstrable benefit, but at considerable cost in time and money. It should be emphasized again that there is no evidence that the teaching of motor skills will have any directly beneficial effects on other learning disabilities such as reading.

Assessment may reveal secondary consequences of clumsiness such as low self-esteem, bullying by peers or unsympathetic attitudes displayed by the child's teachers. These will need addressing directly.

Attention-deficit disorder and hyperactivity

The term 'hyperactive' is commonly used as a synonym for excitable, naughty, restless or boisterously overexuberant; any young child confined in inadequate accommodation may seem hyperactive to the parents. It is also sometimes applied loosely to the aimless and exasperating repetitive activities of learning-disabled children, the irritability induced by some anticonvulsant drugs such as phenobarbitone, the disinhibition syndrome seen after frontal lobe injury (p. 298) and agitated restlessness as a sign of anxiety.

There is a group of truly hyperactive children who are inattentive and restless in all or most situations, commonly have a low-normal or borderline IQ, make poor peer relationships and have a high rate of behaviour disorders. These children have a rather poor prognosis for educational progress and adjustment to adult life. This clinical picture has been called pervasive or generalized hyperkinesis and is a precondition for the diagnosis of a hyperkinetic disorder (ICD-10) and attention deficit/hyperactivity disorder (DSM-IV). See Table 16.4 for diagnostic criteria.

These children have an unusual demeanour which is recognizable from infancy in many cases, with restlessness, excessive irritability and colic. Sleep disturbances are quite often reported and, while not constantly present, may be extreme when they are. Some such children are reported to have needed only 3 hours sleep per night or never to have sustained sleep for more than 20 minutes. Motor milestones are often achieved very early. In early and mid-childhood, motor restlessness is accompanied by poorly modulated behaviour with a lack of persistence in activities requiring thinking, so that tasks are frequently not completed. Parents comment on impulsiveness, lack of awareness of danger with failure to learn from previous painful experiences, a low tolerance of frustration, some social disinhibition and a short attention span. This picture is much commoner in boys than in girls.

In the classroom, these children fail to stay on one task and have difficulty in the organization and completion of their work, which is

Table 16.4 Diagnostic criteria for attention-deficit/ hyperactivity disorder. From DSM-IV (American Psychiatric Association, 1994)

A Either **1** or **2** (note: ICD-10 requires symptoms on both **1** and **2** for the diagnosis of hyperkinetic disorder, which is thus a more severe and less common condition):
1 Six (or more) of the following symptoms of *inattention* have persisted for at least 6 months to a degree that is maladaptive and inconsistent with developmental level:

Inattention
(a) often fails to give close attention to details or makes careless mistakes in schoolwork, work, or other activities
(b) often has difficulty sustaining attention in tasks or play activities
(c) often does not seem to listen when spoken to directly
(d) often does not follow through on instructions and fails to finish schoolwork, chores, or duties in the workplace (not due to oppositional behaviour or failure to understand instructions)
(e) often has difficulty organizing tasks and activities
(f) often avoids, dislikes, or is reluctant to engage in tasks that require sustained mental effort (such as schoolwork or homework)
(g) often loses things necessary for tasks or activities (e.g. toys, school assignments, pencils, books or tools)
(h) is often easily distracted by extraneous stimuli
(i) is often forgetful in daily activities

2 Six (or more) of the following symptoms of *hyperactivity–impulsivity* have persisted for at least 6 months to a degree that is maladaptive and inconsistent with developmental level:

Hyperactivity
(a) often fidgets with hands or feet or squirms in seat
(b) often leaves seat in classroom or in other situations in which remaining seated is expected
(c) often runs about or climbs excessively in situations in which it is inappropriate (in adolescents or adults, this may be limited to subjective feelings of restlessness)
(d) often has difficulty playing or engaging in leisure activities quietly
(e) is often 'on the go' or often acts as if 'driven by a motor'
(f) often talks excessively

Impulsivity
(g) often blurts out answers before questions have been completed
(h) often has difficulty awaiting turn
(i) often interrupts or intrudes on others (e.g. butts into conversations or games)

Continued

Table 16.4 (*continued*)

B Some hyperactive-impulsive or inattentive symptoms that caused impairment were present before age 7 years

C Some impairment from the symptoms is present in two or more settings (e.g. at school or work and at home)

D There must be clear evidence of clinically significant impairment in social, academic or occupational functioning

E The symptoms do not occur exclusively during the course of a pervasive developmental disorder, schizophrenia or other psychotic disorder and are not better accounted for by another mental disorder (e.g. mood disorder, anxiety disorder, dissociative disorder or a personality disorder)

characterized by sloppy presentation, omissions and insertions of irrelevant material. They give the impression of not listening to instructions and they misinterpret advice, even when apparently interested in the subject. Group situations are particularly demanding and attentional difficulties are exaggerated when other children are working in close proximity, but during a brief examination in the consulting-room their problems may seem rather trivial.

Defining the condition

The problems of these children can be seen either as an excess of activity or as a deficit of concentration and application; hence the linking of the two concepts in DSM-IV and 'hyperactivity disorder' in ICD-10.

Although the description given above suggests that hyperactivity is a definite entity, there has been much debate as to whether this is actually so. Some of the difficulty in diagnosis and classification derives from the problems of measuring hyperactivity. Numerous techniques have been used and they often correlate rather poorly with each other. Thus a child may appear hyperactive on one measure but not on another.

Often these children have only minimal deficits in sustained attention and vigilance, and they do not have particular problems in ignoring distracting stimuli. The most striking feature is a relative inability to inhibit a response to a stimulus; the child lacks the ability to stop and reflect before responding. This impulsive responsiveness is to some extent situation-specific and can be controlled in a one-to-one activity where an adult can supervise the child's behaviour. There is a further problem in that specific developmental disorders of scholastic skills commonly coexist and there is a confusing comorbidity with conduct disorder (severe antisocial behaviour).

Causes of hyperactivity

The early onset and pervasiveness of inattentive restlessness in the hyperactivity disorder suggest a constitutional element and there is some good evidence for a genetic factor, at least in older children. Asking parents about their own disposition as children can often lead to helpful revelations and make the child feel less persecuted by criticism of their behaviour.

With the possible exception of the rare cases associated with temporal lobe epilepsy, there is no evidence that the syndrome is caused by brain damage. There may be neurophysiological abnormalities; for example, a disorder of monoamine metabolism has been postulated. Minor defects of vision or hearing may impair concentration in school and present as 'hyperactivity', but are not a sufficient cause of hyperactivity disorder. The possibility of lead intoxication should be considered, particularly in the learning-disabled child with pica, but in practice this seems to be a rare cause. Undoubtedly environmental factors may contribute to the extent and severity of the problem but are not always present, and there are also wide variations in adult tolerance of behaviour disorders.

Dietary factors are often blamed, probably wrongly, for attentional problems, learning difficulties and hyperactivity (see below).

Assessment

Attempts should be made to define the situations

in which problems of attention and impulse control particularly occur, and associated learning difficulties should be investigated. The family may require advice on associated conduct problems and aggression, which may be more important in the long run than the hyperactivity. Psychosocial factors interact with the inherited temperamental characteristics of the child, and these should be taken into account when arranging appropriate help for the child and family.

The child's self-esteem should be estimated, since a poor sense of self-worth is a common consequence. This can be done by asking the child questions such as what he/she likes doing and what he/she is good at, how schoolwork is going and what their best subjects are, and inviting the child to draw a picture of him/herself. Throughout this, an acute ear will pick up the terms the child uses to describe him/herself. A direct enquiry ('Do you sometimes think you are useless at everything?') which yields a confirmatory response needs to be met with reassurance from the doctor that the child is indeed competent at some things. A failure to correct the child's judgement of him/herself will come across as confirmation of their incompetence.

Management

Advice to parents

In many cases parents only require a diagnosis, together with reassurance that they are managing the child correctly and are not making the situation worse by their actions.

There are three ground rules for parents.
1 Revise expectations so that the child is not placed in situations with which he/she cannot cope (protracted meals, long church services, etc.).
2 Curb the amount of negative comment or criticism. Hyperactive children live their lives to a constant soundtrack of adult complaints about them and their self-esteem suffers accordingly.
3 Encourage and praise persistence at sedentary

self-occupation (jigsaws, Lego, computer games, etc.).

In mild cases, a simple energy-consuming activity, which can be shared between parent and child, such as swimming, is sometimes surprisingly effective in restoring a deteriorating relationship between parent and child, although it will not eliminate restlessness at other times.

Advice to teachers

It makes sense to help hyperactive children develop their attention. Teachers can be advised to provide them with tasks or games which require sedentary self-occupation and praise them for their persistence at these. Identifying which elements in the environment are powerful sources of distraction may lead to suggestions as to how the environment can usefully be amended to promote task completion.

Behavioural treatments

Formal behaviour modification can formalize and extend these measures, but is time-consuming. Older children can be taught cognitive routines to help them think about their actions and act less impulsively or to organize and complete a task; but these interventions are the preserve of a child psychiatrist or clinical psychologist with a special interest in the topic.

Medication

In many instances, school-age children with a hyperactivity disorder will require medication in order for the situation to calm down and to allow parents and teachers to help the child develop skills in deficient areas (such as attention, reading, self-esteem or peer relationships). No drug treatment is curative, but it can provide a powerful effect on attention and motor overactivity for the duration of its prescription. This allows associated deficiencies to be corrected by training or maturation, whilst preventing the accumulation of secondary handicaps.

Amphetamine-like stimulant drugs such as methylphenidate have a calming effect in most children with hyperactivity disorder. Some children tolerate them well; their hyperactivity decreases dramatically and their learning may also be improved. High doses can produce a zombie-like state or even a depressed mood, which is usually intolerable as far as the parents are concerned. A few hyperactive children seem totally unaffected by the drug.

Stimulants are most commonly used for children in the 5–11-year bracket, but they may also be effective in adolescents; indeed, there are reports of their successful use in adults. Hyperactive children who also have general learning disabilities do not respond so predictably to stimulant drugs, but occasional successes justify a trial of therapy. These drugs have many side-effects (Table 16.5), but none is unmanageable and the benefits usually far outweigh the adverse effects.

The possibility that addiction to the stimulant agent or misuse of other drugs might occur has been extensively studied and no evidence has been found to substantiate this concern.

Many parents and teachers are quite disturbed by the prospect of manipulating behaviour by means of drugs. Their fears must be acknowledged and a plan agreed for a short therapeutic trial of fixed duration. The drug is then withdrawn and it immediately becomes obvious whether the effects have been beneficial.

The initial dose of methylphenidate is half of the 10 mg tablet in the morning and then a repeat dose at midday. The dose is increased slowly. Further benefit is rarely seen beyond 60 mg/day. The duration of action may only be a couple of hours so that more frequent doses may be needed. Dextro-amphetamine or pemoline may also be used; they often have a longer duration of action per dose. In children who develop insomnia on stimulants, even with doses given no later than midday, imipramine is an alternative. It is wise to involve a child psychiatrist when using this drug.

Haloperidol and clonidine have also been used in the treatment of hyperactivity in this situation, but their side-effects are considerable and their

Table 16.5 Side-effects of stimulant drugs

Stomach-aches
A common side-effect in the first few weeks, but they wear off

Insomnia
A virtually universal problem if the drug is given after mid-afternoon

Anorexia
Occasionally associated with diminished growth velocity. This is not a major problem but monitoring of growth is advisable. Catch-up growth occurs when the drug is stopped

Tics
A few children develop tics. This is an indication for the advice of a child psychiatrist as medication changes may be needed. Usually it is safe to continue

Epilepsy
Stimulants can be given to children with epilepsy. They are not generally thought to be epileptogenic, although isolated case reports suggest that they can occasionally exacerbate fits

effectiveness limited. Sulthiame is occasionally useful but has many side-effects, similar to those of acetazolamide. Again, it is wise to obtain the advice of a child psychiatrist if contemplating the use of any of these drugs.

Whatever approach is adopted, the school must be involved, since the teachers must carry out any behavioural treatment and can help in assessing the effectiveness of drug therapy.

It is good practice to discontinue medication once each year, to see if the drug is still required. Many hyperactive children no longer benefit from medication after the age of 12 or so.

Food allergies, diets and hyperactivity

The possibility that hyperactivity might arise as an adverse reaction to certain foods has been given massive publicity so that most hyperactive children will already have received some sort of diet before they are seen in a clinic. The evidence that diet is relevant is inconsistent.

The early claims by Feingold that hyperactivity was an allergic response to artificial food colourants and preservatives are without scientific basis. No allergic mechanism has been demonstrated, and diets which exclude additives (sometimes referred to by parents as 'E numbers') have been found to be no better than placebo in the treatment of hyperactivity disorder. The same applies to the wilder claims concerning tap-water allergy and the like. Gluten-free and sugar-free diets are also no more effective than placebo.

A more refined hypothesis is that hyperactivity results from an adverse reaction to certain foods on an idiosyncratic basis. This is the reasoning behind the oligoantigenic diet, now increasingly known as the few-foods diet since no allergic mechanism has been demonstrated.

The child is put on a very simple diet containing one meat, one vegetable and one fruit, with only water to drink. This is sustained for 3 weeks. If there is improvement, single foods are introduced one by one and, if hyperactive behaviour recurs, it is assumed to be an adverse reaction to that particular food, which is henceforth excluded from the child's diet. Thus a full picture of dietary tolerance and intolerance is built up.

There is a little evidence that such an approach can be effective for some hyperactive children. How many respond is arguable. In our experience it is only a small subgroup, so that across the board we have not had much success, but enthusiasts claim better results. It is an arduous technique for most families to implement, is not cheap and is hard to carry out in residential settings such as boarding-schools. A clear-cut adverse response to a dietary constituent such as bananas or Coca-Cola is sometimes volunteered in the history and can be tested empirically without the full paraphernalia of a few-foods diet. If the parents are unwilling to comply with a provocation test, they are usually right!

Adverse effects of diets

Diets are not an easy option. The cruder exclusion diets are potentially dangerous and can be experienced by the children as punitive. If they behave badly under provocation, they are accused of breaking their diet. Diets can restrict social activities such as parties or outings for children who are already likely to have difficulties with peer relationships. Usually the whole family has to go on the diet and this is hard to sustain. Lastly, the effects of diets when they do work are smaller than the effect of medication. For such reasons we do not recommend diets routinely, although we are prepared to be supportive of parents who wish to try them. They will need regular supervision by a dietitian and it is wise to build in review interviews with the child in order to gain an impression of the social impact of the restrictions.

Rather similar remarks apply to dietary supplements. Evening primrose oil and megavitamins are quite widely used by parents but there is no evidence that they work, nor is the rationale advanced for their inclusion at all convincing. Awkwardly, the magazine articles about fashionable 'treatments' for hyperactivity which are read by parents and teachers usually portray scepticism among doctors as evidence of reactionary attitudes and ignorance.

The bright child

Giftedness can be defined as an IQ of 135 or greater. Around $2\frac{1}{2}\%$ of children have IQs between 135 and 150, while a very small number have an IQ substantially higher than this and can be regarded as exceptionally gifted or 'geniuses'. The figure would be significantly higher if children are included who have exceptional talents or skills in one particular field. Giftedness can be classified as follows: global (generally high IQ); specific academic ability; creative thinking; leadership; visual or performing arts; and psychomotor — sports and manual skills.

Some caution is wise when interpreting IQ figures. They may have been obtained from a poorly standardized or casually applied test. The Stanford–Binet may yield unstable IQs at its upper scoring limit.

Bright children often have a history of achieving milestones early. They learn to read quickly and have a large vocabulary for their age. They are more likely to come from upper-class homes and, contrary to popular belief, tend to be physically large and healthy (although they are often the youngest in their class and therefore are wrongly thought to be small). They choose playmates on the basis of mental rather than chronological age and often become leaders of their peer group.

It is unfortunate that for some children high intelligence can actually be a disability. They may come to professional attention because for them the normal school curriculum is intolerably slow-moving and boring. Usually teachers recognize that the child is bright, but do not appreciate how bright.

The presenting problems include disruptive behaviour in class, avoidance of school, anxiety or psychosomatic problems and even poor academic performance. The children may lack interest in what they perceive as uninteresting, elementary classwork and fail to perform. They are often aware of their superior intelligence, and react either by deliberately underachieving to retain peer approval, or become immersed in subjects such as mathematics or science, sometimes to the exclusion of broader activities. Children who have adequate stimulation at home may cope well with their frustrations, although the label of 'gifted' often adds to their problems when conferred by parents who are concerned for the child to make full use of their talents. Hypersensitivity to criticism, and perfectionism may be observed in such cases.

There are three approaches to management. None is ideal. The children can be segregated in a specialized school or unit; they can be offered an enriched curriculum; or they can be accelerated ahead of their peer group, working with older children. However, children promoted ahead of their peers often lack the social maturity to enjoy the company of the older children and may behave oddly to secure peer approval. On the other hand, if they are moved to a specialist school or unit they may lose touch with their peers at home.

Paradoxically, recognition and management of bright children are far inferior to those regarding children with other learning disabilities. Parents who recognize their children's needs for a more demanding curriculum often find that the educational authorities, though sympathetic, are unable to help because resources are inadequate. The normal school finds these children disruptive and difficult. Unless special provision can be made by the school or the parents, their talents are likely to be wasted.

References and further reading

American Psychiatric Association (1994) *Diagnostic and Statistical Manual of Mental Disorders*, (4th edn). American Psychiatric Association, Washington, DC.

Audit Commission. (1992) *Getting in on the Act*. HMSO, London.

Audit Commission. (1992) *Getting the Act Together*. HMSO, London.

Bishop, D.V.M. (1989) Unfixed reference, monocular occlusion, and developmental dyslexia — a critique. *British Journal of Ophthalmology*, **73**, 209–15.

Bishop, D.V.M. (1990) *Handedness and Development Disorder*. Clinics in Developmental Medicine, No. 110. Mackeith Press, London.

Bryant, P. and Bradley, L. (1985) *Children's Reading Problems*. Blackwell Scientific Publications, Oxford.

Dawkins, J.L. and Hill, P. (1994) Bullying: another form of abuse? In *Recent Advances in Paediatrics*, Vol. 13, (ed. T.J. David). Churchill Livingstone, Edinburgh.

Farrell, P. (1995) *Children with Emotional and Behavioural Difficulties*. Falmer Press, London.

Freeman, J. (1995) Recent studies of giftedness in children. *Journal of Child Psychology and Psychiatry*, **36**(4), 531–48.

Gordon, N. (1992) Children with developmental dyscalculia. *Developmental Medicine and Child Neurology*, **34**(5), 459–63.

Hannon, P. (1995) *Literacy, Home and School*. Falmer Press, London.

Hellgren, L. (1993) Children with deficits in attention, motor control and perception (DAMP) almost grown up: general health at 16 years. *Developmental Medicine and Child Neurology*, **35**(10), 881–92.

Henderson, S.E. (1992) Clumsiness or developmental coordination disorder in children: a neglected handicap. *Current Paediatrics*, **2**(3), 158–62.

Holt, J. (1969) *How Children Fail*. Pelican Books, Harmondsworth.

Holt, J. (1970) *How Children Learn*. Pelican Books, Harmondsworth.

Jenkins, R. and Mowbray, J.F. (1991) *Post Viral Fatigue Syndrome*. John Wiley & Sons Ltd, Chichester.

Kazdin, A.E. (1990) Childhood depression. *Journal of Child Psychology and Psychiatry*, **31**, 29–41.

Kowal, A. and Pritchard, K. (1990) Psychological characteristics of children who suffer from headache. *Journal of Child Psychology and Psychiatry*, **31**, 637–49.

Leverton, T.J. and Lask, B. (1991) Postviral fatigue syndrome. *Current Paediatrics*, **1**(4), 231–2.

Maughan, B. (1995) Long-term outcomes of developmental reading problems. *Journal of Child Psychology and Psychiatry*, **36**(3), 357–72.

O'Hare, A.E. and Brown, J.K. (1989) Childhood dysgraphia. Part 1. An illustrated clinical classification. *Child: Care, Health and Development*, **15**, 79–104.

O'Hare, A.E. and Brown, J.K. (1989) Childhood dysgraphia. Part 2. A study of hand function. *Child: Care, Health and Development*, **15**, 151–60.

Ounsted, C., Lindsey, J. and Richards, P. (1987) *Temporal Lobe Epilepsy 1948–1986: A Biographical Study*. Clinics in Developmental Medicine, No. 103. Mackeith Press, London.

Rasmussen, P. (1993) Persistent mirror movement: a clinical study of 17 children, adolescents and young adults. *Developmental Medicine and Child Neurology*, **35**(8), 699–707.

Richman, N. (1993) Children in situations of political violence. *Journal of Child Psychology and Psychiatry*, **34**(8), 1286–1303.

Schachar, R. (1991) Childhood hyperactivity. *Journal of Child Psychology and Psychiatry*, **32**, 155–91.

Shalev, R., Manor, O., Amir, N. and Gross-Tsur, V. (1993) The acquisition of arithmetic in normal children: assessment by a cognitive model of dyscalculia. *Developmental Medicine and Child Neurology*, **35**(7), 593–601.

Smyth, T.R. (1991) Abnormal clumsiness in children: a defect of motor programming? *Child: Care, Health and Development*, **17**, 283–94.

Snowling, M.J. (1991) Developmental reading disorders. *Journal of Child Psychology and Psychiatry*, **32**, 49–77.

Stanovich, K.E. (1994) Does dyslexia exist? *Journal of Child Psychology and Psychiatry*, **35**(4), 579–97.

Taylor, E.A. (1986) *The Overactive Child*. Clinics in Developmental Medicine, No. 97. Mackeith Press, London.

World Health Organization (1992) *ICD-10: The ICD-10 Classification of Mental and Behavioural Disorders: Clinical Descriptions and Diagnostic Guidelines*, Chapter V. World Health Organization, Geneva.

CHAPTER 17

Fits, Faints and Funny Turns

Epilepsy is commoner among children with a disability than in the general population. It may be a trivial problem, or a major cause of disability in its own right. Overdiagnosis and excessively vigorous treatment may cause iatrogenic disability. 'Funny turns' should not automatically be assumed to be epileptic just because the child has some other neurological impairment.

Fits and epilepsy

A fit or seizure is a clinical event in which there is a sudden disturbance of neurological function in association with altered activity of cortical neurons. A convulsion is an attack of involuntary muscle contraction, either sustained (tonic) or interrupted (clonic). In epilepsy, there is a tendency to recurrent fits, resulting from abnormal and excessive activity of a more or less extensive collection of neurons. The fit or seizure may be convulsive in type; it may consist of other behavioural or psychic experiences; there may be negative phenomena, for instance loss of awareness or of muscle tone.

Sudden changes of cerebral blood flow, oxygenation or glucose supply may all produce an alteration of consciousness or motor function, culminating in a convulsion with a brief episode of stiffening (the 'tonic' phase), followed by some 'clonic jerks'. It may be very difficult to differentiate epileptic seizures from other causes of 'funny turns', particularly if the attacks terminate with a tonic–clonic episode; the brain has only a limited repertoire of responses to acute insults. For this reason, great importance is attached to the events occurring immediately before and after the period of dramatic neurological disturbance.

Causes of epilepsy

Genetic predisposition

This contributes to the development of epilepsy. There are over 100 named single-gene disorders in which epilepsy may occur, but in total these account for no more than 1% of all people with epilepsy. Some forms of epilepsy are inherited as autosomal dominant or recessive conditions, whereas in others the genetic influence is less well defined. The electroencephalogram (EEG) features seen in children with genetically determined epilepsies, such as absence attacks and benign focal epilepsy, may also be found in recordings from their relatives who never have seizures.

Cerebral lesions

Epileptic activity may originate in damaged areas of brain, usually in the cortex and rarely, if ever, in the brainstem. The damage may be focal or diffuse. The seizure risk is determined by the site, nature and rate of evolution of the lesion, in combination with the underlying level of genetic predisposition. Rarely, a degenerative process or a metabolic abnormality may be responsible. Tumours account for only a tiny proportion of cases.

Physiological and psychological factors

These do not provoke fits, but may explain why fits occur at a particular time. There is a close relationship between epilepsy and sleep. Some seizure types occur predominantly during sleep, others very rarely. Abnormal EEG activity is often only manifest during sleep. Fits occur most often after going to sleep, and just before and just after awakening. Their frequency is probably greater after sleep deprivation, a phenomenon which can be utilized to reveal EEG abnormalities which are not otherwise apparent. All antiepileptic drugs can increase seizure frequency in certain individuals; increased sleepiness or sedation may be one of the mechanisms involved.

In young children with a genetic predisposition to febrile fits, fever is the trigger. Some disabled children show a gradual evolution from apparently typical febrile fits to afebrile epileptic fits; during this period the role of fever seems to become progressively less important. Many disabled children have an increase in fit frequency when they are unwell. Febrile illnesses appear to be a significant provoking factor in young children with epilepsy, although it is not always clear whether it is the fever itself which is responsible. Not surprisingly, therefore, the distinction between febrile fits and epilepsy in disabled children can be difficult or impossible.

Boredom and stress both increase the number of fits, and interesting activities have the opposite effect. Some children only have fits under conditions of extreme excitement, for example on Christmas Eve or the first day of a holiday. Others have fits when intensely stimulating activity suddenly stops. Anxiety can lead to hyperventilation and mild hypocapnia (low carbon dioxide (CO_2)), which itself lowers seizure threshold. In reflex epilepsy, seizures only occur in response to a specific stimulus. The best known is photosensitive epilepsy.

Biochemical effects

Progestogens have a mild anticonvulsant effect and fits occur in some women only at the time of menstruation (catamenial epilepsy), when the hormone level falls. Electrolyte imbalance, low blood sugar or calcium, alcohol, and some drugs, such as phenothiazines, tricyclic antidepressants, some antihistamines and (rarely) methylphenidate may also alter seizure threshold.

The phenomenon of 'kindling'

Repeated electrical stimulation of the rat brain produces seizures of increasing intensity and duration. The stimulus strength required to produce them declines, until eventually spontaneous fits occur, as if the brain is 'learning' to have fits. Kindling has not been demonstrated in higher mammals and its relevance to humans is uncertain.

Classification

There is no completely satisfactory classification of seizure types or of epileptic syndromes. A distinction is made between the type of seizure, based on the clinical event as described by the patient or observer, and the epileptic syndrome (Table 17.1)

Epileptic syndromes are characterized by the clustering of symptoms, signs and EEG phenomena, although they do not necessarily have a single aetiology. They can also be classified by age of onset and by the extent to which a good outcome can be anticipated — 'benign' and 'severe'. A further important distinction is made between generalized and partial seizures. The former have an onset deep in the central areas of the brain and involve both cerebral hemispheres simultaneously and symmetrically. Partial seizures have a focal onset; the electrical discharges may be confined to one area throughout or may spread to involve both hemispheres, resulting in a generalized fit — this is called secondary generalization.

Prevalence

The prevalence in the population as a whole is probably around 0.5–1.0%. It is much higher in people with learning difficulties; estimates range from around 60% for those with profound learning disability to 7 or 8% for those with mild learning disability. Epilepsy is also more common in people with some forms of cerebral palsy, occurring in 50–90% of those with quadriplegia and 15–40% of those with hemiplegia or

Table 17.1 Proposed classification of epilepsies. After Aicardi (1986), courtesy of Raven Press, New York

GENERALIZED EPILEPSIES

Primary generalized epilepsies (or functional or benign) of childhood and adolescence
Petit mal absence epilepsy
Petit mal myoclonic epilepsy
Grand mal epilepsy
Combined petit mal and grand mal epilepsy

Secondary generalized epilepsies (or lesional or malignant) of infancy, childhood and adolescence
Epilepsies secondary to specific encephalopathy
Epilepsies secondary to nonspecific encephalopathy
    West's syndrome
    Lennox–Gastaut syndrome
    Related syndromes

PARTIAL EPILEPSIES

Primary partial epilepsies (or functional or benign) of late childhood and adolescence
Motor epilepsy with centro-midtemporal spikes
Affective epilepsy with midtemporal spikes
Sensorimotor epilepsy with parietal spikes
Visual epilepsy with occipital spike–waves

Secondary partial epilepsies (or lesional or severe) occurring at all ages but especially in adults
Partial epilepsy with elementary symptomatology
Partial epilepsy with complex symptomatology

---

athetosis, but is uncommon in those with classic diplegia.

The generalized epilepsies

Infantile spasms (West's syndrome)

This usually begins in the first year of life with a peak around 3–7 months. The incidence is between 0.2 and 0.4 per 1000. The condition is commoner in males. A family history of the disorder is rarely obtained but there is a small increase in the familial incidence of other types of epilepsy.

The attacks consist of sudden, violent symmetrical contraction of muscles, usually affecting the flexor groups. The trunk, neck and limbs flex and stiffen, the hands clench, and there may be a cry and a change in facial expression and awareness. Irregular breathing, unusual eye movements, smiling, laughing, etc. may be observed. Occasionally, the attacks are asymmetrical or unilateral, or extensor spasms may predominate. The episodes are often mistaken for colic or a startle reflex, but the distinguishing feature is the tendency to occur in clusters. Sometimes the spasms are so mild that they are overlooked, but West's syndrome should always be considered in any infant with a history of developmental deterioration.

Developmental regression and subsequent severe impairments are commonly associated. Motor and cognitive deficits may occur and sometimes autistic features are prominent. The child may lose motor skills and becomes irritable and withdrawn, and many months may elapse before any recovery or developmental progress is seen. In about one-third of cases, the child was normal prior to the onset of the spasms and neurological investigation is unrevealing; such cases are described as 'cryptogenic'. In the remaining two-thirds of cases, the attacks occur in a baby who either is already suspected to be developmentally abnormal because of previous cerebral insults or has some clearly identifiable neurological lesion. In this 'symptomatic group', the insult may be perinatal or postnatal brain injury, hypoglycaemia, meningitis or an intrauterine infection; untreated phenylketonuria, cerebral malformations, tuberose sclerosis, Aicardi's syndrome and metabolic and degenerative conditions should be excluded. The role of pertussis immunization is discussed on p. 167.

Investigation

The EEG shows gross disorganization and continuous abnormal discharges; the pattern is called hypsarrhythmia, although this term is often used, incorrectly, for the clinical syndrome. Records with periods of more normal activity interspersed with the hypsarrhythmia seem to have little influence on prognosis. The EEG usually improves with treatment but deteriorates with clinical relapse.

Occasional infants present with jerks which mimic infantile spasms, but they have a normal EEG and a good prognosis; this phenomenon has been called benign myoclonus of early infancy and needs no treatment. Infantile spasms should also be distinguished from true early myoclonic epilepsy, in which short bursts of EEG abnormalities appear on a normal background tracing.

A computerized tomography (CT) or magnetic resonance imaging (MRI) scan should be arranged. Congenital infections, inherited metabolic disorders, pyridoxine dependency (which may present after the neonatal period) and neurodegenerative conditions should be excluded. The parents should be examined for stigmata of tuberose sclerosis.

Treatment of infantile spasms

Adenocorticotrophic hormone (ACTH) or prednisolone improves the EEG and often controls the spasms, but there is little evidence that either improves the long-term prognosis. It is uncertain whether ACTH is superior to oral prednisolone and there is no consensus regarding the dose regime, duration of therapy or role of alternate-day treatment. ACTH, which is given in a dose of 20−40 units/day, causes a number of complications, including severe hypertension, hypokalemia and infection. Prednisolone, 2 mg/kg/day, is an acceptable alternative.

If steroid therapy does not produce a response in 3 or 4 weeks, it should be discontinued. If the infant does improve, a 6−8-week course is probably sufficient, although relapses are common as the dose of ACTH or prednisolone is reduced. Nitrazepam, initially 1.5−2.5 mg b.d., is often useful in controlling the spasms. Valproate (40−100 mg/kg/day) has also been used with varying success. Vigabatrin (50−200 mg/kg/day) may be effective. Children with symptomatic infantile spasms respond better than those with cryptogenic fits. In particular, those with tuberose sclerosis

often do well, although the spasms may be replaced by partial seizures, which will need treatment in their own right.

It is not known whether the length of time elapsing between onset of the spasms and the start of treatment has any effect on prognosis, but in cryptogenic cases it is wise to start ACTH therapy or prednisolone as soon as possible. In symptomatic cases, however, the potential hazards of steroid therapy may outweigh the benefits, and a trial of nitrazepam, vigabatrin or valproate may be preferable, keeping prednisolone in reserve for intractable cases.

Prognosis

In the symptomatic group there is a high risk (70−90%) of subsequent learning disability, cerebral palsy, autism, hyperkinetic syndrome and other behavioural and psychiatric syndromes. The spasms cease, usually by the second birthday, but other seizure types appear in at least 50%. The cryptogenic group do rather better, with 30−50% making a full recovery.

General management

The visible developmental regression that affects the more severe cases is very distressing for parents. Careful judgement is needed about the introduction of physiotherapy and other supporting services. Although in most cases there is a low recurrence risk in subsequent children, intense anxiety is usual as later children reach the age at which the spasms began, and this needs sympathetic handling.

Lennox−Gastaut syndrome and myoclonic epilepsies of early childhood

This is a mixed group containing both idiopathic and symptomatic seizures. They have in common an early onset (1−6 years), a strong association with organic brain disease or damage, and often an EEG superficially similar to that seen in classic petit mal. Seizure types include atypical absences, with clouding rather than loss of consciousness; atonic−akinetic attacks, in which sudden falls occur with immediate recovery; or there may be only head dropping and myoclonic flexion jerks. In atonic attacks there is suppression of normal muscle activity, whereas a true myoclonic jerk is accompanied by an electrical discharge from the muscle as it contracts. Generalized tonic or tonic−clonic seizures may also occur. Absence status is more common in these types of epilepsy than in true petit mal and may last from hours to days or even weeks (p. 340).

The term 'Lennox−Gastaut syndrome' is used when there are several seizure types, associated with diffuse slow spike−wave pattern on the EEG (1−2.5 Hz); whereas the term 'myoclonic epilepsy' refers to the predominant or exclusive occurrence of myoclonic jerks, usually with a faster spike−wave pattern (3 Hz or faster). However, many cases defy classification.

Causes

Lennox−Gastaut syndrome may be preceded by infantile spasms and is often associated with a wide range of brain insults and disorders. Some rare degenerative conditions may present with myoclonic epilepsy. Genetic factors may play a part in idiopathic cases.

Diagnosis

The atonic−akinetic attacks are usually easy to recognize, but other epileptic syndromes may be suspected if they are not the dominant feature. The EEG findings may be helpful, although the EEG may be normal for some months after the seizures have appeared. There is often excess slow activity, and there are spike−waves and multiple spike complexes, usually with a rate of 1.5−2.5 Hz. These abnormalities are usually present between seizures but occasionally prolonged or ambulatory recording may be required.

Management

Benzodiazepines are sometimes effective in the myoclonic epilepsies. Clonazepam or clobazam are preferable to diazepam. Sodium valproate may also be useful, as may a ketogenic diet. ACTH, phenytoin, vigabatrin and many other drugs have all been used in resistant cases which, unfortunately, are common. Lamotrigine is very effective in some cases, with substantial reduction in the number of seizures and a remarkable increase in alertness and well-being, probably associated with a reduction in interictal EEG abnormality. Felbamate may also be valuable in some cases. A protective helmet is essential for children with atonic−akinetic attacks if they do not respond quickly to treatment. Many of these children have other disabilities and need supporting services.

Prognosis

Prognosis for seizure control and future intellectual development is guarded, particularly in cases associated with other neurological abnormalities. Good prognostic features are normal development prior to onset of epilepsy, absence of other neurological disorder, older age of onset and quick response to treatment. Children with myoclonic jerks but no other seizure types may also have a better prognosis.

Typical absence seizures − 'classic petit mal'

The term 'petit mal' has been widely misused to denote any epileptic attack with rather minor symptoms, and the preferred designation now is 'typical absence seizure'. This epileptic syndrome is defined by the association of absence attacks with an EEG showing symmetrical spike−wave discharges recurring regularly at about 3 Hz. This is mainly a disorder of childhood, occurring usually between 4 and 12 years of age. It accounts for 3−4% of all child epilepsies and is commoner in girls. It is only rarely associated with organic brain damage or with significant physical or mental disability.

The attacks have a sudden onset and termination, without any warning or postical confusion. In a simple typical absence, the child's normal activity ceases, the eyes stare and may drift up and the eyelids flicker. Complex typical absences also occur with automatisms, such as pulling at clothes or chewing movements, or autonomic phenomena, such as pallor, changes in heart rate and urinary incontinence. These automatisms are usually relatively minor and they stop abruptly as the EEG discharge ends. There are usually many attacks each day, but the duration of each is rarely more than 20 or 30 seconds. Up to half of all children with typical absence attacks also develop generalized tonic−clonic seizures.

Causes

The typical EEG abnormality is inherited, although the exact mode of transmission is disputed.

Diagnosis

The differential diagnosis from myoclonic epilepsy and complex partial seizures (see below) is summarized in Table 17.2. This distinction is not always easy. People working with children who have other disabilities often suspect 'petit mal' on the basis of attention lapses, staring, self-stimulating behaviours or changes of muscle tone. In this situation, if there are genuine absences or jerks, a myoclonic epilepsy is more likely. Day-dreaming children are sometimes referred by teachers as having 'suspected petit mal'.

Table 17.2 Comparison of three seizure types with related clinical features

	Typical absence attacks	Myoclonic epilepsies	Complex partial seizures
Age of onset (years)	4−12	1−6	Any time in childhood
Association with other impairments	Rare	Common	Minority of cases
Frequency of attacks	Often many per day — dozens or hundreds	Very variable	Variable, rarely more than three or four per day
Duration of attacks	Rarely > 30 s	Very variable	Often > 30 s, may be several minutes
Aura	No	No	Common
Behaviour during attacks	Cessation of activity, stares, mumbling, fiddling, rarely more complex behaviour	Atypical absences, often with clouding of consciousness, atonic attacks, myoclonic jerks	Various meaningless activities, often complex
Recovery	Sudden and complete	Depends on duration and type	Gradual, often postictal confusion, headache
EEG	3 per second spike−wave during attacks and often between attacks	1.5−2.5 per second spike−wave polyspikes, irregular slow activity	Temporal spikes between attacks

EEG, electroencephalogram.

Hyperventilation for 20–30 deep breaths will often elicit an attack. In typical absence attacks, the EEG is nearly always diagnostic, with a spike–wave complex in both hemispheres at 3 Hz simultaneously with clinically obvious attacks and also in bursts with no apparent clinical manifestation.

Educational effects

Bursts of spike–waves in the EEG, even without apparent clinical manifestations, interrupt the child's concentration. Unrecognized absence seizures are a rare but important cause of educational underachievement.

Treatment

Ethosuximide and sodium valproate are both highly effective. They may be given together in resistant cases. Sodium valproate has the advantage of also providing protection against tonic–clonic attacks. Many children cannot tolerate ethosuximide. Satisfactory treatment should be verified by the absence of spike–waves on the EEG. A few children are resistant to standard drugs and for these a trial of lamotrigine is indicated. In some cases there is a dramatic fall in the number of spike–wave episodes and this may have a beneficial effect on concentration and learning.

Prognosis

In children with typical absence seizures who have a good response to treatment, a normal intelligence quotient (IQ) and no other seizure types, the outlook for remission of the absence attacks before adult life is very good. Up to half of all patients with a history of typical absence seizures will experience major seizures in adolescence or adult life.

Non-convulsive status, petit mal status

These terms are often used as if synonymous, but they are in fact distinct entities. Petit mal status is simply a series of typical absences occurring in such rapid succession as to form a continuous attack. Non-convulsive status (minor epileptic status) includes conditions of diverse aetiology. It is characterized by dazed withdrawal, lack of spontaneity, confusion, apparent intellectual deterioration and myoclonic twitches, with a variety of EEG changes. Complex partial status can occur in children who have suffered from complex partial seizures. Non-convulsive status should always be considered in any child with a history of intellectual deterioration.

Epilepsies with generalized tonic–clonic seizures

The generalized tonic–clonic seizure is the layman's 'typical' epilepsy, but such seizures may occur in many epileptic syndromes. Status epilepticus consists of a series of tonic–clonic attacks without recovery of consciousness between seizures.

Attacks which are generalized from the start are likely to be a manifestation of a primary idiopathic epilepsy, often with a genetic component. Alternatively, they may result from secondary generalization (i.e. spread of abnormal electrical activity) of a focal seizure, of either simple or complex type (see below). Occasionally, generalized epilepsy may originate from multiple independent foci, usually in association with other seizure types.

In the tonic phase, the patient loses consciousness and falls, often causing injury, and lies in a rigid extended posture; the tonic contraction of the diaphragm causes interruption of breathing and cyanosis may occur. After some seconds, clonic jerking begins, affecting both sides of the body symmetrically. As the attack progresses, the rate of jerking slows but each jerk becomes more violent. The tonic phase in children is often more prominent than the clonic phase, and the violent muscular contractions rarely lead to bony injury in childhood, although they may do so in adolescents and adults. The pupils are often dilated.

Stertorous respiration, biting of the tongue and inner cheek, urinary and occasionally faecal incontinence, and increased salivation may occur.

The patient may apparently recover awareness and then go to sleep for up to several hours, after which there may be a postictal headache. Full recovery may take some hours or even many days. In particular, a slight postictal ataxia often disappears very slowly, raising fears of a progressive lesion or drug intoxication. Similarly, extensor plantar responses may also persist for a time.

The juvenile myoclonic epilepsy syndromes

As yet there is no consensus on the precise classification of these epilepsies. Commonly used terms include benign juvenile epilepsy of Janz, myoclonic epilepsy of adolescence and primary generalized epilepsy of adolescence. Similar seizure patterns may also occur in younger children.

Typically, attacks begin in late childhood or the early teens and occur in the first half-hour after waking, although they can also occur during sleep. (In contrast, myoclonic jerks evident as the child falls asleep are almost invariably benign and are not epileptic.) Sleep deprivation, the 3 days prior to menstruation, natural photic stimuli (e.g. sunlight on water, discos, TV, video games) and perhaps excess alcohol act as trigger factors. Some of these patients also have myoclonic jerks which affect the upper body more than the legs and may continue over several minutes or even hours (myoclonic status). The jerks can be violent and result in objects being dropped or thrown. A minority of children suffer in addition from absence attacks.

Causes

There is an inherited predisposition in combination with other cerebral disturbances or lesions. Progress has been made in identifying at least one of the genes for juvenile myoclonic epilepsy.

Investigation

The EEG can be completely normal, but often shows spike–waves or polyspikes, which may be at a rate of three per second, or can be faster at four to six per second — this is said to be virtually pathognomonic of these primary generalized epilepsies. CT scanning need only be done if there is doubt about the diagnosis of a primary generalized epilepsy. It is wise to check the serum calcium and to exclude renal failure. Random blood glucose levels are useless.

Treatment

Valproate is probably the drug of first choice, although carbamazepine is also widely used. Other options include phenobarbitone, phenytoin, primidone, vigabatrin and benzodiazepines, alone or in various combinations. Juvenile myoclonic epilepsies respond to valproate, lamotrigine or clonazepam, although the latter has too many adverse effects for routine use. Carbamazepine and vigabatrin may cause deterioration and even non-convulsive status in these patients.

Prognosis

Primary generalized epilepsies starting in mid- or late childhood or in adolescence have a moderately good prognosis; deterioration rarely occurs and the prospects for seizure control are good, but relapse is frequent if medication is withdrawn. There is a reasonable chance of remission in adult life. The prognosis of epilepsy associated with multiple foci is less satisfactory. Non-febrile seizures following on from febrile convulsions are common and may be a different entity; they often remit by the age of 9 or 10 and the majority seem to have a fairly good prognosis.

The siblings of a child with primary generalized tonic–clonic epilepsy have a significant risk of developing epilepsy themselves; the risk is greater if the onset of the epilepsy was at an early age and if the sibling's EEG shows spike–wave activity.

Partial seizures

Simple partial seizures

These are seizures in which the phenomena are restricted to motor or sensory symptoms; this excludes those in which there are also changes in perception, mood or mental function (complex partial seizures (CPS) (see below)). The abnormal neuronal discharges which cause partial seizures originate in localized areas of the brain, but may sometimes spread, terminating in a generalized tonic–clonic seizure with loss of consciousness (secondary generalization). The spread of convulsive activity may be slow and orderly, as in the classic Jacksonian march from the extremity to the proximal part of the limb, but this is uncommon. More often, the propagation is difficult to follow precisely.

In versive (adversive) attacks, there is conjugate deviation of the head and eyes, sometimes accompanied by movements of the arm. There may be loss of ability to speak while full consciousness is preserved. Sensory seizures involve paraesthesiae or visual, auditory, olfactory or vertiginous symptoms.

Older children may be able to describe the preliminary symptoms or aura but, if they cannot do this, evidence of fear or strange behaviour before the onset of the fit may hint at its focal origin. The seizure itself may cause amnesia for the few moments preceding the loss of consciousness. In some cases neither the patient nor the observers may identify the focal onset, because the secondary generalization is too rapid.

The seizure may involve tonic or, more often, clonic movements of the face, tongue, larynx or limbs. Postictal hemiparesis (Todd's palsy) may follow a focal motor seizure; the limb is hypotonic and hyporeflexic and full recovery may take from minutes to several days.

Benign partial epilepsy of childhood with Rolandic spikes (BPERS)

BPERS accounts for about 20% of epilepsies in school-age children. It has several other names, including benign focal nocturnal epilepsy of childhood and sylvian epilepsy. It is thought to be a clinical expression of a dominantly inherited temporary focal cortical hyperexcitability, linked to brain maturation and with no identifiable localized lesion. The seizures usually begin between 3 and 11 years in a child who is otherwise normal. The attacks are simple motor seizures affecting typically one side of the face, the mouth and pharynx (causing loss of speech with various grunts and gurgles), and the arm, but the leg is rarely involved. The child often retains awareness and may complain of unpleasant sensations in the mouth and throat. Most children with this condition have many or most of their fits during sleep, and the frequency of fits is low; indeed, some only have one or two attacks.

If the clinical picture is typical, there are no other symptoms or signs and the EEG shows spikes in the Rolandic area, there is no need to undertake further investigations. If treatment is required, carbamazepine is probably the drug of choice, although valproate may also be used. However, the prognosis is excellent; the fits usually stop by the mid-teens and drug treatment is not essential.

Simple partial seizures with brain lesions

A wide variety of brain lesions may be associated with simple partial seizures. Some of these patients have multiple independent foci of epileptic discharges and may have more than one seizure type. Partial seizures may originate in cerebral scars caused by trauma, meningitis, febrile convulsive status, encephalitis, valves inserted for hydrocephalus, cysts, angiomata and hamartomata, the lesions of tuberose sclerosis, etc. Cerebral palsy, particularly spastic hemiplegia, is often associated with this type of epilepsy. Tumours rarely present with seizures, and do not necessarily cause severe or deteriorating epilepsy. Conversely, epilepsy is rarely due to a tumour. Nevertheless, a CT scan should be carried out in any child who has had one or more simple partial seizures, unless there is an obvious cause or a confident diagnosis of BPERS can be made.

The treatment of children with partial epilepsy associated with brain lesions is difficult and unsatisfactory. It is important to follow therapeutic rules systematically (p. 350). A few patients may benefit from neurosurgery.

Epilepsia partialis continua

In this rare form of epilepsy there is a focal motor seizure, lasting for hours, days or even years. It is often associated with progressive brain disease.

Fits with complex symptomatology

These attacks are also known as psychomotor fits, affective–psychic seizures and temporal lobe epilepsy; but the term 'complex partial seizure' (CPS) is now preferred. The attacks originate in a limited area of the cortex (not necessarily the temporal lobe) and are associated with impairment of responsiveness or awareness. This is a common seizure type and is often difficult to control. The onset may be at any time in childhood, but the diagnosis is often overlooked in the very young, who cannot describe their subjective experiences adequately.

The attacks usually begin with a brief subjective experience known as the 'aura'. There may be an unpleasant epigastric sensation, a nasty smell or taste, complex auditory or visual hallucinations or distorted perception, a feeling of 'having been there before' (*déjà vu*), a disturbance of speech, vertigo, tachycardia, syncope or one of many other similar experiences. The child may behave strangely, sometimes performing complex actions in a disjointed fashion. The child may mumble or talk repetitive nonsense and is likely to be rather 'aggressive' or confused. Laughing or smiling may occur as part of the attack, particularly in profoundly disabled children. (Fits in which laughter is a very prominent manifestation occur in gelastic epilepsy, which is associated with a benign cyst of the third ventricle.) Secondary generalization may occur, causing a 'grand mal' or

tonic–clonic seizure. At the end of the attack, recovery is gradual and there may be postictal confusion, sleepiness and headache.

Frontal lobe seizures

These are an unusual form of CPS. They are associated with complicated motor automatisms such as thrashing or cycling movements, accompanied by vocalizations. They tend to be frequent and often occur during sleep. The attacks may be so bizarre that they are mistaken for hysterical behaviour or sleep disorders.

Behavioural aspects of CPS

A variety of behavioural and personality disorders may be associated with CPS. Hyperactivity and outbursts of rage are more common in children whose epilepsy is associated with other evidence of brain injury and it is not certain how closely they are related to the epilepsy itself. Some children become more irritable and restless prior to a fit, with a remarkable improvement in mood after the seizure. Sometimes it may be difficult to decide whether difficult behaviour is due to a particular anticonvulsant or to the successful abolition of seizures by the medication.

Children with a history of episodic outbursts of undesirable behaviour are sometimes referred with a request to exclude CPS as the immediate cause. In a primary behavioural problem, episodes are usually precipitated by some environmental trigger, however trivial; the behaviour is not bizarre or stereotyped; there is no postictal confusion or headache. It may be tempting to attribute the child's bad behaviour to an organic brain lesion, particularly if the child also has epilepsy or a past history of some cerebral insult, or if the EEG reveals abnormalities.

In reality, however, behaviour problems are very unlikely to be epileptic in origin and a cautious trial of anticonvulsant medication is justified only rarely. It is important to ensure careful monitoring of the problematic behaviour, agree on an endpoint to the trial and avoid periods of time when there are other major changes in the child's life, such as the start of a new school year or change of school placement. A diagnostic label of epilepsy should be avoided unless there is very clear evidence. The alternative diagnosis of episodic dyscontrol syndrome should also be considered; psychiatric advice will be needed if this is suspected.

Complaints of odd psychic experiences, such as depersonalization or *déjà vu*, may be due to CPS, but are much more commonly a manifestation of anxiety. They can follow illnesses such as glandular fever and may also be due to drug misuse, particularly cannabis derivatives or hallucinogens.

Emotional and behavioural disturbances of all kinds are more common in children with epilepsy than in the general population, and this is particularly true of CPS; but there is no specific pattern and no such thing as an 'epileptic personality' in childhood. CPS are, however, associated with an increased incidence of psychiatric illness in adult life. There is a tendency for patients with left hemisphere lesions to develop schizophrenia, while right-sided lesions are said to predispose to affective disorders. Hyposexuality is common in adults with CPS of childhood onset.

Causes

CPS may arise from any localized cerebral lesion and can occur in association with other neurological impairments. Mesial temporal sclerosis may occur secondary to ischaemia caused by febrile status, and epilepsy due to this lesion appears to have a better prognosis. A congenital hamartomatous malformation and indolent tumours account for some cases. Scans sometimes reveal focal or generalized cerebral atrophy with corresponding dilatation of one or both ventricles. Genetic predisposition does not play a large part in CPS.

Diagnosis

Accurate diagnosis is important (see Table 17.2). In CPS, the EEG during an attack may show multiple spikes, slow-wave activity, low-voltage fast activity, flattening of the record, or occasionally 3 Hz spike–wave complexes. Sometimes, however, the attacks arise in deep cortical structures and recording over the scalp surface does not show any abnormality. Thus a normal record, even during an attack, does not completely rule out the diagnosis. Hyperventilation is less likely to induce an attack than in patients with typical absences.

Between attacks, only a third to a half of recordings show spike discharges. These may be unilateral or bilateral and the yield of abnormalities is doubled if recordings are also made during sleep. There may be focal slow-wave activity. Although the EEG more often reveals abnormalities during sleep, CPS are rare in sleep and hardly ever occur exclusively in sleep. Frontal lobe seizures, BPERS and parasomnias (p. 357) should be considered in such cases.

A CT or MRI scan should be performed routinely in any patient with a confident clinical diagnosis of CPS, whatever the EEG findings.

Treatment

The drug of first choice is probably carbamazepine. If this is not effective on its own, it may be combined with sodium valproate, phenytoin or acetazolamide. Vigabatrin is a useful alternative and may become the preferred option. Primidone, phenobarbitone or lamotrigine may also be tried in resistant cases.

Prognosis

Overall, the prognosis for CPS is less good than for primary generalized seizures. A rapid response to therapy is an encouraging sign. Early onset (before 28 months), intellectual retardation and resistant fits indicate that prognosis for recovery and adjustment in adult life should be guarded.

Reflex epilepsies

Of these, photosensitive epilepsy is by far the commonest. Photosensitivity is to some extent an inherited phenomenon, but other factors determine whether the photosensitive individual has clinical epilepsy. Attacks usually begin between the ages of 6 and 15. The usual stimulus is the normal flicker of the TV screen (black-and-white or colour), not a fault in the set. The flicker becomes a more potent stimulus with close proximity. Some children insist on sitting close to the set, presumably finding the sensation pleasant. Occasionally, other sources of flicker, such as sunlight through trees, moving escalators, zebra crossings or striped patterns may cause attacks. It is important for parents to appreciate that, although these stimuli may provoke a seizure, they do not cause the photosensitivity or epilepsy.

Attacks and funny turns that occur in front of the TV or in the disco are not necessarily due to photosensitivity and, indeed, modern disco lights are rarely, if ever, responsible. Other types of epilepsy and syncopal attacks induced by stress, fatigue, alcohol or unpleasant pictures should be considered.

The EEG shows polyspike or spike—wave discharges in response to flicker and these persist after the stimulus has stopped. Treatment is summarized in Table 17.3.

Rarely, other stimuli such as patterns, eye closure, reading, music, arithmetic or immersion in water may cause fits. Fits evoked by sudden noise or touch ('startle epilepsy') occur in children with organic brain damage and in Tay—Sachs disease. Sudden movement may cause dystonic posturing in paroxysmal choreoathetosis. Some children appear to deliberately elicit reflex seizures by various manoeuvres. This 'self-induced' epilepsy is more likely to occur in children with learning disabilities.

Febrile convulsions

Unlike epilepsy, febrile convulsions are unlikely to cause significant disability in their own right.

Table 17.3 Advice and treatment for photosensitive epilepsy

Watch TV from at least 3 m
Room should be well lit, the TV/monitor screen not too bright
Computer/video games hazardous because of intensity of exposure, same pattern for long periods
Do not play computer games when very tired
Use remote control or let someone else adjust set
For very sensitive people, cover one eye with hand if forced to approach set
Polarized sunglasses in bright sunlight
Cinema is safe; very small risk in discos
If above advice not effective: sodium valproate

Developmental disorders later in childhood are often wrongly attributed to 'brain damage' caused by febrile fits. Rarely, prolonged fits (febrile status) may cause brain injury and repeated febrile fits may have some adverse effects on the development of children with pre-existing neurodevelopmental abnormalities, but in most cases the fits are a reflection of the impairment rather than its cause.

Febrile fits are more frequent and more severe in children with pre-existing neurological disorders (cerebral palsy, learning disability syndromes, etc.). Febrile fits in disabled children have a substantial risk of recurrence and are associated with an increased risk of epilepsy.

Management

The risk that the child may develop epilepsy is probably not altered by prophylactic treatment. The best approach is to provide rectal diazepam (5 mg under the age of 3, 10 mg over 3), to be given as soon as the child has an attack, or 12-hourly while the child is unwell. However, anticonvulsant treatment may be justified if the child has several risk factors, particularly pre-existing developmental abnormalities, or if the parents cannot cope with rectal diazepam; in these circumstances, sodium valproate is probably the drug of choice.

The EEG

Parents imagine the EEG answers all questions relating to brain damage, funny turns and even intelligence and personality. The impressive machinery and the chaotic tracing enhance the magic. Some parents confuse it with electric shock therapy. It is important to tell parents in advance the limitations of the investigation and the decisions which will or will not be based on it. They need to know that up to 15% of the general population have an abnormal EEG and up to 40% of people with epilepsy have a normal interictal EEG.

The parents and child should know what to expect; a picture of the EEG room may help. Some children may need heavy sedation (trimeprazine 2–4 mg/kg, or sodium amylobarbitone if a sleep EEG is needed in older children, at least 90 minutes beforehand). If possible, the EEG should be performed before starting anticonvulsants but it is unnecessary to withdraw therapy for performance of an EEG.

The EEG report

The EEG is invaluable in typical absence seizures, Lennox–Gastaut syndrome, infantile spasms or benign focal epilepsy, and may be helpful in the diagnosis of complex partial seizures. However, spike or spike–wave discharges may occur in children who have never had fits and must never be taken as firm evidence of epilepsy when the clinical history is equivocal. Excessive slow activity and unusual responses to hyperventilation or drowsiness are often reported as 'an abnormal record compatible with epilepsy', but they are not themselves sufficient justification for anticonvulsant treatment.

The EEG does not predict the future occurrence of epilepsy. It is of little value in deciding when to stop treatment or in the evaluation of behaviour disorders, learning disability, clumsiness or 'minimal brain dysfunction'.

Special EEG investigations

The EEG (and the electrocardiogram (ECG) if cardiac disorders are a possibility) can be recorded continuously, by telemetry or by a portable cassette-recorder with simultaneous video-recording. Diagnostic problems should be referred to a team with these facilities; too many children are subjected to open-ended trials of drug therapy as a substitute for accurate diagnosis.

Management of epilepsy

An accurate diagnosis is the first essential, since this will influence the advice offered to the parents and teachers. It is better to wait than to make a wrong diagnosis of epilepsy. To the layman, epilepsy can seem a disastrous diagnosis and misconceptions are not confined to the uneducated. The onset of epilepsy in a child who is already disabled may not always create such alarm, as many parents know of the increased risk, but they may still have an exaggerated idea of its significance.

When to start treatment

Some children may have a single seizure due to a combination of circumstances and, if potential trigger factors can be identified, a 'wait and see' policy is usually welcomed by the parents. There are particular problems with undiagnosable 'funny turns' in toddlers, but follow-up shows that these usually have a good prognosis.

Where the diagnosis is uncertain or the fits are very infrequent, parents may be reluctant to start regular medication. Rectal diazepam for emergency seizure control offers a reasonable alternative for preschool children but many teachers worry about its safety and fear possible accusations of sexual abuse, and may therefore refuse to give this in school.

Many severely disabled children have sudden outbursts of crying, unexplained staring or occasional jerking movements. Careful observation over a prolonged period is often more useful than the EEG in such children. Nothing will be lost by waiting and many children will be saved from unnecessary treatment.

Parents' views on treatment

Parents must understand the reasons for treatment and its minimum duration. If they are worried about the fits and want treatment, they can be relied on to give it regularly but, if they are more afraid of the side-effects (real or imagined) than of the fits, compliance is likely to be poor. Therapeutic trials must be carefully planned; the criteria for success must be established and treatment must be stopped if these are not met.

Most parents believe (correctly) that all drugs have side-effects, and it is usually best to tell them the main unwanted actions of the drug(s), describe the excellent safety record of anticonvulsants and invite them to phone if they suspect any problems. This offer is very rarely abused, but gives the parents confidence and acts as a safety mechanism for early detection of serious side-effects.

Epilepsy is a chronic disorder and the patient's records rapidly become incomprehensible. Parents can help by keeping a record of seizure frequency themselves, perhaps using a diary. A tabular or computer-based record simplifies management; one can see at a glance what changes in therapy have been made, and why. Clinic visits can be reduced by judicious use of the telephone and by agreeing in advance whether, and how much, the parents can adjust dosage themselves. It is unreasonable for parents to waste half a day just to report that a child is well and seizure-free. Children with seizures need to be cared for by one doctor, to avoid multiple or ill-judged changes of medication.

Effects of epilepsy on the child

Parents and teachers often believe that emotional upsets or tantrums may precipitate further fits, so they relax their previous levels of discipline, and

behaviour problems may result. The fear that the child may die in a seizure also changes their attitude. In particular, they worry about the possibility of death during sleep and may change their sleeping arrangements, with adverse effects on their own health and their marriage. An additional, often unrecognized, source of transient behaviour disorder is hospitalization. Many of the problems attributed to fits or drugs may simply be a reaction to hospitalization and the associated disruption of relationships, routines and education. Counselling of the child and parents can avoid many problems (Table 17.4).

Educational problems

The paediatrician must decide with the parents what information should be given to the child's headteacher. Most schools will cope very well with a child with epilepsy, provided that they know what to expect, what to do in the event of a seizure and what activities are forbidden, particularly in sports and swimming. A letter to the headteacher, with copies to the school doctor, the GP and the parents, makes it quite clear that responsibility for the child's well-being is shared with the paediatrician and is a great help in integrating the child into mainstream school.

Children with epilepsy are more likely to suffer from educational problems, including poor progress in reading, lack of attention, and behaviour disorders. Several factors may account for these observations. Firstly, the cerebral lesion which gives rise to the epilepsy may also interfere with learning. Secondly, anticonvulsant drugs may impair concentration and learning. Thirdly, there are subtle social and emotional changes both in the children's view of themselves and in the way others treat them. Teachers may set lower standards of behaviour and achievement for children with epilepsy.

When a child with epilepsy is failing in school, several possibilities should be considered including inadequate control of fits, drug intoxication, excessive time off school, underlying progressive brain disease and unrelated problems such as

Table 17.4 Counselling: points for discussion with children and teenagers with epilepsy

- What happens when you have an attack? (child's fantasy may be much worse than the reality — books and videos available to assist in giving this information)
- What should you/your friends/your parents/teachers do if you have an attack?
- What can you do to reduce/avoid attacks? e.g. behavioural methods, getting enough sleep, care with alcohol, discos, etc.
- What can be done to reduce injury if you have an attack? e.g. recognizing premonitory symptoms; reduce risk of burns and fires — plastic kettles, microwave ovens safer than cookers, self-sealing deep-fat fryers, radiator guards, care with bonfires and cigarettes
- Should you wear a bracelet/pendant giving details of your condition?
- What should you do to have the best chance of getting a driving licence? e.g. careful timing of trials of discontinuing therapy (person should be free of fits — on or off treatment — for 1 year; or have fits only occurring in sleep for the past 3 years; for further details contact DVLA Medical Advisory Group, Swansea SA99 1TU.)
- Is it safe to cycle on main roads?
- What sports should you avoid? e.g. caving, hang-gliding, rock-climbing, scuba-diving
- What contraceptives can you use? (danger of enzyme-inducing drugs reducing effectiveness of contraceptive pill; increased dose may be needed)
- What are your chances of passing on your epilepsy to your children?
- What should you tell a prospective college principal or employer?
- What are the dangers of anticonvulsant drugs if you get pregnant?

Advice about swimming and bathing
- Many more deaths occur in the bath than while swimming
- Water in bathtub should not be more than 7.5 cm deep
- Young children should not bath alone
- Older children should not lock the bathroom door
- Showering while sitting in the bath with the drain open is safe
- Showering while standing in a glass-enclosed shower cubicle is not advised
- It is safe to sit on a low stool in the shower cubicle
- Occasional seizures: child may swim with lifeguard or competent swimmer available. Diving is forbidden
- Frequent seizures: child may swim at shallow end only with immediate and constant individual surveillance

---

hearing loss. When these have been eliminated, the problem must be assessed on its educational aspects alone. Although underachievement in children with epilepsy is common, true intellectual deterioration is rare, but it may occur with un-recognized progressive brain disease, episodes of prolonged status and prolonged high blood levels of drugs such as phenobarbitone or phenytoin.

Drug treatment of epilepsy

There is a vast literature on the pharmacology of anticonvulsant drugs, and this section offers only a brief summary of the most important practical points. Data on the standard anticonvulsants are summarized in Appendix 17.1. Carbamazepine and sodium valproate can be regarded as first-line drugs. The newer options such as vigabatrin and lamotrigine have gradually moved from being add-on drugs for intractable seizures to a more established second-line role. Phenytoin and phenobarbitone should now be relegated to a third-line position.

New drugs

Gabapentin has been introduced as a therapy for partial seizures. Felbamate has a spectrum similar to that of valproate or lamotrigine. At the time of writing, their role in paediatric epilepsy has yet to be established.

A treatment plan

If several changes of dosage or medication are needed in order to achieve control of seizures, parents rapidly lose confidence in both the drugs and the doctor. It is therefore helpful to explain how difficult it is to predict which drug will work for a particular child and at what dose, and to set out a treatment plan in the form of a letter, which is given to the family doctor, the parents and (with the parents' permission) to the school. Figure 17.1 suggests a logical approach to the use of anticonvulsants.

Giving medication can be tedious and the regimen needs to be as simple as possible. Many disabled children can be given tablets crushed up in food. If liquids are preferred, extra care with dental hygiene is needed, as most medicines contain sugars. Putting medicine in a feeding-bottle is unwise as the infant may learn to associate the bottle with an unpleasant taste, causing a feeding problem.

Drug level monitoring

Drug level monitoring is neither necessary nor valid in every child with epilepsy (see Table 17.5). The relationship between dose and blood level (Fig. 17.2) is for many drugs reasonably predictable, whereas that between blood level, clinical benefit and adverse effects is often weak. Furthermore, many patients can tolerate, and benefit from, levels that are above the so-called 'normal' range.

If there is an upper limit to the body's ability to metabolize the substance, then, when that limit is reached, a small increase in dose will cause a large rise in blood level. The main example of this is phenytoin, and the level of this drug must always be monitored as it is so unpredictable. In particular, it must be rechecked after adjusting the dose (allowing adequate time to reach a new equilibrium, which may take 2 weeks).

Carbamazepine levels may be checked 3 months after starting therapy, as the drug induces its own metabolism and levels may fall by up to 30%,

Table 17.5 Situations where drug level monitoring may be helpful

All patients on phenytoin
Doubtful compliance
Uncontrolled seizures
High doses, or previous levels near toxic range
Suspected toxic effects
Severely disabled children — toxicity hard to recognize
Multiple drug therapy
Other systemic disease (liver, kidneys, etc.)

leading to breakthrough seizures. Barbiturate monitoring may be useful as it may be difficult to recognize toxicity in the special circumstances where it is used, for example in the profoundly multiply disabled child or the terminally ill (p. 113). Valproate levels are rarely helpful as they have little relationship with therapeutic effect. There is no role for monitoring the levels of vigabatrin, lamotrigine or benzodiazepines.

The need for a blood level should always be considered critically (see Table 17.5). Local anaesthetic cream ('EMLA', Astra pharmaceuticals) can be very useful for apprehensive children who need repeated venepunctures. Saliva sampling has proved to be unexpectedly troublesome in paediatrics and is not widely used. Rapid assay methods (25 minutes) are useful since the result is available while the child is still in the clinic.

Interactions

Anticonvulsants interact with each other, with other drugs and with endogenous substances. Mechanisms include liver enzyme induction and inhibition, and competition for binding sites on plasma proteins (Table 17.6).

Metabolic bone disease

Enzyme-inducing anticonvulsants, particularly phenytoin and barbiturates, accelerate vitamin D metabolism and may cause osteomalacia and bone pain, which may be overlooked in those who are

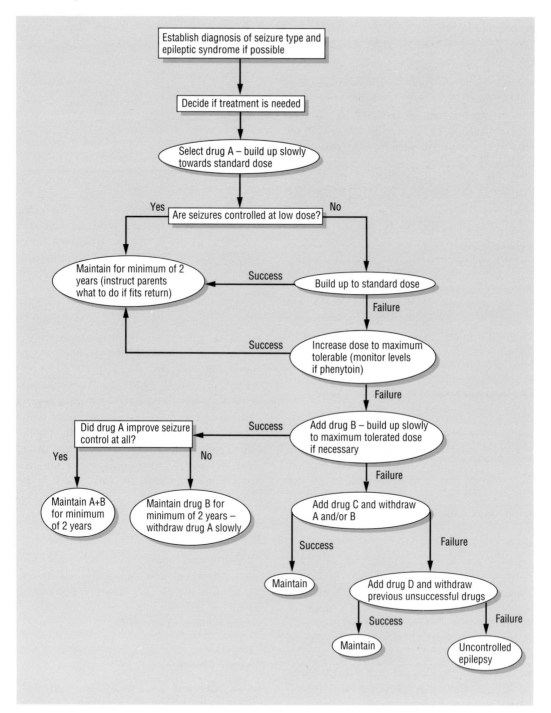

Fig. 17.1 A decision algorithm for difficult epilepsy.

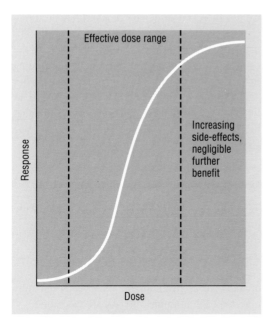

Fig. 17.2 For all drugs, there is a dose–response curve. With very low levels the effect is negligible. At high levels, little extra therapeutic effect is gained by further increases in dosage, but there is often a rapid increase in toxicity. Between these extremes an increase in dose increases the response. In some cases seizures may be abolished with levels at the low end of the range, whereas others may only respond to high levels.

profoundly disabled. Multiple drug therapy, inadequate exposure to sunlight, poor nutrition and muscular inactivity are important predisposing factors. Routine prophylaxis with vitamin D is not recommended but, in high-risk children, the calcium and alkaline phosphatase levels should be checked every 2 years.

Stopping treatment

It is reasonable to try withdrawing treatment if the child has been free of fits for 2 years if the seizures were few in number and easily controlled and for 3 years if the seizures were initially very resistant to treatment. Medication should be reduced slowly (3–6 months) to avoid the risk of withdrawal seizures. The probability of relapse depends on a number of factors (Table 17.7).

The significance of puberty as a cause of increased fit frequency is uncertain, although in autism the onset at puberty of occasional tonic–clonic fits in a previously fit-free child are well documented. Freedom from seizures (on or off drugs) for 1 year is essential before a driving-licence is granted (Table 17.4). Thus it may be more sensible to discontinue medication at age 14 than at 15 so that, if relapse occurs, one fit-free year can still be attained by the age of 16. Some teenagers prefer to continue therapy until they have obtained a licence and completed their education. Their care should be transferred to an adult neurology service; the timing of the hand-over should be decided with the patient.

Table 17.6 Interactions of potential importance in children and teenagers with epilepsy

Carbamazepine, phenytoin, phenobarbitone, primidone (all enzyme-inducers): usually reduced levels when combined
Enzyme-inducers accelerate metabolism of lamotrigine
Sodium valproate inhibits metabolism of lamotrigine
Sodium valproate increases free phenytoin levels; toxicity occurs at lower phenytoin levels
Sulthiame raises phenobarbitone and phenytoin levels by inhibiting metabolism
Enzyme-inducers accelerate metabolism of oral contraceptives: risk of pregnancy
Omeprazole, cimetidine (not ranitidine), cotrimoxazole and isoniazid elevate phenytoin levels
Erythromycin and cimetidine inhibit carbamazepine metabolism; former may raise levels to toxic range in < 5 days
Lamotrigine may produce carbamazepine intoxication in spite of normal levels (due to raised epoxide level)
Aminophylline reduces phenytoin levels
Major tranquillizers are epileptogenic

Table 17.7 Risk of relapse when stopping anticonvulsants

Risk of relapse increased by
Learning disability
Other neurological disease
Difficulty in controlling seizures; large number of seizures
Need for high blood levels of drugs; more than one drug needed
Partial, myoclonic or tonic−clonic seizures
Abnormal EEG*

Relapse rates
Overall relapse rate: 10−30%
Range from 5 to 80% dependent on number of risk factors
Half of all relapses occur in first 3 months
Three-quarters occur in first year

---

* Although the EEG result may increase prognostic accuracy, it is unlikely to change the decision about a trial of anticonvulsant withdrawal.
EEG, electroencephalogram.

Uncontrolled epilepsy

Good control does not necessarily mean total abolition of seizures; this may not be possible, or may only be achieved at the price of severe side-effects. The epilepsy is uncontrolled when the frequency or severity of the seizures or the unwanted drug effects are unacceptable to the child, parents or carers. When a child with epilepsy fails to respond to therapy with first one and then two drugs (as set out in Fig. 17.1) in spite of good compliance, the routine in Table 17.8 is suggested.

Repeated fits with degenerative disease

Recurrent intractable seizures may occur in children with advanced degenerative brain disease. Multiple drug therapy is seldom effective and it may be better to slowly withdraw or at least reduce maintenance therapy; the seizures will probably not get worse and the child may be more responsive and have a better quality of life. Phenobarbitone may be very useful in these patients.

Individual fits can, when necessary, be con-trolled by rectal diazepam or paraldehyde; however, repeated rectal treatment may produce a proctitis, which results in rapid expulsion of the drug solution by the irritable rectum. Continuing fits are distressing for the parents and carers but may not in fact upset the child. It is important, as in other terminal care situations, to ensure that the treatment is not worse than the disease. See also p. 113.

Genetic advice

Teenagers may appreciate information about the inheritance of epilepsy. When the epilepsy is caused by a known neurological disorder, genetic guidance is dependent on the nature of the underlying disease or malformation. The transmission of most forms of idiopathic epilepsy is not fully understood but empirical risks are available.

The teratogenic effects of anticonvulsants have been extensively investigated. There is a small increase in the risk of malformations in children born to epileptic mothers and, possibly, epileptic fathers. It is still uncertain whether the cause of this increase is the epilepsy itself or the use of anticonvulsants, but the use of the latter is undoubtedly preferable to uncontrolled epilepsy. Phenytoin in particular may cause growth deficiency, facial anomalies, digit-nail hypoplasia, and possible orofacial clefts and heart defects. Similar teratogenic effects have been reported with carbamazepine. Valproate therapy is associated with a significant increase in the risk of spina bifida and screening should be offered. Facial and cardiac defects and a variety of developmental and growth problems may also occur.

Non-epileptic 'funny turns'

There are many non-epileptic causes of transient disturbances of behaviour or consciousness. Disabled children are at particular risk of being wrongly diagnosed as having epilepsy.

Table 17.8 An approach to intractable epilepsy

---

1 Review the diagnosis. The child may not have epilepsy at all. The epilepsy may be a different type from that first suspected. Consider pseudoseizures and Meadow's syndrome (p. 359)

2 Is there an underlying focal lesion? Consider a CT scan to exclude this. Is there any evidence of a degenerative metabolic or progressive neurological disease?

3 Examine the child's seizure diary. Did deterioration coincide with introduction of a new anticonvulsant (e.g. carbamazepine can produce minor status)? or an increase in total anticonvulsant load producing sedation? or some other drug given for unrelated reasons (e.g. ciprofloxacin, methylphenidate)? Have the various drug changes made any significant difference to the seizure frequency? If in doubt, consider withdrawal of each drug in turn. Some children actually improve when this is done; many are certainly no worse. Very few patients experience better control on three drugs then they did on two

4 When the diary shows that fits cluster at a particular time of day, a change in dosage times may help, particularly with drugs that have a short half-life. Slow-release preparations may be useful

5 A ketogenic diet is occasionally useful; the advice of a dietitian should be obtained if this is contemplated

6 A therapeutic 'holiday' may restore the effectiveness of benzodiazepines. The drug dosage is reduced over a few weeks, discontinued for 2–3 weeks, then restarted at a low dose. Unfortunately, tolerance usually recurs before very long

7 In some children, notably those with complex partial seizures, full control cannot be achieved even with the most meticulous care. The possibility of neurosurgical treatment should be considered, and advice obtained from a centre specializing in epilepsy surgery. Because of recent technical advances, patients who were thought unsuitable for surgery in the past may now merit re-evaluation

8 In patients with migraine and epilepsy, an oligoantigenic diet may deserve a trial (this is unlikely to help in patients with epilepsy but with no history of migraine)

9 Behavioural measures may be useful in patients whose fits are self-induced, or who have sufficient aura to recognize the onset of an attack. Biofeedback methods have been tried

10 Sometimes the quality of life for child and family may be improved by acceptance of the situation. A fruitless search for a cure may prevent the family from making appropriate plans for the child's future

11 Placement in a special school or unit for children with epilepsy may offer opportunities to make a more precise diagnosis and to undertake further manipulations of therapy in safe surroundings. The relaxed atmosphere where fits are accepted as a fact of life, combined with a regular lifestyle and reliable drug administration, may produce a marked improvement even without changes of medication. Logically, such placements should be funded jointly by health and education authorities

12 Even intractable epilepsy sometimes goes into remission and the family should not be given a completely hopeless prognosis, however discouraged they become

---

CT, computerized tomography.

Breath-holding attacks and reflex anoxic seizures

The most familiar type of breath-holding attack is the *blue, cyanotic* or *type I pattern*. This affects some 5% of children, typically starts in the second year of life, occasionally earlier, and is triggered by angry frustration, injury or a fright so that the toddler cries violently. After a few howls there is silence as breath is held in expiration while the body stiffens in tonic rigidity, rapidly followed by limp immobility. If apnoea is prolonged beyond a few seconds, cyanosis develops and, if protracted, mild clonic movements may occur. Recovery is rapid and complete.

Such attacks may occur when the child is

playing on their own, in which case the diagnosis may be missed. Although the attacks are commonly described as manipulative or 'attention-seeking', they can occur when a parent is not present, and they virtually always subside by the age of 5, irrespective of how parents have reacted. The mechanism is physiological rather than psychological: crying causes hypocapnia, which reduces cerebral blood flow and respiratory arrest. Breath held in expiration is equivalent to a Valsalva manoeuvre and reduces cardiac output. Attacks are more common in anaemic children and may follow a cyclical pattern in children dependent upon periodic blood transfusions, as in sickle-cell disease or thalassaemia.

Less common are *reflex anoxic seizures*, also known as white or type II breath-holding attacks. Sudden pain or fright, particularly in a febrile child, produces an immediate apnoeic collapse, striking pallor and quite often a tonic–clonic seizure secondary to cerebral anoxia. There may be no initial cry at all. The mechanism is bradycardia or asystole caused by vagal inhibition, something which can be simulated by pressing on the eyeballs and demonstrated on an ECG. A reflex anoxic seizure is not epilepsy but its occurrence during a febrile illness can give rise to a misdiagnosis of a febrile seizure. The outcome of a seizure is prompt recovery of breathing and rapid return of consciousness. In the longer term many such children develop syncopal attacks in adolescence.

Breath-holding is generally regarded as a benign problem and treatment is not needed. It is doubtful whether a slap or other painful stimuli are helpful. The child should be left lying flat, in the semiprone position. If the child is picked up and held vertical, cerebral blood flow is reduced further and it seems that the attacks then last longer and recovery is delayed. Telling the parents to ignore the attacks is fruitless and impossible for any parent to follow; it is outdated advice based on a misconception that the attacks are due to attention-seeking behaviour.

Episodes of apnoea and/or bradycardia, and other *apparent life-threatening events* (the so-called

'near-miss cot death' syndrome) should be distinguished from true breath-holding attacks. Admission for observation and investigation may be required. One possibility is episodes of attempted smothering by the mother. This is one form of Meadow's syndrome (Munchausen's syndrome by proxy) (p. 359).

Fainting

If a child faints during prolonged standing, for example in school assembly or waiting in the queue for an immunization, the diagnosis is rarely difficult, but some faints occur without apparent reasons. There is usually, but not always, a preliminary warning of light-headedness or dizziness (not vertigo). Incontinence, tongue-biting and even a brief tonic–clonic episode can occur. If the events preceding the 'blackout' offer no clue, it is worth enquiring about the child's personality. 'Very sensitive', 'squeamish', 'fussy', 'anxious', 'tense' or 'nervy' are all adjectives which are often used to describe children who faint frequently. The parents' own view of what caused the attack may also be useful.

Migraine

Migraine is a familial disorder characterized by recurrent attacks of headache which are widely variable in intensity, frequency and duration. The headache may be accompanied by a variety of focal neurological features, gastrointestinal symptoms and autonomic disturbances.

Common migraine consists of recurrent episodes of headache with nausea or vomiting. In *classical migraine* these features are preceded or accompanied by focal neurological disturbance. *Complicated migraine* refers to cases where there is a neurological deficit which is prolonged beyond the duration of the headache. Young children cannot localize or describe their pain. Abdominal discomfort may be the main complaint and in some cases headache may not be a prominent symptom or may even be absent. Diagnosis may cause particular difficulty in children with hydro-cephalus (p. 159). Migraine-like episodes may also occur in alternating hemiplegia, mitochondrial disorders, and possibly in some metabolic disorders (see Glossary).

The pathogenesis of migraine is very complex and not fully understood. The trigger for the individual attack may be emotion, anxiety, hyperventilation, hormonal changes, intense light or, occasionally, minor trauma to the head (footballer's migraine). The role of foods and food allergies is still uncertain but 'exclusion' diets appear to have some effect on the frequency of attacks.

Focal features include hemiparesis, hemisensory disturbances, ophthalmoplegia, vertigo, visual defects, speech involvement, and drowsiness with mental confusion. The distinction from partial seizures may be difficult, particularly if the child is seen after the attack is over. The evolution of the attack is usually slower than in epilepsy. The headache is likely to occur early in the attack, whereas in epilepsy the headache is postictal. Migraine attacks last longer then epileptic seizures but postictal sleep may confuse the issue. The child with migraine usually retains some degree of rational action, although rarely may present with bizarre behaviour or become unconscious. A positive family history of migraine is helpful, particularly in the case of hemiplegic migraine.

The relationship between migraine and epilepsy is uncertain. They may occasionally coexist, raising the remote possibility of an angioma. Migraine may also provoke a seizure, although this is rare. The EEG is unlikely to clarify the situation as it may also be abnormal in migraine. Also controversial are the links (if any) between migraine, recurrent abdominal pain with vomiting, travel sickness and 'abdominal epilepsy'.

Agonizing continuous or intermittent headaches, with no physical signs and negative investigations, may cause considerable diagnostic problems. Often underlying psychological disturbances can be identified by detailed interviewing, though they may be denied initially.

Headache may also be caused by purely psychological factors, trauma, extra-ocular muscle imbalance, refractive errors, sinusitis, temporomandibular joint dysfunction associated with tension, anxiety and depression, hydrocephalus, tumour, infection, and metabolic disorders.

Management

Emotional disturbance and anxiety, particularly about school, may be amenable to simple advice and discussion and this, coupled with reassurance that the attacks are not of sinister significance, may be all that is needed. Physical examination should include fundoscopy and blood-pressure. However, the diagnosis of migraine rests primarily on the episodic and recurring nature of the symptoms and long-term follow-up may be advisable if there is any doubt about this.

A CT scan should be considered if: the child is very young; the symptoms are unusual or not readily explained; the child is unwell between attacks; the pattern of headache is changing; there is developmental or educational regression; the child is not growing or has a large head.

Treatment

Most children with migraine require only symptomatic treatment such as paracetamol and perhaps an antiemetic such as metoclopramide. Ergotamine by nebulizer is occasionally useful. The role of sumatriptan in childhood is still uncertain. Children whose attacks are frequent and disabling or who have alarming focal features may require prophylactic therapy. Many drugs have been tried; currently the most popular are propranolol and pizotifen.

Hypoglycaemia

Hypoglycaemia in childhood is most often encountered in the following situations: (i) the neonatal period; (ii) various metabolic and endocrine disorders, usually but not always presenting early in life; and (iii) insulin overdosage in diabetic children. Provided that all children with un-explained coma or fits have a blood glucose estimation during the episode, the recognition of hypoglycaemia presents no problem.

Children are often suspected of having hypo-glycaemia as a cause of non-specific symptoms. Apparent recovery with a biscuit or sweet drink is often cited as evidence of hypoglycaemia but this is unwise, for often these children are simply responding to attention or diversion and their symptoms have an emotional basis. If doubt remains after a careful history, arrangements should be made for the child to be seen immediately next time an attack occurs.

Emotional causes of 'funny turns'

Emotional problems are responsible for many unexplained symptoms. The diagnosis is often missed in children with severe intellectual impairment because it is wrongly assumed that such children are not capable of experiencing intense emotions. The presenting complaint may be 'absence attacks' or outbursts of overactivity or aggression. Functional abdominal pain may cause inexplicable misery, pallor and restlessness in young or non-communicating children and may be accompanied by vomiting.

Diagnosis may be complicated because hyper-ventilation — a common response to anxiety — produces a variety of symptoms and may even provoke seizures and possibly migraine in suscep-tible subjects. It takes only a few deep breaths to produce alkalosis, hypocapnia and cerebral vaso-constriction. Symptoms include light-headedness or dizziness (not vertigo), non-specific visual disturbance ('eyes go funny'), a feeling of vague respiratory difficulty, tachycardia, tingling around the mouth and in the extremities, and general anxiety. Dramatic hyperventilation followed by tetany, as described in most textbooks, is relatively rare and represents only the tip of the iceberg of this syndrome.

Common emotional problems which should be considered include: recent separation or other family disruption; change of respite care arrange-ments; bereavement or illness in family or friends; school problems, particularly academic difficult-ies; and relative school failure, where the child is making adequate progress as far as the teacher is concerned but is failing to reach the standards set by the parents or, very often, by the child him/herself. This situation is particularly a problem for the child who has difficulty in communicating their feelings because of mental or physical disability. Lack of friends, boredom, social isolation and depression should be sought in teenagers, particularly those with learning difficulties or communication disorders.

Cardiac disorders

Cardiac arrhythmias should be considered in any child who has unexplained disturbances of consciousness, particularly if associated with exercise. Resting and exercise ECG recordings may be necessary. The QT interval should be measured (see also pp. 211 and 214). Aortic stenosis, cardiac tumours, cardiomyopathy and coronary ischaemia can also occur in children.

Behavioural disturbances

Infantile masturbation occurs mainly in girls. The child looks red in the face, has a glassy expression and perspires, while making violent rocking movements with her hand between her legs. Apart from checking for sources of perineal irritation such as pinworms or chemical irritation (bubble-bath, etc.), no treatment other than distraction and rearrangement of routine is necessary or effective. The activity is quite harmless and eventually subsides. If it is bothersome to adults, the child should be told to do it in private. Attempts to stop it altogether are futile. Worries about child sexual abuse are understandable but usually groundless. Infantile masturbation should not be confused with epilepsy at any age since rocking movements have not been described as a seizure manifestation.

Other so-called gratification phenomena include moving round in small circles and flapping the hands, often with a glazed or self-absorbed expression. Rocking, hand-flapping, eye-poking, head-banging and other self-stimulating behaviours are discussed on pp. 193 and 232. They are only likely to be mistaken for seizures by those unfamiliar with disabled children, but occasionally a sudden break in the activity, associated with a staring expression, may raise the question of absence attacks. Usually they turn out to be a purely behavioural phenomenon.

Tics

These are quick, sudden, repetitive, co-ordinated movements which recur in the same place in the body, always taking the same form. They can be imitated by the child but many children are too embarrassed to do so to order. Common forms include symmetrical eye-blinking, frowning, sniffing, grunting, throat-clearing, head-flicking, shoulder-shrugging and flicking movements of arms or legs. The child can suppress them, especially if on best behaviour, but at the expense of mounting tension, which can only be released by a burst of tics. Thus if tics are suspected in a child who does not manifest them during an interview in the clinic, they can often be seen as the child leaves the room and walks down the corridor. Typically, tics are most likely when the child is passive, as when watching TV or on long car journeys. Correspondingly, they can disappear when the child is engrossed or concentrating hard. Many children show an increase in tics with stress or anxiety but tics are not a symptom of emotional disorder. They seldom present diagnostic difficulty but can be confused with myoclonic jerks, chorea or absence attacks.

Tics are common in normal children between the ages of 6 and 10. A single tic usually subsides over a period of months and can thus be dealt with by explanation and reassurance to both parent and child. Some children have several tics and give a story of one tic fading away over months to be replaced by another one elsewhere in the body. This is the disorder of *chronic multiple tics*, which ultimately has a good prognosis but

can cause the child years of misery through teasing at school and irritable criticism at home. It is hard to treat, although attempts should be made to increase the amount of time the child is actively absorbed and minimize the amount of time watching TV or sitting around. A few children improve through self-monitoring but others find that thinking about the tic brings it on. Haloperidol or clonidine may be effective but many children and families find medication and its side-effects more trouble than they are worth.

Gilles de la Tourette syndrome

This is uncommon. It usually first presents in childhood. It consists of multiple motor tics, of which some are vocal. These can be simple hoots or yelps, but classically (though not constantly) involve swearing. Probably an extreme form of a tic disorder with a strong genetic basis and an association with obsessional disorder, Tourette's syndrome can present with both tics and other complex behaviours, such as compulsions to repeat or copy the utterances or movements of others, carrying out complex movements such as pirouetting or squatting, overactivity or compulsive touching. Although haloperidol, pimozide and clonidine provide good suppression of both tics and complex behaviours, treatment is best supervised by a specialist clinic and the Tourette's Society have a list of such centres.

Sleep disturbances

Simple nightmares are commonplace. They are frightening dreams which can be recalled by the child. Only if occurring several times a week or possessing a repetitive theme should they be considered abnormal and indicative of an emotional disorder.

Night terrors are sometimes described by parents as 'nightmares' but are qualitatively different. They are parasomnias (disturbances of the architecture of sleep) and are precipitated by an explosive emergence from deep (stage IV) sleep into a condition physiologically like wakefulness but actually a dissociated state with disorientation. Thus, after being asleep for about 90 minutes, the child suddenly screams out and may get out of bed. The parents rush in to find the child wide-eyed, evidently terrified, possibly hallucinating and pushing imaginary people (or dinosaurs) away. They cannot get through to the child to comfort or communicate with him/her but may notice that the child's pulse is racing. After a few minutes, the child settles back to sleep and has no recollection of the episode the next day.

Night terrors are more common than often supposed and should usually be met by reassurance (for the parents; the child does not need it, being amnesic for the episode). They do not usually indicate an emotional disorder, although stress can increase their frequency. If troublesome, the parents ensure that the child is settled to sleep at a standard time and time the occurence of the night terror. Once this can be predicted, they wake the child 15 minutes before it is due and keep the child awake for a few minutes before allowing him/her to lapse back into sleep. This is done every night for a week. If it proves impossible to predict a time, an alternative is to suppress stage IV sleep with 2–4 mg of diazepam before bedtime for a month or so to break the cycle.

Some children have difficulty settling themselves to sleep and develop surprisingly violent rocking, head-rolling or head-banging habits which effectively soothe them. Children ordinarily wake at least once during the night but usually settle back to sleep. Those who have difficulty doing so may head-bang during the night too. Occasionally one meets young children who have serious difficulty maintaining sleep and wake frequently during the night, sometimes every 20 minutes. They tend to cry for their parents but may also develop rhythmic habits to settle themselves, usually with the effect of waking the whole household. These self-comforting rhythmic habits subside with time but can be quite disruptive. A metronome set to the frequency of the rocking and slowed gradually night after night can be helpful. Sometimes trimeprazine will gain a short respite but needs to be given no less than 1 hour before bedtime.

Narcolepsy

This commonly starts in adolescence. The characteristic complaint — episodes of irresistible daytime sleep — is unlikely to be missed, although some parents will minimize its significance, blaming it on late nights. The patient should be questioned about cataplexy — a sudden loss of muscle tone causing a fall but no loss of consciousness — which is typically triggered by laughter (or masturbation). There may well be episodes of sleep paralysis at the onset of sleep, which are caused by rapid eye movement (REM) sleep occurring at this time. Surprisingly, teenagers with narcolepsy may complain of poor quality of night-time sleep and the unwary doctor may be misled by such a complaint of insomnia. Further diagnosis and treatment are discussed by Ferber and Kryger (1995).

A few myoclonic jerks at the onset of sleep are a normal phenomenon, as are ritualistic movements of the head or hands while falling asleep. Rhythmic head movements throughout the night are less common (jactatio capitis nocturna).

Vertigo

Benign paroxysmal vertigo is an unusual disorder affecting mainly young children. The attacks of vertigo are sudden and severe but rarely last more than a couple of minutes. There may be pallor, vomiting, sweating and nystagmus. Consciousness is seldom impaired. The child is frightened and remains still, unable to move. Recovery is rapid and complete. The diagnosis is easy if the child can describe their symptoms but is more difficult in the very young. There is no treatment, but the prognosis is excellent. The cause is unknown, although it may be associated with middle-ear disorders in some cases.

Pseudoseizures

Simulated fits are less common in children than in adolescents and adults, but have been observed as early as 4 years of age. They often occur in children who also have genuine epilepsy. Although less common in the intellectually disabled, they may occur in this group. They may be a response to stress or abuse of various kinds. Typically the attacks are generalized clonic rather than partial seizures, but unresponsiveness with loss of postural tone is seen occasionally. Urination, tongue-biting and postictal drowsiness are rare. The serum prolactin does not rise as it does in genuine seizures, but as a distinguishing feature this is not totally reliable. It is important to consider the diagnosis and discuss the possibility before the behaviour pattern becomes entrenched. The advice of a child psychiatrist or psychologist may be required.

Pseudoseizures must be distinguished from factitious epilepsy, in which one parent (nearly always the mother) fabricates a story of seizures, which are never actually observed by anyone else and which do not respond to any standard therapeutic approach. This is one variant of Meadow's syndrome (Munchausen's syndrome by proxy).

References and further reading

Aicardi, J. (1986) *Epilepsy in Children*. Raven Press, New York.

British Medical Association and Royal Pharmaceutical Society of Great Britain (1994) *British National Formulary*, 26. British Medical Association and The Pharmaceutical Press, London.

Buchanan, N. (1994) New choices in anti-epileptic therapy. *Current Paediatrics*, 4(4), 250–3.

Deonna, T. (1993) Cognitive and behavioural correlates of epileptic activity in children. *Journal of Child Psychology and Psychiatry*, 34(5), 611–20.

Ferber, R. and Kryger, M. (1995) *Principles and Practice of Sleep Medicine in the Child*. W.B. Saunders, Philadelphia.

Fish, D. (1992) The place of epilepsy surgery in children. *Current Paediatrics*, 2(2), 73–7.

Hill, P. (1991) Tics and how to handle them. *Current Paediatrics*, 1(1), 36–7.

Hockaday, J.M. (1988) *Migraine in Childhood*. Butterworths, London.

Meadow, R. (1991) Anticonvulsants in pregnancy. *Archives of Disease in Childhood*, 66, 62–5.

O'Donohoe, N.V. (1993) *Epilepsies of Childhood*, (3rd edn). Butterworth-Heinemann, Oxford.

Robb, S.A. and Boyd, S.G. (1991) Which children need an EEG? *Current Paediatrics*, 1(1), 38–9.

Robertson, M.M. (1994) Gilles de la Tourette syndome — an update. *Journal of Child Psychology and Psychiatry*, 35(4), 597–612.

Stephenson, J.B.P. (1990) *Fits and Faints*. Clinics in Developmental Medicine, No. 110. Mackeith Press, London.

Verity, C.M. and Golding, J. (1991) Risk of epilepsy after febrile convulsions: a national cohort study. *BMJ*, 303, 1373–6.

Verity, C.M., Ross, E.M. and Golding, J. (1993) Outcome of childhood status epilepticus and lengthy febrile convulsions: findings of national cohort study. *BMJ*, 307, 225–8.

Wilson, J. (1992) Migraine and epilepsy. *Developmental Medicine and Child Neurology*, 34(7), 645–51.

Appendix 17.1

Drug	Presentation	Dose regimen and levels	Unwanted effects	Comments: use, interactions, etc.
Sodium valproate	Tablets 200 mg, 500 mg. Crushable tablets 100 mg. Syrup and sugar-free liquid, both 200 mg/5 ml. IV also available	10–20 mg/kg/day, increasing to 40 mg/kg/day if necessary. Usually given in two divided doses but many children tolerate and do well on a single daily dose. *Levels*: little correlation between dose and level or between seizure control and level. Rarely helps in assessing compliance or toxicity	Gastrointestinal effects; increased appetite and weight gain; transient hair loss followed by regrowth of more curly hair; oedema; mild bleeding tendency; ataxia and tremor; drowsiness and behavioural changes. Rare: rashes, pancreatitis, blood dyscrasias, gynaecomastia. Increased risk of fetal abnormality, particularly neural tube defects. Teenagers should be warned about this. Liver failure (see comments)	Most children tolerate it well, and side-effects are usually transient and minor, apart from a very rare syndrome of liver damage and encephalopathy. Almost all instances have been in children with pre-existing severe neurological or developmental disorder as well as epilepsy, and usually valproate has been administered in combination with at least one other anticonvulsant. This syndrome usually occurs within the first few months of therapy, and there is a prodromal phase, which usually consists of increased seizures, a flu-like illness, right hypochondrial pain, gastrointestinal disturbance and drowsiness. Some children have had identifiable conditions (e.g. Alper's disease, progressive hepatocerebral degeneration, Huttenlocher's syndrome, ornithine transcarbamylase deficiency). This problem cannot be anticipated by outpatient monitoring of liver function tests and the best protection is probably to warn the parents of this extremely rare complication and to see the child at once if the prodromal features appear
Carbamazepine	Tablets 100 mg, 200 mg, 400 mg. Chewtablets 100 mg, 200 mg. Liquid 100 mg/5 ml. Suppositories 125 mg, 250 mg. Retard tablets 200 mg, 400 mg	Starting dose 5 mg/kg/day, rising slowly if necessary to 20 mg/kg/day. *Levels* vary; recommended therapeutic range 4–13 mg/l (20–50 µmol/l) but some children are drowsy on lower levels and some get optimal control on higher levels. Therefore monitoring is usually of limited value	Gastrointestinal effects. Drowsiness, dizziness, ataxia, behavioural and psychological changes. Visual disturbances at high doses. Leucopenia. Aplastic anaemia. Rash. Liver dysfunction, Stevens–Johnson syndrome, arthralgia, hyponatraemia, cardiac rhythm disturbances. Deterioration of epilepsy; precipitation of non-convulsive status	A first-choice drug for partial seizures and is often useful in generalized epilepsies. Most patients tolerate it well but drowsiness can be troublesome even at standard doses. It is important to start with a small dose and increase over at least 3 or 4 weeks
Phenytoin	Tablets 50 mg, 100 mg. Chewtablets 50 mg. Capsules 25 mg, 50 mg, 100 mg, 300 mg. Suspension 30 mg/5 ml	Starting dose usually 3–4 mg/kg/day, rising to 8 mg/kg/day or more if necessary to maintain levels. Young children better on two doses per day, older children usually tolerate one dose per day. Long half-life, therefore may take up to 2 weeks	Psychological and behavioural changes. Headache. Ataxia, nystagmus and slurred speech in overdose, rashes, acne and coarsening of features, hirsutism, gingival hypertrophy (partially avoidable by good dental hygiene –	Numerous side-effects, in particular the effect on physical appearance. Many drug interactions. Because regular monitoring of blood levels is needed, phenytoin is not a first choice, but is useful when other agents have failed

Drug	Preparations	Dose	Adverse effects	Comments
		to reach steady state before levels meaningful *Monitoring essential. Levels should be* between 10 and 20 mg/l (40–80 μmol/l); for some patients optimal control is only obtained at the upper end of the range, giving a narrow margin between control and toxicity	refer all patients to dentist), megaloblastic anaemia, lymphadenopathy. Rickets and osteomalacia	
Phenobarbitone	Tablets 15 mg, 30 mg, 60 mg. Elixir 15 mg/5 ml	5–8 mg/kg/day. One or two doses per day Monitoring useful in severely disabled children or children on multiple drugs. *Levels* usually 15–40 mg/l (60–180 μmol/l)	Drowsiness, lethargy, depression, hyperactivity and behavioural changes, impaired learning. Rashes, megaloblastic anaemia	Rarely used, as it causes irritability and behaviour change, and probably impairs learning. Better drugs are available. It is cheap and is therefore sometimes the only accessible drug in developing countries
Primidone	Tablets 250 mg. Suspension 250 mg/5 ml	20–30 mg/kg/day in two doses. *Levels*: indications as for phenobarbitone. Usually range is stated as for phenobarbitone	As for phenobarbitone. Rashes may settle on continued administration	Metabolized to phenobarbitone and phenylethylmalonamide. It is only occasionally effective where other drugs have failed
Ethosuximide	Capsules 250 mg. Syrup 250 mg/5 ml	Start at 250 mg/day, can increase slowly to 1.5 g/day if necessary. *Levels* of limited value; usual range 40–100 mg/l (300–700 μmol/l)	Gastro-intestinal effects. Drowsiness, ataxia, headache. Rashes, blood dyscrasias rare.	Used for typical absence seizures. It is cheaper than sodium valproate but provides no protection against tonic–clonic fits. Many children complain of drowsiness, depression and headache, which recover quickly when the drug is stopped
Clonazepam	Tablets 500 μg, 2 mg. Injection available	Start at 125 μg daily and increase very slowly until control obtained. No 'correct' dose of clonazepam; some seizures are controlled with tiny doses. When this happens, the parents should be told that relapse may occur and that they can increase the dose by 0.125 mg (¼ tablet) increments every few days if necessary *Levels* not readily available and of no proven value	Drowsiness, behavioural changes, hypotonia, hypersalivation and bronchial secretion, irritability, withdrawn behaviour	May be effective in various seizure types, particularly the Lennox–Gastaut syndrome. In children with hypertonia, it has the additional benefit of reducing spasticity, although hypersalivation and bronchial hypersecretion are often troublesome. Success with this drug has been limited for two reasons. Firstly, a wide variety of behavioural disturbances occur. This problem can be reduced, but not eliminated, by building up the dose very slowly. Secondly, after a few weeks or months of good control, seizures often recur, and the dose has to be increased, with more risk of behaviour change and decreasing seizure control. A drug 'holiday' sometimes restores effectiveness to some extent. Withdraw slowly (over several weeks) to avoid withdrawal fits. Wait 2 weeks, then restart at 125 μg again

Appendix 17.1 (*continued*)

Drug	Presentation	Dose regimen and levels	Unwanted effects	Comments: use, interactions, etc.
Clobazam	Capsules 10 mg	10−20 mg as single dose in evening *Levels* not available as routine service, not useful	Drowsiness, ataxia, behavioural changes, etc.	Used occasionally for fits with a clearly predictable pattern, e.g. premenstrual, usually only for a short period of time
Vigabatrin	Tablets 500 mg. Sachet 500 mg	Start around 40 mg/kg/day in one or two doses. Exact dose difficult because limited range of preparations but this does not seem to matter. Up to 100 mg/day, more in infantile spasms *Levels* not available or useful	Drowsiness, headache, behavioural changes. Weight gain and gastrointestinal effects. Occasional deterioration in epilepsy (especially myoclonic)	Acts on the GABA enzyme system. It has been used for a range of seizure types, but its main value is for infantile spasms and partial seizures. Behavioural changes are occasionally troublesome and may necessitate withdrawal of the drug. They mainly occur in individuals with a previous history of behavioural or psychological problems. A slow introduction with gradual building up of the dose is essential. Experimental animals show myelin changes but no evidence that this is a problem in humans
Lamotrigine	Tablets 25 mg, 50 mg. Dispersible tablets 5 mg, 25 mg, 100 mg	*Not on valproate:* 2 mg/kg/day in two doses for 14 days, then 5 mg/kg/day for 14 days; maintain usually at 5−15 mg/kg/day *On valproate:* 200 μg/kg/day for 14 days (if calculated dose very small can be given on alternate days), then 500 μg/kg/day for 14 days; maintain at 1−5 mg/kg/day *On phenytoin:* dose may need to be increased *Levels* not available or useful	Malaise, drowsiness, fever, behavioural changes, rash, liver dysfunction, blood dyscrasias, gastrointestinal disturbances. Rarely, rapidly progressive illness with status, multiple organ dysfunction and disseminated intravascular coagulation (uncertain whether caused by lamotrigine)	Acts by preventing the release of excess excitatory amino acids, especially glutamate. It was introduced as a second-line drug for use in partial seizures but is also valuable in children with Lennox−Gastaut syndrome, resistant primary generalized epilepsy, and seizures associated with brain damage. In the latter, cognitive function is sometimes enhanced. The dose adjustments needed when it is used with other anticonvulsants are complicated and it is important to follow the recommended regimen carefully

NB. Mothers taking any of these drugs *except* phenobarbitone can usually continue breast-feeding (*British National Formulary*, 1994). GABA, gamma-aminobutyric acid.

Glossary

Note. With over 2000 syndromes now described, and more added to the list each year, no one person can hope to keep up to date with the literature. The *London Dysmorphology Database* is the best source of information about dysmorphic syndromes. See also Jones (1988), *Smith's Recognisable Patterns of Human Malformation.*

This glossary is included primarily to describe conditions mentioned in the text because of particular diagnostic pitfalls or management implications. Details of organizations and contacts for people with a wide range of disorders and syndromes can be obtained from Contact A Family (address on p. 375).

Abetalipoproteinaemia (Bassen–Kornzweig disease) Coeliac-like syndrome in first year of life; may be accompanied by mild developmental delay. Sensory ataxia. Retinal degeneration with abnormal electroretinogram (ERG). Acanthocytes (burr-like projections on red cells). Low cholesterol. Autosomal recessive. Treatment with vitamin E may arrest progression.

Absence of corpus callosum A computerized tomography (CT) scan finding, not a diagnosis, often with other malformations; many associated conditions and syndromes; occasionally an incidental finding with no developmental abnormalities. If not part of recognized syndrome, mostly sporadic.

Acetazolamide-responsive ataxia Episodes of ataxia, very variable age of onset, frequency and duration. May be normal or mildly ataxic between episodes. Responds dramatically to acetazolamide.

Adrenoleucodystrophy (previously 'Schilder's disease') Demyelinating disease; onset may be sudden, slowly progressive or fluctuating; developmental, behavioural or psychiatric disturbance, followed by spasticity, cortical blindness, seizures. Associated adrenal insufficiency, which may be severe or subclinical. Peroxisomal disorder; elevated levels of very-long-chain fatty acids (VLCFA), abnormal computerized tomography (CT) and magnetic resonance imaging (MRI) scans, visual evoked response (VER) reduced; elevated plasma adrenocorticotrophic hormone (ACTH). Sex-linked recessive. (Treatment with 'Lorenzo's oil' and a diet low in VLCFA still controversial.)

Aicardi's syndrome Infantile spasms with variable electroencephalogram (EEG) changes, lacunar retinopathy looking like Swiss cheese, agenesis of corpus callosum. Other cerebral malformations. Severe psychomotor retardation. Sporadic, only occurs in girls.

Albright's hereditary osteodystrophy See Pseudohypoparathyroidism.

Alexander's disease Onset first year. Macrocephaly. Seizures. Deterioration at variable speed, can be very insidious. Precise cause unknown, may be autosomal recessive.

Alpers' disease Grey-matter degeneration. Some have liver disease. Vomiting, intractable seizures, often myoclonic; spasticity; mental deterioration. Probably includes several conditions, e.g. Huttenlocher's syndrome, which may be underlying diagnosis in valproate-associated liver failure.

Alpha-thalassaemia mental handicap syndrome Severe to profound mental handicap. Mild and variable anaemia. Haemoglobin H (HbH) inclusion bodies staining with brilliant orthocresol blue. Hypertelorism, small nose, carp mouth with tendency to dribble, small genitals, club feet. X-linked. Female carriers have normal intellect but may have minor physical features and subtle blood findings.

Alport syndrome Deafness presenting in late childhood or adult life; microscopic haematuria, nephritis, renal failure in fifth decade.

Alternating hemiplegia Migraine-like condition with onset before 18 months of age; attacks of hemiplegia affecting either side of body; mental deterioration; permanent deficits. May respond to flunarizine.

Angelman's syndrome (previously 'happy puppet syndrome') Delayed development from infancy, late walking, jerky ataxia, prominent lower jaw, wide mouth, tongue thrusting, happy disposition with unprovoked laughter, disproportionately severe impairment of speech and communication, typical EEG abnormalities, onset of fits often by 2 years of age, small head, hypopigmentation. Fifteen per cent are familial cases; some sporadic cases have deletion on maternally derived chromosome 15q11–13.

Apert's syndrome Craniosynostosis, particularly of coronal suture. Syndactyly. Small nose. Narrow or cleft palate. Variable degree of learning disability. Numerous other occasional anomalies. Dominant; most cases are new mutations.

Ataxia–telangiectasia syndrome (Louis–Bar syndrome) Progressive ataxia and involuntary movements, abnormal eye movements. Immunoglobulin A (IgA) deficiency, respiratory and ear infections, telangiectasia on conjunctiva and later on nose, elbows, etc. Lymphoma. Poor growth. Variable learning disability. Investigations: low IgA, elevated α-fetoprotein, abnormal sensitivity to radiation of cultured fibroblasts. Autosomal recessive.

Bardet–Biedl syndrome See Laurence–Moon–Biedl syndrome.

Basal cell naevus syndrome (Gorlin syndrome) Jaw cysts and abnormal teeth; prominent forehead and wide face; various learning difficulties; unusual tumours of ovaries, brain, other organs; skin pits, basal cell naevi in childhood with risk of carcinomatous change; may have macrocephaly, with calcified falx; numerous other features. Autosomal dominant. Gene mapped to chromosome 9q.

Bassen–Kornzweig disease See Abetalipoproteinaemia.

Batten's disease see Neuronal ceroid lipofuscinosis.

Beckwith–Wiedemann syndrome (EMG syndrome — exomphalos, macroglossia, giantism) Birth weight averages 4 kg; rapid growth, severe neonatal hypoglycaemia, large tongue, omphalocele, creases in ear lobules. Occasional hemihypertrophy, tumours. Learning disability variable, possibly related to hypoglycaemia. Sporadic, or autosomal dominant with variable penetrance.

Behr syndrome Bilateral optic atrophy, spastic diplegia, learning disability with onset in early infancy, may remain static for many years. Autosomal recessive.

Biotinidase deficiency Early onset of convulsions resistant to therapy but improving spontaneously; hypotonia, ataxia, regression, alopecia, skin rash. Later deafness and optic atrophy. May be missed by other metabolic 'screening' tests, specific test available. Biotin is effective treatment if given early.

Blepharophimosis syndrome Ptosis, widely separated inner canthi, short palpebral fissures. Intelligence quotient (IQ) usually normal. Two types, female infertile in type 1. Both autosomal dominant.

Branchio-otorenal syndrome (Melnick–Fraser syndrome) Hearing loss (sensorineural, conductive or mixed). Preauricular ear pits. Branchial fistula or cysts. Renal anomalies. (NB. Preauricular pits alone are common.) Check kidney function if syndrome suspected. Autosomal dominant, variable expression.

Canavan's disease Spongiform leucodystrophy. Onset first few months. Delayed development, optic atrophy, hypotonia. Macrocephaly. Abnormal computerized tomography (CT). Aspartoacylase deficiency. Autosomal recessive.

Cerebral giantism See Soto's syndrome.

CHARGE association Colobomata (isolated defects to anophthalmos); heart defect; atresia choanae; retarded growth, usually postnatal, and retarded psychomotor development; genital anomalies and/or hypogonadism; ear anomalies and/or deafness. Usually sporadic but occasional recurrence in same family; cause unknown.

Cockayne's syndrome Onset at 2–4 years of age. Growth failure, deafness, retinal degeneration, photosensitive rash, etc. Appearance of premature ageing. Deterioration in gait and intellect. Computerized tomography (CT) shows atrophy, basal ganglia calcification. Increased sensitivity of fibroblasts to ultraviolet (UV) light. Autosomal recessive.

Coffin–Lowry syndrome Learning disability, coarse facies, large hands with tapering fingers, abnormal vertebrae. Risk of paraplegia and epilepsy later in life. X-linked semidominant inheritance.

Congenital chorea Choreiform movements commencing early in life, non-progressive, not associated with any other handicap. Can be recessive or dominant.

Congenital cytomegalovirus infection The features are low birth weight, microcephaly, periventricular intracranial calcification, spasticity, retardation, deafness, chorioretinitis, hepatomegaly, splenomegaly, anaemia and thrombocytopenia, pneumonitis, bone lesions.

Congenital insensitivity to pain Now regarded as a subtype of hereditary sensory neuropathy (q.v.).

Congenital myopathies A heterogeneous group of conditions with abnormal muscle structure and function. Includes: central core disease, minicore disease, nemaline myopathy, congenital fibre-type disproportion and many others. Also metabolic disorders such as glycogenoses.

Congenital pseudobulbar palsy Caused by bilateral upper motor neuron lesions of the motor tracts supplying the lower cranial nerve nuclei. There is gross incompetence of all movements of lips, tongue and palate. Dribbling is a persistent problem. The lesion may predominantly affect the palate, in which case the picture is that of cleft palate speech without a cleft palate. The brisk jaw jerk distinguishes this disorder from those caused by nuclear agenesis or lower motor neuron lesions.

Congenital rubella infection The general features are intrauterine growth retardation and delayed postnatal growth. Nervous system: microcephaly; severe learning disability; spastic diplegia; hearing loss (may progress in first 2 years); autism, and other communication impairments, disproportionate to hearing and vision defects;

retinopathy ('pepper and salt') — does not impair vision; microphthalmia; cataract; glaucoma; hydrocephalus (very rare); subacute sclerosing panencephalitis (SSPE)-like illness (very rare). Heart: patent ductus; pulmonary stenosis; aortic stenosis; renal artery stenosis; ventricular septal defect (VSD); myocarditis. Other features include thrombocytopenia, hepatosplenomegaly, hepatitis and jaundice, bone lesions, pneumonitis, rash, adenopathy, hypogammaglobulinaemia, abnormal dermatoglyphics, diarrhoea, diabetes, growth hormone deficiency, pancreatic deficiency, hypothyroidism. For risks of congenital infection, see Table G1.

Congenital varicella Unusual outcome of maternal varicella between 8 and 19 weeks' gestation. Hypoplasia of limb. Cutaneous scars. Chorioretinitis. Growth deficiency. Learning disability.

Cornelia de Lange syndrome Pre- and postnatal growth retardation. Learning disability (often severe). Bushy eyebrows meeting in midline. Thin lips with midline 'beak' of upper lip. Limb deficiencies, and hirsutism. Mild cases are difficult to diagnose with confidence. High risk of aspiration pneumonia in infancy (associated with pyloric stenosis) and of other infections. Sporadic; recurrent risk small; various chromosome defects such as micro-deletions have been observed to produce phenocopies.

Craniofacial dysostosis See Crouzon's syndrome.

Cri-du-chat syndrome (Partial deletion short arm chromosome 5, 5p−syndrome) Low birth weight, slow growth, cat-like cry, round facies, developmental retardation, microcephaly. Many other features described.

Crouzon's syndrome (Craniofacial dysostosis) Craniosynostosis, hypoplasia of maxilla, parrot-like nose, shallow orbits, abnormal teeth, deafness. Learning disability not a major feature. Dominant, with variable expression. Shallow orbits may be the only feature. May be new mutation.

Dandy−Walker syndrome Hydrocephalus and cystic dilatation of the fourth ventricle associated with obstruction of the outlet foramina. Large, sometimes transilluminable posterior fossa. Other cerebral malformations. Congenital heart disease. Sporadic or recessive.

Devic's disease (Neuromyelitis optica) Optic neuritis and transverse myelitis causing paraparesis, occurring together or in succession.

DIDMOAD syndrome Diabetes insipidus, diabetes mellitus, optic atrophy and deafness. Autosomal recessive.

Dopa-responsive dystonia (Segawa's syndrome, Hereditary progressive dystonia with diurnal variation) Onset between 1 and 10 years; equinovarus posturing and gait disturbance, frequent falls, starts in one limb and spreads slowly to others. No intellectual deterioration. Symptoms briefly relieved by sleep (but this feature may be absent). With early onset, has been mistaken for ataxic or spastic diplegic cerebral palsy. Responds to L-dopa 5−30 mg/kg/day, with carbidopa. Usually quick response but may need 1−2-month trial. No easy diagnostic test other than therapeutic trial. Probably autosomal dominant.

Dystonia musculorum deformans Variable onset, rarely before age 3. Bizarre posturing of feet, wrist, neck,

Table G1 Congenital rubella: risk of infection and of defects

	Risk of congenital infection (%)
If mother symptomatic in first trimester	> 80
Asymptomatic proven rubella in first trimester	Exact risk uncertain but much less
Maternal infection 13−16 weeks	∼ 50
Maternal infection 17−36 weeks	∼ 40
Maternal infection 36 weeks−term	∼ 100

	Risk of defects caused by congenital infection (% of infected babies)
Infection in weeks 2−11	> 90
Infection in weeks 12−16	± 30
Infection beyond week 17	Very low

Type of defect
Multiple defects:	infection before 8 weeks
Cardiac defects:	only if infection occurs before 11 weeks
Isolated deafness:	13−17 weeks, extremely low risk 17−22 weeks

trunk. Involuntary movements increasingly severe. Early stages easily mistaken for hysteria. Several variants: recessive form (mainly Ashkenazi Jews); dominant form — all races. Stereotactic surgery may help.

Dystrophia myotonica Congenital form: hypotonic infant. Flat immobile face with open triangular mouth. Talipes, dislocated hips and other joint deformities. Feeding problems. High diaphragm. High mortality in first 18 months of life. Learning disability common but not invariable. Myotonia unusual in childhood. Constipation, reflex anal dilatation. Muscle weakness and poor muscle bulk. Cardiac arrhythmia predictable by regular electrocardiogram (ECG). Increased risk of anaesthetic death. Mother often has myotonia, abnormal electromyogram (EMG) and raised creatine phosphokinase (CPK) levels. Tends to improve in first decade but weakness and myotonia progress later. Gene location, 19q13: the gene is an unstable deoxyribonucleic acid (DNA) triplet (cytosine—thymine—guanine (CTG)) which is grossly expanded (cf. fragile-X).

Ectodermal dysplasia Abnormalities of sweating, nails, hair and teeth. Hyperthermia, which may cause learning disability. Language defect. Several forms with variable inheritance.

Edwards' syndrome (Trisomy 18) Incidence 1:3000 births, female:male ratio is 3:1. Growth deficiency (mean birth weight 2340 g), polyhydramnios, small placenta, single umbilical artery. Severely delayed development, hypertonicity. Low-set ears, short palpebral fissures, small mouth and jaw. Clenched hands, index finger overrides third and fifth overrides fourth. Small nipples, herniae, diastasis recti. Reduced hip abduction. Cryptorchidism. Redundant skin. Congenital heart disease. Many other anomalies described. Severe failure to thrive. Probably less than 10% survive first year. Most cases are full trisomy 18 but translocation cases occur. Partial trisomy is associated with less severe features and longer survival.

EEC syndrome Ectrodactyly (limb reduction defects), ectodermal dysplasia, cleft lip and palate. Abnormalities of teeth, hair, occasional deafness. Intelligence usually normal or near-normal. Autosomal dominant.

Ehlers—Danlos syndrome Hyperextensible joints and skin, easy bruising, slow wound-healing with tissue-paper scars, subcutaneous mobile nodules, fragility of blood-vessels. At least 12 types known, with variable severity and inheritance, but likely to be reclassified when basic defects identified.

EMG syndrome See Beckwith—Weidemann syndrome.

Facioauriculovertebral anomalad (First and second arch syndrome, Goldenhaar's syndrome). Asymmetric or unilateral anomalies of mouth, face, pinna, inner ear,

hemivertebrae. Dermoid cysts of eyes. Microphthalmos. Mild learning disability. Usually sporadic.

Familial dysautonomia (Riley—Day syndrome) Virtually confined to Jews from Eastern Europe. Disorder of autonomic nervous system. Neonatal problems. Absent tears. Unstable blood-pressure and temperature control. Dysphagia. Psychomotor retardation. Corneal ulcers. Reduced pain sensitivity. Anaesthesia hazardous. Autosomal recessive. Several other forms of indifference to pain.

Familial myoclonus epilepsy Onset in mid-childhood. Severe myoclonic epilepsy. Dementia. Recessive. (Several other syndromes including myoclonic epilepsy are known.)

Fanconi's syndrome Small stature, microcephaly, learning disability. Various central nervous system (CNS) anomalies including hydrocephalus. Thumb and other limb abnormalities, pancytopenia, skin pigmentation. Poor growth and tendency to infections. High risk of leukaemia. Autosomal recessive.

Fetal alcohol syndrome The features are pre- and postnatal growth deficiency, average intelligence quotient (IQ) 63, fine motor incoordination, microcephaly, short palpebral fissures, ptosis, maxillary hypoplasia, joint anomalies, thin vermilion upper lip with absent philtrum.

FG syndrome Hypotonia, short stature, megalencephaly with or without hydrocephalus (postnatal onset). Hypertelorism, short palpebral fissures, small ears, narrow palate. Imperforate anus and other bowel defects, cardiac defect. X-linked recessive.

First and second arch syndrome See Facioauriculovertebral anomalad.

Floating Harbour syndrome Short stature, characteristic facies, severe expressive language delay. Cause unknown.

Franceschetti—Klein syndrome See Treacher—Collins syndrome.

Friedreich's ataxia The commonest hereditary spinocerebellar degeneration. Presenting sign is often ataxic gait. Dysarthria, nystagmus, clumsy hands. Pes cavus (may rarely be presenting feature and only sign for many years). Absent or reduced tendon jerks with extensor plantars. Abnormal sensory nerve conduction. Kyphoscoliosis. Wasting of small muscles of hands. Cardiomegaly and arrhythmmias. Diabetes. Mean age of onset 10 years. Become wheelchair-dependent, usually in adult life. Recessive; gene on chromosome 9.

Galactokinase deficiency Cause of cataracts early in life without other features of galactosaemia. Incidence 1:100 000—150 000 births. Autosomal recessive.

Galactosaemia Severe neonatal illness with liver dysfunction and cataracts. Dietary treatment involves elimination of lactose and galactose from diet. Even with early treatment there is slight reduction of intelligence quotient (IQ), visual perceptual skills and 50% have speech−language problems. Incidence 1:60 000 births. Autosomal recessive.

GM2 gangliosidosis See Tay−Sachs disease.

Goldenhaar's syndrome See Facioauriculovertebral anomalad.

Gorlin syndrome see Basal cell naevus syndrome.

Hallermann−Streiff syndrome Small stature, micrognathia, small nose, cataract and microphthalmos, hypoplasia of skin, hair and teeth. Variable intellect, may be normal or retarded. Probably dominant; most cases are new mutations.

Hallervorden−Spatz disease Foot deformity, abnormal gait, rigidity, athetosis, intellectual deterioration, dysarthria. Autosomal recessive.

Happy puppet syndrome See Angelman's syndrome.

HARD ± E syndrome See Warburg syndrome.

Hartnup disease Intermittent cerebellar ataxia and other personality and behavioural changes. Retardation variable. Photosensitive rash. Aminoaciduria. Defective transport of tryptophan and other neutral amino acids.

Hereditary arthro-ophthalmopathy See Stickler syndrome.

Hereditary sensory neuropathy At least five subtypes described and many very rare variants. Sensory neuropathy; some have hearing loss and/or learning disability. Indolent ulcers on fingers and feet, neuropathic joints. Self-mutilation in some types. Familial dysautonomia is type III. Variable progression and inheritance.

Homocystinuria Variable psychomotor retardation, sometimes waddling gait. Vascular occlusions with infarcts. Malar flush, livedo reticularis (mottling over shins). Fair skin and hair. Ectopia lentis and iridodonesis (wobbly iris). Osteoporosis. Arachnodactyly in some. Can be mistaken for Marfan's. Autosomal recessive. Dietary changes and vitamin supplements may help.

Huntington's chorea About 5% of cases begin in childhood and arise from paternal transmission. Rigidity. Reduced movements. Chorea. Dementia. Seizures (may be main symptom) and mental retardation. Ataxia. Rapid deterioration. Dominant; due to expanded triplet repeat.

Hypoparathyroidism Cataract, photophobia, ridging of teeth, tetany, fits, extrapyramidal disease, mental deterioration.

Hypothyroidism Neonatal features: characteristic facies (can be mistaken for Down's syndrome), macroglossia, underdeveloped nasal ridge between eyes, umbilical hernia, oedema, goitre, large fontanelles, bradycardia, prolonged jaundice. First few months: lethargic, slow to feed, constipation, cold peripheries, respiratory infections, hypothermia, deafness. Later: short stature, mental retardation, delayed bone age, squint, abnormal gait; pyramidal signs, tremor, skeletal muscle abnormalities, ataxia, 'clumsiness'.

Immotile cilia syndrome See Primary ciliary dyskinesia.

Incontinentia pigmenti Bullous skin lesions in infancy progressing to variable hyperpigmented areas. Fits; learning disability; eye, teeth and hair defects. Sporadic or X-linked dominant. Chromosome mosaicism in skin cell lines.

Jervell Lange Nielsen syndrome Deafness; potentially lethal cardiac arrhythmias associated with prolonged corrected QT interval, QT_c (should not exceed 0.425).

$$QT_c = \sqrt{\frac{QT \text{ measured}}{\text{cycle length (R-R interval)}}}$$

Joubert's syndrome Episodic hyperpnoea (intermittent shallow respiration at a rate of up to 180, like a dog panting) and jerky eye movements, in early infancy; movement disorder, predominantly ataxic in type with cerebellar vermis hypoplasia; learning difficulties; may be associated with retinal dystrophy as in Leber's retinal dystrophy. Autosomal recessive.

Kinky hair disease See Menkes' disease.

Kjellin syndrome Spastic diplegia, distal amyotrophy, macular degeneration.

Klinefelter's syndrome (XXY syndrome) Tall, slim with long limbs. Mild reduction in intelligence quotient (IQ) (average 10−15 points below siblings). Speech and language problems. Fine intention tremor. Behavioural and social problems. Hypogonadism, infertility. Gynaecomastia.

Klippel−Feil syndrome Low posterior hairline, short neck, limited neck movements, fusion of cervical vertebrae. Scoliosis. Sprengel shoulder (abnormal and high scapula). Renal anomalies. Synkinesia. Ptosis. Mirror movements. Cleft palate. Sporadic. May be associated with deafness and Duane's syndrome (Wildervall syndrome).

Krabbe's disease Globoid body leucodystrophy. Infantile form: early onset of vomiting, failure to thrive, crying, slow development followed by regression. May be exaggerated startle. Peripheral neuropathy with reduced reflexes. Progressive deterioration. Can be mistaken for cerebral palsy initially. Abnormal computerized tomography (CT), reduced nerve conduction velocity, elevated cerebrospinal fluid (CSF) protein, reduced galactocerebrosidase activity. Autosomal recessive.

Larsen's syndrome Multiple joint dislocation, shortened nails and metacarpals, flattened facies, foot deformities.

Normal intellect. Inheritance may be either dominant or recessive.

Laurence−Moon−Biedl syndrome (Bardet−Biedl syndrome) Obesity, polydactyly, learning difficulties (not universal), retinitis pigmentosa, hypogonadism. Renal hypoplasia, hydronephrosis, hypertension. Less common: ataxia, deafness, macrocephaly, syndactyly. Probably autosomal recessive.

Leber's disease (NB. Do not confuse with Leber's amaurosis.) Sudden loss of vision, usually in second decade but may present in early childhood; cerebellar signs, spasticity, seizures, learning disability. Due to mitochondrial mutation.

Leigh's disease (Necrotizing encephalomyelopathy) Early onset. Hypotonia with brisk reflexes. Abnormal eye movements. Elevated lactic and pyruvic acids.

Leopard syndrome See Multiple lentigines syndrome.

Lesch−Nyhan syndrome A sex-linked disorder of hypoxanthine metabolism. Excessive production of uric acid. Psychomotor retardation in first year, extrapyramidal movements in second year, progressive spasticity later in life. Severe involuntary self-mutilation (this does not respond to behavioural methods of treatment; restraint, tooth guards and similar measures are necessary). Renal disease and gouty arthritis. Learning disability variable, not severe. Diagnosed by serum uric acid or (better) by uric acid : creatinine ratio in urine.

Leucodystrophy A general term for a group of disorders characterized by widespread and usually symmetrical demyelination of brain white matter. Includes metachromatic leucodystrophy, Krabbe's disease, adrenoleucodystrophy.

Louis−Bar syndrome See Ataxia−telangiectasia syndrome.

Lowe's syndrome (Oculocerebrorenal syndrome) Severe psychomotor retardation; hypotonia; glaucoma and/or cataract; aminoaciduria. Sex-linked recessive.

Mandibulofacial dysostosis See Treacher−Collins syndrome.

Maple syrup urine disease See Organic acidaemias.

Marfan's syndrome Tall stature with span greater than height, arachnodactyly, joint laxity, scoliosis, narrow face, upwards dislocation of lens, myopia, aortic valve abnormalities, dissecting aneurysm of ascending aorta. Normal intelligence. Gene located on chromosome 15; abnormal protein (fibrillin). Autosomal dominant with variable expression. Can be mistaken for homocystinuria. (Marfanoid body build also seen in normals, particularly in Negroid subjects.)

Marinesco−Sjögren syndrome Cerebellar ataxia, weakness, cataracts, scoliosis. Autosomal recessive.

McArdle's disease (Type V glycogen storage disease) Rapid fatigue and cramps on exercise, recovering after rest. Raised creatine phosphokinase (CPK) levels. Autosomal recessive.

Meckel−Gruber syndrome Encephalocele, other craniofacial malformations; polydactyly; renal dysplasia; many other lesions described. Short survival. Main importance is inheritance − autosomal recessive − in contrast to isolated encephalocele.

Megalencephaly Large head due to hamartomatous malformation of brain with hydrocephalus. Psychomotor retardation, occasionally progressive. Fits. Other congenital anomalies. Uncertain whether it is a single entity. Important to exclude other causes of macrocephaly. Probably sporadic in most cases. Occasional reports of dominant or recessive inheritance.

Melnick−Fraser syndrome See Branchio-otorenal syndrome.

Menkes' disease (Kinky hair disease) Seizures and rapid psychomotor deterioration in early infancy. Sparse, short, lightly pigmented abnormal hair. Abnormal copper metabolism. X-linked recessive.

Metachromatic leucodystrophy Several variants: may present in toddlers with gait disorder and deterioration; or in early-school-age children with either gait or intellectual deterioration. Absent ankle reflexes with pyramidal signs often found. Aryl sulphatase deficiency. Autosomal recessive.

Miller−Dieker syndrome Microcephaly, abnormal brain development with lissencephaly (smooth brain); psychomotor retardation and seizures. Poor prognosis. Deletion of chromosome 17p.

Mitochondrial cytopathies A group of disorders characterized by abnormal mitochondria on muscle biopsy. Kearns Sayre syndrome − progressive ophthalmoplegia, ptosis, retinitis pigmentosa, short stature, hearing loss, ataxia, weakness, learning disability. May be multisystem disorder affecting cardiac function, endocrine glands, kidneys, etc. Inherited by maternally derived mitochondrial deoxyribonucleic acid (DNA). Can be associated with stroke-like episodes or with myoclonic epilepsy and ataxia. 'Ragged red' fibres on muscle biopsy.

Möbius (Moebius) syndrome Congenital facial diplegia and bilateral external rectus muscle palsy. There may also be paresis of tongue, palate and larynx, with gross dysarthria. The clinical signs vary considerably. A few cases have also had limb anomalies such as talipes, absence of the pectoralis muscle, deafness, cleft palate, mild pyramidal signs and mild mental handicap. Although there are at least two recorded cases of familial occurrence, in the vast majority the condition appears to be sporadic.

Moya-moya syndrome An angiographic diagnosis; dilatation of small blood-vessels, forming a collateral circulation, in association with carotid occlusion.

Mucopolysaccharidoses (MPS) A group of storage disorders with deficient activity of lysosomal enzymes, leading to accumulation of complex polysaccharides in various organs. All autosomal recessive, except MPS II (Hunter's), which is X-linked.

MPS I (Hurler) is best known: early onset of facial coarsening, lumbar kyphosis, stiff joints and contractures, corneal clouding, enlarged liver and spleen, psychomotor deterioration. Arachnoid cysts, may cause visual impairment. Hearing loss (conductive or sensorineural). Cardiac disorders.

MPS II (Hunter): mid-childhood regression and apathy, deafness, no corneal clouding, unexplained diarrhoea; otherwise similar to MPS I.

MPS III (Sanfilippo): early childhood regression with mobility retained and often hyperactive or aggressive behaviour, but physical features less obvious, no corneal clouding. Unexplained diarrhoea.

MPS IV (Morquio): intellect not affected, severe dwarfing, kyphosis, knock-knees, conductive deafness, late sensorineural deafness and corneal clouding, risk of atlantoaxial subluxation with gradual cord compression (avoid head stands and diving: may need surgical stabilization), carpal tunnel syndrome. Heart lesions.

Many other types and subtypes of MPS (e.g. Scheie, Maroteaux–Lamy); mucolipidoses and GM1 gangliosidosis share some features. NB. will not be detected by mucopolysaccharide urine screening test.

All MPS types Diagnosis by urinary mucopolysaccharide measurement and specific enzyme assays. Monitor for neurosurgical complications as listed, vision and hearing loss, cardiac defects. Arachnoid cysts treatable but corneal grafting not successful. Upper airway problems common; expert anaesthesia essential. Treatment prospects progressing rapidly — contact bone marrow transplant centre, clinical geneticist or voluntary organization for advice and literature.

Multiple lentigines syndrome (Leopard syndrome) Multiple 1–5-mm dark skin lesions; pulmonary stenosis; deafness; variable retardation. Dominant.

Muscular dystrophies Disorders characterized by degenerative process in muscle fibres. (The term myopathy refers to any primary disorder of muscle.) Duchenne and Becker: see pp. 290–2.

Emery–Dreifuss muscular dystrophy: wasting of the upper arm muscles and leg muscles, particularly the peronei; elbow contractures developing early in the course of the disease; cardiomyopathy with conduction defects and increased risk of sudden death. Onset can be in early childhood; the myopathy progresses slowly. X-linked recessive.

Facioscapulohumeral dystrophy: facial weakness from infancy, unable to close eyes; immobile upper lip with fancy, unable to close eyes; immobile upper lip with speech impairment and pouting expression; shoulder girdle and upper arm weakness; foot drop and tight heel cords. Spinal deformity. Raised creatine phosphokinase (CPK). Dominant or sporadic. Several other forms, less well defined.

Nectrotizing encephalomyelopathy See Leigh's disease.

Neurofibromatosis Two types: Table G2 shows features of NF1. NF2 is much less common — associated with familial acoustic neuromas (rare in childhood).

Neuromyelitis optica See Devic's disease.

Neuronal ceroid lipofuscinosis (Batten's disease) Late infantile form (Bielschowsky–Jansky): presents typically at the end of the second year with regression followed by fits. Characteristic electroencephalogram (EEG) and visual evoked response (VER). Juvenile form is more common (Spielmeyer–Vogt): visual failure with pigmentary retinopathy between 5 and 8 years of age; fits; gradual dementia and loss of mobility; episodes of anxiety in teens. Death in teens or early 20s. Abnormal EEG and electroretinogram (ERG), rectal biopsy to confirm. Gene for Batten's located on chromosome 16. Autosomal recessive.

Neuronal migration disorders Disturbance of the process whereby nerve cells migrate from their origins in the ventricular zones to their permanent orderly layers, reaching its peak between third and fifth months. Many possible causes (neurocutaneous syndromes, other single-gene disorders, congenital infections, intrauterine hypoxia, teratogenic agents), but often unknown. In order of decreasing severity: schizencephaly (cleft brain); lissencephaly (smooth brain); pachygyria (decreased number of thickened gyri); polymicrogyria (wrinkled cortex with small folds); neuronal heterotopias (small collections of neurons in subcortical white matter). Often found on computerized tomography/magnetic resonance imaging (CT/MRI) scans in children with learning difficulties, epilepsy, cerebral palsy.

Non-ketotic hyperglycinaemia May present with severe neonatal illness; fits and slow development; or learning difficulties. Detected by amino acid studies.

Noonan's syndrome The main features are the following. Congenital heart defects — often asymptomatic: pulmonary valve stenosis, atrial septal defect (ASD), ventricular septal defect (VSD), hypertrophic cardiomyopathy (not associated with increased risk of sudden death). Facial characteristics: ptosis, large downward slanting eyes, hypertelorism; short neck and webbing of skin on back of neck; low hairline; low-set ears with posteriorly rotated lobes; flat bridge of nose; pronounced top lip with deep cleft. Shortness of stature: normal body proportions; delayed puberty growth spurt; role of growth hormone not yet certain. Psychological development: variable intelligence quotient (IQ), usually in low part of normal

Table G2 Features of neurofibromatosis type 1 (NF1)

Skin
Café au lait patches: begin in first year, increase in size and number, usually present by 6 years of age. Axillary and inguinal freckling. Cutaneous fibromas, usually after puberty

Eye
Lisch nodules on iris, seen only with slit lamp. Present in most cases

Learning disabilities
Severe global learning disability uncommon (3%) but specific learning disabilities common (up to 50%); include reading and writing problems, dyspraxia or clumsiness and attention deficits

Nervous system tumours
Optic glioma presenting with poor vision in one eye or proptosis: incidence and need for scanning of asymptomatic individuals controversial. Spinal tumours, brain tumours of various types: less than 5%. Acoustic neuroma not associated with NF1

Orthopaedic problems
Scoliosis — may develop in childhood or adolescence. Pseudoarthrosis of tibia — high risk of fracture which may remain non-united. Congenital absence of sphenoid wing causing eye to protrude

Other complications
Hypertension due to phaeochromocytoma or renal artery stenosis. Epilepsy (4%). Unexplained short stature. Macrocephaly. Plexiform neurofibromas. Miscellaneous malignancies

Diagnostic criteria
Two or more must be present.
1 Six or more *café au lait* patches, the greatest diameter of which is more than 5 mm in prepubertal children and more than 15 mm in postpubertal subjects
2 Two or more neurofibromas of any type or one plexiform neurofibroma
3 Axillary or inguinal freckling
4 Optic glioma
5 Two or more Lisch nodules
6 A characteristic bone lesion
7 A first-degree relative with NF1

Continued

Table G2 (*continued*)

Routine monitoring
Mandatory: blood-pressure; inspect spine for scoliosis with forward-bending test; visual acuity. Also consider visual fields; school progress; growth. CT or MRI if any new signs or symptoms. Consider possibility of NF complication with any unusual complaint.

CT, computerized tomography; MRI, magnetic resonance imaging.

range but may be global or specific learning difficulties; poor co-ordination; speech and language impairment; tendency to stubbornness and repetitive behaviour. Other problems include oedema in neonatal period; prominent early feeding difficulties; forceful vomiting in infancy; variety of visual defects; a conductive hearing loss; abnormal sternum (pigeon or funnel chest); hypotonia; scoliosis; undescended testes; kidney anomalies; high-arched palate; easy bruising — a variety of clotting abnormalities; abnormal lymphatics; freckles (possible overlap with Leopard syndrome and neurofibromatosis). The gene is mapped to chromosome 11.

Oculocerebrorenal syndrome See Lowe's syndrome.

Opercular syndrome A cortical type of pseudobulbar palsy. Caused by bilateral lesions in opercular region (region covering the insula). Loss of voluntary functions of facial, tongue and bulbar muscles; intelligence preserved; may be transient hemiparesis. Reported in childhood after meningitis.

Organic acidaemias An imprecise term covering a wide variety of metabolic disorders. May present with severe neonatal illness; failure to thrive, with vomiting, anorexia and hypotonia; encephalopathy with acidosis (easily misdiagnosed as encephalitis or Reye's syndrome and may be followed by a spastic, ataxic or athetoid movement disorder and/or intellectual retardation); various non-specific and chronic developmental problems, movement disorders or fits; unusual odour. Diagnosis: may be elevated ammonia and acidosis if acutely ill; amino acid studies not diagnostic; organic acid studies needed but diagnosis easily missed if child not acutely ill. Valproate therapy can cause misleading results.

Otahara's syndrome Early infantile epileptic encephalopathy. Seizures resistant to treatment. May evolve to other seizure syndromes. Many aetiologies. Usually severe psychomotor retardation.

Paroxysmal choreoathetosis Sudden onset of dystonia and abnormal postures, often precipitated by movements. Ataxia. Slow progression. Sex-linked recessive and dominant forms.

Partial deletion short arm chromosome 5, 5p–

syndrome, See Cri-du-chat syndrome.

Patau's syndrome (Trisomy 13) Midline defects: holo-prosencephaly, seizures, cleft lip and palate. Fits. Severe psychomotor retardation. Deafness. Microcephaly, scalp defects. Microphthalmia, colobomata. Ear anomalies. Capillary haemangiomata. Flexed fingers, may overlap, polydactyly. Prominent heels. Single umbilical artery. Cryptorchidism. Cardiac defects. Many other anomalies described. Less than one-fifth survive first year. Usually full trisomy 13, can be translocation, mosaic or partial.

Pelizaeus–Merzbacher disease Early onset but very variable rate of progression. Various abnormal eye movements; often stridor. Psychomotor deterioration, optic atrophy. Abnormal computerized tomography (CT) and magnetic resonance imaging (MRI). No neuropathy. X-linked.

Pena–Shokeir phenotype Arthrogryposis with decreased fetal movements; a heterogeneous condition and not a syndrome.

Pendred syndrome Hearing loss present from birth. Mondini malformation of cochlea visible on computerized tomography (CT) scan. Goitre (may not be large in infancy). Euthyroid; TSH and T3 may be marginally elevated but definitive diagnosis requires perchlorate discharge test. Autosomal recessive.

Peroxisomal disorders Peroxisomes are subcellular organelles; functions include fatty acid and bile acid metabolism, peroxide catabolism. May be reduction in one or many peroxisomal enzymes and functions. Elevated levels of very-long-chain fatty acids (VLCFA). Peroxisomal disorders include adrenoleucodystrophy, infantile Refsum's, Zellweger's diseases.

Phenylketonuria (PKU) Learning disability; infantile spasms, fair hair and blue eyes, dry skin with eczema. Cerebral palsy unusual, but often restless, hyperkinetic. Untreated patients now very rare because of neonatal screening. Mother with poorly controlled or unsuspected PKU may have child with microcephaly.

Poland's anomaly Unilateral hypoplasia or absence of part of the pectoralis muscle, sometimes also involving the breast; there may be underdevelopment of hand.

Pompe's disease (Type II glycogen storage disease) Severe hypotonia in infancy resembling Werdnig–Hoffmann disease, cardiac abnormalities. Autosomal recessive.

Prader–Willi syndrome See Table G3.

Primary ciliary dyskinesia (Immotile cilia syndrome) Chest infections leading to bronchiectasis. Sinusitis. Fifty per cent of patients have situs inversus. Chronic middle ear disease.

Pseudohypoparathyroidism (Albright's hereditary osteodystrophy) Short stature, obesity, learning disability. Hypoplasia of teeth enamel. Short fourth and fifth

Table G3 Features of Prader–Willi syndrome

BIRTH TO 3 YEARS

Major criteria
Neonatal hypotonia, poor sucking, lethargy
Feeding problems and failure to thrive
Characteristic facies: dolichocephaly, almond-shaped eyes, narrow face, small mouth with down-turned corners
Genital hypoplasia:
    Female — hypoplasia of labia minora or clitoris
    Male — cryptorchidism, small penis, scrotal hypoplasia
Global developmental delay
Excessive weight gain after 12 months of age

Minor criteria
Weak cry < 6 months
Squint

3 YEARS TO ADULT LIFE

Major criteria
As for birth to 3 years plus:
Obesity beginning between ages 1 and 6 years if no intervention
Incomplete pubertal development without intervention:
    Female — amenorrhoea/oligomenorrhoea after age 16
    Male — decreased facial and body hair, lack of voice change
    Interested in opposite sex, but fertility unknown
Mild to moderate learning disability
Hyperphagia/foraging for food/obsession with food

Minor criteria
Behaviour problems: tantrums, violent outbursts, obsessive/compulsive behaviour, oppositional, rigid, possessive, stubborn, steals and lies
Sleep disturbance or sleep apnoea
Short stature (for genetic background)
Tendency to fair skin and hair
Small hands and/or feet
Narrow hands
Squint and myopia
Thick viscous saliva with crusting at corners of mouth
Articulation defects
Skin-picking habit

MAY ALSO HAVE THE FOLLOWING
High pain threshold (can mask illness or injury), decreased vomiting, altered temperature sensitivity, scoliosis, kyphosis, early adrenarche, osteoporosis. Diabetes.
Increased incidence of breech birth

metacarpals. Calcification in basal ganglia; variable hypocalcaemia.

Rasmussen's disease Intractable focal seizures and progressive hemiparesis, pathological picture of chronic encephalitis but no viral agent identified.

Riley—Day syndrome see Familial dysautonomia.

Robin anomalad (Pierre Robin syndrome) Mandibular retrognathia, glossoptosis, cleft palate. Limb anomalies. Cardiovascular defects. Various eye disorders including Stickler syndrome (q.v.). Intellect usually normal. Respiratory difficulties in infancy — may need nursing in prone position.

Rubinstein—Taybi syndrome Broad thumbs and toes, maxillary hypoplasia and down-slanting palpebral fissures, short stature. Head is often small. Testes are undescended. Microdeletions of 16p; recurrence risk is small.

Russell—Silver syndrome Low birth weight, short stature, skeletal asymmetry, small face with appearance of large head, tendency to hypoglycaemia, early psychomotor retardation but intelligence quotient (IQ) usually normal. If not, exclude other diagnoses, e.g. chromosome disorder 18p−. May be growth-hormone-deficient. Sporadic; may be dominant.

Schilder's disease see Adrenoleucodystrophy

Seckel syndrome Also known as 'bird-headed dwarf'. Severe growth deficiency. Microcephaly and learning disability. Prominent beaked nose. Joint dislocation. Probably autosomal recessive.

Segawa's syndrome See Dopa-responsive dystonia.

Shprintzen syndrome see Velocardiofacial syndrome.

Sjögren—Larsson syndrome Spastic diplegia, learning disability; ichthyosis, thin brittle hair, short stature. Defect of fatty alcohol oxido-reductase. Autosomal recessive.

Smith—Lemli—Opitz syndrome Pre- and postnatal growth deficiency, psychomotor retardation, failure to thrive, microcephaly, ptosis, syndactyly of second/third toes; males have cryptorchidism, hypospadias. Autosomal recessive.

Sotos' syndrome (Cerebral giantism) Excessive growth, advanced bone age, large hands and feet, macrocephaly, mild to moderate learning disability, poor co-ordination, seizures. No endocrine abnormality established. Adult height not excessive because growth slows in mid- to late childhood. Tendency to difficult behaviour — tantrums, destructiveness, eating and sleeping problems. Exclude fragile-X syndrome, which can look similar. Most cases sporadic, although parents often have large heads, possibility of dominant inheritance.

Sprengel deformity Congenital upward displacement of the scapula.

Stickler syndrome (Hereditary arthro-ophthalmopathy)

Flat nasal bridge, cleft palate, small jaw, hearing loss, severe myopia, retinal detachment, cataract, hyperextensible joints, severe arthropathy, vertebral dysplasia, scoliosis. Autosomal dominant.

Stiff-baby syndrome Attacks of stiffness precipitated by surprise or minor physical contact. Can be mistaken for spasticity. Abnormal muscle activity abolished by diazepam. Probably dominant.

Subacute sclerosing panencephalitis (SSPE) Slowly progressive degenerative brain disease caused by previously acquired measles infection. Presents with intellectual deterioration, myoclonic jerks, occasionally major fits, typical electroencephalogram (EEG) features. Raised measles antibody titre in cerebrospinal fluid (CSF). No established treatment; interferon under trial.

Tay—Sachs disease (GM2 gangliosidosis) Early onset; never sit, or lose ability to sit. Blindness, spasticity, seizures, exaggerated startle response, laughing episodes. Cherry-red spot at macula. Large head. Diagnosis by hexosaminidase assay. Mean age of death 30 months. Autosomal recessive, gene frequency higher in Ashkenazi Jews (screening programme available for heterozygote status).

Treacher—Collins syndrome (Mandibulofacial dysostosis, Franceschetti—Klein syndrome) Antimongoloid palpebral fissures, hypoplasia of cheek and maxilla, small mandible, coloboma of lower eyelid, malformed external ears, conductive deafness, cleft palate; numerous other rare anomalies, intellect usually normal. Autosomal dominant; 60% of cases are fresh mutations. Gene maps to 5q.

Trisomy 13 see Patau's syndrome.

Trisomy 18 see Edward's syndrome.

Tuberose sclerosis see Table G4.

Turner's syndrome (XO syndrome) Small at birth. Small stature (special growth chart available). Tendency to obesity. Ovarian dysgenesis. Transient congenital lymphoedema. Widely spaced nipples. Narrow palate and small mandible. Short neck, often webbed. Narrow hyperconvex nails. Elbow and knee anomalies. Renal anomalies. Coarctation of aorta and other cardiac defects. Sensorineural deafness. Mild learning disability, mean intelligence quotient (IQ) 95 but performance score lower than verbal.

Urea cycle disorders Include argininosuccinic aciduria, citrullinaemia; severe motor forms of hyperammonaemia. Clinical features variable; may be abnormal pale brittle hair; seizures; retardation; episodic headache, vomiting and stupor. Amino acid studies and ammonia levels before and after protein loading for diagnosis.

Usher syndrome Occurs in 3−10% of profoundly deaf children. Autosomal recessive. Type 1: profound deafness, absent vestibular response; delayed motor milestones

Table G4 Features of tuberose sclerosis (TS)

Seizures in 75%: infantile spasms, myoclonic
fits, partial seizures, generalized tonic–
clonic attacks
Learning disabilities — may be mild, moderate
or severe; often with 'autistic' features.
Associated behavioural problems
Movement problems, mainly secondary to
learning disability
CT scan: can be normal, particularly in first
6 months of life. Subependymal glial nodules
along lateral walls of lateral ventricles in
80%. Lesion at foramen of Munro causing
hydrocephalus. Giant astrocytomas (enhance
with contrast), previously called tubers. MRI
may show demyelinated areas

Skin
Angiofibromas in 85% (previously called
adenoma sebaceum): small erythematous
lesions appearing at any age, rarely before 2.
Butterfly facial distribution, many on nasal
folds and chin but spare upper lip. Superficial
similarity to acne. May respond to argon laser
treatment
Hypomelanic patches: ash-leaf depigmented
patches in 80%. May be present in first year;
8 per 1000 normal newborns also have them.
Best seen in ultraviolet light ('Woods' light).
Usually 1 cm to several cm, oval, long axis in
line of dermatome. Scars and skin abrasion
can look similar
Forehead fibrous plaques — 25%. Shagreen
patches — 40%: thickened discoloured skin
on lower lumbar area to one side of midline.
Fibromas — 50%: on nails of hands and feet,
can cause grooves on nails even if not visible.
Gum fibromas. Molluscum fibrosum
pendulum — skin tags around shoulders and
back of neck. Pitted teeth

Eyes
Phacomas — retinal hamartomas, in 50%.
Visual acuity rarely affected

Heart
Rhabdomyomas — 60% of children.
Arrhythmias; cardiac failure which may
improve as the child gets older

Continued

Table G4 (*continued*)

Kidney
Angiomyolipomas in 60%. Usually bilateral.
May cause bleeding or loin pain. Cystic
disease, hypertension

Other
Bone cysts, sclerosis; cystic lung disease (adult
females); rectal polyps

Diagnostic features
1 Primary features: definite diagnosis can
usually be made if only one present
Shagreen patches; ungual fibroma; retinal
hamartomas; facial angiofibromas;
subependymal nodules; renal — more than
one angiomyolipomata
2 Secondary features: at least two features
required to make a diagnosis
Hypomelanic nodules; polycystic kidneys;
cardiac rhabdomyoma; cortical 'tubers';
honeycomb lungs; infantile spasms;* other
seizure types; first-degree relative with TS;
forehead plaque; isolated angiomyolipoma

---

* Caution is required when the child has fits
and hypomelanic nodules because the latter are
not rare and the combination cannot be
considered diagnostic.
CT, computerized tomography; MRI, magnetic
resonance imaging.

(mean age of walking 22 months) and unsteady gait,
retinitis pigmentosa with visual symptoms appearing on
average at age 8. Gene mapped to chromosome 4q.
Type 2: high frequency deafness, no motor delay, visual
symptoms appear later. Chromosome 1q.

Van der Woude syndrome (Lip pit–cleft lip syndrome)
Small pits in lower lip, dental abnormalities, cleft lip
with or without cleft palate. Autosomal dominant.

VATER association Vertebral defects, anal atresia,
tracheo-oesophageal fistula, radial and renal dysplasia.
Cardiac defects, single umbilical artery. Many other
defects described.

Velocardiofacial syndrome (Shprintzen syndrome) Cleft
palate. Prominent nose. Narrow palpebral fissures. Small
mandible. Heart defects (ventricular septal defect)
(VSD), right aortic arch, Fallot's tetralogy, aberrant left
subclavian artery). Short stature. Mild learning disability.
Autosomal dominant. Molecular deletions on chromosome 22 reported.

Waardenburg syndrome Occurs in 2−5% of deaf children. Two types. Both autosomal dominant. Deafness; lateral displacement of medial canthi, heterochromia iridis, white forelock or premature greying, confluent eyebrows, prominent nasal root. Variable penetrance of all features. Type 1 gene mapped to 2q35−37.

Warburg syndrome (HARD ± E syndrome) Hydrocephalus, agyria, retinal dysplasia, with or without encephalocele. Dandy−Walker cyst, other eye anomalies. Diagnosis easily missed because of variable severity. Autosomal recessive.

Williams' syndrome Severe feeding difficulties in first year − vomiting, constipation, refusal to feed. Typical facies, often described as elfin. Anteverted nostrils, prominent lips with open mouth, irregular teeth, aortic stenosis and other heart defects, variable hypercalcaemia in infancy. Nephrocalcinosis. Palpitations, arrhythmias, hypertension later in life. Presence or absence of hypercalcaemia does not alter other features. Tendency to early puberty; obesity in late teens. Growth deficiency (average adult height for males 5′6″ (168 cm), for females 5′ (152 cm)). Mild-to-moderate learning disability with distinctive pattern often found: superfical well-developed chatter with stereotyped phrases and limited understanding. Sociable, out-going, hyperactive, difficulty in maintaining friendships, exaggerated emotional responses. Obsessional interests. Anxious, hypersensitive to noise. Visuospatial and motor difficulties; fear of heights. Sporadic, cause unknown; mutations in elastin have been reported.

Wilson's disease Disorder of copper metabolism. May present as acute or chronic liver disease or haemolytic anaemia. Kayser−Fleischer ring of corneal pigment. Neurological symptoms (deterioration of school performance, dysarthria, drooling, tremor, various involuntary movements) are rare before age 10−12. Usually insidious but can be acute. Gene: chromosome 13q. Autosomal recessive. Treatment with chelating agents.

XO syndrome See Turner's syndrome.

XXY syndrome See Klinefelter's syndrome.

XYY syndrome Rapid growth in mid-childhood. Tall stature. Poor muscle strength and co-ordination. Prominent glabella, long areas, long fingers. Dull intellect. Behavioural problems, aggression. Severe acne at adolescene. Note: XYY individuals may show no abnormalities.

Zellweger syndrome Peroxisomal disorder (q.v.). Hypotonia, severe learning disability, large liver with cirrhotic changes, albuminuria, visual impairment with retinal dystrophy; many other defects described. Breech presentation, early failure to thrive, early death. Can be mistaken for Down's syndrome. Autosomal recessive.

References and further reading

Baraitser, M. and Winter, R. *London Dysmorphology Database**. Oxford Medical Databases, Oxford.

Baraitser, M. and Winter, R. *London Neurogenetics Database**. Oxford Medical Databases, Oxford.

Beighton, P. (1993) *McKusick's Heritable Disorders of Connective Tissue*. Mosby Year Books Europe, Aylsford, Kent.

Jones, K.L.J. (1988) *Smith's Recognizable Patterns of Human Malformation*. W.B. Saunders, Philadelphia.

* Updated regularly.

Addresses for Equipment

NFER Nelson, Darville House, 2 Oxford Road East, Windsor, Berkshire SL4 1DF (for a wide range of psychometric tests and equipment including Portage).

Test Agency, Cournswood House, Clappins Lane, North Dean, High Wycombe HP14 4NW (also a wide range of test materials including the Denver developmental screening test).

Child Growth Foundation, 2 Mayfield Avenue, London W4 1PW (for scales, measuring devices, growth charts, etc.).

Contact A Family, 170 Tottenham Court Road, London, W1P 0HA, telephone: 0171 3833555, fax: 0171 3830259 (for finding out whether and where there is a parent organization or individual with virtually any disorder or syndrome).

Segufix-Bandagen das Humane system, PO Box 50 1364, D2000 Hamburg 50, Germany (for elasticated body-belts).

S.R. Holbrook Ltd, Jackson Road, Coventry CV6 47Y, telephone: 01203 667576, fax: 01203 637543 (for Decubicare fleece products).

Arthrodax Surgical Ltd, Great Western Court, Ashburton, Ross on Wye, Herefordshire, HR9 7XP (for the Haberman feeder).

Index

For specific conditions please also
refer to the Glossary

abetalipoproteinaemia   170, 229
abuse
  physical   111
  sexual   111
  substance   165–6
acceptance   108
acetazolamide   331
achromatopsia   91, 229
acousticopalpebral reflex (APR)   72
acquired immunodeficiency syndrome
      (AIDS)   163
acrocephaly   162
ACTH   191, 337
Acuity Card Procedure   98
acute infantile hemiplegia syndrome
      242
adrenoleucodystrophy   195
Adult Training Centres   129, 196
affectionless psychopathy   25
aggressive behaviour in nursery or
      playgroup   142–3
Aicardi's syndrome   336
albinism   91, 227
alcohol   165
Alport's syndrome   213
alternating squint   89
amblyopia   91–2, 226
amnesia, post-traumatic   302
anal stimulation (anal masturbation)
      142
anencephaly   277
Angelman's syndrome   169, 188,
      254
aniridia   244
anisometropia   87
ankle-foot orthoses (AFOs)   291
Apert's syndrome   162
aphakia   88, 226
aphasia   174, 190–1
  acquired receptive   196
  Broca's   188
  expressive   188
  Wernicke's (fluent)   188
arithmetic problems (dyscalculia)
      315, 324

Arnold–Chiari malformation   159,
      278, 279
arthogryposis   296–8
artificial urinary sphincter (AUS)
      286
Asperger's syndrome (mild autism)
      174, 185, 192, 197, 325
assessment   7–14
  introduction to the family   51–2
    assessment at home   53
    difficult children   52
    video- and tape-recording
      52–3
  methods   9–13
    information from other sources
      13
    using parents as a source of
      information   9–10
    psychological tests   10–12
    tests available to doctors   13
    misconceptions about   13–14
  non-attendance and non-
      compliance   53
  organization   51
  reasons for   9
  structure of the interview   53–65
    background history   54–7
      development history   56
      family relationships   54–5
      family structure   54
      important events   56
      interview with the child
        56–7
      obstetric history   55–6
      past medical history   56
      social background   54
    developmental assessment
      57–9
    definition of the problem   53–4
    neurological examination
      59–65
      cranial nerves   60–1
      examination of the limbs
        61–2
      neurodevelopmental
        examination   65
      orthopaedic examination
        63–5
      preliminary observations   60

primitive reflexes   61
problems of measurement
  control   62
protective and postural reflexes
  61
sensation   62–3
physical examination   59
  physical anomalies   59, 60
astigmatism   88
asymmetric tonic neck reflex (ATNR)
      247, 250
asymmetric tonic reflex posture   46,
      47
athetosis   124, 250
atropine   87
attachment   24–5, 38
attention, cognitive development and
      41
attention control, cognitive
      development and   41
attention-deficit disorder and
      hyperactivity   41, 42,
      327–32
  assessment   32
  causes   329
  defining the condition   328–9
  food allergies, diets and   331–2
  management   329–31
attention difficulties, fragile-X
      syndrome and   156
atypical child   197
auditory agnosia   174, 186
augmentative and alternative means of
      communication (AAC)
      202, 203
autism   143
  adolescence and adult life   196
  atypical   192
  causes   196–7
  childhood-onset   195–6
  classical   192–5
    in infancy   192–4
    language development   194
    rituals, obsessions and
      stereotypies   194–5
    social behaviour   195
  communication disorder in   174,
      191–8
  continuum   185, 193

autism (*cont.*):
definitions   192
early infantile   191
features   192
management   200
prevalence   192
psychometric assessment   196
self-injurious behaviour   143–4
traits   192
see also Asperger's syndrome; Rett's
syndrome
autistic psychopathy   197

Babinski responses   62
backward chaining   135
baclofen   269
Becker's muscular dystrophy   291
Beckwith's syndrome   180, 244
bed wetting (nocturnal enuresis)
141, 288
Behaviour Assessment Battery   236
behaviour problems (challenging
behaviours)   131, 356–7
behavioural psychology   131–3
common types   139–5
behaviour therapy   133–4
eliminating unwanted behaviour
136–9
cognitive therapy   138–9
extinction   137
phobias   138
reinforcement of desirable
behaviour   138
restraint   138
restitution   138
restructuring the environment
136–7
time out   137
treatment of life-threatening
disorder   138
increasing wanted behaviour
134–6
reinforcement   134–5
shaping, prompting, chaining,
modelling   135
tokens   135–6
parental support   134
Behr's syndrome   229, 254
benign familial megencephaly   158
benign myoclonus of early infancy
337
benign partial epilepsy of childhood
with Rolandic spikes
(BPERS)   342
benzodiazepines   165
bereavement reaction   105–7
bilingualism   190

binocular single vision (BSV)   89
bladder exstrophy   289
blindisms   232–3
Bliss symbols   202
bonding   21–5
effect of disability on   23
infant's contribution to   23–4
neonatal   22
parental responses to the infant
22–3
primary maternal preoccupation
22
bottom-shuffling   47, 240
bow legs (genu varum)   49, 63–5
brain injury, acquired   299–302
management   299–301
prognosis   301–2
brainstem-evoked response (BSER)
audiometry   68
Brantley Scott urinary sphincter   286
British Ability Scales   269
British Sign Language for the Deaf
(BSL)   205, 218, 236
brittle bone disease   302–4
Broca's aphasia   188
bullying   311, 312
buphthalmos (infantile glaucoma)
227

café au lait spots   310
see also neurofibromatosis in
Glossary
Callier–Azusa observational
scales   234, 236
Cambridge Crowding Cards   98
carbamazepine   349
cardiac disorders   356
casting   42
cataract   94, 225–7
Catford drum   93
cavus feet   63
cerebral palsies   149, 176–7
adult with   274–5
bilateral signs: hypertonia   239,
244–5
care problems   271–4
classification   237–9
constipation   274
depression   274
dribbling   273–4
epidemiology   240
feeding   271–3
chewing and swallowing   271
food intake   271
gastro-oesophageal reflux   272
gastrostomy   273
management   272

management of regurgitation and
rumination without reflux
273
seating   272
table feeding   272–3
treatment of reflux   273
videofluoroscopy   271–2
hemiplegia   240–4
acquired   242
atypical   242
causes   242–3
congenital   240–2
early development   240
differential diagnosis   243–4
other impairments   242
upper limb function   240–2
hypotonic   253–5
life expectancy   274
management   255–71
activities of daily living   259
communication   261
drug treatment   269
early   255–6
early recognition by development
surveillance   256
education   270–1
foot and ankle deformity   266,
267
gait analysis   265
hip deformity   265–6, 266–7,
268
knee deformity   266, 267
mobility   259, 260–1
orthopaedic considerations in
total body involvement
266–9
psychological assessment
269–70
role of orthopaedic surgery
262–9
role of the therapist   256–7
seating clinic   258
sitting and standing   257–8
scoliosis   267–9
thumb in palm deformity   265
upper limb surgery   265
precocious puberty   144
primitive reflexes in   61
protective and postural reflexes in
61
spastic diplegia   245–9, 254
associated impairments   248–9
early mobility   247–8
prognosis for walking   248
surgery   265–6
upper limb involvement   245–6
terminology   237
total body involvement (four-limb

cerebral palsy) 249–53
  causes 251–3
  diagnosis and investigations
    253
  dyskinetic cerebral palsies
    250–1
  four-limb spastic/rigid
    quadriplegias 251
  impairments associated with
    athetosis 251
  intrapartum asphyxia 251
  prenatal and perinatal causes
    251–3
  wheelchair selection 263
  windswept hip deformity 263,
    266
CHARGE association 230
chickenpox 163
Child Assessment Centres 116
Child Development Centre (CDC)
  51, 173, 198, 233
  evolution of 116
  as information resource 120
Child Development Team (CDT)
  108, 124, 130, 233
Child Health Surveillance programme
  120–1, 215
child psychiatry services 120,
  311–12
Children Act 1989 118, 119
chronic fatigue syndrome (myalgic
  encephalomyelitis) 312–13
circular definitions 15
City University colour test 100
clasp-knife phenomenon 62
cleft lip 177–80
cleft palate 177–80
clinical genetics service 122
clonazepam 269
clonidine 330
clubfoot 63
clumsy child *see* motor disability
cocaine 15
cochlear implants 213, 216
cocktail party syndrome 160, 182
cognitive development, normal
  38–44
  acquisition of concepts and skills
    39–41
    causality 40
    generalization 41
    object permanence 39–40
  attention and attention control 41
  clinical assessment 42–3
  importance of vision 39
  learning in infancy 38–9
  play 41–2
  self-representation 43–4

coloboma 230
Columbia Mental Maturity Scale
  234, 269
Communication Aids Centre 202
communication disorders 173–208
  assessment 176
  augmentation and alternative means
    of communication 201–2
  in autism 174, 191–8
  comorbidity with psychiatric
    disorder 176
  continuum of impairment 174–5
  management 198–201
    assessment and investigation
      198–9
    of autism 200
    counselling 198
    education 198
    explanation to parents 199
    integration 198
    magic cures 201
    neurological examination and
      investigation 198
    nurseries and schools 200
    school placement 198
    speech and language therapy
      199–200
  methods of communication
    202–8
    communication aid technology
      205–8
    Makaton vocabulary 202–5
    object and picture boards 202
    Paget–Gorman Sign System
      (PGSS) 205
    reading 208
    symbols 202
  multiaxial description 175
  patterns 176–98
  terminology 173–6
Community Team 130
complex partial seizure (CPS) 343
computer technology 205
concentration difficulties in fragile-X
  syndrome 156
concomitant squint 89
congenital dislocation of the hip 243
congenital infections 163–5
congenital limb deficiencies 293–6
congenital nystagmus 227–8
congenital palatal incompetence (cleft
  palate speech without cleft
  palate) 179–80
congenital pseudobulbar palsy 177
consonant sounds 30–1
constipation 142, 274
contraception 145
corneal opacities 225–7

Cornelia de Lange syndrome
  143–4, 166
cortical visual impairment (CVI)
  230–1
craniopharyngioma 95
craniosynostosis (craniostenosis)
  162–3
critical period 18
Crouzon's syndrome 162
crowding phenomenon 98
cryptophthalmos 227
cyclopentoate 87
cycloplegia 87
cyproterone acetate 144
cytomegalovirus (CMV) 163, 164,
  210, 213, 219

dantrolene sodium 269
day nursery facilities 122
daytime urinary incontinence
  141–2
  in disabled child 289
  in normal children 288–9
deaf–blind child 235–6
death of disabled child 113–15
definitions 1–3
déja vu 343
delayed visual maturation (DVM)
  231
delusional system 10
dental care 121
Denver developmental screening test
  57, 58
depression 274
  postnatal 56
deprivation, specific language
  impairment and 189–90
desmopressin spray 141
detrusor sphincter dyssynergia
  (DSD) 285
developmental chart 103
developmental delay 102, 147–8
developmental disorder
  definition 15
  of motor function 325
dextro-amphetamine 330
diabetes insipidus/diabetes mellitus/
  optic atrophy/deafness
  (DIDMOAD) syndrome
  229
diarrhoea 142
diazepam 269
differential reinforcement of other
  behaviour (DRO) 138
diphtheria immunization 121
disability
  cause 104

disability (*cont.*):
　definition 1
　diagnosis 102–4
　feelings of disabled person
　　　110–11
　functional effects 104
　type of 102–3
disadvantage, definition 1
disequilibrium syndrome 254
disinhibition syndrome 327
disorder, definition 1
District Handicap Team 116
Doman–Delcato method 125–6
Down's syndrome 149–54
　behaviour 153
　bonding and 23
　clinical features 152–3
　development 153
　macroglossia in 180
　management 152
　puberty and adult life 153
dribbling 273–4
drinking, excessive 288
drowsiness 139
drugs, teratogenic 165
dry bed training 141
Duane's retraction syndrome 89
Duchenne muscular dystrophy 13,
　　　169, 198, 290–2, 293
dysarthria 176–7, 184
dyscalculia 315, 324
dysfluency 181
dysgraphia 315, 323
dyslexia 147, 314, 315, 316
dysmenorrhoea 145
dysmorphic syndrome 316
dysphasia 173, 188, 189, 315
dysphonia 181
dyspraxia 173, 183–4, 315
dyssomnias 139

E numbers 331
ear wax 223
echolalia 34
　delayed 182
ectodermal dysplasia 188
education 126–30
　boarding-schools 128
　curriculum needs 127–8
　early school placement 126
　integration 129
　leaving school 129–30
　preschool teaching services 126
　special schools 126–8
Education Acts
　1971 147
　1981 128–9, 147

1993 128–9
Education Reform Act 1993 129
educational model 15–16
educational underachievement
　　　306–33
　assessment 306–13
　　background history 309
　　defining the terms 307
　　discussion of findings with
　　　parents 310
　　evolution of the problem
　　　307–8
　　interviews with parents and child
　　　308
　　loss of skills 307
　　multiple causes 306–7
　　physical examination 309–10
　psychological assessment 310–13
　　child psychiatry 311–12
　　chronic fatigue syndrome
　　　(myalgic encephalomyelitis)
　　　312–13
　　depression 312
　　IQ testing 311
　　school attendance problems
　　　312
　see also specific learning disability
educationally subnormal (mild)
　　　(ESNM) 147
educationally subnormal (severe)
　　　(ESNS) 147
Ehlers–Danlos syndrome 255
elective mutism 181–2
electrical response testing 186
electroretinogram (ERG) 98
EMLA cream 349
emmetropia 88
empathy 34
epilepsia partialis continua 343
epilepsy 334–6
　causes 334–5
　in cerebral palsy 242
　classification 335
　generalized 336–41
　　epilepsies with generalized
　　　tonic–clonic seizures
　　　340–1
　　infantile spasms (West's
　　　syndrome) 336–7
　　Lennox–Gastaut syndrome
　　　337–8
　　myoclonic epilepsies of early
　　　childhood 337–8
　　non-convulsive status (petit mal
　　　status) 340
　　typical absence seizures (classic
　　　petit mal) 338–40
　management 346–52

counselling 348
drug level monitoring 349
drug treatment 348
educational problems 347–8
effects of epilepsy on the child
　　347
genetic advice 352
　parents' views on treatment
　　347
starting treatment 346–7
stopping treatment 351–2
treatment plan 349–51
uncontrolled epilepsy 352
partial seizures 342–4
　benign partial epilepsy of
　　childhood with Rolandic
　　spikes (BPERS) 342
　complex partial seizure (CPS)
　　343
　fits with complex symptomatology
　　343–4
　simple 342–3
photosensitive 345
prevalence 335–6
reflex 345
startle 345
use of EEG 346
epilepsy aphasia syndrome 191
Erb's palsy 243
ergotamine 355
ethosuximide 340
evolutionary diagnosis 105
expressive aphasia 188
extinction 140

Fabry's disease 157
facioauriculovertebral anomalad 178
faecal smearing 142
faecal soiling 142
fainting 354
Family Fund 122
family therapy 124
Farnsworth–Munsell 100-hue test
　　100
febrile convulsions 345
Feingold diet 126
felbamate 348
fetal alcohol syndrome 165, 166,
　　178
α-fetoprotein (AFP) 287
FG, hydrocephalus in 160
financial help 122
finger-nose test 62
finger-spelling 218
fits *see* epilepsy
flat feet 63
Floating Harbour syndrome 188

fluphenazine 143
food allergies 331−2
fragile-X deoxyribonucleic acid
        (DNA) test 169, 197
fragile-X mental retardation 1
        (FMR-1) 154
fragile-X syndrome 151, 155−7,
        187, 197
    variants 156
Friedreich's ataxia 59
Frisby test 95
funny turns, non-epileptic 352−9
    behavioural disturbances 356−7
    breath-holding attacks 353−4
    cardiac disorders 356
    emotional causes 356
    fainting 354
    hypoglycaemia 355−6
    migraine 354−6
    pseudoseizures 358−9
    reflex anoxic seizures 354
    sleep disturbances 357−8
    tics 357
    vertigo 358

gabapentin 348
Gaucher's disease 158
general (global) learning disability 3
Genie 19
genu valgum (knock knees) 49,
        63−5
genu varum (bow legs) 49, 63−5
Gerstmann syndrome 324
giftedness 332−3
giggle micturition 288
Gilles de la Tourette syndrome 357
Glasgow Acuity Cards 98
glaucoma 227
global learning disabilities 148
glucose-6-phosphate dehydrogenase
        (G6PD) deficiency 253
glutaric aciduria 190
Goldenhaar syndrome 213
goodness of fit concept 26
Gower's manoeuvre 61, 290
graded change 140
graphaesthesia 63
gratification phenomena 356
Griffiths test 13
Guide to Movement Skills (GEMS)
        127

Haberman feeder 178
habituation 39
Haemophilus influenzae type b (Hib)
        immunization 121

haloperidol 143, 330
hand regard 42
hand use in infancy 46−7
handicap, definition 1
HARD ± E syndrome, hydrocephalus
        in 160
hard of hearing 210
head circumference 65−6
Head Start programme 17
hearing 67−85
    acoustic and phonetic principles
        67−70
    characteristics of non-speech
        sounds 69
    frequency and pitch 67−8
    intensity and loudness 68
    measurement of intensity 68
    noise 67
    pure tone 67
    speech sounds 68−9
    see also hearing loss; hearing tests
hearing loss 70, 211−23
    acquired and progressive sensorial
        219
    audiometry 70
    conductive 220−3
        acquired 220−2
        congenital forms 220
    congenital bilateral sensorineural
        210−19
        causes 210−12
            hypoxia and asphyxia 212
            jaundice 212
            perinatal causes 211−12
            prematurity 211−12
        development 212−13
        epidemiology 210
        management 213−19
            counselling and support
                215
            diagnosis and investigation
                213−14
            education 217−18
            hearing-aids 215−17
            psychological assessment
                218−19
    speech discrimination 70
    unilateral 219−20
hearing tests 57−9
    audiometry 70
    blink reflex 72
    cooperative testing 76−8
        disabled children 77
        speech discrimination tests
            77−8
        test procedures 77−8
        unilateral or asymmetric hearing
            loss 76

distraction testing and visual-
        response audiometry
        73−6
    distractor 73−5
    frequency and intensity 76
    technique 73
    unilateral hearing loss 76
    visual alertness 75−6
    visual reinforcement 76
early detection of hearing defects
        82−5
    neonatal screening 83
    school entrant test 84
    screening 83
    vigilance 84
electrical response audiometry
        80−2
    brain-evoked response (BSER)
        80, 81
    electrocochleography (ECoG)
        82
    evoked otoacoustic emissions
        (EOAE) 80
    impedance 82
history 72
practical aspects 72
in preschool children 70−1
    background noise 71
    sound-field testing 70−1
pure-tone audiometry 78−9
    air and bone conduction 79
    masking 79
    pitfalls 79
speech tests — 5 years and upwards
        79−80
hearing-impaired 210
hemihypertrophy 244
hemimegalencephaly 244
hemiplegia 95, 240−4, 262−5
hemisyndromes 61
hepatitis B 164, 165
Hermensky−Pudlak syndrome 227
heroin abuse 165
herpes simplex 163, 195
heterotropia 89−90
hip rotation 63, 64
Hiskey−Nebraska test 219
holophrases 31
homocystinuria 169, 227, 229
Horner's syndrome 92
human immunodeficiency virus (HIV)
        163, 164, 165, 195
Hunter's disease 157, 180
hydranencephaly 58−9
hydrocephalus 159−60, 254
    precocious puberty 144
hydrolethalus 160
hydromyelia 278

hyperactivity   41, 42
hyperbilirubinaemia   253
hypermetropia   88, 90
    in infants   97
hyperthyroidism   154
hypertonia   239, 244–5
hypoarrhythmia   169
hypoglycaemia   355–6
hyporhinophonia   180
hypothyroidism   165
    congenital   154
    macroglossia in   180
hypotonia   253–5
hypoxic-ischaemic encephalopathy
        (HIE)   243, 252

idiot savant   4
illiterate E test   98
imipramine   141
immunization   121, 167
impairment, definition   1
incontinence, urinary   288–9
Individual Family Service Plan (IFSP)
        (USA)   118
infantile glaucoma (buphthalmos)
        227
infantile neuronal ceroid
        lipofuscinosis   169
infantile spasms (West's syndrome)
        149, 336–7
inherited metabolic disorder 157
        (IMD)   157
intelligence
    definition   4
    environmental influences   7
    genetic contribution   4
    pathological influences   5–7
intelligence quotient (IQ)
    in cerebral palsy   242
    heredity   4
    tests   4, 10, 128, 311
interaction   7
intersubjectivity   22
intervention   16–19
    effectiveness   16–18
        benefits of preschool nursery
            experience   18
        effectiveness of therapy   18
        learning disability   18
        role of the school   18
        subcultural deprivation   17–18
    sensitive period for   18–19
intoeing   63
intrapartum asphyxia   166
iron deficiency   140
Ishihara plates   99–100

jactactio capitis nocturnal   358
jaws, malocclusion of   180
Jervell–Lange–Nielsen syndrome
        213
Joubert's syndrome   229, 254
juvenile myoclonic epilepsy
            syndromes   341
juvenile neuronal ceroid lipofuscinosis
        229

Kanner's syndrome   191–5
kernicterus   252
kindling   335
Kleinfelter's disease   154
knock knees (genu valgum)   49,
        63–5
Koluchova twins   19
Kousseff's syndrome   278
Kugelberg–Welander syndrome
        292

labelling   15
lamtrigine   191
Landau reaction   61
Landau–Kleffner syndrome   186,
        191
Lang test   95
language acquisition device   32
language delay, definition   174
language development
    in autism   194
    clinical assessment of
            communicative ability
            36–7
    consonant sounds   30–1
    deviant social behaviour   36–7
    factors affecting   34–5
    in fragile-X syndrome   156
    non-verbal communication   35
    normal   29–37
    origins   31–4
        acquisition of grammar   31–3
        baby talk ('motherese')   31
        higher levels of language learning
            34
        overgeneralization of word
            meanings   32
        parent–child conversation
            33–4
        plurals   33
        referential looking   31
    relevance of linguistic research   36
    speech sounds   29–31
    variations in language acquisition
        35
language disorder, definition   174

language test   15
language therapy in cleft lip and cleft
        palate   178–9
Language units   200
Larsen syndrome   255
latent squint (heterophoria)   89
Laurence–Moon–Biedl syndrome
        229
laxatives   142
lead
    intoxication   140
    poisoning   167–8
lead-pipe rigidity   62
learning disability   3, 147–71
    causes   149–68
        abnormal size or shape of head
            158–63
        chromosome disorders   151–7
        congenital infections   163–5
        dystrophic syndromes   149–51
        environmental   168
        in fragile-X syndrome   155–7
        perinatal   166
        postnatal   166–8
        prenatal   165–6
        sex chromosome disorders
            154–5
        single-gene defects   157–8
    classification   147, 150
    definition   147
    epidemiology   148
    genetic aspects   170
    investigation   168–70
    life expectancy   171
    management   171
    other checks   170
    presentation   148–9
    prognosis   170–1
    terminology   168
    types   319–24
Leber's amaurosis   229, 232
Leber's optic atrophy   229
Leiter scale   219
Lennox–Gastaut syndrome   337–8,
        346
Lesch–Nyhan syndrome   143–4,
        170
letter-matching tests   98
life expectancy
    in cerebral palsy   274
    learning disability and   171
    in Werdig Hoffmann disease   113
limb deficiencies, congenital   293–6
lip-reading   218
listeriosis   163
litigation   107
long-term care   123
loperamide   142

low birth weight, cerebral palsy and 251
Lowe and Costello Symbolic Play test 42
Lowe's syndrome 227
lymphocytic choriomeningitis 163
lysosomal storage diseases (LSDs) 157, 169

macroglossia 180
Makaton symbols 202, 205
Marcus Gunn phenomenon (jaw winking) 92
Marfan's syndrome 227, 229, 255, 326
Marinesco–Sjögren's syndrome 254
masturbation 145
    anal 142
    infantile 356
McCormick toy discrimination test 77
Meadow's syndrome (Munchausen's syndrome by proxy) 354, 359
mean length of utterance (MLU) 35
measles immunization 121
Meckel's syndrome 287
medical model of disease 14
medroxyprogesterone acetate 144
megalencephaly 158
MELAS syndrome 355
Melnick–Fraser syndrome 213
meningitis, bacterial 219
Menkes' syndrome 169
menstruation, management of 145
mental impairment 3
mental retardation *see* learning disability
MERFF syndrome 355
Merrill–Palmer test 218
mesh 22
metachromatic leucodystrophy 190, 195
metatarsus adductus (varus) 63
methylphenidate 330
metoclopramide 355
Metrofanoff procedure 286
microcephaly 149, 160–2, 170
microphthalmia 227
microsquint 89
micturition, frequency of 288
    see also daytime urinary incontinence; nocturnal enuresis (bed wetting)
migraine 354–6
    classical 354

common 354–5
complicated 354–5
footballer's 355
management 355
treatment 355
mineral supplements 126
minimal brain dysfunction (MBD) 15, 315
Moebius syndrome 61, 177
molybdenum cofactor deficiency 170
mongolism *see* Down's syndrome
Moor House reading scheme 208
Moro reflex 247
morphia 165
mosaicism 151
motor development 44–9
    factors affecting 47–8
    first six months 46–7
    motor learning 47
    variations in 48, 49
motor disability (clumsiness) 184, 324–7
    assessment 326–7
    causes 326
    intelligence and achievement 326
    management 327
    presenting features 325
    subgroups 325–6
Movement Assessment Battery for Children 327
mucopolysaccharides screening test 158
mucopolysaccharidosis (MPS) 142
multiply handicapped visually impaired (MHVI) 225
mumps 219
    immunization 121
Munchausen's syndrome by proxy 354, 359
myalgic encephalomyelitis 312–13
mydriasis 87
myelomeningocoele 278
myeloschisis 278
myoclonic epilepsies of early childhood 337–8
myopia 88, 90, 228

naltrexone 143
narcolepsy 358
nasal obstruction 180
National Curriculum 128
near-miss cot death syndrome 354
neural tube defects 277–89
    spina bifida cystica 277–88
    spina bifida occulta 289
neurofibromatosis 227, 316

neurogenic bladder 289
neuromas, acoustic 219
neuropathic bladder 284
night terrors 357–8
nightmares 357
nitrazepam 337
nocturnal enuresis (bed wetting) 141, 288
non-convulsive status 169
non-verbal communication 35, 43
    assessment of 57
Noonan's syndrome 151, 188, 326
normal development 21–49
    bonding and attachment 21–5
    child's place in the family 21
    language development 29
    social and interpersonal behaviour 21–9
    temperament and personality 25
    development from 1 to 5 28–9
    early school years 29
    genetic factor 27–8
Norrie's disease 232
nursery school 18, 122, 142–3, 200
nystagmus 91

occult spinal dysraphism 243
occupational therapy
    in cerebral palsy 256–7
    for motor disability 327
ocular albinism 227
ocular dysmetria 228
oculomotor apraxia 228
oligoantigenic diet 331
opercular syndrome 177
ophthalmic investigation
    colour vision 99–100
    computerized tomography/ magnetic resonance imaging (CT/MRI) scanning 99
    electrophysiological techniques 98–9
optic atrophy 229
optic nerve hypoplasia 230
ORAC 207
oscillopsia 227
osteogenesis imperfecta (OI) ('brittle bone disease') 302–4
outcome measures 124
outtoeing 63
overprotection 108

Paget–Gorman Sign System (PGSS) 205, 236
paracetamol 355
paralytic (incomitant) squint 89

paraplegia, acquired 298
parasomnias 139
parents and family
  acceptance 108
  bereavement reaction 105–7
  coping 109–11
    cognitive reframing 109–10
    emotion-focused coping 109
    problem-focused coping 108
  differences in reactions 110
  effect of disability on 108–10
  effect on siblings 110
  further crises 112
  information about disability
    102–4, 118
  litigation 107
  news-breaking to 101–2
  overprotection 108
  problem of uncertainty 104–5
  rejection 108
  second opinions 107–8
  self-deception 10
  services needed by 118–23
    child health surveillance
      120–1
    child psychiatry 120
    clinical genetics service 122
    dental care 121
    financial help 122
    follow-up consultations
      118–20
    immunization 121
    long-term care 123
    psychology services 120
    respite care 122
    support 120
  written reports 103
partially hearing units 217
parvovirus B19 163
pemoline 330
Pendred's syndrome 213
periconceptional vitamins 278
peripatetic teachers 126
peroxisomal disorder 170
persistent rumination and vomiting
    138
persistent vegetative state (PVS) 302
personality 25
pertussis immunization 121, 167
pervasive developmental disorders
    (PDDs) 192
pes cavus 59
phenobarbitone 327
phenylalanine 170
phenylketonuria 157
phenytoin 349, 352
phobias 138, 312
phocomelia 323

physiotherapy in cerebral palsy
    256–7
pica 140–1, 167
picture vocabulary tests 270
Pierre Robin syndrome 178
plagiocephaly 162, 243
play
  cognitive development and 41–2
  role of parents 41–2
  persistence of immature patterns
    42
playgroups, aggressive behaviour in
    142–3
Poland's anomaly 244
policy statements 124
poliomyelitis 243, 298
  immunization 121
porencephaly 251
Portage system 10, 124, 126, 236
postnatal depression 56
post-traumatic amnesia 302
practice toileting 141
Prader–Willi syndrome 121, 144,
    166
prednisolone 337
professional reactions to disability
    112
prostheses for limb deficiencies
    295–6
pseudobulbar palsy 249
pseudohypertrophy 290
pseudohypoparathyroidism 169
pseudoseizures 359
pseudosquint 89, 90
psychology services 120, 124
psychometric tests and scales
    11–12
psychomotor retardation 147
ptosis 92
puberty 144–5
  onset 144
  precocious 144–5
pure-tone audiometry (PTA) 68, 70

quadriplegia, acquired 298

randomized controlled trial (RCT)
    16
Randot test 95
rapid eye movement (REM) sleep
    358
Raven's progressive matrices 219
REACH 293
reading
  in communication disorders 208
  in hearing loss 213

tests 10
  see also reading disability
reading disability 318–22
  component skills and reading
    readiness 320
  as a heterogeneous condition
    319–20
  learning to read 319
  management 322
  nature of deficit 320
  orthoptic treatment 322
  parent involvement 322
  reading failure 319
  reading recovery 322
  subgroups of reading problems
    320–1
    developmental classification
      321–2
    linguistic deficits 320–1
    visual defects 321
Rebus method 202
reciprocating gait orthosis 282
recruitment 212
reflex anoxic seizures 354
reflexes
  acousticopalpebral (APR) 72
  asymmetric tonic neck (ATNR)
    247, 250
  blink 72
  Moro 247
  postural 61
  primitive 44–5, 61
  protective 46, 61
refractive error 228–9
Refsum's disease 229, 235
reinforcement 142
rejection 108
residential care 112
resilience 7
respite care 108, 122, 123
restitution 142
retinal disorders 229
retinitis pigmentosa (RP) 229
  electroretinogram (ERG) 98
retinoblastoma 228
retinopathy of prematurity (retrolental
    fibroplasia) 228
Rett's syndrome 190, 197–8
Reynell–Zinkin test 15, 233, 234,
    236
Rieger's syndrome 227
Rosti feeder 178
rubella
  congenital 163, 196, 210, 213,
    219, 227, 235
  immunization 121
Russell–Silver syndrome 121, 244

Sanfilippo's syndrome 142, 169, 190, 195
scaphocephaly 162
scene-setting 135, 140
schizoid personality 197
school phobia 138, 312
school refusal 312
SCOPE (Spastics Society) 275
secretory otitis media (SOM) (glue ear, otitis with effusion) 142, 196, 220–3
    clinical importance 221–2
    management 222–3
    screening 83
    specific language impairment and 189
Segufix–Bandagen das Humane System 139
selective mutism 52, 53
self-esteem 44
self-injurious behaviour (SIB) (self-mutilation) 138, 143–4
sensation level 70
separation anxiety 24
services for disabled children 116–30
    changing ideas about 116–18
sexual behaviour, inappropriate 145
sexual relationships 124, 287
sexuality 144–5
shape-matching test 98
Sheridan–Gardiner test 98
shyness 181–2
sickle-cell anaemia 190
signing 215, 218
sleep apnoea 139
sleep disturbance 135, 139–40, 357–8
slit-ventricle syndrome 281
Snellen letter chart 86, 87, 91, 96, 97
Snellen pseudofraction 86
Snijders–Oomen test 219
social class
    language development and 4
    social behaviour and 27
social interaction 38
sodium valproate 340, 349
Sonksen Picture Test 98
Sonksen–Silver Acuity System (SSAS) 98
spastic diplegia 245–9, 254
Special Needs Planning Group 116, 128
specific language impairment (SLI) 174, 182–91
    causes 187–90
        bilingualism 190

brain lesions, dysphasia and 188, 189
        chromosomal influences 187
        dysmorphic syndromes 188
        genetic factors 188
        impaired processing 189
        inadequate input 189
        normal variation 187
        secretory otitis media 189
        severe deprivation 189–90
        spurious factors 190
    loss of speech 190–1
        acquired receptive aphasia 190–1
        disintegrative processes 190
        links to other conditions 191
    predicting outcome 186–7
    prevalence and definition 182–3
    subtypes 183–6
        articulatory dyspraxia 183–4
        comprehension deficit 186
        congenital auditory imperception (auditory agnosia) 186
        lexical-syntactic deficit 184
        overlap between categories 185–6
        phonological-syntactic deficit 183
        semantic-pragmatic deficit 184–5
        simple expressive language delay 183
specific learning disability 3, 148, 312–18
    causes 314
    definition 313–14
    emotional and environmental influences 318
    genetic and developmental aspects 316
    neuropsychological hypotheses 316–18
        hemisphere dominance 316–17
        information-processing models 318
        miscellaneous 318
        organic brain disorders 314–16
    origin of the term 313
    prevalence 314
speech
    fragile-X syndrome 156
    in hearing loss 212
    normal sounds 29–31
    see also language development
speech therapy
    in cleft lip and cleft palate 178–9
spelling 322–3

spina bifida 124
spina bifida cystica 277–88
    bladder and urinary tract 284–6
    bowel problems 286–7
    complications of paraplegia 283–4
    epidemiology, aetiology and genetics 278
    general problems 287
    hydrocephalus 280–2
    operative procedures 283
    orthopaedic management 282–3
    preliminary management 278–9
    prevention 287–8
    selection for treatment 279–80
    sexual problems 287
    treatment 280
    urinary incontinence 288–9
spina bifida occulta 289
spinal cord injury without radiographic abnormality (SCIWORA) 298
spinal muscular atrophies 292–3
SPOD (Sexual Problems of the Disabled) 124
Sprengel's shoulder 244
squint *see* strabismus
strabismus
    causes 89–90
    management 90
    test in infancy 94–5
staff, care for 124
stammering 181
Standford–Binet test 218, 332
Staphylococcus albus (epidermidis) 281
star chart system 135, 141
Statement of Special Educational Need 129
statutory allowances 122
STEPS 293
stereognosis 63
steroids 191
Stickler syndrome 178
stigma attached to disability 1
Stott–Henderson Test of Motor Impairment 327
strephosymbolia 316
stress 118
stuttering 181
Stycar graded balls test 97
Stycar miniature toys test 98
substance abuse 165–6
sweep test 84
syphilis 163
syringomyelia 278

TAR syndrome 294

Tay−Sachs disease 345
teenagers, disabled 123−4
    with communication disorders,
        counselling of 199
temperament 7, 25
terminal illness 113−14
Test for Reception of Grammar 270
tetanus immunization 121
thalidomide 293
theory of mind 22
tibial torsion 63, 64
tics 357
time out 142
Titmus fly test 95
Todd's palsy 342
toes
    clawing of 63
    overriding of fifth over fourth 63
toileting, practice 141
tones 68
tongue-tie 180
tonic labyrinthine reflex (TLR) 247
TORCH screen 170
touching, inappropriate 145
Tourette's syndrome 357
toxoplasmosis 163
trace element supplements 126
tracheostomy 180−1
Treacher−Collins syndrome 178,
        213, 220
trimeprazine (Vallergan) 140
triple test 152
trisomy 18 278
tuberose sclerosis 196
turn-taking 23
    language and 31
    non-verbal communication and
        35
    visions and 39
Turner's syndrome 154

unilateral tiptoe gait 243
uniocular squint 89
unorthodox or alternative medicine
        124−6
urinary incontinence 288−9
Usher's syndrome 213, 229, 235

VACTERL association 294
Vallergan 140
Valproate 337
Van der Woude's syndrome 178
velocardiofacial syndrome 178
vertigo 358
very-low-birth-weight (VLBW) babies
        166
vesicoureteric reflux (VUR) 285
viagtrin 337
videourodynamic study (VDU) 285
Vineland Scale 269
viral encephalitis 195
vision
    colour 99−100
    early development 86
    eye movements 90−1
    importance in cognitive
        development 39
    visual acuity 86−9, 224
        measurement 87−9, 96−7
        refraction and refractive error
            87
    visual field
        in infancy 73, 75
        testing 94−5
    see also ophthalmic investigation;
        vision, testing; and under
        names of defects of vision
vision, testing
    colour 99−100
    early detection of defects 100
    information from parents 92−3
    minimum observable tests 96,
        97−8
    minimum separable tests 96, 98
        Acuity Card Procedure 98
        letter-matching tests 98
        Stycar miniature toys test 98
    near vision 97−8
    qualitative assessment in infancy
        93−7
    systematic examination 94
    test for squint 94−5
        corneal reflections 94
        cover tests 95
        eye movements 94−5
        head tilt 94
        nystagmoid jerks 95

stereo tests 95
visual fields 94−5
visual acuity 87−9, 96−7
visual axis 89
visual evoked response (VER) 99
visual impairment 224−36
    deaf−blind child 235−6
    development of baby with 231−3
    education 233−5
    employment 235
    epidemiology 224−5
    eye disorders, classification
        225−31
    management 233
    mobility training 235
vitamin supplements 126

Waardenburg's syndrome 213
Walker−Warburg syndrome 160
Warburg syndrome 230
Warnock Report 1978 128−9
Wechsler intelligence scale for
        children (WISC) 218
Werdnig−Hoffmann disease 62,
        255, 292
    ataxic 254
    life expectancy 113
Wernicke's (fluent) aphasia 188
West's syndrome (infantile spasms)
        149, 336−7
Williams Test 234
Williams' syndrome 151, 188
Wilson's disease 190, 195
word-blindness (dyslexia) 147, 314,
        315, 316
writing problems (dysgraphia) 315,
        323
writing tests 10

X-linked retardation 187
XXX syndrome 154
XYY syndrome 154

Zellweger's syndrome 229
zopiclone 140